5-STAR
BABY NAME
ADVISOR

Bruce Lansky

 Meadowbrook Press
Distributed by Simon & Schuster
New York

Library of Congress Cataloging-in-Publication Data

Lansky, Bruce.   APR 2 4 2008
.5-star baby name advisor / Bruce Lansky.
    p. cm.
 ISBN-10 0-88166-533-9, ISBN-13 978-0-88166-533-8 (Meadowbrook Press)
 ISBN-10 0-684-05784-0, ISBN-13 978-0-684-05784-2 (Simon & Schuster)
 1. Names, Personal--Dictionaries. I. Title. II. Title: Five-star baby name advisor.
CS2377.L335 2008
929.4'4--dc22

                    2007039053

Researchers: Megan McGinnis, Angela Wiechmann, Alicia Ester
Production Manager: Paul Woods
Graphic Design Manager: Tamara Peterson
Typesetting: Danielle White
Proofreading: Christine Zuchora-Walske
Cover Photo: Comstock, Corbis, Paul Woods

Published by Meadowbrook Press, 5451 Smetana Drive, Minnetonka, Minnesota 55343

www.meadowbrookpress.com

BOOK TRADE DISTRIBUTION by Simon and Schuster, a division of Simon and Schuster, Inc.,
1230 Avenue of the Americas, New York, New York 10020

11 10 09 08 10 9 8 7 6 5 4 3 2 1

Printed in the United States of America

Dedication

This book is dedicated to expectant parents who take the responsibility of selecting a name for their baby seriously.

With this book, you'll find that the process of searching for a name has changed from finding a name that *you* like to finding a name that will give your child a head start in life and be a pleasure for him or her—and you—to live with.

Because this book will improve your skill at weighing the pros and cons of names, it can help you make a more intelligent choice, and I think it'll also make the process of discussing names with your partner, friends, and family a lot more productive.

Contents

Introduction

Have you ever opened a dictionary-style baby name book and wanted more? Not more *names*—more *guidance*. Of course, it's great to have a large number of names at your fingertips, but so many options may make it difficult to find a name that will work for you and your baby. By that I mean:

- a name both you and your partner will love
- a name your child will find a pleasure to live with
- a name that will give your child a head start in life

If you want a better, smarter way to choose your baby's name, *5-Star Baby Name Advisor* is for you. It features a wide selection of names complete with origins and meanings—information found in many dictionary-style books. But what makes it truly unique is that it also provides practical information and advice that will help you make a wise selection you and your child won't regret later on.

In this book I rate each name based on six important factors: first impression, gender association, popularity and trend, spelling, pronunciation, and versatility. The cumulative score for each name is reflected in a star rating. (5 stars is the highest rating; 1 star is the lowest.) I then conclude each name profile with brief commentary detailing my final thoughts or concerns.

Although it is impossible to completely avoid subjectivity in the rating process, I used strict criteria to make it as objective as possible. The criteria are based on the common-sense values of parents concerned about the happiness and success of their children. This book is the product of my experience advising parents about names for more than thirty years.

As you browse each name in this book (or scan the quick-and-easy Star Search feature), try not to interpret the star rating in terms of how "good" or "bad" a name is. Instead, the rating is intended to answer these two questions: How comfortable will your child be with that name? How positive an impression will that name make for him or her?

Of course, your own preferences will play a key role in the process of choosing a name. You want to select a name that you will be happy with. But with this book in your hands, you can select a name that will also benefit your child. (Many outrageous celebrity baby names seem to be ego trips for the parents—no matter what kind of burden they might inflict on the children.)

If you ultimately choose a name with a low score, for whatever reason, at least you'll be aware of its potential to inconvenience your child daily and send strange vibes to others. Knowing that, I'm hoping you'll select a higher-rated middle name to give your child a fallback option.

Now I'll discuss the six criteria I used to rate every name in this book.

First Impression

Famous people often affect the first impressions names make. Picture someone named Elvis. (Did the image of Elvis Presley immediately come to mind?) Now picture someone named Gwyneth. (Did Gwyneth Paltrow come to mind?) Although we don't always realize it, names can create vivid images in our minds. Some names (e.g., Elvis and

Gwyneth) immediately remind us of famous name-sakes; other names suggest specific physical, psychological, or social attributes (e.g., Bertha = oversized; Gaylord = wimpy; Pansy = timid; Buffy = snooty; Archie = goofy; and Bartholomew = rich).

Even names you've never heard of still make a strong impression on you. Imagine you're a kindergarten teacher taking attendance on the first day of school—a school attended by the children of celebrities. When you call their names—Apple, Dweezil, Audio Science, Daisy Boo, and Moxie CrimeFighter—how will their classmates respond? Now imagine you're an employer: If you received a resumé from a job applicant with one of those names, how would you respond?

For each name in this book, you'll find a first impression based on data from thousands of parents and parents-to-be about the images they associate with names. Before you settle on a name, consider what impression it will make on your child's future friends, teachers, employers, and acquaintances. Will the name give him or her a head start in life? Will people hear the name and assume your child is smart, attractive, or friendly—or will they assume he or she is snobby, dumb, or nerdy?

When rating names, I favor those that create positive impressions over those that create negative or strange impressions.

Gender Association

Al is a name used by boys. Alex is used by boys and girls—but mostly boys. Alix is used by boys and girls—but mostly girls. Alexa is a name used by girls. All names—even those within the same name "family"—have unique gender associations.

Will teachers know your child's gender when they see his or her name on the class list? Later in life, will potential employers know whether your child is a man or woman when they read a resumé? Will your child's mail be addressed to "Ms." instead of "Mr." or vice versa? These are real-life situations in which gender association comes into play. Although current naming trends suggest some parents like names that blur gender lines, other parents like names with crystal-clear gender association.

When rating names, I prefer those with clear gender association. I understand that a masculine-sounding name can "strengthen" a girl's image and a feminine-sounding name can "soften" a boy's image, but I also understand that children can be quite sensitive about gender issues.

Popularity and Trend

Because Emily and Jacob are so popular, it's possible there might be two or three children with those names in your child's daycare class. That's the downside to choosing names high on the U.S. Social Security Administration's (SSA) list of the thousand most popular boys' and girls' names. If you choose a name lower on the list, your child is less likely to share that name with a classmate. But a name's ubiquity isn't the only issue to consider when it comes to popularity rankings—quality is key, too. Keep in mind that the lower you go on the SSA list, the more likely you are to encounter unusual variations of popular names (like Kayli) or names that seem dated and old fashioned (like Clarence or Elmer).

The popularity of names, like the length of hemlines and the width of ties, is subject to change. That's clearly demonstrated in the yearly SSA rankings. Even if you're not a slave to "fashion," it's wise to consider a name's popularity (where it falls in the SSA rankings) and its trend (whether it has risen or fallen in popularity over the years) before bestowing it upon your child. Doing so can help you avoid choosing an outdated, unfashionable name, but it can just as easily help you avoid the name du jour.

That's why I've listed popularity and trend information for each name. Many names include SSA data from today and 2000, indicating the trend thus far in the decade. As you'll see, other names haven't appeared in the SSA's Top 1000 in decades. Still other names have never appeared on the Top 1000 list at any time.

When rating names, I agree with psychologists who say children with popular names have better odds of success than children with uncommon names—unless the name is so popular that the child may not feel unique.

Spelling

Some parents think their child will be special if they give him or her a special name—a goal they often try to accomplish by starting with a name they like (e.g., Cathleen) and giving it an unusual spelling (e.g., Catheleene). If you open a copy of *100,000+ Baby Names*, you'll discover how popular it is for parents to choose unusual spellings for common (or even uncommon) names. There you'll find sixty-two variations of Cathleen. That number doesn't even include the thirty-nine variations of Cafleen, nor does it include the sixteen variations of Kathleen and the thirty-nine variations of Kafleen.

Many parents alter a name's spelling without a second thought to the consequences. In my opinion,

spelling isn't a factor you should ignore. How you spell your child's name will affect him or her for life. Creative spelling is an easy way to personalize a name, but the more creative you get, the more problems other people will have with the name. Having a name that's hard to spell could be a daily inconvenience to your child. If your child's name is Mikal, he'll either need to correct people who spell it Michael or will have to spell it letter by letter every time he gives his name. Don't forget that a hard-to-spell name is probably also hard to pronounce. Worse yet, a silly "alphabet soup" spelling might create an equally silly impression of your child.

When rating names, I favor the most common and easy-to-spell names over more esoteric variations.

Pronunciation

Which syllable(s) should you emphasize when calling Philomena? Is Alicia pronounced "a-LEE-see-ya," "a-LISH-a," or "a-LEE-sha"? People in Ireland may know how to pronounce Siobhan, but do you? (You'll find the correct pronunciation on page 168.)

Most parents think pronunciation is more important than spelling. The sound of a name is its true essence—it's what makes a name a *name*. As a parent, you can choose to pronounce your child's name however you want. But will a teacher be able to pronounce your child's name on the first day of school? How will a nurse pronounce it in the waiting room at the doctor's office? How will a potential employer pronounce it when calling for an interview?

No matter what pronunciation you choose for your baby's name, you need to keep in mind how other people may pronounce it based on spelling alone. If you select a difficult-to-pronounce name or a more obscure pronunciation for a classic name, don't be surprised if your child spends the rest of his or her life correcting people.

When rating names, I favor names that have simple, common pronunciations and/or are easy to pronounce phonetically.

Versatility

To illustrate the importance of versatility, let's use the name Elizabeth: You can call her by her given name, or you can call her Liz, Lizzie, Lisa, Liza, Eliza, Beth, Betsy, Betty, Bess, or Bessie. It's like getting eleven names in one. (To see the nickname options for Elizabeth or any other name, check out the "Common Nicknames" section of the profile.)

But versatility is more than just the number of nicknames—it's how well a name can adapt to various social situations throughout your child's life. With its great versatility, William will serve your son well in any situation at any point in time. He can be Billy as little boy, Will in high school, William when applying to law school, and "just plain Bill" when he runs for public office.

Different names have different degrees of versatility. Some have only one common nickname, such as Gabriel (Gabe) and Joshua (Josh). Other names have no nicknames at all, such as my own name, Bruce. While Bruce or Gabriel aren't as flexible as William or Elizabeth, they're still appropriate for both formal and informal use.

At the bottom of the versatility scale are names traditionally used as nicknames rather than legal, given names. (These names are defined as "familiar forms" or "short forms" of other names in their respective profiles.) Take Lizzie and Timmy: They're approachable and youthful, but they're also very

informal and juvenile. They don't create a mature impression when your child graduates from high school, applies to college, or goes on a job interview. Even Liz and Tim are more versatile, but they, too, are not formal enough for situations requiring authority or ceremony.

When rating names for versatility, I prefer names with many options appropriate for both informal and formal use. From an opposite perspective, versatility is important to consider if you don't like nicknames at all. In that case, don't pick a name with lots of nickname options. You can call your child by any name you want, but you can't control what your family calls him or her (unless you want to spend every breath correcting them). More importantly, you'll have absolutely no control over what schoolmates call him or her. Bottom line: If you don't want your William to become Billy, choose another name.

Now that you're familiar with all of the criteria, you'll be able to understand how I arrived at the star rankings for each name. And you'll be better prepared to assess any name that strikes your fancy.

I hope you thoroughly enjoy the process of searching for a name that will work well for both you and your child. I hope you'll pick a name you love—while keeping in mind how the name you select will affect your child's happiness and success.

Pick a winner!

Bruce Lansky

Bruce Lansky

Star Search

Girls' Names

5 Stars

Abigail
Allison
Amber
Amelia
Angela
Angelina
Anna
Ashlyn
Audrey
Bella
Brooke
Cadence
Charlotte
Christine
Diana
Ella
Emma
Faith
Florence
Gabriela
Gabrielle
Grace
Gracie
Harmony
Isabel
Jacqueline
Jade
Janelle
Jenna

Josephine
Julia
Julie
Juliet
Katherine
Kylie
Lauren
Leah
Lillian
Lily
Lucille
Lucy
Maya
Megan
Melody
Natalie
Olive
Olivia
Piper
Rachel
Rebecca
Samantha
Sara
Sarah
Savannah
Serenity
Vanessa
Violet

4 Stars

Abby
Ada
Addie
Adelaide

Aileen
Aimee
Alana
Alexa
Alexandria
Alexis
Alice
Alicia
Alissa
Allie
Alma
Alyssa
Amanda
Amy
Ana
Anastasia
Andrea
Angie
Anita
Ann
Annie
Anya
April
Aretha
Ariel
Ashley
Asia
Athena
Aubrey
Aurora
Autumn
Ava
Belle
Bernice

Beth
Bethany
Betsy
Bianca
Bliss
Brenda
Brenna
Briana
Brianna
Bridget
Caitlyn
Callidora
Callie
Camille
Camryn
Capri
Caprice
Carissa
Carla
Carlen
Carlotta
Carly
Carol
Carolina
Caroline
Casey
Cassandra
Cassidy
Catherine
Celeste
Charisma
Charisse
Charity
Charlene

Chastity
Chelsea
Cheyenne
Chloe
Christina
Cicely
Claire
Clara
Cora
Cordelia
Corinne
Daisy
Dakota
Danica
Danielle
Darla
Delilah
Delta
Destiny
Dianne
Dixie
Dolly
Dora
Dorothy
Ebony
Eileen
Eldora
Eleanor
Elise
Elizabeth
Ellen
Ellie
Emily
Erin

Estelle
Eva
Eve
Fantasia
Felicity
Florida
Francine
Frida
Gabriella
Georgina
Gina
Giselle
Glenda
Gloria
Greta
Hannah
Hayley
Hazel
Heidi
Holly
Hope
India
Iris
Isabella
Ivy
Jada
Jana
Jane
Janet
Janna
Jasmine
Jayne
Jena
Jenay

Jennifer
Jenny
Jessica
Jill
Jillian
Jocelyn
Jolene
Jolie
Jordan
Josie
Journey
Joy
Judith
Juliana
Justine
Kate
Katharine
Kathleen
Katrina
Kay
Kayla
Kaylee
Kelsey
Kendra
Kenya
Kessie
Kimberly
Kira
Koren
Kristin
Kristina
Kyla
Lacey
Lainey
Larissa
Laura
Laurel

Leandra
Leilani
Liberty
Lila
Linda
Lola
Lolly
Lonna
Lorraine
Louisa
Luna
Lyla
Mackenzie
Madeline
Madison
Magdalen
Mallory
Marcella
Margaret
Maria
Mariah
Marie
Mariel
Marietta
Marissa
Marit
Martha
Martina
Mary
Mary Ellen
Matilda
Melanie
Melissa
Mia
Michaela
Michelle
Miranda

Modesta
Modesty
Molly
Montana
Nadia
Nancy
Nanette
Naomi
Natalia
Nessa
Nicole
Nina
Olympia
Oprah
Paige
Patience
Patricia
Paula
Pauline
Penelope
Phoebe
Posy
Priscilla
Reba
Reese
Regina
Renee
Roberta
Rochelle
Roma
Rosa
Rosalie
Rose
Rosemary
Ruth
Sable
Sabrina

Samara
Sandra
Savanna
Scarlett
Selena
Serena
Shelby
Shirley
Sierra
Skye
Sofia
Sophia
Sophie
Stella
Stephanie
Stockard
Summer
Susan
Susannah
Suzanne
Sydney
Tabitha
Tamara
Tatiana
Taylor
Tessa
Tia
Trinity
Trista
Valerie
Verena
Victoria
Virginia
Vivian
Wanda
Wilhelmina
Willow

Yolanda
Zoe
Zola

3 Stars

Aaliyah
Abira
Adele
Adeline
Adora
Adrienne
Agnes
Akiko
Akina
Alexandra
Alisha
Allegra
Alyson
Amaya
Anezka
Angelica
Angelique
Anika
Annette
Annika
Antoinette
Antonia
Aria
Ariana
Arlene
Astra
Audra
Avril
Babette
Bailey
Baka
Barbara

Beatrice
Becca
Becky
Belinda
Benita
Berkley
Bernadette
Bess
Bette
Betty
Beverly
Blanca
Blanche
Bonita
Bonnie
Breanna
Bree
Breena
Brigitte
Britta
Brittney
Buffy
Caitlin
Camilla
Candace
Candida
Candra
Cara
Carina
Carlene
Carmen
Carrie
Cassie
Cecelia
Celine
Chanel
Chantal

Charmaine	Elaine	Hanna	Katelyn	Lisa	May
Chavi	Electra	Harriet	Kathy	Liz	McKayla
Chaya	Elena	Heather	Katie	Lois	Meredith
Cheryl	Eliza	Helen	Katina	Loretta	Mickie
Chika	Elsie	Henrietta	Katy	Lori	Mildred
Chiquita	Erica	Hilary	Kaya	Louise	Millie
Christy	Esmeralda	Ilene	Kerry	Lucia	Mindy
Cindy	Esperanza	Imogene	Kiara	Lucie	Minka
Clare	Ethel	Inga	Kim	Lucinda	Minnie
Clarissa	Evelyn	Ingrid	Kirsten	Lulu	Miriam
Claudia	Evie	Irene	Kora	Lupita	Missy
Colleen	Fawn	Italia	Krista	Lydia	Mona
Connie	Felice	Ivory	Kristen	Lynette	Monica
Constance	Felicia	Jackie	Kristine	Lynn	Monique
Consuelo	Fiona	Jaclyn	Krystal	Maddie	Morgan
Cori	Flannery	Jaime	Kyra	Maggie	Muriel
Corrina	Fran	Janae	Laila	Maisie	Mya
Courtney	Frances	Janie	Lakeisha	Malana	Natasha
Cristy	Francesca	Janine	Lana	Mandy	Neena
Crystal	Gaby	Jeanette	Lane	Mansi	Nerissa
Cynthia	Gail	Jelena	Latonya	Mara	Nia
Daphne	Gemma	Jessie	Latoya	Marcia	Nicolette
Darcy	Genevieve	Joan	Laurie	Marcy	Nikita
Darlene	Georgette	Joanna	Laverne	Margarita	Noel
Dawn	Georgia	Joni	Lawanda	Marguerite	Nola
Deirdre	Gillian	Joyce	Lea	Marilyn	Nora
Della	Ginger	Judy	Leigh	Marjorie	Norma
Denise	Ginny	Julianne	Leila	Marlene	Nyssa
Desiree	Giovana	June	Lenora	Marley	Octavia
Diamond	Glenna	Kacey	Letitia	Marlo	Oletha
Diane	Greer	Kali	Lia	Marsha	Onella
Doris	Gretchen	Kameko	Lilac	Marta	Opal
Dottie	Gretel	Kanika	Lilah	Mary Beth	Ophelia
Eartha	Gwen	Karen	Lilith	Maura	Pamela
Eden	Gwendolyn	Kari	Lina	Maureen	Paris
Edith	Gwyneth	Kass	Lindsay	Mauve	Patrice
Ela	Hallie	Katarina	Lindsey	Maxine	Paulette

Pavla	Shakila	Tisha	Billie	Eugenia	Kitra
Paz	Shakira	Torie	Blair	Geraldine	Kona
Pearl	Shanna	Torrance	Blythe	Germaine	Kristi
Peggy	Shannon	Tova	Brandy	Ghita	Lacy
Pennie	Sharon	Tracy	Brie	Gladys	Lara
Petula	Shauna	Trish	Britany	Glory	Laveda
Phylicia	Sheba	Trudy	Brittany	Guadalupe	Leona
Polly	Sheena	Tyne	Bunny	Guinevere	Libby
Poria	Shelly	Tyra	Calantha	Haley	Linnea
Prudence	Sherry	Vanna	Caley	Hasana	Liza
Rae	Shonda	Veda	Carey	Hedda	Lorna
Ramona	Shoshana	Velma	Cathleen	Hedwig	Mabel
Reagan	Simone	Vera	Cathy	Helga	Mae
Reanna	Sondra	Verna	Celia	Hermosa	Maira
Regan	Stacy	Veronica	Cheri	Honora	Maire
Rhea	Storm	Wendy	Christa	Hortense	Marnie
Rhiannon	Sue	Whitney	Clementine	Huberta	Maud
Rhoda	Sunny	Winifred	Collette	Ida	Mead
Rhonda	Sunshine	Winona	Cyndi	Iman	Meka
Ricki	Suzette	Winter	Dana	Irma	Melinda
Riona	Suzie	Yoko	Dani	Janis	Mercedes
Rita	Sylvia	Zahara	Deborah	Jean	Meryl
Robyn	Taffy	Zaida	Dee Dee	Jeri	Millicent
Rori	Taka	Zaza	Delia	Jessamine	Milly
Rosalyn	Tameka	Zelia	Delores	Jezebel	Mimi
Roseanna	Tammy		Delphine	Jo	Mireille
Roseanne	Tara	**2 Stars**	Demi	Jodi	Misty
Roxanna	Taryn	Adena	Dena	Juanita	Mitzi
Rue	Tasha	Agatha	Dina	Kala	Moira
Sabina	Tatum	Alberta	Dominique	Kalare	Myra
Sabra	Tess	Alena	Donna	Kalinda	Nadine
Sagara	Thea	Ali	Doreen	Kaliska	Nailah
Sage	Theresa	Andreana	Doria	Kelby	Narcissa
Sally	Therese	Aolani	Drusilla	Kelly	Nevaeh
Sandy	Thomasina	Bambi	Edna	Kimi	Nidia
Sarina	Tiffany	Barbie	Enid	Kimmy	Nike
Selina	Tina	Bertha	Ester	Kishi	Nikki

Noreen	Racquel	Stevie	Uriana	Chiara	Myrna
Norell	Randi	Stormy	Ursula	Chris	Nellie
Nyx	Raven	Sybil	Vicki	Donata	Pandita
Oceana	Reilly	Sylvana	Yasmine	Eunice	Pat
Odele	Romola	Tanya	Yvonne	Fifi	Pythia
Odera	Sapphire	Tawny	Zena	Fleta	Qadira
Olga	Sasha	Tegan	Zephyr	Helene	Siobhan
Orella	Shari	Terri	Zizi	Heloise	Svetlana
Othelia	Sharlene	Theone		Iolanthe	Tanith
Pansy	Sheila	Tierney		Isi	Thema
Patti	Sissy	Toni		Jody	Winda
Phaedra	Sonya	Tonya		Lizina	Yvette
Phyllis	Stacey	Tricia		Lorena	
Portia	Stacia	Trina		Margaux	
Rachael	Starr	Urania		Margot	

1 Star

Anais
Baba
Blinda
Cai
Candi

Boys' Names

5 Stars

Abraham
Adam
Alexander
Andrew
Angel
Asher
Austin
Benjamin
Brian
Bryson
Caleb
Carlos
Carson
Carter
Charles
Chase
Christian
Christopher
Daniel
David
Dominic
Edward
Elijah
Gabriel
Hayden
Henry
Isaac
Jack
Jackson
James
Jason
Joel
John
Joseph
Joshua
Jude
Kenneth
Kevin
Logan
Lucas
Luke
Matthew
Maxwell
Moses
Nathan
Nicholas
Oliver
Owen
Paul
Ricardo
Robert
Ronald
Steven
Thomas
Timothy
William

4 Stars

Aaron
Abel
Abram
Adler
Adrian
Adriel
Aidan
Aladdin
Albert
Alberto
Alec
Alex
Andre
Ansel
Anthony
Antonio
Armen
Arthur
Arturo
August
Augustus
Barton
Bennett
Benson
Bill
Blaine
Bond
Brad
Brant
Brayden
Brendan
Brent
Brett
Bryan
Bryce
Caden
Calvin
Cameron
Campbell
Carl
Carlo
Chad
Chance
Chandler
Clark
Clay
Clayton
Cliff
Clint
Cole
Connor
Constantine
Cooper
Craig
Curt
Dakota
Dale
Danny
Darius
Dave
Deangelo
Denver
Derek
Desmond
Diego
Donald
Donovan
Douglas
Drake
Drew
Duncan
Dustin
Dylan
Earl
Edgar
Edwin
Eli
Elvis
Emerson
Emmanuel
Eric
Ethan
Evan
Fletcher
Gage
Garrett
Garrison
Garth
Gavin
Grady
Grant
Grayson
Greg
Gregory
Griffin
Guy
Harmon
Harrison
Heath
Hector
Horace
Houston
Hunter
Isaiah
Israel
Jacob
Jaden
Jake
Jamison
Jasper
Jay
Jayden
Jeff
Jefferson
Jeremiah
Jesse
Jesus
Joe
Jonah
Jonas
Jonathan
Jordan
Jose
Josh
Josiah
Justin
Keith
Kellan
Kelvin
Ken
Kent
Kermit
Kirk
Kyle
Lance
Landon
Leon
Levi
Louis
Manuel
Marc
Marco
Marcus
Mario
Marlon
Marshall
Martin
Mason
Merlin
Michael
Miles
Myles
Nathaniel
Nick
Noah
Nolan
Orlando
Orson
Pablo

Parker	Tremaine	Aron	Clifford	Elton	Harry
Patrick	Trent	Ashton	Clinton	Emery	Harvey
Peter	Tristan	Aubrey	Colby	Emil	Herbert
Porter	Tyler	Avery	Colin	Emilio	Herman
Quincy	Victor	Barak	Collin	Emmett	Holden
Quinn	Vince	Barry	Corey	Enrique	Homer
Ranger	Vincent	Beaman	Cornelius	Ephraim	Howard
Raymond	Walter	Beau	Cory	Ernest	Hubert
Reggie	Will	Ben	Curtis	Ernie	Hugh
Ricky	Wilson	Bentley	Cyrus	Ezekiel	Hugo
Roberto	Winston	Bernard	Dalton	Ezra	Humphrey
Rodney	Wood	Blake	Dan	Fabian	Ian
Roland	Wyatt	Bo	Dante	Ferdinand	Ira
Roman	Zachary	Bob	Darby	Fernando	Irving
Ross	Zane	Bobby	Darren	Finnegan	Ivan
Roy		Braden	Darrius	Forrest	Jamal
Ruben	**3 Stars**	Bradford	Daryl	Francis	Jared
Ryan	Ace	Bradley	Dennis	Franklin	Jed
Sam	Addison	Brady	Denny	Fred	Jeffrey
Samuel	Akeem	Brandon	Devin	Frederick	Jeremy
Saul	Alden	Breck	Dexter	Frick	Jeriah
Seth	Alejandro	Brock	Dick	Fritz	Jermaine
Shane	Alfonso	Bruce	Dirk	Fynn	Jerome
Shepherd	Alfred	Bud	Don	Gabe	Jimmy
Silas	Alfredo	Buddy	Dorian	Gareth	Joey
Simba	Ali	Byron	Doyle	Gary	Johann
Skipper	Allen	Caesar	Dudley	Gaylord	Johnny
Skyler	Alvin	Carlton	Duff	Gene	Jorge
Spencer	Amos	Carrick	Dusty	George	Juan
Stephen	Anders	Casey	Eddie	Gerald	Judd
Sutherland	Andy	Casper	Edmund	Gerard	Jules
Sylvester	Angus	Cedric	Eduardo	Gideon	Julian
Tanner	Antoine	Charlie	Elias	Gilbert	Julius
Teddy	Archie	Charlton	Elliot	Godfrey	Kale
Theo	Argus	Chester	Ellis	Gordon	Keaton
Theodore	Armando	Chris	Elmer	Graham	Keelan
Toby	Arnold	Chuck	Elmo	Harold	Keenan

Keene	Miguel	Ringo	Sundeep	Wilbert	Bern
Kelly	Mike	Robbie	Tad	Wilbur	Bert
Kenny	Milton	Rocky	Tate	Wilfred	Billy
Kerry	Montgomery	Rodrigo	Taylor	Willard	Bjorn
Kieran	Monty	Roger	Ted	Willis	Blade
Kim	Morgan	Rolando	Terrell	Xander	Boris
King	Morris	Ron	Terrence	Xavier	Bram
Kohana	Muhammed	Roosevelt	Terry	Zachariah	Brooklyn
Kurt	Navin	Royce	Tevin	Zedekiah	Butch
Lane	Nelson	Rudolph	Thaddeus	Zeke	Cain
Larry	Noel	Rudy	Tim	Zeno	Carey
Leif	Norman	Russell	Titus	Zephyr	Carmel
Leo	Ollie	Rusty	Tobias		Cecil
Leonard	Omar	Sadler	Todd	**2 Stars**	Chet
Leroy	Oscar	Salvador	Tom	Adolf	Clarence
Lester	Oz	Sammy	Tomlin	Adon	Claude
Lewis	Paddy	Samson	Tommy	Ahmad	Clyde
Liam	Pedro	Santiago	Tony	Ajay	Cody
Lionel	Philip	Sawyer	Travis	Alcott	Conrad
Lister	Pin	Scott	Trayton	Alistair	Corbin
Lonnie	Preston	Sean	Trenton	Alphonse	Damian
Lorenzo	Quentin	Sebastian	Trevor	Amir	Darryl
Lorne	Quinlan	Senior	Trey	Angelo	Devlin
Luther	Raheem	Sergio	Troy	Arlen	Dimitri
Lyle	Ralph	Shavar	Tucker	Arnie	Dunn
Lyndon	Ramon	Shawn	Ty	Auden	Dwayne
Mack	Randy	Sherman	Tyree	Aurek	Dwight
Malcolm	Raul	Sidney	Tyrone	Axel	Ed
Marion	Ray	Simon	Tyson	Bailey	Eldon
Mark	Reese	Slade	Vance	Baron	Elvin
Marvin	Regis	Soloman	Vaughn	Barrett	Ennis
Mateo	Reid	Stanislav	Vernon	Bart	Ervin
Matt	Rex	Stanley	Wade	Bartholomew	Eugene
Maurice	Rhett	Sterling	Wallace	Basil	Ewan
Max	Richard	Steve	Waylon	Baul	Fabio
Melvin	Rick	Stuart	Wesley	Benny	Fergus
Mervin	Riley	Sullivan	Weston	Berk	Ferguson

Fidel	Kadar	Morton	Purdy	Thornton	Dorcas
Floyd	Kareem	Murray	Quintin	Timmy	Geraldo
Flynn	Karl	Myron	Randolph	Tracy	Giuseppe
Ford	Kendall	Neal	Raphael	Tymon	Gunther
Frank	Kenley	Nigel	Rashad	Tyrel	Gwidon
Freddie	Kipp	Nodin	Reginald	Ulysses	Hakim
Gino	Kiros	Norton	Reilly	Upton	Hussein
Glen	Kris	Obert	Reynold	Vic	Ignatius
Gomer	Lamar	Octavius	Robin	Vijay	Ittamar
Grimshaw	Lars	Og	Rocco	Vinny	Jan
Grover	Lawrence	Orien	Rock	Virgil	Kane
Habib	Lee	Oswald	Rollo	Vito	Kelsey
Ham	Lenny	Otis	Roscoe	Vladimir	Laramie
Hank	Leslie	Otto	Rufus	Warren	Llewellyn
Hans	Lex	Ottokar	Rush	Wayne	Mandek
Harley	Lincoln	Palmer	Ruskin	Wendell	Rei
Herschel	Lloyd	Paolo	Saburo	Willie	Reynard
Hilario	Lowell	Park	Santos	Xerxes	Rhys
Ike	Luc	Pascale	Scotty	Yoshi	Rico
Jacques	Luis	Pat	Serge		Ronnie
Jagger	Malik	Payton	Shakir	**1 Star**	Sarngin
Jamie	Marcel	Percy	Sharif	Armand	Schuyler
Jarl	Marty	Perry	Sheldon	Arsen	Seamus
Javier	Mathias	Pete	Sherrod	Ballard	Sinclair
Jedidiah	Maximilian	Phineas	Slater	Bane	Stefan
Jerry	Maynard	Pierce	Steel	Bilal	Thanos
Jibril	Mikhail	Pierre	Stefano	Cletus	Wiley
Jim	Milt	Poni	Stevie	Coty	Yakov
Jock	Mitch	Prince	Tan	Darrion	
Julio	Mitchell	Pryor	Tariq	Deman	

Profiles of
Girls' Names

Aaliyah ★★★

(Hebrew) a form of Aliya.

First Impression: People over-whelmingly picture Aaliyah as an African American singer with long hair and a willowy frame, much like the late R&B star of the same name.

Gender Association: Used for girls

Popularity and Trend: #91 (#211 in 2000)

Risk of Misspelling: High

Risk of Mispronunciation: High

Famous Namesakes: Singer Aaliyah Haughton

Common Nicknames: Liya

Common Variations: Aliya

Consider This: Although a lot of people will know this name because of the late singer Aaliyah, many will still have trouble spelling and pronouncing it.

Abby ★★★★

(Hebrew) a familiar form of Abigail.

First Impression: Thanks to famous advice columnist "Dear Abby," people think Abby is happy to lend an ear.

Gender Association: Used for girls

Popularity and Trend: #205 (#205 in 2000)

Risk of Misspelling: Fairly low

Risk of Mispronunciation: Low

Famous Namesakes: Advice columnist Abigail "Abby" Van Buren; character Abby Lockhart (ER)

Common Nicknames: None

Common Variations: Abbey, Abbi, Abbie

Consider This: People are likely to mistake Abby for a nickname instead of a given name in its own right.

Abigail ★★★★★

(Hebrew) father's joy.

First Impression: Abigail is described as kind, gentle, and humble, not to mention pretty.

Gender Association: Used for girls

Popularity and Trend: #6 (#14 in 2000)

Risk of Misspelling: Fairly low

Risk of Mispronunciation: Low

Famous Namesakes: First lady Abigail Adams; columnist Abigail Van Buren; actress Abigail Breslin

Common Nicknames: Abby, Gail

Common Variations: Abbigail

Consider This: Abigail is a classic, versatile name, but it may be *too* popular for some parents' tastes.

Abira ★★★

(Hebrew) my strength.

First Impression: People imagine that Abira's beauty is rivaled only by her kindness.

Gender Association: Used for girls

Popularity and Trend: Never been ranked in Top 1000

Risk of Misspelling: Average

Risk of Mispronunciation: Average

Famous Namesakes: None

Common Nicknames: Abeer

Common Variations: None

Consider This: This unusual name can be pronounced "ah-BEE-rah" or "ah-BYE-rah."

Ada ★★★★

(German) a form of Adelaide. (English) prosperous; happy. (Hebrew) a form of Adah.

First Impression: Ada is considered an older woman who's stunningly beautiful and elegant.

Gender Association: Used for girls

Popularity and Trend: #715 (#852 in 2004)

Risk of Misspelling: Fairly low

Risk of Mispronunciation: Fairly low

Famous Namesakes: Writer Ada Louise Huxtable; character Ada Monroe (*Cold Mountain*)

Common Nicknames: None

Common Variations: Aida

Consider This: Ada isn't very versatile, but it seems elegant.

Addie ★★★★

(Greek, German) a familiar form of Adelaide, Adrienne.

First Impression: People use words that end in *y* to describe Addie: *bubbly*, *witty*, and *spunky*.

Gender Association: Used for girls

Popularity and Trend: Last ranked in the Top 1000 in the 1960s

Risk of Misspelling: Fairly low

Risk of Mispronunciation: Low

Famous Namesakes: Civil rights figure Addie Mae Collins; character Addie (*American Girl* series)
Common Nicknames: None
Common Variations: Addy
Consider This: Addie hasn't been popular for a long time, which makes it seem a bit unique.

Adelaide ★★★★
(German) noble and serene.
First Impression: People say Adelaide is friendly, pleasant, and eager to make you feel right at home.
Gender Association: Used for girls
Popularity and Trend: #921 (#900 in 2005)
Risk of Misspelling: Average
Risk of Mispronunciation: Fairly low
Famous Namesakes: Character Miss Adelaide (*Guys and Dolls*)
Common Nicknames: Ada, Addie, Della
Common Variations: Adelaida
Consider This: Although Adelaide and its many nicknames (Ada, Addie, Della) are uncommon, people have mostly positive impressions of them.

Adele ★★★
(English) a form of Adelaide, Adeline.
First Impression: Folks think Adele is nerdy, shy, and not very pretty, but she's most likely quite sweet.
Gender Association: Used for girls
Popularity and Trend: Last ranked in the Top 1000 in the 1960s

Risk of Misspelling: Average
Risk of Mispronunciation: Low
Famous Namesakes: Character Adele (*Die Fledermaus*); character Adele (*Jane Eyre*)
Common Nicknames: Della
Common Variations: Adela
Consider This: This old-fashioned name seems too nerdy for most people.

Adeline ★★★
(English) a form of Adelaide.
First Impression: Adeline is pictured as an uptight and conservative small-town girl who's likely shy and polite, but boring.
Gender Association: Used for girls
Popularity and Trend: #467 (#806 in 2000)
Risk of Misspelling: Fairly low
Risk of Mispronunciation: Average
Famous Namesakes: Actress Adeline Blondieau
Common Nicknames: Ada, Addie, Addy
Common Variations: Adelina, Adilene
Consider This: This name's popularity is surging, but its stiff image may hold it back.

Adena ★★
(Hebrew) noble; adorned.
First Impression: Adena isn't considered the brightest bulb, but people feel there's never a dull moment when you're around her.
Gender Association: Used for girls
Popularity and Trend: Never been ranked in Top 1000

Risk of Misspelling: Average
Risk of Mispronunciation: Average
Famous Namesakes: Singer Adena Howard
Common Nicknames: Dena
Common Variations: Adina
Consider This: People's unfamiliarity with this name may cause some pronunciation and spelling trouble.

Adora ★★★
(Latin) beloved.
First Impression: Adora may be adorable in many ways, but many think she's also odd.
Gender Association: Used for girls
Popularity and Trend: Never been ranked in Top 1000
Risk of Misspelling: Fairly low
Risk of Mispronunciation: Fairly low
Famous Namesakes: Character Princess Adora (*She-Ra: Princess of Power*)
Common Nicknames: Dora
Common Variations: None
Consider This: This name has never been ranked in the Top 1000, which may be why some find it odd.

Adrienne ★★★
(Greek) rich. (Latin) dark.
First Impression: To many, Adrienne is a sweet, caring woman who's always there for her loved ones.
Gender Association: Used for girls
Popularity and Trend: #736 (#530 in 2000)
Risk of Misspelling: Average
Risk of Mispronunciation: Fairly low

Famous Namesakes: Poet Adrienne Rich; designer Adrienne Vittadini

Common Nicknames: Addie, Ade

Common Variations: Adriane, Adrienna

Consider This: Adrienne's popularity peaked in the '80s, and now it's falling fast. Its pronunciation is also the same as that for Adrian, a popular name for boys, which may cause gender confusion.

Agatha ★★

(Greek) good, kind.

First Impression: Most people picture Agatha as an old, wrinkled mother-in-law who's a cranky, know-it-all nag.

Gender Association: Used for girls

Popularity and Trend: Last ranked in the Top 1000 in the 1940s

Risk of Misspelling: Low

Risk of Mispronunciation: Low

Famous Namesakes: Author Agatha Christie; saint Agatha

Common Nicknames: Aggie

Common Variations: Agathe

Consider This: Despite its well-loved namesakes, Agatha comes across as old—and awful.

Agnes ★★★

(Greek) pure.

First Impression: People think Agnes is introverted and nerdy with glasses and a matronly, homely appearance.

Gender Association: Used for girls

Popularity and Trend: Last ranked in the Top 1000 in the 1960s

Risk of Misspelling: Fairly low

Risk of Mispronunciation: Low

Famous Namesakes: Dancer Agnes de Mille; actress Agnes Moorhead

Common Nicknames: Aggie

Common Variations: Anessa

Consider This: Popular from the 1890s to the 1920s but never since, Agnes seems old-fashioned and nerdy.

Aileen ★★★★

(Scottish) light bearer. (Irish) a form of Helen.

First Impression: Aileen is thought to be fun-loving and bubbly, but also insightful and intelligent.

Gender Association: Used for girls

Popularity and Trend: #537 (#526 in 2000)

Risk of Misspelling: Average

Risk of Mispronunciation: Fairly low

Famous Namesakes: Infamous killer Aileen Wuornos

Common Nicknames: None

Common Variations: Aline

Consider This: If you have Irish or Scottish roots, Aileen may be a good fit for you. But some people don't know it's pronounced "AY-leen."

Aimee ★★★★

(Latin) a form of Amy. (French) loved.

First Impression: Folks say Aimee is a sweetheart—and spunky to boot.

Gender Association: Used for girls

Popularity and Trend: #763 (#556 in 2000)

Risk of Misspelling: Average

Risk of Mispronunciation: Low

Famous Namesakes: Singer Aimee Mann; actress Amy Irving; singer Amy Grant; singer Amy Winehouse; actress Amy Adams; actress Amy Sedaris; actress Amy Brennemen; comedian Amy Poehler; novelist Amy Tan

Common Nicknames: None

Common Variations: Amy, Aimie

Consider This: Aimee is a French form of Amy, and most people are likely to pronounce it like "Amy" and spell it that way, too.

Akiko ★★★

(Japanese) bright light.

First Impression: People think of Akiko as a friendly free spirit of Japanese or Hawaiian descent.

Gender Association: Used for girls

Popularity and Trend: Never been ranked in Top 1000

Risk of Misspelling: Average

Risk of Mispronunciation: Average

Famous Namesakes: Actress Akiko Wakabayashi; comic book character Akiko

Common Nicknames: None

Common Variations: None

Consider This: This Japanese name may sound odd with certain surnames.

Akina ★★★

(Japanese) spring flower.

First Impression: Akina is imagined to be either shy, submissive, and intelligent or bubbly, confident, and spunky.

Gender Association: Used for girls

Popularity and Trend: Never been ranked in Top 1000

Risk of Misspelling: Average

Risk of Mispronunciation: Average

Famous Namesakes: Singer Akina Nakamori

Common Nicknames: None

Common Variations: None

Consider This: Like Akiko, this Japanese name may not fit with some surnames.

Alana ★★★★

(Irish) attractive; peaceful. (Hawaiian) offering.

First Impression: People regard Alana as an exotic and glamorous woman whom men can't help but find attractive.

Gender Association: Used for girls

Popularity and Trend: #166 (#254 in 2000)

Risk of Misspelling: Average

Risk of Mispronunciation: Average

Famous Namesakes: Model Alana Stewart; actress Alana De La Garza

Common Nicknames: Lana

Common Variations: Alanah, Alanna

Consider This: This attractive name just keeps getting more popular.

Alberta ★★

(German, French) noble and bright.

First Impression: Alberta, Canada, is often envisioned as a cold, hard region, and Alberta is likewise imagined to be a cold, hard woman.

Gender Association: Used for girls

Popularity and Trend: Last ranked in the Top 1000 in the 1970s

Risk of Misspelling: Low

Risk of Mispronunciation: Low

Famous Namesakes: Blues singer Alberta Hunter; actress Alberta Watson

Common Nicknames: Bertha

Common Variations: Elberta

Consider This: Alberta may have to suffer through "Canada, eh?" jokes all her life.

Alena ★★

(Russian) a form of Helen.

First Impression: Alena is thought to have a nasty and wicked temper that flares up on short notice.

Gender Association: Used for girls

Popularity and Trend: #665 (#722 in 2000)

Risk of Misspelling: Average

Risk of Mispronunciation: Average

Famous Namesakes: Model Alena Seredova

Common Nicknames: Lena

Common Variations: Alina

Consider This: This Russian name is exotic and likely to cause spelling and pronunciation problems. Many people may not realize it can be "ah-LEE-nah" or "ah-LAY-nah."

Alexa ★★★★

(Greek) a form of Alexandra.

First Impression: Alexa gives the impression of a spoiled rich girl with a sports car, cell phone, and a free ride to a fancy college.

Gender Association: Used for girls

Popularity and Trend: #39 (#87 in 2000)

Risk of Misspelling: Fairly low

Risk of Mispronunciation: Low

Famous Namesakes: Politican Alexa McDonough; star kid Alexa Ray Joel; actress Alexa Vega

Common Nicknames: Lex, Lexi

Common Variations: Alexsa

Consider This: This name is every bit as popular as Alexandra, but it isn't nearly as versatile.

Alexandra ★★★

(Greek) a form of Alexander.

First Impression: Alexandra seems to carry herself like royalty—and expects others to regard her as such.

Gender Association: Used mostly for girls

Popularity and Trend: #40 (#36 in 2000)

Risk of Misspelling: Fairly low

Risk of Mispronunciation: Fairly low

Famous Namesakes: Actress Alexandra Paul; empress Alexandra Fyodorovna

Common Nicknames: Alex, Alexa, Lex, Lexi, Xandra, Sandra, Sandy, Sasha

Common Variations: Alessandra, Aleksandra, Alexandria

Consider This: Alexandra is a very popular and versatile name with an unfortunately snobby image.

Alexandria ★★★★

(Greek) a form of Alexandra.

First Impression: Alexandria appears to have posh possessions to go with her posh personality.

Gender Association: Used for girls

Popularity and Trend: #147 (#91 in 2000)

Risk of Misspelling: Fairly low

Risk of Mispronunciation: Fairly low

Famous Namesakes: Star kid Alexandria Zahra Bowie

Common Nicknames: Alex, Lex, Lexi, Sandra, Sandy, Sasha

Common Variations: Alexandrea, Alixandria, Alexia

Consider This: Alexandria is just as versatile as Alexandra, but it's a little more unique.

Alexis ★★★★

(Greek) a form of Alexandra.

First Impression: Alexis is considered a sexy and seductive knockout.

Gender Association: Used mostly for girls

Popularity and Trend: #14 (#6 in 2000)

Risk of Misspelling: Fairly low

Risk of Mispronunciation: Low

Famous Namesakes: Actress Alexis Bledel; actress Alexis Arquette

Common Nicknames: Lex, Lexi

Common Variations: Alexus, Lexis, Lexus

Consider This: The most popular name in the Alexandra family, Alexis may be *too* popular for some parents' tastes.

Ali ★★

(Greek) a familiar form of Alice, Alicia, Alisha, Alison.

First Impression: People say Ali is a kindhearted, unselfish, and well-liked girl.

Gender Association: Used mostly for boys

Popularity and Trend: Last ranked #926 in 2000

Risk of Misspelling: Fairly high

Risk of Mispronunciation: Fairly low

Famous Namesakes: Actress Ali MacGraw; actress Ally Sheedy; television character Ally McBeal; actress Ali Larter

Common Nicknames: Al

Common Variations: Ally

Consider This: This spelling is used mostly for boys. Ally and Allie are less ambiguous and more popular options for girls.

Alice ★★★★

(Greek) truthful. (German) noble.

First Impression: People think Alice is a cute blond who's kind and meek, but eager to have a wonderful adventure.

Gender Association: Used for girls

Popularity and Trend: #383 (#421 in 2000)

Risk of Misspelling: Low

Risk of Mispronunciation: Low

Famous Namesakes: Character Alice (*Alice's Adventures in Wonderland*); author Alice Walker; character Alice Nelson (*The Brady Bunch*); character Alice Hyatt (*Alice*); writer Alice B. Toklas

Common Nicknames: Ali

Common Variations: Alyce

Consider This: A Top 100 name for the first half of the twentieth century, Alice has become significantly less popular, though it still ranks in the Top 500.

Alicia ★★★★

(English) a form of Alice.

First Impression: Alicia is believed to be a popular, confident, and perky party girl.

Gender Association: Used for girls

Popularity and Trend: #167 (#121 in 2000)

Risk of Misspelling: Fairly low

Risk of Mispronunciation: Fairly high

Famous Namesakes: Actress Alicia Silverstone; singer Alicia Keys; actress Alicia Witt

Common Nicknames: Ali, Licia

Common Variations: Alisha, Aleecia

Consider This: Alicia is a fairly popular name, but its many pronunciations ("ah-LEE-shah," "ah-LISH-ah," and "ah-LEE-cee-ah") may create daily hassle.

Alisha ★★★

(Greek) truthful. (German) noble. (English) a form of Alicia.

First Impression: People agree Alisha is pretty, but they aren't sure whether she's friendly and helpful or bossy and stubborn.

Gender Association: Used for girls

Popularity and Trend: #584 (#401 in 2000)

Risk of Misspelling: Average

Risk of Mispronunciation: Average

Famous Namesakes: Singer Alicia Keys; actress Alicia Silverstone; actress Alicia Witt

Common Nicknames: Ali, Lisha

Common Variations: Aleesha

Consider This: Most people lean toward the phonetic "ah-LISH-ah" for this spelling, but some may pronounce it "ah-LEE-shah."

Alissa ★★★★

(Greek) a form of Alice, Alyssa.

First Impression: Folks say Alissa is charming, outgoing, and quite an alluring flirt.

Gender Association: Used for girls

Popularity and Trend: #377 (#279 in 2000)

Risk of Misspelling: Average

Risk of Mispronunciation: Low

Famous Namesakes: Actress Alyssa Milano

Common Nicknames: Lissa

Common Variations: Elissa

Consider This: Alissa is not nearly as popular as Top 20–name Alyssa, but it has a slightly more positive image.

Allegra ★★★

(Latin) cheerful.

First Impression: People think Allegra is a dark beauty with hippie-like, freewheeling tendencies.

Gender Association: Used for girls

Popularity and Trend: Never been ranked in Top 1000

Risk of Misspelling: Fairly low

Risk of Mispronunciation: Fairly low

Famous Namesakes: Heiress Allegra Versace; ballerina Allegra Kent

Common Nicknames: None

Common Variations: Allegria

Consider This: Although some people will think of allergy medication when they hear this name, more will think of a cheerful free spirit.

Allie ★★★★

(Greek) a familiar form of Alice, Alicia, Alisha, Alison.

First Impression: Allie calls to mind a perky and cheerful girl who loves to kid around.

Gender Association: Used for girls

Popularity and Trend: #229 (#392 in 2000)

Risk of Misspelling: Average

Risk of Mispronunciation: Low

Famous Namesakes: Actress Ally Sheedy; television character Ally McBeal; actress Ali MacGraw; actress Ali Larter

Common Nicknames: Al

Common Variations: Ali, Alli, Ally

Consider This: Allie is fairly popular in its own right, but even so, people are likely to think it's a nickname for Alice, Alicia, or Alison.

Allison ★★★★★

(English) a form of Alison.

First Impression: Allison is described as a sweet and personable woman who's full of compliments and eager to make others happy.

Gender Association: Used mostly for girls

Popularity and Trend: #46 (#44 in 2000)

Risk of Misspelling: Average

Risk of Mispronunciation: Low

Famous Namesakes: Actress Allison Munn; actress Allison Janney; singer Alison Moorer; musician Allison Kraus

Common Nicknames: Ali, Allie, Al

Common Variations: Alison, Alyson

Consider This: Although the traditional spelling of this name is "Alison," Allison is far more popular and has ranked in the Top 50 since the '80s.

Alma ★★★★

(Arabic) learned. (Latin) soul.

First Impression: Alma means "soul" in Latin, and people think Alma is a charitable and soulful Latina who's spiritually and emotionally strong.

Gender Association: Used for girls

Popularity and Trend: #616 (#491 in 2000)

Risk of Misspelling: Fairly low

Risk of Mispronunciation: Fairly low

Famous Namesakes: Prophet Alma the Younger

Common Nicknames: None

Common Variations: None

Consider This: Alma is neither popular nor versatile, but it has a very positive image.

Alyson ★★★

(English) a form of Alison.

First Impression: Some say Alyson is angelic and kindhearted, but others say she's controlling and spoiled.

Gender Association: Used for girls

Popularity and Trend: #471 (#461 in 2000)

Risk of Misspelling: Average

Risk of Mispronunciation: Low

Famous Namesakes: Actress Alyson Hannigan; actress Allison Munn; actress Allison Janney; singer Allison Moorer; musician Allison Kraus

Common Nicknames: Ali

Common Variations: Alison, Allison

Consider This: There's a good chance people will spell this name as "Alison" or "Allison," which are much more popular.

Alyssa ★★★★

(Greek) rational.

First Impression: Like Alyssa Milano, Alyssa is pictured as a beautiful, dainty woman with dark features and so much confidence, she borders on being arrogant and temperamental.

Gender Association: Used for girls

Popularity and Trend: #19 (#12 in 2000)

Risk of Misspelling: Fairly low

Risk of Mispronunciation: Low

Famous Namesakes: Actress Alyssa Milano

Common Nicknames: Lyssa

Common Variations: Alissa, Allysa

Consider This: Alyssa has been a Top 20 name since 1997, though it may be cooling off.

Amanda ★★★★

(Latin) lovable.

First Impression: People think Amanda will smile to your face, but watch out when you turn your back.

Gender Association: Used mostly for girls

Popularity and Trend: #102 (#32 in 2000)

Risk of Misspelling: Low

Risk of Mispronunciation: Low

Famous Namesakes: Swimmer Amanda Beard; actress Amanda Peet; actress Amanda Bynes; gymnast Amanda Borden; actress Amanda Plummer

Common Nicknames: Manda, Mandy

Common Variations: Amanada

Consider This: Amanda was a Top 10 name throughout the '80s and '90s, but it's falling steadily now.

Amaya ★★★

(Japanese) night rain.

First Impression: Amaya is regarded as a caring sweetheart who's dreamy and peaceful.

Gender Association: Used for girls

Popularity and Trend: #215 (#196 in 2000)

Risk of Misspelling: Average

Risk of Mispronunciation: Average

Famous Namesakes: Journalist Amaya Brecher

Common Nicknames: None

Common Variations: None

Consider This: This unique Japanese name seemingly came out of nowhere to become a Top 200 name in 2000, and it's held steady ever since. Pronunciation and spelling may be a little tricky, though.

Amber ★★★★★

(French) amber.

First Impression: Amber is considered a soft-spoken and shy girl who's well liked by everyone.

Gender Association: Used mostly for girls
Popularity and Trend: #136 (#46 in 2000)
Risk of Misspelling: Low
Risk of Mispronunciation: Low
Famous Namesakes: Actress Amber Tamblyn; actress Amber Benson; model Amber Valletta
Common Nicknames: Amberlee
Common Variations: Ambar, Ambyr
Consider This: Amber has been a popular name for over thirty years, but now its popularity may be descending.

Amelia ★★★★★

(German) hardworking. (Latin) a form of Emily.
First Impression: People say Amelia is intelligent, independent, successful, and very classy— like aviator Amelia Earhart.
Gender Association: Used for girls
Popularity and Trend: #82 (#207 in 2000)
Risk of Misspelling: Fairly low
Risk of Mispronunciation: Fairly low
Famous Namesakes: Aviator Amelia Earhart; children's book character Amelia Bedelia; beauty queen Amelia Vega
Common Nicknames: Melia, Millie
Common Variations: Amalia, Amilia
Consider This: People still associate Amelia Earhart with this strong, classic name that's becoming quite popular again.

Amy ★★★★

(Latin) beloved.
First Impression: Amy is seen as a friendly and perky gal who loves to join in the fun.
Gender Association: Used for girls
Popularity and Trend: #128 (#107 in 2000)
Risk of Misspelling: Fairly low
Risk of Mispronunciation: Low
Famous Namesakes: Actress Amy Irving; singer Amy Grant; singer Amy Winehouse; actress Amy Adams; actress Amy Sedaris; singer Aimee Mann; actress Amy Brennemen; comedian Amy Poehler; novelist Amy Tan
Common Nicknames: None
Common Variations: Aimee
Consider This: Amy was the second most popular name of the '70s, and it shows: It has many famous namesakes.

Ana ★★★★

(Hawaiian, Spanish) a form of Hannah.
First Impression: Ana calls to mind a woman who's pretty, happy, compassionate, and full of life.
Gender Association: Used for girls
Popularity and Trend: #143 (#136 in 2000)
Risk of Misspelling: Average
Risk of Mispronunciation: Average
Famous Namesakes: Comedian Ana Gasteyer; singer Ana Johnsson; poet Ana Castillo
Common Nicknames: None
Common Variations: Anna
Consider This: Ana has become a fairly popular name, but pronunciation ("Is it 'ANN-ah' or 'AHN-ah?'") and spelling ("One *n* or two?") may raise questions.

Anais ★

(Hebrew) gracious.
First Impression: People envision Anais as snobby, judgmental, and the center of the arty, cool crowd.
Gender Association: Used for girls
Popularity and Trend: #869 (#995 in 2003)
Risk of Misspelling: Fairly high
Risk of Mispronunciation: Fairly high
Famous Namesakes: Writer Anaïs Nin
Common Nicknames: None
Common Variations: None
Consider This: Some people may be familiar with Anais because of writer Anaïs Nin, but most will have trouble spelling and pronouncing it.

Anastasia ★★★★

(Greek) resurrection.
First Impression: Anastasia is considered as kind as she is pretty.
Gender Association: Used for girls
Popularity and Trend: #288 (#309 in 2000)
Risk of Misspelling: Average

Risk of Mispronunciation: Fairly high

Famous Namesakes: Grand duchess Anastasia of Russia; singer Anastacia

Common Nicknames: Ana, Stacy, Stacia

Common Variations: Anastacia, Nastasia

Consider This: Anastasia may seem too elaborate for some parents, but it has several nicknaming options. Pronunciation may be a problem with "ann-ah-STAY-zhah," "ann-ah-STAH-shah," and "ann-ah-STAH-zee-ah" as options.

Andrea ★★★★

(Greek) strong; courageous.

First Impression: Andrea comes across as a confident and intelligent achiever.

Gender Association: Used mostly for girls

Popularity and Trend: #59 (#55 in 2000)

Risk of Misspelling: Fairly low

Risk of Mispronunciation: Fairly low

Famous Namesakes: Journalist Andrea Mitchell; character Andrea Zuckerman (*Beverly Hills, 90210*); comedian Andrea Martin; actress Andrea Thompson; singer Andrea Corr

Common Nicknames: Andee

Common Variations: Andria, Andreana

Consider This: Most people pronounce this name "ANN-dree-ah," so if you choose the rarer forms of "AHN-dree-ah" or "ahn-DREY-

ah," your daughter will need to correct people.

Andreana ★★

(Greek) a form of Andrea.

First Impression: People think Andreana is a gregarious and witty woman with a fun smile, but she has a mean, self-centered side.

Gender Association: Used for girls

Popularity and Trend: Never been ranked in Top 1000

Risk of Misspelling: Fairly high

Risk of Mispronunciation: Fairly high

Famous Namesakes: None

Common Nicknames: Andee

Common Variations: Andreanna

Consider This: This variation of Andrea is more unique, but also more difficult to spell and pronounce.

Anezka ★★★

(Czech) a form of Hannah.

First Impression: Anezka is pictured as beautiful and worldly inside and out.

Gender Association: Used for girls

Popularity and Trend: Never been ranked in Top 1000

Risk of Misspelling: Fairly high

Risk of Mispronunciation: Fairly high

Famous Namesakes: None

Common Nicknames: None

Common Variations: None

Consider This: People like this Czech name, though they may have a hard time identifying its origin— let alone pronouncing it.

Angela ★★★★★

(Greek) angel; messenger.

First Impression: People see Angela as a kind and polite woman who surprises people with her street smarts and straightforward honesty.

Gender Association: Used for girls

Popularity and Trend: #114 (#79 in 2000)

Risk of Misspelling: Low

Risk of Mispronunciation: Low

Famous Namesakes: Actress Angela Lansbury; actress Angela Bassett; chancellor Angela Merkel; activist Angela Davis

Common Nicknames: Angie, Angel

Common Variations: Angelica, Angelina, Angeline, Angelique

Consider This: Angela is a very versatile name that has ranked in the Top 200 since the '40s.

Angelica ★★★

(Greek) a form of Angela.

First Impression: Many picture Angelica as a hurtful, conniving girl who's spoiled, bratty, and used to things going her way.

Gender Association: Used for girls

Popularity and Trend: #208 (#138 in 2000)

Risk of Misspelling: Fairly low

Risk of Mispronunciation: Low

Famous Namesakes: Actress Angelica Huston; character Angelica Pickles (*Rugrats*)

Common Nicknames: Angelic, Angie, Angel

Common Variations: Anjelica

Consider This: Angelina and Angela are similar names with much more positive first impressions than Angelica.

Angelina ★★★★★

(Russian) a form of Angela.

First Impression: People see Angelina as an angelic, sympathetic, and giving woman who can also be fiery and spontaneous, like actress Angelina Jolie.

Gender Association: Used for girls

Popularity and Trend: #48 (#157 in 2000)

Risk of Misspelling: Low

Risk of Mispronunciation: Low

Famous Namesakes: Actress Angelina Jolie; abolitionist Angelina Grimke; character Angelina Johnson (*Harry Potter* series)

Common Nicknames: Gina, Angie, Angel

Common Variations: None

Consider This: This name's image is linked very closely to Angelina Jolie's. Most people tend to view her positively, but if you don't, you should probably pick another name.

Angelique ★★★

(French) a form of Angela.

First Impression: Many people think Angelique is prissy, mean, and pampered, but she may be delicate, sweet, and gentle.

Gender Association: Used for girls

Popularity and Trend: #693 (#466 in 2000)

Risk of Misspelling: Average

Risk of Mispronunciation: Average

Famous Namesakes: Singer Angelique Kidjo

Common Nicknames: Angie, Angel

Common Variations: None

Consider This: This French form of Angela could give some spelling trouble.

Angie ★★★★

(Greek) a familiar form of Angela.

First Impression: Angie is seen as a funny, happy-go-lucky gal who loves to gossip.

Gender Association: Used for girls

Popularity and Trend: #389 (#499 in 2000)

Risk of Misspelling: Low

Risk of Mispronunciation: Low

Famous Namesakes: Actress Angie Dickinson; actress Angie Harmon; model Angie Everheart; singer Angie Stone; rapper Angie Martinez

Common Nicknames: None

Common Variations: None

Consider This: There are a lot of famous Angies, though some may find it too informal as a given name.

Anika ★★★

(Czech) a form of Anna.

First Impression: People see Anika as a free spirit who's expressive, artistic, and sensitive.

Gender Association: Used for girls

Popularity and Trend: #485 (#625 in 2000)

Risk of Misspelling: Average

Risk of Mispronunciation: Fairly high

Famous Namesakes: Actress Anika Noni Rose

Common Nicknames: None

Common Variations: Anica

Consider This: Although Anika looks like Annika, some people may not realize it's pronounced "ah-NEE-kah."

Anita ★★★★

(Spanish) a form of Ann, Anna.

First Impression: Anita is regarded as a warm and friendly woman who's often brave with her sharp tongue.

Gender Association: Used for girls

Popularity and Trend: Last ranked in the Top 1000 in the 1980s

Risk of Misspelling: Fairly low

Risk of Mispronunciation: Low

Famous Namesakes: Singer Anita Bryant; singer Anita Baker; character Anita (*West Side Story*); actress Anita Ekberg

Common Nicknames: Nita

Common Variations: Aneta

Consider This: Anita hasn't been a popular name since the '80s, and all of the famous namesakes are older women.

Ann ★★★★

(English) gracious.

First Impression: To many people, Ann carries herself with well-mannered poise.

Gender Association: Used for girls

Popularity and Trend: #731 (#493 in 2000)

Risk of Misspelling: Average

Risk of Mispronunciation: Low

Famous Namesakes: Columnist Ann Landers; actress Ann-Margaret; singer Anne Murray; writer Ann Coulter; politician Ann Richards; diarist Anne Frank; comedian Anne Meara; actress Ann Bancroft; author Anne Rice

Common Nicknames: Annie

Common Variations: Anne

Consider This: While Anna is still very popular, both Ann's and Anne's popularity are spiraling downward. Most famous Anns are middle aged.

Anna ★★★★★

(German, Italian, Czech, Swedish) gracious.

First Impression: In most people's minds, Anna has so much to offer—personality, brains, looks, and more.

Gender Association: Used for girls

Popularity and Trend: #23 (#22 in 2000)

Risk of Misspelling: Fairly low

Risk of Mispronunciation: Fairly low

Famous Namesakes: Actress Anna Paquin; model Anna Nicole Smith; tennis player Anna Kournikova; columnist Anna Quindlin; actress Anna Faris; designer Anna Sui; editor Anna Wintour

Common Nicknames: Ann, Annie

Common Variations: Ana, Anya

Consider This: Anna is a classic, versatile name that has left the Top 100 only once in over a hundred years.

Annette ★★★

(French) a form of Ann.

First Impression: Annette is pictured as the high-school band majorette who's kindhearted but a little geeky.

Gender Association: Used for girls

Popularity and Trend: #881 (#744 in 2000)

Risk of Misspelling: Fairly low

Risk of Mispronunciation: Fairly low

Famous Namesakes: Actress Annette Bening; actress Annette Funicello

Common Nicknames: Nettie

Common Variations: None

Consider This: Popular from the '40s to the '60s, Annette is likely to slip off the Top 1000 list soon.

Annie ★★★★

(English) a form of Ann.

First Impression: Like Annie "Little Sure Shot" Oakley, Annie is imagined to be spunky, brave, and joyful.

Gender Association: Used for girls

Popularity and Trend: #398 (#306 in 2000)

Risk of Misspelling: Low

Risk of Mispronunciation: Low

Famous Namesakes: Comic strip character Little Orphan Annie; cowgirl Annie Oakley; singer Annie Lennox; photographer Annie Leibovitz; writer Annie Proulx

Common Nicknames: None

Common Variations: None

Consider This: Annie is a more casual and youthful form of Ann, though well-respected women like Annie Leibovitz and Annie Proulx use it professionally.

Annika ★★★

(Russian) a form of Ann. (Swedish) a form of Anneka.

First Impression: Annika Sörenstam affects this name's image, making people think of Annika as a competitive and athletic woman with a Scandinavian appearance.

Gender Association: Used for girls

Popularity and Trend: #335 (#446 in 2000)

Risk of Misspelling: Average

Risk of Mispronunciation: Average

Famous Namesakes: Golfer Annika Sörenstam; character Annika Hansen (*Star Trek: Voyager*)

Common Nicknames: Annik

Common Variations: Anika

Consider This: Annika may fit well with a Scandinavian or Russian surname. Pronunciation will be divided between "ANN-eh-kah" and "AHN-eh-kah."

Antoinette ★★★

(French) a form of Antonia.

First Impression: People see Antoinette as regal, classy, and wealthy, but also snobby, pompous, and prissy.

Gender Association: Used for girls

Popularity and Trend: Last ranked in the Top 1000 in the 1980s

Risk of Misspelling: Average

Risk of Mispronunciation: Average

Famous Namesakes: Queen Marie Antoinette; minister Antoinette Blackwell

Common Nicknames: Nettie, Toinette, Toni, Ann

Common Variations: Antonette

Consider This: With famous namesake Marie Antoinette, this name may seem lofty, but there are plenty of friendly nicknames to use.

Antonia ★★★

(Greek) flourishing. (Latin) praiseworthy.

First Impression: Antonia is pictured as a natural leader who's confident and commanding.

Gender Association: Used mostly for girls

Popularity and Trend: Last ranked in the Top 1000 in the 1980s

Risk of Misspelling: Fairly low

Risk of Mispronunciation: Fairly high

Famous Namesakes: Poet Antonia Byatt; character Antonia Shimerda (*My Antonia*); author Antonia Fraser; film director Antonia Bird

Common Nicknames: Toni

Common Variations: Antonina, Antoinette

Consider This: Antonia may be pronounced "ann-toh-NEE-ah" by some and "ann-TOH-nee-ah" by others.

Anya ★★★★

(Russian) a form of Anna.

First Impression: People see Anya as a strong character who believes in herself.

Gender Association: Used for girls

Popularity and Trend: #405 (#586 in 2000)

Risk of Misspelling: Fairly low

Risk of Mispronunciation: Fairly low

Famous Namesakes: Character Anya (*Buffy the Vampire Slayer*)

Common Nicknames: None

Common Variations: Anja

Consider This: This Russian name is rising in popularity, but it may not work with every surname. Pronunciation could pose a slight challenge for those who don't realize it's "AHN-yah" instead of "ANN-yah."

Aolani ★★

(Hawaiian) heavenly cloud.

First Impression: Aolani is said to be a soft-spoken Hawaiian woman who's warm, peaceful, and fond of golden sunsets viewed from the beach.

Gender Association: Used for girls

Popularity and Trend: Never been ranked in Top 1000

Risk of Misspelling: Fairly high

Risk of Mispronunciation: Fairly high

Famous Namesakes: None

Common Nicknames: None

Common Variations: None

Consider This: This Hawaiian name will be tricky for the average person to spell and pronounce.

April ★★★★

(Latin) opening.

First Impression: April is considered soft and sweet, but still outgoing and popular.

Gender Association: Used for girls

Popularity and Trend: #319 (#214 in 2000)

Risk of Misspelling: Low

Risk of Mispronunciation: Low

Famous Namesakes: Character April O'Neil (*Teenage Mutant Ninja Turtles*); actress April Grace

Common Nicknames: None

Common Variations: Avril

Consider This: April had its heyday in the '70s and '80s, but now it's falling fast.

Aretha ★★★★
(Greek) virtuous.

First Impression: Thanks to Aretha Franklin, Aretha is seen as a strong, gifted, and loud African American singer.

Gender Association: Used for girls

Popularity and Trend: Last ranked in the Top 1000 in the 1970s

Risk of Misspelling: Low

Risk of Mispronunciation: Low

Famous Namesakes: Singer Aretha Franklin

Common Nicknames: Retha

Common Variations: Oretha

Consider This: There's no separating this name's image from Aretha Franklin's.

Aria ★★★
(Hebrew) a form of Ariel.

First Impression: People think Aria is a talented and intelligent woman who's creative, charming, and a little eccentric.

Gender Association: Used mostly for girls

Popularity and Trend: #661 (#957 in 2000)

Risk of Misspelling: Fairly low

Risk of Mispronunciation: Fairly low

Famous Namesakes: None

Common Nicknames: None

Common Variations: Arya, Ariah

Consider This: This musical name is unique, but definitely on the rise.

Ariana ★★★
(Greek) holy.

First Impression: Ariana may be independent and self-centered, or she may be compassionate and sensitive.

Gender Association: Used for girls

Popularity and Trend: #78 (#109 in 2000)

Risk of Misspelling: Average

Risk of Mispronunciation: Fairly high

Famous Namesakes: Columnist Arianna Huffington

Common Nicknames: Ari

Common Variations: Arianna, Arianne

Consider This: There are several pronunciation combinations because "Ari-" can be said "AIR-ee" or "AR-ee" and "-ana" can be "ANN-ah" or "AHN-ah."

Ariel ★★★★
(Hebrew) lioness of God.

First Impression: Most people think of Ariel as an innocent (perhaps naïve) princess who often has her head in the clouds, like a certain little mermaid.

Gender Association: Used mostly for girls

Popularity and Trend: #202 (#184 in 2000)

Risk of Misspelling: Fairly low

Risk of Mispronunciation: Low

Famous Namesakes: Character Ariel (*The Tempest*); character Princess Ariel (*The Little Mermaid*)

Common Nicknames: Ari

Common Variations: Arial, Ariele

Consider This: Most Americans think of this as a girls' name because of *The Little Mermaid*, but it is also used for Jewish boys.

Arlene ★★★
(Irish) pledge.

First Impression: Arlene's friends always look to her for advice—but not when it comes to fashion.

Gender Association: Used for girls

Popularity and Trend: Last ranked in the Top 1000 in the 1980s

Risk of Misspelling: Fairly low

Risk of Mispronunciation: Low

Famous Namesakes: Actress Arlene Dahl; television personality Arlene Francis

Common Nicknames: None

Common Variations: Arleen, Arlena

Consider This: Arlene hasn't been a Top 1000 name since the '80s, and that shows in its somewhat frumpy image.

Ashley ★★★★
(English) ash-tree meadow.

First Impression: Most people think of Ashley as a bubbly and innocent cheerleader, but others say she's a picky and snobby rich girl.

Gender Association: Used mostly for girls

Popularity and Trend: #12 (#4 in 2000)

Risk of Misspelling: Fairly low

Risk of Mispronunciation: Low

Famous Namesakes: Actress Ashley Olsen; singer Ashlee Simpson; actress Ashley Judd; singer Ashley Tisdale

Common Nicknames: Ash, Lee

Common Variations: Ashlee, Ashleigh

Consider This: Although not quite as popular as it was a few years ago, Ashley is still popular enough that your daughter will likely share the name with a classmate.

Ashlyn ★★★★★

(English) ash-tree pool. (Irish) vision, dream.

First Impression: Ashlyn is imagined to be a "good girl" who's tender, gracious, and a little naïve.

Gender Association: Used for girls

Popularity and Trend: #140 (#178 in 2000)

Risk of Misspelling: Fairly low

Risk of Mispronunciation: Low

Famous Namesakes: None

Common Nicknames: Ash

Common Variations: Aislynn, Ashlin

Consider This: Ashlyn is more unique than similar-sounding Ashley, but it's still popular.

Asia ★★★★

(Greek) resurrection. (English) eastern sunrise. (Swahili) a form of Aisha.

First Impression: In appearance and personality, Asia is seen as an exotic and mysterious woman.

Gender Association: Used for girls

Popularity and Trend: #332 (#220 in 2000)

Risk of Misspelling: Low

Risk of Mispronunciation: Low

Famous Namesakes: Actress Asia Argento

Common Nicknames: None

Common Variations: Asiah

Consider This: Place names are hit-or-miss, but this place name seems to be a hit.

Astra ★★★

(Greek) star.

First Impression: Astra is perceived as a free-spirited flirt, a warm mother, or a mysterious introvert.

Gender Association: Used for girls

Popularity and Trend: Never been ranked in Top 1000

Risk of Misspelling: Fairly low

Risk of Mispronunciation: Fairly low

Famous Namesakes: Comic book character Astra; character Princess Astra (Dr. Who)

Common Nicknames: None

Common Variations: Aster

Consider This: People don't know what to think about this unusual name, but they are generally positive about it.

Athena ★★★★

(Greek) wise.

First Impression: Like a goddess, Athena is thought to be a brave heroine with a statuesque physique.

Gender Association: Used for girls

Popularity and Trend: #504 (#528 in 2000)

Risk of Misspelling: Fairly low

Risk of Mispronunciation: Low

Famous Namesakes: Mythological figure Athena; heiress Athina Onassis de Miranda

Common Nicknames: None

Common Variations: Athina

Consider This: This is a very strong name, which may make it hard for your daughter if she turns out to be quiet or shy. It is also very Greek.

Aubrey ★★★★

(German) noble; bearlike. (French) blond ruler; elf ruler.

First Impression: People think Aubrey may be shy or flirty, but either way, she's a loving soul.

Gender Association: Used mostly for girls

Popularity and Trend: #92 (#223 in 2000)

Risk of Misspelling: Fairly low

Risk of Mispronunciation: Low

Famous Namesakes: Singer Aubrey O'Day; artist Aubrey Beardsley

Common Nicknames: None

Common Variations: Aubree, Avery

Consider This: Aubrey was mostly considered a boys' name until the '80s. Now it's used almost exclusively for girls, ranking in the Top 100.

Audra ★★★

(French) a form of Audrey.

First Impression: Audra may be considered a ritzy eccentric who's stuck-up and rude, or she's a good-natured soul who loves both kids and animals.

Gender Association: Used for girls

Popularity and Trend: Last ranked in the Top 1000 in the 1990s

Risk of Misspelling: Low

Risk of Mispronunciation: Low

Famous Namesakes: Actress Audra Lindley; actress Audra McDonald

Common Nicknames: None

Common Variations: None

Consider This: This French form of Audrey has never been very popular, and it has a mixed first impression.

Audrey ★★★★★

(English) noble strength.

First Impression: Audrey makes people think of an elegant, graceful, and beautiful woman like Audrey Hepburn.

Gender Association: Used mostly for girls

Popularity and Trend: #68 (#115 in 2000)

Risk of Misspelling: Low

Risk of Mispronunciation: Low

Famous Namesakes: Actress Audrey Hepburn; actress Audrey Tautou

Common Nicknames: Audey

Common Variations: Audra, Audree

Consider This: This classic, elegant name has never been unpopular, but it's having a comeback of sorts.

Aurora ★★★★

(Latin) dawn.

First Impression: People say Aurora has a strong sense of self and a stronger presence.

Gender Association: Used for girls

Popularity and Trend: #312 (#488 in 2000)

Risk of Misspelling: Fairly low

Risk of Mispronunciation: Fairly low

Famous Namesakes: Goddess Aurora; character Princess Aurora (*Sleeping Beauty*)

Common Nicknames: Rori

Common Variations: None

Consider This: Aurora means "dawn," and just as the sun keeps rising at dawn, this name keeps rising in popularity.

Autumn ★★★★

(Latin) autumn.

First Impression: Some say Autumn is cheerful and talkative, while others say she's uppity and reserved.

Gender Association: Used for girls

Popularity and Trend: #95 (#77 in 2000)

Risk of Misspelling: Low

Risk of Mispronunciation: Low

Famous Namesakes: Actress Autumn Reeser

Common Nicknames: None

Common Variations: Autum

Consider This: As season names go, Autumn is more popular than Summer and Winter.

Ava ★★★★

(Greek) a form of Eva.

First Impression: Much like silver-screen siren Ava Gardner, Ava is seen as a bombshell who comes across as confident and glamorous.

Gender Association: Used for girls

Popularity and Trend: #5 (#180 in 2000)

Risk of Misspelling: Fairly low

Risk of Mispronunciation: Fairly low

Famous Namesakes: Actress Ava Gardner; country singer Ava Barber

Common Nicknames: None

Common Variations: Eva

Consider This: This glamorous name has skyrocketed in popularity over the past few years.

Avril ★★★

(French) a form of April.

First Impression: Perhaps thinking of pop sensation Avril Lavigne, people say Avril is a wild and opinionated rock star with lots of creativity and spunk.

Gender Association: Used for girls

Popularity and Trend: Never been ranked in Top 1000

Risk of Misspelling: Average

Risk of Mispronunciation: Average

Famous Namesakes: Singer Avril Lavigne

Common Nicknames: None
Common Variations: April
Consider This: Most people will know this French form of April thanks to Avril Lavigne, but it's still not a Top 1000 name.

Baba ★
(African) born on Thursday.
First Impression: Folks believe Baba may be the "black sheep" of her family—a heavyset simpleton who's immature and shy.
Gender Association: Used for girls
Popularity and Trend: Never been ranked in Top 1000
Risk of Misspelling: Average
Risk of Mispronunciation: Average
Famous Namesakes: Character Ali Baba (*The Book of One Thousand and One Nights*)
Common Nicknames: None
Common Variations: None
Consider This: Too many people associate this African name with "Baa, Baa, Black Sheep" for it to be a smart choice.

Babette ★★★
(French, German) a form of Barbara.
First Impression: People think Babette is charismatic, confident, and stylish.
Gender Association: Used for girls
Popularity and Trend: Last ranked in the Top 1000 in the 1960s
Risk of Misspelling: Low
Risk of Mispronunciation: Low

Famous Namesakes: Character Babette (*Babette's Feast*)
Common Nicknames: Babs, Bette
Common Variations: None
Consider This: Once a nickname for Barbara, Babette makes a decent given name by itself.

Bailey ★★★
(English) bailiff.
First Impression: Most people picture Bailey as playful, happy, and charming. Others see her as cranky and stubborn.
Gender Association: Used mostly for girls
Popularity and Trend: #112 (#68 in 2000)
Risk of Misspelling: Fairly low
Risk of Mispronunciation: Low
Famous Namesakes: Character Miranda Bailey (*Grey's Anatomy*); singer Corinne Bailey Rae
Common Nicknames: None
Common Variations: Baylee, Bayley, Bailee
Consider This: This unisex name is used more often for girls than boys, but it has a young feel either way.

Baka ★★★
(Hindi) crane.
First Impression: Baka is thought to be a sweet, kind foreigner who's pudgy but strong.
Gender Association: Used for girls

Popularity and Trend: Never been ranked in Top 1000
Risk of Misspelling: Average
Risk of Mispronunciation: Average
Famous Namesakes: Deity Baka Brahma
Common Nicknames: None
Common Variations: None
Consider This: Baka is a Hindi name that may sound unusual with some surnames.

Bambi ★★
(Italian) child.
First Impression: Disney's Bambi was an innocent fawn, but people think a woman with this name is probably far from innocent.
Gender Association: Used for girls
Popularity and Trend: Last ranked in the Top 1000 in the 1980s
Risk of Misspelling: Low
Risk of Mispronunciation: Low
Famous Namesakes: Film character Bambi
Common Nicknames: None
Common Variations: None
Consider This: If your daughter's name is Bambi, people will think she's a deer or a stripper.

Barbara ★★★
(Latin) stranger, foreigner.
First Impression: Barbara is pictured as witty, but she may also be grouchy or gullible.
Gender Association: Used for girls

Popularity and Trend: #561 (#521 in 2000)

Risk of Misspelling: Fairly low

Risk of Mispronunciation: Fairly low

Famous Namesakes: Journalist Barbara Walters; singer Barbra Streisand; actress Barbara Stanwyck; singer Barbara Mandrell; author Barbara Kingsolver; senator Barbara Boxer; first lady Barbara Bush; actress Barbara Hershey

Common Nicknames: Babe, Babette, Babs, Barb, Barbie, Bobbi, Bebe

Common Variations: Barbra

Consider This: The most famous Barbaras are older women, but the name has plenty of younger-sounding nicknames. Keep in mind that some people pronounce this with three syllables and others pronounce it with two.

Barbie ★★

(American) a familiar form of Barbara.

First Impression: People think Barbie has a reputation for being a ditzy drama queen who's as conceited, attention starved, and unlikable as she is dumb.

Gender Association: Used for girls

Popularity and Trend: Last ranked in the Top 1000 in the 1960s

Risk of Misspelling: Low

Risk of Mispronunciation: Low

Famous Namesakes: Famous doll Barbie; centerfold Barbie Benton

Common Nicknames: None

Common Variations: None

Consider This: It's almost impossible to separate this name from the famous doll, which a lot of people view negatively.

Beatrice ★★★

(Latin) blessed; happy; bringer of joy.

First Impression: Beatrice is regarded as old, matronly, and plump, as well as grouchy and rude.

Gender Association: Used for girls

Popularity and Trend: #966 (#971 in 2000)

Risk of Misspelling: Fairly low

Risk of Mispronunciation: Low

Famous Namesakes: Actress Beatrice Arthur; character Beatrice (*Much Ado about Nothing*); character Beatrice Portinari (*The Divine Comedy*); actress Beatrice Strait; princess Beatrice of York

Common Nicknames: Bea, Bee, Trixie, Tricia

Common Variations: Beatris, Beatriz

Consider This: Although Beatrice is perceived as an old-lady name, Paul McCartney recently named his daughter Beatrice.

Becca ★★★

(Hebrew) a short form of Rebecca.

First Impression: Becca is pictured as sunny, sweet, demure, and honest.

Gender Association: Used for girls

Popularity and Trend: Never been ranked in Top 1000

Risk of Misspelling: Fairly low

Risk of Mispronunciation: Low

Famous Namesakes: None

Common Nicknames: None

Common Variations: Becka

Consider This: Despite its wonderful image, this nickname for Rebecca has never been ranked in the Top 1000.

Becky ★★★

(American) a familiar form of Rebecca.

First Impression: Positively perky and popular is how folks picture Becky.

Gender Association: Used for girls

Popularity and Trend: Last ranked in the Top 1000 in the 1990s

Risk of Misspelling: Low

Risk of Mispronunciation: Low

Famous Namesakes: Character Becky Sharp (*Vanity Fair*); character Becky Thatcher (*The Adventures of Tom Sawyer*); actress Becky Ann Baker; character Becky Conner (*Roseanne*)

Common Nicknames: None

Common Variations: None

Consider This: Although it may be too informal as a given name, this nickname belongs to two famous literary characters: Becky Sharp (*Vanity Fair*) and Becky Thatcher (*The Adventures of Tom Sawyer*).

Belinda ★★★

(Spanish) beautiful.

First Impression: People see Belinda as a gentle and sensitive girl with unattractive looks.

Gender Association: Used for girls

Popularity and Trend: #809 (#730 in 2005)

Risk of Misspelling: Low

Risk of Mispronunciation: Low

Famous Namesakes: Singer Belinda Carlisle

Common Nicknames: Belle

Common Variations: Blinda

Consider This: It's ironic that a name meaning "beautiful" makes people think of someone so physically unattractive.

Bella ★★★★★

(Latin) beautiful.

First Impression: To many, Bella's personality is as beautiful as her name suggests.

Gender Association: Used for girls

Popularity and Trend: #181 (#748 in 2000)

Risk of Misspelling: Low

Risk of Mispronunciation: Low

Famous Namesakes: Feminist Bella Abzug

Common Nicknames: Belle

Common Variations: None

Consider This: Bella hadn't been ranked for eighty years when it reemerged in 2000 at #748. It

has shot up from there and is likely to get even more popular.

Belle ★★★★

(French) beautiful.

First Impression: Belle is considered a sweet, angelic woman who's sensitive, affectionate, and caring.

Gender Association: Used for girls

Popularity and Trend: Last ranked in the Top 1000 in the 1930s

Risk of Misspelling: Fairly low

Risk of Mispronunciation: Low

Famous Namesakes: Character Belle (*Beauty and the Beast*); character Belle Black (*Days of Our Lives*)

Common Nicknames: Billie

Common Variations: Bel

Consider This: Belle hasn't been ranked since the '30s, but it sounds a lot like Bella, a similar name that has suddenly become popular. People will know Belle from *Beauty and the Beast*.

Benita ★★★

(Spanish) a form of Benedicta.

First Impression: Benita is seen as diligent and serious at times, and at other times she's cheerful and playful.

Gender Association: Used for girls

Popularity and Trend: Last ranked in the Top 1000 in the 1970s

Risk of Misspelling: Fairly low

Risk of Mispronunciation: Fairly low

Famous Namesakes: Athlete Benita Fitzgerald Mosley; singer Benita Hill; novelist Benita Brown

Common Nicknames: Nita

Common Variations: None

Consider This: This Spanish name may sound strange with non-Latino surnames.

Berkley ★★★

(Scottish, English) birch-tree meadow.

First Impression: Berkley is imagined to be a liberal, hippie activist who's well educated and strong-minded.

Gender Association: Used about equally for girls and boys

Popularity and Trend: Never been ranked in Top 1000

Risk of Misspelling: Average

Risk of Mispronunciation: Low

Famous Namesakes: Choreographer Busby Berkeley

Common Nicknames: None

Common Variations: Berkeley

Consider This: This unisex name is strongly associated with its namesake, the very liberal University of California, Berkeley.

Bernadette ★★★

(French) a form of Bernadine.

First Impression: Bernadette is thought to be a kind, honest, and hardworking older woman.

Gender Association: Used for girls

Popularity and Trend: Last ranked in the Top 1000 in the 1990s

Risk of Misspelling: Low

Risk of Mispronunciation: Low

Famous Namesakes: Actress Bernadette Peters
Common Nicknames: Berni
Common Variations: Nadette
Consider This: Bernadette isn't as versatile as Bernice, which has a similar sound.

Bernice ★★★★
(Greek) bringer of victory.
First Impression: People see Bernice as an older homemaker who's thought to be a great cook.
Gender Association: Used for girls
Popularity and Trend: Last ranked in the Top 1000 in the 1980s
Risk of Misspelling: Low
Risk of Mispronunciation: Low
Famous Namesakes: Songwriter Bernice Williams
Common Nicknames: Berni, Berry, Bunny
Common Variations: Vernice
Consider This: Bernice may be old-fashioned, but it has a surprising number of nicknames.

Bertha ★★
(German) bright; illustrious; brilliant ruler.
First Impression: Bertha is described first and foremost as obese, but she's also thought to be unfriendly, rude, and slow.
Gender Association: Used for girls
Popularity and Trend: Last ranked in the Top 1000 in the 1980s
Risk of Misspelling: Low

Risk of Mispronunciation: Low
Famous Namesakes: Tennis player Bertha Townsend
Common Nicknames: Birdie
Common Variations: Berta
Consider This: Bertha is one of the most negatively received names out there.

Bess ★★★
(Hebrew) a short form of Bessie.
First Impression: Bess is viewed as a motherly, caring woman with laughing eyes and a wide smile.
Gender Association: Used for girls
Popularity and Trend: Last ranked in the Top 1000 in the 1920s
Risk of Misspelling: Low
Risk of Mispronunciation: Low
Famous Namesakes: First lady Bess Wallace Truman; character Bess (*Porgy & Bess*); actress Bess Armstrong
Common Nicknames: None
Common Variations: None
Consider This: Bess hasn't been a popular name since the '20s, which may give it a dated feel.

Beth ★★★★
(Hebrew, Aramaic) house of God. A form of Bethany, Elizabeth.
First Impression: Beth is thought to be a kind and sensitive young woman who's meek and shy.
Gender Association: Used for girls
Popularity and Trend: Last ranked in the Top 1000 in the 1990s

Risk of Misspelling: Low
Risk of Mispronunciation: Low
Famous Namesakes: Character Beth March (*Little Women*); playwright Beth Henley; comedian Beth Littleford
Common Nicknames: None
Common Variations: None
Consider This: Both Beth and Bethany make very quiet first impressions.

Bethany ★★★★
(Aramaic) house of figs.
First Impression: Bethany is typically imagined to be a quiet girl, but others believe she has some pep.
Gender Association: Used for girls
Popularity and Trend: #244 (#151 in 2000)
Risk of Misspelling: Low
Risk of Mispronunciation: Low
Famous Namesakes: Surfer Bethany Hamilton; actress Bethany Joy Lenz
Common Nicknames: Beth
Common Variations: Bethani
Consider This: Bethany is a biblical place name, so some people may see Bethany as a religious girl.

Betsy ★★★★
(American) a familiar form of Elizabeth.
First Impression: People see Betsy as wacky, silly, wild, and loud.
Gender Association: Used for girls
Popularity and Trend: #743 (last ranked #990 in 1994)

Risk of Misspelling: Low

Risk of Mispronunciation: Low

Famous Namesakes: Flag maker Betsy Ross; designer Betsy Johnson

Common Nicknames: None

Common Variations: None

Consider This: Betsy peaked in the '50s, but it may be on the rise again.

Bette ★★★

(French) a form of Betty.

First Impression: Bette evokes the image of a quiet, serious, and compassionate girl with curly brown hair and a pretty face.

Gender Association: Used for girls

Popularity and Trend: Last ranked in the Top 1000 in the 1960s

Risk of Misspelling: Average

Risk of Mispronunciation: Average

Famous Namesakes: Entertainer Bette Midler; actress Bette Davis

Common Nicknames: None

Common Variations: Betty

Consider This: Bette can be pronounced either "bet" (like Bette Midler) or "BEH-tee" (like Bette Davis), which may prove challenging.

Betty ★★★

(Hebrew) consecrated to God. (English) a familiar form of Elizabeth.

First Impression: With so many famous Bettys—from Betty Boop to Betty Crocker—people say Betty could be perky or conservative.

Gender Association: Used for girls

Popularity and Trend: Last ranked in the Top 1000 in the 1990s

Risk of Misspelling: Fairly low

Risk of Mispronunciation: Low

Famous Namesakes: Actress Betty White; feminist Betty Friedan; cartoon character Betty Boop; actress Betty Grable; character Betty (*Archie* comic book series); first lady Betty Ford; character Betty Rubble (*The Flintstones*); character Betty Suarez (*Ugly Betty*)

Common Nicknames: None

Common Variations: Bette

Consider This: There are a lot of famous women named Betty, but most of them are elderly or deceased.

Beverly ★★★

(English) beaver field.

First Impression: Beverly is seen as either perpetually disapproving or lots of fun.

Gender Association: Used mostly for girls

Popularity and Trend: Last ranked in the Top 1000 in the 1990s

Risk of Misspelling: Fairly low

Risk of Mispronunciation: Low

Famous Namesakes: Actress Beverly D'Angelo; author Beverly Cleary; actress Beverly Mitchell; opera singer Beverly Sills

Common Nicknames: Bev, Buffy

Common Variations: Beverley

Consider This: Beverly is a versatile name, but it has an ambiguous image.

Bianca ★★★★

(Italian) white.

First Impression: Bianca is envisioned as a self-assured, bold, and successful businesswoman.

Gender Association: Used for girls

Popularity and Trend: #182 (#170 in 2000)

Risk of Misspelling: Fairly low

Risk of Mispronunciation: Average

Famous Namesakes: Character Bianca (*Othello*); character Bianca (*The Taming of the Shrew*); jetsetter Bianca Jagger

Common Nicknames: Binney

Common Variations: Bianka, Blanche

Consider This: Bianca can be pronounced "bee-ANN-kah" or "bee-AHN-kah."

Billie ★★

(English) strong willed. (German, French) a familiar form of Belle, Belinda, Wilhelmina.

First Impression: Billie is imagined to be a country girl who's unsophisticated and uneducated, but a lot of fun.

Gender Association: Used mostly for girls

Popularity and Trend: Last ranked in the Top 1000 in the 1990s

Risk of Misspelling: Average

Risk of Mispronunciation: Low

Famous Namesakes: Actress Billie Piper; tennis player Billie Jean King; singer Billie Holliday; actress Billie Burke

Common Nicknames: None
Common Variations: Billi, Billy
Consider This: Billie isn't exactly an urbane name, but it could work for a country girl. However, its pronunciation is the same as Billy, a popular nickname for boys, which may cause gender confusion.

Blair ★★

(Scottish) plains dweller.
First Impression: Many people see Blair as pretty but snobby, much like Blair of TV's *The Facts of Life*.
Gender Association: Used about equally for girls and boys
Popularity and Trend: Last ranked in the Top 1000 in the 1990s
Risk of Misspelling: Fairly low
Risk of Mispronunciation: Low
Famous Namesakes: Character Blair Warner (*The Facts of Life*); prime minister Tony Blair
Common Nicknames: None
Common Variations: Blaire
Consider This: Blair is the quintessential snobby '80s name. Today, it's used equally for boys and girls, which may pose a problem for some parents searching for names with clear gender associations.

Blanca ★★★

(Italian) a form of Bianca.
First Impression: Blanca is pictured as a pale and blue-eyed society matron who's famous for her work with children's charities.

Gender Association: Used for girls
Popularity and Trend: #800 (#644 in 2000)
Risk of Misspelling: Fairly low
Risk of Mispronunciation: Average
Famous Namesakes: Actress Blanca Portillo
Common Nicknames: None
Common Variations: Bianca, Blanche
Consider This: Blanca is a unique name that comes across as elegant.

Blanche ★★★

(French) a form of Bianca.
First Impression: People say Blanche is an older woman who's flamboyant, confident, attractive, and still man-hungry, much like the character Blanche of TV's *The Golden Girls*.
Gender Association: Used for girls
Popularity and Trend: Last ranked in the Top 1000 in the 1960s
Risk of Misspelling: Low
Risk of Mispronunciation: Low
Famous Namesakes: Character Blanche DuBois (*A Streetcar Named Desire*); jazz singer Blanche Calloway; character Blanche Devareaux (*The Golden Girls*)
Common Nicknames: None
Common Variations: Bianca
Consider This: Thanks to namesakes Blanche Devereaux and Blanche DuBois, this name is perfect for a man-hungry Southern belle—but perhaps no one else.

Blinda ★

(American) a form of Belinda.
First Impression: Blinda is seen as a mousy and often bullied pushover who lacks self-esteem.
Gender Association: Used for girls
Popularity and Trend: Never been ranked in Top 1000
Risk of Misspelling: Average
Risk of Mispronunciation: Average
Famous Namesakes: None
Common Nicknames: None
Common Variations: Belinda
Consider This: This short form of Belinda has a mousy image like its root name, and it may be too unusual for most people.

Bliss ★★★★

(English) blissful, joyful.
First Impression: People understandably think Bliss is happy, sweet, and quiet—and a pleasure to be around.
Gender Association: Used mostly for girls
Popularity and Trend: Never been ranked in Top 1000
Risk of Misspelling: Low
Risk of Mispronunciation: Low
Famous Namesakes: Poet Bliss Carman
Common Nicknames: None
Common Variations: None
Consider This: People may find Bliss a somewhat odd name, but they think a girl named Bliss would indeed be blissful.

Blythe ★★

(English) happy, cheerful.

First Impression: Blythe is pictured as either the classiest woman in the arty crowd or the artiest woman in the classy crowd.

Gender Association: Used mostly for girls

Popularity and Trend: Never been ranked in Top 1000

Risk of Misspelling: Average

Risk of Mispronunciation: Average

Famous Namesakes: Actress Blythe Danner

Common Nicknames: None

Common Variations: None

Consider This: Although people think Blythe is a classy name, some may not know it's pronounced "BLIE-th."

Bonita ★★★

(Spanish) pretty.

First Impression: People see Bonita as a beautiful Spanish woman who may be outgoing and spunky, but often rude.

Gender Association: Used for girls

Popularity and Trend: Last ranked in the Top 1000 in the 1970s

Risk of Misspelling: Fairly low

Risk of Mispronunciation: Fairly low

Famous Namesakes: Actress Bonita Granville

Common Nicknames: Bonnie

Common Variations: None

Consider This: Bonita is a pretty name for a pretty Latina, but it may sound strange with certain surnames.

Bonnie ★★★

(English, Scottish) beautiful, pretty. (Spanish) a form of Bonita.

First Impression: Be careful if you sit by Bonnie—people say she'll talk your ear off.

Gender Association: Used for girls

Popularity and Trend: Last ranked #974 in 2003

Risk of Misspelling: Low

Risk of Mispronunciation: Low

Famous Namesakes: Bank robber Bonnie Parker; singer Bonnie Raitt; actress Bonnie Hunt

Common Nicknames: None

Common Variations: Bunny

Consider This: Bonnie was quite popular for most of the twentieth century, but it was out of the Top 1000 by 2000, and it probably won't come back.

Brandy ★★

(Dutch) an after-dinner drink made from distilled wine.

First Impression: Although popular, Brandy is curiously seen as mean and self-centered.

Gender Association: Used mostly for girls

Popularity and Trend: #801 (#399 in 2000)

Risk of Misspelling: Fairly low

Risk of Mispronunciation: Low

Famous Namesakes: Singer Brandy Norwood; basketball player Brandy Reed; singer Brandi Carlile

Common Nicknames: None

Common Variations: Brandi, Brandie

Consider This: Besides the fact that its popularity is plummeting, you may want to think twice before naming your daughter after an alcoholic beverage.

Breanna ★★★

(Irish) a form of Briana.

First Impression: People think Breanna likes herself a lot more than others like her.

Gender Association: Used for girls

Popularity and Trend: #126 (#80 in 2000)

Risk of Misspelling: Fairly high

Risk of Mispronunciation: Average

Famous Namesakes: Reporter Brianna Keilar

Common Nicknames: Brea, Bree

Common Variations: Breana, Briana, Brianna

Consider This: There are many variations of this name, which is bad for spelling. In addition, the confusion between "bree-ANN-ah" or "bree-AHN-ah" is bad for pronunciation.

Bree ★★★

(English) broth. (Irish) power. A form of Breann.

First Impression: Bree is pictured as an outgoing but snobby fashionista.

Gender Association: Used for girls
Popularity and Trend: #955 (last ranked #973 in 1992)
Risk of Misspelling: Fairly low
Risk of Mispronunciation: Low
Famous Namesakes: Character Bree Van De Kamp (*Desperate Housewives*)
Common Nicknames: None
Common Variations: Brie
Consider This: Blame Bree from *Desperate Housewives* for the name's snobby come-off.

Breena ★★★

(Irish) fairy palace.
First Impression: Some imagine Breena as a compassionate, loving girl, but others believe she's headstrong and self-absorbed.
Gender Association: Used for girls
Popularity and Trend: Never been ranked in Top 1000
Risk of Misspelling: Average
Risk of Mispronunciation: Low
Famous Namesakes: Author Breena Clarke
Common Nicknames: Bree
Common Variations: None
Consider This: This never-been-ranked Irish name is similar to Brenna and Brenda.

Brenda ★★★★

(Irish) little raven. (English) sword.
First Impression: Brenda is described as an extroverted and confident

woman who's hardworking, capable, and assertive.
Gender Association: Used for girls
Popularity and Trend: #239 (#172 in 2000)
Risk of Misspelling: Low
Risk of Mispronunciation: Low
Famous Namesakes: Comic strip character Brenda Starr; actress Brenda Fricker; actress Brenda Strong; character Brenda Walsh (*Beverly Hills, 90210*); singer Brenda Lee
Common Nicknames: None
Common Variations: Brena, Brenna
Consider This: Hugely popular from the '40s to the '70s, Brenda's popularity is slowly descending.

Brenna ★★★★

(Irish) a form of Brenda.
First Impression: People picture Brenna as a cute and confident cheerleader.
Gender Association: Used for girls
Popularity and Trend: #381 (#310 in 2000)
Risk of Misspelling: Fairly low
Risk of Mispronunciation: Low
Famous Namesakes: Singer Brenna Gethers
Common Nicknames: None
Common Variations: Brena, Brenda
Consider This: Brenna is similar to Brenda and Briana, but more unique.

Briana ★★★★

(Irish) strong; virtuous, honorable.
First Impression: Briana is seen as a sweet, cheery, and dependable woman who can be whiny and bossy at rare times.
Gender Association: Used for girls
Popularity and Trend: #121 (#83 in 2000)
Risk of Misspelling: Average
Risk of Mispronunciation: Average
Famous Namesakes: Reporter Brianna Keilar
Common Nicknames: Bri, Brina
Common Variations: Breana, Breanna, Briahna, Brianna, Briann
Consider This: "Briana" is the root spelling of the name, but Brianna is more popular, which could create spelling confusion. There may also be pronunciation trouble with people divided between "bree-ANN-ah" and "bree-AHN-ah."

Brianna ★★★★

(Irish) a form of Briana.
First Impression: People see Brianna as a sweetie who's good-willed and bighearted.
Gender Association: Used for girls
Popularity and Trend: #20 (#15 in 2000)
Risk of Misspelling: Average
Risk of Mispronunciation: Average
Famous Namesakes: Reporter Brianna Keilar
Common Nicknames: Bri, Brina

Common Variations: Briana, Breanna, Briannah, Breana, Briann

Consider This: "Brianna" is the most popular spelling of this name, but with so many variations, spelling will still be confused. As with Briana, people will pronounce it "bree-ANN-ah" and "bree-AHN-ah."

Bridget ★★★★

(Irish) strong.

First Impression: Blame it on Bridget Jones: People envision Bridget as a comical and sometimes flighty Englishwoman who's blond and just a little plump.

Gender Association: Used for girls

Popularity and Trend: #347 (#273 in 2000)

Risk of Misspelling: Fairly low

Risk of Mispronunciation: Fairly low

Famous Namesakes: Actress Bridget Fonda; actress Bridgette Wilson-Sampras; character Bridget Jones (*Bridget Jones' Diary*); actress Bridget Moynahan

Common Nicknames: Bridge, Gitta

Common Variations: Bridgette, Birgette, Bedelia, Brigit, Brigitte

Consider This: If you don't like Bridget Jones, you may want to consider one of Bridget's many variations.

Brie ★★

(French) a type of cheese. (Irish) a form of Bree.

First Impression: Most people see Brie as a wispy, pretty thing who can be funny and flirty, but also mean and moody.

Gender Association: Used for girls

Popularity and Trend: Never been ranked in Top 1000

Risk of Misspelling: Average

Risk of Mispronunciation: Average

Famous Namesakes: Character Bree Van De Kamp (*Desperate Housewives*)

Common Nicknames: None

Common Variations: Bree

Consider This: Brie is certainly more unique than Bree, but it may make people think of cheese.

Brigitte ★★★

(French) a form of Bridget.

First Impression: Brigitte is pictured as a sexy and long-legged European who's ambitious and in charge, much like sexy namesakes Brigitte Bardot and Brigitte Nielsen.

Gender Association: Used for girls

Popularity and Trend: Last ranked in the Top 1000 in the 1970s

Risk of Misspelling: Average

Risk of Mispronunciation: Average

Famous Namesakes: Actress Brigitte Nielsen; actress Brigitte Bardot

Common Nicknames: Gitta

Common Variations: Bridget

Consider This: Brigitte is a French name that may fit better with

some surnames than with others. Another problem is that some people may pronounce it the same as Bridget, but the French pronunciation is "breh-ZHEET."

Britany ★★

(English) from Britain.

First Impression: People think Britany seems adorable, but this girl's got sass.

Gender Association: Used for girls

Popularity and Trend: Last ranked in the Top 1000 in the 1990s

Risk of Misspelling: Fairly high

Risk of Mispronunciation: Low

Famous Namesakes: Actress Brittany Snow; actress Brittany Murphy; singer Britney Spears; actress Brittney Powell

Common Nicknames: Britta, Brit, Bret

Common Variations: Brittany, Brittney

Consider This: This is the traditional spelling of a name with many popular variations, but it hasn't been ranked since the '90s. People will likely confuse it for a number of other spellings.

Britta ★★★

(Swedish) strong. (Latin) a form of Britany.

First Impression: This name calls to mind a kind, classy, and beautiful woman who's completely comfortable and confident at social gatherings.

Gender Association: Used for girls

Popularity and Trend: Never been ranked in Top 1000
Risk of Misspelling: Average
Risk of Mispronunciation: Fairly high
Famous Namesakes: Saint Britta
Common Nicknames: Britt
Common Variations: Brita
Consider This: This Swedish name has never been ranked, and pronunciation is tougher than it looks. Some say "BRIH-tah," others say "BREE-tah," and still others say "BRY-tah."

Brittany ★★

(English) from Britain.
First Impression: Brittany is believed to be a cliquish and snobby teen who's self-absorbed, shallow, and mean.
Gender Association: Used for girls
Popularity and Trend: #318 (#61 in 2000)
Risk of Misspelling: Average
Risk of Mispronunciation: Low
Famous Namesakes: Actress Brittany Snow; actress Brittany Murphy; singer Britney Spears; actress Brittney Powell
Common Nicknames: Britta, Brit, Bret
Common Variations: Britany, Brittney
Consider This: This is the most popular spelling in the Britany family, but even it has taken a nosedive since 2000. (Blame Britney Spears.)

Brittney ★★★

(English) a form of Britany.
First Impression: Many think Brittney is a spunky and bubbly blond who loves parties and clubs, but she's also a bit spacey.
Gender Association: Used for girls
Popularity and Trend: #626 (#147 in 2000)
Risk of Misspelling: Fairly high
Risk of Mispronunciation: Low
Famous Namesakes: Actress Brittany Snow; actress Brittany Murphy; singer Britney Spears; actress Brittney Powell
Common Nicknames: Britta, Brit, Bret
Common Variations: Britany, Brittany
Consider This: This spelling of Britany is the closest to Britney Spears's, and its popularity seems to be going down as fast as her career.

Brooke ★★★★★

(English) brook, stream.
First Impression: Most people see Brooke as carefree, spirited, and talkative.
Gender Association: Used mostly for girls
Popularity and Trend: #44 (#51 in 2000)
Risk of Misspelling: Fairly low
Risk of Mispronunciation: Low
Famous Namesakes: Model Brooke Shields; model Brooke Burke; actress Brooke Burns; singer Brooke Hogan
Common Nicknames: None
Common Variations: Brook, Brooks
Consider This: In the Top 100 since the '80s, Brooke's popularity continues to rise.

Buffy ★★★

(American) buffalo; from the plains.
First Impression: When some people hear this name, they think of a snooty Valley girl, but others picture a blond who kills blood-sucking vampires in her spare time.
Gender Association: Used for girls
Popularity and Trend: Last ranked in the Top 1000 in the 1970s
Risk of Misspelling: Low
Risk of Mispronunciation: Low
Famous Namesakes: Character Buffy Summers (*Buffy the Vampire Slayer*); singer-songwriter Buffy Sainte-Marie
Common Nicknames: None
Common Variations: None
Consider This: *Buffy the Vampire Slayer* may have changed this name's image, but it didn't make it any more popular.

Bunny ★★

(Greek) a familiar form of Bernice. (English) little rabbit.
First Impression: People think Bunny is a big-haired and dimwitted blonde who models for *Playboy*.
Gender Association: Used for girls

Popularity and Trend: Never been ranked in Top 1000
Risk of Misspelling: Low
Risk of Mispronunciation: Low
Famous Namesakes: Character Bunny Lake (*Bunny Lake Is Missing!*); character Bunny Lebowski (*The Big Lebowski*); character Bunny MacDougal (*Sex and the City*)
Common Nicknames: None
Common Variations: None
Consider This: People think Bunny is a stripper or a prostitute, so avoid this name, even if you think it sounds cute.

Cadence ★★★★
(Latin) rhythm.
First Impression: Cadence is imagined to be a well-liked and joyful young girl.
Gender Association: Used for girls
Popularity and Trend: #214 (#959 in 2002)
Risk of Misspelling: Low
Risk of Mispronunciation: Low
Famous Namesakes: None
Common Nicknames: Cady
Common Variations: Kadence, Kaydence, Caydence
Consider This: Cadence and its many variations first entered the Top 1000 in 2002 and have zoomed up the list. It's no wonder the name sounds young to so many people.

Cai ★
(Vietnamese) feminine.
First Impression: People think Cai has a unique blend of good looks, kindness, and drive.
Gender Association: Used mostly for boys
Popularity and Trend: Never been ranked in Top 1000
Risk of Misspelling: High
Risk of Mispronunciation: High
Famous Namesakes: Inventor Cai Lun
Common Nicknames: None
Common Variations: Kai
Consider This: Although it looks as though it should be pronounced "kye," this Asian name is pronounced "sye."

Caitlin ★★★
(Irish) pure.
First Impression: Caitlin is well-to-do, but she's not well thought of—people imagine she's egocentric, snobby, and spoiled.
Gender Association: Used for girls
Popularity and Trend: #207 (#75 in 2000)
Risk of Misspelling: Average
Risk of Mispronunciation: Low
Famous Namesakes: Figure skater Caitlyn "Kitty" Carruthers; swimmer Kaitlin Sandeno; character Caitlin Cooper (*The O.C.*)
Common Nicknames: Cait, Catie

Common Variations: Caitlyn, Kaitlin, Katelyn
Consider This: "Caitlin" is the root spelling of this name, but there are so many variations that any Caitlin will find herself having to spell out her name more often than not.

Caitlyn ★★★★
(Irish) a form of Caitlin, Kaitlan.
First Impression: People see Caitlyn as a rich preppy who's motivated, caring, and popular.
Gender Association: Used for girls
Popularity and Trend: #199 (#118 in 2000)
Risk of Misspelling: Fairly high
Risk of Mispronunciation: Low
Famous Namesakes: Figure skater Caitlyn "Kitty" Carruthers; swimmer Kaitlin Sandeno; character Caitlin Cooper (*The O.C.*)
Common Nicknames: Cait, Catie
Common Variations: Caitlin, Kaitlyn, Katelyn
Consider This: This spelling isn't as common as "Caitlin," but it has a more positive first impression.

Calantha ★★
(Greek) beautiful blossom.
First Impression: Calantha is pictured as either a weird but intelligent goth or a lively and energetic ditz.
Gender Association: Used for girls

Popularity and Trend: Never been ranked in Top 1000
Risk of Misspelling: Average
Risk of Mispronunciation: Fairly low
Famous Namesakes: None
Common Nicknames: None
Common Variations: None
Consider This: This Greek name has never been in the Top 1000, which is probably why some people think it's strange.

Caley ★★
(American) a form of Caeley.
First Impression: Caley is thought to be a kindhearted and positive goody-goody with a comforting smile, but she may come across as a bore.
Gender Association: Used mostly for girls
Popularity and Trend: Never been ranked in Top 1000
Risk of Misspelling: Fairly high
Risk of Mispronunciation: Average
Famous Namesakes: None
Common Nicknames: None
Common Variations: Caeley, Caylee, Kaylee
Consider This: This name's spelling and pronunciation are quite tricky. If you see it, you may not know whether it's "CAL-ee" or "CAY-lee." If you hear the name, you may not come up with this particular spelling, as there are so many variations like it.

Callidora ★★★★
(Greek) gift of beauty.
First Impression: Callidora is seen as either a sweet, quiet woman who works with kids, or a lively woman who works in the entertainment industry.
Gender Association: Used for girls
Popularity and Trend: Never been ranked in Top 1000
Risk of Misspelling: Average
Risk of Mispronunciation: Fairly low
Famous Namesakes: Character Callidora Black (*Harry Potter* series)
Common Nicknames: Callie, Dora
Common Variations: None
Consider This: This unusual name can be shortened easily, and many will know it, thanks to *Harry Potter* character Callidora Black.

Callie ★★★★
(Greek, Arabic) a form of Cala, Calista.
First Impression: People think Callie is a sporty gal who's cheery, funny, and popular.
Gender Association: Used for girls
Popularity and Trend: #303 (#321 in 2000)
Risk of Misspelling: Average
Risk of Mispronunciation: Fairly low
Famous Namesakes: Screenwriter Callie Khouri; character Callie Torres (*Grey's Anatomy*)
Common Nicknames: None
Common Variations: Calie, Cally, Cali
Consider This: Callie has fairly easy pronunciation compared to many names in the Callie/Caley family, but spelling may still be a problem.

Camilla ★★★
(Italian) a form of Camille.
First Impression: Although Camilla appears demure and ladylike, people think she's actually stuck-up, stiff, and adulterous—perhaps like Camilla, the Duchess of Cornwall.
Gender Association: Used for girls
Popularity and Trend: #825 (#875 in 2005)
Risk of Misspelling: Fairly low
Risk of Mispronunciation: Low
Famous Namesakes: Duchess Camilla Parker-Bowles; actress Camilla Belle
Common Nicknames: Cami, Millie
Common Variations: Camila
Consider This: While people think Camilla is a snobbish name, Camille is much more liked.

Camille ★★★★
(French) young ceremonial attendant.
First Impression: People see Camille as blessed with elegance and many talents.
Gender Association: Used mostly for girls

Popularity and Trend: #308
(#269 in 2000)
Risk of Misspelling: Fairly low
Risk of Mispronunciation: Fairly low
Famous Namesakes: Composer
Camille Saint-Saëns; author
Camille Paglia
Common Nicknames: Cami, Millie
Common Variations: Camylle
Consider This: Camille isn't quite as
popular now as it was in the '90s,
but with its versatility and great
first impression, it's still a good
choice.

Camryn ★★★★
(American) a form of Cameron.
First Impression: Camryn is
considered a lovable mischief
maker.
Gender Association: Used mostly
for girls
Popularity and Trend: #216
(#183 in 2000)
Risk of Misspelling: Average
Risk of Mispronunciation: Low
Famous Namesakes: Actress Camryn
Manheim; actress Cameron Diaz
Common Nicknames: Camry
Common Variations: Kamryn, Cameron
Consider This: Cameron is traditionally
a boys' name, but the "Camryn"
spelling is used more for girls.

Candace ★★★
(Greek) glittering white; glowing.
First Impression: People see Candace
as a popular, fun, and perky

cheerleader whose nonstop pep
and ditziness get annoying
quickly.
Gender Association: Used for girls
Popularity and Trend: Last ranked in
the Top 1000 in the 1980s
Risk of Misspelling: Fairly low
Risk of Mispronunciation: Low
Famous Namesakes: Actress Candice
Bergen; actress Candace Cameron;
wrestler Candice Michelle
Common Nicknames: Candy
Common Variations: Candice, Kandace
Consider This: Candace and variation
Candice both peaked in the '80s
and now have a dated feel.

Candi ★
(American) a familiar form of
Candace, Candice, Candida.
First Impression: Candi is seen as a
dimwitted bimbo who most
likely enjoys her work as an
exotic dancer.
Gender Association: Used for girls
Popularity and Trend: Last ranked in
the Top 1000 in the 1980s
Risk of Misspelling: Average
Risk of Mispronunciation: Low
Famous Namesakes: Singer Candi
Staton; drag queen Candy
Darling; actress Candy Clark
Common Nicknames: None
Common Variations: Candy, Candie
Consider This: Everyone assumes
Candi is a stripper, so perhaps
stick to Candace instead.

Candida ★★★
(Latin) bright white.
First Impression: Candida is pictured as
an energetic and vibrant woman.
Gender Association: Used for girls
Popularity and Trend: Last ranked in
the Top 1000 in the 1970s
Risk of Misspelling: Average
Risk of Mispronunciation: Average
Famous Namesakes: Novelist Candida
Crewe
Common Nicknames: Candy
Common Variations: None
Consider This: People may have
trouble spelling and pronouncing
this name. Plus, it's also the name
of the yeast that causes some
yeast infections.

Candra ★★★
(Latin) glowing.
First Impression: People view Candra
as a strong woman, but she has
to be careful not to seem *too*
strong at times.
Gender Association: Used for girls
Popularity and Trend: Never been
ranked in Top 1000
Risk of Misspelling: Average
Risk of Mispronunciation: Average
Famous Namesakes: Emperor Candra
Gupta I
Common Nicknames: Candy
Common Variations: Kandra
Consider This: For such an unusual
name, Candra has a mostly
positive first impression.

Capri ★★★★

(Italian) a short form of Caprice.

First Impression: Capri is seen as a friendly, innocent, and light-hearted pixie who loves to go on adventures.

Gender Association: Used for girls

Popularity and Trend: Never been ranked in Top 1000

Risk of Misspelling: Fairly low

Risk of Mispronunciation: Fairly low

Famous Namesakes: Senator Capri Cafaro

Common Nicknames: None

Common Variations: Kapri

Consider This: Capri is an island famous for its sun and good times, and that influence is clear in Capri's image. It's perhaps not the most professional name, however.

Caprice ★★★★

(Italian) fanciful.

First Impression: People imagine Caprice as a lively, fun-loving, and strong-willed party girl.

Gender Association: Used for girls

Popularity and Trend: Never been ranked in Top 1000

Risk of Misspelling: Fairly low

Risk of Mispronunciation: Fairly low

Famous Namesakes: Model Caprice Bourret

Common Nicknames: Capri

Common Variations: None

Consider This: The name Caprice is glamorous, but understandably, it also has a capricious connotation, which isn't necessarily a good thing.

Cara ★★★

(Latin) dear. (Irish) friend.

First Impression: Cara is seen as a rebel with a cause, but some may not care for her antics.

Gender Association: Used for girls

Popularity and Trend: #559 (#393 in 2000)

Risk of Misspelling: Fairly low

Risk of Mispronunciation: Average

Famous Namesakes: Actress Irene Cara; actress Cara Buono

Common Nicknames: Carey

Common Variations: Carra, Caralee

Consider This: Cara can be pronounced two ways: "CAR-ah" or "CARE-ah."

Carey ★★

(Welsh) a form of Cara, Caroline, Karen, Katherine.

First Impression: People don't know whether Carey is a boy or a girl, and they also can't decide whether Carey is a bookworm or a joker.

Gender Association: Used about equally for girls and boys

Popularity and Trend: Last ranked in the Top 1000 in the 1980s

Risk of Misspelling: Fairly high

Risk of Mispronunciation: Low

Famous Namesakes: Actress Carey Lowell; character Carrie White (*Carrie*); character Carrie Bradshaw (*Sex and the City*); actress Carrie Fisher; actress Carrie-Anne Moss; actress Kerry Washington; actress Kari Wührer; actress Keri Russell

Common Nicknames: None

Common Variations: Carrie, Cary, Karey

Consider This: This spelling is used equally for boys and girls, which could lead to gender confusion. There are plenty of other variations of Carey that are used for just girls.

Carina ★★★

(Italian) dear little one. (Greek) a form of Cora. (Swedish) a form of Karen.

First Impression: Carina is pictured as a friendly, shy woman with a secret wild side.

Gender Association: Used for girls

Popularity and Trend: #864 (#566 in 2000)

Risk of Misspelling: Fairly low

Risk of Mispronunciation: Low

Famous Namesakes: Actress Carina Lau

Common Nicknames: None

Common Variations: Caren, Carine

Consider This: Carina has Italian, Greek, and Swedish meanings, so it has a multicultural feel.

Carissa ★★★★

(Greek) beloved.

First Impression: Carissa is said to be upbeat, fun, cool, and well liked.

Gender Association: Used for girls

Popularity and Trend: #585 (#411 in 2000)

Risk of Misspelling: Fairly low

Risk of Mispronunciation: Low

Famous Namesakes: Surfer Carissa Moore

Common Nicknames: None

Common Variations: Carisa, Karissa

Consider This: Carissa scores better than other "-issa" names, like Clarissa and Larissa.

Carla ★★★★

(German) farmer. (English) strong. (Latin) a form of Carol, Caroline.

First Impression: Folks say Carla is a loud and lively woman full of sarcasm, spunk, and wit.

Gender Association: Used for girls

Popularity and Trend: #501 (#404 in 2000)

Risk of Misspelling: Fairly low

Risk of Mispronunciation: Low

Famous Namesakes: Actress Carla Gugino; model Carla Bruni; character Carla Tortelli (*Cheers*)

Common Nicknames: None

Common Variations: Karla

Consider This: Carla has German and English origins as well as Latin, but it tends to come across as purely Italian, thanks to Carla Tortelli from TV's *Cheers*.

Carlen ★★★★

(English) a form of Caroline.

First Impression: People see Carlen as an attentive, diplomatic, and outgoing leader.

Gender Association: Used for girls

Popularity and Trend: Never been ranked in Top 1000

Risk of Misspelling: Average

Risk of Mispronunciation: Low

Famous Namesakes: Country singer Carlene Carter

Common Nicknames: None

Common Variations: Carlene, Carleen

Consider This: Some people may think this variation of Carlene is spelled like the surname "Carlin."

Carlene ★★★

(English) a form of Caroline.

First Impression: Carlene is considered a loud and brash gal who's tough but friendly.

Gender Association: Used for girls

Popularity and Trend: Last ranked in the Top 1000 in the 1970s

Risk of Misspelling: Fairly low

Risk of Mispronunciation: Low

Famous Namesakes: Country singer Carlene Carter

Common Nicknames: None

Common Variations: Karlene

Consider This: This form of Caroline hasn't been popular for several decades, but its root name is still in the Top 100.

Carlotta ★★★★

(Italian) a form of Charlotte.

First Impression: People envision Carlotta as a giving and thoughtful Latina with a ton of charm and a ton of friends.

Gender Association: Used for girls

Popularity and Trend: Last ranked in the Top 1000 in the 1960s

Risk of Misspelling: Fairly low

Risk of Mispronunciation: Low

Famous Namesakes: Journalist Carlotta Gall; ballerina Carlotta Grisi

Common Nicknames: Lottie, Lola

Common Variations: Carlita

Consider This: Carlotta is an Italian name, but it also may work well with any Latino surname.

Carly ★★★★

(English) a form of Caroline, Charlotte.

First Impression: Folks think it's so easy to like Carly, a talkative, carefree, and sometimes silly woman.

Gender Association: Used for girls

Popularity and Trend: #251 (#169 in 2000)

Risk of Misspelling: Fairly low

Risk of Mispronunciation: Low

Famous Namesakes: Musician Carly Simon; gymnast Carly Patterson

Common Nicknames: None

Common Variations: Carley, Carlie, Karly

Consider This: Carly is a nickname for Caroline or Charlotte, but it sometimes stands alone as a given name, too.

Carmen ★★★

(Latin) song.

First Impression: Carmen is imagined to be a dark-haired, dark-eyed beauty who's passionate and full of life.

Gender Association: Used mostly for girls

Popularity and Trend: #258 (#271 in 2000)

Risk of Misspelling: Low

Risk of Mispronunciation: Low

Famous Namesakes: Opera character Carmen; actress Carmen Electra; character Carmen Sandiego (*Where in the World Is Carmen Sandiego?*)

Common Nicknames: None

Common Variations: Carman, Charmaine

Consider This: Although climbing the Top 1000, Carmen may fit best with Latino surnames.

Carol ★★★★

(German) farmer. (French) song of joy. (English) strong.

First Impression: Carol is thought to be a friendly joker with a big smile.

Gender Association: Used for girls

Popularity and Trend: #968 (#726 in 2000)

Risk of Misspelling: Fairly low

Risk of Mispronunciation: Low

Famous Namesakes: Comedian Carol Burnett; actress Carole Lombard; actress Carol Channing

Common Nicknames: Carrie

Common Variations: Carole, Karol

Consider This: Many of Carol's namesakes are funny women, but they're all older. At #968, it's almost out of the Top 1000.

Carolina ★★★★

(Italian) a form of Caroline.

First Impression: Carolina is regarded as a high-spirited and vibrant charmer with talent, drive, and ambition.

Gender Association: Used for girls

Popularity and Trend: #281 (#267 in 2000)

Risk of Misspelling: Low

Risk of Mispronunciation: Average

Famous Namesakes: Designer Carolina Herrera

Common Nicknames: Carrie, Lina, Carol

Common Variations: Karolina

Consider This: This Italian name can be pronounced "care-oh-LEEN-ah" or "care-oh-LINE-ah."

Caroline ★★★★

(French) little and strong.

First Impression: Caroline strikes people as a logical and practical bookworm who's timid, a little boring, but sweet nonetheless.

Gender Association: Used for girls

Popularity and Trend: #89 (#65 in 2000)

Risk of Misspelling: Fairly low

Risk of Mispronunciation: Average

Famous Namesakes: First daughter Caroline Kennedy Schlossberg; princess Caroline of Monaco; comedian Caroline Rhea

Common Nicknames: Carrie, Carly, Carol

Common Variations: Carolina, Carolyn, Karoline

Consider This: Caroline is a classic, popular name with many variations, but it does have a pronunciation problem: Some say "CARE-oh-line" and others say "CARE-oh-lin."

Carrie ★★★

(English) a form of Carol, Caroline.

First Impression: Many people think Carrie is an awkward outcast who uses her telekinetic powers in a rampage, much like Stephen King's *Carrie*.

Gender Association: Used for girls

Popularity and Trend: #859 (#503 in 2000)

Risk of Misspelling: Average

Risk of Mispronunciation: Low

Famous Namesakes: Character Carrie White (*Carrie*); character Carrie Bradshaw (*Sex and the City*); actress Carrie Fisher; actress Carrie-Anne Moss; actress Kerry Washington; actress Kari

Wührer; actress Keri Russell; actress Carey Lowell
Common Nicknames: None
Common Variations: Carey, Cary, Kerry, Keri
Consider This: This is the most common spelling of Carrie and the only one still in the Top 1000, but it's falling fast. Still, it was a Top 200 name for almost all of the twentieth century.

Casey ★★★★
(Irish) brave. (Greek) a form of Acacia.
First Impression: Casey is described as a popular, friendly, and good-humored gal.
Gender Association: Used about equally for girls and boys
Popularity and Trend: #411 (#208 in 2000)
Risk of Misspelling: Fairly low
Risk of Mispronunciation: Low
Famous Namesakes: Singer Kasey Chambers; actor Casey Affleck; radio personality Casey Kasem
Common Nicknames: Case
Common Variations: Kacey, Kasey
Consider This: Casey is used equally for girls and boys, which could cause gender confusion.

Cassandra ★★★★
(Greek) helper of men.
First Impression: People think Cassandra is either shy or outgoing, but an upstanding woman either way.

Gender Association: Used for girls
Popularity and Trend: #219 (#100 in 2000)
Risk of Misspelling: Fairly low
Risk of Mispronunciation: Average
Famous Namesakes: Author Cassandra King; mythological figure Cassandra
Common Nicknames: Cass, Cassie, Sandy
Common Variations: Casandra, Cassondra, Cassaundra, Sandra
Consider This: Cassandra is a very versatile name that's slowly losing popularity.

Cassidy ★★★★
(Irish) clever.
First Impression: Many believe Cassidy could be bubbly and charming or snobby and rich.
Gender Association: Used mostly for girls
Popularity and Trend: #198 (#105 in 2000)
Risk of Misspelling: Fairly low
Risk of Mispronunciation: Low
Famous Namesakes: Actress Cassidy Rae; rapper Cassidy
Common Nicknames: Cass, Cassie
Common Variations: Kassidy
Consider This: Cassidy is also a common Irish surname.

Cassie ★★★
(Greek) a familiar form of Cassandra, Catherine.

First Impression: Cassie is seen as a rambunctious and chatty working-class hero.
Gender Association: Used mostly for girls
Popularity and Trend: #732 (#347 in 2000)
Risk of Misspelling: Average
Risk of Mispronunciation: Low
Famous Namesakes: R&B singer Cassie
Common Nicknames: Cass
Common Variations: Cassey, Cassy
Consider This: A sinking nickname for Cassandra, Cassie has a working-class feel.

Catherine ★★★★
(Greek) pure. (English) a form of Katherine.
First Impression: Catherine is portrayed as a demure girl with classy, traditional manners.
Gender Association: Used mostly for girls
Popularity and Trend: #122 (#81 in 2000)
Risk of Misspelling: Average
Risk of Mispronunciation: Low
Famous Namesakes: Actress Catherine Zeta-Jones; actress Catherine O'Hara; singer Katherine McPhee; actress Catherine Bell; empress Catherine the Great; actress Catherine Deneuve; actress Katharine Hepburn; publisher Katharine Graham; actress Katherine Heigl

Common Nicknames: Cate, Cathy, Cassie

Common Variations: Catharine, Katherine, Cathrine

Consider This: This variation of Katherine ranked in the Top 100 for all of the twentieth century, but is slipping now. Because Katherine continues to be very popular, people may assume Catherine is spelled that way.

Cathleen ★★

(Irish) a form of Catherine.

First Impression: People say Cathleen is a smart, avid reader, but they also feel she's dull and afraid to take risks.

Gender Association: Used for girls

Popularity and Trend: Last ranked in the Top 1000 in the 1980s

Risk of Misspelling: Average

Risk of Mispronunciation: Low

Famous Namesakes: Actress Kathleen Turner; actress Cathleen Nesbitt; actress Kathleen Robertson

Common Nicknames: Cathy

Common Variations: Kathleen

Consider This: This name peaked in the '50s, and today Kathleen with a K is the more popular spelling.

Cathy ★★

(Greek) a familiar form of Catherine, Cathleen.

First Impression: People see Cathy as a mousy introvert, an even-tempered teetotaler, or a chatty secretary.

Gender Association: Used for girls

Popularity and Trend: Last ranked in the Top 1000 in the 1990s

Risk of Misspelling: Average

Risk of Mispronunciation: Low

Famous Namesakes: Comic strip character Cathy; actress Kathy Bates; model Kathy Ireland; cartoonist Cathy Guisewite; television host Kathie Lee Gifford

Common Nicknames: None

Common Variations: Cathi, Kathy

Consider This: Cathy isn't as popular as its root names, Catherine or Cathleen, or even Kathy, another variation.

Cecelia ★★★

(Latin) a form of Cecilia.

First Impression: People believe Cecelia is a mysterious, possible religious, woman who's so shy and strange, she's hard to read.

Gender Association: Used for girls

Popularity and Trend: #669 (#778 in 2000)

Risk of Misspelling: Average

Risk of Mispronunciation: Low

Famous Namesakes: Saint Cecilia; opera singer Cecilia Bartoli; artist Cecilia Rodhe

Common Nicknames: Cissy, Celia

Common Variations: Cecilia, Cecile, Cicely

Consider This: Namesake Saint Cecilia may be the reason people find this name religious.

Celeste ★★★★

(Latin) celestial, heavenly.

First Impression: Most think Celeste is a hoot, but some find her zaniness annoying.

Gender Association: Used for girls

Popularity and Trend: #327 (#274 in 2000)

Risk of Misspelling: Fairly low

Risk of Mispronunciation: Low

Famous Namesakes: Actress Celeste Holm; author Celeste Bradley

Common Nicknames: None

Common Variations: Celestine, Celesta

Consider This: Celeste almost cracked the Top 200 in 2004, but it fell again and looks to be heading toward the middle of the Top 1000, where it's been for most of the past one hundred years.

Celia ★★

(Latin) a form of Cecilia.

First Impression: Celia is pictured as a spoiled and snobby preppy who has a lot of snooty friends.

Gender Association: Used for girls

Popularity and Trend: #707 (#620 in 2000)

Risk of Misspelling: Fairly low

Risk of Mispronunciation: Low

Famous Namesakes: Singer Celia Cruz; actress Celia Weston

Common Nicknames: None

Common Variations: None
Consider This: The image of Celia and its root name, Cecelia, are both negative—but very different. Compare them to Cicely, a similar name that makes a more positive impression.

Celine ★★★

(Greek) a form of Celena.

First Impression: Like Celine Dion, Celine is pictured as a singer with a beautiful voice, beautiful face, but emaciated figure.

Gender Association: Used for girls

Popularity and Trend: Last ranked #677 in 2000

Risk of Misspelling: Fairly low

Risk of Mispronunciation: Low

Famous Namesakes: Singer Celine Dion

Common Nicknames: None

Common Variations: Selene

Consider This: Celine's image is highly associated with Celine Dion's, but it doesn't share her popularity.

Chanel ★★★

(English) channel.

First Impression: People feel Chanel is a stylish and sophisticated model.

Gender Association: Used for girls

Popularity and Trend: #917 (#819 in 2000)

Risk of Misspelling: Fairly low

Risk of Mispronunciation: Fairly low

Famous Namesakes: Designer Coco Chanel; model Chanel Iman

Common Nicknames: None

Common Variations: Chanell, Chanelle, Shanel

Consider This: It can be risky to name your daughter after a brand, especially one as chic as Chanel.

Chantal ★★★

(French) song.

First Impression: People agree Chantal is a pretty woman with an elegant, sophisticated fashion sense, which makes her a great fashion magazine writer.

Gender Association: Used for girls

Popularity and Trend: Last ranked in the Top 1000 in the 1990s

Risk of Misspelling: Average

Risk of Mispronunciation: Fairly low

Famous Namesakes: Singer Chantal Kreviazuk; singer Chantal Goya

Common Nicknames: None

Common Variations: Chantel, Chauntel

Consider This: A few people may pronounce this name "chan-TALL" instead of "shan-TALL."

Charisma ★★★★

(Greek) the gift of leadership.

First Impression: People think Charisma's name seems to announce her personality: She's charming, magnetic, and likable.

Gender Association: Used for girls

Popularity and Trend: Never been ranked in Top 1000

Risk of Misspelling: Low

Risk of Mispronunciation: Low

Famous Namesakes: Actress Charisma Carpenter

Common Nicknames: None

Common Variations: None

Consider This: Someone named Charisma is expected to be charming and outgoing. If your daughter ends up shy, this name could be a burden.

Charisse ★★★★

(Greek) a form of Charity.

First Impression: Charisse evokes the image of a lovable, affable, and desirable French charmer.

Gender Association: Used for girls

Popularity and Trend: Last ranked in the Top 1000 in the 1970s

Risk of Misspelling: Average

Risk of Mispronunciation: Average

Famous Namesakes: Actress Cyd Charisse

Common Nicknames: None

Common Variations: None

Consider This: This Greek name has a French-sounding twist. The fact that it's "shah-REESE" and not "chah-REESE" may trip up some people.

Charity ★★★★

(Latin) charity, kindness.

First Impression: People naturally think Charity is charitable, describing her as helpful, kind, and always wanting to make a difference.

Gender Association: Used for girls

Popularity and Trend: #673 (#459 in 2000)

Risk of Misspelling: Low

Risk of Mispronunciation: Low

Famous Namesakes: Character Charity Standish (*Passions*)

Common Nicknames: Cherry

Common Variations: None

Consider This: This name is becoming less popular with parents, despite its sweet image.

Charlene ★★★★

(English) a form of Caroline.

First Impression: Like any Southern woman, Charlene is seen as full of charm.

Gender Association: Used for girls

Popularity and Trend: Last ranked in the Top 1000 in the 1990s

Risk of Misspelling: Fairly low

Risk of Mispronunciation: Low

Famous Namesakes: Actress Charlene Tilton; fitness guru Charlene Prickett; singer Sharlene Spiteri

Common Nicknames: Charlie

Common Variations: Charleen, Sharlene

Consider This: Charlene has always been more popular than variation Sharlene, but both are out of the Top 1000 now.

Charlotte ★★★★★

(French) a form of Caroline.

First Impression: People get the impression Charlotte is a calm and collected thinker with sexy allure.

Gender Association: Used for girls

Popularity and Trend: #123 (#289 in 2000)

Risk of Misspelling: Low

Risk of Mispronunciation: Low

Famous Namesakes: Character Charlotte York (*Sex and the City*); author Charlotte Brontë; author Charlotte Perkins Gilman; singer Charlotte Church; actress Charlotte Rae; actress Charlotte d'Amboise; actress Charlotte Gainsbourg

Common Nicknames: Carly, Lotte, Lottie

Common Variations: Carlotta, Sharlotte

Consider This: Charlotte is an old-fashioned name that's never been unpopular, though it hit a low in the '90s. Now it's on the rise again.

Charmaine ★★★

(French) a form of Carmen.

First Impression: Charmaine is pictured as outgoing, outspoken, and fun, but she's suspected to have a quick temper.

Gender Association: Used for girls

Popularity and Trend: Last ranked in the Top 1000 in the 1990s

Risk of Misspelling: Average

Risk of Mispronunciation: Low

Famous Namesakes: Character Charmaine Bucco (*The Sopranos*); singer Charmaine Neville

Common Nicknames: None

Common Variations: Sharmaine

Consider This: Charlotte is a similar-sounding name with much more appeal. It's possible that Charmaine could turn into toilet-tissue "Charmin" during playground teasing.

Chastity ★★★★

(Latin) pure.

First Impression: Most people think Chastity is an angelic, virginal girl, but others think she's a devilish flirt.

Gender Association: Used for girls

Popularity and Trend: Last ranked in the Top 1000 in the 1990s

Risk of Misspelling: Low

Risk of Mispronunciation: Low

Famous Namesakes: Activist Chastity Bono

Common Nicknames: None

Common Variations: Chasidy

Consider This: Chastity may get teased for this name in middle school. Try Charity, a safer virtue name, instead.

Chavi ★★★

(Roma) girl.

First Impression: Chavi is viewed as kind, caring, and so small that she's affectionately called a pipsqueak.

Gender Association: Used for girls

Popularity and Trend: Never been ranked in Top 1000

Risk of Misspelling: Average

Risk of Mispronunciation: Average

Famous Namesakes: Actress Chavi Mittal

Common Nicknames: None

Common Variations: None

Consider This: Chavi is Roma, but people may think it's a Latino name.

Chaya ★★★

(Hebrew) life; living.

First Impression: Chaya is imagined to be a beautiful and friendly African American woman who's a fun people-person.

Gender Association: Used for girls

Popularity and Trend: #785 (#779 in 2000)

Risk of Misspelling: Fairly high

Risk of Mispronunciation: Fairly high

Famous Namesakes: Composer Chaya Arbel

Common Nicknames: None

Common Variations: None

Consider This: Chaya is a Hebrew name, but people tend to associate it with African Americans. While it looks like "CHAY-ah," it's pronounced either "CHAH-yah" or "HAH-yah."

Chelsea ★★★★

(English) seaport.

First Impression: Chelsea is described by most as personable and popular, but others see her as jealous and mean.

Gender Association: Used for girls

Popularity and Trend: #192 (#140 in 2000)

Risk of Misspelling: Fairly low

Risk of Mispronunciation: Low

Famous Namesakes: First daughter Chelsea Clinton; actress Chelsea Noble; actress Chelsea Handler

Common Nicknames: None

Common Variations: Chelsey, Kelsey

Consider This: Although still popular, this name has fallen quite a way from its peak of #34 in the '90s.

Cheri ★★

(French) a form of Cher.

First Impression: People think Cheri's happy disposition is perfect for someone who looks after others.

Gender Association: Used for girls

Popularity and Trend: Last ranked in the Top 1000 in the 1980s

Risk of Misspelling: Fairly high

Risk of Mispronunciation: Fairly high

Famous Namesakes: Comedian Cheri Oteri; actress Sherry Stringfield; actress Shari Belafonte

Common Nicknames: None

Common Variations: Cherie, Cherri

Consider This: For a seemingly simple name, pronunciation and spelling are big problems. It's typically pronounced "shah-REE," "SHAIR-ee," or "SHER-ee." When they hear the name, they may spell it "Sherry" or "Cherie."

Cheryl ★★★

(French) beloved.

First Impression: Folks believe Cheryl could be a sweet and feminine priss, a cranky and sarcastic barmaid, or a smart and organized leader.

Gender Association: Used for girls

Popularity and Trend: Last ranked in the Top 1000 in the 1990s

Risk of Misspelling: Average

Risk of Mispronunciation: Low

Famous Namesakes: Actress Cheryl Hines; model Cheryl Tiegs; singer Sheryl Crow; actress Cheryl Ladd

Common Nicknames: None

Common Variations: Sheryl

Consider This: This spelling has been more popular than "Sheryl," but neither is in the Top 1000.

Cheyenne ★★★★

(Cheyenne) a tribal name.

First Impression: Cheyenne is thought to be a happy, popular girl who's responsible and caring but perhaps a bit arrogant and self-centered at times.

Gender Association: Used mostly for girls

Popularity and Trend: #171
(#99 in 2000)
Risk of Misspelling: Average
Risk of Mispronunciation: Low
Famous Namesakes: Singer Cheyenne
Kimball
Common Nicknames: None
Common Variations: Chyenne,
Sheyenne
Consider This: This tribal name, which
is sometimes used for boys, may
have hit its peak a few years ago.

Chiara ★

(Italian) a form of Clara.
First Impression: Chiara is described as
a gossiper who's sometimes sweet
and sometimes not.
Gender Association: Used for girls
Popularity and Trend: Never been
ranked in Top 1000
Risk of Misspelling: High
Risk of Mispronunciation: High
Famous Namesakes: Actress Chiara
Caselli
Common Nicknames: None
Common Variations: Clara
Consider This: This Italian variation
has a mostly negative first impres-
sion plus two pronunciation
options: "key-AIR-ah" and
"key-AR-ah."

Chika ★★★

(Japanese) near and dear.
First Impression: Chika is pictured
as spunky, opinionated, and
outspoken.

Gender Association: Used for girls
Popularity and Trend: Never been
ranked in Top 1000
Risk of Misspelling: Average
Risk of Mispronunciation: Average
Famous Namesakes: Author Chika
Unigwe
Common Nicknames: None
Common Variations: None
Consider This: Chika is a unique name
that creates a spunky image.

Chiquita ★★★

(Spanish) little one.
First Impression: People think Chiquita
is a wild and colorful Latina
dancer.
Gender Association: Used for girls
Popularity and Trend: Last ranked in
the Top 1000 in the 1980s
Risk of Misspelling: Average
Risk of Mispronunciation: Average
Famous Namesakes: Banana mascot
Miss Chiquita
Common Nicknames: None
Common Variations: Shiquita
Consider This: When people hear this
name, they think only of banana
mascot Miss Chiquita.

Chloe ★★★★

(Greek) blooming, verdant.
First Impression: People agree on
Chloe's looks, but they can't
agree whether she's a charmer,
a fashionista, a follower, or an
intellectual.

Gender Association: Used for girls
Popularity and Trend: #18
(#38 in 2000)
Risk of Misspelling: Fairly low
Risk of Mispronunciation: Low
Famous Namesakes: Actress Chloe
Sevigny; character Chloe
O'Brian (24)
Common Nicknames: None
Common Variations: Cloe, Kloe
Consider This: Chloe has become
incredibly popular, and it may
keep rising. People don't know
what to think about the name,
but that's probably because they
don't know any Chloes…yet.

Chris ★

(Greek) a short form of Christina,
Christine.
First Impression: Chris is imagined
to be an arrogant, obnoxious
dullard.
Gender Association: Used mostly
for boys
Popularity and Trend: Last ranked in
the Top 1000 in the 1970s
Risk of Misspelling: Average
Risk of Mispronunciation: Low
Famous Namesakes: Tennis player
Chris Evert
Common Nicknames: Chrissy
Common Variations: Cris, Kris
Consider This: Chris is used much
more often for boys, and it's
much more casual than
Christine or Christina.

Christa ★★

(German) a form of Christina.

First Impression: People see Christa as a wild child with a short attention span and a dislike of school.

Gender Association: Used for girls

Popularity and Trend: Last ranked in the Top 1000 in the 1980s

Risk of Misspelling: Average

Risk of Mispronunciation: Low

Famous Namesakes: Teacher Christa McAuliffe; actress Christa Miller; actress Krista Allen

Common Nicknames: Christy

Common Variations: Crista, Krista

Consider This: Because Christa is imagined as a party girl who isn't college material, Christina is a better option.

Christina ★★★★

(Greek) Christian; anointed.

First Impression: Christina is considered either kind and soft-spoken or snobby and bratty.

Gender Association: Used for girls

Popularity and Trend: #158 (#73 in 2000)

Risk of Misspelling: Fairly low

Risk of Mispronunciation: Low

Famous Namesakes: Singer Christina Aguilera; actress Christina Applegate; actress Christina Ricci; singer Christina Milian; character Christina Yang (*Grey's Anatomy*)

Common Nicknames: Chrissy, Christy, Chris, Tina

Common Variations: Cristina, Kristina, Christine, Christa

Consider This: This versatile name was very popular from the '60s through the '90s, but it's slowly slipping now.

Christine ★★★★★

(French, English) a form of Christina.

First Impression: Christine is regarded as a good-humored woman who's strong-willed and career minded.

Gender Association: Used for girls

Popularity and Trend: #437 (#217 in 2000)

Risk of Misspelling: Fairly low

Risk of Mispronunciation: Low

Famous Namesakes: Actress Christine Taylor; actress Christine Lahti; actress Christine Baranski; speed skater Kristine Holzer

Common Nicknames: Chrissy, Christy, Chris

Common Variations: Cristine, Christina, Kristine, Christa

Consider This: A form of Christina, Christine is also versatile. It has a more positive image than Christina, but it's not nearly as popular.

Christy ★★★

(English) a short form of Christina, Christine.

First Impression: Christy is seen as a fun and flirty party girl by most, but others say she's a snobby model or actress.

Gender Association: Used for girls

Popularity and Trend: Last ranked in the Top 1000 in the 1980s

Risk of Misspelling: Average

Risk of Mispronunciation: Low

Famous Namesakes: Model Christie Brinkley; model Christy Turlington; actress Kristy McNichol; actress Kristy Swanson; figure skater Kristi Yamaguchi; singer Cristy Lane

Common Nicknames: None

Common Variations: Cristy, Kristy, Kristi, Christie

Consider This: This nickname for Christina and Christine peaked in the '70s and has been falling ever since. This spelling is the most common of several variations.

Cicely ★★★★

(English) a form of Cecilia.

First Impression: People think Cicely is a bubbly and adventurous girl who's flirty and funny.

Gender Association: Used for girls

Popularity and Trend: Never been ranked in Top 1000

Risk of Misspelling: Average

Risk of Mispronunciation: Fairly low

Famous Namesakes: Actress Cicely Tyson; illustrator Cicely Mary Barker

Common Nicknames: Cissy

Common Variations: Cecelia

Consider This: Cicely has never been a popular name, but people may know it if they're familiar with actress Cicely Tyson. Others may try to spell it "Sicily," like the island.

Cindy ★★★

(Greek) moon. (Latin) a form of Cynthia.

First Impression: Perky, bossy, or snobby—folks believe Cindy's personality can run the gamut.

Gender Association: Used for girls

Popularity and Trend: #365 (#262 in 2000)

Risk of Misspelling: Fairly low

Risk of Mispronunciation: Low

Famous Namesakes: Model Cindy Crawford; character Cindy Brady (*The Brady Bunch*); singer Cyndi Lauper

Common Nicknames: None

Common Variations: Cindi, Cyndi

Consider This: This form of Cindy scores better than Cyndi, but they're both dated.

Claire ★★★★

(French) a form of Clair.

First Impression: Claire is pictured as attractive, sweet, and perfect in every way.

Gender Association: Used for girls

Popularity and Trend: #86 (#86 in 2000)

Risk of Misspelling: Average

Risk of Mispronunciation: Low

Famous Namesakes: Actress Claire Danes; actress Claire Bloom; character Claire Bennett (*Heroes*); saint Clare of Assisi; playwright Clare Boothe Luce

Common Nicknames: None

Common Variations: Clair, Clare, Clara, Klaire

Consider This: Claire is an old-fashioned name that rose dramatically in the '80s and '90s and has stayed steadily popular ever since. It's "perfect" image probably has something to do with that.

Clara ★★★★

(Latin) clear; bright.

First Impression: Clara is regarded as a beautiful and dainty old woman.

Gender Association: Used for girls

Popularity and Trend: #233 (#354 in 2000)

Risk of Misspelling: Fairly low

Risk of Mispronunciation: Fairly low

Famous Namesakes: Nurse Clara Barton; character Clara (*The Nutcracker*)

Common Nicknames: None

Common Variations: Clair, Claire, Clare, Klara

Consider This: Clara was a Top 100 name from the 1890s to the 1930s, which is probably why people think it's an old lady's name. It's been rising fast since 2000, though.

Clare ★★★

(English) a form of Clara.

First Impression: Clare is imagined to be a smart and sophisticated scholar who's introspective and serious.

Gender Association: Used mostly for girls

Popularity and Trend: #663 (#537 in 2000)

Risk of Misspelling: Average

Risk of Mispronunciation: Low

Famous Namesakes: Saint Clare of Assisi; playwright Clare Boothe Luce; actress Claire Danes; actress Claire Bloom; character Claire Bennett (*Heroes*)

Common Nicknames: None

Common Variations: Clair, Claire, Clara, Klare

Consider This: This Clare has a positive image like Claire, but it loses points on spelling and popularity.

Clarissa ★★★

(Greek) brilliant. (Italian) a form of Clara.

First Impression: People see Clarissa as a spoiled brat who needs a lot of attention.

Gender Association: Used for girls

Popularity and Trend: #468 (#325 in 2000)

Risk of Misspelling: Fairly low

Risk of Mispronunciation: Low

Famous Namesakes: Character Clarissa Darling (*Clarissa Explains It All*); character Clarissa Dalloway (*Mrs. Dalloway*); character Clarissa Harlowe (*Clarissa*)

Common Nicknames: None

Common Variations: Clarisa

Consider This: Clarissa has a bratty image, but Carissa is a sound-alike name that comes across much better.

Claudia ★★★

(Latin) a form of Claude.

First Impression: Many think Claudia may be a kind bookworm, a standoffish prude, or a spoiled diva.

Gender Association: Used for girls

Popularity and Trend: #339 (#200 in 2000)

Risk of Misspelling: Fairly low

Risk of Mispronunciation: Low

Famous Namesakes: Model Claudia Schiffer; character Claudia Salazar (*24*)

Common Nicknames: Claudie

Common Variations: Klaudia, Claudette

Consider This: Nobody knows what kind of first impression Claudia makes, but its popularity is certainly sinking.

Clementine ★★

(Latin) merciful.

First Impression: Clementine is thought to be quiet, shy, dull, and stodgy.

Gender Association: Used for girls

Popularity and Trend: Last ranked in the Top 1000 in the 1950s

Risk of Misspelling: Fairly low

Risk of Mispronunciation: Fairly low

Famous Namesakes: Character Clementine Kruczynski (*Eternal Sunshine of the Spotless Mind*); baroness Clementine Spencer-Churchill

Common Nicknames: None

Common Variations: Clementina, Klementine

Consider This: Maybe Clementine hasn't been a Top 1000 name since the '50s because people think it's so sad and dull.

Colleen ★★★

(Irish) girl.

First Impression: Colleen strikes people as bashful and bookish, but once she comes out of her shell, she's sweet and playful.

Gender Association: Used for girls

Popularity and Trend: #902 (#455 in 2000)

Risk of Misspelling: Fairly low

Risk of Mispronunciation: Low

Famous Namesakes: Actress Colleen Dewhurst

Common Nicknames: None

Common Variations: Coleen, Kolleen

Consider This: This Irish name may disappear from the Top 1000 soon.

Collette ★★

(Greek, French) a form of Nicole.

First Impression: Collette comes across as coy and coquettish, but people think this Southern socialite also has a stubborn side that causes a lot of trouble.

Gender Association: Used for girls

Popularity and Trend: Last ranked in the Top 1000 in the 1970s

Risk of Misspelling: Average

Risk of Mispronunciation: Low

Famous Namesakes: Actress Toni Colette; designer Collette Dinnigan

Common Nicknames: None

Common Variations: Colette, Kollette

Consider This: Collette is a nickname for Nicole, but some parents may think it's formal enough to stand on its own.

Connie ★★★

(Latin) a familiar form of Constance.

First Impression: Connie is seen as either the weak, mousy type or a perky and outgoing optimist.

Gender Association: Used mostly for girls

Popularity and Trend: Last ranked in the Top 1000 in the 1990s

Risk of Misspelling: Low

Risk of Mispronunciation: Low

Famous Namesakes: Actress Connie Britton; news anchor Connie Chung; singer Connie Frances;

actress Connie Selleca; singer Connie Stevens; actress Connie Nielsen

Common Nicknames: None

Common Variations: None

Consider This: There are a lot of famous Connies, but they're all middle aged or older.

Constance ★★★

(Latin) constant; firm.

First Impression: Constance is described as an educated woman who's serious and shy.

Gender Association: Used for girls

Popularity and Trend: Last ranked in the Top 1000 in the 1990s

Risk of Misspelling: Fairly low

Risk of Mispronunciation: Low

Famous Namesakes: Actress Constance Towers; actress Constance Marie

Common Nicknames: Connie

Common Variations: Konstance

Consider This: Constance is more formal than Connie, but perhaps they'd work well together as a given name and nickname pairing.

Consuelo ★★★

(Spanish) consolation.

First Impression: Folks think Consuelo's smile is as pleasant as she is.

Gender Association: Used for girls

Popularity and Trend: Last ranked in the Top 1000 in the 1980s

Risk of Misspelling: Fairly high

Risk of Mispronunciation: Fairly high

Famous Namesakes: Aristocrat Consuelo Vanderbilt

Common Nicknames: None

Common Variations: Consuela

Consider This: A common name in Latino families, Consuelo may be hard for others to spell and pronounce.

Cora ★★★★

(Greek) maiden.

First Impression: People believe Cora may be classy, but that doesn't stop her from being difficult and demanding.

Gender Association: Used for girls

Popularity and Trend: #384 (#482 in 2000)

Risk of Misspelling: Fairly low

Risk of Mispronunciation: Low

Famous Namesakes: Actress Cora Witherspoon

Common Nicknames: Corey, Coretta, Corissa

Common Variations: Kora

Consider This: For such a short name, Cora has a good number of nicknames.

Cordelia ★★★★

(Latin) warmhearted. (Welsh) sea jewel.

First Impression: Cordelia is pictured as a gentle, old-fashioned woman with a generous heart.

Gender Association: Used for girls

Popularity and Trend: Last ranked in the Top 1000 in the 1950s

Risk of Misspelling: Fairly low

Risk of Mispronunciation: Fairly low

Famous Namesakes: Character Queen Cordelia (*King Lear*); character Cordelia Chase (*Buffy the Vampire Slayer*)

Common Nicknames: Delia, Della

Common Variations: Kordelia

Consider This: Cordelia hasn't been ranked since the '50s, which is probably why people think it has an old-fashioned first impression.

Cori ★★★

(Irish) a form of Corey.

First Impression: People describe Cori as a mischievous and fun-loving tomboy with red hair and freckles.

Gender Association: Used mostly for girls

Popularity and Trend: Last ranked in the Top 1000 in the 1990s

Risk of Misspelling: Fairly high

Risk of Mispronunciation: Low

Famous Namesakes: Model Cory Kennedy

Common Nicknames: None

Common Variations: Corey, Cory

Consider This: "Cori" may be a more feminine spelling, but it isn't as popular as "Corey" or "Cory," which are both used more for boys and thus could cause both spelling trouble *and* gender confusion.

Corinne ★★★★

(Greek) maiden.

First Impression: People think Corinne is either a sweet, helpful librarian or a graceful and outgoing Southerner.

Gender Association: Used for girls

Popularity and Trend: #826 (#546 in 2000)

Risk of Misspelling: Average

Risk of Mispronunciation: Low

Famous Namesakes: Singer Corinne Bailey Rae

Common Nicknames: Cory

Common Variations: Corrine, Corrina

Consider This: Corinne's popularity is sinking fast, but the name's first impression is still mostly positive.

Corrina ★★★

(Greek) a form of Corinne.

First Impression: People say Corrina is lovable, boisterous, and sometimes silly.

Gender Association: Used for girls

Popularity and Trend: Never been ranked in Top 1000

Risk of Misspelling: Average

Risk of Mispronunciation: Fairly low

Famous Namesakes: Ancient poet Corinna

Common Nicknames: Cory

Common Variations: Corrine

Consider This: This name has never been in the Top 1000, but it has a fun image.

Courtney ★★★

(English) from the court.

First Impression: Quite a contrast here: Some think Courtney is a tease, and others think she's a goody-goody.

Gender Association: Used mostly for girls

Popularity and Trend: #190 (#59 in 2000)

Risk of Misspelling: Fairly low

Risk of Mispronunciation: Low

Famous Namesakes: Singer Courtney Love; actress Courteney Cox

Common Nicknames: None

Common Variations: Cortney, Kourtney, Kortney

Consider This: Although Courtney is still a Top 200 name, it has fallen quite a bit from its high of #22 in the '90s.

Cristy ★★★

(English) a familiar form of Cristina.

First Impression: Folks believe Cristy always looks on the bright side of life and always radiates good feelings.

Gender Association: Used for girls

Popularity and Trend: Last ranked in the Top 1000 in the 1980s

Risk of Misspelling: Fairly high

Risk of Mispronunciation: Low

Famous Namesakes: Singer Cristy Lane; figure skater Kristi Yamaguchi; model Christie Brinkley; model Christy Turlington; actress Kristy McNichol; actress Kristy Swanson

Common Nicknames: None

Common Variations: Christie, Christy, Kristy, Kristi

Consider This: This version of Christy is not common, which could cause spelling troubles, but it has the most positive first impression of any of the name's variations.

Crystal ★★★

(Latin) clear, brilliant glass.

First Impression: People see Crystal as nice but trashy.

Gender Association: Used for girls

Popularity and Trend: #201 (#132 in 2000)

Risk of Misspelling: Fairly low

Risk of Mispronunciation: Low

Famous Namesakes: Actress Krystal Bernard; singer Crystal Gayle; gospel singer Crystal Lewis

Common Nicknames: Crys, Cristy

Common Variations: Cristal, Chrystel, Krystal

Consider This: Although Crystal is thought trashy by many, it remains relatively popular.

Cyndi ★★

(Greek) a form of Cindy.

First Impression: Cyndi is considered to be an eccentric, opinionated, and boyish punk rocker, like Cyndi Lauper.

Gender Association: Used for girls

Popularity and Trend: Last ranked in the Top 1000 in the 1960s

Risk of Misspelling: Fairly high

Risk of Mispronunciation: Low

Famous Namesakes: Singer Cyndi Lauper; model Cindy Crawford; character Cindy Brady (*The Brady Bunch*)

Common Nicknames: None

Common Variations: Cindy, Cindi

Consider This: Unless you're a big Cyndi Lauper fan, you'll want to avoid this variation of Cindy.

Cynthia ★★★

(Greek) moon.

First Impression: Some people think Cynthia is bubbly and cheery, but just as many think she's stiff and snobby.

Gender Association: Used for girls

Popularity and Trend: #240 (#164 in 2000)

Risk of Misspelling: Fairly low

Risk of Mispronunciation: Low

Famous Namesakes: Designer Cynthia Rowley; actress Cynthia Nixon; actress Cynthia Watros

Common Nicknames: Cindy

Common Variations: Cinthia

Consider This: Popular from the '40s to the '70s, Cynthia feels a bit dated.

Daisy ★★★★

(English) day's eye.

First Impression: Daisy is thought to be sunny, sociable, and happy-go-lucky.

Gender Association: Used for girls

Popularity and Trend: #149 (#141 in 2000)

Risk of Misspelling: Low

Risk of Mispronunciation: Low

Famous Namesakes: Character Daisy Buchanan (*The Great Gatsby*); fiction character Daisy Miller; character Daisy Duke (*The Dukes of Hazzard*); Disney character Daisy Duck

Common Nicknames: None

Common Variations: Daisey

Consider This: Daisy makes a positive—but not particularly serious—first impression.

Dakota ★★★★

(Dakota) a tribal name.

First Impression: People consider Dakota to be a nice tomboy who loves sports and the outdoors.

Gender Association: Used mostly for boys

Popularity and Trend: #191 (#295 in 2000)

Risk of Misspelling: Low

Risk of Mispronunciation: Low

Famous Namesakes: Actress Dakota Fanning

Common Nicknames: None

Common Variations: Dakotah

Consider This: Because it's used more for boys, people think Dakota has a tomboy vibe. But Dakota Fanning may change that perception.

Dana ★★

(English) from Denmark; bright as day.

First Impression: To some, Dana is mean and insecure, but others believe she's lively and strong-minded—though still annoying.

Gender Association: Used mostly for girls

Popularity and Trend: #395 (#311 in 2000)

Risk of Misspelling: Fairly low

Risk of Mispronunciation: Low

Famous Namesakes: Character Dana Scully (*The X-Files*); actress Dana Delaney; actress Dana Reeve; actress Dana "Queen Latifah" Owens

Common Nicknames: None

Common Variations: Daina, Dayna

Consider This: Dana probably won't match its '70s popularity anytime soon.

Dani ★★

(Hebrew) a familiar form of Danielle.

First Impression: Dani reminds people of a bubbly, active sports nut.

Gender Association: Used for girls

Popularity and Trend: Never been ranked in Top 1000

Risk of Misspelling: Average
Risk of Mispronunciation: Fairly low
Famous Namesakes: Character Dani Beck (*Law & Order: Special Victims Unit*)
Common Nicknames: None
Common Variations: Danni
Consider This: This familiar form of Danielle creates a sporty image, most likely because it sounds like the boys' name Danny.

Danica ★★★★
(Slavic) morning star. (Hebrew) a form of Danielle.
First Impression: Danica is pictured as bursting with life—and chatter.
Gender Association: Used for girls
Popularity and Trend: #352 (#610 in 2005)
Risk of Misspelling: Fairly low
Risk of Mispronunciation: Low
Famous Namesakes: Racecar driver Danica Patrick; actress Danica McKellar
Common Nicknames: Dani
Common Variations: Dannica
Consider This: Racecar driver Danica Patrick is probably responsible for this name's huge jump in popularity from 2005 to 2006.

Danielle ★★★★
(Hebrew, French) God is my judge.
First Impression: Danielle is imagined to be good-natured, helpful, and funny.

Gender Association: Used mostly for girls
Popularity and Trend: #116 (#48 in 2000)
Risk of Misspelling: Fairly low
Risk of Mispronunciation: Low
Famous Namesakes: Novelist Danielle Steel; model Danielle Evans
Common Nicknames: Dani
Common Variations: Daniell, Danyel, Daniella
Consider This: A Top 20 name throughout the '80s and '90s, the very versatile Danielle is slowly falling.

Daphne ★★★
(Greek) laurel tree.
First Impression: Daphne is described as an affectionate and nonjudgmental confidante who has tall, model-like looks and lots of patience.
Gender Association: Used for girls
Popularity and Trend: #606 (#632 in 2000)
Risk of Misspelling: Fairly low
Risk of Mispronunciation: Fairly low
Famous Namesakes: Actress Daphne Zuniga; character Daphne Blake (*Scooby Doo*); actress Daphne Maxwell Reid; actress Daphne Ashbrook
Common Nicknames: None
Common Variations: Daphnee, Dafny
Consider This: This name's popularity peaked in the '60s, but it's slowly rising again.

Darcy ★★★
(Irish) dark. (French) fortress.
First Impression: Some see Darcy as a mousy and lonely nerd, but others see her as an out-of-control wild girl.
Gender Association: Used mostly for girls
Popularity and Trend: Last ranked in the Top 1000 in the 1990s
Risk of Misspelling: Fairly low
Risk of Mispronunciation: Low
Famous Namesakes: Musician D'arcy Wretzky
Common Nicknames: None
Common Variations: Darci, Darcie
Consider This: Whether it's considered nerdy or wild, Darcy doesn't seem to have a positive image.

Darla ★★★★
(English) a form of Darlene.
First Impression: Darla is seen as a charismatic, adorable youth.
Gender Association: Used for girls
Popularity and Trend: Last ranked in the Top 1000 in the 1980s
Risk of Misspelling: Low
Risk of Mispronunciation: Low
Famous Namesakes: Character Darla (*Buffy the Vampire Slayer*); character Darla (*The Little Rascals*)
Common Nicknames: None
Common Variations: Darlene
Consider This: Darla is pictured as a child, which will be fine when your daughter is young, but a problem as she gets older.

Darlene ★★★

(French) little darling.

First Impression: Darlene is pictured as a rough and rude loudmouth with lots to say and lots of spunk.

Gender Association: Used for girls

Popularity and Trend: Last ranked in the Top 1000 in the 1980s

Risk of Misspelling: Low

Risk of Mispronunciation: Low

Famous Namesakes: Singer Darlene Love; character Darlene Conner (*Roseanne*); tennis player Darlene Hard

Common Nicknames: Darla

Common Variations: Darlin

Consider This: This name's first impression is likely too negative to make it a choice for most people.

Dawn ★★★

(English) sunrise, dawn.

First Impression: People think Dawn's luminous name gives her a sunny image.

Gender Association: Used for girls

Popularity and Trend: Last ranked in the Top 1000 in the 1980s

Risk of Misspelling: Low

Risk of Mispronunciation: Low

Famous Namesakes: Actress Dawn French

Common Nicknames: None

Common Variations: Dawna

Consider This: Dawn was a Top 100 name throughout the '60s and '70s, but it may be too dated for today's parents. Plus, its pronunciation sounds similar to Don, a traditional boys' name, which may cause gender confusion.

Deborah ★★

(Hebrew) bee.

First Impression: Although Deborah is considered very social, she isn't easy to get along with.

Gender Association: Used for girls

Popularity and Trend: #676 (#497 in 2000)

Risk of Misspelling: Average

Risk of Mispronunciation: Average

Famous Namesakes: Actress Debra Winger; singer Deborah Gibson; journalist Deborah Norville; actress Deborah Kerr; singer Deborah Harry; singer Deborah Cox

Common Nicknames: Deb, Debbie

Common Variations: Debra

Consider This: Deborah was very popular in the '50s and '60s, but it's much less so today. There may be pronunciation problems because some say "DEB-rah," some say "DEB-oh-rah," and a small handful even say "dah-BORE-ah."

Dee Dee ★★

(Welsh) black, dark.

First Impression: People say Dee Dee is friendly and outspoken, but also annoying and childish.

Gender Association: Used for girls

Popularity and Trend: Last ranked in the Top 1000 in the 1960s

Risk of Misspelling: Average

Risk of Mispronunciation: Low

Famous Namesakes: Radio personality Dee Dee Bridgewater

Common Nicknames: Dee

Common Variations: DeeDee

Consider This: Despite its seeming simplicity, people may not know to spell out this name.

Deirdre ★★★

(Irish) sorrowful; wanderer.

First Impression: Folks believe Deirdre isn't always talkative, but she's always a good friend.

Gender Association: Used for girls

Popularity and Trend: Last ranked in the Top 1000 in the 1990s

Risk of Misspelling: Average

Risk of Mispronunciation: Average

Famous Namesakes: Actress Deirdre Hall; author Deirdre Coleman Imus

Common Nicknames: Dee Dee

Common Variations: Deidra, Diedra

Consider This: Now a Top 1000 dropout, people may assume Deirdre is middle aged.

Delia ★★

(Greek) visible; from Delos, Greece. (German, Welsh) a form of Adelaide, Cordelia.

First Impression: To many, Delia may be a snobby, greedy ice queen.

Gender Association: Used for girls
Popularity and Trend: Last ranked in the Top 1000 in the 1980s
Risk of Misspelling: Average
Risk of Mispronunciation: Average
Famous Namesakes: Journalist Delia Gallagher; television chef Delia Smith
Common Nicknames: None
Common Variations: None
Consider This: Delia has quite a negative image, and people may confuse it for "DELL-ee-ah" instead of "DEAL-ee-ah." Delilah is a similar name that scores much better.

Delilah ★★★★

(Hebrew) brooder.
First Impression: Caring, friendly, and humorous, Delilah is pictured as the life of the party.
Gender Association: Used for girls
Popularity and Trend: #548 (#673 in 2000)
Risk of Misspelling: Fairly low
Risk of Mispronunciation: Low
Famous Namesakes: Biblical figure Delilah; radio personality Delilah
Common Nicknames: Lila
Common Variations: None
Consider This: The hit song "Hey There Delilah" by the Plain White T's may have a future effect on this name's popularity.

Della ★★★

(English) a form of Adelaide, Cordelia, Delaney.
First Impression: Della comes across as a kind but ditzy and distracted waitress.
Gender Association: Used for girls
Popularity and Trend: Last ranked in the Top 1000 in the 1970s
Risk of Misspelling: Low
Risk of Mispronunciation: Low
Famous Namesakes: Actress Della Reese
Common Nicknames: None
Common Variations: None
Consider This: Because Della comes across as unintelligent, try Adelaide, Cordelia, or Delaney, which are Della's root names.

Delores ★★

(Spanish) a form of Dolores.
First Impression: Most people think of Delores as troubled and unhappy.
Gender Association: Used for girls
Popularity and Trend: Last ranked in the Top 1000 in the 1980s
Risk of Misspelling: Average
Risk of Mispronunciation: Fairly low
Famous Namesakes: Fiction character Dolores Claiborne; character Dolores Umbridge (*Harry Potter* series)
Common Nicknames: Lola
Common Variations: Deloris, Dolores
Consider This: *Harry Potter*'s Dolores Umbridge hasn't helped this name's perception. Plus, it doesn't help that Dolores, the root name, means "suffering."

Delphine ★★

(Greek) from Delphi, Greece.
First Impression: Delphine is imagined to be an attention-seeking motor mouth who loves to gossip.
Gender Association: Used for girls
Popularity and Trend: Last ranked in the Top 1000 in the 1960s
Risk of Misspelling: Average
Risk of Mispronunciation: Fairly low
Famous Namesakes: Businesswoman Delphine Arnault; actress Delphine Seyrig
Common Nicknames: None
Common Variations: Delfina
Consider This: This very Greek name peaked in the '20s and hasn't been ranked since the '60s.

Delta ★★★★

(Greek) door.
First Impression: People imagine Delta as a quick-witted social butterfly with Southern charm.
Gender Association: Used for girls
Popularity and Trend: Last ranked in the Top 1000 in the 1910s
Risk of Misspelling: Low
Risk of Mispronunciation: Low
Famous Namesakes: Singer Delta Goodrem; actress Delta Burke
Common Nicknames: None
Common Variations: None

Consider This: Delta has never been a popular name, but people will know it because of Delta Burke, to whom the first impression is very closely tied.

Demi ★★

(French) half. (Greek) a form of Demetria.

First Impression: Demi is thought to have actress Demi Moore's beauty, but she could be funny and cheerful, spoiled and self-involved, or mysterious and independent.

Gender Association: Used for girls

Popularity and Trend: Last ranked in the Top 1000 in the 1990s

Risk of Misspelling: Fairly low

Risk of Mispronunciation: Fairly high

Famous Namesakes: Actress Demi Moore

Common Nicknames: None

Common Variations: None

Consider This: People know this name because of Demi Moore, but it's still thought to be unusual and somewhat hard to pronounce as "deh-MEE," not "DEM-ee."

Dena ★★

(English, Native American) valley. (Hebrew) a form of Dinah.

First Impression: Dena is pictured as an artistic and free-spirited mother.

Gender Association: Used for girls

Popularity and Trend: Last ranked in the Top 1000 in the 1990s

Risk of Misspelling: Fairly high

Risk of Mispronunciation: Average

Famous Namesakes: Basketball player Dena Head

Common Nicknames: None

Common Variations: Deena, Dina, Dee

Consider This: When people see this name, they may mistakenly pronounce it "DEH-nah" instead of "DEE-nah," and when they hear it, they may mistakenly spell it "Dina."

Denise ★★★

(French) follower of Dionysus, the god of wine.

First Impression: Denise is seen as either a friendly busybody or a wallflower.

Gender Association: Used for girls

Popularity and Trend: #379 (#328 in 2000)

Risk of Misspelling: Fairly low

Risk of Mispronunciation: Low

Famous Namesakes: Actress Denise Richards; singer Denise Williams; fitness guru Denise Austin; character Denise Huxtable (*The Cosby Show*)

Common Nicknames: None

Common Variations: Denice

Consider This: Denise was very popular from the '50s to the '70s, but feels a bit dated now.

Desiree ★★★

(French) desired, longed for.

First Impression: People think Desiree's looks may be desirable, but her personality may be conceited and rude or caring and quiet.

Gender Association: Used for girls

Popularity and Trend: #300 (#181 in 2000)

Risk of Misspelling: Average

Risk of Mispronunciation: Average

Famous Namesakes: Singer Desiree

Common Nicknames: Desi

Common Variations: Desirae

Consider This: People may mistakenly pronounce it "dez-uh-REE" instead of "dez-uh-RAY."

Destiny ★★★★

(French) fate.

First Impression: Destiny is pictured as a chatty and vivacious go-getter, but she also has a sweet, dreamy side.

Gender Association: Used for girls

Popularity and Trend: #37 (#24 in 2000)

Risk of Misspelling: Low

Risk of Mispronunciation: Low

Famous Namesakes: Actress Destiny "Miley" Cyrus

Common Nicknames: None

Common Variations: Destinee

Consider This: A lot of people are making a date with Destiny: The name has remained in the Top 40 since 2000.

Diamond ★★★

(Latin) precious gem.

First Impression: People describe Diamond as spoiled, vain, and as elegant as her name suggests.

Gender Association: Used mostly for girls

Popularity and Trend: #316 (#162 in 2000)

Risk of Misspelling: Low

Risk of Mispronunciation: Low

Famous Namesakes: Singer Neil Diamond; actor Lou Diamond Phillips

Common Nicknames: Di

Common Variations: None

Consider This: Diamond's vain image may be what's causing it to lose popularity.

Diana ★★★★★

(Latin) divine.

First Impression: Not surprisingly, Diana is described as a sweet, generous, and poised princess.

Gender Association: Used for girls

Popularity and Trend: #120 (#106 in 2000)

Risk of Misspelling: Fairly low

Risk of Mispronunciation: Low

Famous Namesakes: Princess Diana; singer Diana Ross; actress Diana Rigg; musician Diana Krall

Common Nicknames: Di

Common Variations: Dianna

Consider This: This name's image is still very closely associated with Princess Diana's.

Diane ★★★

(Latin) a form of Diana.

First Impression: Diane is pictured as full of confidence, but she sometimes seems a little haughty.

Gender Association: Used for girls

Popularity and Trend: Last ranked in the Top 1000 in the 1980s

Risk of Misspelling: Fairly low

Risk of Mispronunciation: Low

Famous Namesakes: Actress Dianne Wiest; actress Diane Keaton; speed skater Dianne Holum; actress Diane Lane; zoologist Dian Fossey; actress Diane Ladd; journalist Diane Sawyer; designer Diane von Furstenberg; senator Diane Feinstein

Common Nicknames: Di

Common Variations: Dianne

Consider This: Diane was as popular as Diana in the middle of the twentieth century, but it fell off the Top 1000 list in the '80s, while Diana got a boost from a certain princess.

Dianne ★★★★

(Latin) a form of Diana.

First Impression: Diana is a goddess in Roman mythology, yet people say it's Dianne who's the charismatic woman with the beauty of a goddess.

Gender Association: Used for girls

Popularity and Trend: Last ranked in the Top 1000 in the 1980s

Risk of Misspelling: Average

Risk of Mispronunciation: Low

Famous Namesakes: Actress Dianne Wiest; actress Diane Keaton; speed skater Dianne Holum; actress Diane Lane; zoologist Dian Fossey; actress Diane Ladd; journalist Diane Sawyer; designer Diane von Furstenberg

Common Nicknames: Di

Common Variations: Diane

Consider This: Dianne has a more positive first impression than Diane, but the spelling is less well known and it's just as unpopular.

Dina ★★

(Hebrew) a form of Dinah.

First Impression: Most people describe Dina as a raspy-voiced woman who loves to drink, smoke, flirt, and have a wild time.

Gender Association: Used for girls

Popularity and Trend: Last ranked in the Top 1000 in the 1990s

Risk of Misspelling: Average

Risk of Mispronunciation: Average

Famous Namesakes: Actress Dina Meyer; singer Dinah Shore; politician Dina Powell; actress Dinah Manhoff; singer Dinah Washington

Common Nicknames: None

Common Variations: Dena, Deena, Dee

Consider This: People may pronounce this name as "DEE-nah" or "DYE-nah."

Dixie ★★★★

(French) tenth. (English) wall; dike.

First Impression: Dixie is described as a giggly, chatty, and ditzy Southerner.

Gender Association: Used for girls

Popularity and Trend: Last ranked in the Top 1000 in the 1980s

Risk of Misspelling: Low

Risk of Mispronunciation: Low

Famous Namesakes: Actress Dixie Carter

Common Nicknames: None

Common Variations: None

Consider This: Dixie is still synonymous with the South for many people, so it may not appeal to parents in other parts of the country.

Dolly ★★★★

(American) a familiar form of Dolores, Dorothy.

First Impression: People say Dolly is a friendly, vivacious, and cheerful country girl, much like country singer Dolly Parton.

Gender Association: Used for girls

Popularity and Trend: Last ranked in the Top 1000 in the 1960s

Risk of Misspelling: Low

Risk of Mispronunciation: Low

Famous Namesakes: First lady Dolly Madison; singer Dolly Parton

Common Nicknames: None

Common Variations: None

Consider This: Most people like Dolly Parton, so most people like the name Dolly. But if you don't want your daughter evoking a country singer with bountiful bosoms, you should pick another name.

Dominique ★★

(French) a form of Dominica.

First Impression: No single image of Dominique is dominant: People think she could be sweet, temperamental, or playful.

Gender Association: Used mostly for girls

Popularity and Trend: #648 (#258 in 2000)

Risk of Misspelling: Average

Risk of Mispronunciation: Average

Famous Namesakes: Actress Dominique Swain; gymnast Dominique Dawes; gymnast Dominique Moceanu

Common Nicknames: None

Common Variations: Domonique

Consider This: Once Olympic gymnasts Dominique Dawes and Dominique Moceanu retired, this name's popularity took a dive.

Donata ★

(Latin) gift.

First Impression: Donata is seen as a moody and dull nag with a bad attitude.

Gender Association: Used for girls

Popularity and Trend: Never been ranked in Top 1000

Risk of Misspelling: Fairly low

Risk of Mispronunciation: Average

Famous Namesakes: None

Common Nicknames: None

Common Variations: Donatila

Consider This: Donata may be a popular and well-liked name in Latin countries, but others have a negative first impression of this unfamiliar name.

Donna ★★

(Italian) lady.

First Impression: There's very little consensus about Donna: She may be shy, outgoing, mean, nice, smart, or ditzy.

Gender Association: Used for girls

Popularity and Trend: #832 (#660 in 2000)

Risk of Misspelling: Fairly low

Risk of Mispronunciation: Low

Famous Namesakes: Actress Donna Reed; singer Donna Summer; designer Donna Karan; singer Donna Lewis; character Donna Martin (*Beverly Hills, 90210*)

Common Nicknames: None

Common Variations: Dona

Consider This: Once *The Donna Reed Show* left the airwaves, this name's popularity started to sink.

Dora ★★★★
(Greek) gift.

First Impression: Like Dora the Explorer, Dora is pictured as a munchkin who's kind, intelligent, pleasant, and adventurous.

Gender Association: Used for girls

Popularity and Trend: Last ranked in the Top 1000 in the 1990s

Risk of Misspelling: Low

Risk of Mispronunciation: Low

Famous Namesakes: Television character Dora the Explorer

Common Nicknames: Dori

Common Variations: Doreen, Doretta

Consider This: Thanks to *Dora the Explorer*, Dora is pictured as an ethnic child, which may or may not fit with your family's background.

Doreen ★★
(Irish) moody, sullen. (French) golden. (Greek) a form of Dora.

First Impression: Doreen is seen as brainy, but also boring and grumpy.

Gender Association: Used for girls

Popularity and Trend: Last ranked in the Top 1000 in the 1970s

Risk of Misspelling: Low

Risk of Mispronunciation: Low

Famous Namesakes: Author Doreen Cronin

Common Nicknames: None

Common Variations: Dora

Consider This: The name is easy to spell and pronounce, but its unpleasant first impression sinks it.

Doria ★★
(Greek) a form of Dorian.

First Impression: People see Doria as a mopey, unpopular wallflower who lives alone with her cats.

Gender Association: Used for girls

Popularity and Trend: Never been ranked in Top 1000

Risk of Misspelling: Fairly low

Risk of Mispronunciation: Fairly low

Famous Namesakes: None

Common Nicknames: Dori

Common Variations: None

Consider This: It's no wonder Doria has never been a popular name: People think it's fit for a frumpy wallflower.

Doris ★★★
(Greek) sea.

First Impression: Doris makes people think of a happy old lady who bakes and knits for her grandchildren.

Gender Association: Used for girls

Popularity and Trend: Last ranked in the Top 1000 in the 1990s

Risk of Misspelling: Low

Risk of Mispronunciation: Low

Famous Namesakes: Actress Doris Day; actress Doris Roberts; author Doris Kearns Goodwin; heiress Doris Duke

Common Nicknames: Dori

Common Variations: None

Consider This: Doris is better suited for a grandma than a child.

Dorothy ★★★★
(Greek) gift of God.

First Impression: Most people describe Dorothy as a kind, forgiving, and hospitable friend.

Gender Association: Used for girls

Popularity and Trend: Last ranked in the Top 1000 in the 1980s

Risk of Misspelling: Low

Risk of Mispronunciation: Low

Famous Namesakes: Character Dorothy Gale (*The Wizard of Oz*); model Dorothy Stratten; character Dorothy Zbornak (*The Golden Girls*); writer Dorothy Parker; actress Dorothy Dandridge; figure skater Dorothy Hamill

Common Nicknames: Dot, Dottie, Dori

Common Variations: Dorothea, Doretta

Consider This: Dorothy feels dated, but with its positive vibe and great versatility, perhaps it could follow the trend of old-fashioned names making comebacks.

Dottie ★★★
(Greek) a familiar form of Dorothy.

First Impression: Dottie is described as a chipper and talkative older woman who's sort of round, very sweet, and not really hip.

Gender Association: Used for girls

Popularity and Trend: Last ranked in the Top 1000 in the 1960s

Risk of Misspelling: Fairly low

Risk of Mispronunciation: Low

Famous Namesakes: Country singer Dottie West; golfer Dottie Pepper

Common Nicknames: Dot

Common Variations: Dotty

Consider This: Dottie isn't formal and it feels old, but it's definitely a cute nickname.

Drusilla ★★

(Latin) descendant of Drusus, the strong one.

First Impression: People think Drusilla is scary, evil, and witchy.

Gender Association: Used for girls

Popularity and Trend: Last ranked in the Top 1000 in the 1910s

Risk of Misspelling: Average

Risk of Mispronunciation: Fairly low

Famous Namesakes: Character Drusilla (*Buffy the Vampire Slayer*)

Common Nicknames: Dru

Common Variations: Drucilla

Consider This: The very negative image and the fact that it hasn't been popular since the 1910s should dissuade parents from choosing this name.

Eartha ★★★

(English) earthy.

First Impression: Eartha is described as a laid-back nature lover.

Gender Association: Used for girls

Popularity and Trend: Last ranked in the Top 1000 in the 1940s

Risk of Misspelling: Low

Risk of Mispronunciation: Fairly low

Famous Namesakes: Actress Eartha Kitt

Common Nicknames: None

Common Variations: None

Consider This: For obvious reasons, Eartha has an earthy image. It's relatively easy to spell and pronounce, too.

Ebony ★★★★

(Greek) a hard, dark wood.

First Impression: Ebony is considered a strong beauty with a strong personality.

Gender Association: Used for girls

Popularity and Trend: Last ranked in the Top 1000 in the 1980s

Risk of Misspelling: Low

Risk of Mispronunciation: Low

Famous Namesakes: Actress Ebony Thomas

Common Nicknames: None

Common Variations: Eboney

Consider This: Ebony comes across as an African American name.

Eden ★★★

(Babylonian) a plain. (Hebrew) delightful.

First Impression: Eden is perceived as a preacher's daughter who seems innocent, but may be more worldly than her daddy realizes.

Gender Association: Used mostly for girls

Popularity and Trend: #320 (#522 in 2000)

Risk of Misspelling: Low

Risk of Mispronunciation: Low

Famous Namesakes: Actress Eden Riegel

Common Nicknames: None

Common Variations: Edin

Consider This: Eden is fast on the rise and seems to be a good name for religious parents.

Edith ★★★

(English) rich gift.

First Impression: People agree that Edith is an old grandmother, but they can't decide whether she's a caring wallflower or a snippy grouch.

Gender Association: Used for girls

Popularity and Trend: #638 (#564 in 2000)

Risk of Misspelling: Low

Risk of Mispronunciation: Low

Famous Namesakes: Character Edith Bunker (*All in the Family*); designer Edith Head; author Edith Wharton

Common Nicknames: Edie

Common Variations: None

Consider This: Edith is a grandmotherly name with a mostly unpleasant first impression.

Edna ★★

(Hebrew) rejuvenation.

First Impression: Edna is thought to be a conservative and mean old spinster who wears horn-rimmed glasses, frumpy cardigans, and a permanent scowl.

Gender Association: Used for girls

Popularity and Trend: Last ranked in the Top 1000 in the 1990s

Risk of Misspelling: Low

Risk of Mispronunciation: Low

Famous Namesakes: Poet Edna St. Vincent Millay; television host Dame Edna Everage; character Edna Krabappel (*The Simpsons*)

Common Nicknames: None

Common Variations: None

Consider This: If you name your daughter Edna, she'll come across as an old spinster when she's still young.

Eileen ★★★★

(Irish) a form of Helen.

First Impression: Most people see Eileen as a smart, bookish woman who can be serious, strict, and well organized when it comes to her work.

Gender Association: Used for girls

Popularity and Trend: #770 (#627 in 2000)

Risk of Misspelling: Fairly low

Risk of Mispronunciation: Low

Famous Namesakes: Modeling agency founder Eileen Ford; actress Eileen Atkins; actress Eileen Davidson; designer Eileen Gray

Common Nicknames: None

Common Variations: Aileen, Ilene

Consider This: Eileen is an old-fashioned name, but Ilene and Aileen are trendier variations.

Ela ★★★

(Polish) a form of Adelaide.

First Impression: Ela is imagined to be a quiet, elderly lady who lives in the country.

Gender Association: Used for girls

Popularity and Trend: Never been ranked in Top 1000

Risk of Misspelling: Average

Risk of Mispronunciation: Average

Famous Namesakes: Singer Ella Fitzgerald; activist Ella Baker

Common Nicknames: Elle

Common Variations: Ella

Consider This: Ella with two *l*'s is a much more popular name, but people may get confused about this variation's spelling and pronunciation.

Elaine ★★★

(French) a form of Helen.

First Impression: Elaine strikes people as a traditional, rigid woman who comes from a rich background.

Gender Association: Used for girls

Popularity and Trend: #719 (#577 in 2000)

Risk of Misspelling: Fairly low

Risk of Mispronunciation: Low

Famous Namesakes: Character Elaine Benes (*Seinfield*); comedian Elayne Boosler; actress Elaine Stritch

Common Nicknames: Lainey

Common Variations: Elayne, Laine, Lane

Consider This: Elaine may have upper-class appeal, but as the first impression proves, that's not always a good thing.

Eldora ★★★★

(Spanish) golden, gilded.

First Impression: People think Eldora is a bold but peculiar character.

Gender Association: Used for girls

Popularity and Trend: Last ranked in the Top 1000 in the 1940s

Risk of Misspelling: Low

Risk of Mispronunciation: Low

Famous Namesakes: None

Common Nicknames: Dora

Common Variations: None

Consider This: Eldora may work best with Spanish, Latino, and Greek surnames.

Eleanor ★★★★

(Greek) light.

First Impression: Eleanor is seen as full of intelligent thoughts, but she keeps them to herself.

Gender Association: Used for girls

Popularity and Trend: #277 (#374 in 2000)

Risk of Misspelling: Fairly low

Risk of Mispronunciation: Low

Famous Namesakes: First lady Eleanor Roosevelt; queen Eleanor of Aquitaine

Common Nicknames: Elle, Ella, Nellie, Nora

Common Variations: Eleanore, Elinor, Ellen, Leanore

Consider This: There are many ways to spell Eleanor, but this classic spelling is the one moving up the Top 1000.

Electra ★★★

(Greek) shining; brilliant.

First Impression: Thanks to Electra's famous namesakes, people think she's an exciting, daring, and electrifying woman.

Gender Association: Used for girls

Popularity and Trend: Never been ranked in Top 1000

Risk of Misspelling: Fairly low

Risk of Mispronunciation: Low

Famous Namesakes: Actress Carmen Electra; mythological figure Electra; comic book character Elektra

Common Nicknames: None

Common Variations: None

Consider This: People will probably know this name because of Carmen Electra and the superhero Elektra, but those figures may be hard for a young girl to live up to.

Elena ★★★

(Greek) a form of Eleanor. (Italian) a form of Helen.

First Impression: Elena is considered bossy, but she's family oriented and faithful.

Gender Association: Used for girls

Popularity and Trend: #187 (#234 in 2000)

Risk of Misspelling: Average

Risk of Mispronunciation: Average

Famous Namesakes: Opera singer Elena Gerhardt

Common Nicknames: None

Common Variations: Ellena, Elina

Consider This: Elena has Greek and Italian origins, but many people may see it as Latino. Pronunciation may be divided between "ee-LAIN-ah" and "ah-LAIN-ah."

Elise ★★★★

(French, English) a form of Elizabeth, Elysia.

First Impression: Elise is pictured as a well-traveled and smart sophisticate who can be sullen and needy at times, but funny and personable at others.

Gender Association: Used for girls

Popularity and Trend: #218 (#253 in 2000)

Risk of Misspelling: Fairly low

Risk of Mispronunciation: Fairly low

Famous Namesakes: Actress Elise Neal

Common Nicknames: Liset, Lissie

Common Variations: Elyse

Consider This: Though not a long name, Elise is surprisingly versatile.

Eliza ★★★

(Hebrew) a form of Elizabeth.

First Impression: Eliza is thought to be a nerdy and dorky bookworm who's funny and nice.

Gender Association: Used for girls

Popularity and Trend: #325 (#380 in 2000)

Risk of Misspelling: Fairly low

Risk of Mispronunciation: Low

Famous Namesakes: Actress Eliza Dushku; character Eliza Doolittle (*My Fair Lady*)

Common Nicknames: None

Common Variations: Aliza

Consider This: Of the many forms of Elizabeth, Eliza seems to be one of the nerdiest.

Elizabeth ★★★★

(Hebrew) consecrated to God.

First Impression: Many people describe Elizabeth as compassionate and demure, but others say she's guarded and a bit snobby.

Gender Association: Used mostly for girls

Popularity and Trend: #11 (#10 in 2000)

Risk of Misspelling: Fairly low

Risk of Mispronunciation: Low

Famous Namesakes: Queens Elizabeth I and II; actress Elizabeth Taylor;

actress Elizabeth Hurley;
activist Elizabeth Cady Stanton;
actress Elizabeth Mitchell; actress
Elizabeth Berkley; senator
Elizabeth Dole

Common Nicknames: Bess, Bessie,
Betsy, Beth, Betty, Libby, Liz,
Lizzie, Lisa, Liza, Eliza

Common Variations: Elisabeth, Elise,
Eliza, Elsa, Liza

Consider This: A fine enough name
for two queens of England, this
classic, versatile name is still very
popular.

Ella ★★★★★

(English) elfin; beautiful fairy-
woman. (Greek) a form of
Eleanor.

First Impression: Ella is seen as a
beautiful, good-natured, and
beloved woman.

Gender Association: Used for girls

Popularity and Trend: #21
(#265 in 2000)

Risk of Misspelling: Low

Risk of Mispronunciation: Low

Famous Namesakes: Singer Ella
Fitzgerald; activist Ella Baker

Common Nicknames: Ellie

Common Variations: None

Consider This: Ella is a classic, well-
liked name that's very easy to
spell and pronounce. It's no
wonder it's regained its early-
twentieth-century popularity.

Ellen ★★★★

(English) a form of Eleanor, Helen.

First Impression: Most people think
of Ellen as a timid and mousy
booklover.

Gender Association: Used for girls

Popularity and Trend: #544
(#451 in 2000)

Risk of Misspelling: Fairly low

Risk of Mispronunciation: Low

Famous Namesakes: Comedian Ellen
DeGeneres; actress Ellen Pompeo;
actress Ellen Barkin

Common Nicknames: Ellie

Common Variations: Ellena, Ellyn

Consider This: Root name Eleanor is
making a comeback, but Ellen
seems to be getting less popular.

Ellie ★★★★

(English) a short form of Eleanor,
Ella, Ellen.

First Impression: Ellie is imagined to
be an overwhelmingly sweet and
adorable Southern girl who's
bubbly and playful, much like
character Elly May Clampett
of TV's *The Beverly Hillbillies*.

Gender Association: Used for girls

Popularity and Trend: #175
(#360 in 2000)

Risk of Misspelling: Fairly low

Risk of Mispronunciation: Low

Famous Namesakes: Character Elly
May Clampett (*The Beverly
Hillbillies*)

Common Nicknames: None

Common Variations: Elly

Consider This: This nickname for
Eleanor, Ella, and Ellen strikes
many as Southern, no doubt
because of *The Beverly Hillbillies*.

Elsie ★★★

(German) a familiar form of Elsa,
Helsa.

First Impression: Elsie is pictured as a
cuddly, loving, and happy girl
with plenty of smiles and giggles.

Gender Association: Used for girls

Popularity and Trend: #879
(#919 in 2005)

Risk of Misspelling: Low

Risk of Mispronunciation: Low

Famous Namesakes: Dairy mascot
Elsie the Cow

Common Nicknames: None

Common Variations: None

Consider This: Although Elsie creates
a cute and happy image, many
people still associate this name
with a cow.

Emily ★★★★

(Latin) flatterer. (German)
industrious.

First Impression: People describe
Emily as shy, soft-spoken, and
poetic, much like poet Emily
Dickinson.

Gender Association: Used mostly
for girls

Popularity and Trend: #1
(#1 in 2000)

Risk of Misspelling: Fairly low

Risk of Mispronunciation: Low

Famous Namesakes: Author Emily Brontë; etiquette expert Emily Post; poet Emily Dickinson; actress Emily VanCamp; actress Emily Blunt

Common Nicknames: Millie, Em

Common Variations: Emilee, Emma, Amelia

Consider This: This number-one name is so popular that any classroom will inevitably have at least one Emily, if not two or three.

Emma ★★★★★

(German) a form of Emily.

First Impression: People think Emma is a beam of happiness and sweetness.

Gender Association: Used for girls

Popularity and Trend: #2 (#17 in 2000)

Risk of Misspelling: Low

Risk of Mispronunciation: Low

Famous Namesakes: Character Emma Woodhouse (*Emma*); actress Emma Thompson; actress Emma Samms; actress Emma Watson; singer Emma Bunton; actress Emma Roberts

Common Nicknames: Emmy

Common Variations: Ema, Emily

Consider This: Emma is a short form of Emily that's just about as popular at number two. (Side note: There are a lot of famous British Emmas, so if you're an Anglophile, this name's for you.)

Enid ★★

(Welsh) life; spirit.

First Impression: People say Enid is soft-spoken, shy, and sometimes fearful.

Gender Association: Used for girls

Popularity and Trend: Last ranked in the Top 1000 in the 1950s

Risk of Misspelling: Fairly low

Risk of Mispronunciation: Fairly low

Famous Namesakes: Author Enid Blyton; author Enid Bagnold

Common Nicknames: None

Common Variations: None

Consider This: Enid is an old-fashioned name that isn't viewed favorably.

Erica ★★★

(Scandinavian) ruler of all. (English) brave ruler.

First Impression: Erica is pictured as successful but unkind.

Gender Association: Used for girls

Popularity and Trend: #222 (#102 in 2000)

Risk of Misspelling: Fairly low

Risk of Mispronunciation: Low

Famous Namesakes: Actress Erica Durance; character Erica Kane (*All My Children*); singer Erykah Badu

Common Nicknames: Riki

Common Variations: Ericka, Erika

Consider This: Erica's image is harsh, which may be why this name has fallen in popularity.

Erin ★★★★

(Irish) peace.

First Impression: Most people see Erica as a leggy, blond activist, much like Erin Brockovich.

Gender Association: Used mostly for girls

Popularity and Trend: #130 (#60 in 2000)

Risk of Misspelling: Fairly low

Risk of Mispronunciation: Low

Famous Namesakes: Activist Erin Brockovich; actress Erin Moran

Common Nicknames: None

Common Variations: Aerin, Erinn, Eryn

Consider This: In 2005, this Irish name left the Top 100 for the first time in over thirty years. Plus, its pronunciation is the same as Aaron, a popular boys' name, which may cause gender confusion.

Esmeralda ★★★

(Greek, Spanish) a form of Emerald.

First Impression: Esmeralda is envisioned as an outrageous woman who's caring but bossy, wise but goofy.

Gender Association: Used for girls

Popularity and Trend: #224 (#195 in 2000)

Risk of Misspelling: Average
Risk of Mispronunciation: Average
Famous Namesakes: Character Esmeralda (*The Hunchback of Notre Dame*); character Esmeralda (*Bewitched*)
Common Nicknames: Esme
Common Variations: Ezmeralda
Consider This: Considering Esmeralda is a bit of a mouthful, it's relatively popular.

Esperanza ★★★
(Spanish) hope.
First Impression: The name Esperanza means "hope," so it isn't a surprise that people see Esperanza as dreamy and hopeful.
Gender Association: Used for girls
Popularity and Trend: #675 (#529 in 2000)
Risk of Misspelling: Fairly high
Risk of Mispronunciation: Average
Famous Namesakes: Jazz musician Esperanza Spalding
Common Nicknames: None
Common Variations: None
Consider This: Esperanza is a very Latino name that could be tricky for some to spell and pronounce.

Estelle ★★★★
(French) a form of Esther.
First Impression: Folks think Estelle has it all: beauty, charisma, intelligence, and poise.
Gender Association: Used for girls

Popularity and Trend: Last ranked in the Top 1000 in the 1960s
Risk of Misspelling: Low
Risk of Mispronunciation: Low
Famous Namesakes: Actress Estelle Getty; actress Estelle Harris
Common Nicknames: Stella
Common Variations: Estée, Estella
Consider This: Although Estelle is a traditional name, the first impression doesn't have a dated feel at all.

Ester ★★
(Persian) a form of Esther.
First Impression: Ester is seen as an elderly woman who's reserved and grouchy.
Gender Association: Used for girls
Popularity and Trend: Last ranked in the Top 1000 in the 1960s
Risk of Misspelling: Average
Risk of Mispronunciation: Low
Famous Namesakes: Biblical figure Esther
Common Nicknames: Essie
Common Variations: Esther, Estée, Estella, Hester
Consider This: Even Madonna (who chose Esther as her Hebrew name when she converted to Kabbalah) can't bring this name back.

Ethel ★★★
(English) noble.
First Impression: People see Ethel as a sweet granny or an old grump.

Gender Association: Used for girls
Popularity and Trend: Last ranked in the Top 1000 in the 1970s
Risk of Misspelling: Low
Risk of Mispronunciation: Low
Famous Namesakes: Socialite Ethel Kennedy; singer Ethel Merman; character Ethel Mertz (*I Love Lucy*); alleged spy Ethel Rosenberg
Common Nicknames: None
Common Variations: None
Consider This: Ethel was a popular name in the early half of the twentieth century, but it may be too old-fashioned for today's parents.

Eugenia ★★
(Greek) born to nobility.
First Impression: Eugenia is regarded as a timid, nerdy math wiz with average, mousy looks and thick glasses.
Gender Association: Used for girls
Popularity and Trend: Last ranked in the Top 1000 in the 1980s
Risk of Misspelling: Average
Risk of Mispronunciation: Average
Famous Namesakes: Model Eugenia Silva
Common Nicknames: Gina
Common Variations: Eugenie
Consider This: People may pronounce this name "you-GENE-ah" or "you-GENE-ee-ah."

Eunice ★
(Greek) happy; victorious.

First Impression: Eunice is pictured as a lonely and nerdy outcast.

Gender Association: Used for girls

Popularity and Trend: Last ranked in the Top 1000 in the 1990s

Risk of Misspelling: Average

Risk of Mispronunciation: Average

Famous Namesakes: Socialite Eunice Kennedy Shriver; character Eunice (*A Streetcar Named Desire*)

Common Nicknames: None

Common Variations: None

Consider This: Eunice is an old-fashioned name that's unfamiliar to many and unattractive to most.

Eva ★★★★
(Greek) a form of Evangelina. (Hebrew) a form of Eve.

First Impression: Eva is described as a woman of strong character.

Gender Association: Used for girls

Popularity and Trend: #124 (#294 in 2000)

Risk of Misspelling: Fairly low

Risk of Mispronunciation: Average

Famous Namesakes: Actress Eva Longoria; actress Eva Gabor; actress Eva Mendes; actress Eva Green; first lady Eva Peron

Common Nicknames: None

Common Variations: Ava

Consider This: While most people will pronounce this name "EE-vah," some may opt for "EH-vah" or even "AY-vah."

Eve ★★★★
(Hebrew) life.

First Impression: People have several images of Eve: She may be a sweetie, rebel, leader, or tomboy.

Gender Association: Used for girls

Popularity and Trend: #590 (#538 in 2000)

Risk of Misspelling: Low

Risk of Mispronunciation: Low

Famous Namesakes: Rapper Eve; biblical figure Eve; actress Eve Arden; actress Eve Plumb

Common Nicknames: Evie

Common Variations: Eva, Evita

Consider This: Eve isn't nearly as popular as Eva, but it scores just as well.

Evelyn ★★★
(English) hazelnut.

First Impression: To many, Evelyn may be rich and sophisticated, but she's rude and stingy with money.

Gender Association: Used mostly for girls

Popularity and Trend: #65 (#150 in 2000)

Risk of Misspelling: Fairly low

Risk of Mispronunciation: Fairly low

Famous Namesakes: Actress Evelyn Keyes; singer Evelyn Champagne King

Common Nicknames: Lyn, Evie

Common Variations: Eveline

Consider This: "EV-ah-lin" is the standard pronunciation, but people may pronounce this name as "EVE-lin," too.

Evie ★★★
(Hungarian) a familiar form of Eve.

First Impression: Folks think Evie has her head in the clouds.

Gender Association: Used for girls

Popularity and Trend: Last ranked in the Top 1000 in the 1940s

Risk of Misspelling: Low

Risk of Mispronunciation: Fairly low

Famous Namesakes: None

Common Nicknames: None

Common Variations: None

Consider This: Because it's a diminutive form of Eve, Evie may come across as a name for a young girl.

Faith ★★★★★
(English) faithful; fidelity.

First Impression: People describe Faith as sweet, angelic, and, of course, faithful.

Gender Association: Used for girls

Popularity and Trend: #64 (#66 in 2000)

Risk of Misspelling: Low

Risk of Mispronunciation: Low

Famous Namesakes: Singer Faith Hill; actress Faith Ford; singer Faith Evans

Common Nicknames: None

Common Variations: Faye

Consider This: Faith has held steadily popular for years and is a great choice if you're religious (or a fan of country music).

Fantasia ★★★★

(Greek) imagination.

First Impression: People think Fantasia is an imaginative and joyful waitress who struggles to make her way as a singer, much like *American Idol*–winner Fantasia Barrino.

Gender Association: Used for girls

Popularity and Trend: Never been ranked in Top 1000

Risk of Misspelling: Fairly low

Risk of Mispronunciation: Fairly low

Famous Namesakes: Singer Fantasia Barrino

Common Nicknames: None

Common Variations: None

Consider This: A lot of people will know and like this name thanks to Fantasia Barrino, but it may seem a bit flamboyant to some.

Fawn ★★★

(French) young deer.

First Impression: People believe Fawn could be as gentle and sweet as a baby deer, or she could be an exotic dancer.

Gender Association: Used for girls

Popularity and Trend: Last ranked in the Top 1000 in the 1980s

Risk of Misspelling: Low

Risk of Mispronunciation: Low

Famous Namesakes: Infamous secretary Fawn Hall

Common Nicknames: None

Common Variations: Fawna

Consider This: Fawn is easy to spell and pronounce, but it makes some people think of strippers.

Felice ★★★

(Latin) a form of Felicia.

First Impression: Many people feel Felice has many wonderful qualities, but she's afraid to show them.

Gender Association: Used for girls

Popularity and Trend: Never been ranked in Top 1000

Risk of Misspelling: Fairly low

Risk of Mispronunciation: Fairly low

Famous Namesakes: None

Common Nicknames: None

Common Variations: Felicia

Consider This: Many people will be able to pronounce this name ("feh-LEESE"), but a few may have trouble.

Felicia ★★★

(Latin) fortunate; happy.

First Impression: Felicia is seen as high energy and high class.

Gender Association: Used for girls

Popularity and Trend: Last ranked in the Top 1000 in the 1980s

Risk of Misspelling: Average

Risk of Mispronunciation: Fairly low

Famous Namesakes: Character Felicia Forrester (*The Bold and the Beautiful*); actress Phylicia Rashad

Common Nicknames: None

Common Variations: Phylicia, Felice, Felicity

Consider This: Felicia hasn't been in the Top 1000 since the '80s, but it's more popular than its variation Phylicia, which has never been ranked.

Felicity ★★★★

(English) a form of Felicia.

First Impression: This name's image is inspired by the title character of TV's *Felicity*, a dreamer who followed her heart.

Gender Association: Used for girls

Popularity and Trend: #617 (#445 in 2000)

Risk of Misspelling: Fairly low

Risk of Mispronunciation: Low

Famous Namesakes: Actress Felicity Huffman; character Felicity Porter (*Felicity*); character Felicity (*American Girl* series)

Common Nicknames: None

Common Variations: None

Consider This: Felicity has been falling ever since *Felicity* left the airwaves, but people still have a great first impression of it.

Fifi ★

(French) a familiar form of Josephine.

First Impression: When people hear this name, they think of a spoiled

French airhead with fluffy hair that may resemble poodle fur.

Gender Association: Used mostly for girls

Popularity and Trend: Never been ranked in Top 1000

Risk of Misspelling: Fairly low

Risk of Mispronunciation: Fairly low

Famous Namesakes: Character Fifi Le Fume (*Looney Tunes*); star kid Fifi Trixibelle Geldof

Common Nicknames: None

Common Variations: None

Consider This: You probably don't want your daughter to remind people of a French poodle.

Fiona ★★★

(Irish) fair, white.

First Impression: People believe singer Fiona Apple—famed for her songwriting talent, waiflike looks, and strong will—influences this name's image.

Gender Association: Used for girls

Popularity and Trend: #333 (#460 in 2000)

Risk of Misspelling: Fairly low

Risk of Mispronunciation: Low

Famous Namesakes: Character Princess Fiona (*Shrek*); singer Fiona Apple; actress Fiona Shaw

Common Nicknames: None

Common Variations: None

Consider This: Although the first impression ties to Fiona Apple, this name has been climbing the Top 1000 ever since Princess Fiona appeared in *Shrek*.

Flannery ★★★

(Irish) redhead.

First Impression: People think Flannery is a socially awkward and quiet loner with a frail figure, glasses, and knobby knees.

Gender Association: Used for girls

Popularity and Trend: Never been ranked in Top 1000

Risk of Misspelling: Fairly low

Risk of Mispronunciation: Fairly low

Famous Namesakes: Author Flannery O'Connor

Common Nicknames: Flanna

Common Variations: None

Consider This: This very Irish name doesn't have a great first impression.

Fleta ★

(English) swift, fast.

First Impression: Fleta is pictured as a grump, either because she's withdrawn or because she's just downright mean.

Gender Association: Used for girls

Popularity and Trend: Last ranked in the Top 1000 in the 1900s

Risk of Misspelling: Average

Risk of Mispronunciation: Average

Famous Namesakes: None

Common Nicknames: None

Common Variations: None

Consider This: Fleta hasn't been a Top 1000 name since the dawn of the twentieth century. The spelling and pronunciation are unclear, too.

Florence ★★★★★

(Latin) blooming; flowery; prosperous.

First Impression: People think Florence is well loved and well read.

Gender Association: Used for girls

Popularity and Trend: Last ranked in the Top 1000 in the 1980s

Risk of Misspelling: Low

Risk of Mispronunciation: Low

Famous Namesakes: Actress Florence Henderson; nurse Florence Nightingale

Common Nicknames: Flo, Florie, Flossie

Common Variations: Flora, Florida

Consider This: Florence may seem old-fashioned to some, but it's versatile, easy to spell and pronounce, and well perceived.

Florida ★★★★

(Spanish) a form of Florence.

First Impression: People claim Florida is a cheerful and bright blond who's talkative, flirty, but perhaps a bit ditzy.

Gender Association: Used for girls

Popularity and Trend: Last ranked in the Top 1000 in the 1920s

Risk of Misspelling: Low

Risk of Mispronunciation: Low

Famous Namesakes: Character Florida Evans (*Good Times*)

Common Nicknames: Flo

Common Variations: Florence

Consider This: People may find Florida a goofy name for a person, but everyone will know how to spell and pronounce it.

Fran ★★★

(Latin) a short form of Frances.

First Impression: Thanks to Fran Drescher, most people think of Fran as funny, loud, cheerful, and kind of obnoxious.

Gender Association: Used mostly for girls

Popularity and Trend: Last ranked in the Top 1000 in the 1960s

Risk of Misspelling: Low

Risk of Mispronunciation: Low

Famous Namesakes: Comedian Fran Drescher; author Fran Leibowitz

Common Nicknames: None

Common Variations: None

Consider This: A nickname for Frances, Fran has a punchy image, but it may be too casual as a given name.

Frances ★★★

(Latin) free; from France.

First Impression: Frances is thought to be an upstanding, smart, and quiet straight shooter.

Gender Association: Used for girls

Popularity and Trend: #779 (#575 in 2000)

Risk of Misspelling: Fairly low

Risk of Mispronunciation: Low

Famous Namesakes: Actress Frances Farmer; actress Frances Bavier; actress Frances McDormand

Common Nicknames: Fran, Frannie, Fannie, Frankie

Common Variations: Francis, Francesca, Francine

Consider This: Frances has been around forever, which makes it classic but dated. Also, its pronunciation is the same as Francis, a traditional boys' name, which may cause gender confusion.

Francesca ★★★

(Italian) a form of Frances.

First Impression: People believe Francesca may be proper and well read, but she's also arrogant.

Gender Association: Used for girls

Popularity and Trend: #428 (#405 in 2000)

Risk of Misspelling: Average

Risk of Mispronunciation: Fairly low

Famous Namesakes: Actress Francesca Annis

Common Nicknames: Fran, Frannie

Common Variations: None

Consider This: This Italian name is not necessarily easy to pronounce, and it has a snobby come-off.

Francine ★★★★

(French) a form of Frances.

First Impression: Francine is seen as an odd old lady.

Gender Association: Used for girls

Popularity and Trend: Last ranked in the Top 1000 in the 1980s

Risk of Misspelling: Low

Risk of Mispronunciation: Low

Famous Namesakes: Character Francine Frensky (*Arthur*)

Common Nicknames: Fran, Francie

Common Variations: None

Consider This: Of all the Frances variations, Francine has the oldest (and oddest) first impression.

Frida ★★★★

(German) a form of Alfreda, Elfrida, Frederica, Sigfreda.

First Impression: Whether calm or fiery, Frida is considered passionate about her art.

Gender Association: Used for girls

Popularity and Trend: #836 (#918 in 2001)

Risk of Misspelling: Fairly low

Risk of Mispronunciation: Fairly low

Famous Namesakes: Artist Frida Kahlo

Common Nicknames: None

Common Variations: Freida

Consider This: Frida is a German name, but many people think it's Latino because of Mexican artist Frida Kahlo.

Gabriela ★★★★★

(Italian) a form of Gabrielle.

First Impression: Gabriela is pictured as a quiet charmer.

Gender Association: Used for girls

Popularity and Trend: #110
(#117 in 2000)

Risk of Misspelling: Average

Risk of Mispronunciation: Low

Famous Namesakes: Poet Gabriela
Mistral; tennis player Gabriela
Sabatini

Common Nicknames: Gaby

Common Variations: Gabriella

Consider This: Gabriela with one *l*
is the classic spelling of the
name, but it's not as popular
as Gabriella.

Gabriella ★★★★

(Italian) a form of Gabriela.

First Impression: Gabriella is envisioned as a beautiful woman
who's warm, confident, elegant,
and intelligent, but occasionally
snobby.

Gender Association: Used for girls

Popularity and Trend: #50
(#98 in 2000)

Risk of Misspelling: Average

Risk of Mispronunciation: Low

Famous Namesakes: Poet Gabriela
Mistral; tennis player Gabriela
Sabatini

Common Nicknames: Gaby

Common Variations: Gabriela

Consider This: Gabriella is more
popular than Gabriela, but
for some reason, it has a snobbier feel.

Gabrielle ★★★★★

(French) devoted to God.

First Impression: Folks see Gabrielle as
a one-woman show who enjoys
singing, dancing, and telling
jokes.

Gender Association: Used mostly
for girls

Popularity and Trend: #62
(#49 in 2000)

Risk of Misspelling: Fairly low

Risk of Mispronunciation: Low

Famous Namesakes: Character
Gabrielle Solis (*Desperate
Housewives*); model Gabrielle
Reese; actress Gabrielle Carteris;
actress Gabrielle Union; actress
Gabrielle Anwar

Common Nicknames: Gaby

Common Variations: Gabriele

Consider This: More popular than
Gabriela but less popular than
Gabriella, Gabrielle is a common
name with an outgoing image.

Gaby ★★★

(French) a familiar form of
Gabrielle.

First Impression: Gaby, people think,
is true to her name: She never
stops talking.

Gender Association: Used for girls

Popularity and Trend: Never been
ranked in Top 1000

Risk of Misspelling: Fairly low

Risk of Mispronunciation: Fairly low

Famous Namesakes: Actress Gaby
Hoffmann

Common Nicknames: None

Common Variations: Gabby

Consider This: Gaby is cute, but it
clearly isn't as versatile as
Gabrielle or Gabriella.

Gail ★★★

(English) merry, lively. (Hebrew) a
form of Abigail.

First Impression: People believe it
takes Gail a little while to warm
up, but she's a sweet and devoted
family woman.

Gender Association: Used for girls

Popularity and Trend: Last ranked in
the Top 1000 in the 1980s

Risk of Misspelling: Fairly low

Risk of Mispronunciation: Low

Famous Namesakes: Runner Gail
Devers

Common Nicknames: None

Common Variations: Gayle

Consider This: Abigail is much more
popular than this shortened
version.

Gemma ★★★

(Latin, Italian) jewel, precious
stone.

First Impression: Gemma is viewed as
the sweetest flower child in the
commune.

Gender Association: Used for girls

Popularity and Trend: Never been
ranked in Top 1000

Risk of Misspelling: Fairly low

Risk of Mispronunciation: Fairly low
Famous Namesakes: Model Gemma
 Ward; singer Gemma Hayes
Common Nicknames: None
Common Variations: Gema
Consider This: This name is much
 more common in the United
 Kingdom.

Genevieve ★★★

(German, French) a form of
 Guinevere.
First Impression: Genevieve is said
 to be a patient, respectful, and
 gentle woman who's bright and
 jovial.
Gender Association: Used for girls
Popularity and Trend: #368
 (#507 in 2000)
Risk of Misspelling: Fairly high
Risk of Mispronunciation: Average
Famous Namesakes: Actress
 Genevieve Bujold; television
 host Genevieve Gorder
Common Nicknames: Gena
Common Variations: Genovieve,
 Geneva
Consider This: Genevieve is a long
 name that may be tricky to spell
 and pronounce.

Georgette ★★★

(French) a form of Georgia.
First Impression: Georgette is pictured
 as a pretty Southerner who's
 vivacious and fun, but perhaps
 desperate for attention.

Gender Association: Used for girls
Popularity and Trend: Last ranked in
 the Top 1000 in the 1970s
Risk of Misspelling: Low
Risk of Mispronunciation: Low
Famous Namesakes: Actress
 Georgette Harvey; character
 Georgette Franklin (*The Mary
 Tyler Moore Show*)
Common Nicknames: Georgie
Common Variations: Georgia
Consider This: Georgette sounds like
 Georgia, which may be why
 people think it has Southern
 charm.

Georgia ★★★

(Greek) farmer.
First Impression: People think Georgia
 is a peach—as long as she's in
 charge.
Gender Association: Used for girls
Popularity and Trend: #273
 (#334 in 2000)
Risk of Misspelling: Low
Risk of Mispronunciation: Low
Famous Namesakes: Actress Georgia
 Bright Engel; artist Georgia
 O'Keeffe; actress Jorja Fox
Common Nicknames: Georgie
Common Variations: Jorja, Georgina,
 Georgette
Consider This: Florida has a more
 positive first impression than
 Georgia, but this state name is
 much more popular.

Georgina ★★★★

(English) a form of Georgia.
First Impression: Georgina is seen as a
 gregarious redhead who's always
 ready for a night on the town.
Gender Association: Used for girls
Popularity and Trend: Last ranked in
 the Top 1000 in the 1990s
Risk of Misspelling: Low
Risk of Mispronunciation: Low
Famous Namesakes: Author Georgina
 Gentry
Common Nicknames: Georgie
Common Variations: Georgia,
 Georgette
Consider This: Georgina isn't as
 popular as Georgia, but its
 first impression may be more
 appealing.

Geraldine ★★

(German) mighty with a spear.
First Impression: Geraldine is viewed
 as a gawky, geeky, and lonely
 old lady.
Gender Association: Used for girls
Popularity and Trend: Last ranked in
 the Top 1000 in the 1990s
Risk of Misspelling: Fairly low
Risk of Mispronunciation: Fairly low
Famous Namesakes: Actress
 Geraldine Sue Page; politician
 Geraldine Ferraro
Common Nicknames: Geri
Common Variations: Jeraldine
Consider This: Geraldine was a big
 name from the 1910s through

the 1940s, but it probably isn't making a comeback anytime soon.

Germaine ★★

(French) from Germany.

First Impression: Folks think Germaine comes on strong, which is exciting for some but too much for others.

Gender Association: Used mostly for boys

Popularity and Trend: Last ranked in the Top 1000 in the 1960s

Risk of Misspelling: Average

Risk of Mispronunciation: Low

Famous Namesakes: Writer Germaine Greer

Common Nicknames: None

Common Variations: Jermaine

Consider This: It may be because of Jermaine Jackson that Germaine is used more often for boys and thought of as African American.

Ghita ★★

(Italian) pearly.

First Impression: Ghita is imagined to be a shy and unassuming schoolgirl who's studious and friendly in her own quiet way.

Gender Association: Used for girls

Popularity and Trend: Never been ranked in Top 1000

Risk of Misspelling: Fairly high

Risk of Mispronunciation: Fairly high

Famous Namesakes: Actress Ghita Norby

Common Nicknames: None

Common Variations: None

Consider This: People will have trouble pronouncing and spelling this very Italian name.

Gillian ★★★

(Latin) a form of Jillian.

First Impression: People envision Gillian as an artist with a wild, far-out imagination.

Gender Association: Used for girls

Popularity and Trend: #758 (#324 in 2000)

Risk of Misspelling: Average

Risk of Mispronunciation: Fairly low

Famous Namesakes: Actress Gillian Anderson; singer Gillian Welch; actress Jillian Barberie

Common Nicknames: Gill, Gilly

Common Variations: Jillian

Consider This: Jillian is a much more popular version of this name, but Gillian has an artier vibe.

Gina ★★★★

(Italian) a form of Angelina, Eugenia, Regina, Virginia.

First Impression: Gina is considered always in charge and always sure of herself.

Gender Association: Used for girls

Popularity and Trend: #712 (#356 in 2000)

Risk of Misspelling: Fairly low

Risk of Mispronunciation: Low

Famous Namesakes: Actress Gina Lollabridga; actress Geena Davis; actress Gina Gershon; actress Gina Rowlands

Common Nicknames: None

Common Variations: Gena, Geena

Consider This: On its own, Gina's popularity is sinking fast. Try one of the names it's derived from instead.

Ginger ★★★

(Latin) flower; spice.

First Impression: People think Ginger could be a hesitant follower, a bratty snob, or a rebellious dropout.

Gender Association: Used for girls

Popularity and Trend: Last ranked in the Top 1000 in the 1980s

Risk of Misspelling: Low

Risk of Mispronunciation: Low

Famous Namesakes: Dancer Ginger Rogers

Common Nicknames: Ginny

Common Variations: None

Consider This: Ginger is easy to spell and pronounce, but this name hasn't been big since the era of *Gilligan's Island*.

Ginny ★★★

(English) a familiar form of Ginger, Virginia.

First Impression: Ginny appears to be in touch with her inner child: She's seen as sweet, playful, and a bit naïve.

Gender Association: Used for girls
Popularity and Trend: Last ranked in
the Top 1000 in the 1960s
Risk of Misspelling: Fairly low
Risk of Mispronunciation: Fairly low
Famous Namesakes: Character Ginny
Weasley (*Harry Potter* series)
Common Nicknames: None
Common Variations: Jinny
Consider This: If you like Ginny,
consider naming your daughter
Virginia. That'll give you a solid
formal name and a cute informal
name for her.

Giovana ★★★

(Italian) a form of Jane.
First Impression: Giovana is most
often thought to be an Italian
woman with a warm personality
and a beautiful face.
Gender Association: Used for girls
Popularity and Trend: Never been
ranked in Top 1000
Risk of Misspelling: Average
Risk of Mispronunciation: Fairly low
Famous Namesakes: Actress Giovanna
Antonelli
Common Nicknames: None
Common Variations: Giovanna,
Giovanni
Consider This: This spelling has never
been ranked, but Giovanna hit
#682 in 2005.

Giselle ★★★★

(German) pledge; hostage.
First Impression: Giselle is pictured
as a nice girl who's misread as
arrogant.
Gender Association: Used for girls
Popularity and Trend: #168
(#212 in 2000)
Risk of Misspelling: Fairly low
Risk of Mispronunciation: Average
Famous Namesakes: Model Gisele
Bündchen
Common Nicknames: None
Common Variations: Gisele, Gisella
Consider This: Model Gisele
Bündchen spells her name with
one *l*, but people may still think
of her when they see the name
Giselle.

Gladys ★★

(Latin) small sword. (Irish) princess.
(Welsh) a form of Claudia.
First Impression: Gladys is seen as
either always complaining or
always gossiping.
Gender Association: Used for girls
Popularity and Trend: Last ranked in
the Top 1000 in the 1990s
Risk of Misspelling: Fairly low
Risk of Mispronunciation: Fairly low
Famous Namesakes: Singer Gladys
Knight; actress Gladys Cooper
Common Nicknames: None
Common Variations: Gladis
Consider This: Gladys has too
negative a first impression to

make it a good choice for most
parents.

Glenda ★★★★

(Welsh) a form of Glenna.
First Impression: Folks see Glenda as a
happy and sweet woman who's
always smiling.
Gender Association: Used for girls
Popularity and Trend: Last ranked in
the Top 1000 in the 1980s
Risk of Misspelling: Low
Risk of Mispronunciation: Low
Famous Namesakes: Actress Glenda
May Jackson
Common Nicknames: None
Common Variations: Glenna
Consider This: Despite being a dated
name, Glenda makes a strongly
positive first impression on
people.

Glenna ★★★

(Irish) valley, glen.
First Impression: It's a tossup to most
people: Glenna may be kind,
dull, or high class.
Gender Association: Used for girls
Popularity and Trend: Last ranked in
the Top 1000 in the 1970s
Risk of Misspelling: Fairly low
Risk of Mispronunciation: Low
Famous Namesakes: None
Common Nicknames: None
Common Variations: Glenda
Consider This: Glenna is a pretty
unique name, but it's easy to
spell and pronounce.

Gloria ★★★★

(Latin) glory.

First Impression: Gloria is viewed as an unpopular geek, but that doesn't stop her from being happy, hyperactive, and nice.

Gender Association: Used for girls

Popularity and Trend: #453 (#358 in 2000)

Risk of Misspelling: Low

Risk of Mispronunciation: Low

Famous Namesakes: Singer Gloria Estefan; singer Gloria Gaynor; activist Gloria Steinem

Common Nicknames: None

Common Variations: Glory

Consider This: Gloria is still in the top half of the Top 1000, but it may feel dated.

Glory ★★

(Latin) a form of Gloria.

First Impression: Glory comes across as a ruthless backstabber who's constantly gossiping.

Gender Association: Used for girls

Popularity and Trend: Never been ranked in Top 1000

Risk of Misspelling: Low

Risk of Mispronunciation: Low

Famous Namesakes: Character Glory (*Buffy the Vampire Slayer*)

Common Nicknames: None

Common Variations: Gloria

Consider This: There's nothing glorious about Glory's image.

Grace ★★★★★

(Latin) graceful.

First Impression: Grace is thought to be compassionate, dedicated, Christian, and—naturally—graceful.

Gender Association: Used for girls

Popularity and Trend: #17 (#19 in 2000)

Risk of Misspelling: Low

Risk of Mispronunciation: Low

Famous Namesakes: Character Grace Adler (*Will & Grace*); actress Grace Kelly; singer Grace Slick; model Grace Jones; author Grace Paley

Common Nicknames: Gracie

Common Variations: Gracia

Consider This: Grace will always be a beloved virtue, so Grace is likely to remain in vogue for a long time.

Gracie ★★★★★

(English) a familiar form of Grace.

First Impression: Gracie is pictured as a sweet girl who wants to save the world.

Gender Association: Used for girls

Popularity and Trend: #103 (#244 in 2000)

Risk of Misspelling: Low

Risk of Mispronunciation: Low

Famous Namesakes: Comedian Gracie Allen

Common Nicknames: None

Common Variations: None

Consider This: Gracie isn't as formal as Grace, but people hold it in the same high esteem.

Greer ★★★

(Scottish) vigilant.

First Impression: People see Greer as a well-bred, attractive woman who comes from old money.

Gender Association: Used for girls

Popularity and Trend: Never been ranked in Top 1000

Risk of Misspelling: Fairly low

Risk of Mispronunciation: Low

Famous Namesakes: Actress Greer Garson; star kid Grier Hammond Henchy

Common Nicknames: None

Common Variations: Grier

Consider This: Greer has never been a Top 1000 name, but it may move up now that Brooke Shields named her daughter Grier.

Greta ★★★★

(German) a form of Gretchen, Margaret.

First Impression: Folks think Greta has success on her mind, and she's determined to get it.

Gender Association: Used for girls

Popularity and Trend: #680 (#756 in 2000)

Risk of Misspelling: Fairly low

Risk of Mispronunciation: Low

Famous Namesakes: News anchor Greta van Susteren; actress Greta Garbo

Common Nicknames: None
Common Variations: None
Consider This: Greta may sound better with a German or Scandinavian surname than with others.

Gretchen ★★★

(German) a form of Margaret.

First Impression: Gretchen seems to feel more comfortable working with algorithms than with other people.
Gender Association: Used for girls
Popularity and Trend: #771 (#742 in 2000)
Risk of Misspelling: Fairly low
Risk of Mispronunciation: Low
Famous Namesakes: Actress Gretchen Mol; singer Gretchen Wilson; news anchor Gretchen Carlson
Common Nicknames: None
Common Variations: Greta
Consider This: Gretchen is a German form of Margaret that hit its peak in the '70s.

Gretel ★★★

(German) a form of Margaret.

First Impression: Gretel is, of course, a young fairytale heroine, which is why people think she's naïve and childlike.
Gender Association: Used for girls
Popularity and Trend: Never been ranked in Top 1000
Risk of Misspelling: Fairly low
Risk of Mispronunciation: Fairly low

Famous Namesakes: Character Gretel (*Hansel and Gretel*)
Common Nicknames: None
Common Variations: None
Consider This: Most people know "Hansel and Gretel," which helps this German name on spelling and pronunciation. But be aware that it may sound odd with some surnames.

Guadalupe ★★

(Arabic) river of black stones.

First Impression: People believe Guadalupe has a kind and happy heart.
Gender Association: Used mostly for girls
Popularity and Trend: #255 (#245 in 2000)
Risk of Misspelling: Fairly high
Risk of Mispronunciation: Fairly high
Famous Namesakes: Religious icon Our Lady of Guadalupe; president Guadalupe Victoria
Common Nicknames: Lupe
Common Variations: None
Consider This: This originally Arabic name is very popular with Latino families due to religious icon Our Lady of Guadalupe.

Guinevere ★★

(French, Welsh) white wave; white phantom.

First Impression: Guinevere is viewed as a vulnerable and fragile woman who has come undone.

Gender Association: Used for girls
Popularity and Trend: Never been ranked in Top 1000
Risk of Misspelling: Fairly high
Risk of Mispronunciation: Average
Famous Namesakes: Legendary figure Guinevere
Common Nicknames: Gwen
Common Variations: Genevieve, Jennifer, Winifred
Consider This: Guinevere's image is beautiful but tragic, and so the name may be too dramatic for some parents.

Gwen ★★★

(Welsh) a short form of Guinevere, Gwendolyn.

First Impression: Gwen reminds most people of a bold and strong-willed blond musician like Gwen Stefani, but others say she's rude and greedy.
Gender Association: Used for girls
Popularity and Trend: Last ranked in the Top 1000 in the 1980s
Risk of Misspelling: Fairly low
Risk of Mispronunciation: Low
Famous Namesakes: Singer Gwen Stefani; character Gwen Stacy (*Spider-Man*)
Common Nicknames: None
Common Variations: None
Consider This: Gwendolyn, the root form of this name, is more popular than Gwen and more versatile, too.

Gwendolyn ★★★

(Welsh) white wave; white browed; new moon.

First Impression: People think Gwendolyn hides a unique personality behind her bashfulness.

Gender Association: Used for girls

Popularity and Trend: #631 (#732 in 2000)

Risk of Misspelling: Fairly low

Risk of Mispronunciation: Fairly low

Famous Namesakes: Poet Gwendolyn Brooks

Common Nicknames: Gwen, Wendy

Common Variations: Gwyneth

Consider This: Gwendolyn is somewhat uncommon, but nicknames Gwen and Wendy make it a versatile pick.

Gwyneth ★★★

(Welsh) a form of Gwendolyn.

First Impression: Gwyneth is seen to always have her pretty nose in the air.

Gender Association: Used for girls

Popularity and Trend: Never been ranked in Top 1000

Risk of Misspelling: Fairly low

Risk of Mispronunciation: Fairly low

Famous Namesakes: Actress Gwyneth Paltrow

Common Nicknames: Gwen, Gwyn, Winnie

Common Variations: Gwendolyn

Consider This: Judging from the first impression, it's hard to say if people think Gwyneth Paltrow is snooty, or if they feel the name itself carries a snooty vibe.

Haley ★★

(Scandinavian) heroine.

First Impression: Haley's perkiness is endearing to most, but some find her annoying.

Gender Association: Used mostly for girls

Popularity and Trend: #75 (#28 in 2000)

Risk of Misspelling: Fairly high

Risk of Mispronunciation: Average

Famous Namesakes: Actress Hayley Mills; swimmer Hayley Lewis; actress Hayley Duff

Common Nicknames: None

Common Variations: Halee, Hallie, Halle, Halley

Consider This: Haley is popular, but so are its many variations, which could cause spelling confusion. There's confusion with pronunciation as well, because people may pronounce it "HAL-lee" instead of "HAY-lee."

Hallie ★★★

(Scandinavian) a form of Haley.

First Impression: People see Hallie as a heartfelt and helpful girl brimming with cheer and wit.

Gender Association: Used for girls

Popularity and Trend: #450 (#297 in 2000)

Risk of Misspelling: Fairly high

Risk of Mispronunciation: Average

Famous Namesakes: Actress Hallie Kate Eisenberg; character Hallie Parker (*The Parent Trap*); actress Halle Berry

Common Nicknames: None

Common Variations: Halee, Halle, Haley, Halley

Consider This: Both Hallie and variation Halle are losing popularity fast. Like most names in this family, it has spelling and pronunciation woes.

Hanna ★★★

(Hebrew) a form of Hannah.

First Impression: Hanna is pictured as a high-powered dynamo.

Gender Association: Used mostly for girls

Popularity and Trend: #269 (#171 in 2000)

Risk of Misspelling: Average

Risk of Mispronunciation: Low

Famous Namesakes: Biblical figure Hannah; actress Daryl Hannah; television character Hannah Montana

Common Nicknames: Nina

Common Variations: Hannah

Consider This: Hanna is less popular than Hannah, so people will probably spell this name with the final *h*.

Hannah ★★★★

(Hebrew) gracious.

First Impression: People think Hannah has the skills and the heart to make the world a better place.

Gender Association: Used mostly for girls

Popularity and Trend: #8 (#2 in 2000)

Risk of Misspelling: Fairly low

Risk of Mispronunciation: Low

Famous Namesakes: Biblical figure Hannah; actress Daryl Hannah; television character Hannah Montana

Common Nicknames: Nina

Common Variations: Hanna

Consider This: Hannah has been very popular for a long time, and with such a positive first impression, it's clear that people aren't tiring of it.

Harmony ★★★★★

(Latin) harmonious.

First Impression: People imagine Harmony as a beautiful, soft-spoken, and sensitive woman who seeks harmony in her life.

Gender Association: Used for girls

Popularity and Trend: #342 (#720 in 2000)

Risk of Misspelling: Low

Risk of Mispronunciation: Low

Famous Namesakes: Character Harmony Kendall (*Buffy the Vampire Slayer*)

Common Nicknames: None

Common Variations: None

Consider This: If you're expecting a singer or just a happy child, you may choose this harmonious name.

Harriet ★★★

(French) ruler of the household. (English) a form of Henrietta.

First Impression: Harriet Nelson will always be one of America's favorite TV mothers, and people still think of Harriet as a caring and thoughtful mom.

Gender Association: Used for girls

Popularity and Trend: Last ranked in the Top 1000 in the 1970s

Risk of Misspelling: Fairly low

Risk of Mispronunciation: Low

Famous Namesakes: Actress Harriet Nelson; abolitionist Harriet Tubman; author Harriet Beecher Stowe; character Harriet Oleson (*Little House on the Prairie*);

Common Nicknames: Hettie

Common Variations: None

Consider This: This old-fashioned name isn't likely to become popular again anytime soon.

Hasana ★★

(Swahili) she arrived first.

First Impression: People imagine Hasana comes from an exotic background, but they aren't sure if she's loud and big-headed or quiet and kind.

Gender Association: Used for girls

Popularity and Trend: Never been ranked in Top 1000

Risk of Misspelling: Average

Risk of Mispronunciation: Average

Famous Namesakes: None

Common Nicknames: None

Common Variations: Huseina

Consider This: Hasana is a Swahili name that sounds as though it could have many different ethnic origins.

Hayley ★★★★

(English) hay meadow.

First Impression: Hayley is considered full of life, surprises, and energy.

Gender Association: Used for girls

Popularity and Trend: #306 (#148 in 2000)

Risk of Misspelling: Fairly high

Risk of Mispronunciation: Low

Famous Namesakes: Actress Hayley Mills; swimmer Hayley Lewis; actress Hayley Duff

Common Nicknames: None

Common Variations: Hailey, Haley

Consider This: Haley is a more popular variation of this name, which means spelling will be a problem. On the plus side, Hayley is more phonetic and thus easier to pronounce than some variations.

Hazel ★★★★

(English) hazelnut tree; commanding authority.

First Impression: Hazel is pictured as a modest woman with modest traits.
Gender Association: Used for girls
Popularity and Trend: #465 (#893 in 2000)
Risk of Misspelling: Low
Risk of Mispronunciation: Low
Famous Namesakes: Star kid Hazel Patricia Moder
Common Nicknames: None
Common Variations: None
Consider This: Hazel was already on the rise when Julia Roberts named her daughter Hazel in 2004, and now the name's surging even more.

Heather ★★★
(English) flowering heather.
First Impression: Heather is seen as your typical snob in the popular crowd.
Gender Association: Used for girls
Popularity and Trend: #341 (#126 in 2000)
Risk of Misspelling: Low
Risk of Mispronunciation: Low
Famous Namesakes: Activist Heather Mills; actress Heather Locklear; actress Heather Graham
Common Nicknames: None
Common Variations: None
Consider This: The teen movie *Heathers* came out in 1989, but people still think Heather is a snobby name to this day.

Hedda ★★
(German) battler.
First Impression: Hedda is described as a big-boned woman who is stern and stubborn.
Gender Association: Used for girls
Popularity and Trend: Never been ranked in Top 1000
Risk of Misspelling: Average
Risk of Mispronunciation: Fairly low
Famous Namesakes: Gossip columnist Hedda Hopper; fiction character Hedda Gabler
Common Nicknames: None
Common Variations: Hetta
Consider This: Hedda means "battler," and people seem to take that meaning literally.

Hedwig ★★
(German) warrior.
First Impression: Folks believe Hedwig is a stout, broad woman as well as a wise and protective mother.
Gender Association: Used about equally for girls and boys
Popularity and Trend: Last ranked in the Top 1000 in the 1920s
Risk of Misspelling: Average
Risk of Mispronunciation: Average
Famous Namesakes: Character Hedwig (*Hedwig and the Angry Inch*); character Hedwig (*Harry Potter* series)
Common Nicknames: None
Common Variations: None

Consider This: Hedwig has a relatively positive first impression for such a harsh-sounding name. Plus, it's used equally for boys and girls, which may pose a problem for parents searching for names with clear gender associations.

Heidi ★★★★
(German) a form of Adelaide.
First Impression: People see Heidi as a sweet friend, a self-absorbed daddy's girl, or a sarcastic dropout.
Gender Association: Used for girls
Popularity and Trend: #295 (#351 in 2000)
Risk of Misspelling: Fairly low
Risk of Mispronunciation: Low
Famous Namesakes: Model Heidi Klum; madam Heidi Fleiss; fiction character Heidi
Common Nicknames: None
Common Variations: None
Consider This: This German name may work best with a German surname, but it seems suitable for nearly any ethnic background.

Helen ★★★
(Greek) light.
First Impression: Helen is pictured as a mature woman who's self-assured and successful, though she was quiet and dorky as a girl.
Gender Association: Used for girls
Popularity and Trend: #343 (#345 in 2000)

Risk of Misspelling: Low
Risk of Mispronunciation: Low
Famous Namesakes: Actress Helen Hunt; mythological figure Helen of Troy; advocate Helen Keller; actress Helen Hayes; singer Helen Reddy; actress Helen Mirren
Common Nicknames: None
Common Variations: Helene, Helena
Consider This: Helen was hugely popular for the first half of the twentieth century, which is undoubtedly why people think the name belongs to an older woman.

Helene ★
(French) a form of Helen.
First Impression: People think Helene may be refined, but she's also aloof.
Gender Association: Used for girls
Popularity and Trend: Last ranked in the Top 1000 in the 1970s
Risk of Misspelling: Fairly high
Risk of Mispronunciation: High
Famous Namesakes: Poet Helene Johnson; mythological figure Helene
Common Nicknames: None
Common Variations: Helen, Helena
Consider This: This French name has a very elegant but very snobby image. It also has many different pronunciations, including "heh-LAHN-ah," "heh-LEN-ee," and "heh-LAIN."

Helga ★★
(German) pious. (Scandinavian) a form of Olga.
First Impression: Everyone says Helga is a brutish, stern, and imposing mountain of a woman who hails from Germany.
Gender Association: Used for girls
Popularity and Trend: Last ranked in the Top 1000 in the 1910s
Risk of Misspelling: Low
Risk of Mispronunciation: Low
Famous Namesakes: Character Helga Hufflepuff (*Harry Potter* series)
Common Nicknames: None
Common Variations: None
Consider This: Like Bertha, Hedda, and Olga, Helga just doesn't sound pleasant.

Heloise ★
(French) a form of Louise.
First Impression: Heloise is seen as an old, dowdy woman who's unsocial, grouchy, and mean.
Gender Association: Used for girls
Popularity and Trend: Never been ranked in Top 1000
Risk of Misspelling: Average
Risk of Mispronunciation: Average
Famous Namesakes: Historical figure Heloise; advice columnist Heloise Evans
Common Nicknames: None
Common Variations: None

Consider This: This name's over-whelmingly negative image seals its fate as a 1-star name.

Henrietta ★★★
(English) ruler of the household.
First Impression: Most people see Henrietta as an awkward introvert, but others say she's a snobby sophisticate.
Gender Association: Used for girls
Popularity and Trend: Last ranked in the Top 1000 in the 1960s
Risk of Misspelling: Fairly low
Risk of Mispronunciation: Fairly low
Famous Namesakes: Gymnast Henrietta Ónodi
Common Nicknames: Etta, Hettie, Hattie
Common Variations: Henriette
Consider This: Henrietta hasn't been a big name since the '60s.

Hermosa ★★
(Spanish) beautiful.
First Impression: Hermosa is regarded as either kind and ambitious or lazy and obnoxious.
Gender Association: Used for girls
Popularity and Trend: Never been ranked in Top 1000
Risk of Misspelling: Fairly high
Risk of Mispronunciation: Fairly high
Famous Namesakes: None
Common Nicknames: None
Common Variations: None
Consider This: Spanish speakers may think Hermosa is "beautiful,"

but it may be too unusual for others. Pronunciation is also a problem because only Spanish speakers may know to pronounce it "er-MOH-sah" instead of "her-MOH-sah."

Hilary ★★★
(Greek) cheerful, merry.
First Impression: Like a certain politician, Hilary is thought to be an opinionated and ambitious woman who some people find bossy and annoying.
Gender Association: Used mostly for girls
Popularity and Trend: Last ranked in the Top 1000 in the 1990s
Risk of Misspelling: Average
Risk of Mispronunciation: Low
Famous Namesakes: Politician Hillary Rodham Clinton; actress Hilary Duff; actress Hilary Burton; actress Hilary Swank
Common Nicknames: None
Common Variations: Hillary
Consider This: Even with the spelling difference, decide whether you're a Hillary Clinton fan before you choose this name.

Holly ★★★★
(English) holly tree.
First Impression: Most people think Holly is an overly sweet, optimistic, and open-minded girl, despite her poor upbringing.
Gender Association: Used for girls

Popularity and Trend: #346 (#189 in 2000)
Risk of Misspelling: Low
Risk of Mispronunciation: Low
Famous Namesakes: Actress Holly Hunter; actress Holly Robinson-Peete
Common Nicknames: None
Common Variations: Hollie
Consider This: The popularity of this name seems to be sinking fast.

Honora ★★
(Latin) honorable.
First Impression: Some believe Honora is a good-natured woman who tends to be a little weird, but others say she's a witchy chatterbox.
Gender Association: Used for girls
Popularity and Trend: Never been ranked in Top 1000
Risk of Misspelling: Average
Risk of Mispronunciation: Fairly low
Famous Namesakes: None
Common Nicknames: Honey, Nora
Common Variations: Onora
Consider This: Honora is Latin for "honorable," but most people seem to think the name is weird.

Hope ★★★★
(English) hope.
First Impression: People say Hope is as gentle a creature as you will find.
Gender Association: Used for girls
Popularity and Trend: #200 (#146 in 2000)

Risk of Misspelling: Low
Risk of Mispronunciation: Low
Famous Namesakes: Comedian Bob Hope; actress Hope Davis; actress Hope Lange
Common Nicknames: None
Common Variations: None
Consider This: Hope is on its way up the Top 1000, and it may be because of its sweet first impression.

Hortense ★★
(Latin) gardener.
First Impression: Hortense is considered so joyless, she's scary to be near.
Gender Association: Used for girls
Popularity and Trend: Last ranked in the Top 1000 in the 1930s
Risk of Misspelling: Fairly low
Risk of Mispronunciation: Low
Famous Namesakes: Author Hortense Calisher
Common Nicknames: None
Common Variations: None
Consider This: Hortense is easy to spell and say, but its very negative first impression sinks it.

Huberta ★★
(German) bright mind; bright spirit.
First Impression: To many, Huberta's enthusiasm sometimes comes across a little strong.
Gender Association: Used for girls
Popularity and Trend: Never been ranked in Top 1000

Risk of Misspelling: Low
Risk of Mispronunciation: Fairly low
Famous Namesakes: None
Common Nicknames: None
Common Variations: None
Consider This: Neither Hubert nor Huberta are Top 1000 names.

Ida ★★

(German) hardworking. (English) prosperous.

First Impression: People picture Ida sitting in her rocking chair with a cup of Postum in hand, a cat in her lap, and a frown on her face.
Gender Association: Used for girls
Popularity and Trend: Last ranked in the Top 1000 in the 1980s
Risk of Misspelling: Fairly low
Risk of Mispronunciation: Fairly low
Famous Namesakes: Activist Ida B. Wells; journalist Ida Tarbell
Common Nicknames: None
Common Variations: Idelle
Consider This: Ida clearly seems fit for a grandmother, not a baby.

Ilene ★★★

(Irish) a form of Helen.

First Impression: Ilene is viewed as not only intelligent, but witty and kind, too.
Gender Association: Used for girls
Popularity and Trend: Last ranked in the Top 1000 in the 1960s
Risk of Misspelling: Average
Risk of Mispronunciation: Fairly low
Famous Namesakes: Television producer Ilene Chaiken; actress Ilene Graff
Common Nicknames: None
Common Variations: Eileen
Consider This: Ilene has never been as popular as Eileen, but people view it quite positively.

Iman ★★

(Arabic) believer.

First Impression: People say Iman is a determined, confident, and successful African model, much like Somalian-born supermodel Iman.
Gender Association: Used mostly for girls
Popularity and Trend: Never been ranked in Top 1000
Risk of Misspelling: Fairly high
Risk of Mispronunciation: Fairly high
Famous Namesakes: Princess Iman bint al-Abdullah; model Iman Abdulmajid
Common Nicknames: None
Common Variations: Imani
Consider This: As the first impression indicates, Iman's image is very closely associated with supermodel Iman Abdulmajid's, but this exotic name will still be unfamiliar to many.

Imogene ★★★

(Latin) image, likeness.

First Impression: People say Imogene may be a schoolmarm or a scientist, but that doesn't mean she can't dish with the best of them.
Gender Association: Used for girls
Popularity and Trend: Last ranked in the Top 1000 in the 1950s
Risk of Misspelling: Average
Risk of Mispronunciation: Average
Famous Namesakes: Actress Imogene Coca; singer Imogen Heap
Common Nicknames: None
Common Variations: Imogen
Consider This: Imogene may give people pause before they try to pronounce it ("IM-oh-jean") or spell it.

India ★★★★

(Sanskrit) river.

First Impression: India calls to mind a reserved yet emotionally strong woman with star quality.
Gender Association: Used for girls
Popularity and Trend: #568 (#395 in 2000)
Risk of Misspelling: Low
Risk of Mispronunciation: Low
Famous Namesakes: Singer India Arie
Common Nicknames: None
Common Variations: Indya
Consider This: India rates well, but keep in mind that people will likely expect someone with this name to have dark skin.

Inga ★★★

(Scandinavian) a form of Ingrid.

First Impression: People think Inga has a soft side, but she can be hardnosed when she needs to be.

Gender Association: Used for girls

Popularity and Trend: Last ranked in the Top 1000 in the 1910s

Risk of Misspelling: Fairly low

Risk of Mispronunciation: Fairly low

Famous Namesakes: Actress Inga Swenson; speed skater Inga Artamonova

Common Nicknames: None

Common Variations: Ingrid

Consider This: This Scandinavian name has been missing from the Top 1000 for a hundred years.

Ingrid ★★★

(Scandinavian) hero's daughter; beautiful daughter.

First Impression: Ingrid is seen as a determined and intelligent woman who's also domineering, humorless, and aloof.

Gender Association: Used for girls

Popularity and Trend: #619 (#856 in 2000)

Risk of Misspelling: Fairly low

Risk of Mispronunciation: Fairly low

Famous Namesakes: Actress Ingrid Bergman

Common Nicknames: Inga

Common Variations: Inga

Consider This: In spite of beloved famous namesake Ingrid Bergman, Ingrid makes a cold first impression.

Iolanthe ★

(English) a form of Yolanda.

First Impression: Iolanthe is depicted as a gentle, sensitive, and bashful loner who many say is strange and weird.

Gender Association: Used for girls

Popularity and Trend: Never been ranked in Top 1000

Risk of Misspelling: High

Risk of Mispronunciation: High

Famous Namesakes: Opera character Iolanthe

Common Nicknames: None

Common Variations: None

Consider This: Most people won't know how to spell or pronounce this name ("eye-oh-LAN-thee"), and many find it weird in general.

Irene ★★★

(Greek) peaceful.

First Impression: Irene is described as kind, practical, and ladylike, but her conservative demeanor makes her a wee bit boring.

Gender Association: Used for girls

Popularity and Trend: #593 (#468 in 2000)

Risk of Misspelling: Low

Risk of Mispronunciation: Low

Famous Namesakes: Singer Irene Cara; actress Irene Dunn

Common Nicknames: None

Common Variations: Irena

Consider This: Iris, another Greek I name, is gaining popularity at about the same rate Irene is losing popularity.

Iris ★★★★

(Greek) rainbow.

First Impression: People think Iris has a bright, creative mind.

Gender Association: Used for girls

Popularity and Trend: #369 (#412 in 2000)

Risk of Misspelling: Low

Risk of Mispronunciation: Low

Famous Namesakes: Mythological figure Iris; writer Iris Murdoch

Common Nicknames: None

Common Variations: None

Consider This: If you're looking for a name that makes a smart first impression, Iris could be a keeper.

Irma ★★

(Latin) a form of Erma. (German) a form of Irmgaard.

First Impression: Irma is described as mousy in both demeanor and appearance.

Gender Association: Used for girls

Popularity and Trend: Last ranked in the Top 1000 in the 1990s

Risk of Misspelling: Average

Risk of Mispronunciation: Fairly low

Famous Namesakes: Singer Irma Thomas; actress Irma P. Hall

Common Nicknames: None

Common Variations: Erma

Consider This: Both Irma and root name Erma have been unpopular for some time.

Isabel ★★★★★

(Spanish) consecrated to God.

First Impression: Folks believe Isabel has inner and outer beauty.

Gender Association: Used for girls

Popularity and Trend: #87 (#93 in 2000)

Risk of Misspelling: Fairly low

Risk of Mispronunciation: Fairly low

Famous Namesakes: Author Isabel Allende; character Isabel Archer (*The Portrait of a Lady*); actress Isabel Sanford; queen Isabel of Spain

Common Nicknames: Belle, Izzy

Common Variations: Isabelle, Isobel, Isabella

Consider This: "Isabel" is the root spelling of this versatile and beautiful-sounding name, but Isabelle is just about as popular, which could cause spelling problems.

Isabella ★★★★

(Italian) a form of Isabel.

First Impression: With Isabella of Castile as a namesake, people believe Isabella has queenly grace and class.

Gender Association: Used for girls

Popularity and Trend: #4 (#45 in 2000)

Risk of Misspelling: Fairly low

Risk of Mispronunciation: Low

Famous Namesakes: Actress Isabella Rossellini; queen Isabella of Castile; model Izabella Miko

Common Nicknames: Bella

Common Variations: Isabela

Consider This: Isabella is a regal-sounding name that has made huge strides in popularity from 2000 to 2006.

Isi ★

(Spanish) a short form of Isabel.

First Impression: Isi is thought to be an eccentric with odd clothes and weird creativity.

Gender Association: Used for girls

Popularity and Trend: Never been ranked in Top 1000

Risk of Misspelling: High

Risk of Mispronunciation: Fairly high

Famous Namesakes: Character Dr. Izzie Stevens (*Grey's Anatomy*)

Common Nicknames: None

Common Variations: Issie

Consider This: This unconventional nickname for Isabel doesn't work well as a given name—nor even a nickname. People will expect it to be pronounced like the word *icy*, or they may expect it to be spelled "Izzy."

Italia ★★★

(Italian) from Italy.

First Impression: Italia is primarily regarded as a snobby and condescending model who's sexy, olive-skinned, and incredibly rich.

Gender Association: Used for girls

Popularity and Trend: Never been ranked in Top 1000

Risk of Misspelling: Fairly low

Risk of Mispronunciation: Fairly low

Famous Namesakes: None

Common Nicknames: None

Common Variations: Italina

Consider This: Italia means "from Italy," so it's great for Italians… but probably only Italians. Also, there may be a trick to pronunciation if people don't realize it's "eh-TAHL-ee-ah" and not "eh-TAL-ee-ah."

Ivory ★★★

(Latin) made of ivory.

First Impression: Ivory is considered a real sweetheart whose looks live up to her name.

Gender Association: Used mostly for girls

Popularity and Trend: Last ranked in the Top 1000 in the 1920s

Risk of Misspelling: Low

Risk of Mispronunciation: Low

Famous Namesakes: Film director James Ivory; professional wrestler Ivory; basketball player Ivory Latta

Common Nicknames: None

Common Variations: None

Consider This: People expect Ivory to have a light complexion. If your family is darker hued, but you like the sound of this name, consider Ivy, instead.

Ivy ★★★★
(English) ivy tree.
First Impression: Ivy is pictured as a sassy, unique spirit everyone loves.
Gender Association: Used mostly for girls
Popularity and Trend: #334 (#352 in 2000)
Risk of Misspelling: Low
Risk of Mispronunciation: Low
Famous Namesakes: Character Poison Ivy (*Batman*)
Common Nicknames: None
Common Variations: Ivey
Consider This: Moderately popular, Ivy comes across as alternative and cool.

Jackie ★★★
(American) a familiar form of Jacqueline.
First Impression: People say Jackie is outgoing—that is, she's usually *out going* to many hotspots.
Gender Association: Used about equally for girls and boys
Popularity and Trend: Last ranked in the Top 1000 in the 1990s
Risk of Misspelling: Fairly low
Risk of Mispronunciation: Low
Famous Namesakes: Film character Jackie Brown; character Jackie Harris (*Roseanne*)

Common Nicknames: None
Common Variations: Jacki, Jacqui
Consider This: People may assume Jackie is short for Jacqueline, a more formal choice. This name is also used equally for boys and girls, which may pose a problem for parents searching for names with clear gender associations.

Jaclyn ★★★
(American) a form of Jacqueline.
First Impression: People think Jaclyn swings between being forceful and being graceful.
Gender Association: Used for girls
Popularity and Trend: #860 (#452 in 2000)
Risk of Misspelling: Average
Risk of Mispronunciation: Fairly low
Famous Namesakes: Actress Jaclyn Smith
Common Nicknames: Jackie
Common Variations: Jacklyn
Consider This: Jaclyn is technically a short form of Jacqueline, but it seems formal and versatile enough to stand on its own.

Jacqueline ★★★★★
(French) supplanter, substitute; little Jacqui.
First Impression: Jacqueline Kennedy Onassis was one of the most iconic women of the twentieth century, so it's only fitting people think Jacqueline has poise and elegance.

Gender Association: Used for girls
Popularity and Trend: #118 (#63 in 2000)
Risk of Misspelling: Fairly low
Risk of Mispronunciation: Fairly low
Famous Namesakes: First lady Jacqueline Kennedy Onassis; actress Jacqueline Bisset
Common Nicknames: Jack, Jackie
Common Variations: Jacquelin, Jackalyn, Jackeline, Jackilyn, Jackolyn
Consider This: This elegant name recently left the Top 100 for the first time in eighty years, but that's likely only due to the rise in variant spellings.

Jada ★★★★
(Hebrew) wise. (Spanish) a form of Jade.
First Impression: Most people see Jada as a hardworking and confident African American woman, although she may be blunt at times.
Gender Association: Used for girls
Popularity and Trend: #93 (#84 in 2000)
Risk of Misspelling: Fairly low
Risk of Mispronunciation: Fairly low
Famous Namesakes: Actress Jada Pinkett Smith
Common Nicknames: None
Common Variations: Jaida, Jayda
Consider This: This Top 100 name's image sounds a lot like namesake Jada Pinkett Smith's.

Jade ★★★★★

(Spanish) jade.

First Impression: Jade is seen as exquisite as the jewel she's named after.

Gender Association: Used mostly for girls

Popularity and Trend: #111 (#116 in 2000)

Risk of Misspelling: Low

Risk of Mispronunciation: Low

Famous Namesakes: Jewelry designer Jade Jagger

Common Nicknames: Jadie

Common Variations: Jaid, Jayde

Consider This: This exotic but easily spelled and pronounced name is on the rise.

Jaime ★★★

(French) I love.

First Impression: Jaime is described as perky and brave, but that doesn't mean she's wild.

Gender Association: Used mostly for boys

Popularity and Trend: Last ranked in the Top 1000 in the 1980s

Risk of Misspelling: Average

Risk of Mispronunciation: Fairly low

Famous Namesakes: Actress Jaime Pressley; actress Jaime King

Common Nicknames: None

Common Variations: Jamie

Consider This: Jamie is much more popular than Jaime. Both spellings are used more often for boys, though.

Jana ★★★★

(Hebrew) gracious, merciful. (Slavic) a form of Jane.

First Impression: People think Jana is an appealing combination of brains and fun.

Gender Association: Used for girls

Popularity and Trend: Last ranked in the Top 1000 in the 1980s

Risk of Misspelling: Average

Risk of Mispronunciation: Average

Famous Namesakes: Tennis player Jana Novotná; model Jana Svenson

Common Nicknames: Jan

Common Variations: Janna

Consider This: This spelling of Jana hasn't been ranked since the '80s, but the name still has a stellar first impression. It's usually pronounced "JAN-ah," but some cultures pronounce it "YON-ah."

Janae ★★★

(American) a form of Jane. (Hebrew) a form of Jana.

First Impression: People imagine this African American woman is sweet, goodhearted, and highly sociable.

Gender Association: Used for girls

Popularity and Trend: #679 (#470 in 2000)

Risk of Misspelling: Average

Risk of Mispronunciation: Average

Famous Namesakes: None

Common Nicknames: None

Common Variations: Jenae, Jenay

Consider This: People may pronounce Janae "jan-EE" or "ja-NAY."

Jane ★★★★

(Hebrew) God is gracious.

First Impression: "Plain Jane" is right: Jane is described as modest, sensible, and plain.

Gender Association: Used for girls

Popularity and Trend: #478 (#435 in 2000)

Risk of Misspelling: Fairly low

Risk of Mispronunciation: Low

Famous Namesakes: Journalist Jane Pauley; actress Jayne Mansfield; actress Jane Seymour; actress Jane Fonda; author Jane Austen; fiction character Jane Eyre; actress Jane Russell

Common Nicknames: Jan, Janie, Janice, Jannie

Common Variations: Jayne

Consider This: Jane may be thought plain, but the name is still a classic.

Janelle ★★★★★

(French) a form of Jane.

First Impression: Janelle is described as flamboyant, and she doesn't care what others think.

Gender Association: Used for girls

Popularity and Trend: #390 (#471 in 2000)

Risk of Misspelling: Fairly low
Risk of Mispronunciation: Fairly low
Famous Namesakes: Model Janelle Perry
Common Nicknames: Jan, Elle
Common Variations: Janel
Consider This: Janelle is thought to be wilder than its plain-Jane root name.

Janet ★★★★
(English) a form of Jane.
First Impression: People say Janet is a helpful girl who's pretty, trustworthy, and funny.
Gender Association: Used for girls
Popularity and Trend: #562 (#413 in 2000)
Risk of Misspelling: Low
Risk of Mispronunciation: Low
Famous Namesakes: Singer Janet Jackson; actress Janet Leigh; attorney general Janet Reno; author Janet Evanovich
Common Nicknames: Jan
Common Variations: None
Consider This: Despite gradually slipping down the Top 1000, Janet is still considered an all-American name for an all-American girl.

Janie ★★★
(English) a familiar form of Jane.
First Impression: Folks say Janie may be an innocent sweetheart or a heartless homewrecker.
Gender Association: Used for girls
Popularity and Trend: Last ranked in the Top 1000 in the 1990s
Risk of Misspelling: Fairly low
Risk of Mispronunciation: Low
Famous Namesakes: Character Janie Crawford (*Their Eyes Were Watching God*); theatre actress Janie Sell
Common Nicknames: None
Common Variations: Janey
Consider This: Compared to other names in this family, Janie sounds very young, and it's not versatile.

Janine ★★★
(French) a form of Jane.
First Impression: Most people say Janine is a snarky, smart comedian (like Janeane Garofalo), but some say she's a sexy, busty porn star (like Janine Lindemulder).
Gender Association: Used for girls
Popularity and Trend: Last ranked in the Top 1000 in the 1990s
Risk of Misspelling: Fairly low
Risk of Mispronunciation: Fairly low
Famous Namesakes: Actress Janine Turner; comedian Janeane Garofalo; adult film star Janine Lindemulder
Common Nicknames: Jan
Common Variations: Janeane, Janeen
Consider This: Janine's famous namesakes leave a strong impression on its image, for better or for worse.

Janis ★★
(Hebrew, English) a form of Janice.
First Impression: People say Janis is a wild, crazy, and cool singer with a hippie lifestyle and, unfortunately, a drug and alcohol problem, much like rock legend Janis Joplin.
Gender Association: Used mostly for girls
Popularity and Trend: Last ranked in the Top 1000 in the 1970s
Risk of Misspelling: Average
Risk of Mispronunciation: Fairly low
Famous Namesakes: Singer Janis Joplin; model Janice Dickinson; singer Janis Ian
Common Nicknames: Jan
Common Variations: Janice
Consider This: Janice is the more popular root spelling of this name, but if you're a fan of Janis Joplin, choose this spelling.

Janna ★★★★
(Arabic) harvest of fruit. (Hebrew) a form of Johana.
First Impression: People say Janna is kind, cheerful, and humorous—a very social gal.
Gender Association: Used for girls
Popularity and Trend: Last ranked in the Top 1000 in the 1990s
Risk of Misspelling: Average
Risk of Mispronunciation: Fairly low
Famous Namesakes: Model Jana Svenson; tennis player Jana Novotná

Common Nicknames: Jan
Common Variations: Jana
Consider This: This spelling of Janna is slightly more popular than Jana, but it hasn't been ranked since the '90s. Like Jana, it may be pronounced "JAN-ah" or "YON-ah."

Jasmine ★★★★

(Persian) jasmine flower.
First Impression: People say Jasmine's personality is most likely as sweet as the scent of her namesake flower.
Gender Association: Used for girls
Popularity and Trend: #29 (#27 in 2000)
Risk of Misspelling: Fairly low
Risk of Mispronunciation: Fairly low
Famous Namesakes: Actress Jasmine Guy; character Princess Jasmine (Aladdin)
Common Nicknames: Jas, Jasma, Jassi
Common Variations: Jasmin
Consider This: Jasmine has been ranked in the Top 30 since the '90s, likely thanks to Disney's Aladdin. Most people pronounce it "JAZZ-min," but a few may opt for "jaz-MEEN."

Jayne ★★★★

(Hindi) victorious. (English) a form of Jane.
First Impression: Jayne is considered a total type A: She's organized,

dependable, intelligent, and tough.
Gender Association: Used for girls
Popularity and Trend: Last ranked in the Top 1000 in the 1970s
Risk of Misspelling: Average
Risk of Mispronunciation: Low
Famous Namesakes: Journalist Jane Pauley; actress Jayne Mansfield; actress Jane Seymour; actress Jane Fonda; author Jane Austen; fiction character Jane Eyre; actress Jane Russell
Common Nicknames: Jan, Janie, Janice, Jannie
Common Variations: Jane
Consider This: Jayne has a more dynamic first impression than Jane, but most people will misspell it.

Jean ★★

(Scottish) God is gracious.
First Impression: Jean is pictured as a goodhearted, religious woman who can be bossy and gossipy from time to time.
Gender Association: Used mostly for boys
Popularity and Trend: Last ranked in the Top 1000 in the 1990s
Risk of Misspelling: Fairly low
Risk of Mispronunciation: Low
Famous Namesakes: Novelist Jean Rhys; actress Jean Simmons; actress Gene Tierney; actress

Jean Stapleton; actress Jean Harlow
Common Nicknames: Jeanie
Common Variations: Jeanne
Consider This: With the French pronunciation "zhawn," this name is clearly used more for boys. However, even when pronounced "jeen," the homonym Gene, a traditional boys' name, may cause gender confusion.

Jeanette ★★★

(French) a form of Jean.
First Impression: Jeanette is thought to be a moody and blunt blue-collar mother.
Gender Association: Used for girls
Popularity and Trend: Last ranked in the Top 1000 in the 1980s
Risk of Misspelling: Fairly low
Risk of Mispronunciation: Fairly low
Famous Namesakes: Actress Jeanette MacDonald; novelist Jeanette Winterson
Common Nicknames: Jean, Jeanie
Common Variations: Jeanetta
Consider This: People may pronounce this as "jean-ETT" or "jah-NET."

Jelena ★★★

(Russian) a form of Helen.
First Impression: The first thing people notice about Jelena is how smiley and friendly she is —she seems to get along with everyone.

Gender Association: Used for girls

Popularity and Trend: Never been ranked in Top 1000

Risk of Misspelling: High

Risk of Mispronunciation: Fairly high

Famous Namesakes: Tennis player Jelena Jankovi; tennis player Jelena Doki

Common Nicknames: None

Common Variations: None

Consider This: Many people won't know the traditional "yay-LAY-nah" pronunciation for this name. Other pronunciations include "jeh-LEE-nah" and "jah-LAY-nah."

Jena ★★★★

(Arabic) a form of Jenna.

First Impression: Jena is viewed as a precocious young lady who's smart and sweet.

Gender Association: Used for girls

Popularity and Trend: Last ranked in the Top 1000 in the 1980s

Risk of Misspelling: Average

Risk of Mispronunciation: Average

Famous Namesakes: Actress Jena Malone; actress Jenna Elfman; actress Jenna Fisher

Common Nicknames: Jen, Jenny

Common Variations: Jenna, Genna

Consider This: Jena is pronounced the same as Jenna, but people may think it's pronounced like Gina.

Jenay ★★★★

(American, Hebrew) a form of Janae.

First Impression: Jenay is most often viewed as a creative, artistic woman—perhaps a dancer or singer—with a toned, tall figure and pretty looks.

Gender Association: Used for girls

Popularity and Trend: Never been ranked in Top 1000

Risk of Misspelling: Average

Risk of Mispronunciation: Fairly low

Famous Namesakes: None

Common Nicknames: Jen

Common Variations: Jenae, Janae

Consider This: While most people will pronounce this name as "jen-AY," some may think it's pronounced like Jenny.

Jenna ★★★★★

(Arabic) small bird. (Welsh) a form of Jennifer.

First Impression: Jenna is thought to be a spirited and humorous party girl with a kind heart.

Gender Association: Used for girls

Popularity and Trend: #88 (#64 in 2000)

Risk of Misspelling: Fairly low

Risk of Mispronunciation: Low

Famous Namesakes: Actress Jena Malone; actress Jenna Elfman; actress Jenna Fisher

Common Nicknames: Jen, Jenny

Common Variations: Jena, Genna

Consider This: Jenna is a very popular form of Jennifer, though it is a bit less formal.

Jennifer ★★★★

(Welsh) white wave; white phantom.

First Impression: Jennifer is seen as ready to take on any challenge.

Gender Association: Used mostly for girls

Popularity and Trend: #51 (#26 in 2000)

Risk of Misspelling: Fairly low

Risk of Mispronunciation: Low

Famous Namesakes: Actress Jennifer Aniston; actress Jennifer Lopez; actress Jennifer Garner; actress Jennifer Connelly; actress Jennifer Tilly; actress Jennifer Jason Leigh; actress Jennifer Love Hewitt; actress Jennifer Hudson; author Jennifer Weiner

Common Nicknames: Jen, Jenny, Jenna

Common Variations: Gennifer, Jenifer

Consider This: Look at all of Jennifer's famous namesakes to see how popular this name has been over the years. It's still a Top 100 name, though it's starting to slip.

Jenny ★★★★

(Welsh) a familiar form of Jennifer.

First Impression: Jenny is described as sunny, fun-loving, perky, and happy to go with the flow.

Gender Association: Used for girls

Popularity and Trend: #475 (#361 in 2000)
Risk of Misspelling: Fairly low
Risk of Mispronunciation: Low
Famous Namesakes: Talk show host Jenny Jones; actress Jennie Garth; actress Jenny McCarthy
Common Nicknames: Jen
Common Variations: Jeni
Consider This: Compared to Jennifer, Jenny is much more casual, much less popular, and much more youthful, but it still has a good vibe.

Jeri ★★

(American) a short form of Jeraldine.
First Impression: People think Jeri could be a vivacious party girl, an angry schemer, or a boring nerd.
Gender Association: Used for girls
Popularity and Trend: Last ranked in the Top 1000 in the 1980s
Risk of Misspelling: Average
Risk of Mispronunciation: Low
Famous Namesakes: Actress Jeri Ryan; singer Geri Halliwell
Common Nicknames: None
Common Variations: Geri
Consider This: Jeri's first impression seems too negative to make this name a good choice. Plus, its pronunciation is the same as Jerry, a popular nickname for boys, which may cause gender confusion.

Jessamine ★★

(French) a form of Jasmine.
First Impression: Folks say Jessamine lives in the lap of luxury, but she's too self-absorbed.
Gender Association: Used for girls
Popularity and Trend: Never been ranked in Top 1000
Risk of Misspelling: Average
Risk of Mispronunciation: Fairly high
Famous Namesakes: None
Common Nicknames: Jessa, Jess, Jessie
Common Variations: None
Consider This: Is Jessamine pronounced "JESS-ah-meen," "JESS-ah-min," or "JESS-ah-mine"? People may not know.

Jessica ★★★★

(Hebrew) wealthy.
First Impression: People believe Jessica bubbles with personality, but she may be untrustworthy and gossipy.
Gender Association: Used mostly for girls
Popularity and Trend: #32 (#8 in 2000)
Risk of Misspelling: Fairly low
Risk of Mispronunciation: Low
Famous Namesakes: Singer Jessica Simpson; actress Jessica Lange; character Jessica Rabbit (*Who Framed Roger Rabbit*); actress Jessica Biel; actress Jessica Alba; model Jessica Stam
Common Nicknames: Jessa, Jess, Jessie
Common Variations: Jesica
Consider This: Jessica was the number-one name for most of the '80s and '90s, but it's slowly starting to slip down the Top 100.

Jessie ★★★

(Hebrew) a short form of Jessica. (Scottish) a form of Janet.
First Impression: Because of Jessie the Yodeling Cowgirl of *Toy Story 2*, Jessie is pictured as a happy-go-lucky and cheerful tomboy.
Gender Association: Used about equally for girls and boys
Popularity and Trend: #558 (#400 in 2000)
Risk of Misspelling: Fairly low
Risk of Mispronunciation: Low
Famous Namesakes: Singer Jessie Daniels
Common Nicknames: Jess
Common Variations: Jessy, Jessi, Jesse
Consider This: Jessie is a well-liked nickname with a fun tomboy feel, but it may have limitations as a given name. Also, it's used equally for boys and girls, which may pose a problem for parents searching for names with clear gender associations.

Jezebel ★★

(Hebrew) unexalted; impure.
First Impression: Because of Jezebel, the infamous biblical figure, this name connotes any wicked woman.

Gender Association: Used for girls

Popularity and Trend: Never been ranked in Top 1000

Risk of Misspelling: Average

Risk of Mispronunciation: Fairly low

Famous Namesakes: Biblical figure Jezebel

Common Nicknames: Belle

Common Variations: None

Consider This: Thanks (or no thanks) to the biblical Jezebel, people have a terrible image of this name. It isn't easy to spell, either.

Jill ★★★★

(English) a form of Jillian.

First Impression: Jill is viewed as always smiling and sweet.

Gender Association: Used for girls

Popularity and Trend: Last ranked in the Top 1000 in the 1980s

Risk of Misspelling: Low

Risk of Mispronunciation: Low

Famous Namesakes: Actress Jill Hennessy; actress Jill Clayburgh; singer Jill Scott

Common Nicknames: None

Common Variations: None

Consider This: Jill is a short form of Jillian, but it seems to stand on its own all right.

Jillian ★★★★

(Latin) youthful.

First Impression: Jillian is a triple threat: She's described as attractive, intelligent, and lovable.

Gender Association: Used for girls

Popularity and Trend: #174 (#120 in 2000)

Risk of Misspelling: Average

Risk of Mispronunciation: Low

Famous Namesakes: Actress Jillian Barberie; actress Gillian Anderson; singer Gillian Welch

Common Nicknames: Jill, Jilly

Common Variations: Gillian

Consider This: Jillian is more popular than Gillian, but both forms make positive first impressions.

Jo ★★

(American) a short form of Joana, Jolene, Josephine.

First Impression: People say Jo has a rugged appeal, perhaps because her name sounds masculine.

Gender Association: Used mostly for girls

Popularity and Trend: Last ranked in the Top 1000 in the 1980s

Risk of Misspelling: Average

Risk of Mispronunciation: Low

Famous Namesakes: Character Jo March (*Little Women*); character Jo Polniaczek (*The Facts of Life*)

Common Nicknames: Joey

Common Variations: None

Consider This: If Jo's masculine image is a problem, save it as a nickname for Joanna, Jolene, or Josephine. Furthermore, its pronunciation is the same as Joe, a popular nickname for boys, which may cause gender confusion.

Joan ★★★

(Hebrew) God is gracious.

First Impression: Joan evokes the image of a brassy, demanding, and perhaps intimidating older woman.

Gender Association: Used mostly for girls

Popularity and Trend: Last ranked in the Top 1000 in the 1990s

Risk of Misspelling: Low

Risk of Mispronunciation: Low

Famous Namesakes: Actress Joan Allen; actress Joan Crawford; saint Joan of Arc; musician Joan Jett; comedian Joan Rivers; singer Joan Baez; actress Joan Collins

Common Nicknames: Jo, Joanie

Common Variations: None

Consider This: This name had its heyday in the '30s and '40s, but it seems dated now.

Joanna ★★★

(English) a form of Joan.

First Impression: People think Joanna will either stab you in the back, regale you with her knowledge, or buy you a beer at the honky-tonk.

Gender Association: Used for girls

Popularity and Trend: #256 (#238 in 2000)

Risk of Misspelling: Fairly low
Risk of Mispronunciation: Low
Famous Namesakes: Biblical figure Joanna; singer Joanna Newsom; actress Joanna Lumley; model Joanna Krupa
Common Nicknames: Jo, Anna
Common Variations: Joana, Johana
Consider This: Joanna's image is mixed, but it's still a relatively popular name.

Jocelyn ★★★★

(Latin) joyous.

First Impression: Folks say Jocelyn's good looks may go with either a charming personality or an uppity one.
Gender Association: Used mostly for girls
Popularity and Trend: #73 (#122 in 2000)
Risk of Misspelling: Average
Risk of Mispronunciation: Fairly low
Famous Namesakes: Singer Jocelyn Brown; surgeon general Jocelyn Elders; socialite Jocelyn Wildenstein
Common Nicknames: Joss, Lynn
Common Variations: Jocelin, Josalyn, Joselin, Joclyn, Joslin
Consider This: There are plenty of ways to spell this name, but this version recently entered the Top 100. The slight problem with pronunciation is that some say it as three syllables ("JOSS-ah-

lyn") and others say it as two ("JOSS-lyn").

Jodi ★★

(American) a familiar form of Judith.

First Impression: Jodi is seen as one tomboy who likes to be in charge.
Gender Association: Used for girls
Popularity and Trend: Last ranked in the Top 1000 in the 1990s
Risk of Misspelling: Fairly high
Risk of Mispronunciation: Low
Famous Namesakes: Writer Jodi Picoult; actress Jodie Foster; singer Jody Watley
Common Nicknames: Jo
Common Variations: Jody, Jodie
Consider This: Jodi is a casual name that could be confused with several variant spellings, including Jody, the name used equally for boys and girls, which could cause gender confusion.

Jody ★

(American) a familiar form of Judith.

First Impression: Jody has people split into two camps: Some say she's quiet, boring, and sensitive. Others say she's loud, crazy, and outspoken.
Gender Association: Used about equally for girls and boys
Popularity and Trend: Last ranked in the Top 1000 in the 1990s

Risk of Misspelling: Average
Risk of Mispronunciation: Low
Famous Namesakes: Singer Jody Watley; actress Jodie Foster; writer Jodi Picoult
Common Nicknames: Jo
Common Variations: Jodi, Jodie
Consider This: Jody is used equally for boys and girls, which may cause confusion.

Jolene ★★★★

(Hebrew) God will add, God will increase. (English) a form of Josephine.

First Impression: People think Jolene works hard all day, but she knows how to kick up her heels when the whistle blows.
Gender Association: Used for girls
Popularity and Trend: Last ranked in the Top 1000 in the 1990s
Risk of Misspelling: Fairly low
Risk of Mispronunciation: Low
Famous Namesakes: Actress Jolene Blalock
Common Nicknames: Jo
Common Variations: Joleen
Consider This: Dolly Parton's song "Jolene" may be a big source for this name's first impression.

Jolie ★★★★

(French) pretty.

First Impression: True to her name's meaning, Jolie is described as "pretty" inside and out.
Gender Association: Used for girls

Popularity and Trend: #614
(#821 in 2000)
Risk of Misspelling: Fairly low
Risk of Mispronunciation: Low
Famous Namesakes: Actress Angelina
Jolie; singer Jolie Holland
Common Nicknames: Jo
Common Variations: Jolee
Consider This: People will know how
to pronounce this "pretty" French
name, thanks to Angelina Jolie.

Joni ★★★
(American) a familiar form of Joan.
First Impression: Joni is imagined to
be a hardworking and deter-
mined woman.
Gender Association: Used for girls
Popularity and Trend: Last ranked in
the Top 1000 in the 1980s
Risk of Misspelling: Average
Risk of Mispronunciation: Fairly low
Famous Namesakes: Singer Joni
Mitchell; character Joanie
Cunningham (*Happy Days*)
Common Nicknames: None
Common Variations: Joanie
Consider This: This spelling is less
common than Joanie, but Joni
Mitchell makes it familiar to
most.

Jordan ★★★★
(Hebrew) descending.
First Impression: People say Jordan is
a talented basketball player with
dark hair and a tall, fit physique,
much like a female version of
sports legend Michael Jordan.
Gender Association: Used mostly
for boys
Popularity and Trend: #97
(#50 in 2000)
Risk of Misspelling: Fairly low
Risk of Mispronunciation: Low
Famous Namesakes: Actress Jordan
Ladd; model Jordan
Common Nicknames: Jori
Common Variations: Jordann, Jordin,
Jorden, Jordon
Consider This: Jordan is used more
often for boys, but it's been a Top
100 girls' name for some time.

Josephine ★★★★★
(French) a form of Joseph.
First Impression: Folks say Josephine's
inner strength is rivaled only by
her beauty.
Gender Association: Used for girls
Popularity and Trend: #221
(#288 in 2000)
Risk of Misspelling: Fairly low
Risk of Mispronunciation: Low
Famous Namesakes: Historical figure
Josephine de Beauharnais; singer
Josephine Baker
Common Nicknames: Jo, Joey, Josie,
Fifi, Josette
Common Variations: Josefine, Josepha,
Josephina
Consider This: Josephine is a strong,
versatile, and classic name that's
becoming popular once again.

Josie ★★★★
(Hebrew) a form of Josephine.
First Impression: People picture Josie
as a spunky, cool, and wild
redhead with a big smile.
Gender Association: Used for girls
Popularity and Trend: #291
(#327 in 2000)
Risk of Misspelling: Fairly low
Risk of Mispronunciation: Low
Famous Namesakes: Character Josie
(*Josie and the Pussycats*); model
Josie Maran; actress Josie Bissett
Common Nicknames: Jo
Common Variations: Josi, Josey
Consider This: Although casual, Josie
is on the rise, and people have a
very positive first impression of it.

Journey ★★★★
(English) journey.
First Impression: People imagine
Journey as a free-spirited hippie
who loves to take adventures
around the world.
Gender Association: Used for girls
Popularity and Trend: #822
(#950 in 2001)
Risk of Misspelling: Low
Risk of Mispronunciation: Low
Famous Namesakes: None
Common Nicknames: None
Common Variations: None
Consider This: This so-called hippie
name has been at the bottom of
the Top 1000 list for a few years.

Joy ★★★★

(Latin) joyous.

First Impression: Joy is viewed as a joyful, content, and smiling young girl.

Gender Association: Used for girls

Popularity and Trend: #507 (#458 in 2000)

Risk of Misspelling: Low

Risk of Mispronunciation: Low

Famous Namesakes: Actress Joy Bryant; comedian Joy Behar

Common Nicknames: None

Common Variations: Joi

Consider This: Most people see Joy as a young girl, though Joy Behar is a well-known older namesake.

Joyce ★★★

(Latin) joyous.

First Impression: People think Joyce does the best she can to provide for her kids.

Gender Association: Used for girls

Popularity and Trend: #831 (#669 in 2000)

Risk of Misspelling: Low

Risk of Mispronunciation: Low

Famous Namesakes: Actress Joyce Dewitt; advice columnist Joyce Brothers; author Joyce Carol Oates

Common Nicknames: None

Common Variations: None

Consider This: According to its image, Joyce reminds people of a mother, so perhaps try Joy instead to create a more youthful impression.

Juanita ★★

(Spanish) a form of Jane, Joan.

First Impression: People imagine Juanita has a bad attitude, a huge ego, and a nasty streak.

Gender Association: Used for girls

Popularity and Trend: Last ranked in the Top 1000 in the 1980s

Risk of Misspelling: Average

Risk of Mispronunciation: Average

Famous Namesakes: Actress Juanita Moore; activist Juanita Craft

Common Nicknames: Juana, Nita

Common Variations: None

Consider This: Juanita is definitely a Latino name.

Judith ★★★★

(Hebrew) praised.

First Impression: Some think Judith is self-confident and strong, but others call her bossy and opinionated.

Gender Association: Used for girls

Popularity and Trend: #577 (#617 in 2000)

Risk of Misspelling: Low

Risk of Mispronunciation: Low

Famous Namesakes: Actress Judith Light; author Judith Krantz; poet Judith Viorst

Common Nicknames: Judy, Jodie

Common Variations: None

Consider This: Judith hearkens back to the '40s and '50s, but it still ranks in the middle of the Top 1000.

Judy ★★★

(Hebrew) a familiar form of Judith.

First Impression: Judy is described as a bubbly and talkative woman with old-fashioned values.

Gender Association: Used for girls

Popularity and Trend: Last ranked in the Top 1000 in the 1990s

Risk of Misspelling: Fairly low

Risk of Mispronunciation: Low

Famous Namesakes: Actress Judy Garland; author Judy Blume; singer Judy Collins; actress Judy Davis; actress Judi Dench; actress Judy Holliday; actress Judy Greer, character Judy Jetson (*The Jetsons*)

Common Nicknames: None

Common Variations: Judi

Consider This: Judy is an old-fashioned name that's not as versatile as Judith.

Julia ★★★★★

(Latin) youthful.

First Impression: People think Julia may be sensitive and graceful, or sassy and stubborn.

Gender Association: Used for girls

Popularity and Trend: #31 (#29 in 2000)

Risk of Misspelling: Low

Risk of Mispronunciation: Low

Famous Namesakes: Actress Julia Stiles; actress Julia Ormond;

actress Julia Roberts; chef Julia Child; actress Julia Louis-Dreyfuss; activist Julia Butterfly Hill

Common Nicknames: Jules, Julie
Common Variations: Julie, Juliana
Consider This: It could be the influence of actress Julia Roberts: This always-popular name has been even more popular the past twenty years.

Juliana ★★★★

(Czech, Spanish) a form of Julia.

First Impression: Juliana is pictured as a kind, graceful, and pleasant woman with a lot of confidence and social savoir-faire.
Gender Association: Used for girls
Popularity and Trend: #162 (#241 in 2000)
Risk of Misspelling: Average
Risk of Mispronunciation: Average
Famous Namesakes: Queen Juliana of the Netherlands; actress Juliana Marguiles
Common Nicknames: Jules, Julia
Common Variations: Julianna, Julieanna
Consider This: People may pronounce this name "joo-lee-AHN-ah" or "joo-lee-ANN-ah." Either way, it's on the rise.

Julianne ★★★

(English) a form of Julia.

First Impression: Folks say Julianne may just be another snobby rich girl.
Gender Association: Used for girls
Popularity and Trend: #884 (#515 in 2000)
Risk of Misspelling: Fairly low
Risk of Mispronunciation: Low
Famous Namesakes: Actress Julianne Moore; actress Julianne Phillips
Common Nicknames: Jules, Julie
Common Variations: Julieanne
Consider This: Juliana ranks much higher than Julianne, especially because of its first impression.

Julie ★★★★★

(English) a form of Julia.

First Impression: Julie is considered to be approachable, empathetic, and loyal.
Gender Association: Used for girls
Popularity and Trend: #296 (#190 in 2000)
Risk of Misspelling: Fairly low
Risk of Mispronunciation: Low
Famous Namesakes: Actress Julie Andrews; actress Julie Newmar; actress Julie Christie
Common Nicknames: Jules
Common Variations: Julee
Consider This: Julie isn't nearly as popular as Julia, but people think Julie's image is just as likable.

Juliet ★★★★★

(French) a form of Julia.

First Impression: Juliet is imagined to be a purehearted and thoughtful young woman with flowing dark hair.
Gender Association: Used for girls
Popularity and Trend: #581 (#623 in 2000)
Risk of Misspelling: Fairly low
Risk of Mispronunciation: Low
Famous Namesakes: Character Juliet (*Romeo and Juliet*); actress Juliette Lewis; actress Juliette Binoche
Common Nicknames: Jules, Julie
Common Variations: Juliette
Consider This: Thanks to Shakespeare, everybody knows this name. And this Shakespearean spelling is considerably more popular than "Juliette."

June ★★★

(Latin) born in the sixth month.

First Impression: June Cleaver from TV's *Leave It to Beaver* epitomized the cheery side of motherhood in the '50s, and June is still regarded as a happy homemaker.
Gender Association: Used for girls
Popularity and Trend: Last ranked in the Top 1000 in the 1980s
Risk of Misspelling: Low
Risk of Mispronunciation: Low
Famous Namesakes: Actress June Allyson; singer June Carter Cash; character June Cleaver (*Leave It to Beaver*)
Common Nicknames: Junie
Common Variations: None
Consider This: On one hand, people associate this name with old-fashioned June Cleaver, which

isn't necessarily a good thing. But on the other hand, June is a snap to spell and pronounce.

Justine ★★★★

(Latin) a form of Justin.

First Impression: Justine is considered the right woman for any job.

Gender Association: Used mostly for girls

Popularity and Trend: #950 (#473 in 2000)

Risk of Misspelling: Low

Risk of Mispronunciation: Low

Famous Namesakes: Actress Justine Bateman; musician Justine Frischmann

Common Nicknames: Justa

Common Variations: Justina

Consider This: The new millennium hasn't been good for Justine's popularity.

Kacey ★★★

(Irish) brave. (American) a form of Casey.

First Impression: People think Kacey has a heart of gold, and that matters more than her ditziness.

Gender Association: Used mostly for girls

Popularity and Trend: Last ranked in the Top 1000 in the 1980s

Risk of Misspelling: Fairly high

Risk of Mispronunciation: Low

Famous Namesakes: Singer Kasey Chambers; actor Casey Affleck; radio personality Casey Kasem

Common Nicknames: None

Common Variations: Kacy, Kasey, Casey

Consider This: Kacey isn't as common as Casey or Kasey, but even though this spelling is used more exclusively for girls, its pronunciation is the same as Casey, which is used equally for boys and girls.

Kala ★★

(Arabic) a form of Kalila.

First Impression: Kala is seen as calm, quiet, and creative.

Gender Association: Used mostly for girls

Popularity and Trend: Last ranked in the Top 1000 in the 1990s

Risk of Misspelling: Average

Risk of Mispronunciation: Average

Famous Namesakes: None

Common Nicknames: None

Common Variations: Kalah

Consider This: Kala is a unique Arabic name that may cause pronunciation problems. (Is it "KAH-lah" or "KAL-ah"?)

Kalare ★★

(Latin, Basque) bright; clear.

First Impression: People think Kalare is a shy and reserved introvert who's quite caring but who's also something of a doormat.

Gender Association: Used for girls

Popularity and Trend: Never been ranked in Top 1000

Risk of Misspelling: Fairly high

Risk of Mispronunciation: Fairly high

Famous Namesakes: None

Common Nicknames: None

Common Variations: None

Consider This: Kalare is an unusual name that sounds like the more conventional Clare. It may be pronounced "kah-LAIR," "kah-LAR," or perhaps even "kah-LAR-ay."

Kali ★★★

(Hindi) the black one. (Hawaiian) hesitating.

First Impression: People say all the girls want to be friends with warmhearted and energetic Kali.

Gender Association: Used mostly for girls

Popularity and Trend: #542 (#427 in 2000)

Risk of Misspelling: Fairly high

Risk of Mispronunciation: Average

Famous Namesakes: Screenwriter Callie Khouri; character Dr. Callie Torres (*Grey's Anatomy*)

Common Nicknames: None

Common Variations: Cali, Kaley, Callie, Kallie

Consider This: A name like Kali is quite a challenge. The Hindi pronunciation is "KAHL-ee," but many people will expect it to be "KAL-ee." Spelling is also tricky because it can be confused with the numerous Callie variations.

Kalinda ★★

(Hindi) sun.

First Impression: To many, Kalinda has high energy but low self-esteem.

Gender Association: Used for girls

Popularity and Trend: Never been ranked in Top 1000

Risk of Misspelling: Fairly low

Risk of Mispronunciation: Fairly low

Famous Namesakes: None

Common Nicknames: Linda

Common Variations: Calinda

Consider This: Kalinda rates high on spelling and pronunciation for a unique name, but the first impression isn't stellar.

Kaliska ★★

(Moquelumnan) coyote chasing deer.

First Impression: People see Kaliska as a talkative and flirty young girl.

Gender Association: Used for girls

Popularity and Trend: Never been ranked in Top 1000

Risk of Misspelling: Average

Risk of Mispronunciation: Fairly low

Famous Namesakes: None

Common Nicknames: None

Common Variations: None

Consider This: Kaliska sounds like Calista, but it's less familiar.

Kameko ★★★

(Japanese) turtle child.

First Impression: Quiet in social situations, Kameko seems to come alive when she's exploring the great outdoors.

Gender Association: Used for girls

Popularity and Trend: Never been ranked in Top 1000

Risk of Misspelling: Average

Risk of Mispronunciation: Average

Famous Namesakes: None

Common Nicknames: None

Common Variations: None

Consider This: Kameko is a Japanese name that may not work as well with non-Japanese surnames.

Kanika ★★★

(Mwera) black cloth.

First Impression: When people say Kanika has a great personality, they mean she's gregarious and kind.

Gender Association: Used for girls

Popularity and Trend: Never been ranked in Top 1000

Risk of Misspelling: Average

Risk of Mispronunciation: Average

Famous Namesakes: Actress Kanika Subramanian

Common Nicknames: None

Common Variations: None

Consider This: People have a good first impression of Kanika, but they may have a little trouble spelling or pronouncing it.

Karen ★★★

(Greek) pure.

First Impression: Karen is described as a kindhearted but mousy teacher's pet.

Gender Association: Used for girls

Popularity and Trend: #173 (#154 in 2000)

Risk of Misspelling: Fairly low

Risk of Mispronunciation: Fairly low

Famous Namesakes: Actress Karen Black; singer Karen Carpenter; actress Karen Allen; character Karen Walker (*Will & Grace*)

Common Nicknames: Kari

Common Variations: Karyn, Karin, Karon

Consider This: A popular name at the tail end of the twentieth century, Karen's popularity is slowly waning.

Kari ★★★

(Greek) pure. (Danish) a form of Caroline, Katherine.

First Impression: People think Kari lives for excitement and fun.

Gender Association: Used for girls

Popularity and Trend: Last ranked in the Top 1000 in the 1980s

Risk of Misspelling: Average

Risk of Mispronunciation: Average

Famous Namesakes: Actress Kari Wührer; actress Keri Russell; character Carrie White (*Carrie*); character Carrie Bradshaw (*Sex and the City*); actress Carrie

Fisher; actress Carrie-Anne Moss; actress Kerry Washington
Common Nicknames: None
Common Variations: Cari
Consider This: Kari was last ranked in the '80s. Danes pronounce it "KAR-ee," but non-Danes are likely to call it "KARE-ee."

Kass ★★★
(Greek) a short form of Kassandra.
First Impression: Kass is considered a go-getter on the road to success.
Gender Association: Used for girls
Popularity and Trend: Never been ranked in Top 1000
Risk of Misspelling: Fairly high
Risk of Mispronunciation: Low
Famous Namesakes: Singer Mama Cass
Common Nicknames: None
Common Variations: Cass
Consider This: People will probably assume this name starts with a *C* and is a nickname for Cassandra.

Katarina ★★★
(Czech) a form of Katherine.
First Impression: Some see Katarina as elegant but cold, but others imagine she's the life of the party.
Gender Association: Used for girls
Popularity and Trend: Last ranked #647 in 2000
Risk of Misspelling: Fairly low
Risk of Mispronunciation: Fairly low
Famous Namesakes: Figure skater Katarina Witt

Common Nicknames: Kat
Common Variations: None
Consider This: A nice idea for families with Eastern European roots.

Kate ★★★★
(Greek) pure. (English) a short form of Katherine.
First Impression: Kate is thought to be lively and fearless with a can-do spirit.
Gender Association: Used for girls
Popularity and Trend: #142 (#225 in 2000)
Risk of Misspelling: Fairly low
Risk of Mispronunciation: Low
Famous Namesakes: Actress Kate Hudson; singer Kate Bush; actress Kate Winslet; actress Kate Jackson; actress Kate Bosworth; model Kate Moss; designer Kate Spade; actress Kate Beckinsale; actress Cate Blanchett
Common Nicknames: Katie
Common Variations: Cate
Consider This: Kate is more casual than Katherine, but it's used often enough that most people won't find it *too* informal.

Katelyn ★★★
(Irish) a form of Katelin.
First Impression: People say Katelyn's parents don't set many limits or rules for their precious, spoiled daughter.
Gender Association: Used for girls

Popularity and Trend: #61 (#54 in 2000)
Risk of Misspelling: Average
Risk of Mispronunciation: Low
Famous Namesakes: Figure skater Caitlin "Kitty" Carruthers; swimmer Katilin Sandeno; character Caitlin Cooper (*The O.C.*)
Common Nicknames: Kate, Katie, Lynn
Common Variations: Kaitlin, Katelin, Catelyn
Consider This: "Katelyn" is the most popular spelling of this name, but with so many variations, people may misspell it anyway.

Katharine ★★★★
(Greek) a form of Katherine.
First Impression: It's hard not to see Hollywood legend Katharine Hepburn in this name's image: Katharine is described as an attractive, hardworking woman with proper manners.
Gender Association: Used for girls
Popularity and Trend: #906 (#668 in 2000)
Risk of Misspelling: Fairly high
Risk of Mispronunciation: Low
Famous Namesakes:
Publisher Katharine Graham; actress Katharine Hepburn; actress Catherine Zeta-Jones; actress Catherine O'Hara; singer Katherine McPhee; actress Catherine Bell; empress Catherine the Great; actress

Catherine Deneuve; actress
Katherine Heigl

Common Nicknames: Kathy, Kassie,
Kate, Katie

Common Variations: Katherine,
Catharine, Catherine, Katheryn

Consider This: Katharine is not
nearly as popular as Katherine
or Catherine, so spelling will
be a problem, but at least pronunciation won't.

Katherine ★★★★★

(Greek) pure.

First Impression: People believe
Katherine is a determined and
bold woman who knows what
she wants and how to get it.

Gender Association: Used for girls

Popularity and Trend: #36
(#33 in 2000)

Risk of Misspelling: Fairly low

Risk of Mispronunciation: Low

Famous Namesakes:
Actress Katherine Heigl;
actress Catherine Zeta-Jones;
actress Catherine O'Hara;
singer Katherine McPhee;
actress Catherine Bell; empress
Catherine the Great; actress
Catherine Deneuve; publisher
Katharine Graham

Common Nicknames: Kathy, Kassie,
Kate, Katie

Common Variations: Katharine,
Catharine, Catherine, Katheryn

Consider This: "Katherine" is the
classic and most popular spelling
of this strong, versatile name.

Kathleen ★★★★

(Irish) a form of Katherine.

First Impression: Folks say Kathleen's
Irish eyes are usually smiling.

Gender Association: Used for girls

Popularity and Trend: #371
(#204 in 2000)

Risk of Misspelling: Fairly low

Risk of Mispronunciation: Low

Famous Namesakes: Actress Kathleen
Turner; actress Kathleen
Robertson

Common Nicknames: Kathy

Common Variations: Cathleen

Consider This: Kathleen rates higher
than Cathleen on first impression
and popularity.

Kathy ★★★

(English) a familiar form of
Katherine, Kathleen.

First Impression: Kathy is described
as a softhearted and motherly
woman who likes to please.

Gender Association: Used for girls

Popularity and Trend: #907
(#653 in 2000)

Risk of Misspelling: Average

Risk of Mispronunciation: Low

Famous Namesakes: Comic strip
character Cathy; actress Kathy
Bates; model Kathy Ireland;
cartoonist Cathy Guisewite;
television host Kathie Lee Gifford

Common Nicknames: None

Common Variations: Kathi, Cathy,
Cathi

Consider This: Kathy may soon fall
off the Top 1000, like Cathy did
in the '80s.

Katie ★★★

(English) a familiar form of Kate.

First Impression: People describe Katie
as perky and spontaneous,
although she often seems silly
and childish.

Gender Association: Used for girls

Popularity and Trend: #107
(#97 in 2000)

Risk of Misspelling: Fairly low

Risk of Mispronunciation: Low

Famous Namesakes: News anchor
Katie Couric; actress Katie
Holmes; model Katie Price

Common Nicknames: None

Common Variations: Kati, Katy

Consider This: Although very popular
on its own, Katie has an immature
come-off because it's traditionally
a nickname.

Katina ★★★

(English, Russian) a form of
Katherine.

First Impression: Katina is often
imagined to be a friendly
chatterbox, or she may be shy,
quiet, and simple.

Gender Association: Used for girls

Popularity and Trend: Last ranked in
the Top 1000 in the 1980s

Risk of Misspelling: Average
Risk of Mispronunciation: Average
Famous Namesakes: Actress Katina Paxinou
Common Nicknames: Kat
Common Variations: Catina
Consider This: Katina sounds like Katrina, but it's much less common.

Katrina ★★★★
(German) a form of Katherine.
First Impression: Katrina is viewed as a bit of a daredevil.
Gender Association: Used for girls
Popularity and Trend: #382 (#236 in 2000)
Risk of Misspelling: Fairly low
Risk of Mispronunciation: Fairly low
Famous Namesakes: Singer Katrina Leskanich
Common Nicknames: Kat, Trina
Common Variations: Catrina
Consider This: Katrina was a big name in the '80s and '90s, but it's been losing steam. It could fall further now that people associate the name with Hurricane Katrina.

Katy ★★★
(English) a familiar form of Kate.
First Impression: People think Katy is cute, sweet, spunky, and active.
Gender Association: Used for girls
Popularity and Trend: Last ranked in the Top 1000 in the 1980s
Risk of Misspelling: Average

Risk of Mispronunciation: Fairly low
Famous Namesakes: News anchor Katie Couric; actress Katie Holmes; model Katie Price
Common Nicknames: None
Common Variations: Katie, Kati
Consider This: Katy is less common than Katie, which means people may misspell it.

Kay ★★★★
(Greek) rejoicer. A familiar form of Katherine. (Teutonic) a fortified place. (Latin) merry.
First Impression: Kay's classmates knew what they were doing when they voted her most likely to succeed.
Gender Association: Used mostly for girls
Popularity and Trend: Last ranked in the Top 1000 in the 1980s
Risk of Misspelling: Low
Risk of Mispronunciation: Low
Famous Namesakes: Senator Kay Bailey Hutchinson
Common Nicknames: None
Common Variations: None
Consider This: Although Kay is a root name, people may assume it's short for Katherine.

Kaya ★★★
(Hopi) wise child. (Japanese) resting place.
First Impression: Kaya is considered polite and friendly on the

surface, but depressed and lonely deep down.
Gender Association: Used for girls
Popularity and Trend: #640 (#757 in 2000)
Risk of Misspelling: Average
Risk of Mispronunciation: Average
Famous Namesakes: Singer Kaya Jones
Common Nicknames: Kay
Common Variations: None
Consider This: Is Kaya pronounced "KAY-ah" or "KYE-ah"? People may not know.

Kayla ★★★★
(Arabic, Hebrew) laurel; crown.
First Impression: People think Kayla has a real innocence about her.
Gender Association: Used for girls
Popularity and Trend: #26 (#13 in 2000)
Risk of Misspelling: Fairly low
Risk of Mispronunciation: Low
Famous Namesakes: Character Kayla Brady (*Days of Our Lives*)
Common Nicknames: Kay
Common Variations: Kaylah
Consider This: Kayla is seen as a name for a young girl, though that perception could change as more Kaylas grow up.

Kaylee ★★★★
(American) a form of Kayla.
First Impression: People say Kaylee usually does a good job of hiding her deep-seated insecurities.

Gender Association: Used for girls

Popularity and Trend: #42
(#72 in 2000)

Risk of Misspelling: Fairly high

Risk of Mispronunciation: Low

Famous Namesakes: None

Common Nicknames: Kay

Common Variations: Kaley, Kayleigh, Caley

Consider This: Kaylee and its variations Kayleigh and Kaley are all rising in popularity, which makes spelling a chore. Spelling is also confounded by the homophones that start with *C*.

Kelby ★★

(German) farm by the spring.

First Impression: Kelby may be confident, but people think conceited may be a better way to describe her.

Gender Association: Used mostly for boys

Popularity and Trend: Never been ranked in Top 1000

Risk of Misspelling: Fairly low

Risk of Mispronunciation: Fairly low

Famous Namesakes: None

Common Nicknames: None

Common Variations: None

Consider This: This name is used more often for boys. Parents searching for names with clear female associations may want to avoid it.

Kelly ★★

(Irish) brave warrior.

First Impression: People see Kelly as a perky and energetic cheerleader who, alas, is also snobby and mean.

Gender Association: Used mostly for girls

Popularity and Trend: #212
(#111 in 2000)

Risk of Misspelling: Fairly low

Risk of Mispronunciation: Low

Famous Namesakes: Talk show host Kelly Ripa; singer Kelly Clarkson; singer Kelly Osbourne; actress Kelly Preston; singer Kelly Rowland; actress Kelly Packard; actress Kelly Reilly

Common Nicknames: None

Common Variations: Kelley, Kelli

Consider This: Kelly was very popular in the '70s and '80s, but it may seem dated now.

Kelsey ★★★★

(Scandinavian, Scottish) ship island. (English) a form of Chelsea.

First Impression: Kelsey is mostly viewed as a fussy and snobby intellectual with a healthy self-esteem.

Gender Association: Used mostly for girls

Popularity and Trend: #184
(#88 in 2000)

Risk of Misspelling: Fairly low

Risk of Mispronunciation: Low

Famous Namesakes: Actor Kelsey Grammer

Common Nicknames: Kelsa

Common Variations: Kelcey

Consider This: Kelsey peaked in the '90s and probably won't have a comeback soon.

Kendra ★★★★

(English) a form of Kenda.

First Impression: Kendra is seen as a strong, straightforward woman who's most likely African American.

Gender Association: Used for girls

Popularity and Trend: #243
(#187 in 2000)

Risk of Misspelling: Fairly low

Risk of Mispronunciation: Low

Famous Namesakes: Model Kendra Wilkinson

Common Nicknames: None

Common Variations: Kindra

Consider This: Kendra seems like an African American name to many, perhaps because it's similar to Kenya.

Kenya ★★★★

(Hebrew) animal horn.

First Impression: Kenya is considered stunningly beautiful with determined confidence, a strong mind, and almost regal grace.

Gender Association: Used mostly for girls

Popularity and Trend: #523
(#508 in 2000)

Risk of Misspelling: Low

Risk of Mispronunciation: Low

Famous Namesakes: Actress Kenya Moore

Common Nicknames: None

Common Variations: Kenia

Consider This: Because of its geographical reference, people will assume someone named Kenya is an African American or a native African.

Kerry ★★★

(Irish) dark-haired.

First Impression: People think Kerry's bubbly spirit is infectious.

Gender Association: Used mostly for girls

Popularity and Trend: Last ranked in the Top 1000 in the 1990s

Risk of Misspelling: Fairly high

Risk of Mispronunciation: Low

Famous Namesakes: Actress Kerry Washington; actress Kari Wührer; actress Keri Russell; movie character Carrie; character Carrie Bradshaw (*Sex and the City*); actress Carrie Fisher; actress Carrie-Anne Moss

Common Nicknames: None

Common Variations: Carey, Keri, Cari, Carrie, Karey

Consider This: Kerry is more unique than Carrie, but people may misspell it.

Kessie ★★★★

(Ashanti) chubby baby.

First Impression: Folks say Kessie leaves everyone smiling and laughing.

Gender Association: Used for girls

Popularity and Trend: Never been ranked in Top 1000

Risk of Misspelling: Fairly low

Risk of Mispronunciation: Low

Famous Namesakes: Disney character Kessie

Common Nicknames: None

Common Variations: Kesse

Consider This: Kessie is an uncommon name, but it should be relatively easy to spell and pronounce.

Kiara ★★★

(Irish) little and dark.

First Impression: Kiara is pictured as self-reliant, but that may be because she's so temperamental, no one wants to deal with her.

Gender Association: Used for girls

Popularity and Trend: #185 (#130 in 2000)

Risk of Misspelling: Fairly high

Risk of Mispronunciation: Fairly high

Famous Namesakes: Actress Kiara Hunger

Common Nicknames: None

Common Variations: Keyara, Kiarra

Consider This: Kiara is an Irish name that may seem very exotic. Maybe too exotic, because it can be

pronounced "kee-AIR-ah," "kee-AR-ah," "kye-AR-ah," or "KEER-ah."

Kim ★★★

(Vietnamese) needle. (English) a short form of Kimberly.

First Impression: Kim is seen as a vivacious and high-spirited gal who likes to take charge.

Gender Association: Used mostly for girls

Popularity and Trend: Last ranked in the Top 1000 in the 1990s

Risk of Misspelling: Low

Risk of Mispronunciation: Low

Famous Namesakes: Actress Kim Basinger; actress Kim Delaney; actress Kim Fields; actress Kim Catrall; actress Kim Novak; singer Kim Gordon; rapper Lil' Kim

Common Nicknames: Kimmy

Common Variations: Kym

Consider This: Kim hasn't been ranked since the '90s, but Kimberly is very popular and much more formal.

Kimberly ★★★★

(English) chief, ruler.

First Impression: To some, Kimberly is a classy but pompous preppy, but others sense she's a sweet and smiley cheerleader.

Gender Association: Used for girls

Popularity and Trend: #58 (#58 in 2000)

Risk of Misspelling: Fairly low

Risk of Mispronunciation: Low

Famous Namesakes: News anchor Kimberly Guilfoyle; actress Kimberly Elise; actress Kimberly Williams; socialite Kimberly Stewart

Common Nicknames: Kim, Kimmy, Kimber

Common Variations: Kimberlee

Consider This: Kimberly was in the Top 40 from the '60s to the '90s and has stayed in the Top 60 since 2000.

Kimi ★★

(Japanese) righteous.

First Impression: To some, Kimi is friendly, peppy, and popular, but others see her as obnoxious and dimwitted.

Gender Association: Used for girls

Popularity and Trend: Never been ranked in Top 1000

Risk of Misspelling: Fairly high

Risk of Mispronunciation: Average

Famous Namesakes: Character Kimmy Gibbler (*Full House*); figure skater Kimmie Meissner

Common Nicknames: Kim

Common Variations: Kimmy, Kimmie

Consider This: Although Kimi is a Japanese name pronounced "KEE-mee," many may think it's a variation of Kimmy.

Kimmy ★★

(English) a familiar form of Kimberly.

First Impression: People say Kimmy shows up at all the parties, even though she's never invited to any of them.

Gender Association: Used for girls

Popularity and Trend: Never been ranked in Top 1000

Risk of Misspelling: Average

Risk of Mispronunciation: Low

Famous Namesakes: Character Kimmy Gibbler (*Full House*); figure skater Kimmie Meissner

Common Nicknames: None

Common Variations: Kimi, Kimmie

Consider This: People see Kimmy as a pest, which may come from *Full House* character Kimmy Gibbler.

Kira ★★★★

(Persian) sun. (Latin) light.

First Impression: Kira is said to be a warmhearted woman with a good future ahead of her because she's bright, skilled, and strong-minded.

Gender Association: Used for girls

Popularity and Trend: #249 (#292 in 2000)

Risk of Misspelling: Fairly high

Risk of Mispronunciation: Average

Famous Namesakes: Character Kira Nerys (*Star Trek: Deep Space Nine*); figure skater Kira Ivanova

Common Nicknames: Kyrie

Common Variations: Keera

Consider This: Keira is a better-known version of this name,

which points to a spelling problem. Pronunciation could also be a problem with people who don't know if it's "KEER-ah" or "KYE-rah."

Kirsten ★★★

(Greek) Christian; anointed. (Scandinavian) a form of Christine.

First Impression: People think Kirsten carries herself above others, which may make her a leader—or a snob.

Gender Association: Used for girls

Popularity and Trend: #407 (#255 in 2000)

Risk of Misspelling: Fairly low

Risk of Mispronunciation: Low

Famous Namesakes: Actress Kirsten Dunst; character Kirsten Cohen (*The O.C.*)

Common Nicknames: Kirsty

Common Variations: Kersten, Kirstan

Consider This: Kirsten is losing popularity at a fast clip, as are similar names Kristen and Kristin.

Kishi ★★

(Japanese) long and happy life.

First Impression: Kishi is seen by most as an innocent and playful Asian girl who may have family troubles.

Gender Association: Used for girls

Popularity and Trend: Never been ranked in Top 1000

Risk of Misspelling: Average

Risk of Mispronunciation: Average
Famous Namesakes: None
Common Nicknames: None
Common Variations: None
Consider This: Kishi is a Japanese name that may not fit well with some surnames.

Kitra ★★

(Hebrew) crowned.
First Impression: Kitra is envisioned as a rebellious girl who's full of life, but also full of nastiness.
Gender Association: Used for girls
Popularity and Trend: Never been ranked in Top 1000
Risk of Misspelling: Average
Risk of Mispronunciation: Average
Famous Namesakes: None
Common Nicknames: None
Common Variations: None
Consider This: Kitra is a very unique name with a mixed first impression. Pronunciation will also be mixed between "KEE-trah" and "KIT-trah."

Kona ★★

(Hawaiian) lady. (Hindi) angular.
First Impression: People think Kona is kind, graceful, and witty with dark hair and coffee-colored skin.
Gender Association: Used mostly for boys
Popularity and Trend: Never been ranked in Top 1000
Risk of Misspelling: Average
Risk of Mispronunciation: Fairly low

Famous Namesakes: None
Common Nicknames: None
Common Variations: None
Consider This: Kona is used more often for boys, but it's so rare that most people aren't even aware of the gender association problem.

Kora ★★★

(Greek) a form of Cora.
First Impression: Kora is seen as one of these traits: pleasant, bland, or bitter.
Gender Association: Used for girls
Popularity and Trend: Never been ranked in Top 1000
Risk of Misspelling: Fairly high
Risk of Mispronunciation: Low
Famous Namesakes: Actress Cora Witherspoon
Common Nicknames: Kory, Corissa, Carina, Koretta
Common Variations: Cora
Consider This: Cora with a C will be more familiar than "Kora," so spelling will definitely be an issue for this name.

Koren ★★★★

(Greek) a form of Karen, Kora, Korin.
First Impression: This name creates the impression of a confident, bold, and can-do woman who doesn't give up easily.
Gender Association: Used for girls

Popularity and Trend: Never been ranked in Top 1000
Risk of Misspelling: Average
Risk of Mispronunciation: Fairly low
Famous Namesakes: Writer Koren Zailckas
Common Nicknames: Kory
Common Variations: None
Consider This: This Greek name is unusual, but it comes across positively.

Krista ★★★

(Czech) a form of Christina.
First Impression: To many, Krista seems like an outgoing and popular young woman of good spirits.
Gender Association: Used for girls
Popularity and Trend: #701 (#408 in 2000)
Risk of Misspelling: Average
Risk of Mispronunciation: Low
Famous Namesakes: Actress Krista Allen; teacher Christa McAuliffe; actress Christa Miller
Common Nicknames: Kris
Common Variations: Christa, Krysta
Consider This: Like Christa, Krista is on its way out.

Kristen ★★★

(Greek) Christian; anointed. (Scandinavian) a form of Christine.
First Impression: People say Kristen won't—or can't—hide the fact that she's a spoiled snob.

Gender Association: Used mostly
for girls
Popularity and Trend: #374
(#142 in 2000)
Risk of Misspelling: Average
Risk of Mispronunciation: Low
Famous Namesakes: Actress Kristen
Bell; actress Kristen Stewart;
actress Kristin Kreuk; actress
Kristin Scott Thomas; actress
Kristin Chenoweth
Common Nicknames: Kris, Kristy
Common Variations: Kristin
Consider This: Although the two
names are very similar, Kristen
comes across as much snobbier
than Kristin.

Kristi ★★

(Scandinavian) a short form of
Kristine.
First Impression: Folks think Kristi is
chatty, but she's also catty.
Gender Association: Used for girls
Popularity and Trend: Last ranked in
the Top 1000 in the 1990s
Risk of Misspelling: Fairly high
Risk of Mispronunciation: Low
Famous Namesakes: Figure skater
Kristi Yamaguchi; model
Christie Brinkley; model Christy
Turlington; actress Kristy
McNichol; actress Kristy
Swanson; singer Cristy Lane
Common Nicknames: None
Common Variations: Kristy, Christy,
Kristi, Christi

Consider This: Kristi is a casual name
with a cutesy spelling that's hard
to take seriously.

Kristin ★★★★

(Scandinavian) a form of Kristen.
First Impression: Kristin is considered
so popular because she's so fun to
be around.
Gender Association: Used for girls
Popularity and Trend: #574
(#301 in 2000)
Risk of Misspelling: Average
Risk of Mispronunciation: Low
Famous Namesakes: Actress Kristin
Scott Thomas; actress Kristin
Chenoweth; actress Kristen Bell;
actress Kristen Stewart; actress
Kristin Kreuk
Common Nicknames: Kris, Kristy
Common Variations: Kristen
Consider This: "Kristen" is the more
popular spelling of this name,
but Kristin is viewed more posi-
tively. Both names are trending
downward.

Kristina ★★★★

(Greek) Christian; anointed.
(Scandinavian) a form of
Christina.
First Impression: People believe
Kristina knows when to cut loose
and when to buckle down.
Gender Association: Used for girls
Popularity and Trend: #404
(#218 in 2000)
Risk of Misspelling: Average

Risk of Mispronunciation: Low
Famous Namesakes: Singer Christina
Aguilera; actress Christina
Applegate; actress Christina
Ricci; singer Christina Milian;
character Christina Yang (Grey's
Anatomy)
Common Nicknames: Kris, Krissa,
Krissie, Tina, Krista, Kristen
Common Variations: Christina,
Cristina
Consider This: Kristina is a more
unique version of Christina that's
used often in Scandinavian
countries.

Kristine ★★★

(Scandinavian) a form of Christine.
First Impression: Kristine is described
as shallow, selfish, and rude, but
she's also smart and successful.
Gender Association: Used for girls
Popularity and Trend: Last ranked in
the Top 1000 in the 1980s
Risk of Misspelling: Average
Risk of Mispronunciation: Low
Famous Namesakes: Speed skater
Kristine Holzer; actress Christine
Taylor; actress Christine Lahti;
actress Christine Baranski
Common Nicknames: Kris, Kristy,
Krissie, Kristen, Kirsten
Common Variations: Christine,
Cristine
Consider This: People have a better
opinion of the name Christine
than of this uncommon variation.

Krystal ★★★

(American) clear, brilliant glass.

First Impression: Krystal is pictured as a social gal who's quick to make friends, but most of those "friends" are men.

Gender Association: Used for girls

Popularity and Trend: #505 (#346 in 2000)

Risk of Misspelling: Average

Risk of Mispronunciation: Low

Famous Namesakes: Actress Krystal Bernard; singer Crystal Gayle; gospel singer Crystal Lewis

Common Nicknames: Krys

Common Variations: Crystal

Consider This: Crystal is more popular than Krystal, but both have less-than-classy images.

Kyla ★★★★

(Irish) lovely. (Yiddish) crown; laurel.

First Impression: People think Kyla is known for her tender heart.

Gender Association: Used for girls

Popularity and Trend: #204 (#235 in 2000)

Risk of Misspelling: Fairly low

Risk of Mispronunciation: Low

Famous Namesakes: Actress Kyla Pratt

Common Nicknames: None

Common Variations: Kylah

Consider This: As with Kylie, people may think Kyla is a name for a young girl.

Kylie ★★★★★

(West Australian Aboriginal) curled stick; boomerang. (Irish) a form of Kyle.

First Impression: Folks say Kylie is 100 percent adorable.

Gender Association: Used for girls

Popularity and Trend: #66 (#104 in 2000)

Risk of Misspelling: Fairly low

Risk of Mispronunciation: Fairly low

Famous Namesakes: Singer Kylie Minogue; model Kylie Bax

Common Nicknames: None

Common Variations: Kylee

Consider This: Kylie is a very youthful-sounding name, but it's quickly becoming popular.

Kyra ★★★

(Greek) noble.

First Impression: Most people say Kyra is a lovable friend who holds secrets in utmost confidence.

Gender Association: Used for girls

Popularity and Trend: #195 (#202 in 2000)

Risk of Misspelling: Fairly high

Risk of Mispronunciation: Average

Famous Namesakes: Actress Kyra Sedgwick

Common Nicknames: Kyrie

Common Variations: Keira, Kira

Consider This: Like Kira, Kyra has problems. People may pronounce it as "KYE-rah" or "KEER-ah," and they may spell it "Kira" or "Keira."

Lacey ★★★★

(Latin) cheerful. (Greek) a form of Larissa.

First Impression: Lacey is considered dedicated to her friends and values.

Gender Association: Used for girls

Popularity and Trend: #446 (#371 in 2000)

Risk of Misspelling: Average

Risk of Mispronunciation: Low

Famous Namesakes: Actress Lacey Chabert; country singer Lacy J. Dalton

Common Nicknames: None

Common Variations: Lacy, Lace

Consider This: This spelling of Lacey is much more popular than Lacy, but people may expect it to be spelled like the word *lacy*.

Lacy ★★

(Latin) cheerful. (Greek) a form of Larissa.

First Impression: People think Lacy knows how to play the part of the likable girl, but deep down, she may be conceited and snobby.

Gender Association: Used mostly for girls

Popularity and Trend: Last ranked in the Top 1000 in the 1990s

Risk of Misspelling: Average

Risk of Mispronunciation: Low

Famous Namesakes: Country singer Lacy J. Dalton; actress Lacey Chabert
Common Nicknames: None
Common Variations: Lacey, Lace
Consider This: This spelling is less popular and less well received than Lacey, but it is spelled the same way as the word *lacy*.

Laila ★★★

(Arabic) a form of Leila.
First Impression: Many say Laila seems nice, but she's so mysterious that it's hard to tell.
Gender Association: Used for girls
Popularity and Trend: #235 (#643 in 2000)
Risk of Misspelling: Fairly high
Risk of Mispronunciation: Average
Famous Namesakes: Boxer Laila Ali
Common Nicknames: None
Common Variations: Layla, Leyla
Consider This: Laila has leapt in popularity recently, but people still may pause for the pronunciation and spelling.

Lainey ★★★★

(French) a familiar form of Elaine.
First Impression: Lainey is described as a hilarious storyteller.
Gender Association: Used for girls
Popularity and Trend: #725 (#925 in 2003)
Risk of Misspelling: Fairly low
Risk of Mispronunciation: Low

Famous Namesakes: Actress Lainie Kazan
Common Nicknames: None
Common Variations: Lainie
Consider This: Lainey isn't very formal, and it's not particularly popular.

Lakeisha ★★★

(American) a combination of the prefix La + Keisha.
First Impression: Lakeisha is viewed as sassy but sweet.
Gender Association: Used for girls
Popularity and Trend: Last ranked in the Top 1000 in the 1990s
Risk of Misspelling: Average
Risk of Mispronunciation: Fairly low
Famous Namesakes: None
Common Nicknames: None
Common Variations: Lakiesha, Lekeisha
Consider This: Lakeisha is almost exclusively seen as an African American name.

Lana ★★★

(Latin) woolly. (Irish) attractive, peaceful. (Hawaiian) floating; bouyant.
First Impression: Lana is pictured as a sexy and slender beauty who's smart, successful, and talented.
Gender Association: Used for girls
Popularity and Trend: #412 (#948 in 2001)
Risk of Misspelling: Average

Risk of Mispronunciation: Average
Famous Namesakes: Actress Lana Turner; character Lana Lang (*Smallville*)
Common Nicknames: Laney
Common Variations: Lanna
Consider This: A fairly popular name in the '40s and '50s, Lana almost disappeared in the '90s, but now it keeps getting more popular. Pronunciation can be a problem, though, with both "LAN-ah" and "LON-ah" as options.

Lane ★★★

(English) narrow road.
First Impression: Lane is thought to be a happily independent woman who would rather advance her career than date.
Gender Association: Used mostly for boys
Popularity and Trend: Never been ranked in Top 1000
Risk of Misspelling: Fairly low
Risk of Mispronunciation: Low
Famous Namesakes: Actress Diane Lane; character Lane Kim (*Gilmore Girls*); character Lois Lane (*Superman*)
Common Nicknames: Laney
Common Variations: Laine
Consider This: Lane is used more often for boys; Elaine, Lainey, and Lana are used exclusively for girls.

Lara ★★

(Greek) cheerful. (Latin) shining; famous.

First Impression: Lara comes across as a responsible bookworm, a self-important know-it-all, or an eccentric neurotic.

Gender Association: Used for girls

Popularity and Trend: #834 (#848 in 2000)

Risk of Misspelling: Average

Risk of Mispronunciation: Fairly high

Famous Namesakes: Character Lara Croft (*Tomb Raider*); actress Lara Flynn Boyle

Common Nicknames: Lari

Common Variations: Laura, Lora

Consider This: People may pronounce Lara as "LORE-ah," "LAR-ah," or "LAIR-ah."

Larissa ★★★★

(Greek) cheerful.

First Impression: People say Larissa is a bright young woman with an impish smile and love of practical jokes.

Gender Association: Used for girls

Popularity and Trend: #633 (#485 in 2000)

Risk of Misspelling: Fairly low

Risk of Mispronunciation: Low

Famous Namesakes: Gymnast Larissa Latynina

Common Nicknames: Lacey, Lara

Common Variations: Larisa, Laryssa

Consider This: Larissa means "cheerful," and the name's image seems to live up to the meaning.

Latonya ★★★

(American) a combination of the prefix La + Tonya. (Latin) a form of Latona.

First Impression: Latonya is seen as headstrong but kindhearted.

Gender Association: Used for girls

Popularity and Trend: Last ranked in the Top 1000 in the 1990s

Risk of Misspelling: Average

Risk of Mispronunciation: Low

Famous Namesakes: Author Latonya Williams

Common Nicknames: Tonya

Common Variations: Latonia

Consider This: Like Latoya, people see Latonya as an African American name.

Latoya ★★★

(American) a combination of the prefix La + Toya.

First Impression: Latoya is described as often unlikable and bossy, but she does redeem herself now and then.

Gender Association: Used for girls

Popularity and Trend: Last ranked in the Top 1000 in the 1990s

Risk of Misspelling: Fairly low

Risk of Mispronunciation: Low

Famous Namesakes: Singer LaToya Jackson

Common Nicknames: Toya

Common Variations: None

Consider This: Before you choose this name, keep in mind that it will conjure up images of namesake LaToya Jackson.

Laura ★★★★

(Latin) crowned with laurel.

First Impression: Laura is depicted as a bone-thin brunette with a big brain.

Gender Association: Used mostly for girls

Popularity and Trend: #172 (#85 in 2000)

Risk of Misspelling: Fairly low

Risk of Mispronunciation: Low

Famous Namesakes: Author Laura Ingalls Wilder; first lady Laura Bush; actress Laura Linney; actress Laura Innes; actress Laura San Giacomo; radio personality Dr. Laura Schlessinger; character Laura Spencer (*General Hospital*)

Common Nicknames: Laurie, Lolly, Loretta

Common Variations: Lara, Lora

Consider This: Laura recently left the Top 100 for the first time in over one hundred years.

Laurel ★★★★

(Latin) laurel tree.

First Impression: This name makes people think of a quiet, gentle woman who's as intelligent as she is caring.

Gender Association: Used for girls

Popularity and Trend: #846
(#565 in 2000)
Risk of Misspelling: Low
Risk of Mispronunciation: Low
Famous Namesakes: Actress Laurel
Holloman
Common Nicknames: Laurie
Common Variations: Lorelle
Consider This: If you want a unique
alternative to Laura or Lauren,
Laurel is for you.

Lauren ★★★★★
(English) a form of Laura.
First Impression: People think Lauren
has wonderful beauty, brains,
and heart.
Gender Association: Used mostly
for girls
Popularity and Trend: #24
(#11 in 2000)
Risk of Misspelling: Fairly low
Risk of Mispronunciation: Low
Famous Namesakes: Actress Lauren
Bacall; actress Lauren Holly;
actress Lauren Graham; singer
Lauryn Hill; reality television
star Lauren Conrad
Common Nicknames: Ren, Laurie
Common Variations: Loren
Consider This: The only problem
with Lauren is that it may be *too*
popular—it has ranked in the
Top 25 since the '80s.

Laurie ★★★
(English) a familiar form of Laura.
First Impression: Everyone seems to
want fun, bubbly Laurie as a
best friend.
Gender Association: Used mostly
for girls
Popularity and Trend: Last ranked in
the Top 1000 in the 1990s
Risk of Misspelling: Fairly low
Risk of Mispronunciation: Low
Famous Namesakes: Actress Laurie
Metcalf; singer Lorrie Morgan;
actress Lori Singer; actress Lori
Laughlin
Common Nicknames: None
Common Variations: Lori
Consider This: People will likely
assume Laurie is a nickname
for Laura or Lauren.

Laveda ★★
(Latin) cleansed, purified.
First Impression: Most people say
Laveda is an overweight and
homely dullard, but she may be
a kind woman with leadership
skills.
Gender Association: Used for girls
Popularity and Trend: Never been
ranked in Top 1000
Risk of Misspelling: Average
Risk of Mispronunciation: Average
Famous Namesakes: None
Common Nicknames: Veda
Common Variations: None

Consider This: Laveda could be
pronounced "lah-VAY-dah" or
"lah-VEE-dah."

Laverne ★★★
(Latin) springtime. (French) grove
of alder trees.
First Impression: Laverne is considered
a matronly church lady with
pursed lips, outdated clothes,
and a grumpy disposition.
Gender Association: Used for girls
Popularity and Trend: Last ranked in
the Top 1000 in the 1970s
Risk of Misspelling: Fairly low
Risk of Mispronunciation: Low
Famous Namesakes: Character
Laverne De Fazio (*Laverne &
Shirley*)
Common Nicknames: Verna
Common Variations: None
Consider This: Laverne was out of the
Top 1000 even before *Laverne &
Shirley* began airing.

Lawanda ★★★
(American) a combination of the
prefix La + Wanda.
First Impression: Lawanda strikes
people as an extrovert with a
flair for fashion and a bit of an
attitude.
Gender Association: Used for girls
Popularity and Trend: Last ranked in
the Top 1000 in the 1980s
Risk of Misspelling: Fairly low
Risk of Mispronunciation: Low

Famous Namesakes: Actress LaWanda Page
Common Nicknames: None
Common Variations: None
Consider This: Lawanda is another *La* name people identify as African American.

Lea ★★★

(Hawaiian) the goddess of canoe makers. (Hebrew) a form of Leah.
First Impression: People think Lea may be a bright artist, a stuck-up whiner, a caring helper, or a spunky charmer.
Gender Association: Used for girls
Popularity and Trend: #613 (#663 in 2000)
Risk of Misspelling: Fairly high
Risk of Mispronunciation: Average
Famous Namesakes: Actress Lea Thompson; singer Lea Salonga
Common Nicknames: Lee
Common Variations: Leah, Leia, Lia
Consider This: Sometimes this name is pronounced like Leah, but other times it's pronounced like Lee. Either way you pronounce it, people may misspell it as one of those other names.

Leah ★★★★★

(Hebrew) weary.
First Impression: Leah is described as a warm woman with natural beauty—and a knack for sticking her foot in her mouth.
Gender Association: Used for girls

Popularity and Trend: #69 (#96 in 2000)
Risk of Misspelling: Fairly low
Risk of Mispronunciation: Low
Famous Namesakes: Actress Leah Remini; biblical figure Leah; model Liya Kebede
Common Nicknames: Lee
Common Variations: Lea, Leia, Lia
Consider This: Leah, a biblical name, has been in the Top 100 since the '90s.

Leandra ★★★★

(Latin) like a lioness.
First Impression: Leandra is pictured as a sweet and stylish trendsetter who's bright and self-sufficient.
Gender Association: Used for girls
Popularity and Trend: Last ranked in the Top 1000 in the 1990s
Risk of Misspelling: Fairly low
Risk of Mispronunciation: Average
Famous Namesakes: None
Common Nicknames: Lee
Common Variations: None
Consider This: Leandra's image is hip, even if the name's popularity isn't.

Leigh ★★★

(English) a form of Lee.
First Impression: Folks say Leigh may come from a well-to-do family, but she doesn't lead a coddled life.
Gender Association: Used mostly for girls

Popularity and Trend: Last ranked in the Top 1000 in the 1990s
Risk of Misspelling: Average
Risk of Mispronunciation: Fairly low
Famous Namesakes: Actress Vivien Leigh
Common Nicknames: None
Common Variations: Lee
Consider This: Most people will pronounce this name "lee," but some may go with "lay."

Leila ★★★

(Hebrew) dark beauty; night. (Arabic) born at night.
First Impression: Leila is seen as a stunning woman who's sweet and affectionate with her children.
Gender Association: Used for girls
Popularity and Trend: #284 (#595 in 2000)
Risk of Misspelling: Fairly high
Risk of Mispronunciation: Fairly high
Famous Namesakes: Actress Leila Shenna
Common Nicknames: None
Common Variations: Laila, Layla, Leyla
Consider This: Like Laila, Leila's popularity has soared, but pronunciation could be tricky ("LEE-lah," "LAY-lah," and "LYE-lah").

Leilani ★★★★

(Hawaiian) heavenly flower; heavenly child.

First Impression: Leilani is described as a lovely, dark-skinned Hawaiian who's caring, good-natured, and irresistibly lovable.
Gender Association: Used for girls
Popularity and Trend: #313 (#523 in 2000)
Risk of Misspelling: Fairly high
Risk of Mispronunciation: Average
Famous Namesakes: Model Leilani Dowding
Common Nicknames: Lani, Lei
Common Variations: None
Consider This: Leilani is a Hawaiian name that's gaining popularity in the other forty-nine states, too.

Lenora ★★★

(Greek, Russian) a form of Eleanor.
First Impression: Lenora makes people think of a librarian who's friendly with children, but shy with adults.
Gender Association: Used for girls
Popularity and Trend: Last ranked in the Top 1000 in the 1970s
Risk of Misspelling: Low
Risk of Mispronunciation: Low
Famous Namesakes: None
Common Nicknames: Nora
Common Variations: None
Consider This: Lenora may seem bookish because it sounds like Lenore, the name used in Edgar Allan Poe's "The Raven."

Leona ★★

(German) brave as a lioness.
First Impression: Leona is thought to be a spiteful, self-centered, and vicious woman with lots of wealth, much like infamous real-estate mogul Leona Helmsley.
Gender Association: Used for girls
Popularity and Trend: Last ranked in the Top 1000 in the 1980s
Risk of Misspelling: Fairly low
Risk of Mispronunciation: Fairly low
Famous Namesakes: Hotel magnate Leona Helmsley; singer Leona Naess
Common Nicknames: Lona, Leonie
Common Variations: Liona, Leonna
Consider This: Leona has a terrible image, but its versatility may attract some parents.

Letitia ★★★

(Latin) a form of Leticia.
First Impression: Letitia is described as either a holy woman or a sex symbol.
Gender Association: Used for girls
Popularity and Trend: Last ranked in the Top 1000 in the 1980s
Risk of Misspelling: Fairly high
Risk of Mispronunciation: Average
Famous Namesakes: Model Laetitia Casta
Common Nicknames: None
Common Variations: None

Consider This: People may mistakenly spell Letitia as "Leticia" or "Leteesha."

Lia ★★★

(Greek) bringer of good news. (Hebrew, Dutch, Italian) dependent.
First Impression: Lia is said to be creative, talented, and intriguing.
Gender Association: Used for girls
Popularity and Trend: #521 (#762 in 2000)
Risk of Misspelling: Fairly high
Risk of Mispronunciation: Average
Famous Namesakes: Model Liya Kebede; actress Leah Remini; biblical figure Leah
Common Nicknames: Lee
Common Variations: Leah, Lea
Consider This: Lia is a unique version of Leah, but some people might pronounce it "LYE-ah."

Libby ★★

(Hebrew) a familiar form of Elizabeth.
First Impression: Libby is depicted as either funny and original or sad and lonely.
Gender Association: Used for girls
Popularity and Trend: #798 (#977 in 2002)
Risk of Misspelling: Fairly low
Risk of Mispronunciation: Low
Famous Namesakes: Character Libby (*Lost*)
Common Nicknames: None

Common Variations: None

Consider This: A nickname for Elizabeth, Libby may come across as too young or too casual.

Liberty ★★★★

(Latin) free.

First Impression: Liberty gives the impression of a free-spirited thrill seeker with sassy independence.

Gender Association: Used for girls

Popularity and Trend: #539 (#754 in 2001)

Risk of Misspelling: Low

Risk of Mispronunciation: Low

Famous Namesakes: None

Common Nicknames: None

Common Variations: None

Consider This: If your child is introverted, a bold name like Liberty may be too hard for her to live up to.

Lila ★★★★

(Arabic) night. (Hindi) free will of God. (Persian) lilac.

First Impression: Lila is seen as successful in social circles as well as business circles.

Gender Association: Used for girls

Popularity and Trend: #329 (#751 in 2000)

Risk of Misspelling: Fairly low

Risk of Mispronunciation: Fairly low

Famous Namesakes: Actress Lila Kedrova; country singer Lyla McCann

Common Nicknames: None

Common Variations: Lilah, Lyla

Consider This: This old-fashioned name is making a comeback.

Lilac ★★★

(Sanskrit) lilac; blue purple.

First Impression: Lilac is considered as sweet, lovely, and earthy as the flower of the same name.

Gender Association: Used for girls

Popularity and Trend: Never been ranked in Top 1000

Risk of Misspelling: Fairly low

Risk of Mispronunciation: Fairly low

Famous Namesakes: None

Common Nicknames: None

Common Variations: None

Consider This: Although Lilac has never been ranked in the Top 1000, other flower names are popular, and this one has a great first impression.

Lilah ★★★

(Arabic, Hindi, Persian) a form of Lila.

First Impression: People think Lilah has culture and character.

Gender Association: Used for girls

Popularity and Trend: #867 (last ranked in the Top 1000 in the 1890s)

Risk of Misspelling: Average

Risk of Mispronunciation: Fairly low

Famous Namesakes: Actress Lila Kedrova; country singer Lyla McCann

Common Nicknames: None

Common Variations: Lila, Lyla

Consider This: Lilah left the Top 1000 in the 1890s then suddenly reappeared at #867 in 2006.

Lilith ★★★

(Arabic) of the night; night demon.

First Impression: Lilith is seen as strong and independent, but she can be stuck-up and snobby.

Gender Association: Used for girls

Popularity and Trend: Never been ranked in Top 1000

Risk of Misspelling: Fairly low

Risk of Mispronunciation: Fairly low

Famous Namesakes: Character Lilith Sternin (*Cheers*); biblical figure Lilith

Common Nicknames: Lily

Common Variations: None

Consider This: Lilith has never been ranked in the Top 1000, but people will probably know it thanks to Lilith from *Cheers* and the Lilith Fair concerts.

Lillian ★★★★★

(Latin) lily flower.

First Impression: Lillian is imagined to be a soft-spoken and soft-mannered woman who's sweet, graceful, and wise.

Gender Association: Used for girls

Popularity and Trend: #38 (#129 in 2000)

Risk of Misspelling: Fairly low

Risk of Mispronunciation: Low

Famous Namesakes: Actress Lillian Gish; author Lillian Hellman

Common Nicknames: Lily, Lian, Lila

Common Variations: Lilian, Lillyann

Consider This: Although Lillian is an old-fashioned name, it's made huge strides in popularity since 2000.

Lily ★★★★★

(Latin, Arabic) a form of Lilly.

First Impression: Folks say Lily has a hard time holding back her love for life.

Gender Association: Used for girls

Popularity and Trend: #33 (#124 in 2000)

Risk of Misspelling: Fairly low

Risk of Mispronunciation: Low

Famous Namesakes: Actress Lily Tomlin; character Lily Potter (*Harry Potter* series); model Lily Cole

Common Nicknames: None

Common Variations: Lilly, Lili

Consider This: Like Lillian, Lily is an old name that has recently become very popular.

Lina ★★★

(Greek) light. (Arabic) tender. (Latin) a form of Lena.

First Impression: To many, Lina seems to be a good, upstanding person.

Gender Association: Used for girls

Popularity and Trend: #981 (#982 in 2002)

Risk of Misspelling: Average

Risk of Mispronunciation: Fairly low

Famous Namesakes: Director Lina Wertmüller

Common Nicknames: None

Common Variations: Lena, Leena

Consider This: Almost off the Top 1000 list at #981, Lina may be too unusual for most people. Lena is slightly more popular.

Linda ★★★★

(Spanish) pretty.

First Impression: No matter what life brings, Linda seems determined to keep smiling.

Gender Association: Used for girls

Popularity and Trend: #462 (#357 in 2000)

Risk of Misspelling: Fairly low

Risk of Mispronunciation: Low

Famous Namesakes: Musician Linda McCartney; actress Linda Hamilton; actress Linda Cardellini; singer Linda Ronstadt; actress Linda Blair

Common Nicknames: Lindy

Common Variations: Lynda

Consider This: Linda was very popular in the middle of the twentieth century, but it's been sliding fast since the '80s.

Lindsay ★★★

(English) a form of Lindsey.

First Impression: Lindsay is imagined to be a loud, lively, and popular girl who's self-absorbed and bratty.

Gender Association: Used mostly for girls

Popularity and Trend: #263 (#179 in 2000)

Risk of Misspelling: Average

Risk of Mispronunciation: Low

Famous Namesakes: Actress Lindsay Lohan; actress Lindsay Wagner; actress Lindsay McKeon; tennis player Lindsey Davenport

Common Nicknames: None

Common Variations: Lindsey, Lyndsay

Consider This: Because of Lindsay Lohan's scandals, be as wary of Lindsay as you are of Britney or Paris.

Lindsey ★★★

(English) linden-tree island; camp near the stream.

First Impression: Lindsey is envisioned as a popular, flirty, and attractive party girl.

Gender Association: Used mostly for girls

Popularity and Trend: #186 (#103 in 2000)

Risk of Misspelling: Average

Risk of Mispronunciation: Low

Famous Namesakes: Actress Lindsay Lohan; actress Lindsay Wagner; actress Lindsay McKeon; tennis player Lindsey Davenport

Common Nicknames: None

Common Variations: Lindsay, Lyndsay

Consider This: Lindsey is slightly more popular than Lindsay, though people tend to associate both with Lindsay Lohan.

Linnea ★★

(Scandinavian) lime tree.

First Impression: If you're looking for straight talk and matter-of-fact thinking, people say Linnea is your woman.

Gender Association: Used for girls

Popularity and Trend: Last ranked in the Top 1000 in the 1950s

Risk of Misspelling: Fairly high

Risk of Mispronunciation: Fairly high

Famous Namesakes: Actress Linnea Quigley

Common Nicknames: Lynn

Common Variations: Lynnea

Consider This: Linnea is unusual enough to cause spelling and pronunciation problems (is it "lin-AY-ah" or "lin-EE-ah"?), but people seem to think of it favorably.

Lisa ★★★

(Hebrew, English) a form of Elizabeth.

First Impression: Many see Lisa as an attention seeker who's reckless and wild, but some imagine her as quiet, serious, and careful.

Gender Association: Used for girls

Popularity and Trend: #503 (#296 in 2000)

Risk of Misspelling: Fairly low

Risk of Mispronunciation: Low

Famous Namesakes: Singer Lisa Marie Presley; character Lisa Simpson (*The Simpsons*); actress Lisa Bonet; actress Lisa Kudrow; actress Lisa Edelstein; actress Lisa Rinna

Common Nicknames: None

Common Variations: Leesa

Consider This: Lisa is technically a short form of Elizabeth, though it seems to stand on its own all right.

Liz ★★★

(English) a short form of Elizabeth.

First Impression: Liz is said to be a brash and headstrong woman who knows all and wants all.

Gender Association: Used for girls

Popularity and Trend: Last ranked in the Top 1000 in the 1960s

Risk of Misspelling: Low

Risk of Mispronunciation: Low

Famous Namesakes: Actress Liz Taylor; designer Liz Claiborne; singer Liz Phair

Common Nicknames: Lizzie

Common Variations: None

Consider This: Liz seems too informal—people will assume your child's given name is Elizabeth.

Liza ★★

(American) a form of Elizabeth.

First Impression: Like Liza Minnelli, Liza is described as a wild free spirit who's confident and fun, yet arrogant and obnoxious.

Gender Association: Used for girls

Popularity and Trend: Last ranked in the Top 1000 in the 1990s

Risk of Misspelling: Average

Risk of Mispronunciation: Average

Famous Namesakes: Singer Liza Minnelli; actress Liza Huber

Common Nicknames: None

Common Variations: Leeza

Consider This: People still associate this name with Liza Minnelli, which is both good and bad. Plus, it can be pronounced as either "LYE-zah" and "LEE-zah."

Lizina ★

(Latvian) a form of Elizabeth.

First Impression: Lizina is considered a shy, withdrawn loner who has trouble making friends.

Gender Association: Used for girls

Popularity and Trend: Never been ranked in Top 1000

Risk of Misspelling: Average

Risk of Mispronunciation: Average

Famous Namesakes: None

Common Nicknames: Lizzie

Common Variations: None

Consider This: Even as a form of Elizabeth, Lizina seems too odd and unique for most people.

Lois ★★★

(German) famous warrior.

First Impression: People say Lois's IQ is phenomenal, but her social skills are disgraceful.

Gender Association: Used for girls

Popularity and Trend: Last ranked in the Top 1000 in the 1980s
Risk of Misspelling: Low
Risk of Mispronunciation: Low
Famous Namesakes: Character Lois Lane (*Superman*); character Lois Griffin (*Family Guy*); actress Lois Chiles; character Lois (*Hi & Lois*)
Common Nicknames: None
Common Variations: None
Consider This: Even Superman can't save Lois's image from geekdom.

Lola ★★★★

(Spanish) a familiar form of Carlotta, Dolores, Louise.
First Impression: Lola is viewed as a cheeky and flamboyant gal who loves to flirt.
Gender Association: Used for girls
Popularity and Trend: #280 (#754 in 2002)
Risk of Misspelling: Low
Risk of Mispronunciation: Low
Famous Namesakes: Character Lola (*Run Lola Run*)
Common Nicknames: Lolita
Common Variations: None
Consider This: Lola is a fun name, which is great in many situations, but it's hard to take Lola seriously.

Lolly ★★★★

(English) sweet; candy.
First Impression: Lolly is seen as a playful and gregarious cutie who laughs a lot.
Gender Association: Used for girls

Popularity and Trend: Never been ranked in Top 1000
Risk of Misspelling: Low
Risk of Mispronunciation: Low
Famous Namesakes: Pop singer Lolly
Common Nicknames: None
Common Variations: None
Consider This: Lolly is a cute name, but not a very serious one.

Lonna ★★★★

(Latin, German, English) a form of Lona.
First Impression: Lonna comes across as a confident woman with a strong will and strong desires.
Gender Association: Used for girls
Popularity and Trend: Last ranked in the Top 1000 in the 1940s
Risk of Misspelling: Average
Risk of Mispronunciation: Low
Famous Namesakes: None
Common Nicknames: None
Common Variations: Lona
Consider This: Although Lonna is a Top 1000 dropout, its first impression doesn't seem dated.

Lorena ★

(English) a form of Lauren.
First Impression: Remember Lorena Bobbitt? People picture Lorena as a tough and stubborn woman who's fiery and sometimes cruel.
Gender Association: Used for girls
Popularity and Trend: #705 (#517 in 2000)
Risk of Misspelling: Average

Risk of Mispronunciation: Average
Famous Namesakes: Singer Lorena McKennitt; angry wife Lorena Bobbitt
Common Nicknames: Lori
Common Variations: None
Consider This: A notorious namesake and somewhat challenging pronunciation ("lore-EE-nah" or "lore-AY-nah") make this a 1-star name.

Loretta ★★★

(English) a form of Laura.
First Impression: Perhaps inspired by country legend Loretta Lynn, people see Loretta as a wild gal who loves drinkin', swearin', and hangin' with men.
Gender Association: Used for girls
Popularity and Trend: Last ranked in the Top 1000 in the 1990s
Risk of Misspelling: Low
Risk of Mispronunciation: Low
Famous Namesakes: Singer Loretta Lynn; actress Loretta Young
Common Nicknames: Lori
Common Variations: None
Consider This: Loretta is a countrified nickname for Laura, but it can stand as a given name on its own.

Lori ★★★

(Latin) crowned with laurel. (French) a short form of Lorraine. (American) a familiar form of Laura.

First Impression: Lori is considered a fun-loving, flirtatious, and well-liked woman who's young at heart.
Gender Association: Used for girls
Popularity and Trend: Last ranked in the Top 1000 in the 1990s
Risk of Misspelling: Average
Risk of Mispronunciation: Low
Famous Namesakes: Actress Laurie Metcalf; singer Lorrie Morgan; actress Lori Singer; actress Lori Laughlin
Common Nicknames: None
Common Variations: Laurie
Consider This: Lori is informal, and it's not used as often as Laurie.

Lorna ★★
(Latin) crowned with laurel.
First Impression: People think Lorna is a mean woman who's snobby, two-faced, and hot-tempered.
Gender Association: Used for girls
Popularity and Trend: Last ranked in the Top 1000 in the 1970s
Risk of Misspelling: Low
Risk of Mispronunciation: Low
Famous Namesakes: Fiction character Lorna Doone; actress Lorna Luft
Common Nicknames: None
Common Variations: None
Consider This: Lorna Luft was always less popular than her half-sister, Liza Minelli, and as names, Lorna is less popular than Liza.

Lorraine ★★★★
(Latin) sorrowful.
First Impression: Lorraine is pictured as an everyday, real woman.
Gender Association: Used for girls
Popularity and Trend: Last ranked in the Top 1000 in the 1990s
Risk of Misspelling: Fairly low
Risk of Mispronunciation: Low
Famous Namesakes: Playwright Lorraine Hansberry; actress Lorraine Bracco
Common Nicknames: Lori, Raina, Rainey
Common Variations: Loraine
Consider This: Lorraine was a big name from the '20s to the '40s, but it seems old-fashioned now.

Louisa ★★★★
(English) a form of Louise.
First Impression: Folks say Louisa is known for her kindness and happiness.
Gender Association: Used for girls
Popularity and Trend: Last ranked in the Top 1000 in the 1960s
Risk of Misspelling: Fairly low
Risk of Mispronunciation: Fairly low
Famous Namesakes: Author Louisa May Alcott
Common Nicknames: None
Common Variations: Luisa
Consider This: Louisa May Alcott makes this currently unranked name well known.

Louise ★★★
(German) famous warrior.
First Impression: Louise is regarded as quick with the sarcasm as she is with a smile.
Gender Association: Used for girls
Popularity and Trend: Last ranked in the Top 1000 in the 1980s
Risk of Misspelling: Low
Risk of Mispronunciation: Fairly low
Famous Namesakes: Actress Louise Brooks; actress Louise Fletcher; actress Louise Lombard
Common Nicknames: Lulu, Luella, Lou, Lola
Common Variations: None
Consider This: Louise was very popular for the first half of the twentieth century, but it's dated today.

Lucia ★★★
(Italian, Spanish) a form of Lucy.
First Impression: People say Lucia has clear morals but ambiguous ethnicity.
Gender Association: Used for girls
Popularity and Trend: #340 (#490 in 2000)
Risk of Misspelling: Fairly high
Risk of Mispronunciation: Fairly high
Famous Namesakes: Actress Lucia Mendez
Common Nicknames: None
Common Variations: None
Consider This: Lucia may work best with Italian or Latino last names, but because it can be

"loo-CHEE-ah," "loo-SEE-ah," or "loo-SHAH," pronunciation may be a problem.

Lucie ★★★
(French) a form of Lucy.
First Impression: Lucie is described as a free-spirited and unconventional young girl.
Gender Association: Used for girls
Popularity and Trend: Last ranked in the Top 1000 in the 1920s
Risk of Misspelling: Average
Risk of Mispronunciation: Low
Famous Namesakes: Actress Lucie Arnaz; actress Lucy Liu; character Lucy (Peanuts); actress Lucy Lawless; activist Lucy Stone
Common Nicknames: None
Common Variations: Lucy, Luci
Consider This: "Lucy" is the far more popular spelling, but Lucie has a positive first impression, too.

Lucille ★★★★★
(English) a form of Lucy.
First Impression: Lucille Ball is the Queen of Comedy, so for most people this name calls to mind a witty, fun-loving comic.
Gender Association: Used for girls
Popularity and Trend: #728 (#937 in 2003)
Risk of Misspelling: Low
Risk of Mispronunciation: Fairly low
Famous Namesakes: Comedian Lucille Ball
Common Nicknames: Lucy, Lulu

Common Variations: None
Consider This: Historically, Lucille was a nickname, but in modern use, it's considered to be more formal than Lucy.

Lucinda ★★★
(Latin) a form of Lucy.
First Impression: Lucinda is described as a bossy know-it-all who demands to know everything about everyone.
Gender Association: Used for girls
Popularity and Trend: Last ranked in the Top 1000 in the 1980s
Risk of Misspelling: Low
Risk of Mispronunciation: Fairly low
Famous Namesakes: Musician Lucinda Williams
Common Nicknames: Cindy, Lucy, Lulu
Common Variations: None
Consider This: Lucinda is a form of Lucy with a not-so-positive first impression.

Lucy ★★★★★
(Latin) light; bringer of light.
First Impression: Lucy strikes people as a playful and wacky comedian who's outgoing, affectionate, peppy, and smart.
Gender Association: Used for girls
Popularity and Trend: #152 (#323 in 2000)
Risk of Misspelling: Fairly low
Risk of Mispronunciation: Low
Famous Namesakes: Actress Lucie Arnaz; actress Lucy Liu;

character Lucy (Peanuts); actress Lucy Lawless; activist Lucy Stone
Common Nicknames: Lucille, Lulu
Common Variations: Lucie, Luci
Consider This: Lucy is a well-regarded, old-fashioned name that has become quite popular once again.

Lulu ★★★
(Arabic) pearl. (English) soothing, comforting. (Latin) a familiar form of Lucy, Lucille, Luna.
First Impression: People envision Lulu as a cheerful, silly, and mischievous girl who's loads of fun to be around.
Gender Association: Used for girls
Popularity and Trend: Last ranked in the Top 1000 in the 1930s
Risk of Misspelling: Fairly low
Risk of Mispronunciation: Fairly low
Famous Namesakes: Comic strip character Little Lulu; singer Lulu
Common Nicknames: None
Common Variations: Loulou
Consider This: Lulu is often used as a nickname for Lu names such as Lucy. If it's used as a given name, people may find it very informal or unprofessional.

Luna ★★★★
(Latin) moon.
First Impression: Luna is depicted as an open-minded artist and an independent spirit.
Gender Association: Used for girls

Popularity and Trend: #516
(#890 in 2003)
Risk of Misspelling: Fairly low
Risk of Mispronunciation: Fairly low
Famous Namesakes: Character Luna
Lovegood (*Harry Potter* series)
Common Nicknames: Lulu
Common Variations: None
Consider This: Luna is a unique
name, and so it creates a unique
first impression. Still, it may be
too different for some people.

Lupita ★★★
(Latin) a form of Lupe.
First Impression: Lupita is seen as a
lively and talented salsa dancer
who hails from Spain or Latin
America.
Gender Association: Used for girls
Popularity and Trend: Never been
ranked in Top 1000
Risk of Misspelling: Average
Risk of Mispronunciation: Average
Famous Namesakes: Actress Lupita
Ferrer; actress Lupita Tovar
Common Nicknames: Lulu
Common Variations: None
Consider This: Lupita is an ethnic
name some may not recognize—
especially since it's never been in
the Top 1000.

Lydia ★★★
(Greek) from Lydia, an ancient
land in Asia.

First Impression: Lydia is pictured as a
mysterious and withdrawn loner
who's thought to be intelligent.
Gender Association: Used for girls
Popularity and Trend: #131
(#149 in 2000)
Risk of Misspelling: Fairly low
Risk of Mispronunciation: Fairly low
Famous Namesakes: Socialite Lydia
Hearst
Common Nicknames: Lyda
Common Variations: Lidia
Consider This: Lydia may have a loner
image, but it keeps getting more
and more popular.

Lyla ★★★★
(French) island.
First Impression: People say Lyla is
sweet and outgoing, and her
charm shines through her
singing.
Gender Association: Used for girls
Popularity and Trend: #639
(#859 in 2005)
Risk of Misspelling: Average
Risk of Mispronunciation: Low
Famous Namesakes: Actress Lila
Kedrova; country singer Lila
McCann
Common Nicknames: None
Common Variations: Lila, Lilah
Consider This: Lyla isn't as popular
as Lila, but it's gaining popu-
larity fast.

Lynette ★★★
(Welsh) idol. (English) a form of
Linette.
First Impression: Folks say Lynette has
a peaceful, easy spirit.
Gender Association: Used for girls
Popularity and Trend: Last ranked in
the Top 1000 in the 1990s
Risk of Misspelling: Fairly low
Risk of Mispronunciation: Low
Famous Namesakes: Character
Lynette Scavo (*Desperate
Housewives*); designer Lynette
Jennings
Common Nicknames: Lynn
Common Variations: Lynnette
Consider This: Although Lynette
has never been a popular name,
people will know it from TV's
Desperate Housewives.

Lynn ★★★
(English) waterfall; pool below a
waterfall.
First Impression: Friendly, easygoing
Lynn is considered the perfect
caregiver.
Gender Association: Used mostly
for girls
Popularity and Trend: Last ranked in
the Top 1000 in the 1990s
Risk of Misspelling: Average
Risk of Mispronunciation: Low
Famous Namesakes: Actress Lynn
Redgrave; singer Loretta Lynn;
actress Lynn Whitfield; second
lady Lynne Cheney

Common Nicknames: None
Common Variations: Lyn, Lynne
Consider This: No spelling of Lynn has been ranked so far this millennium.

Mabel ★★

(Latin) lovable.

First Impression: Mabel is seen as a crotchety old lady with orthopedic shoes and a miserable attitude.
Gender Association: Used for girls
Popularity and Trend: Last ranked in the Top 1000 in the 1960s
Risk of Misspelling: Fairly low
Risk of Mispronunciation: Average
Famous Namesakes: Actress Mabel King
Common Nicknames: Maybelline, Belle, May
Common Variations: Mabelle, Mabella
Consider This: Mabel hasn't been ranked in such a long time that it seems unfamiliar and dated.

Mackenzie ★★★★

(Irish) child of the wise leader.

First Impression: Mackenzie is described as a pleasant girl who has a tomboyish, sporty streak that makes her hyper.
Gender Association: Used mostly for girls
Popularity and Trend: #53 (#43 in 2000)
Risk of Misspelling: Average
Risk of Mispronunciation: Low

Famous Namesakes: Actress Mackenzie Phillips
Common Nicknames: Kenzie, Mac
Common Variations: Mackenzy, Makenzie, Mckenzie, Mackensie
Consider This: "Mackenzie" is the classic spelling of this very popular name, but with so many variations, people may still misspell it.

Maddie ★★★

(English) a familiar form of Madeline.

First Impression: Maddie is viewed as a pretty girl with a great smile and a perky swing to life.
Gender Association: Used for girls
Popularity and Trend: Never been ranked in Top 1000
Risk of Misspelling: Average
Risk of Mispronunciation: Low
Famous Namesakes: Character Maddie Hayes (*Moonlighting*); actress Maddie Corman
Common Nicknames: None
Common Variations: Maddy
Consider This: If used as a given name, Maddie will be mistaken for a short form of Madeline or Madison.

Madeline ★★★★

(Greek) high tower.

First Impression: Madeline strikes people as a wealthy, sophisticated brunette who's nice but demure.

Gender Association: Used for girls
Popularity and Trend: #71 (#56 in 2000)
Risk of Misspelling: Average
Risk of Mispronunciation: Fairly low
Famous Namesakes: Secretary of state Madeleine Albright; actress Madeline Stowe; actress Madeline Kahn; author Madeline L'Engle; singer Madeline Peyroux; fiction character Madeline
Common Nicknames: Maddy, Madge, Maud
Common Variations: Madeleine, Madaline, Madalyn, Madelaine
Consider This: Madeline is a very popular name with many variations.

Madison ★★★★

(English) good; child of Maud.

First Impression: Above all, people think Madison is immensely entertaining. She's also said to be loving, devoted, and open-minded.
Gender Association: Used mostly for girls
Popularity and Trend: #3 (#3 in 2000)
Risk of Misspelling: Fairly low
Risk of Mispronunciation: Low
Famous Namesakes: First lady Dolly Madison; novelist Madison Smartt Bell; singer Madison Cross; character Madison (*Splash*)
Common Nicknames: Maud

Common Variations: Maddisen, Madysen, Mattison

Consider This: Madison is a popular (maybe *too* popular) name that's been stuck at number-three for years.

Mae ★★

(English) a form of May.

First Impression: Mae is regarded as harsh, mean, and shamefully manipulative.

Gender Association: Used for girls

Popularity and Trend: Last ranked in the Top 1000 in the 1960s

Risk of Misspelling: Average

Risk of Mispronunciation: Fairly low

Famous Namesakes: Actress Mae West; character Aunt May (*Spider-Man*); character May Welland (*The Age of Innocence*); model May Anderson

Common Nicknames: None

Common Variations: May

Consider This: May comes across with a much more positive image than Mae.

Magdalen ★★★★

(Greek) high tower.

First Impression: People say Magdalen is a devout, caring, graceful, and intelligent woman with dark hair, perhaps like biblical Mary Magdalene.

Gender Association: Used for girls

Popularity and Trend: Last ranked in the Top 1000 in the 1920s

Risk of Misspelling: Fairly low

Risk of Mispronunciation: Average

Famous Namesakes: Biblical figure Mary Magdalene

Common Nicknames: Mada, Magda, Maggie, Mala, Malena

Common Variations: Magdalena, Magdalene

Consider This: Magdalen is very versatile and a fine name for a religious family.

Maggie ★★★

(Greek) pearl. (English) a familiar form of Magdalen, Margaret.

First Impression: Maggie is considered either a bland woman stuck in her dull ways or a sharp-tongued, working-class waitress.

Gender Association: Used for girls

Popularity and Trend: #189 (#198 in 2000)

Risk of Misspelling: Fairly low

Risk of Mispronunciation: Low

Famous Namesakes: Actress Maggie Gyllenhaal; character Maggie the Cat (*Cat on a Hot Tin Roof*); actress Maggie Smith; character Maggie Simpson (*The Simpsons*)

Common Nicknames: None

Common Variations: Maggy

Consider This: People have mixed reactions to this nickname for Margaret, but the name keeps getting more popular anyway.

Maira ★★

(Irish) a form of Mary.

First Impression: Although some see Maira as snippy and humorless, others see her as caring and social.

Gender Association: Used for girls

Popularity and Trend: Last ranked in the Top 1000 in the 1990s

Risk of Misspelling: Fairly high

Risk of Mispronunciation: Fairly high

Famous Namesakes: None

Common Nicknames: None

Common Variations: Mara

Consider This: Pronounced "MARE-ah," "MAY-rah," or "MY-rah," this name is a spelling and pronunciation challenge.

Maire ★★

(Irish) a form of Mary.

First Impression: Many describe Maire as an older woman who's short on confidence, but others say she's strong-willed and eager to lead.

Gender Association: Used for girls

Popularity and Trend: Never been ranked in Top 1000

Risk of Misspelling: Fairly high

Risk of Mispronunciation: Average

Famous Namesakes: Folk singer Maire Brennan

Common Nicknames: None

Common Variations: Mare

Consider This: Maire has an average risk of mispronunciation because it can be pronounced two ways—one easy, one difficult. The easy option: Pronouncing it phonetically, like the word *mare*. The difficult option: Using the traditional Irish pronunciation "MOY-ah."

Maisie ★★★

(Scottish) a familiar form of Margaret.

First Impression: Maisie is described as a friendly and gentle girl who's funny, lots of fun, and full of contagious smiles.

Gender Association: Used for girls

Popularity and Trend: Never been ranked in Top 1000

Risk of Misspelling: Average

Risk of Mispronunciation: Fairly low

Famous Namesakes: Fiction character Maisie Dobbs

Common Nicknames: None

Common Variations: Maizie, Maisey

Consider This: Maisie is a cute, fun name that's too informal. Use it as a nickname for Margaret instead.

Malana ★★★

(Hawaiian) bouyant, light.

First Impression: People say Malana has boundless beauty, but a humble personality.

Gender Association: Used for girls

Popularity and Trend: Never been ranked in Top 1000

Risk of Misspelling: Fairly low

Risk of Mispronunciation: Fairly low

Famous Namesakes: Character Malena Scordia (*Malena*)

Common Nicknames: Mal

Common Variations: None

Consider This: This Hawaiian name gives very positive vibes, and most people will correctly pronounce it as "mah-LAH-nah."

Mallory ★★★★

(German) army counselor. (French) unlucky.

First Impression: Mallory may have the classic beauty of a model, but she's said to be a smart-mouthed rebel.

Gender Association: Used mostly for girls

Popularity and Trend: #234 (#213 in 2000)

Risk of Misspelling: Fairly low

Risk of Mispronunciation: Low

Famous Namesakes: Character Mallory Keaton (*Family Ties*); model Mallory Snyder

Common Nicknames: Mal, Mallie

Common Variations: Malerie

Consider This: Mallory has roughly held the same ranking since the '80s.

Mandy ★★★

(Latin) a familiar form of Amanda.

First Impression: Mandy is pictured as the most popular girl in school, but she may be perky and sweet or snobby and cruel.

Gender Association: Used for girls

Popularity and Trend: Last ranked in the Top 1000 in the 1980s

Risk of Misspelling: Fairly low

Risk of Mispronunciation: Low

Famous Namesakes: Actress and singer Mandy Moore

Common Nicknames: None

Common Variations: Mandi, Mandee

Consider This: Amanda is much more formal than Mandy, which is best used as a nickname.

Mansi ★★★

(Hopi) plucked flower.

First Impression: Mansi comes across as a free-spirited, strong-willed, and happy-go-lucky African American woman.

Gender Association: Used for girls

Popularity and Trend: Never been ranked in Top 1000

Risk of Misspelling: Fairly high

Risk of Mispronunciation: Fairly high

Famous Namesakes: None

Common Nicknames: None

Common Variations: None

Consider This: This Hopi name will be unfamiliar to most people, and most won't know to pronounce it "MAHN-see," but it still has a very positive first impression.

Mara ★★★

(Hebrew) melody. (Greek) a form of Amara. (Slavic) a form of Mary.

First Impression: Mara is viewed as an insightful, diligent, and intelligent bookworm who's probably on the speech team.

Gender Association: Used for girls

Popularity and Trend: #681 (#606 in 2000)

Risk of Misspelling: Fairly low

Risk of Mispronunciation: Fairly low

Famous Namesakes: Actress Mara Wilson; character Marah Lewis (*Guiding Light*)

Common Nicknames: None

Common Variations: Marah

Consider This: Most people will know this name is pronounced "MAR-ah," but perhaps a few may mistake it for "MARE-ah."

Marcella ★★★★

(Latin) martial, warlike.

First Impression: Emotionally and physically, Marcella is seen as always composed.

Gender Association: Used for girls

Popularity and Trend: Last ranked in the Top 1000 in the 1990s

Risk of Misspelling: Fairly low

Risk of Mispronunciation: Fairly low

Famous Namesakes: Chef Marcella Hazan

Common Nicknames: Marcy

Common Variations: Marcela

Consider This: Marcella peaked in the '20s, but Latino families should still consider this name.

Marcia ★★★

(Latin) martial, warlike.

First Impression: Like her or not, Marcia is often described as a wild and crazy gal.

Gender Association: Used for girls

Popularity and Trend: Last ranked in the Top 1000 in the 1990s

Risk of Misspelling: Average

Risk of Mispronunciation: Fairly low

Famous Namesakes: Actress Marsha Mason; character Marcia Brady (*The Brady Bunch*); actress Marcia Cross; actress Marcia Gay Harden

Common Nicknames: Marcy

Common Variations: Marsha

Consider This: Neither Marcia nor Marsha have been ranked since the '90s.

Marcy ★★★

(English) a familiar form of Marcella, Marcia.

First Impression: People say Marcy knows all the scuttlebutt in her suburban neighborhood.

Gender Association: Used for girls

Popularity and Trend: Last ranked in the Top 1000 in the 1980s

Risk of Misspelling: Fairly low

Risk of Mispronunciation: Low

Famous Namesakes: Character Marcy (*Peanuts*); actress Marcy Walker

Common Nicknames: None

Common Variations: Marci

Consider This: People may mistake this as a nickname and not a given name.

Margaret ★★★★

(Greek) pearl.

First Impression: Margaret has a kind soul, but some say she's timid, and others say she's bossy.

Gender Association: Used for girls

Popularity and Trend: #161 (#110 in 2000)

Risk of Misspelling: Fairly low

Risk of Mispronunciation: Low

Famous Namesakes: Prime minister Margaret Thatcher; author Margaret Mitchell; anthropologist Margaret Mead; writer Margaret Atwood; activist Margaret Sanger; comedian Margaret Cho

Common Nicknames: Peggy, Marge, Margie, Maretta, Mamie, Maisey, Maggie, Madge, Gretel, Greta

Common Variations: Margret, Margarit, Marguerite, Margarita

Consider This: Margaret is a classic name with a great deal of versatility.

Margarita ★★★

(Italian, Spanish) a form of Margaret.

First Impression: With this name, it's pretty easy to see how people can imagine a wild and fun-loving Latina who likes to drink and party.

Gender Association: Used for girls

Popularity and Trend: #944
(#654 in 2000)

Risk of Misspelling: Fairly low

Risk of Mispronunciation: Low

Famous Namesakes: Designer
Margarita Missoni

Common Nicknames: Rita

Common Variations: Margaret,
Marguerite

Consider This: This name is primarily
used by Latino families, but
everyone should think twice
before they let their daughter
share a name with a cocktail.

Margaux ★

(French) a form of Margaret.

First Impression: People get the
impression that Margaux is a
cold, uptight, but beautiful
French model.

Gender Association: Used for girls

Popularity and Trend: Never been
ranked in Top 1000

Risk of Misspelling: Fairly high

Risk of Mispronunciation: Fairly high

Famous Namesakes: Model Margaux
Hemingway; actress Margot
Kidder; ballerina Margot Fonteyn

Common Nicknames: None

Common Variations: Margot, Margo

Consider This: Margaux is not only
fairly difficult to spell with its
"-aux" ending, but it's also
linked to a tragic namesake,
Margaux Hemingway.

Margot ★

(French) a form of Margaret.

First Impression: Snooty and rude,
Margot seems to like books much
more than she likes people.

Gender Association: Used for girls

Popularity and Trend: Last ranked in
the Top 1000 in the 1960s

Risk of Misspelling: Fairly high

Risk of Mispronunciation: Fairly high

Famous Namesakes: Actress Margot
Kidder; ballerina Margot
Fonteyn; model Margaux
Hemingway

Common Nicknames: None

Common Variations: Margaux, Margo

Consider This: With a silent t, this
French name is hard to spell
and pronounce.

Marguerite ★★★

(French) a form of Margaret.

First Impression: Although she's an
older woman, Marguerite is still
considered a class act.

Gender Association: Used for girls

Popularity and Trend: Last ranked in
the Top 1000 in the 1970s

Risk of Misspelling: Average

Risk of Mispronunciation: Fairly low

Famous Namesakes:
Writer Marguerite Duras;
physicist Marguerite Perey;
actress Marguerite Moreau

Common Nicknames: Rita

Common Variations: Margaret

Consider This: Although Marguerite
has some style, it's still an old-
fashioned name.

Maria ★★★★

(Hebrew) bitter; sea of bitterness.
(Italian, Spanish) a form of Mary.

First Impression: Maria is seen as
tough as she is tender.

Gender Association: Used for girls

Popularity and Trend: #47
(#41 in 2000)

Risk of Misspelling: Low

Risk of Mispronunciation: Low

Famous Namesakes: Opera singer
Maria Callas; character Maria
(West Side Story); character Maria
(The Sound of Music); journalist
Maria Shriver; tennis player
Maria Sharapova; actress Maria
Bello; television host Maria
Menounos

Common Nicknames: None

Common Variations: Mariah

Consider This: Maria does have an
ethnic connotation, but overall,
it's a classic name suitable for
any culture.

Mariah ★★★★

(Hebrew) a form of Mary.

First Impression: People imagine
Mariah as an arrogant and
sometimes mean diva with a
sexy appearance and dynamic
singing talent, much like
megastar Mariah Carey.

Gender Association: Used for girls
Popularity and Trend: #81
   (#76 in 2000)
Risk of Misspelling: Fairly low
Risk of Mispronunciation: Low
Famous Namesakes: Singer Mariah
   Carey
Common Nicknames: None
Common Variations: Maria
Consider This: This name scores well,
   but keep in mind that Mariah
   Carey's reputation gives it a
   high-maintenance vibe.

Marie ★★★★

(French) a form of Mary.
First Impression: Marie is said to be
   a loving and kind middle-aged
   Latina who finds herself clinging
   to old-fashioned morals.
Gender Association: Used for girls
Popularity and Trend: #578
   (#373 in 2000)
Risk of Misspelling: Low
Risk of Mispronunciation: Low
Famous Namesakes: Queen Marie
   Antoinette; physicist Marie
   Curie; singer Marie Osmond
Common Nicknames: None
Common Variations: Maree
Consider This: Compared to Maria,
   the first impression for Marie
   calls to mind an elderly woman,
   which may mean it's a dated
   name.

Mariel ★★★★

(German, Dutch) a form of Mary.
First Impression: Folks warn not to let
   Mariel's meek demeanor fool
   you—she's quite sharp.
Gender Association: Used for girls
Popularity and Trend: Last ranked in
   the Top 1000 in the 1990s
Risk of Misspelling: Fairly low
Risk of Mispronunciation: Low
Famous Namesakes: Actress Mariel
   Hemingway
Common Nicknames: Mare, Mary
Common Variations: None
Consider This: Mariel came on the
   scene in the '80s, but fell off the
   radar by the '90s.

Marietta ★★★★

(Italian) a form of Marie.
First Impression: Marietta is viewed as
   a lighthearted lady, even though
   she's not very smart.
Gender Association: Used for girls
Popularity and Trend: Last ranked in
   the Top 1000 in the 1960s
Risk of Misspelling: Fairly low
Risk of Mispronunciation: Fairly low
Famous Namesakes: Opera singer
   Marietta Alboni; humorist
   Marietta Holley
Common Nicknames: Mare, Mary
Common Variations: None
Consider This: Like many names with
   the "-etta" suffix, Marietta seems
   old-fashioned.

Marilyn ★★★

(Hebrew) Mary's line of descen-
   dants.
First Impression: People say Marilyn is
   sweet, ditzy, and spontaneous,
   but unfortunately also troubled
   with mental problems and drug
   addiction, much like cultural
   icon Marilyn Monroe.
Gender Association: Used for girls
Popularity and Trend: #514
   (#510 in 2000)
Risk of Misspelling: Fairly low
Risk of Mispronunciation: Low
Famous Namesakes: Actress Marilyn
   Monroe; musician Marilyn
   Manson; columnist Marilyn
   vos Savant
Common Nicknames: Mare
Common Variations: Marilyne,
   Marylin
Consider This: Marilyn's first impression places more emphasis on
   psychological problems than on
   physical beauty. In addition to a
   troublesome image, the name
   seems dated.

Marissa ★★★★

(Latin) a form of Maris, Marisa.
First Impression: People think Marissa
   knows just how to brighten
   someone's day.
Gender Association: Used for girls
Popularity and Trend: #104
   (#78 in 2000)
Risk of Misspelling: Average

Risk of Mispronunciation: Low

Famous Namesakes: Actress Marisa Tomei; character Marissa Cooper (*The O.C.*); actress Marissa Jaret Winokur; model Marissa Miller

Common Nicknames: None

Common Variations: Marisa

Consider This: The "One *s* or two?" spelling problem may cause some trouble for Marissa.

Marit ★★★★

(Aramaic) lady.

First Impression: Folks can listen—and laugh—to Marit's stories all night.

Gender Association: Used for girls

Popularity and Trend: Never been ranked in Top 1000

Risk of Misspelling: Fairly low

Risk of Mispronunciation: Fairly low

Famous Namesakes: Singer Marit Larsen

Common Nicknames: None

Common Variations: Marita, Maritsa

Consider This: For an uncommon name, Marit conjures up a fun, cool first impression. Most people should know it's pronounced "MARE-it."

Marjorie ★★★

(Greek) a form of Margaret. (Scottish) a form of Mary.

First Impression: Marjorie is considered either quick to chat or quick to cave in to others' demands.

Gender Association: Used for girls

Popularity and Trend: Last ranked in the Top 1000 in the 1990s

Risk of Misspelling: Fairly low

Risk of Mispronunciation: Low

Famous Namesakes: Novelist Marjorie Kinnan Rawlings

Common Nicknames: Marge, Margie

Common Variations: Margery

Consider This: This variation of Margaret and Mary doesn't come across as well as either of its root names.

Marlene ★★★

(Greek) high tower. (Slavic) a form of Magdalen.

First Impression: People say Marlene may be dull with an unpleasant demeanor, or she may be playful with a carefree attitude.

Gender Association: Used for girls

Popularity and Trend: #515 (#513 in 2000)

Risk of Misspelling: Fairly low

Risk of Mispronunciation: Low

Famous Namesakes: Actress Marlene Dietrich; painter Marlene Dumas

Common Nicknames: Marley

Common Variations: Marlena, Marleen

Consider This: Marlene and Maureen rate about the same, but Marlene is still in the Top 1000.

Marley ★★★

(English) a form of Marlene.

First Impression: Marley is imagined to be a gifted and artistic musician who's spiritual, independent, fearless, and definitely not conservative, much like reggae legend Bob Marley.

Gender Association: Used mostly for girls

Popularity and Trend: #415 (#695 in 2000)

Risk of Misspelling: Average

Risk of Mispronunciation: Low

Famous Namesakes: Actress Marley Shelton; actress Marlee Matlin

Common Nicknames: None

Common Variations: Marli, Marlee

Consider This: Before you choose this name, carefully consider how you feel about Bob Marley's music and politics, given that both affect the name's image.

Marlo ★★★

(English) a form of Mary.

First Impression: Folks believe Marlo has a kind heart to soften her big mouth.

Gender Association: Used about equally for girls and boys

Popularity and Trend: Last ranked in the Top 1000 in the 1970s

Risk of Misspelling: Fairly low

Risk of Mispronunciation: Low

Famous Namesakes: Actress Marlo Thomas

Common Nicknames: None

Common Variations: None

Consider This: This name was popular when actress Marlo Thomas was TV's *That Girl* in the late '60s–early '70s. Today, it's used equally for boys and girls, which may pose a problem for parents searching for names with clear gender associations.

Marnie ★★

(Hebrew) a form of Marnina.

First Impression: Marnie is described as selfish and full of herself, but frankly, people find her to be nothing special at all.

Gender Association: Used for girls

Popularity and Trend: Last ranked in the Top 1000 in the 1970s

Risk of Misspelling: Fairly low

Risk of Mispronunciation: Low

Famous Namesakes: Film character Marnie; singer Marni Nixon

Common Nicknames: None

Common Variations: Marni

Consider This: Marnie has been off the popularity radar for years, and gauging by the first impression, that comes as no surprise.

Marsha ★★★

(English) a form of Marcia.

First Impression: Marsha is seen as either prissy or popular.

Gender Association: Used for girls

Popularity and Trend: Last ranked in the Top 1000 in the 1990s

Risk of Misspelling: Average

Risk of Mispronunciation: Low

Famous Namesakes: Actress Marsha Mason; character Marcia Brady (*The Brady Bunch*); actress Marcia Cross; actress Marcia Gay Harden

Common Nicknames: Marcy

Common Variations: Marcia

Consider This: Spelling will be a bit of a problem for this name, with people wondering if it's the "-sha" version or "-cia" version. And despite the spelling difference, this variation of Marcia still carries some Marcia Brady baggage.

Marta ★★★

(English) a form of Martha, Martina.

First Impression: People say Marta doesn't realize what a good person she is.

Gender Association: Used for girls

Popularity and Trend: Last ranked in the Top 1000 in the 1980s

Risk of Misspelling: Low

Risk of Mispronunciation: Low

Famous Namesakes: Singer Marta Sanchez

Common Nicknames: None

Common Variations: None

Consider This: Marta is techincally a short form of Martha and Martina, but it's strong enough to stand on its own.

Martha ★★★★

(Aramaic) lady; sorrowful.

First Impression: Pop icon Martha Stewart inspires a contradicting image of a charming homemaker and ruthless businesswoman.

Gender Association: Used for girls

Popularity and Trend: #526 (#375 in 2000)

Risk of Misspelling: Low

Risk of Mispronunciation: Low

Famous Namesakes: First lady Martha Washington; entrepreneur Martha Stewart; choreographer Martha Graham; biblical figure Martha; character Martha Kent (*Superman*); singer Martha Reeves

Common Nicknames: Marti, Mattie

Common Variations: Marta

Consider This: This name has taken a nosedive in popularity, most likely due to Martha Stewart's rollercoaster public image.

Martina ★★★★

(Latin) martial, warlike.

First Impression: This name's image has a sporty but serious edge, thanks to tennis stars Martina Hingis and Martina Navratilova.

Gender Association: Used for girls

Popularity and Trend: Last ranked in the Top 1000 in the 1980s

Risk of Misspelling: Low

Risk of Mispronunciation: Low

Famous Namesakes: Tennis player Martina Hingis; singer Martina McBride; tennis player Martina Navratilova

Common Nicknames: Marti, Tina, Marta

Common Variations: Martine

Consider This: With a martial meaning and with two determined tennis stars as namesakes, Martina isn't a "soft" name.

Mary ★★★★

(Hebrew) bitter; sea of bitterness.

First Impression: Because of the biblical mother of Jesus, people picture Mary as a nurturing and gentle mother who's religious, traditional, and simple.

Gender Association: Used for girls

Popularity and Trend: #84 (#47 in 2000)

Risk of Misspelling: Low

Risk of Mispronunciation: Low

Famous Namesakes: Biblical figure Mary; Mary Queen of Scots; fiction character Mary Poppins; biblical figure Mary Magdalene; singer Mary J. Blige; reporter Mary Hart; character Mary Jane Watson (*Spider-Man*); entrepreneur Mary Kay Ash; artist Mary Cassatt

Common Nicknames: Molly

Common Variations: Merry

Consider This: Mary had been the number one girls' name for many decades, but it's now sliding down the Top 100.

Mary Beth ★★★

(American) a combination of Mary + Beth.

First Impression: Mary Beth is described as a sensitive and sweet woman who's old-fashioned, quiet, and intelligent.

Gender Association: Used for girls

Popularity and Trend: Last ranked in the Top 1000 in the 1960s

Risk of Misspelling: Fairly low

Risk of Mispronunciation: Low

Famous Namesakes: Political figure Mary Beth Cahill; actress Mary Beth Evans; actress Mary Beth Hurt; actress Mary Beth McDonough

Common Nicknames: None

Common Variations: Maribeth

Consider This: Both Mary and Beth create gentle images, so it's no surprise that the image for Mary Beth is mousy, too.

Mary Ellen ★★★★

(American) a combination of Mary + Ellen.

First Impression: Mary Ellen is viewed as a pleasant young woman who happens to like staying home on Saturday nights.

Gender Association: Used for girls

Popularity and Trend: Last ranked in the Top 1000 in the 1960s

Risk of Misspelling: Low

Risk of Mispronunciation: Low

Famous Namesakes: Photographer Mary Ellen Mark

Common Nicknames: None

Common Variations: None

Consider This: Like Mary and Mary Beth, Mary Ellen has a quiet image.

Matilda ★★★★

(German) powerful battler.

First Impression: Matilda is pictured as a curious, lively girl.

Gender Association: Used for girls

Popularity and Trend: Last ranked in the Top 1000 in the 1960s

Risk of Misspelling: Fairly low

Risk of Mispronunciation: Low

Famous Namesakes: Character Matilda Wormwood (*Matilda*)

Common Nicknames: Mattie, Maud, Tilda, Tillie

Common Variations: Mathilde

Consider This: For a name that's been out of the Top 1000 for quite some time, Matilda certainly has a fun, youthful first impression.

Maud ★★

(English) a form of Madeline, Matilda.

First Impression: People describe Maud as a homely, masculine-looking grouch.

Gender Association: Used for girls

Popularity and Trend: Last ranked in the Top 1000 in the 1930s

Risk of Misspelling: Average

Risk of Mispronunciation: Low

Famous Namesakes: Actress Maud Adams; character Maude Findlay (*Maude*)

Common Nicknames: None

Common Variations: Maude

Consider This: Maud has been unpopular for many decades, even when TV's *Maude* aired in the '70s.

Maura ★★★

(Irish) dark. A form of Mary, Maureen.

First Impression: Some people call Maura self-assured and determined, but others label her as bratty, full of herself, and short-tempered if she doesn't get her way.

Gender Association: Used for girls

Popularity and Trend: #922 (#750 in 2000)

Risk of Misspelling: Fairly low

Risk of Mispronunciation: Fairly low

Famous Namesakes: Author Maura Murphy; actress Maura Tierney; actress Maura West

Common Nicknames: None

Common Variations: Moira

Consider This: If trends continue, Maura may soon slip out of the Top 1000.

Maureen ★★★

(French) dark. (Irish) a form of Mary.

First Impression: People say Maureen may be an older churchgoer who plays bingo and lives alone with her cats, or a young beauty who's cool, fashionable, popular, and funny.

Gender Association: Used for girls

Popularity and Trend: Last ranked in the Top 1000 in the 1990s

Risk of Misspelling: Low

Risk of Mispronunciation: Low

Famous Namesakes: Tennis player Maureen Connolly; actress Maureen O'Hara; Maureen O'Sullivan; actress Maureen McCormick

Common Nicknames: Mo

Common Variations: None

Consider This: While Maura is barely hanging in the Top 1000, Maureen has fallen out of it.

Mauve ★★★

(French) violet colored.

First Impression: No middle ground for Mauve—folks say she's either a recluse or a party animal.

Gender Association: Used for girls

Popularity and Trend: Never been ranked in Top 1000

Risk of Misspelling: Low

Risk of Mispronunciation: Low

Famous Namesakes: None

Common Nicknames: None

Common Variations: None

Consider This: Unlike Scarlett or Ruby, Mauve is color name that may never catch on, perhaps because similar-sounding names like Maud are unpopular as well.

Maxine ★★★

(Latin) greatest.

First Impression: Middle-aged and beautiful, Maxine is most likely a rich and spoiled divorcée, but deep down, people think she wants the best for everyone.

Gender Association: Used for girls

Popularity and Trend: Last ranked in the Top 1000 in the 1970s

Risk of Misspelling: Low

Risk of Mispronunciation: Low

Famous Namesakes: Poet Maxine Kumin; singer Maxine Nightingale

Common Nicknames: Maxie

Common Variations: Maxime

Consider This: Because it hasn't been popular for many years, Maxine is more suitable for a middle-aged woman than a newborn.

May ★★★

(Latin) great. (Arabic) discerning. (English) flower; month of May.

First Impression: May strikes people as a pleasant, demure, but simple-minded housewife.

Gender Association: Used for girls

Popularity and Trend: Last ranked in the Top 1000 in the 1960s

Risk of Misspelling: Fairly low

Risk of Mispronunciation: Low

Famous Namesakes: Character Aunt May (*Spider-Man*); character May Welland (*The Age of Innocence*); actress Mae West; model May Anderson

Common Nicknames: None

Common Variations: Mae

Consider This: Interestingly, people view both May and June as housewives.

Maya ★★★★★

(Hindi) God's creative power. (Greek) mother; grandmother. (Latin) great.

First Impression: People say Maya knows how to have fun while getting things done.

Gender Association: Used for girls

Popularity and Trend: #57 (#113 in 2000)

Risk of Misspelling: Fairly low

Risk of Mispronunciation: Fairly low

Famous Namesakes: Poet Maya Angelou; comedian Maya Rudolph

Common Nicknames: None

Common Variations: Maija, Mya

Consider This: While most will get it right, for a few people, pronunciation could be a problem with this name ("MY-ah" or "MAY-ah"?).

McKayla ★★★

(American) a form of Michaela.

First Impression: McKayla is seen as a charming little lady.

Gender Association: Used for girls

Popularity and Trend: #579 (#430 in 2000)

Risk of Misspelling: Fairly high

Risk of Mispronunciation: Low

Famous Namesakes: None

Common Nicknames: Mickie, Kayla

Common Variations: Michaela, Mackayla, Makayla, Mekayla, Mickayla

Consider This: McKayla may get lost in the sea of Michaela variations, especially because it's stylized like a surname: *Mc* and capital *K*.

Mead ★★

(Greek) honey wine.

First Impression: Simply put, Mead is considered a social misfit.

Gender Association: Used mostly for boys

Popularity and Trend: Never been ranked in Top 1000

Risk of Misspelling: Fairly low

Risk of Mispronunciation: Low

Famous Namesakes: Anthropologist Margaret Mead

Common Nicknames: None

Common Variations: None

Consider This: Perhaps the awkward image of Mead relates to the brilliant yet unpolished image of anthropologist Margaret Mead. Furthermore, this name is used more for boys than girls, which may repel parents searching for names with clear feminine association.

Megan ★★★★★

(Greek) pearl; great. (Irish) a form of Margaret.

First Impression: Megan is imagined to be a kind and caring woman with a pretty smile and pretty complexion.

Gender Association: Used mostly for girls

Popularity and Trend: #60 (#18 in 2000)

Risk of Misspelling: Fairly low

Risk of Mispronunciation: Low

Famous Namesakes: Actress Megan Mullally; actress Megan Ward; author Megan McCafferty

Common Nicknames: Meg, Meggie

Common Variations: Meghan, Meagan

Consider This: A Top 20 name in the '90s, Megan is experiencing a slight a drop in popularity this decade.

Meka ★★

(Hebrew) a familiar form of Michaela.

First Impression: This name sounds like *meek*, so people say she's shy and passive but still quite happy.

Gender Association: Used mostly for girls

Popularity and Trend: Never been ranked in Top 1000

Risk of Misspelling: Average

Risk of Mispronunciation: Average

Famous Namesakes: Journalist Meka Nichols

Common Nicknames: None

Common Variations: None

Consider This: This nickname for Michaela doesn't work overly well as a given name. Pronunciation

("MEE-kah" or "MECK-ah") is a little tricky, as is spelling.

Melanie ★★★★

(Greek) dark-skinned.

First Impression: This name calls to mind a loving and sweet mother who's fun, confident, and free spirited.

Gender Association: Used for girls

Popularity and Trend: #83 (#114 in 2000)

Risk of Misspelling: Fairly low

Risk of Mispronunciation: Low

Famous Namesakes: Actress Melanie Griffith; character Melanie Wilkes (*Gone with the Wind*); singer Melanie Brown; singer Melanie Chisholm

Common Nicknames: Mel

Common Variations: Malanie, Melaney

Consider This: Melanie has been a steady Top 200 name for several decades.

Melinda ★★

(Greek) honey.

First Impression: People describe Melinda as a nervous, jumpy hypochondriac.

Gender Association: Used for girls

Popularity and Trend: Last ranked in the Top 1000 in the 1980s

Risk of Misspelling: Fairly low

Risk of Mispronunciation: Low

Famous Namesakes: Philanthropist Melinda Gates

Common Nicknames: Linda, Mandy, Melina, Mindy

Common Variations: Malinda

Consider This: Strangely, Melinda creates a rather negative first impression.

Melissa ★★★★

(Greek) honey bee.

First Impression: Melissa is seen as high energy and high-class.

Gender Association: Used for girls

Popularity and Trend: #117 (#71 in 2000)

Risk of Misspelling: Fairly low

Risk of Mispronunciation: Low

Famous Namesakes: TV commentator Melissa Rivers; musician Melissa Manchester; actress Melissa Joan Hart; singer Melissa Etheridge; actress Melissa George

Common Nicknames: Elissa, Missy, Millie

Common Variations: Melisa

Consider This: Melissa has seen a drop in popularity since the '70s, when it was as high as number two.

Melody ★★★★★

(Greek) melody.

First Impression: Melody is pictured as sweet as a song.

Gender Association: Used for girls

Popularity and Trend: #299 (#398 in 2000)

Risk of Misspelling: Low

Risk of Mispronunciation: Low

Famous Namesakes: Actress Melody Scott Thomas

Common Nicknames: None

Common Variations: Melodie

Consider This: This pretty name's popularity usually hovers in the Top 200 to 400 range. Spelling and pronunciation will be easy.

Mercedes ★★

(Latin) reward, payment. (Spanish) merciful.

First Impression: People think *fast and furious* describes Mercedes's approach to life; she may be a stripper.

Gender Association: Used for girls

Popularity and Trend: #440 (#285 in 2000)

Risk of Misspelling: Fairly low

Risk of Mispronunciation: Fairly low

Famous Namesakes: Actress Mercedes Ruehl

Common Nicknames: None

Common Variations: Marcedes

Consider This: Mercedes-Benz may be a classy, refined line of automobiles, but that positive association unfortunately doesn't apply when Mercedes is used as a girls' name.

Meredith ★★★

(Welsh) protector of the sea.

First Impression: Folks think snobby and moody Meredith doesn't win many people over.

Gender Association: Used mostly for girls

Popularity and Trend: #310 (#293 in 2000)

Risk of Misspelling: Fairly low

Risk of Mispronunciation: Low

Famous Namesakes: Character Meredith Grey (*Grey's Anatomy*); actress Meredith Baxter; journalist Meredith Vieira; singer Meredith Brooks

Common Nicknames: Merry

Common Variations: Meridith

Consider This: Even with popular namesakes like Meredith Vieira and *Grey's Anatomy* character Meredith Grey, this name conjures up a negative first impression.

Meryl ★★

(German) famous. (Irish) shining sea.

First Impression: Meryl is thought to be an incredibly mean and arrogant bully.

Gender Association: Used for girls

Popularity and Trend: Last ranked in the Top 1000 in the 1950s

Risk of Misspelling: Fairly low

Risk of Mispronunciation: Low

Famous Namesakes: Actress Meryl Streep

Common Nicknames: None

Common Variations: Merril, Marel

Consider This: Meryl Streep is a 5-star actress, but this is a 2-star name.

Mia ★★★★

(Italian) mine.

First Impression: Mia is pictured as a fascinating original.

Gender Association: Used for girls

Popularity and Trend: #13 (#94 in 2000)

Risk of Misspelling: Fairly low

Risk of Mispronunciation: Average

Famous Namesakes: Actress Mia Farrow; soccer player Mia Hamm; model Mia Tyler

Common Nicknames: None

Common Variations: Miah

Consider This: This name is pronounced "MEE-ah," but some may mistake it for "MY-ah."

Michaela ★★★★

(Hebrew) a form of Michael.

First Impression: People describe Michaela as an attractive brunette who's feminine but physically strong.

Gender Association: Used for girls

Popularity and Trend: #331 (#153 in 2000)

Risk of Misspelling: Average

Risk of Mispronunciation: Fairly low

Famous Namesakes: Character Michaela Quinn (*Dr. Quinn, Medicine Woman*)

Common Nicknames: Mia, Mickie, Meka

Common Variations: McKayla, Mackayla, Makayla, Mekayla, Mickayla

Consider This: Michaela is a classic name that's often passed over in favor of its variations, like Makayla, which creates all sorts of spelling woes.

Michelle ★★★★

(French) who is like God?

First Impression: Michelle is viewed as brainy and headstrong, but possibly too strong at times.

Gender Association: Used for girls

Popularity and Trend: #80 (#52 in 2000)

Risk of Misspelling: Fairly low

Risk of Mispronunciation: Low

Famous Namesakes: Actress Michelle Pfieffer; singer Michelle Branch; actress Michelle Phillips; actress Michelle Lee; figure skater Michelle Kwan; actress Michelle Williams; actress Michelle Trachtenberg

Common Nicknames: Shelly, Mia

Common Variations: Michele

Consider This: Michelle saw huge popularity in the '70s and '80s, and although it's slipping, it's still a common name.

Mickie ★★★

(American) a familiar form of Michaela.

First Impression: People expect fun, not depth, from someone with this bubbly name.

Gender Association: Used for girls

Popularity and Trend: Last ranked in the Top 1000 in the 1950s

Risk of Misspelling: Average

Risk of Mispronunciation: Low

Famous Namesakes: Professional wrestler Mickie James; cartoon character Mickey Mouse

Common Nicknames: None

Common Variations: Micki, Mickey

Consider This: As with many names traditionally used as nicknames, Mickie seems very casual and silly. Plus, its pronunciation is the same as that for Mickey, a traditional nickname for boys, which may cause gender confusion.

Mildred ★★★

(English) gentle counselor.

First Impression: Mildred is considered a grandma on the go.

Gender Association: Used for girls

Popularity and Trend: Last ranked in the Top 1000 in the 1980s

Risk of Misspelling: Low

Risk of Mispronunciation: Low

Famous Namesakes: Film character Mildred Pierce; author Mildred Taylor

Common Nicknames: Millie

Common Variations: None

Consider This: As the first impression clearly states, people assume anyone named Mildred is a silvery old lady—not a newborn.

Millicent ★★

(English) industrious. (Greek) a form of Melissa.

First Impression: Unfortunately, Millicent is depicted as either evil or nerdy.

Gender Association: Used for girls

Popularity and Trend: Last ranked in the Top 1000 in the 1960s

Risk of Misspelling: Average

Risk of Mispronunciation: Fairly low

Famous Namesakes: Activist Millicent Garrett Fawcett

Common Nicknames: Millie, Missy

Common Variations: Milicent

Consider This: Perhaps Millicent gets its evil image from the similar-sounding Maleficent, the villain of Disney's *Sleeping Beauty*.

Millie ★★★

(English) a familiar form of Amelia, Emily, Mildred, Millicent.

First Impression: Folks say Millie is an innocent and sweetly naïve woman who's easy to take advantage of.

Gender Association: Used for girls

Popularity and Trend: Last ranked in the Top 1000 in the 1960s

Risk of Misspelling: Fairly low

Risk of Mispronunciation: Low

Famous Namesakes: Actress Millie Perkins; singer Millie Jackson; character Millie Dillmount (*Thoroughly Modern Millie*)

Common Nicknames: None

Common Variations: Milly

Consider This: Because Millie is a fun nickname for Emily, Amelia, and so on, it doesn't seem smart to use it as a given name.

Milly ★★

(English) a familiar form of Amelia, Emily, Mildred, Millicent.

First Impression: A regular at the coffee klatch, Milly is said to be a warmhearted, intelligent, and old-fashioned woman who's chubby, dowdy, and short.

Gender Association: Used for girls

Popularity and Trend: Never been ranked in Top 1000

Risk of Misspelling: Average

Risk of Mispronunciation: Low

Famous Namesakes: Actress Millie Perkins; singer Millie Jackson; character Millie Dillmount (*Thoroughly Modern Millie*)

Common Nicknames: None

Common Variations: Millie

Consider This: If you *must* choose between Millie and Milly as a given name (a decision already fraught with problems), avoid Milly for its less-common spelling.

Mimi ★★

(French) a familiar form of Miriam.

First Impression: Mimi is considered either a sweet old lady or a boorish character.

Gender Association: Used for girls

Popularity and Trend: Last ranked in the Top 1000 in the 1960s

Risk of Misspelling: Fairly low

Risk of Mispronunciation: Fairly low

Famous Namesakes: Actress Mimi Rogers; character Mimi Bobeck (*The Drew Carey Show*)

Common Nicknames: None

Common Variations: None

Consider This: Mimi experienced a blip in popularity in the Baby Boom years, but today it's mostly associated with the flamboyant secretary on TV's *The Drew Carey Show*.

Mindy ★★★

(Greek) a familiar form of Melinda.

First Impression: People say Mindy's bouncy personality can go two ways: She's either a fun flirt or a snobby ditz.

Gender Association: Used for girls

Popularity and Trend: Last ranked in the Top 1000 in the 1990s

Risk of Misspelling: Fairly low

Risk of Mispronunciation: Low

Famous Namesakes: Character Mindy McConnell (*Mork & Mindy*); actress Mindy Cohn; singer Mindy McCready

Common Nicknames: None

Common Variations: Mindi

Consider This: Mindy is what you call a "cheerleader" name, which you may find appealing—or not.

Minka ★★★

(Polish) a short form of Wilhelmina.

First Impression: Minka is pictured as a playful minx.

Gender Association: Used for girls

Popularity and Trend: Never been ranked in Top 1000

Risk of Misspelling: Fairly low

Risk of Mispronunciation: Fairly low

Famous Namesakes: Actress Minka Kelly

Common Nicknames: None

Common Variations: None

Consider This: For an unusual name, Minka seems free spirited and fun.

Minnie ★★★

(American) a familiar form of Mina, Minerva, Minna, Wilhelmina.

First Impression: People think Minnie ranges from bashful to ditzy.

Gender Association: Used for girls

Popularity and Trend: Last ranked in the Top 1000 in the 1960s

Risk of Misspelling: Fairly low

Risk of Mispronunciation: Low

Famous Namesakes: Disney character Minnie Mouse; actress Minnie Driver; comedian Minnie Pearl; singer Minnie Ripperton

Common Nicknames: None

Common Variations: Minny

Consider This: Because Minnie has its limitations, consider using it as a nickname rather than a given name.

Miranda ★★★★

(Latin) strange; wonderful; admirable.

First Impression: Miranda is considered a complex personality because she's sociable, shy, and bossy at different times.

Gender Association: Used for girls

Popularity and Trend: #139 (#112 in 2000)

Risk of Misspelling: Fairly low

Risk of Mispronunciation: Low

Famous Namesakes: Character Miranda Hobbes (*Sex and the City*) actress Miranda Richardson; character Miranda Bailey (*Grey's Anatomy*); singer Miranda Lambert; model Miranda Kerr; actress Miranda Otto

Common Nicknames: Randi, Mira

Common Variations: Meranda

Consider This: After being in the Top 100 in the '90s, Miranda's popularity has slipped a bit this decade.

Mireille ★★

(Hebrew) God spoke. (Latin) wonderful.

First Impression: This name reminds people of a studious and bookish wallflower.

Gender Association: Used for girls

Popularity and Trend: Never been
ranked in Top 1000
Risk of Misspelling: High
Risk of Mispronunciation: High
Famous Namesakes: Singer Mireille
Mathieu
Common Nicknames: None
Common Variations: Mirella
Consider This: Beware of spelling
and pronunciation trouble with
this tricky name pronounced
"meer-AY."

Miriam ★★★

(Hebrew) bitter; sea of bitterness.
First Impression: Miriam is seen as a
grandmother who lives a simple,
moral, and sometimes boring life.
Gender Association: Used for girls
Popularity and Trend: #292
(#281 in 2000)
Risk of Misspelling: Fairly low
Risk of Mispronunciation: Fairly low
Famous Namesakes: Biblical figure
Miriam; actress Miriam Margoyles
Common Nicknames: Mimi, Miri,
Mitzi
Common Variations: Mariam
Consider This: This form of Mary
sounds somewhat old-fashioned,
though it's moderately popular
today.

Missy ★★★

(English) a familiar form of
Melissa, Millicent.

First Impression: Some say Missy is
annoying and some say she's big-
hearted.
Gender Association: Used for girls
Popularity and Trend: Last ranked in
the Top 1000 in the 1980s
Risk of Misspelling: Low
Risk of Mispronunciation: Low
Famous Namesakes: Singer Missy
Higgins; rapper Missy Elliot;
model Missy Rayder
Common Nicknames: None
Common Variations: None
Consider This: Not surprisingly, Missy
is best reserved as a nickname.

Misty ★★

(English) shrouded by mist.
First Impression: People think Misty
is a trampy and trashy Las Vegas
stripper who has stringy, bleached-
blond hair with dark roots.
Gender Association: Used for girls
Popularity and Trend: Last ranked in
the Top 1000 in the 1980s
Risk of Misspelling: Low
Risk of Mispronunciation: Low
Famous Namesakes: Singer Misty
Edwards
Common Nicknames: None
Common Variations: Misti
Consider This: Yikes! Do you want
people to automatically assume
your daughter is a stripper?

Mitzi ★★

(German) a familiar form of Mary,
Miriam.

First Impression: Mitzi is described as
a dumb but sweet blond who's
thin, short, and blue-eyed.
Gender Association: Used for girls
Popularity and Trend: Last ranked in
the Top 1000 in the 1970s
Risk of Misspelling: Average
Risk of Mispronunciation: Low
Famous Namesakes: Actress Mitzi
Kapture; actress Mitzi Gaynor
Common Nicknames: None
Common Variations: None
Consider This: Mitzi's dumb blond
image may be the reason this
name dropped off the Top 1000
list decades ago.

Modesta ★★★★

(Italian, Spanish) a form of
Modesty.
First Impression: People say Modesta
proves that modesty and confi-
dence aren't mutually exclusive
qualities.
Gender Association: Used for girls
Popularity and Trend: Never been
ranked in Top 1000
Risk of Misspelling: Fairly low
Risk of Mispronunciation: Fairly low
Famous Namesakes: Saint Modesta
Common Nicknames: None
Common Variations: None
Consider This: Although it's a unique
name, Modesta creates good
vibes because it makes such a
positive impression.

Modesty ★★★★

(Latin) modest.

First Impression: It's no surprise people think Modesty is coy, sweet, innocent, and, of course, modest.

Gender Association: Used for girls

Popularity and Trend: Never been ranked in Top 1000

Risk of Misspelling: Low

Risk of Mispronunciation: Low

Famous Namesakes: Comic strip character Modesty Blaise

Common Nicknames: None

Common Variations: Modesta, Modestine

Consider This: Like Modesta, Modesty gives off good vibes, but it benefits from having easier spelling and pronunciation.

Moira ★★

(Irish) great. A form of Mary.

First Impression: Moira is imagined to be a dorky math wiz loaded with book smarts and logic.

Gender Association: Used for girls

Popularity and Trend: Last ranked in the Top 1000 in the 1960s

Risk of Misspelling: Average

Risk of Mispronunciation: Average

Famous Namesakes: Actress Moira Shearer; actress Moira Kelly

Common Nicknames: None

Common Variations: Maura

Consider This: Spelling and pronunciation may be a bit tricky for this name.

Molly ★★★★

(Irish) a familiar form of Mary.

First Impression: Molly is considered delightfully demure.

Gender Association: Used for girls

Popularity and Trend: #105 (#95 in 2000)

Risk of Misspelling: Fairly low

Risk of Mispronunciation: Low

Famous Namesakes: Actress Molly Ringwald; comedian Molly Shannon

Common Nicknames: None

Common Variations: Molli

Consider This: Technically a nickname for Mary, Molly is a popular name in its own right—even if it is a bit casual.

Mona ★★★

(Irish) noble. (Greek) a form of Monica, Ramona, Rimona.

First Impression: Forget her old age—people say Mona is alive and kickin'.

Gender Association: Used mostly for girls

Popularity and Trend: Last ranked in the Top 1000 in the 1980s

Risk of Misspelling: Low

Risk of Mispronunciation: Low

Famous Namesakes: Character Mona Robinson (*Who's the Boss?*)

Common Nicknames: None

Common Variations: Muna

Consider This: Here's a name that's perfect for a granny, but not a baby.

Monica ★★★

(Greek) solitary. (Latin) advisor.

First Impression: Monica primarily comes across as a vain, selfish, and manipulative princess. But she can be fun, popular, and even sweet.

Gender Association: Used for girls

Popularity and Trend: #250 (#167 in 2000)

Risk of Misspelling: Fairly low

Risk of Mispronunciation: Low

Famous Namesakes: Character Monica Gellar (*Friends*); R&B singer Monica; infamous White House intern Monica Lewinsky; actress Monica Potter; actress Monica Bellucci

Common Nicknames: Mona

Common Variations: Monika

Consider This: Monica has been sliding in popularity since the turn of the millennium, despite the positive namesake of Monica Geller from TV's *Friends*.

Monique ★★★

(French) a form of Monica.

First Impression: Folks advise to take Monique as she comes—the good and the bad.

Gender Association: Used for girls

Popularity and Trend: #655 (#342 in 2000)

Risk of Misspelling: Fairly low
Risk of Mispronunciation: Low
Famous Namesakes: Comedian Mo'Nique; designer Monique Lhuillier
Common Nicknames: None
Common Variations: None
Consider This: Originally a French name, Monique now has African American associations, perhaps because of comedian Mo'Nique.

Montana ★★★★

(Spanish) mountain.
First Impression: People say Montana is sassy and strong, and she doesn't like to be cooped up indoors.
Gender Association: Used mostly for girls
Popularity and Trend: #868 (#593 in 2000)
Risk of Misspelling: Low
Risk of Mispronunciation: Low
Famous Namesakes: Television character Hannah Montana
Common Nicknames: Monti
Common Variations: None
Consider This: Girls' names don't come more rugged than this one, but it still has some feminine charm.

Morgan ★★★

(Welsh) seashore.
First Impression: Morgan strikes people as a beautiful, wealthy woman who's strong to the point of being bossy and snobby to the point of being rude.
Gender Association: Used mostly for girls
Popularity and Trend: #35 (#25 in 2000)
Risk of Misspelling: Fairly low
Risk of Mispronunciation: Low
Famous Namesakes: Actress Morgan Fairchild; mythological figure Morgan le Fay
Common Nicknames: None
Common Variations: Morgen
Consider This: Morgan is a popular name, but it has a hardnosed image.

Muriel ★★★

(Arabic) myrrh. (Irish) shining sea.
First Impression: Muriel is pictured as a fun-loving and charming woman that everyone loves to be around—despite the fact that she's nerdy and unattractive with a big nose and buckteeth.
Gender Association: Used for girls
Popularity and Trend: Last ranked in the Top 1000 in the 1960s
Risk of Misspelling: Average
Risk of Mispronunciation: Average
Famous Namesakes: Character Muriel Heslop (*Muriel's Wedding*)
Common Nicknames: None
Common Variations: Meryl
Consider This: If it's a tossup between Muriel and Meryl, Muriel has a better first impression, but Meryl fares better with pronunciation.

Mya ★★★

(Burmese) emerald. (Italian) a form of Mia.
First Impression: Everyone sees Mya in a unique way, from wise and quiet to perky and loud.
Gender Association: Used for girls
Popularity and Trend: #101 (#175 in 2000)
Risk of Misspelling: Average
Risk of Mispronunciation: Average
Famous Namesakes: Singer Mya; poet Maya Angelou; comedian Maya Rudolph
Common Nicknames: None
Common Variations: Maya, Maija
Consider This: Some people might not know to pronounce this "MY-ah," and some may mistakenly spell it "Maya."

Myra ★★

(Latin) fragrant ointment.
First Impression: People say Myra proves that old brainiacs never die, they just get dorkier.
Gender Association: Used for girls
Popularity and Trend: Last ranked in the Top 1000 in the 1980s
Risk of Misspelling: Fairly low
Risk of Mispronunciation: Low
Famous Namesakes: Fiction character Myra Breckenridge
Common Nicknames: None
Common Variations: None
Consider This: This name's first impression says it all.

Myrna ★

(Irish) beloved.

First Impression: People perceive Myrna to be a cranky and rude woman with no qualms about bossing others around.

Gender Association: Used for girls

Popularity and Trend: Last ranked in the Top 1000 in the 1970s

Risk of Misspelling: Average

Risk of Mispronunciation: Average

Famous Namesakes: Actress Myrna Loy

Common Nicknames: None

Common Variations: None

Consider This: Myrna is even less desirable than Myra, due to tricky spelling and pronunciation. (While Myra is phonetically pronounced "MY-rah," Myrna is pronounced "MUR-nah.")

Nadia ★★★★

(French, Slavic) hopeful.

First Impression: Nadia is thought to be friendly and gentle but determined and focused, much like gymnast Nadia Comaneci.

Gender Association: Used for girls

Popularity and Trend: #188 (#256 in 2000)

Risk of Misspelling: Fairly low

Risk of Mispronunciation: Fairly low

Famous Namesakes: Gymnast Nadia Comaneci; character Nadia Yassir (24); character Nadia Santos (Alias); actress Nadia Bjorlin

Common Nicknames: None

Common Variations: Nadja

Consider This: The popularity of this name has climbed since Nadia Comaneci appeared at the 1976 Montreal Olympics. Pronunciation will be a minor problem between those who say "NAHD-yah" and those who say "NAH-dee-ah."

Nadine ★★

(French, Slavic) a form of Nadia.

First Impression: Nadine is regarded as a shy and aloof homebody who's single and friendless.

Gender Association: Used for girls

Popularity and Trend: Last ranked in the Top 1000 in the 1980s

Risk of Misspelling: Fairly low

Risk of Mispronunciation: Fairly low

Famous Namesakes: Novelist Nadine Gordimer; singer Nadine Coyle; actress Nadine Velazquez

Common Nicknames: None

Common Variations: Nadeen

Consider This: Without an influential namesake, this name is less popular than Nadia.

Nailah ★★

(Arabic) a form of Naila.

First Impression: People think Nailah isn't just a fashion model—she's a role model.

Gender Association: Used mostly for girls

Popularity and Trend: Never been ranked in Top 1000

Risk of Misspelling: Fairly high

Risk of Mispronunciation: Fairly high

Famous Namesakes: None

Common Nicknames: None

Common Variations: None

Consider This: Nailah is a pretty name with ugly spelling and pronunciation ("nah-EE-lah") problems.

Nancy ★★★★

(English) a form of Ann.

First Impression: Nancy is thought to be smart, curious, and hard-working, much like fictional sleuth Nancy Drew.

Gender Association: Used for girls

Popularity and Trend: #326 (#233 in 2000)

Risk of Misspelling: Fairly low

Risk of Mispronunciation: Low

Famous Namesakes: Speaker of the house Nancy Pelosi; fiction character Nancy Drew; first lady Nancy Reagan; figure skater Nancy Kerrigan; musician Nancy Wilson; talk show host Nancy Grace

Common Nicknames: None

Common Variations: Nanci

Consider This: Nancy has tumbled in popularity since the '50s, as it has become more dated.

Nanette ★★★★

(French) a form of Nancy.

First Impression: Nanette may be a polite hometown girl, but people say she won't get pushed around.

Gender Association: Used for girls

Popularity and Trend: Last ranked in the Top 1000 in the 1970s

Risk of Misspelling: Low

Risk of Mispronunciation: Fairly low

Famous Namesakes: Designer Nanette Lepore

Common Nicknames: Nettie

Common Variations: None

Consider This: This form of Nancy has a French twist, but it hasn't been popular for quite some time.

Naomi ★★★★

(Hebrew) pleasant, beautiful.

First Impression: People think Naomi is charming and as beautiful as supermodel Naomi Campbell.

Gender Association: Used for girls

Popularity and Trend: #129 (#185 in 2000)

Risk of Misspelling: Average

Risk of Mispronunciation: Average

Famous Namesakes: Actress Naomi Watts; model Naomi Campbell; singer Naomi Judd; writer Naomi Wolf

Common Nicknames: None

Common Variations: Naomie

Consider This: Naomi poses a slight challenge with spelling and pronunciation, but it helps that

there are many famous namesakes in pop culture.

Narcissa ★★

(Greek) daffodil.

First Impression: Not surprisingly, people say Narcissa is a narcissist.

Gender Association: Used for girls

Popularity and Trend: Never been ranked in Top 1000

Risk of Misspelling: Fairly low

Risk of Mispronunciation: Fairly low

Famous Namesakes: Character Narcissa Malfoy (*Harry Potter* series)

Common Nicknames: None

Common Variations: Narissa

Consider This: This name comes from the narcissus flower (which is good), but most people unfortunately think it means "narcissist" (which is bad).

Natalia ★★★★

(Russian) a form of Natalie.

First Impression: Natalia is seen as a happy woman with a quiet air of mystery.

Gender Association: Used for girls

Popularity and Trend: #94 (#219 in 2000)

Risk of Misspelling: Fairly low

Risk of Mispronunciation: Fairly low

Famous Namesakes: Ballerina Natalia Romanovna Makarova; model Natalia Vodianova

Common Nicknames: Talia

Common Variations: Natalya, Nathalia

Consider This: This beautiful variation of Natalie is quickly rising in popularity.

Natalie ★★★★★

(Latin) born on Christmas day.

First Impression: Folks think Natalie has brains behind her beauty.

Gender Association: Used for girls

Popularity and Trend: #16 (#34 in 2000)

Risk of Misspelling: Fairly low

Risk of Mispronunciation: Low

Famous Namesakes: Actress Natalie Wood; actress Natalie Portman; singer Natalie Imbruglia; singer Natalie Merchant

Common Nicknames: Natie, Nata

Common Variations: Natalee, Nathalie

Consider This: Natalie earns a near-perfect rating, but it loses points because its many common variations create spelling problems.

Natasha ★★★

(Russian) a form of Natalie.

First Impression: Natasha is thought to be a cruel, ruthless woman who's self-centered and spoiled. This name is also used stereotypically for Russian femme fatales, like Natasha of TV's *The Rocky and Bullwinkle Show*.

Gender Association: Used for girls

Popularity and Trend: #357 (#280 in 2000)

Risk of Misspelling: Fairly low

Risk of Mispronunciation: Fairly low

Famous Namesakes: Actress Natassja Kinski; actress Natasha Richardson; actress Natasha Henstridge; singer Natasha Bedingfield

Common Nicknames: Tasha, Stacy

Common Variations: Natascha

Consider This: While it earns a high rating, Natasha suffers a bit because it's often the name for stereotypical Russian villainesses in pop culture.

Neena ★★★

(Spanish) a form of Nina.

First Impression: Neena is pictured as either a sweetheart or a gold digger.

Gender Association: Used for girls

Popularity and Trend: Never been ranked in Top 1000

Risk of Misspelling: Average

Risk of Mispronunciation: Low

Famous Namesakes: Actress Neena Gupta; designer Nina Ricci; singer Nina Persson; singer Nina Gordon; singer Nina Simone

Common Nicknames: None

Common Variations: Nina

Consider This: With its uncommon spelling, Neena doesn't fare as well as Nina.

Nellie ★

(English) a familiar form of Cornelia, Eleanor, Helen, Prunella.

First Impression: Nellie is described as a bossy, snotty, and selfish blond with ringlets, much like character Nellie Oleson of TV's *Little House on the Prairie*.

Gender Association: Used mostly for girls

Popularity and Trend: Last ranked in the Top 1000 in the 1970s

Risk of Misspelling: Average

Risk of Mispronunciation: Low

Famous Namesakes: Character Nellie Oleson (*Little House on the Prairie*); journalist Nellie Bly; singer Nellie McKay; singer Nelly Furtado

Common Nicknames: None

Common Variations: Nelly

Consider This: It's amazing to think that *Little House on the Prairie* character Nellie Oleson still affects this name's image. Also, spelling may be a problem, with people not knowing whether it's "Nellie" or "Nelly."

Nerissa ★★★

(Greek) sea nymph.

First Impression: People say Nerissa is a dainty, sexy woman with dark hair and dark skin.

Gender Association: Used for girls

Popularity and Trend: Never been ranked in Top 1000

Risk of Misspelling: Fairly low

Risk of Mispronunciation: Fairly low

Famous Namesakes: Character Nerissa (*The Merchant of Venice*)

Common Nicknames: Rissa

Common Variations: Narissa

Consider This: Only Shakespeare buffs are familiar with this name.

Nessa ★★★★

(Scandinavian) promontory. (Greek) a form of Agnes.

First Impression: Opinions are split: Nessa could be caring, melancholy, or spunky.

Gender Association: Used for girls

Popularity and Trend: Never been ranked in Top 1000

Risk of Misspelling: Low

Risk of Mispronunciation: Low

Famous Namesakes: Singer Nessa Morgan

Common Nicknames: Nessie

Common Variations: Nesha

Consider This: Head to head, Nessa rates higher than Nerissa, possibly because it's easier to spell and pronounce.

Nevaeh ★★

(American) the word heaven spelled backward.

First Impression: Some say Nevaeh is smart; others say she's not a great thinker.

Gender Association: Used for girls

Popularity and Trend: #43 (#266 in 2001)

Risk of Misspelling: Fairly high

Risk of Mispronunciation: High

Famous Namesakes: None

Common Nicknames: None

Common Variations: None

Consider This: With Nevaeh's hellish pronunciation (it could be "NEV-ah," "neh-VAY-ah," or "neh-VYE-ah") and spelling, why not just choose the name Heaven over this backward variation?

Nia ★★★
(Irish) a form of Neila.
First Impression: Nia is viewed as a soft-spoken college student.
Gender Association: Used for girls
Popularity and Trend: #380 (#307 in 2000)
Risk of Misspelling: Fairly low
Risk of Mispronunciation: Fairly low
Famous Namesakes: Actress Nia Long; actress Nia Peeples
Common Nicknames: None
Common Variations: Nya
Consider This: This name is pronounced "NEE-ah," but some may mistake it for "NYE-ah."

Nicole ★★★★
(French) a form of Nicholas.
First Impression: Nicole is described as a stuck-up, rude, and intolerable woman who doesn't have many friends.
Gender Association: Used mostly for girls
Popularity and Trend: #74 (#31 in 2000)
Risk of Misspelling: Fairly low
Risk of Mispronunciation: Low
Famous Namesakes: Actress Nicole Kidman; socialite Nicole Richie; singer Nicole Scherzinger; designer Nicole Miller
Common Nicknames: Nikki, Colette, Nico, Colie
Common Variations: Nichol, Nicolette, Nickole, Nicola
Consider This: Nicole has a wide variety of nicknames, and perhaps that versatility adds to its popularity.

Nicolette ★★★
(French) a form of Nicole.
First Impression: People see Nicolette as a blond who could be ditzy, independent, snooty, or wild.
Gender Association: Used for girls
Popularity and Trend: #997 (#589 in 2000)
Risk of Misspelling: Fairly low
Risk of Mispronunciation: Low
Famous Namesakes: Actress Nicolette Sheridan
Common Nicknames: Colette, Nikki, Nico, Colie
Common Variations: Nicholette, Nikolette
Consider This: Considering that Nicole is such a popular name, it's surprising that this variation barely makes the Top 1000.

Nidia ★★
(Latin) nest.
First Impression: No matter how unpleasant she may be, people can't get enough of this popular party girl.
Gender Association: Used for girls
Popularity and Trend: Never been ranked in Top 1000
Risk of Misspelling: Average
Risk of Mispronunciation: Average
Famous Namesakes: Professional wrestler Nidia
Common Nicknames: None
Common Variations: None
Consider This: Nidia is uncommon but not unheard of, so it's odd that it's never made the Top 1000. Some may pronounce it "NID-ee-ah," but others pronounce it "NEE-dee-ah."

Nike ★★
(Greek) victorious.
First Impression: It may seem obvious, but people imagine Nike is a sports nut who's cocky, bull-headed, and competitive.
Gender Association: Used about equally for girls and boys
Popularity and Trend: Never been ranked in Top 1000
Risk of Misspelling: Fairly low
Risk of Mispronunciation: Fairly low
Famous Namesakes: Mythological figure Nike
Common Nicknames: None
Common Variations: None
Consider This: Nike is synonymous with sports, and judging from the first impression, the bad side of sports. Plus, it's used equally for boys and girls, which may

pose a problem for parents searching for names with clear gender associations.

Nikita ★★★

(Russian) victorious people.

First Impression: Nikita is seen as a gorgeous Russian woman who's self-possessed and cool.

Gender Association: Used mostly for girls

Popularity and Trend: Last ranked #883 in 2000

Risk of Misspelling: Fairly low

Risk of Mispronunciation: Fairly low

Famous Namesakes: Character Nikita (*La Femme Nikita*); premier Nikita Khrushchev

Common Nicknames: Nikki, Nik

Common Variations: Nakita, Nikkita

Consider This: Because Nikita is primarily thought to be a Russian name, you may need to consider its fit with your last name and family heritage.

Nikki ★★

(American) a familiar form of Nicole.

First Impression: Nikki is considered the picture-perfect mean girl.

Gender Association: Used mostly for girls

Popularity and Trend: Last ranked in the Top 1000 in the 1980s

Risk of Misspelling: Fairly high

Risk of Mispronunciation: Low

Famous Namesakes: Model Niki Taylor; actress Nikki Cox; poet Nikki Giovanni; actress Nikki Reed

Common Nicknames: Nik

Common Variations: Niki, Nicky, Nicki

Consider This: Nikki conjures up images of a teenage diva you probably don't want your daughter to become. Spelling will be a problem as well, given that there are many ways to spell this familiar form of Nicole.

Nina ★★★★

(Spanish) girl. (Native American) mighty. (Hebrew) a form of Hannah.

First Impression: This lively Latina is regarded as a real firecracker.

Gender Association: Used for girls

Popularity and Trend: #272 (#221 in 2000)

Risk of Misspelling: Fairly low

Risk of Mispronunciation: Low

Famous Namesakes: Singer Nina Simone; actress Neena Gupta; designer Nina Ricci; singer Nina Persson; singer Nina Gordon

Common Nicknames: None

Common Variations: Neena

Consider This: No doubt because *niña* means "girl" in Spanish, this name has a Latino association.

Noel ★★★

(Latin) Christmas.

First Impression: People think Noel uses her talents and gifts for her faith.

Gender Association: Used mostly for boys

Popularity and Trend: Last ranked in the Top 1000 in the 1990s

Risk of Misspelling: Average

Risk of Mispronunciation: Average

Famous Namesakes: Musician Noel Gallagher; composer Noel Coward

Common Nicknames: Noely

Common Variations: Noelle

Consider This: Noel ("noh-ELL"), the girls' name, could be confused for Noel ("NOH-ell"), the boys' name.

Nola ★★★

(Latin) small bell. (Irish) famous; noble.

First Impression: She may be smart and sweet, but people believe Nola is paralyzed by anxiety.

Gender Association: Used for girls

Popularity and Trend: Last ranked in the Top 1000 in the 1960s

Risk of Misspelling: Low

Risk of Mispronunciation: Low

Famous Namesakes: Actress Nola Fairbanks

Common Nicknames: None

Common Variations: Nolana

Consider This: Nola seems to be a mousy name, especially compared to the similar-sounding Lola.

Nora ★★★
(Greek) light.

First Impression: Nora is viewed as either boring or dry, and because of writers Nora Roberts and Nora Ephron, she's likely the literary type.

Gender Association: Used for girls

Popularity and Trend: #245 (#501 in 2000)

Risk of Misspelling: Fairly low

Risk of Mispronunciation: Low

Famous Namesakes: Author Nora Roberts; writer Nora Ephron; singer Norah Jones

Common Nicknames: None

Common Variations: Norah

Consider This: Nora has made a huge leap in popularity since 2000, and thanks to singer Norah Jones, both spellings are moving up.

Noreen ★★
(Irish) a form of Eleanor, Nora. (Latin) a form of Norma.

First Impression: Noreen is seen simply as a dweeb.

Gender Association: Used for girls

Popularity and Trend: Last ranked in the Top 1000 in the 1970s

Risk of Misspelling: Low

Risk of Mispronunciation: Low

Famous Namesakes: Author Noreen Ayres

Common Nicknames: None

Common Variations: None

Consider This: Ouch! The first impression of Noreen is definitely not cool.

Norell ★★
(Scandinavian) from the north.

First Impression: Folks think Norell may be friendly and sporty or bland and dorky.

Gender Association: Used for girls

Popularity and Trend: Never been ranked in Top 1000

Risk of Misspelling: Average

Risk of Mispronunciation: Average

Famous Namesakes: None

Common Nicknames: None

Common Variations: None

Consider This: Most often used as a last name, Norell may give off mixed vibes as a first name. Some people may pronounce it "NOR-ell" instead of "noh-RELL."

Norma ★★★
(Latin) rule, precept.

First Impression: It may be hard for people to see Norma as anything but a pill.

Gender Association: Used for girls

Popularity and Trend: Last ranked in the Top 1000 in the 1980s

Risk of Misspelling: Low

Risk of Mispronunciation: Low

Famous Namesakes: Actress Norma Jean Baker, birth name of Marilyn Monroe; designer Norma Kamali; movie character Norma Rae

Common Nicknames: None

Common Variations: None

Consider This: Norma is thought to be an outdated name with a cranky image.

Nyssa ★★★
(Greek) beginning.

First Impression: People say Nyssa makes a good impression at work, at home, and on the street.

Gender Association: Used for girls

Popularity and Trend: Never been ranked in Top 1000

Risk of Misspelling: Average

Risk of Mispronunciation: Average

Famous Namesakes: Character Nyssa of Traken (*Dr. Who*)

Common Nicknames: None

Common Variations: Nyasia

Consider This: Compared to Nerissa and Nessa, Nyssa has a good vibe, but it does pose spelling and pronunciation problems. It may be pronounced "NISS-ah" or "NYE-sah."

Nyx ★★
(Greek) night.

First Impression: Nyx is pictured as a dark mystery who may be depressed and lonely.

Gender Association: Used for girls

Popularity and Trend: Never been ranked in Top 1000

Risk of Misspelling: Average

Risk of Mispronunciation: Low
Famous Namesakes: Mythological figure Nyx
Common Nicknames: None
Common Variations: None
Consider This: Whether it's a conscious or subconscious nod to the Greek goddess of night, people conjure up dark, mysterious, and ultimately sad images of Nyx.

Oceana ★★

(Greek) ocean.
First Impression: Oceana is viewed as quiet and a little mysterious, which leads people to wonder whether she's a hippie, mermaid, or normal gal.
Gender Association: Used for girls
Popularity and Trend: Never been ranked in Top 1000
Risk of Misspelling: Fairly low
Risk of Mispronunciation: Average
Famous Namesakes: None
Common Nicknames: None
Common Variations: None
Consider This: For such a seemingly simple name, pronunciation ("oh-shee-AHN-ah") may not be as easy as you'd think.

Octavia ★★★

(Latin) eighth.
First Impression: Folks find the word *sharp* describes Octavia in several ways, because she's smart, fearless, and somewhat surly.

Gender Association: Used for girls
Popularity and Trend: Last ranked in the Top 1000 in the 1990s
Risk of Misspelling: Fairly low
Risk of Mispronunciation: Fairly low
Famous Namesakes: Historical figure Octavia Minor; social reformer Octavia Hill
Common Nicknames: None
Common Variations: Otavia, Octaviana
Consider This: Octavia is a name full of leadership and strength, but as the first impression shows, sometimes power can be seen as a negative trait.

Odele ★★

(Greek) melody, song.
First Impression: People think this little old lady may be shy or jolly.
Gender Association: Used for girls
Popularity and Trend: Never been ranked in Top 1000
Risk of Misspelling: Average
Risk of Mispronunciation: Fairly low
Famous Namesakes: None
Common Nicknames: None
Common Variations: Odelette
Consider This: One may expect to spell this "Odelle," so "Odele" has a slightly counterintuitive spelling with only one *l*.

Odera ★★

(Hebrew) plough.
First Impression: Odera is described as a creative—if not bizarre—woman with an open mind, a warm heart, and perhaps a tough childhood.
Gender Association: Used for girls
Popularity and Trend: Never been ranked in Top 1000
Risk of Misspelling: Average
Risk of Mispronunciation: Fairly low
Famous Namesakes: None
Common Nicknames: None
Common Variations: None
Consider This: Playground teasing alert—think twice about naming your daughter something that sounds so similar to the word *odor*.

Oletha ★★★

(Scandinavian) nimble.
First Impression: Oletha is considered a family-oriented woman who's loving but often too critical and old-fashioned.
Gender Association: Used for girls
Popularity and Trend: Never been ranked in Top 1000
Risk of Misspelling: Fairly low
Risk of Mispronunciation: Fairly low
Famous Namesakes: None
Common Nicknames: None
Common Variations: Yaletha
Consider This: The first impression indicates that people find this uncommon name to be old-fashioned, much like Odele.

Olga ★★
(Scandinavian) holy.

First Impression: People say Olga is a big, burly, and homely foreigner whose personality matches her appearance.

Gender Association: Used for girls

Popularity and Trend: Last ranked in the Top 1000 in the 1990s

Risk of Misspelling: Low

Risk of Mispronunciation: Low

Famous Namesakes: Gymnast Olga Korbut

Common Nicknames: None

Common Variations: None

Consider This: Olga is one of those names that brings to mind shot-putting foreigners with stern faces.

Olive ★★★★★
(Latin) olive tree.

First Impression: Olive is seen as cheery and maybe a little cheeky.

Gender Association: Used for girls

Popularity and Trend: Last ranked in the Top 1000 in the 1950s

Risk of Misspelling: Low

Risk of Mispronunciation: Low

Famous Namesakes: Character Olive Oyl (*Popeye*); character Olive (*Little Miss Sunshine*)

Common Nicknames: Ollie, Liv

Common Variations: Olivia

Consider This: Olive is very similar to Olivia in many respects, but it's not on the Top 1000 list while Olivia is #7. Comparing famous namesake Olive Oyl with Olivia Newton-John may explain the huge difference in popularity.

Olivia ★★★★★
(Latin) a form of Olive. (English) a form of Olga.

First Impression: Most people—but not all—say there's everything to like about Olivia.

Gender Association: Used for girls

Popularity and Trend: #7 (#16 in 2000)

Risk of Misspelling: Fairly low

Risk of Mispronunciation: Low

Famous Namesakes: Singer Olivia Newton-John; R&B singer Olivia; actress Olivia de Havilland; actress Olivia Hussey; actress Olivia Wilde

Common Nicknames: Ollie, Liv, Livia

Common Variations: Alivia, Olyvia

Consider This: Olivia gets good scores all around, which is why it's a Top 10 name.

Olympia ★★★★
(Greek) heavenly.

First Impression: The first Olympic Games were held in the ancient city of Olympia, Greece, which means this name's image carries an athletic spirit.

Gender Association: Used for girls

Popularity and Trend: Never been ranked in Top 1000

Risk of Misspelling: Low

Risk of Mispronunciation: Low

Famous Namesakes: Actress Olympia Dukakis; social reformer Olympia de Gouges; senator Olympia Snowe

Common Nicknames: None

Common Variations: None

Consider This: Olympia has never been ranked in the Top 1000, perhaps because it's a rather lofty name for a small child.

Onella ★★★
(Hungarian) a form of Helen.

First Impression: Onella is viewed as a groovy "granola" gal.

Gender Association: Used for girls

Popularity and Trend: Never been ranked in Top 1000

Risk of Misspelling: Fairly low

Risk of Mispronunciation: Fairly low

Famous Namesakes: None

Common Nicknames: None

Common Variations: None

Consider This: The hippie image for this uncommon name is positive, but it does suggest that people feel Onella is…different.

Opal ★★★
(Hindi) precious stone.

First Impression: Opal is considered either a mousy older lady sitting on a park bench, or a high-strung career woman sitting in a board-room.

Gender Association: Used for girls

Popularity and Trend: Last ranked in the Top 1000 in the 1960s

Risk of Misspelling: Low

Risk of Mispronunciation: Low

Famous Namesakes: Character Opal Gardner (*All My Children*)

Common Nicknames: None

Common Variations: Opalina

Consider This: The first impression paints pictures of two very different women, which means this name is hard to classify.

Ophelia ★★★

(Greek) helper.

First Impression: With Shakespeare's Ophelia from *Hamlet* in mind, people say she's vulnerable and tragic, yet loyal.

Gender Association: Used for girls

Popularity and Trend: Last ranked in the Top 1000 in the 1950s

Risk of Misspelling: Fairly low

Risk of Mispronunciation: Fairly low

Famous Namesakes: Character Ophelia (*Hamlet*)

Common Nicknames: None

Common Variations: Ofelia

Consider This: Even Shakespeare buffs may be wary of choosing this name and all its tragic connotations.

Oprah ★★★★

(Hebrew) a form of Orpah.

First Impression: There's no doubt people think of talk show queen Oprah Winfrey when they hear this name.

Gender Association: Used for girls

Popularity and Trend: Never been ranked in Top 1000

Risk of Misspelling: Low

Risk of Mispronunciation: Low

Famous Namesakes: Talk show host Oprah Winfrey

Common Nicknames: None

Common Variations: None

Consider This: Oprah Winfrey is one of the most positive role models in pop culture, yet this name has never made the Top 1000.

Orella ★★

(Latin) announcement from the gods; oracle.

First Impression: People say Orella is a dumb country girl who found herself a rich husband (thanks to her sexy figure).

Gender Association: Used for girls

Popularity and Trend: Never been ranked in Top 1000

Risk of Misspelling: Fairly low

Risk of Mispronunciation: Fairly low

Famous Namesakes: None

Common Nicknames: None

Common Variations: None

Consider This: Head to head with the first impression for Onella, Orella certainly comes out on the bottom.

Othelia ★★

(Spanish) rich.

First Impression: To many, Othelia may be a shy loner or a domineering drama teacher.

Gender Association: Used for girls

Popularity and Trend: Never been ranked in Top 1000

Risk of Misspelling: Fairly low

Risk of Mispronunciation: Fairly low

Famous Namesakes: None

Common Nicknames: None

Common Variations: None

Consider This: Othelia has a vibe much like Ophelia, but it lacks literary cachet.

Paige ★★★★

(English) young child.

First Impression: For being so young, Paige is seen as quite poised.

Gender Association: Used mostly for girls

Popularity and Trend: #76 (#69 in 2000)

Risk of Misspelling: Fairly low

Risk of Mispronunciation: Low

Famous Namesakes: TV host Paige Davis; actress Paige Moss; actress Paige Turco

Common Nicknames: None

Common Variations: Payge, Page

Consider This: True to its definition, Paige has a positive, youthful connotation that's typically achieved only by nicknames.

Pamela ★★★

(Greek) honey.

First Impression: People immediately imagine Pamela as dense and dumb, but also sweet and funny in a perky way, perhaps like sex symbol Pamela Anderson.

Gender Association: Used for girls

Popularity and Trend: #530 (#456 in 2000)

Risk of Misspelling: Low

Risk of Mispronunciation: Low

Famous Namesakes: Actress Pamela Anderson; actress Pamela Reed; author Pamela Des Barres; actress Pamela Sue Martin

Common Nicknames: Pam, Pammy

Common Variations: None

Consider This: Although Pamela isn't a stripper stage name like Bambi or Misty, it clearly makes people think of sex-symbol Pamela Anderson, which may be an uncomfortable burden for your daughter.

Pandita ★

(Hindi) scholar.

First Impression: People may think of *bandida* when they hear the name Pandita—why else would they imagine a cunning and sneaky Mexican thief?

Gender Association: Used for girls

Popularity and Trend: Never been ranked in Top 1000

Risk of Misspelling: Fairly high

Risk of Mispronunciation: Fairly high

Famous Namesakes: Social reformer Pandita Ramabai

Common Nicknames: None

Common Variations: None

Consider This: This Hindi name is closely related to and pronounced much like the English word *pundit*, but people seem to think it's like the Spanish word *bandida*.

Pansy ★★

(Greek) flower; fragrant. (French) thoughtful.

First Impression: Folks say Pansy lives up—or perhaps *down*—to her wimpy name.

Gender Association: Used for girls

Popularity and Trend: Last ranked in the Top 1000 in the 1950s

Risk of Misspelling: Low

Risk of Mispronunciation: Low

Famous Namesakes: Character Pansy Parkinson (*Harry Potter* series)

Common Nicknames: None

Common Variations: None

Consider This: Don't count on anyone to remember a pansy is a flower—most people say it's slang for *wimp*.

Paris ★★★

(French) the capital of France.

First Impression: Socialite Paris Hilton is famous simply for being famous, and it's hard for people to separate this name's image from hers.

Gender Association: Used mostly for girls

Popularity and Trend: #260 (#474 in 2000)

Risk of Misspelling: Low

Risk of Mispronunciation: Low

Famous Namesakes: Socialite Paris Hilton; character Paris (*Romeo and Juliet*); mythological figure Paris

Common Nicknames: None

Common Variations: Parris

Consider This: Although this name is more popular today than in 2000, recently it has slid from its peak at #157 in 2004, thanks to Paris Hilton's scandals.

Pat ★

(Latin) a short form of Patricia, Patsy.

First Impression: Like the androgynous sketch character played by Julia Sweeney on *Saturday Night Live*, people say Pat is a frumpy, friendless woman.

Gender Association: Used about equally for girls and boys

Popularity and Trend: Last ranked in the Top 1000 in the 1960s

Risk of Misspelling: Low

Risk of Mispronunciation: Low

Famous Namesakes: First lady Pat Nixon; *Saturday Night Live* character Pat

Common Nicknames: None

Common Variations: None

Consider This: With the unforgettable *SNL* character Pat, this name has become synonymous with androgyny. It's used equally for boys and girls, which may pose a problem for parents searching for names with clear gender associations.

Patience ★★★★

(English) patient.

First Impression: People believe Patience hides away in the periodicals, but she's a gentle soul when you get to know her.

Gender Association: Used for girls

Popularity and Trend: #580 (#897 in 2000)

Risk of Misspelling: Low

Risk of Mispronunciation: Low

Famous Namesakes: Character Patience Phillips (*Catwoman*)

Common Nicknames: Patia

Common Variations: None

Consider This: This virtue name is gaining popularity, but it has a mousier image than, say, Hope or Charity.

Patrice ★★★

(French) a form of Patricia.

First Impression: Folks believe Patrice has quiet kindness.

Gender Association: Used mostly for girls

Popularity and Trend: Last ranked in the Top 1000 in the 1990s

Risk of Misspelling: Fairly low

Risk of Mispronunciation: Fairly low

Famous Namesakes: Prime minister Patrice Lumumba

Common Nicknames: Pat, Patty

Common Variations: None

Consider This: Aside from the fact that Patrice has dropped out of the Top 1000, there's not much difference between Patricia and this French variation.

Patricia ★★★★

(Latin) noblewoman.

First Impression: Patricia strikes people as a calm, comforting woman with green eyes, blond hair, and a short, stocky build.

Gender Association: Used for girls

Popularity and Trend: #413 (#228 in 2000)

Risk of Misspelling: Fairly low

Risk of Mispronunciation: Low

Famous Namesakes: Actress Patricia Heaton; actress Patricia Arquette; singer Patricia Kaas; designer Patricia Field; model Patricia Velasquez

Common Nicknames: Pat, Patty, Tricia, Patia, Patsy, Trish

Common Variations: Patrisha, Patrice

Consider This: Patricia enjoyed Top 20 popularity from the '30s through the '60s, now making it seem "old" to contemporary parents' ears.

Patti ★★

(English) a familiar form of Patricia.

First Impression: People say Patti may be a funny gal, a mean backstabber, or a withdrawn wallflower.

Gender Association: Used for girls

Popularity and Trend: Last ranked in the Top 1000 in the 1970s

Risk of Misspelling: Average

Risk of Mispronunciation: Low

Famous Namesakes: Actress Patty Duke; heiress Patty Hearst; singer Patti LaBelle; singer Patty Griffin; musician Patti Smith

Common Nicknames: None

Common Variations: Patty

Consider This: Patti has two main trouble spots: It's tricky to spell because Patty is an equally popular variation, and it's quite casual as a diminutive form of Patricia.

Paula ★★★★

(Latin) small.

First Impression: Paula is considered so smart, she may be nerdy, and so polite, she may be rigid.

Gender Association: Used for girls

Popularity and Trend: #671 (#572 in 2000)

Risk of Misspelling: Low

Risk of Mispronunciation: Low

Famous Namesakes: Singer Paula Abdul; news anchor Paula Zahn;

cook Paula Deen; actress Paula Patton; singer Paula Cole

Common Nicknames: Paulette, Polly

Common Variations: Paulina, Pauline

Consider This: Like many names that begin "Pa-," Paula creates a first impression of a withdrawn woman.

Paulette ★★★

(Latin) a form of Paula.

First Impression: People think Paulette may be a smart but withdrawn geek, a caring and friendly kindergarten teacher, or a snooty and posh Parisian.

Gender Association: Used for girls

Popularity and Trend: Last ranked in the Top 1000 in the 1980s

Risk of Misspelling: Low

Risk of Mispronunciation: Low

Famous Namesakes: Actress Paulette Goddard; country singer Paulette Carlson

Common Nicknames: Polly

Common Variations: None

Consider This: The image for Paulette seems as nerdy as Paula's and as affectionate as Pauline's, but the "-ette" suffix gives it a French air.

Pauline ★★★★

(French) a form of Paula.

First Impression: This name gives the impression of an affectionate, caring, and jolly woman who's most likely a nurse.

Gender Association: Used for girls

Popularity and Trend: Last ranked in the Top 1000 in the 1990s

Risk of Misspelling: Low

Risk of Mispronunciation: Low

Famous Namesakes: Critic Pauline Kael; poet Pauline Johnson; actress Pauline Collins

Common Nicknames: Polly

Common Variations: Paulina

Consider This: Compared to Paula and Paulette, Pauline gives off positive vibes.

Pavla ★★★

(Czech, Russian) a form of Paula.

First Impression: Pavla is perceived as a strong, practical Russian woman with self-control.

Gender Association: Used for girls

Popularity and Trend: Never been ranked in Top 1000

Risk of Misspelling: Fairly low

Risk of Mispronunciation: Fairly low

Famous Namesakes: Filmmaker Pavla Fleischer

Common Nicknames: None

Common Variations: None

Consider This: As the first impression suggests, Pavla is primarily thought of as an ethnic name.

Paz ★★★

(Spanish) peace.

First Impression: People think Paz is good-humored and jolly, but she's also as passive and peaceful as her name suggests.

Gender Association: Used mostly for girls

Popularity and Trend: Never been ranked in Top 1000

Risk of Misspelling: Average

Risk of Mispronunciation: Average

Famous Namesakes: Actress Paz Vega; poet Octavio Paz

Common Nicknames: None

Common Variations: None

Consider This: Spanish for "peace," Paz is most likely used by Latino families. Some people unfamiliar with Spanish may not realize it's pronounced "pahs."

Pearl ★★★

(Latin) jewel.

First Impression: Pearl is viewed as either a little old lady who'll invite you for tea, or she's an outspoken waitress who'll top off your coffee.

Gender Association: Used for girls

Popularity and Trend: Last ranked in the Top 1000 in the 1980s

Risk of Misspelling: Low

Risk of Mispronunciation: Low

Famous Namesakes: Author Pearl S. Buck; singer Pearl Bailey

Common Nicknames: Pearlie

Common Variations: Perla

Consider This: For such a pretty name, Pearl has elderly and rough working-class connotations.

Peggy ★★★

(Greek) a familiar form of Margaret.

First Impression: Peggy is described as naïve and happy, but she sometimes rubs people the wrong way.

Gender Association: Used for girls

Popularity and Trend: Last ranked in the Top 1000 in the 1990s

Risk of Misspelling: Low

Risk of Mispronunciation: Low

Famous Namesakes: Columnist Peggy Noonan; actress Peggy Lipton; singer Peggy Lee

Common Nicknames: Peg

Common Variations: None

Consider This: Quite popular from the '30s to the '60s, this nickname for Margaret has fallen off the radar as a given name.

Penelope ★★★★

(Greek) weaver.

First Impression: This name calls to mind an adventurous, intelligent woman with childlike energy and a love for exploring.

Gender Association: Used for girls

Popularity and Trend: #481 (#944 in 2001)

Risk of Misspelling: Fairly low

Risk of Mispronunciation: Fairly low

Famous Namesakes: Actress Penelope Cruz; actress Penelope Ann Miller; character Penelope (The Odyssey)

Common Nicknames: Pennie

Common Variations: None

Consider This: After falling out of the Top 1000 in the '80s, Penelope has made a huge surge recently.

Pennie ★★★

(Greek) a familiar form of Penelope, Peninah.

First Impression: Some may say this loving and spirited Pennie is from heaven.

Gender Association: Used for girls

Popularity and Trend: Last ranked in the Top 1000 in the 1960s

Risk of Misspelling: Average

Risk of Mispronunciation: Low

Famous Namesakes: Director Penny Marshall; photographer Pennie Smith; character Penny Lane (Almost Famous)

Common Nicknames: None

Common Variations: Penny

Consider This: Pennie isn't popular as a given name, but its positive image still shines through. Spelling may be confused for "Penny."

Petula ★★★

(Latin) seeker.

First Impression: People say Petula is sweet yet meek and wholesome yet gullible.

Gender Association: Used for girls

Popularity and Trend: Never been ranked in Top 1000

Risk of Misspelling: Fairly low

Risk of Mispronunciation: Fairly low

Famous Namesakes: Singer Petula Clark

Common Nicknames: None

Common Variations: None

Consider This: Petula's image doesn't recall singer Petula Clark, its one and only namesake, which suggests that the sound of the name itself invokes an impression.

Phaedra ★★

(Greek) bright.

First Impression: Deep down, Phaedra is depicted as a passionate go-getter, but she comes across as reserved.

Gender Association: Used for girls

Popularity and Trend: Never been ranked in Top 1000

Risk of Misspelling: Fairly high

Risk of Mispronunciation: Average

Famous Namesakes: Mythological figure Phaedra

Common Nicknames: None

Common Variations: None

Consider This: Because most people aren't familiar with Phaedra from mythology, spelling this name is daunting.

Phoebe ★★★★

(Greek) shining.

First Impression: Phoebe is described as bohemian and scatterbrained, yet funny, much like Phoebe Buffay of TV's Friends.

Gender Association: Used for girls

Popularity and Trend: #366
(#440 in 2000)
Risk of Misspelling: Fairly low
Risk of Mispronunciation: Fairly low
Famous Namesakes: Character Phoebe
Buffay (*Friends*); actress Phoebe
Cates
Common Nicknames: None
Common Variations: Phebe
Consider This: Phoebe from *Friends*
gives this old-fashioned name a
wacky yet hip appeal.

Phylicia ★★★

(Latin) fortunate; happy. (Greek) a
form of Felicia.

First Impression: People imagine
Phylicia to be a dark-haired and
attractive African American
woman who's ambitious, profes-
sional, and always in charge.
Gender Association: Used for girls
Popularity and Trend: Last ranked in
the Top 1000 in the 1990s
Risk of Misspelling: Average
Risk of Mispronunciation: Fairly low
Famous Namesakes: Actress Phylicia
Rashád; character Felicia Forrester
(*The Bold and the Beautiful*)
Common Nicknames: None
Common Variations: Philicia, Felicia
Consider This: Both Phylicia and
Felicia (which may be easier to
spell) have African American
associations.

Phyllis ★★

(Greek) green bough.
First Impression: People think Phyllis
may get meaner with age, or she
may be goodhearted and witty.
Gender Association: Used for girls
Popularity and Trend: Last ranked in
the Top 1000 in the 1980s
Risk of Misspelling: Fairly low
Risk of Mispronunciation: Low
Famous Namesakes: Comedian
Phyllis Diller; activist Phyllis
Schlafly; character Phyllis
Lindstrom (*The Mary Tyler
Moore Show*)
Common Nicknames: None
Common Variations: Phylis
Consider This: Phyllis is most defi-
nitely an old-lady name that
hasn't made any sort of
comeback.

Piper ★★★★★

(English) pipe player.
First Impression: Piper is seen as perky,
but she's also a warmhearted
leader.
Gender Association: Used for girls
Popularity and Trend: #246
(#509 in 2000)
Risk of Misspelling: Low
Risk of Mispronunciation: Low
Famous Namesakes: Actress Piper
Laurie; actress Piper Perabo
Common Nicknames: None
Common Variations: None

Consider This: Trade names are
trendy, and this one is making a
climb up the popularity charts.

Polly ★★★

(Latin) a familiar form of Paula,
Pauline.

First Impression: Polly is imagined to
be peppy, perky, cheery, and
smiley—maybe too much so.
Gender Association: Used for girls
Popularity and Trend: Last ranked in
the Top 1000 in the 1970s
Risk of Misspelling: Fairly low
Risk of Mispronunciation: Low
Famous Namesakes: Entertainer Polly
Bergen; actress Polly Holliday;
actress Polly Walker
Common Nicknames: None
Common Variations: Pollie
Consider This: Polly is a fun nickname,
but it's perhaps too casual for a
given name.

Poria ★★★

(Hebrew) fruitful.
First Impression: People primarily
imagine Poria as a heavyset girl
who's content with her life but
is a bit shy.
Gender Association: Used for girls
Popularity and Trend: Never been
ranked in Top 1000
Risk of Misspelling: Average
Risk of Mispronunciation: Average
Famous Namesakes: None
Common Nicknames: None
Common Variations: None

Consider This: Poria scores slightly better than Portia. Pronunciation is challenging, though, with both "PORE-ee-ah" and "pore-EYE-ah" as options.

Portia ★★
(Latin) offering.

First Impression: If you feel the temperature fluctuate, people say it's just Portia—she's an icy snob, yet she's also hotly strong-willed.

Gender Association: Used for girls

Popularity and Trend: Last ranked in the Top 1000 in the 1990s

Risk of Misspelling: Average

Risk of Mispronunciation: Average

Famous Namesakes: Character Portia (*The Merchant of Venice*); actress Portia de Rossi

Common Nicknames: None

Common Variations: Porscha, Porsche, Porsha

Consider This: Even with namesake Portia de Rossi, this name is now off the Top 1000 list, and a few people may not realize it's pronounced "PORE-shah."

Posy ★★★★
(English) flower, small bunch of flowers.

First Impression: People think Posy inspires a delightful, free-spirited image.

Gender Association: Used for girls

Popularity and Trend: Never been ranked in Top 1000

Risk of Misspelling: Fairly low

Risk of Mispronunciation: Low

Famous Namesakes: Actress Parker Posey; cartoonist Posy Simmonds

Common Nicknames: None

Common Variations: Posie, Posey

Consider This: While Posy creates a pleasant first impression, it's a hard name to take seriously.

Priscilla ★★★★
(Latin) ancient.

First Impression: Most people say Priscilla is an obnoxious, scatter-brained gossip.

Gender Association: Used for girls

Popularity and Trend: #372 (#275 in 2000)

Risk of Misspelling: Fairly low

Risk of Mispronunciation: Low

Famous Namesakes: Actress Priscilla Presley

Common Nicknames: Prissy, Cilla

Common Variations: Pricilla, Priscila

Consider This: Although Priscilla has never been a superstar name, it's seen modest popularity for over one hundred years.

Prudence ★★★
(Latin) cautious; discreet.

First Impression: Here's an obvious image: Prudence is considered a prude.

Gender Association: Used for girls

Popularity and Trend: Last ranked in the Top 1000 in the 1940s

Risk of Misspelling: Low

Risk of Mispronunciation: Low

Famous Namesakes: Activist Prudence Crandall; singer Prudence Johnson

Common Nicknames: Prudy, Pru

Common Variations: None

Consider This: Virtue names are *usually* appealing, but Prudence sounds old-fashioned and, well, prudish.

Pythia ★
(Greek) prophet.

First Impression: Pythia's life is regarded as pitiful and bleak, but she draws upon it as a gifted songwriter and singer.

Gender Association: Used for girls

Popularity and Trend: Never been ranked in Top 1000

Risk of Misspelling: Fairly high

Risk of Mispronunciation: Fairly high

Famous Namesakes: Mythological figure Pythia

Common Nicknames: None

Common Variations: None

Consider This: Not only is this name hard to spell and pronounce, but it also seems to conjure up the word *pitiful*.

Qadira ★
(Arabic) powerful.

First Impression: Folks say Qadira would rather observe than join in.

Gender Association: Used for girls

Popularity and Trend: Never been ranked in Top 1000

Risk of Misspelling: High
Risk of Mispronunciation: High
Famous Namesakes: None
Common Nicknames: None
Common Variations: None
Consider This: Often pronounced "kah-DEER-ah," this Arabic name may be difficult to spell and pronounce for anyone outside that culture.

Rachael ★★

(Hebrew) a form of Rachel.
First Impression: People think Rachael is a loud and talkative receptionist with a brash laugh.
Gender Association: Used for girls
Popularity and Trend: #392 (#227 in 2000)
Risk of Misspelling: Average
Risk of Mispronunciation: Low
Famous Namesakes: Actress Rachael Leigh Cook; talk show host Rachael Ray; actress Rachael Harris; character Rachel Green (*Friends*); actress Rachel McAdams; actress Rachel Weisz; actress Rachel Bilson
Common Nicknames: Rae
Common Variations: Rachel, Racheal
Consider This: What a difference an *a* makes—Rachael scores much lower than Rachel.

Rachel ★★★★★

(Hebrew) female sheep.
First Impression: Rachel is seen as a strong-minded, assertive, and independent woman, but she's also caring and nurturing.
Gender Association: Used mostly for girls
Popularity and Trend: #49 (#21 in 2000)
Risk of Misspelling: Fairly low
Risk of Mispronunciation: Low
Famous Namesakes: Character Rachel Green (*Friends*); actress Rachel McAdams; actress Rachel Weisz; actress Rachel Bilson; actress Rachael Leigh Cook; talk show host Rachael Ray; actress Rachael Harris
Common Nicknames: Rae
Common Variations: Rachael, Racheal
Consider This: This 5-star name has seen a gentle slide in popularity.

Racquel ★★

(French) a form of Rachel.
First Impression: People say Racquel has sex appeal, but there's little appeal to her personality.
Gender Association: Used for girls
Popularity and Trend: Last ranked in the Top 1000 in the 1970s
Risk of Misspelling: Average
Risk of Mispronunciation: Low
Famous Namesakes: Actress Raquel Welch
Common Nicknames: None
Common Variations: Raquel
Consider This: Spelling differences aside, Raquel Welch casts a sexy but otherwise negative shadow on this name's image.

Rae ★★★

(English) doe. (Hebrew) a form of Rachel.
First Impression: People say Rae is a small-town mom who's outgoing, active, and adventurous.
Gender Association: Used for girls
Popularity and Trend: Last ranked in the Top 1000 in the 1970s
Risk of Misspelling: Fairly low
Risk of Mispronunciation: Low
Famous Namesakes: Movie character Norma Rae; actress Rae Dawn Chong; actress Charlotte Rae
Common Nicknames: None
Common Variations: None
Consider This: As indicated in the first impression, Rae has a small-town, if not country, appeal. However, its pronunciation is the same as that for Ray, a popular name for boys, which may cause gender confusion.

Ramona ★★★

(Spanish) mighty; wise protector.
First Impression: Ramona is imagined to be a mischievous and silly brunette who some may call an annoying, immature pest, much like Ramona Quimby, the pesky character from a series of children's books by Beverly Cleary.
Gender Association: Used for girls
Popularity and Trend: Last ranked in the Top 1000 in the 1980s
Risk of Misspelling: Low

Risk of Mispronunciation: Low

Famous Namesakes: Fiction character Ramona Quimby

Common Nicknames: Mona

Common Variations: None

Consider This: Spelling, pronunciation, and versatility are fine, but first impression and popularity hurt this name's appeal and score.

Randi ★★

(English) a familiar form of Miranda, Randall.

First Impression: Randi is viewed as a cynical and jaded introvert with a rebellious edge.

Gender Association: Used for girls

Popularity and Trend: Last ranked in the Top 1000 in the 1980s

Risk of Misspelling: Average

Risk of Mispronunciation: Low

Famous Namesakes: Radio personality Randi Rhodes

Common Nicknames: None

Common Variations: Randy

Consider This: Randi is doubly casual—it's traditionally a nickname, and it has an "-i" ending that's especially cutesy and hard to spell. Plus, its pronunciation is the same as that for Randy, a popular name for boys, which may cause gender confusion.

Raven ★★

(English) blackbird.

First Impression: People say Raven's personality and appearance are as dark as her name suggests.

Gender Association: Used mostly for girls

Popularity and Trend: #441 (#216 in 2000)

Risk of Misspelling: Low

Risk of Mispronunciation: Low

Famous Namesakes: Actress Raven Symone

Common Nicknames: None

Common Variations: Ravon, Ravin

Consider This: Ravens have dark, gothic connotations, and the name Raven is no different.

Reagan ★★★

(Irish) little ruler.

First Impression: Reagan is described as a cheerful chatterbox or an articulate woman.

Gender Association: Used mostly for girls

Popularity and Trend: #155 (#286 in 2000)

Risk of Misspelling: Fairly low

Risk of Mispronunciation: Average

Famous Namesakes: President Ronald Reagan

Common Nicknames: None

Common Variations: Regan, Reganne

Consider This: If you choose this name for your daughter, be ready to answer "Did you name her after Ronald Reagan?" Also be ready for pronunciation problems: It can be either "REE-gan" or "RAY-gan."

Reanna ★★★

(German, English) a form of Raina. (American) a form of Raeann.

First Impression: When Reanna's friends need help, people say she's the first one they call.

Gender Association: Used for girls

Popularity and Trend: Last ranked #863 in 2000

Risk of Misspelling: Fairly low

Risk of Mispronunciation: Average

Famous Namesakes: Model Reanna Taylor

Common Nicknames: None

Common Variations: Reanne

Consider This: Reanna is usually pronounced "ree-ANN-ah," but a few may mistake it for "ree-AHN-ah" or "REEN-ah."

Reba ★★★★

(Hebrew) fourth-born child.

First Impression: People think Reba is a red-haired country singer who's assertive and outspoken, sweet and lovable, outgoing and funny, much like country star Reba McEntire.

Gender Association: Used for girls

Popularity and Trend: Last ranked in the Top 1000 in the 1960s

Risk of Misspelling: Low

Risk of Mispronunciation: Low
Famous Namesakes: Singer Reba McEntire
Common Nicknames: None
Common Variations: Reva
Consider This: Because Reba McEntire is such a famous namesake, this name definitely has a country twang.

Rebecca ★★★★★
(Hebrew) tied, bound.
First Impression: Folks say Rebecca has a great personality and great looks.
Gender Association: Used for girls
Popularity and Trend: #96 (#39 in 2000)
Risk of Misspelling: Fairly low
Risk of Mispronunciation: Low
Famous Namesakes: Fiction character Rebecca; actress Rebecca De Mornay; fiction character Rebecca of Sunnybrook Farm; actress Rebecca Romijn; actress Rebecca Gayheart; biblical figure Rebecca
Common Nicknames: Becca, Becky, Reba, Reva
Common Variations: Rebecka, Rebekah
Consider This: Talk about timeless: Rebecca has been in the Top 100 since 1940 and in the Top 200 since 1890.

Reese ★★★★
(Welsh) a form of Reece.
First Impression: People think Reese is confident, spunky, and energetic as well as friendly, fun, and good-humored, just like actress Reese Witherspoon.
Gender Association: Used for girls
Popularity and Trend: #159 (#886 in 2000)
Risk of Misspelling: Fairly low
Risk of Mispronunciation: Low
Famous Namesakes: Actress Reese Witherspoon
Common Nicknames: None
Common Variations: Reece
Consider This: Reese's surge in popularity proves how much impact a celebrity can have on a name. Just keep in mind that while this spelling is used mostly for girls, "Reece" and "Rhys" are used mostly for boys.

Regan ★★★
(Irish) a form of Reagan.
First Impression: People think Regan approaches life with great sincerity.
Gender Association: Used mostly for girls
Popularity and Trend: #567 (#467 in 2000)
Risk of Misspelling: Average
Risk of Mispronunciation: Average
Famous Namesakes: Character Regan MacNeil (*The Exorcist*)
Common Nicknames: None
Common Variations: Reagan, Reganne
Consider This: Although it's traditionally pronounced "REE-gan," some may pronounce this name "RAY-gan" instead.

Regina ★★★★
(Latin) queen. (English) king's advisor.
First Impression: Regina is envisioned as confident, strong, and—of course—regal.
Gender Association: Used for girls
Popularity and Trend: #603 (#531 in 2000)
Risk of Misspelling: Low
Risk of Mispronunciation: Fairly low
Famous Namesakes: Actress Regina King; actress Regina Hall; musician Regina Spektor; singer Regina Belle
Common Nicknames: Gina, Rain, Raina, Rainee, Reggie, Rainey
Common Variations: Regine
Consider This: On occasions when Regina seems too regal, use one of its many great nicknames.

Reilly ★★
(Irish) a form of Riley.
First Impression: People aren't sure if Reilly is a name for a girl or a boy, and they also aren't sure if Reilly is polite, popular, or rowdy.
Gender Association: Used mostly for boys

Popularity and Trend: Last ranked #793 in 2000

Risk of Misspelling: Average

Risk of Mispronunciation: Low

Famous Namesakes: Actress Kelly Reilly

Common Nicknames: None

Common Variations: Riley, Rylie, Ryley

Consider This: Gender association and spelling may become daily inconveniences for Reilly.

Renee ★★★★

(French) a form of Renée.

First Impression: Renee is said to be a droll and clever brown-haired beauty.

Gender Association: Used mostly for girls

Popularity and Trend: #582 (#362 in 2000)

Risk of Misspelling: Fairly low

Risk of Mispronunciation: Low

Famous Namesakes: Actress Renee Zellweger; actress Renee Russo; opera singer Renee Fleming

Common Nicknames: None

Common Variations: Renae, Rene

Consider This: Renee scores well, but it's relatively low in popularity—perhaps because it had its prime in the '60s and '70s.

Rhea ★★★

(Greek) brook, stream.

First Impression: People consider Rhea to be a grumpy yet funny smart aleck who's well loved for being so bold, much like Rhea Perlman who played feisty waitress Carla on TV's *Cheers*.

Gender Association: Used for girls

Popularity and Trend: Last ranked in the Top 1000 in the 1950s

Risk of Misspelling: Fairly low

Risk of Mispronunciation: Low

Famous Namesakes: Actress Rhea Perlman; model Rhea Durham

Common Nicknames: None

Common Variations: Rheanna

Consider This: Because of Rhea's connection to character Carla from TV's *Cheers*, it has working-class sass.

Rhiannon ★★★

(Welsh) witch; nymph; goddess.

First Impression: Rhiannon is pictured as an expressive spirit with some mystery to her.

Gender Association: Used for girls

Popularity and Trend: #738 (#454 in 2000)

Risk of Misspelling: Average

Risk of Mispronunciation: Fairly low

Famous Namesakes: None

Common Nicknames: Rhian

Common Variations: Rheannon

Consider This: The dreamy image for this name is perhaps influenced by the Fleetwood Mac song "Rhiannon."

Rhoda ★★★

(Greek) from Rhodes, Greece.

First Impression: Rhoda is regarded as secure in her solitary lifestyle.

Gender Association: Used for girls

Popularity and Trend: Last ranked in the Top 1000 in the 1960s

Risk of Misspelling: Fairly low

Risk of Mispronunciation: Low

Famous Namesakes: Character Rhoda Morgenstern (*Rhoda*)

Common Nicknames: None

Common Variations: None

Consider This: Sometimes pop culture doesn't affect names: *Rhoda*, the TV sitcom, didn't do anything to resurrect this name's popularity.

Rhonda ★★★

(Welsh) grand.

First Impression: People think Rhonda speaks her mind, for good or bad.

Gender Association: Used for girls

Popularity and Trend: Last ranked in the Top 1000 in the 1990s

Risk of Misspelling: Fairly low

Risk of Mispronunciation: Low

Famous Namesakes: TV host Rhonda Shear; actress Rhonda Fleming

Common Nicknames: Ronnette

Common Variations: Ronda

Consider This: When the Beach Boys' hit "Help Me, Rhonda" was hot, so was this name. Now the song and the name are both off the charts, and the name sounds dated.

Ricki ★★★

(American) a familiar form of Erica, Frederica, Ricarda.

First Impression: Folks say Ricki has a soft side and a rugged side.

Gender Association: Used mostly for girls

Popularity and Trend: Never been ranked in Top 1000

Risk of Misspelling: Fairly high

Risk of Mispronunciation: Low

Famous Namesakes: Talk show host Ricki Lake

Common Nicknames: None

Common Variations: Riki, Rikki, Ricky

Consider This: Like Nikki, Ricki has two strikes against it: People will likely think it's a nickname, and they're likely to misspell it, thanks to the many other variations of this name. Plus, its pronunciation is the same as that for Ricky, a common nickname for boys, which may cause gender confusion.

Riona ★★★

(Irish) saint.

First Impression: Riona is considered to be a quiet introvert who's calm, peaceful, and blissfully laid-back.

Gender Association: Used for girls

Popularity and Trend: Never been ranked in Top 1000

Risk of Misspelling: Average

Risk of Mispronunciation: Average

Famous Namesakes: None

Common Nicknames: None

Common Variations: None

Consider This: Because Riona is such an uncommon name, it may pose a pronunciation challenge to those who don't know it's "ree-OH-nah." Spelling could be tricky, too.

Rita ★★★

(Sanskrit) brave; honest. (Greek) a form of Margarita.

First Impression: Be prepared—people say Rita is a bit forward.

Gender Association: Used for girls

Popularity and Trend: Last ranked in the Top 1000 in the 1980s

Risk of Misspelling: Low

Risk of Mispronunciation: Low

Famous Namesakes: Actress Rita Wilson; actress Rita Hayworth; actress Rita Moreno; news anchor Rita Cosby

Common Nicknames: None

Common Variations: None

Consider This: Rita has spunk, but being a Top 1000 dropout means it's dated.

Roberta ★★★★

(English) a form of Robert.

First Impression: Because the name Roberta is a version of the name Robert, people find her to be a strong-willed, manly woman in a leadership position.

Gender Association: Used for girls

Popularity and Trend: Last ranked in the Top 1000 in the 1990s

Risk of Misspelling: Low

Risk of Mispronunciation: Low

Famous Namesakes: Singer Roberta Flack

Common Nicknames: Berta, Bobbette, Bobbi, Robbi

Common Variations: None

Consider This: Although Roberta is clearly a girls' name, it still creates a masculine first impression, which may or may not be a positive.

Robyn ★★★

(English) a form of Robin.

First Impression: People think Robyn's finer traits balance out her rougher ones.

Gender Association: Used mostly for girls

Popularity and Trend: Last ranked in the Top 1000 in the 1980s

Risk of Misspelling: Average

Risk of Mispronunciation: Low

Famous Namesakes: Actress Robin Givens; radio personality Robin Quivers; choreographer Robin Antin

Common Nicknames: Robinette

Common Variations: Robin, Robynn

Consider This: Because of the *y*, people likely see "Robyn" as a more feminine spelling than "Robin." It may cause some problems with spelling, though.

Rochelle ★★★★

(French) large stone. (Hebrew) a form of Rachel.

First Impression: Rochelle's kindness is considered admirable, but it makes her somewhat vulnerable, too.

Gender Association: Used for girls

Popularity and Trend: Last ranked in the Top 1000 in the 1990s

Risk of Misspelling: Fairly low

Risk of Mispronunciation: Low

Famous Namesakes: None

Common Nicknames: Shelly

Common Variations: Rochel

Consider This: Rochelle doesn't have the assertiveness that Rachel has.

Roma ★★★★

(Latin) from Rome.

First Impression: Roma is imagined to be an ambitious, intelligent, and self-confident businesswoman who'd rather have a career than a family.

Gender Association: Used for girls

Popularity and Trend: Last ranked in the Top 1000 in the 1940s

Risk of Misspelling: Low

Risk of Mispronunciation: Low

Famous Namesakes: Actress Roma Downey

Common Nicknames: Romy

Common Variations: None

Consider This: Although it's been off the Top 1000 list for decades, Roma doesn't seem dated. It has a very strong image for such an uncommon name.

Romola ★★

(Latin) a form of Roma.

First Impression: People think Romola's multifaceted personality makes her hard to read.

Gender Association: Used for girls

Popularity and Trend: Never been ranked in Top 1000

Risk of Misspelling: Average

Risk of Mispronunciation: Average

Famous Namesakes: Actress Romola Garai

Common Nicknames: Romy

Common Variations: None

Consider This: An uncommon name, Romola sounds foreign. It may look as though it's pronounced "roh-MOLE-ah," but it's "ROME-oh-lah."

Rori ★★★

(Irish) famous brilliance; famous ruler.

First Impression: Rori can be quite stubborn, but people say she's a good person.

Gender Association: Used for girls

Popularity and Trend: Never been ranked in Top 1000

Risk of Misspelling: Average

Risk of Mispronunciation: Low

Famous Namesakes: Character Rory Gilmore (*Gilmore Girls*); film maker Rory Kennedy

Common Nicknames: None

Common Variations: Rory

Consider This: Rori is a variation of Rory, a common boys' name. This could make spelling—and gender association—a problem.

Rosa ★★★★

(Italian, Spanish) a form of Rose.

First Impression: People see Rosa as kind and caring, hardworking and determined, serene and laid-back, happy and spirited, or shy and mysterious.

Gender Association: Used for girls

Popularity and Trend: #400 (#316 in 2000)

Risk of Misspelling: Low

Risk of Mispronunciation: Low

Famous Namesakes: Civil rights icon Rosa Parks

Common Nicknames: Rosie

Common Variations: Roza

Consider This: Compared to Rose, Rosa has more diverse ethnic associations.

Rosalie ★★★★

(English) a form of Rosalind.

First Impression: People say Rosalie keeps an even keel, even when she's having fun.

Gender Association: Used for girls

Popularity and Trend: Last ranked in the Top 1000 in the 1980s

Risk of Misspelling: Fairly low

Risk of Mispronunciation: Low

Famous Namesakes: Sculptor Rosalie Gascoigne

Common Nicknames: Rosa, Rosie
Common Variations: None
Consider This: Rosalie is a fun, yet not too casual, member of the Rose family.

Rosalyn ★★★

(Spanish) a form of Rosalind.

First Impression: This name makes people think of a gentle and caring grandmother who's classy, sophisticated, and rich.
Gender Association: Used for girls
Popularity and Trend: Last ranked in the Top 1000 in the 1980s
Risk of Misspelling: Average
Risk of Mispronunciation: Fairly low
Famous Namesakes: First lady Rosalyn Carter; actress Roselyn Sanchez
Common Nicknames: Rosa, Roz, Rosie
Common Variations: Rosalind, Rosalin
Consider This: Like Rose, Rosalyn is associated with an older woman, which suggests it's a dated name.

Rose ★★★★

(Latin) rose.

First Impression: Rose is the picture of poise and grace.
Gender Association: Used for girls
Popularity and Trend: #350 (#299 in 2000)
Risk of Misspelling: Low
Risk of Mispronunciation: Low
Famous Namesakes: Character Rose Nylund (*The Golden Girls*);

actress Rose McGowan; matriarch Rose Kennedy
Common Nicknames: Rosie
Common Variations: Rosa, Rosetta
Consider This: Rose would be a 5-star name if it weren't for its low popularity and grandmotherly connotation, which seem to go hand in hand.

Roseanna ★★★

(English) a combination of Rose + Anna.

First Impression: Roseanna is imagined by many people as a sassy and sarcastic comedian who borders on being rude and annoying. Sounds a lot like Roseanne Barr, doesn't it?
Gender Association: Used for girls
Popularity and Trend: Last ranked in the Top 1000 in the 1950s
Risk of Misspelling: Fairly low
Risk of Mispronunciation: Low
Famous Namesakes: Actress Rosanna Arquette
Common Nicknames: Rosie, Rose, Anna
Common Variations: None
Consider This: Roseanne Barr makes such an impact, she influences the name Roseanna, too.

Roseanne ★★★

(English) a combination of Rose + Ann.

First Impression: People overwhelmingly picture Roseanne with a chubby stature and round

cheeks, just like comedian Roseanne Barr.
Gender Association: Used for girls
Popularity and Trend: Last ranked in the Top 1000 in the 1960s
Risk of Misspelling: Fairly low
Risk of Mispronunciation: Low
Famous Namesakes: Comedian Roseanne Barr
Common Nicknames: Rosie, Rose, Anne
Common Variations: None
Consider This: There's little difference between this name and its sister, Roseanna, except it lacks that final syllable.

Rosemary ★★★★

(English) a combination of Rose + Mary.

First Impression: Rosemary comes across as caring and kindhearted, but she's also very quiet.
Gender Association: Used for girls
Popularity and Trend: #703 (#634 in 2000)
Risk of Misspelling: Low
Risk of Mispronunciation: Low
Famous Namesakes: Character Rosemary Woodhouse (*Rosemary's Baby*); singer Rosemary Clooney
Common Nicknames: Rosie, Rose, Mary, Romy
Common Variations: None
Consider This: The first impression for Rosemary is no surprise considering Rose is an old-fashioned, gentle name, and so is Mary.

Roxanna ★★★

(Persian) a form of Roxann.

First Impression: When people hear this name, they think of an insecure, codependent hair-dresser or a cocktail waitress who's gossipy, loud, and looking for true love.

Gender Association: Used for girls

Popularity and Trend: Last ranked in the Top 1000 in the 1990s

Risk of Misspelling: Low

Risk of Mispronunciation: Low

Famous Namesakes: None

Common Nicknames: Roxie, Anna

Common Variations: Roxanne

Consider This: Maybe blame it on the sound—the name Roxanna evokes the image of a woman on the "rocks."

Rue ★★★

(German) famous. (French) street. (English) regretful; strong-scented herbs.

First Impression: Rue is seen as a small woman with a big attitude.

Gender Association: Used for girls

Popularity and Trend: Never been ranked in Top 1000

Risk of Misspelling: Fairly low

Risk of Mispronunciation: Low

Famous Namesakes: Actress Rue McClanahan

Common Nicknames: None

Common Variations: None

Consider This: Rue McClanahan and Rhea Perlman played very memorable characters on TV. Just as the name Rhea takes on Carla's image from *Cheers*, the name Rue takes on Blanche's image from *The Golden Girls*.

Ruth ★★★★

(Hebrew) friendship.

First Impression: Many people think Ruth is helpful, gentle, faithful, and honorable. But others say she's confident, bold, boisterous, and larger than life.

Gender Association: Used for girls

Popularity and Trend: #373 (#344 in 2000)

Risk of Misspelling: Low

Risk of Mispronunciation: Low

Famous Namesakes: Biblical figure Ruth; judge Ruth Bader Ginsburg; actress Ruth Gordon; actress Ruth Hussey

Common Nicknames: Ruthie

Common Variations: None

Consider This: Judging from the first impression, Ruth seems to be a hard name to put one's finger on.

Sabina ★★★

(Latin) a form of Sabine.

First Impression: People think Sabina is friendly, but she also needs some time alone with her thoughts.

Gender Association: Used for girls

Popularity and Trend: Last ranked in the Top 1000 in the 1920s

Risk of Misspelling: Fairly low

Risk of Mispronunciation: Fairly low

Famous Namesakes: Character Sabina (*The Unbearable Lightness of Being*); singer Sabina Sciubba

Common Nicknames: Bina

Common Variations: None

Consider This: Although it's been off the Top 1000 for almost ninety years, Sabina doesn't seem as dated as other names from its era.

Sable ★★★★

(English) sable; sleek.

First Impression: A sable is a luxurious fur, which may explain why people think Sable has posh, fashionable flair.

Gender Association: Used for girls

Popularity and Trend: Never been ranked in Top 1000

Risk of Misspelling: Low

Risk of Mispronunciation: Low

Famous Namesakes: Professional wrestler Sable

Common Nicknames: None

Common Variations: None

Consider This: Sable has a high-class style that may—or may not—make it a good option for your daughter.

Sabra ★★★

(Hebrew) thorny cactus fruit. (Arabic) resting.

First Impression: Folks think Sabra has a spirited personality, for better or worse.

Gender Association: Used for girls

Popularity and Trend: Never been ranked in Top 1000
Risk of Misspelling: Fairly low
Risk of Mispronunciation: Fairly low
Famous Namesakes: Mythological figure Princess Sabra
Common Nicknames: None
Common Variations: Sabria
Consider This: Typically pronounced "SAY-brah," people may pronounce this name "SAH-bra," like the term for a native-born Israeli.

Sabrina ★★★★
(Latin) boundary line. (English) princess. (Hebrew) a form of Sabra.
First Impression: People say Sabrina's lack of verbosity may stem from shyness, although some believe she's secretive or perhaps even frightened in social situations.
Gender Association: Used mostly for girls
Popularity and Trend: #197 (#92 in 2000)
Risk of Misspelling: Fairly low
Risk of Mispronunciation: Low
Famous Namesakes: Character Sabrina Spellman (*Sabrina the Teenage Witch*); character Sabrina Fairchild (*Sabrina*); actress Sabrina Lloyd
Common Nicknames: Brina, Rena
Common Variations: Sabreena

Sagara ★★★
(Hindi) ocean.
First Impression: Sagara is said to be a proud, strong, and perhaps even regal Indian woman with dark eyes, skin, and hair.
Gender Association: Used for girls
Popularity and Trend: Never been ranked in Top 1000
Risk of Misspelling: Average
Risk of Mispronunciation: Average
Famous Namesakes: Anime character Sanosuke Sagara
Common Nicknames: None
Common Variations: None
Consider This: This Hindi name creates a beautiful first impression, but it's pronunciation may be tricky. It's pronounced "sah-GAH-rah," but some may think it's "sah-GARE-ah" or "sah-GAR-ah."

Sage ★★★
(English) wise.
First Impression: Few people see Sage's true personality through her irresponsible behavior.
Gender Association: Used about equally for girls and boys
Popularity and Trend: #417 (#489 in 2000)
Risk of Misspelling: Low
Risk of Mispronunciation: Low

Consider This: If you're looking for a solid name that's not overly popular, Sabrina is a nice choice.

Famous Namesakes: Musician Sage Francis
Common Nicknames: None
Common Variations: Saige
Consider This: Keep in mind that this name is used equally for girls and boys.

Sally ★★★
(English) princess.
First Impression: This name reminds people of a sociable and very chatty housewife.
Gender Association: Used for girls
Popularity and Trend: Last ranked in the Top 1000 in the 1980s
Risk of Misspelling: Fairly low
Risk of Mispronunciation: Low
Famous Namesakes: Actress Sally Struthers; talk show host Sally Jessy Raphael; actress Sally Field; runner Sally Gunnell; astronaut Sally Ride
Common Nicknames: None
Common Variations: Sallie
Consider This: Sally is not only outdated, but it's also as casual as a name can get without being a nickname.

Samantha ★★★★★
(Aramaic) listener. (Hebrew) told by God.
First Impression: By night, Samantha is said to be a sociable, vivacious woman who loves to party and loves life in general.

Gender Association: Used mostly for girls
Popularity and Trend: #10 (#7 in 2000)
Risk of Misspelling: Fairly low
Risk of Mispronunciation: Low
Famous Namesakes: Character Samantha Jones (*Sex and the City*); character Samantha Stephens (*Bewitched*); singer Samantha Mumba; actress Samantha Morton; TV host Samantha Harris
Common Nicknames: Sam, Sammy
Common Variations: Sammantha
Consider This: Samantha is a Top 10 name, meaning its only downside is that it may be *too* popular.

Samara ★★★★
(Latin) elm-tree seed.
First Impression: Samara is described as a Middle Eastern woman who's bubbly, fun-loving, and always wearing a big smile.
Gender Association: Used for girls
Popularity and Trend: #351 (#889 in 2000)
Risk of Misspelling: Fairly low
Risk of Mispronunciation: Average
Famous Namesakes: Character Samara Morgan (*The Ring*)
Common Nicknames: Mara
Common Variations: Samarah
Consider This: Interestingly, Samara jumped in popularity after the release of the film *The Ring*, yet

no one associates that ghostly character with the name. The typical pronunciation is "sah-MARE-ah," though people may think it's "sah-MAR-ah."

Sandra ★★★★
(Greek) defender of mankind.
First Impression: Sandra is considered independent, assertive, and quite confident.
Gender Association: Used for girls
Popularity and Trend: #364 (#257 in 2000)
Risk of Misspelling: Low
Risk of Mispronunciation: Average
Famous Namesakes: Actress Sandra Dee; actress Sandra Bullock; judge Sandra Day O'Connor; author Sandra Cisneros; actress Sandra Oh; comedian Sandra Bernhard
Common Nicknames: Sandy
Common Variations: None
Consider This: The pronunciation debate ("SAN-drah" versus "SAHN-drah") is a problem for this name.

Sandy ★★★
(Greek) a familiar form of Cassandra, Sandra.
First Impression: People say we should all strive to be as generous and kind as Sandy.
Gender Association: Used mostly for girls

Popularity and Trend: Last ranked in the Top 1000 in the 1980s
Risk of Misspelling: Fairly low
Risk of Mispronunciation: Low
Famous Namesakes: Actress Sandy Duncan; character Sandy Olsson (*Grease*); actress Sandy Dennis
Common Nicknames: None
Common Variations: Sandee, Sandi
Consider This: The first impression suggests Sandy is a great option as a nickname, but it's very casual for a given name.

Sapphire ★★
(Greek) blue gemstone.
First Impression: Folks think Sapphire sure has sex appeal, but not many other positive qualities.
Gender Association: Used for girls
Popularity and Trend: Never been ranked in Top 1000
Risk of Misspelling: Average
Risk of Mispronunciation: Low
Famous Namesakes: None
Common Nicknames: None
Common Variations: Saphire, Sapphira
Consider This: Like Bambi, Sapphire unfortunately seems like stage name for a stripper. Also, some people may forget the second *p* when they spell this name.

Sara ★★★★★
(Hebrew) a form of Sarah.
First Impression: Sara is considered a wonderful person to know.
Gender Association: Used for girls

Popularity and Trend: #72
(#57 in 2000)

Risk of Misspelling: Average

Risk of Mispronunciation: Low

Famous Namesakes: Actress Sara Gilbert; actress Sarah Michelle Gellar; actress Sara Ramirez; biblical figure Sara; duchess Sarah Ferguson; singer Sarah McLachlan; actress Sarah Jessica Parker; actress Sarah Bernhardt; singer Sara Evans; actress Sarah Chalke

Common Nicknames: Sadie, Sarina, Sarita

Common Variations: Sarah

Consider This: Although Sara is a popular name, people may spell it with a final *h* because Sarah is more popular and more established as the classic spelling.

Sarah ★★★★★

(Hebrew) princess.

First Impression: People think every little thing about Sarah is gentle.

Gender Association: Used mostly for girls

Popularity and Trend: #15
(#5 in 2000)

Risk of Misspelling: Fairly low

Risk of Mispronunciation: Low

Famous Namesakes: Actress Sara Gilbert; actress Sarah Michelle Gellar; actress Sara Ramirez; biblical figure Sara; duchess Sarah Ferguson; singer Sarah

McLachlan; actress Sarah Jessica Parker; actress Sarah Bernhardt; singer Sara Evans; actress Sarah Chalke

Common Nicknames: Sadie, Sarina, Sarita

Common Variations: Sara

Consider This: After about twenty-five years in the Top 10, Sarah's popularity is ever-so-gradually slipping.

Sarina ★★★

(Hebrew) a form of Sarah.

First Impression: People aren't sure if Sarina has a fine character to match her fine leadership skills.

Gender Association: Used for girls

Popularity and Trend: Last ranked #827 in 2000

Risk of Misspelling: Average

Risk of Mispronunciation: Fairly low

Famous Namesakes: Singer Sarina Paris; tennis player Serena Williams; character Serena (*Bewitched*)

Common Nicknames: Rina

Common Variations: Sarena

Consider This: Compared to Serena, Sarina has a few downsides, including a less favorable first impression and a greater possibility of being misspelled—which may have affected the popularity of this name.

Sasha ★★

(Russian) a familiar form of Alexandra.

First Impression: Sasha is pictured as a gloomy, eccentric, and tortured artist.

Gender Association: Used mostly for girls

Popularity and Trend: #336
(#476 in 2000)

Risk of Misspelling: Fairly low

Risk of Mispronunciation: Low

Famous Namesakes: Actress Sasha Alexander; comedian Sacha Baron Cohen; figure skater Sasha Cohen

Common Nicknames: None

Common Variations: Sacha

Consider This: Sasha is sometimes used as a boys' variation of Alexander, and although it's still mostly used for girls, perhaps the gender association will be affected by comedian Sacha Baron Cohen's fame.

Savanna ★★★★

(Spanish) a form of Savannah.

First Impression: Savanna is viewed as a gentle spirit with a fiery passion for saving the earth.

Gender Association: Used for girls

Popularity and Trend: #230
(#210 in 2000)

Risk of Misspelling: Average

Risk of Mispronunciation: Low

Famous Namesakes: Character Savannah Jackson (*Waiting to Exhale*)

Common Nicknames: Vanna

Common Variations: Savannah, Savana

Consider This: Savanna scores relatively well, but it loses a few points as a less popular spelling of Savannah.

Savannah ★★★★★

(Spanish) treeless plain.

First Impression: People say Savannah is not afraid to tell it like it is.

Gender Association: Used for girls

Popularity and Trend: #30 (#37 in 2000)

Risk of Misspelling: Fairly low

Risk of Mispronunciation: Low

Famous Namesakes: Character Savannah Jackson (*Waiting to Exhale*)

Common Nicknames: Vanna

Common Variations: Savanna, Savana

Consider This: This name is loaded with Southern charm, thanks to the city of Savannah, Georgia.

Scarlett ★★★★

(English) bright red.

First Impression: Like *Gone with the Wind* heroine Scarlett O'Hara, Scarlett is thought to be a conceited and snappy vixen who's wealthy, headstrong, and precocious.

Gender Association: Used for girls

Popularity and Trend: #297 (#941 in 2000)

Risk of Misspelling: Fairly low

Risk of Mispronunciation: Low

Famous Namesakes: Actress Scarlett Johansson; character Scarlett O'Hara (*Gone with the Wind*)

Common Nicknames: None

Common Variations: Scarlet

Consider This: This name's surging popularity has more to do with actress Scarlett Johansson than character Scarlett O'Hara, but either way, people may forget the last *t* when spelling this name.

Selena ★★★★

(Greek) a form of Selene.

First Impression: This name's image recalls the charm of Selena Quintanilla-Pérez, the late Tejano singer who was murdered at the height of her stardom.

Gender Association: Used for girls

Popularity and Trend: #285 (#194 in 2000)

Risk of Misspelling: Fairly low

Risk of Mispronunciation: Low

Famous Namesakes: Singer Selena Quintanilla-Pérez; character Selina Kyle (*Batman*)

Common Nicknames: Sela, Sena

Common Variations: Celena, Selina

Consider This: Because the first impression links to Selena, the singer, this name has a Latino association.

Selina ★★★

(Greek) a form of Celina, Selena.

First Impression: People say Selina's rough life forced her to develop hardnosed traits.

Gender Association: Used for girls

Popularity and Trend: #901 (#812 in 2000)

Risk of Misspelling: Average

Risk of Mispronunciation: Low

Famous Namesakes: Character Selina Kyle (*Batman*); singer Selena Quintanilla-Pérez

Common Nicknames: Sela, Sena

Common Variations: Celena, Selena

Consider This: For whatever reason, Selina creates a tough, perhaps even underprivileged, first impression.

Serena ★★★★

(Latin) peaceful.

First Impression: Aptly, Serena is seen as a gentle, easy soul.

Gender Association: Used for girls

Popularity and Trend: #396 (#209 in 2000)

Risk of Misspelling: Fairly low

Risk of Mispronunciation: Low

Famous Namesakes: Tennis player Serena Williams; character Serena (*Bewitched*); singer Sarina Paris

Common Nicknames: Rena

Common Variations: Serene, Serina

Consider This: Spelling matters: Serena and Sarina look similar, but Serena has a positive first impression because its spelling conjures up the word *serene*.

Serenity ★★★★★
(Latin) peaceful.

First Impression: Fittingly, people say, Serenity brings quietude and calm to those around her.

Gender Association: Used for girls

Popularity and Trend: #135 (#433 in 2000)

Risk of Misspelling: Low

Risk of Mispronunciation: Low

Famous Namesakes: None

Common Nicknames: None

Common Variations: None

Consider This: Like many virtue names, Serenity has a pleasant appeal, not to mention familiar spelling and pronunciation.

Shakila ★★★
(Arabic) pretty.

First Impression: Folks think Shakila's warm heart gives her a special place in the eyes of her friends and family.

Gender Association: Used for girls

Popularity and Trend: Never been ranked in Top 1000

Risk of Misspelling: Average

Risk of Mispronunciation: Fairly high

Famous Namesakes: Singer Shakila

Common Nicknames: None

Common Variations: None

Consider This: Shakila may be associated with either Arabic or African American ethnicity.

Shakira ★★★
(Arabic) thankful.

First Impression: This image calls to mind Colombian singer Shakira, who's an international sensation thanks largely to her seductive belly-dancing.

Gender Association: Used for girls

Popularity and Trend: #791 (#844 in 2000)

Risk of Misspelling: Average

Risk of Mispronunciation: Average

Famous Namesakes: Singer Shakira Ripoll

Common Nicknames: None

Common Variations: Shakyra, Shaquira

Consider This: The name Shakira crosses ethnic lines: The name is Arabic, but it's associated with Latino singer Shakira (whose father has Lebanese heritage).

Shanna ★★★
(Irish) a form of Shana, Shannon.

First Impression: Shanna is depicted as an outgoing woman who intricately and diligently plans every part of her week.

Gender Association: Used for girls

Popularity and Trend: Last ranked in the Top 1000 in the 1990s

Risk of Misspelling: Fairly high

Risk of Mispronunciation: Fairly high

Famous Namesakes: Actress Shanna Moakler

Common Nicknames: Shan

Common Variations: Shana

Consider This: When people see this name, they may mistakenly pronounce it "SHAN-nah" instead of "SHAWN-ah," and when they hear it, they may mistakenly spell it "Shauna."

Shannon ★★★
(Irish) small and wise.

First Impression: People say Shannon is wild, confident, and fearless, perhaps like actress Shannen Doherty.

Gender Association: Used mostly for girls

Popularity and Trend: #359 (#152 in 2000)

Risk of Misspelling: Fairly low

Risk of Mispronunciation: Low

Famous Namesakes: Gymnast Shannon Miller; actress Shannon Elizabeth; actress Shannen Doherty; actress Shannon Tweed; actress Shannyn Sossamon

Common Nicknames: None

Common Variations: Shannen

Consider This: If you're drawn to "Sha-" names, Shannon is more popular than both Shanna and Sharon.

Shari ★★
(French) beloved, dearest. (Hungarian) a form of Sarah.

First Impression: Shari is pictured as
an energetic and witty waitress
who works hard and has a
hard life.
Gender Association: Used for girls
Popularity and Trend: Last ranked in
the Top 1000 in the 1990s
Risk of Misspelling: Fairly high
Risk of Mispronunciation: Low
Famous Namesakes: Puppeteer Shari
Lewis; actress Sherry Stringfield;
actress Shari Belafonte; comedian
Cheri Oteri
Common Nicknames: None
Common Variations: Sherry, Sheri,
Cheri
Consider This: With so many sound-
alike variations of this name,
Shari will be tricky to spell.

Sharlene ★★

(French) little and strong.
First Impression: Sharlene comes
across as an untrusting, watchful,
and cautious woman.
Gender Association: Used for girls
Popularity and Trend: Last ranked in
the Top 1000 in the 1970s
Risk of Misspelling: Average
Risk of Mispronunciation: Low
Famous Namesakes: Actress Charlene
Tilton; fitness guru Charlene
Prickett; singer Sharlene Spiteri
Common Nicknames: Sharla
Common Variations: Charlene,
Sharleen

Consider This: Compared to Charlene,
Sharlene inspires a not-so-positive
first impression.

Sharon ★★★

(Hebrew) desert plain.
First Impression: People can't decide if
Sharon is a crabby perfectionist, a
fun-loving adventurer, or a sweet
introvert, but they agree that
she's middle aged.
Gender Association: Used for girls
Popularity and Trend: #623
(#420 in 2000)
Risk of Misspelling: Fairly low
Risk of Mispronunciation: Low
Famous Namesakes: Actress Sharon
Stone; actress Sharon Tate;
personality Sharon Osbourne;
actress Sharon Case
Common Nicknames: Shara
Common Variations: Sharen, Sharron
Consider This: Although this name
hasn't dropped out of the Top
1000, be aware that it does have
a dated sound.

Shauna ★★★

(Hebrew, Irish) a form of Shana,
Shaun.
First Impression: Shauna is seen as
outgoing and self-assured, but
she can be a little wild at times.
Gender Association: Used for girls
Popularity and Trend: Last ranked in
the Top 1000 in the 1990s
Risk of Misspelling: Fairly high
Risk of Mispronunciation: Low

Famous Namesakes: Model Shauna
Sand; actress Shauna Kain
Common Nicknames: None
Common Variations: Shawna, Seana,
Shona, Shanna
Consider This: While easy to pro-
nounce, Shauna could be hard
to spell based on the number of
variations for this feminine form
of Sean.

Sheba ★★★

(Hebrew) a form of Bathsheba.
First Impression: People picture Sheba
as "the Queen of Sheba"—that
is, she's a powerful, assertive, and
willful woman.
Gender Association: Used for girls
Popularity and Trend: Never been
ranked in Top 1000
Risk of Misspelling: Fairly low
Risk of Mispronunciation: Fairly low
Famous Namesakes: Biblical figure
the Queen of Sheba
Common Nicknames: None
Common Variations: None
Consider This: Naming your
daughter Sheba may seem
presumptuous, considering its
high-and-mighty association.

Sheena ★★★

(Hebrew) God is gracious. (Irish) a
form of Jane.
First Impression: People think Sheena
knows how to bat her eyelashes
in a flirty yet sweet way.
Gender Association: Used for girls

Popularity and Trend: Last ranked in the Top 1000 in the 1990s
Risk of Misspelling: Fairly low
Risk of Mispronunciation: Low
Famous Namesakes: Singer Sheena Easton; comic book character Sheena, Queen of the Jungle
Common Nicknames: None
Common Variations: Shena
Consider This: The name Sheena was popular in the '80s, when singer Sheena Easton was popular, but neither the singer nor the name is big anymore.

Sheila ★★
(Latin) blind. (Irish) a form of Cecelia.
First Impression: Sheila is considered either an arrogant blond or a boring nerd.
Gender Association: Used for girls
Popularity and Trend: #946 (#690 in 2000)
Risk of Misspelling: Fairly low
Risk of Mispronunciation: Low
Famous Namesakes: Musician Sheila E; activist Sheila Wellstone
Common Nicknames: None
Common Variations: None
Consider This: Sheila's first impression has two attributes, but they're both negative. On the positive side, most people should pronounce it correctly as "SHEE-lah."

Shelby ★★★★
(English) ledge estate.
First Impression: Folks say Shelby shoots the breeze with every person she passes on the street.
Gender Association: Used mostly for girls
Popularity and Trend: #133 (#70 in 2000)
Risk of Misspelling: Fairly low
Risk of Mispronunciation: Low
Famous Namesakes: Character Shelby Eatenton Latcherie (*Steel Magnolias*); singer Shelby Lynne
Common Nicknames: Shel
Common Variations: Chelby
Consider This: With namesakes like country singer Shelby Lynne and *Steel Magnolias* character Shelby Eatenton, this name has a Southern sound.

Shelly ★★★
(English) meadow on the ledge. (French) a form of Michelle.
First Impression: Most say Shelly is kind and likable, but others say she's timid and bland.
Gender Association: Used for girls
Popularity and Trend: Last ranked in the Top 1000 in the 1990s
Risk of Misspelling: Low
Risk of Mispronunciation: Low
Famous Namesakes: Author Mary Wollstonecraft Shelley; actress Shelly Long
Common Nicknames: None
Common Variations: None
Consider This: Shelly loses out to Shelby, thanks to the latter name's better first impression, popularity, and versatility.

Sherry ★★★
(French) beloved, dearest.
First Impression: Most people believe Sherry is silly, loud, and fun, but perhaps selfish and insecure as well. A few people claim, however, that she's insecure, shy, and quiet.
Gender Association: Used for girls
Popularity and Trend: Last ranked in the Top 1000 in the 1990s
Risk of Misspelling: Average
Risk of Mispronunciation: Low
Famous Namesakes: Actress Sherry Stringfield; actress Shari Belafonte; comedian Cheri Oteri; puppeteer Shari Lewis
Common Nicknames: None
Common Variations: Shari, Sheri, Cheri
Consider This: Like Shelly, Sherry dropped out of the Top 1000 in the '90s, which means they're dated names.

Shirley ★★★★
(English) bright meadow.
First Impression: People think Shirley is a happy, cheerful, and helpful woman.
Gender Association: Used for girls

Popularity and Trend: Last ranked in the Top 1000 in the 1980s
Risk of Misspelling: Low
Risk of Mispronunciation: Low
Famous Namesakes: Actress Shirley MacLaine; actress Shirley Jones; singer Shirley Manson; actress Shirley Temple; author Shirley Jackson; singer Shirley Bassey
Common Nicknames: None
Common Variations: None
Consider This: Shirley is both young and old: Most people picture an older woman when they hear this name, yet the name also calls to mind the eternal youth of Shirley Temple.

Shonda ★★★
(Irish) a form of Shona.
First Impression: People say Shonda is a highly motivated and hard-working African American woman, much like Shonda Rhimes, creator of TV's *Grey's Anatomy*.
Gender Association: Used for girls
Popularity and Trend: Last ranked in the Top 1000 in the 1980s
Risk of Misspelling: Fairly high
Risk of Mispronunciation: Low
Famous Namesakes: Writer Shonda Rhimes
Common Nicknames: None
Common Variations: Shaunda, Shawnda

Consider This: With a number of sound-alike variations, this name will cause spelling problems.

Shoshana ★★★
(Hebrew) a form of Susan.
First Impression: People think Shoshana has all the right stuff for success.
Gender Association: Used for girls
Popularity and Trend: Never been ranked in Top 1000
Risk of Misspelling: Average
Risk of Mispronunciation: Fairly low
Famous Namesakes: Actress Shoshannah Stern; designer Shoshanna Lonstein Gruss
Common Nicknames: None
Common Variations: None
Consider This: Although Shoshana is a Hebrew name often used by Jewish families, it seems suitable for many cultural backgrounds.

Sierra ★★★★
(Irish) black. (Spanish) saw toothed.
First Impression: Folks believe Sierra pushes herself to achieve amazing goals.
Gender Association: Used mostly for girls
Popularity and Trend: #141 (#53 in 2000)
Risk of Misspelling: Fairly low
Risk of Mispronunciation: Low
Famous Namesakes: None
Common Nicknames: None
Common Variations: Siera

Consider This: After being in the Top 100 for over a decade, Sierra is now sliding lower in popularity.

Simone ★★★
(Hebrew) she heard.
First Impression: Simone is thought to be a sexy and lithe woman who's as kind and considerate as she is beautiful.
Gender Association: Used for girls
Popularity and Trend: #564 (#583 in 2000)
Risk of Misspelling: Fairly low
Risk of Mispronunciation: Fairly low
Famous Namesakes: Writer Simone de Beauvoir; actress Simone Simon; character Simone Deveaux (*Heroes*)
Common Nicknames: None
Common Variations: Symone
Consider This: This feminine version of Simon has a posh, French flair.

Siobhan ★
(Irish) a form of Joan.
First Impression: People can't agree if Siobhan is elegant, dependent, or intelligent.
Gender Association: Used for girls
Popularity and Trend: Last ranked in the Top 1000 in the 1980s
Risk of Misspelling: High
Risk of Mispronunciation: High
Famous Namesakes: Actress Siobhán McKenna; actress Siobhan Fallon; singer Siobhan Donaghy
Common Nicknames: None
Common Variations: None

Consider This: No, this isn't pronounced "SEE-oh-ban." It's "shih-VAHN."

Sissy ★★

(American) a familiar form of Cecelia.

First Impression: This name gives the impression of a whiny, prissy wimp who's shy, timid, and quick to submit.

Gender Association: Used for girls

Popularity and Trend: Never been ranked in Top 1000

Risk of Misspelling: Low

Risk of Mispronunciation: Low

Famous Namesakes: Actress Sissy Spacek

Common Nicknames: None

Common Variations: None

Consider This: With its wimpy connotation, Sissy doesn't work well even as a nickname—unless you use it for your little sister.

Skye ★★★★

(Arabic) water giver. (Dutch) a form of Skyler.

First Impression: Skye's good will is considered as big as the sky.

Gender Association: Used mostly for girls

Popularity and Trend: #433 (#480 in 2000)

Risk of Misspelling: Fairly low

Risk of Mispronunciation: Low

Famous Namesakes: Singer Skye Sweetnam; character Skye Chandler Quartermaine (*General Hospital*); actress Ione Skye

Common Nicknames: None

Common Variations: Sky

Consider This: Skye is a pretty nature name, but it may trip up those who forget to spell it with a final *e*.

Sofia ★★★★

(Greek) a form of Sophia.

First Impression: Sofia may be soft spoken, but people say she's no wallflower.

Gender Association: Used for girls

Popularity and Trend: #56 (#161 in 2000)

Risk of Misspelling: Average

Risk of Mispronunciation: Low

Famous Namesakes: Director Sofia Coppola; actress Sophia Loren; actress Sophia Bush; actress Sofia Vergara; actress Sophia Myles; character Sophia Petrillo (*The Golden Girls*)

Common Nicknames: Sofie

Common Variations: Sophia

Consider This: Sophia may be the more established and popular spelling, but Sofia gets the scoring edge.

Sondra ★★★

(Greek) defender of mankind.

First Impression: People say Sondra is an arrogant and bossy know-it-all.

Gender Association: Used for girls

Popularity and Trend: Last ranked in the Top 1000 in the 1980s

Risk of Misspelling: Fairly low

Risk of Mispronunciation: Low

Famous Namesakes: Character Sondra Huxtable Tibideaux (*The Cosby Show*)

Common Nicknames: None

Common Variations: Saundra, Sandra

Consider This: Sondra is easier to pronounce than Sandra, but it loses points for first impression, popularity, and versatility.

Sonya ★★

(Greek) wise. (Russian, Slavic) a form of Sophia.

First Impression: People believe Sonya could be a popular people-person or a dramatic snob.

Gender Association: Used for girls

Popularity and Trend: Last ranked in the Top 1000 in the 1980s

Risk of Misspelling: Average

Risk of Mispronunciation: Average

Famous Namesakes: Figure skater Sonja Henie; actress Sonya Smith

Common Nicknames: None

Common Variations: Sonia, Sonja

Consider This: With both "SOHN-yah" and "SAHN-yah" as options, pronunciation will likely be a problem.

Sophia ★★★★

(Greek) wise.

First Impression: Sophia is described as sweet natured and elegant, though perhaps a bit prim unless she lets her hair down.

Gender Association: Used for girls

Popularity and Trend: #9 (#42 in 2000)

Risk of Misspelling: Fairly low

Risk of Mispronunciation: Low

Famous Namesakes: Director Sofia Coppola; actress Sophia Loren; actress Sophia Bush; actress Sofia Vergara; actress Sophia Myles; character Sophia Petrillo (*The Golden Girls*)

Common Nicknames: Sophie

Common Variations: Sofia

Consider This: Sophia narrowly misses the 5-star score, thanks to its prim first impression and its overexposure as a Top 10 name.

Sophie ★★★★

(Greek) a form of Sophia.

First Impression: Sophie is seen as a cultured and refined woman.

Gender Association: Used for girls

Popularity and Trend: #125 (#160 in 2000)

Risk of Misspelling: Fairly low

Risk of Mispronunciation: Low

Famous Namesakes: Actress Sophie Marceau; singer Sophie Ellis Bextor; activist Sophie Scholl; model Sophie Dahl; character Sophie Zawistowski (*Sophie's Choice*)

Common Nicknames: None

Common Variations: Sofie

Consider This: Sophie doesn't seem overly casual as a given name, even though it's sometimes used as a nickname for Sophia.

Stacey ★★

(Greek) resurrection. (Irish) a form of Anastasia, Eustacia, Natasha.

First Impression: Stacey has two images straight from a typical junior high school setting: She's either a klutzy nerd or a boy-crazy airhead.

Gender Association: Used mostly for girls

Popularity and Trend: #976 (#682 in 2000)

Risk of Misspelling: Average

Risk of Mispronunciation: Low

Famous Namesakes: Actress Stacy Dash; actress Stacy Keibler; TV host Stacy London; singer Stacy "Fergie" Ferguson

Common Nicknames: None

Common Variations: Stacy, Stacee

Consider This: Both Stacey and Stacy have image problems, but for whatever reason, Stacey is associated with adolescent stereotypes.

Stacia ★★

(English) a form of Anastasia.

First Impression: People think Stacia may be a wild party girl or a prim and delicate dancer.

Gender Association: Used for girls

Popularity and Trend: Last ranked in the Top 1000 in the 1980s

Risk of Misspelling: Average

Risk of Mispronunciation: Fairly high

Famous Namesakes: None

Common Nicknames: None

Common Variations: Stasya

Consider This: Stacia inspires a slightly more positive image, but many people still lump it into the same "party girl" camp as Stacy. Pronunciation could be challenging: "STAY-shah" versus "STAH-shah" versus "STAH-shee-ah."

Stacy ★★★

(Greek) resurrection. (Irish) a form of Anastasia, Eustacia, Natasha.

First Impression: Stacy may have a good time, but folks say she has not-so-good qualities, like being self-centered and ditzy.

Gender Association: Used mostly for girls

Popularity and Trend: #672 (#597 in 2000)

Risk of Misspelling: Fairly low

Risk of Mispronunciation: Low

Famous Namesakes: Actress Stacy Dash; actress Stacy Keibler; TV host Stacy London; singer Stacy "Fergie" Ferguson

Common Nicknames: None

Common Variations: Stacey, Stacee

Consider This: In the "Stacy versus Stacey" debate, this spelling scores better, but it rates only 3 stars.

Starr ★★

(English) star.

First Impression: It's a tossup for most people: Starr could be obnoxious, arty, or trashy.

Gender Association: Used mostly for girls

Popularity and Trend: Last ranked in the Top 1000 in the 1980s

Risk of Misspelling: Average

Risk of Mispronunciation: Low

Famous Namesakes: TV host Star Jones

Common Nicknames: None

Common Variations: Star

Consider This: An unconventional noun name like Starr often stands out and evokes strong first impressions—which, as you can see, aren't always positive.

Stella ★★★★

(Latin) star. (French) a form of Estelle.

First Impression: People say Stella is more than just a pretty face; she has a pretty personality, too.

Gender Association: Used for girls

Popularity and Trend: #241 (#656 in 2000)

Risk of Misspelling: Low

Risk of Mispronunciation: Low

Famous Namesakes: Designer Stella McCartney; character Stella Kowalski (*A Streetcar Named Desire*); actress Stella Adler

Common Nicknames: None

Common Variations: None

Consider This: It's no surprise that Stella is gaining popularity—it's a pleasant name with very few downsides.

Stephanie ★★★★

(Greek) crowned.

First Impression: People believe Stephanie can have just about any personality: perky, witchy, sweet, ditzy, boring, or simply average.

Gender Association: Used mostly for girls

Popularity and Trend: #70 (#40 in 2000)

Risk of Misspelling: Fairly low

Risk of Mispronunciation: Low

Famous Namesakes: Actress Stephanie Powers; model Stephanie Seymour; actress Stephanie Zimbalist; radio personality Stephanie Miller

Common Nicknames: Steffi, Stevie

Common Variations: Stephani, Stefani

Consider This: Stephanie certainly has a mixed bag of first impressions, but it's still a Top 100 name.

Stevie ★★

(Greek) a familiar form of Stephanie.

First Impression: People think Stevie is quite nice, so she'd be better off if she acted like herself and didn't try to be "cool."

Gender Association: Used mostly for girls

Popularity and Trend: Last ranked in the Top 1000 in the 1990s

Risk of Misspelling: Fairly low

Risk of Mispronunciation: Low

Famous Namesakes: Singer Stevie Nicks

Common Nicknames: None

Common Variations: Stevi

Consider This: Stevie may be a fun nickname for Stephanie, but many people may perceive it as a nickname for Steve or Steven.

Stockard ★★★★

(English) stockyard.

First Impression: Stockard may be proper, but people believe she has a sense of humor—much as actress Stockard Channing has.

Gender Association: Used for girls

Popularity and Trend: Never been ranked in Top 1000

Risk of Misspelling: Fairly low

Risk of Mispronunciation: Low

Famous Namesakes: Actress Stockard Channing

Common Nicknames: None

Common Variations: None

Consider This: Because this name evokes Stockard Channing's bold, unique persona, it's important to consider how it may fit your child's future personality.

Storm ★★★

(English) storm.

First Impression: Thanks to the *X-Men* comics and films, many people believe Storm is a courageous superhero who's strong, powerful, and ready to help the less fortunate.

Gender Association: Used for girls

Popularity and Trend: Never been ranked in Top 1000

Risk of Misspelling: Low

Risk of Mispronunciation: Low

Famous Namesakes: Character Storm (*X-Men*)

Common Nicknames: None

Common Variations: Stormy

Consider This: Think twice about this name: One, do you really want your daughter associated with a superhero? Two, do you really want her associated with a weather pattern known for destruction and danger?

Stormy ★★

(English) impetuous by nature.

First Impression: Like a storm rising on an otherwise perfect day, people say Stormy can quickly move from pleasant to unpleasant.

Gender Association: Used mostly for girls

Popularity and Trend: Never been ranked in Top 1000

Risk of Misspelling: Low

Risk of Mispronunciation: Low

Famous Namesakes: None

Common Nicknames: None

Common Variations: Storm

Consider This: While Storm benefits from the superhero connection, Stormy has nothing but a volatile, impetuous first impression.

Sue ★★★

(Hebrew) a short form of Susan, Susana.

First Impression: Sue is viewed as likable, but she has her issues.

Gender Association: Used for girls

Popularity and Trend: Last ranked in the Top 1000 in the 1980s

Risk of Misspelling: Low

Risk of Mispronunciation: Low

Famous Namesakes: Author Sue Taylor Grafton; author Sue Townsend; designer Sue Wong; talk show host Sue Johanson; character Sue Richards (*The Fantastic Four*)

Common Nicknames: Susie

Common Variations: None

Consider This: Sue works well as a nickname and an easy, accessible given name, though it lacks the gravitas of Susan.

Summer ★★★★

(English) summertime.

First Impression: Summer is pictured as warm and carefree as the season that shares her name.

Gender Association: Used for girls

Popularity and Trend: #154 (#145 in 2000)

Risk of Misspelling: Low

Risk of Mispronunciation: Low

Famous Namesakes: Character Summer Roberts (*The O.C.*); swimmer Summer Sanders

Common Nicknames: None

Common Variations: None

Consider This: Like Autumn, this season name is popular for good reason. And it's a smart alternative to names like Sunny and Sunshine.

Sunny ★★★

(English) sunny; bright, cheerful. A familiar form of Sunshine.

First Impression: Fittingly enough, people think Sunny has a sunny disposition (though she's likely not the most intelligent person in the room).

Gender Association: Used about equally for girls and boys

Popularity and Trend: Last ranked in the Top 1000 in the 1980s

Risk of Misspelling: Low

Risk of Mispronunciation: Low

Famous Namesakes: Character Sunny Beaudelaire (*Lemony Snicket* series)

Common Nicknames: None

Common Variations: None

Consider This: Sunny certainly is "bright, cheerful," but it may be too cheery to be taken seriously. Plus, it's used equally for boys and girls, which may pose a problem for parents searching for names with clear gender associations.

Sunshine ★★★

(English) sunshine.

First Impression: Sunshine is considered a cheerful, peppy girl with lots of smiles and giggles, but not a lot of intelligence.

Gender Association: Used for girls

Popularity and Trend: Last ranked in the Top 1000 in the 1980s

Risk of Misspelling: Low

Risk of Mispronunciation: Low

Famous Namesakes: R&B singer Sunshine Anderson

Common Nicknames: Sunny

Common Variations: None

Consider This: Like Sunny, Sunshine is clouded by a lack of seriousness.

Susan ★★★★

(Hebrew) lily.

First Impression: People believe Susan's strong personality is sometimes misconstrued, but she's actually a great friend.

Gender Association: Used for girls

Popularity and Trend: #611 (#422 in 2000)

Risk of Misspelling: Fairly low

Risk of Mispronunciation: Low

Famous Namesakes: Actress Susan Sarandon; activist Susan B. Anthony; actress Susan Lucci; actress Susan Dey; author Susan Cheever

Common Nicknames: Suze, Sue, Susie, Sukey, Suzette, Zanna, Zsa Zsa

Common Variations: Susana, Susanne, Suzan, Suzanne

Consider This: The main drawback to Susan is its falling popularity, which suggests it's starting to sound dated.

Susannah ★★★★

(Hebrew) a form of Susan.

First Impression: Susannah is imagined to be a friendly and fun free spirit who loves big gatherings and music.

Gender Association: Used for girls

Popularity and Trend: Last ranked in the Top 1000 in the 1970s

Risk of Misspelling: Average

Risk of Mispronunciation: Low

Famous Namesakes: Actress Susannah York; character Susannah Polk (*Susannah*); screenwriter Susannah Grant; singer Susannah Hoffs

Common Nicknames: Suze, Sue, Susie, Suzette, Anna

Common Variations: Susana, Suzannah

Consider This: Thanks to "Oh! Susanna," Susannah is the folksy member of the Susan family.

Suzanne ★★★★

(English) a form of Susan.

First Impression: Folks say Suzanne walks into a conference room feeling self-assured and ready to succeed.

Gender Association: Used for girls

Popularity and Trend: Last ranked in the Top 1000 in the 1990s

Risk of Misspelling: Fairly low

Risk of Mispronunciation: Low

Famous Namesakes: Actress Suzanne Somers; actress Suzanne Pleshette; singer Suzanne Vega

Common Nicknames: Suze, Sue, Susie, Zanna, Zsa Zsa, Suzette

Common Variations: Susanne, Suzan

Consider This: Like many Susan variations, Suzanne is a Top 1000 dropout, but it does garner a positive first impression. Most people will likely know to pronounce it "soo-ZAN."

Suzette ★★★

(French) a form of Susan.

First Impression: Suzette is depicted as ditzy and childish, but she certainly has her share of fun.

Gender Association: Used for girls

Popularity and Trend: Last ranked in the Top 1000 in the 1970s

Risk of Misspelling: Fairly low

Risk of Mispronunciation: Low

Famous Namesakes: Beauty queen Suzette Charles

Common Nicknames: Sue, Suze

Common Variations: None

Consider This: The "-ette" ending seems to give this name a youthful, almost flirty, vibe that may not be a plus.

Suzie ★★★

(American) a familiar form of Susan, Susana.

First Impression: Suzie is sociable, or at least that's what most people say.

Gender Association: Used for girls

Popularity and Trend: Last ranked in the Top 1000 in the 1960s

Risk of Misspelling: Average

Risk of Mispronunciation: Low

Famous Namesakes: Musician Suzie Quatro

Common Nicknames: None

Common Variations: Susie

Consider This: Suzie is a friendly name, but it's best to use it as a nickname for Susan or Suzanne.

Svetlana ★

(Russian) bright light.

First Impression: This name reminds folks of Russian gymnast Svetlana Khorkina, who's as famous for her testy behavior as she is for her athletic prowess.

Gender Association: Used for girls

Popularity and Trend: Never been ranked in Top 1000

Risk of Misspelling: Fairly high

Risk of Mispronunciation: Fairly high

Famous Namesakes: Gymnast Svetlana Khorkina

Common Nicknames: Lana

Common Variations: None

Consider This: Some people may find it difficult to spell and pronounce this Russian name ("svyet-LAHN-ah").

Sybil ★★

(Greek) prophet.

First Impression: Thanks to *Sybil*, the popular book and miniseries based on the life of a woman with multiple personalities, people imagine Sybil as a fragile, brittle woman with intense mood and personality swings.

Gender Association: Used for girls

Popularity and Trend: Last ranked in the Top 1000 in the 1960s

Risk of Misspelling: Average

Risk of Mispronunciation: Low

Famous Namesakes: Patriot Sybil Ludington; actress Cybil Shepherd

Common Nicknames: None

Common Variations: Cybil

Consider This: Sybil was off the Top 1000 list long before the book and miniseries *Sybil* made it synonymous with split personalities.

Sydney ★★★★

(French) from Saint-Denis, France.

First Impression: People say Sydney has some spunk—and some wit.

Gender Association: Used mostly for girls

Popularity and Trend: #34 (#23 in 2000)

Risk of Misspelling: Average

Risk of Mispronunciation: Low

Famous Namesakes: Character Sydney Bristow (*Alias*); actress Sydney Tamiia Poitier

Common Nicknames: Syd

Common Variations: Sidney

Consider This: Sydney is much more popular than Sidney, but the existence of two spelling options may cause spelling problems.

Sylvana ★★

(Latin) forest.

First Impression: Folks think Sylvana has a mysterious, exotic quality.

Gender Association: Used for girls

Popularity and Trend: Never been ranked in Top 1000

Risk of Misspelling: Average

Risk of Mispronunciation: Average

Famous Namesakes: Actress Sylvana Simons

Common Nicknames: None

Common Variations: Silvana

Consider This: Sylvana has a heavy—perhaps even foreign—sound, which creates mystery that may or may not be beneficial. In addition, pronunciation may differ between "sill-VAHN-ah" and "sill-VAN-ah."

Sylvia ★★★

(Latin) forest.

First Impression: People imagine Sylvia as a depressed, mentally unstable, and deeply intelligent writer, much like tragic poet Sylvia Plath.

Gender Association: Used for girls
Popularity and Trend: #524
(#505 in 2000)
Risk of Misspelling: Fairly low
Risk of Mispronunciation: Low
Famous Namesakes: Author Sylvia Plath; author Sylvia Browne
Common Nicknames: Sylvie
Common Variations: Silvia
Consider This: Sylvia Plath is indeed a tragic figure, but she's also a respected literary figure, which may explain why this name lands somewhere in the middle of the Top 1000.

Tabitha ★★★★
(Greek, Aramaic) gazelle.
First Impression: Tabitha is pictured as most likely fun-loving and clever.
Gender Association: Used for girls
Popularity and Trend: #534
(#319 in 2000)
Risk of Misspelling: Fairly low
Risk of Mispronunciation: Low
Famous Namesakes: Biblical figure Tabitha; character Tabitha (*Bewitched*)
Common Nicknames: Tabby
Common Variations: Tabatha, Tabbitha
Consider This: After peaking in the '80s, Tabitha is now gradually slipping in popularity.

Taffy ★★★
(Welsh) a familiar form of Taffline.
First Impression: People describe Taffy as bubbly, fun, and silly, not to mention sweet and lovable.
Gender Association: Used mostly for girls
Popularity and Trend: Never been ranked in Top 1000
Risk of Misspelling: Low
Risk of Mispronunciation: Low
Famous Namesakes: None
Common Nicknames: None
Common Variations: None
Consider This: The first impression is quite clear: This name is sweet, but has little substance.

Taka ★★★
(Japanese) honored.
First Impression: People say Taka may be strong, but she's not stern.
Gender Association: Used for girls
Popularity and Trend: Never been ranked in Top 1000
Risk of Misspelling: Average
Risk of Mispronunciation: Average
Famous Namesakes: None
Common Nicknames: None
Common Variations: None
Consider This: Taka (pronounced "TAH-kah") is a seemingly simple name, but because most people aren't familiar with it, it may cause mild spelling and pronunciation problems.

Tamara ★★★★
(Hebrew) palm tree.
First Impression: People think Tamara has a sassy, fun side.
Gender Association: Used for girls
Popularity and Trend: #678
(#417 in 2000)
Risk of Misspelling: Fairly low
Risk of Mispronunciation: Fairly high
Famous Namesakes: Actress Tamera Mowry; singer Tamyra Grey; actress Tamara Tunie
Common Nicknames: Tammy, Tamar, Mara
Common Variations: Tamarah, Tamera
Consider This: Pronunciation holds this name back. It could be pronounced "tah-MAIR-ah," "tah-MAR-ah," "TAM-rah," or even "TAM-ah-rah."

Tameka ★★★
(Aramaic) twin.
First Impression: Tameka is said to be a spirited and vibrant African American woman.
Gender Association: Used for girls
Popularity and Trend: Last ranked in the Top 1000 in the 1990s
Risk of Misspelling: Average
Risk of Mispronunciation: Average
Famous Namesakes: TV host Tamika Ray; stylist Tameka Foster
Common Nicknames: None
Common Variations: Timeka
Consider This: Tameka is often used by African American families.

Pronunciation could be tricky for some people who don't know that it's pronounced "tah-MEEK-ah."

Tammy ★★★
(English) a familiar form of Thomasina. (Hebrew) a familiar form of Tamara.

First Impression: Tammy is thought to be a nurturing, sensitive, and patient woman who loves to help others.

Gender Association: Used mostly for girls

Popularity and Trend: Last ranked in the Top 1000 in the 1990s

Risk of Misspelling: Fairly low

Risk of Mispronunciation: Low

Famous Namesakes: Singer Tammy Wynette; personality Tammy Faye Bakker

Common Nicknames: None

Common Variations: Tami

Consider This: Tammy is a great nickname with a positive vibe, but its low popularity suggests it's a not-so-great given name.

Tanith ★
(Phoenician) goddess of love.

First Impression: Tanith is seen as a fast-talking extrovert who can sometimes be short-tempered.

Gender Association: Used for girls

Popularity and Trend: Never been ranked in Top 1000

Risk of Misspelling: High

Risk of Mispronunciation: High

Famous Namesakes: Ice dancer Tanith Belbin

Common Nicknames: None

Common Variations: None

Consider This: To anyone unfamiliar with Phoenician mythology (which is most of us), Tanith may seem like an odd name. It may also be hard to pronounce ("tah-NEET").

Tanya ★★
(Russian, Slavic) fairy queen.

First Impression: Tanya strikes people as a bossy and sometimes even nasty bleached-blond country gal, perhaps thanks to country music star Tanya Tucker.

Gender Association: Used for girls

Popularity and Trend: #746 (#573 in 2000)

Risk of Misspelling: Average

Risk of Mispronunciation: Average

Famous Namesakes: Actress Tanya Roberts; singer Tanya Tucker

Common Nicknames: Tana

Common Variations: Tania, Tonya

Consider This: Aside from the troublesome first impression, Tanya suffers from pronunciation problems ("TAN-yah" versus "TAHN-yah").

Tara ★★★
(Aramaic) throw; carry. (Irish) rocky hill. (Arabic) a measurement.

First Impression: Tara is said to be a fun, bold, and self-indulgent woman who's known for her crazy antics, much like Tara Reid, one of Hollywood's wildest party girls.

Gender Association: Used for girls

Popularity and Trend: #463 (#239 in 2000)

Risk of Misspelling: Fairly low

Risk of Mispronunciation: Average

Famous Namesakes: Actress Tara Reid; figure skater Tara Lipinski; beauty queen Tara Conner

Common Nicknames: Tari

Common Variations: Tarah, Tera

Consider This: Tara poses a challenge for pronunciation because both "TAIR-ah" and "TAR-ah" are popular.

Taryn ★★★
(Irish) a form of Tara.

First Impression: Taryn is pictured as a wacky but cool character.

Gender Association: Used mostly for girls

Popularity and Trend: #444 (#447 in 2000)

Risk of Misspelling: Average

Risk of Mispronunciation: Average

Famous Namesakes: Actress Taryn Manning

Common Nicknames: None

Common Variations: Tarin, Taran

Consider This: This variation of Tara has the same pronunciation problem as its root name.

Tasha ★★★

(Greek) born on Christmas day. (Russian) a form of Natasha.

First Impression: People think Tasha seems to participate in every extracurricular activity.

Gender Association: Used for girls

Popularity and Trend: Last ranked in the Top 1000 in the 1990s

Risk of Misspelling: Average

Risk of Mispronunciation: Average

Famous Namesakes: Actress Tasha Smith; character Tasha Yar (*Star Trek: The Next Generation*)

Common Nicknames: None

Common Variations: Tosha

Consider This: Tasha could be tricky to pronounce for those who don't realize it's "TAH-shah," a short form of Natasha.

Tatiana ★★★★

(Slavic) fairy queen.

First Impression: Many people envision Tatiana as an intelligent and literary woman, perhaps even a professor.

Gender Association: Used for girls

Popularity and Trend: #283 (#252 in 2000)

Risk of Misspelling: Average

Risk of Mispronunciation: Average

Famous Namesakes: Grand duchess Tatiana Nikolaievna of Russia

Common Nicknames: Tata, Tiana

Common Variations: Tatianna, Tatyana

Consider This: Tatiana is a Top 300 name with a positive first impression. Pronunciation can be a mouthful ("tah-tee-AHN-ah").

Tatum ★★★

(English) cheerful.

First Impression: People disagree as to whether Tatum exudes confidence or insecurity.

Gender Association: Used mostly for girls

Popularity and Trend: #349 (#419 in 2000)

Risk of Misspelling: Fairly low

Risk of Mispronunciation: Low

Famous Namesakes: Actress Tatum O'Neal

Common Nicknames: Tate

Common Variations: None

Consider This: Tatum has gradually risen in popularity recently.

Tawny ★★

(Gypsy) little one. (English) brownish yellow, tan.

First Impression: People say Tawny is a sassy, rebellious, and flirty stripper with fake breasts, fake blond hair, and a fake tan, perhaps like actress-model Tawny Kitaen.

Gender Association: Used for girls

Popularity and Trend: Never been ranked in Top 1000

Risk of Misspelling: Low

Risk of Mispronunciation: Low

Famous Namesakes: Actress-model Tawny Kitaen

Common Nicknames: None

Common Variations: Tawnee

Consider This: Tawny Kitaen isn't the world's greatest role model, as the first impression suggests.

Taylor ★★★★

(English) tailor.

First Impression: People describe Taylor as cheerful, playful, flirty, and fun-loving.

Gender Association: Used mostly for girls

Popularity and Trend: #22 (#9 in 2000)

Risk of Misspelling: Fairly low

Risk of Mispronunciation: Low

Famous Namesakes: Singer Taylor Swift; singer Taylor Hicks; singer Taylor Dayne

Common Nicknames: Taye

Common Variations: Tayler, Tayla

Consider This: Taylor was a Top 10 name for the better part of the '90s, and although it's dropped a bit, it's still very popular.

Tegan ★★

(Welsh) a form of Teagan.

First Impression: People believe Tegan may have a geeky career, but she's no social misfit.

Gender Association: Used mostly for girls

Popularity and Trend: Never been ranked in Top 1000

Risk of Misspelling: Average

Risk of Mispronunciation: Average

Famous Namesakes: Singer Tegan
Quin; character Tegan Jovanka
(*Dr. Who*)

Common Nicknames: None

Common Variations: Teagan

Consider This: This particular spelling has never been ranked in the
Top 1000, but the "Teagan"
spelling is #425.

Terri ★★

(Greek) a familiar form of Theresa.

First Impression: Terri is seen as a
cheerful, perky, and fun-loving
gal who chatters nonstop.

Gender Association: Used for girls

Popularity and Trend: Last ranked in
the Top 1000 in the 1990s

Risk of Misspelling: Fairly high

Risk of Mispronunciation: Low

Famous Namesakes: Actress Teri
Garr; actress Teri Hatcher;
actress Teri Polo

Common Nicknames: None

Common Variations: Teri, Terry

Consider This: With downsides in
popularity, spelling, and versatility, Terri doesn't have many
upsides. Plus, its pronunciation is
the same as that for Terry, a common nickname for boys, which
may cause gender confusion.

Tess ★★★

(Greek) a short form of Quintessa,
Theresa.

First Impression: Tess is depicted as a
well-rounded mom.

Gender Association: Used for girls

Popularity and Trend: #734
(#549 in 2000)

Risk of Misspelling: Low

Risk of Mispronunciation: Low

Famous Namesakes: Character
Tess Durbeyfield (*Tess of the
d'Urbervilles*); actress Tess Harper

Common Nicknames: None

Common Variations: None

Consider This: Tess would have a better score if it weren't traditionally
used as a nickname.

Tessa ★★★★

(Greek) reaper.

First Impression: Folks say Tessa may
not be the brightest bulb, but
she's happy she married into an
upscale lifestyle.

Gender Association: Used for girls

Popularity and Trend: #252
(#266 in 2000)

Risk of Misspelling: Low

Risk of Mispronunciation: Low

Famous Namesakes: None

Common Nicknames: Tess

Common Variations: None

Consider This: Even with a less positive first impression, Tessa has a
better score than Tess, 4 stars to
3, thanks to its versatility.

Thea ★★★

(Greek) goddess.

First Impression: Thea is thought to
be a compassionate, loyal, and
intelligent woman.

Gender Association: Used for girls

Popularity and Trend: Last ranked in
the Top 1000 in the 1950s

Risk of Misspelling: Average

Risk of Mispronunciation: Average

Famous Namesakes: Comedian Thea
Vidale; jazz singer Thea Gill;
mythological figure Thea

Common Nicknames: None

Common Variations: None

Consider This: Thea is sometimes
associated with African American
ethnicity. It's often pronounced
"THEE-ah," but it can also be
"TAY-ah."

Thema ★

(African) queen.

First Impression: Despite her ability to
command others, Thema is said
to be cold and detached, prefer-
ring isolation.

Gender Association: Used for girls

Popularity and Trend: Never been
ranked in Top 1000

Risk of Misspelling: Fairly high

Risk of Mispronunciation: High

Famous Namesakes: None

Common Nicknames: None

Common Variations: None

Consider This: This name has a
special problem with pronunciation: Most people will likely
pronounce it "THEME-ah," but
the original African pronunciation is "TAY-mah."

Theone ★★

(Greek) gift of God.

First Impression: Theone is said to be a modern-day Greek goddess who's lovely, tall, sweet, and congenial.

Gender Association: Used for girls

Popularity and Trend: Never been ranked in Top 1000

Risk of Misspelling: Fairly high

Risk of Mispronunciation: Fairly high

Famous Namesakes: None

Common Nicknames: None

Common Variations: None

Consider This: This Greek name may sound like that of a goddess, but it's ungodly to spell and pronounce ("thee-OHN-ee").

Theresa ★★★

(Greek) reaper.

First Impression: People say Theresa either pushes others around or gets pushed around herself.

Gender Association: Used for girls

Popularity and Trend: #717 (#416 in 2000)

Risk of Misspelling: Fairly low

Risk of Mispronunciation: Average

Famous Namesakes: Nun Mother Teresa; actress Theresa Russell; actress Theresa Randle

Common Nicknames: Resi, Reza, Terri, Tess, Tessie, Tracy, Tressa

Common Variations: Teresa, Therese

Consider This: While most people pronounce it "teh-REE-sah," some may go with "teh-RAY-sah" or "teh-REZ-ah."

Therese ★★★

(Greek) a form of Theresa.

First Impression: People think Therese has a prestigious upbringing and career.

Gender Association: Used for girls

Popularity and Trend: Last ranked in the Top 1000 in the 1980s

Risk of Misspelling: Average

Risk of Mispronunciation: Fairly high

Famous Namesakes: Saint Therese of Lisieux

Common Nicknames: Terri, Tess, Tessie

Common Variations: None

Consider This: Like Theresa, Therese can be pronounced several ways, including "teh-REESE," "teh-REESE-ah," or "teh-REZ."

Thomasina ★★★

(Hebrew) twin.

First Impression: Thomasina is perceived as a self-centered, prissy, and uptight bookworm.

Gender Association: Used for girls

Popularity and Trend: Never been ranked in Top 1000

Risk of Misspelling: Fairly low

Risk of Mispronunciation: Low

Famous Namesakes: Cook Thomasina Miers

Common Nicknames: Tammy, Tamsin, Tommie

Common Variations: None

Consider This: This feminine version of Thomas doesn't give off good vibes.

Tia ★★★★

(Greek) princess. (Spanish) aunt.

First Impression: Tia is said to be an outgoing, charming, and popular woman who's a good communicator.

Gender Association: Used for girls

Popularity and Trend: #608 (#406 in 2000)

Risk of Misspelling: Fairly low

Risk of Mispronunciation: Fairly low

Famous Namesakes: Actress Tia Carrere

Common Nicknames: None

Common Variations: Teah

Consider This: Unlike Mia, Tia seems to have clear pronunciation, with most people knowing to pronounce it "TEE-ah."

Tierney ★★

(Irish) noble.

First Impression: People say Tierney sometimes lets her emotions run away.

Gender Association: Used mostly for girls

Popularity and Trend: Never been ranked in Top 1000

Risk of Misspelling: Average

Risk of Mispronunciation: Fairly low

Famous Namesakes: Actress Gene Tierney; actress Maura Tierney; jazz singer Tierney Sutton

Common Nicknames: None
Common Variations: None
Consider This: Last names used as first names are popular, but Tierney is a lesser-known name in that category. Some people may pronounce it "TEER-nee" and others may pronounce it "TEER-er-nee."

Tiffany ★★★

(Latin) trinity. (Greek) a form of Theophania.
First Impression: Tiffany is overwhelmingly seen as a dimwitted and flighty blond Valley girl.
Gender Association: Used for girls
Popularity and Trend: #210 (#101 in 2000)
Risk of Misspelling: Fairly low
Risk of Mispronunciation: Low
Famous Namesakes: Singer Tiffany; actress Tiffani Thiessen
Common Nicknames: Tiff
Common Variations: Tiffani
Consider This: Despite having a totally '80s vibe, Tiffany is still fairly popular.

Tina ★★★

(Spanish, American) a form of Augustine, Martina, Christina, Valentina.
First Impression: People describe Tina as a bubbly, talkative gal who never stops yapping.
Gender Association: Used for girls

Popularity and Trend: #932 (#574 in 2000)
Risk of Misspelling: Fairly low
Risk of Mispronunciation: Low
Famous Namesakes: Actress Tina Louise; singer Tina Turner; actress Tina Yothers; comedian Tina Fey
Common Nicknames: None
Common Variations: Teena
Consider This: Tina has nearly fallen out of the Top 1000, but it's a popular nickname for many other names.

Tisha ★★★

(Latin) joy.
First Impression: Tisha is said to be a kind and caring African American cutie with a lot of friends.
Gender Association: Used mostly for girls
Popularity and Trend: Last ranked in the Top 1000 in the 1980s
Risk of Misspelling: Average
Risk of Mispronunciation: Average
Famous Namesakes: Actress Tisha Campell
Common Nicknames: Tish
Common Variations: None
Consider This: Although many people may assume it's pronounced "TISH-ah," this short form of Leticia is often pronounced "TEE-shah."

Toni ★★

(Greek, Latin) a familiar form of Antonia, Antoinette.
First Impression: More likely than not, Toni is regarded as the bright spot in someone's day.
Gender Association: Used mostly for girls
Popularity and Trend: #819 (#545 in 2000)
Risk of Misspelling: Average
Risk of Mispronunciation: Low
Famous Namesakes: Author Toni Morrison; singer Toni Braxton; actress Toni Collette; singer Toni Basil
Common Nicknames: None
Common Variations: Tonie, Tony
Consider This: Because Toni is often used as a nickname for Antonia and Antoinette, people may assume it's not a given name. Plus, its pronunciation is the same as that for Tony, a popular nickname for boys, which may cause gender confusion.

Tonya ★★

(Slavic) fairy queen.
First Impression: Because of figure skater Tonya Harding—one of history's most infamous Olympians—Tonya is seen as a jealous, selfish woman with poor self-esteem.
Gender Association: Used for girls

Popularity and Trend: Last ranked in the Top 1000 in the 1990s
Risk of Misspelling: Average
Risk of Mispronunciation: Low
Famous Namesakes: Figure skater Tonya Harding; actress Tonya Pinkins
Common Nicknames: None
Common Variations: Tonia, Tanya
Consider This: Tonya Harding's image does affect this name, but it was declining in popularity before the infamous skater became a household name.

Torie ★★★

(English) a form of Tori, Tory.
First Impression: Torie is seen as a wild, fun punk, but she's also a good person.
Gender Association: Used for girls
Popularity and Trend: Never been ranked in Top 1000
Risk of Misspelling: Fairly high
Risk of Mispronunciation: Low
Famous Namesakes: Actress Tori Spelling
Common Nicknames: None
Common Variations: Tori, Tory
Consider This: With so many ways to spell this name, Torie may be confused for Tori or Tory.

Torrance ★★★

(Irish) a form of Torrence.
First Impression: People say Torrance comes at people with a torrent of willpower.

Gender Association: Used for girls
Popularity and Trend: Never been ranked in Top 1000
Risk of Misspelling: Fairly low
Risk of Mispronunciation: Low
Famous Namesakes: Character Torrance Shipman (*Bring It On*)
Common Nicknames: Torie
Common Variations: None
Consider This: This old-fashioned name has a youthful namesake with Kirsten Dunst's character from the movie *Bring It On*.

Tova ★★★

(Hebrew) a form of Tovah.
First Impression: Folks think Tova may be free spirited, open minded, or perhaps a little slow.
Gender Association: Used for girls
Popularity and Trend: Never been ranked in Top 1000
Risk of Misspelling: Average
Risk of Mispronunciation: Low
Famous Namesakes: Actress Tovah Feldshuh
Common Nicknames: None
Common Variations: Tovah
Consider This: Tova is most likely used by Jewish families, and this particular spelling is not as common as "Tovah."

Tracy ★★★

(Latin) warrior. (Greek) a form of Theresa.

First Impression: People say Tracy is a battler—they say she's courageous, brave, and hardworking.
Gender Association: Used mostly for girls
Popularity and Trend: Last ranked in the Top 1000 in the 1980s
Risk of Misspelling: Fairly low
Risk of Mispronunciation: Low
Famous Namesakes: Actress Tracy Gold; actress Tracy Ellis Ross; actress Tracy Ullman; designer Tracy Reese; singer Tracy Chapman
Common Nicknames: None
Common Variations: Tracey, Traci
Consider This: Perhaps because Tracy is sometimes used as a male name, it creates a powerful impression even when used as a female name.

Tricia ★★

(Latin) a form of Patricia.
First Impression: People believe Tricia's perky image has a seedy side that only a few see.
Gender Association: Used for girls
Popularity and Trend: Last ranked in the Top 1000 in the 1990s
Risk of Misspelling: Average
Risk of Mispronunciation: Low
Famous Namesakes: First daughter Tricia Nixon; model Tricia Helfer
Common Nicknames: Trish
Common Variations: Trisha
Consider This: Spelling and versatility are problems because "Tricia" is a

variant spelling of Trisha, and it's often used as a nickname for Patricia.

Trina ★★

(Greek) pure.

First Impression: People say Trina is a small girl with a big foul mouth, a penchant for starting fights, and a wild sense of style.

Gender Association: Used for girls

Popularity and Trend: Last ranked in the Top 1000 in the 1990s

Risk of Misspelling: Fairly low

Risk of Mispronunciation: Low

Famous Namesakes: Rapper Trina

Common Nicknames: None

Common Variations: None

Consider This: The rapper Trina inspires a mixed reaction, but the name Trina has been off the Top 1000 since the '90s—long before the rapper appeared on the scene.

Trinity ★★★★

(Latin) triad.

First Impression: Trinity is viewed as either a smart lawyer who just passed the bar or a wild cowgirl who works at the Bar-T Ranch.

Gender Association: Used mostly for girls

Popularity and Trend: #63 (#74 in 2000)

Risk of Misspelling: Low

Risk of Mispronunciation: Low

Famous Namesakes: Character Trinity (*The Matrix*)

Common Nicknames: Trini

Common Variations: None

Consider This: Trinity catapulted in popularity after character Trinity appeared in the *Matrix* movies, but the first impression doesn't link to that character at all.

Trish ★★★

(Latin) a familiar form of Beatrice, Patricia, Trisha.

First Impression: People find that Trish is a bubbly, happy extrovert who's sexy, blond, and busty. She's also honest, respectful, and kind.

Gender Association: Used for girls

Popularity and Trend: Never been ranked in Top 1000

Risk of Misspelling: Low

Risk of Mispronunciation: Low

Famous Namesakes: Professional wrestler Trish Stratus

Common Nicknames: None

Common Variations: None

Consider This: Since Trisha is technically a nickname, its short form, Trish, sounds even more casual.

Trista ★★★★

(Latin) a form of Tristan.

First Impression: People imagine Trista as a vibrant cheerleader who's fun, flirty, and almost too sweet, perhaps like reality-TV star Trista Rehn-Sutter.

Gender Association: Used for girls

Popularity and Trend: #812 (#967 in 2002)

Risk of Misspelling: Low

Risk of Mispronunciation: Low

Famous Namesakes: Reality-TV star Trista Rehn-Sutter

Common Nicknames: None

Common Variations: None

Consider This: Because this name is tied to reality TV, which will always be identified as a 2000s concept, it may sound dated as the years go by.

Trudy ★★★

(German) a familiar form of Gertrude.

First Impression: Trudy is considered just like any other little girl—playful and innocent.

Gender Association: Used for girls

Popularity and Trend: Last ranked in the Top 1000 in the 1970s

Risk of Misspelling: Fairly low

Risk of Mispronunciation: Low

Famous Namesakes: Actress Trudie Styler

Common Nicknames: None

Common Variations: Trudel, Trudie

Consider This: This nickname for Gertrude creates a youthful impression that unfortunately won't grow with your daughter.

Tyne ★★★

(English) river.

First Impression: Tyne is said to be an assertive, strong-willed woman who sometimes seems over-bearing, stubborn, and even mean, much like characters played by feisty actress Tyne Daly of TV's *Cagney & Lacey* and *Judging Amy*.

Gender Association: Used for girls
Popularity and Trend: Never been ranked in Top 1000
Risk of Misspelling: Fairly low
Risk of Mispronunciation: Low
Famous Namesakes: Actress Tyne Daly
Common Nicknames: None
Common Variations: None
Consider This: Actress Tyne Daly is a positive namesake overall, but she—and therefore this name—is identified as middle aged.

Tyra ★★★
(Scandinavian) battler.
First Impression: People say Tyra is a gorgeous and leggy African American model who's successful and confident, just like supermodel and talk show host Tyra Banks.
Gender Association: Used for girls
Popularity and Trend: #662 (#448 in 2000)
Risk of Misspelling: Fairly low
Risk of Mispronunciation: Low
Famous Namesakes: Model Tyra Banks
Common Nicknames: None
Common Variations: Tyrah

Consider This: Because of Tyra Banks, some people may associate this name with African Americans more than any other ethnic group.

Urania ★★
(Greek) heavenly.
First Impression: Urania is pictured as an antisocial and depressed loner who's not happy with her life.
Gender Association: Used for girls
Popularity and Trend: Never been ranked in Top 1000
Risk of Misspelling: Average
Risk of Mispronunciation: Average
Famous Namesakes: Mythological figure Urania
Common Nicknames: None
Common Variations: None
Consider This: If you want to name your daughter after a planet with mythological roots, name her Venus. Stay away from Uranus; she'll be the butt of jokes.

Uriana ★★
(Greek) heaven; the unknown.
First Impression: Uriana is depicted as funny, although perhaps in a laughing-*at*-her way, a not laughing-*with*-her way.
Gender Association: Used for girls
Popularity and Trend: Never been ranked in Top 1000
Risk of Misspelling: Average
Risk of Mispronunciation: Average

Famous Namesakes: None
Common Nicknames: None
Common Variations: None
Consider This: With a very similar spelling, it's no shock that Uriana rates just as poorly as Urania does. Pronunciation could be tricky with both "ur-ee-AHN-ah" and "ur-ee-ANN-ah" as options.

Ursula ★★
(Greek) little bear.
First Impression: People overwhelmingly think Ursula is a horrible, evil, and witchlike woman who's power hungry and quick to trample anyone in her path, much like Ursula the Sea Witch of Disney's *The Little Mermaid*.
Gender Association: Used for girls
Popularity and Trend: Last ranked in the Top 1000 in the 1980s
Risk of Misspelling: Fairly low
Risk of Mispronunciation: Low
Famous Namesakes: Actress Ursula Andress; character Ursula the Sea Witch (*The Little Mermaid*); character Ursula Buffay (*Mad about You*)
Common Nicknames: Sula, Ursa
Common Variations: Ursula
Consider This: It's never good to be named after a villain, especially a plump sea witch.

Valerie ★★★★

(Latin) strong.

First Impression: People think Valerie could be stuck-up, meek, or compassionate.

Gender Association: Used for girls

Popularity and Trend: #127 (#166 in 2000)

Risk of Misspelling: Fairly low

Risk of Mispronunciation: Low

Famous Namesakes: Actress Valarie Rae Miller; actress Valerie Bertinelli; actress Valerie Harper

Common Nicknames: Val, Valli

Common Variations: Valarie, Valery, Valorie

Consider This: People can't quite agree on Valerie's image, which may or may not be a plus.

Vanessa ★★★★★

(Greek) butterfly.

First Impression: Vanessa has a healthy self-esteem, and for good reason: She's perceived as an ambitious, smart, and sophisticated woman.

Gender Association: Used for girls

Popularity and Trend: #79 (#62 in 2000)

Risk of Misspelling: Fairly low

Risk of Mispronunciation: Low

Famous Namesakes: Actress Vanessa Williams; TV host Vanessa Minnello; actress Vanessa Redgrave; singer Vanessa Carlton

Common Nicknames: Nessa, Nessie, Van, Vanna

Common Variations: Vanesa, Venessa

Consider This: A strong 5-star name, Vanessa has few downsides.

Vanna ★★★

(Cambodian) golden. (Greek) a form of Vanessa.

First Impression: Vanna strikes people as a spoiled yet glamorous blond aristocrat who's snooty and full of herself.

Gender Association: Used for girls

Popularity and Trend: Never been ranked in Top 1000

Risk of Misspelling: Low

Risk of Mispronunciation: Low

Famous Namesakes: Game show host Vanna White

Common Nicknames: None

Common Variations: None

Consider This: Vanna not only has a poor first impression, but it also sounds straight out of the '80s.

Veda ★★★

(Sanskrit) sacred lore; knowledge.

First Impression: Veda is described as a creative and worldly ad exec who's as sophisticated as she is intelligent.

Gender Association: Used for girls

Popularity and Trend: Last ranked in the Top 1000 in the 1960s

Risk of Misspelling: Fairly high

Risk of Mispronunciation: Fairly high

Famous Namesakes: None

Common Nicknames: None

Common Variations: Vida

Consider This: A Veda is an ancient Sanskrit text, but this name doesn't necessarily have a Hindu association. What it does have is a pronunciation problem: Many people may expect it to be pronounced "VED-ah," but it's either "VEE-dah" or "VAY-dah."

Velma ★★★

(German) a form of Vilhelmina.

First Impression: Most people imagine Velma is a dull, humorless, and bookish geek in raggedy clothes.

Gender Association: Used for girls

Popularity and Trend: Last ranked in the Top 1000 in the 1970s

Risk of Misspelling: Low

Risk of Mispronunciation: Low

Famous Namesakes: Character Velma Dinkley (Scooby-Doo); character Velma Kelly (Chicago)

Common Nicknames: None

Common Variations: None

Consider This: Velma is old-fashioned and nerdy—not the best combination.

Vera ★★★

(Latin) true. (Slavic) faith.

First Impression: People think Vera is a sophisticated and graceful professional with creative vision, strong confidence, and powerful determination.

Gender Association: Used for girls

Popularity and Trend: Last ranked in the Top 1000 in the 1980s

Risk of Misspelling: Fairly low
Risk of Mispronunciation: Average
Famous Namesakes: Designer Vera Wang; actress Vera Farmiga; film character Vera Drake
Common Nicknames: None
Common Variations: None
Consider This: Like Velma, Vera is an old name, but designer Vera Wang puts it in a contemporary context. Pronunciation could be a problem, though, with "VEER-ah" or "VAIR-ah" as options.

Verena ★★★★

(Latin) truthful.
First Impression: People say Verena is well known for her ladylike disposition and style.
Gender Association: Used for girls
Popularity and Trend: Never been ranked in Top 1000
Risk of Misspelling: Fairly low
Risk of Mispronunciation: Fairly low
Famous Namesakes: Saint Verena
Common Nicknames: None
Common Variations: Vera, Verna
Consider This: Verena has never been ranked in the Top 1000, but it seems to create an elegant image. Most people will likely pronounce it correctly as "veh-REEN-ah."

Verna ★★★

(Latin) springtime. (French) a form of Laverne.
First Impression: Folks say Verna has a logical mind but a laid-back vibe.

Gender Association: Used for girls
Popularity and Trend: Last ranked in the Top 1000 in the 1970s
Risk of Misspelling: Low
Risk of Mispronunciation: Low
Famous Namesakes: Actress Verna Bloom
Common Nicknames: None
Common Variations: None
Consider This: Verna is much like Velma; it seems dated and bland.

Veronica ★★★

(Latin) true image.
First Impression: Veronica isn't thought to be *entirely* bad, but she is a brat.
Gender Association: Used for girls
Popularity and Trend: #211 (#143 in 2000)
Risk of Misspelling: Fairly low
Risk of Mispronunciation: Low
Famous Namesakes: Reporter Veronica Guerin; TV character Veronica Mars; character Veronica Lodge (*Archie* comic book series)
Common Nicknames: Roni, Ronica, Vera
Common Variations: Veronika
Consider This: This name loses some points, thanks to Veronica Lodge from the *Archie* comics, who most likely gives it a spoiled image.

Vicki ★★

(Latin) a familiar form of Victoria.
First Impression: Vicki is seen as a people-person with a few foibles.
Gender Association: Used for girls
Popularity and Trend: Last ranked in the Top 1000 in the 1980s
Risk of Misspelling: Average
Risk of Mispronunciation: Low
Famous Namesakes: Comedian Vicki Lawrence; actress Vicki Lewis
Common Nicknames: None
Common Variations: Vicky, Vikki
Consider This: Because Victoria scores so much better, it's smart to use Vicki as a nickname and not a given name.

Victoria ★★★★

(Latin) victorious.
First Impression: With such a regal name, Victoria is considered a strong but uppity woman.
Gender Association: Used for girls
Popularity and Trend: #28 (#20 in 2000)
Risk of Misspelling: Fairly low
Risk of Mispronunciation: Low
Famous Namesakes: Queen Victoria; singer Victoria Beckham; actress Victoria Principal; actress Victoria Rowell; model Victoria Silvstedt
Common Nicknames: Tori, Vicky
Common Variations: Viktoria
Consider This: The only strike against this popular name is the mixed

first impression, which suggests Victoria is strong (good), but arrogant (bad).

Violet ★★★★★
(French) a plant with purplish blue flowers.

First Impression: Everything about this name calls to people's minds a delicate violet in a sunny field.

Gender Association: Used for girls

Popularity and Trend: #261 (#741 in 2000)

Risk of Misspelling: Low

Risk of Mispronunciation: Low

Famous Namesakes: Star kid Violet Anne Affleck; character Violet Beauregarde (*Charlie and the Chocolate Factory*)

Common Nicknames: Vi

Common Variations: Violeta

Consider This: One may think the surge in Violet's popularity is due to star kid Violet Affleck, but this name had actually been on the rise for years before she was born in 2005.

Virginia ★★★★
(Latin) pure, virginal.

First Impression: Folks think you'll probably find Virginia with a cup of tea, a far-off look, and a smile on her face.

Gender Association: Used for girls

Popularity and Trend: #511 (#366 in 2000)

Risk of Misspelling: Low

Risk of Mispronunciation: Low

Famous Namesakes: Writer Virginia Woolf; actress Virginia Madsen; actress Virginia McKenna

Common Nicknames: Gina, Ginny, Ginger

Common Variations: Virginie

Consider This: If it weren't for Virginia's relatively low popularity—which suggests it may be a bit old-fashioned—it would be a 5-star name.

Vivian ★★★★
(Latin) full of life.

First Impression: Vivian is viewed as either zesty or nerdy.

Gender Association: Used for girls

Popularity and Trend: #223 (#272 in 2000)

Risk of Misspelling: Fairly low

Risk of Mispronunciation: Low

Famous Namesakes: Actress Vivian Leigh; actress Vivian Vance; designer Vivienne Westwood

Common Nicknames: Viv, Viva

Common Variations: Viviane, Vivien

Consider This: Vivian is a solid 4-star name, held back only because it seems slightly dated.

Wanda ★★★★
(German) wanderer.

First Impression: Wanda seems to be a loud and silly party girl with a hearty—and most likely obnoxious—laugh.

Gender Association: Used for girls

Popularity and Trend: Last ranked in the Top 1000 in the 1990s

Risk of Misspelling: Low

Risk of Mispronunciation: Low

Famous Namesakes: Comedian Wanda Sykes; singer Wanda Jackson

Common Nicknames: None

Common Variations: None

Consider This: Unlike Wendy, Wanda has fallen out of the Top 1000.

Wendy ★★★
(Welsh) white; light-skinned. A familiar form of Gwendolyn, Wanda.

First Impression: Wendy is known as a caring and kind woman who's eager to lend a hand wherever and however she can.

Gender Association: Used for girls

Popularity and Trend: #354 (#317 in 2000)

Risk of Misspelling: Fairly low

Risk of Mispronunciation: Low

Famous Namesakes: Character Wendy Darling (*Peter Pan*); playwright Wendy Wasserstein; radio personality Wendy Williams

Common Nicknames: None

Common Variations: Wendi

Consider This: Wendy rates relatively well, but perhaps it's best used as a nickname rather than as a given name.

Whitney ★★★

(English) white island.

First Impression: People think Whitney could be perky and preppy or spiteful and selfish.

Gender Association: Used mostly for girls

Popularity and Trend: #531 (#270 in 2000)

Risk of Misspelling: Fairly low

Risk of Mispronunciation: Low

Famous Namesakes: Singer Whitney Houston

Common Nicknames: Whit

Common Variations: Whitnee

Consider This: The mixed reaction in Whitney's first impression may relate to Whitney Houston and her ups and downs as a celebrity.

Wilhelmina ★★★★

(German) a form of Wilhelm

First Impression: Wilhelmina is depicted as a large and plump woman who's caring, sweet, and eager to listen.

Gender Association: Used for girls

Popularity and Trend: Last ranked in the Top 1000 in the 1950s

Risk of Misspelling: Average

Risk of Mispronunciation: Average

Famous Namesakes: Character Wilhelmina Slater (*Ugly Betty*); model Wilhelmina Cooper

Common Nicknames: Billie, Helma, Minka, Minnie, Mina, Willa, Willette, Willie, Wilma

Common Variations: Vilhelmina

Consider This: Wilhelmina hasn't been popular for generations, but it is one of the most versatile names you can find. Pronunciation could be a mouthful: "will-eh-MEEN-ah."

Willow ★★★★

(English) willow tree.

First Impression: A name like Willow creates such a lovely picture of a demure, waiflike lady.

Gender Association: Used for girls

Popularity and Trend: #529 (#760 in 2000)

Risk of Misspelling: Low

Risk of Mispronunciation: Low

Famous Namesakes: Character Willow Rosenberg (*Buffy the Vampire Slayer*); TV host Willow Bay

Common Nicknames: None

Common Variations: None

Consider This: Where Starr, Sunny, and Storm fail as nature names, Willow succeeds because it creates such a pleasant first impression.

Winda ★

(Swahili) hunter.

First Impression: People resoundingly agree Winda is unlikable, saying she's anything from dumb to nasty to dull.

Gender Association: Used for girls

Popularity and Trend: Never been ranked in Top 1000

Risk of Misspelling: Fairly high

Risk of Mispronunciation: Fairly high

Famous Namesakes: Writer Winda Benedetti

Common Nicknames: None

Common Variations: None

Consider This: This name may look as though it's pronounced "WIN-dah," but the traditional pronunciation is "WEEN-dah."

Winifred ★★★

(German) peaceful friend. (Welsh) a form of Guinevere.

First Impression: Winifred is described as an old bookworm with old money and old-fashioned ideals.

Gender Association: Used for girls

Popularity and Trend: Last ranked in the Top 1000 in the 1960s

Risk of Misspelling: Fairly low

Risk of Mispronunciation: Fairly low

Famous Namesakes: TV producer Winifred Hervey

Common Nicknames: Winnie, Freddie, Win

Common Variations: None

Consider This: As the first impression clearly states, Winifred is a very old-fashioned name.

Winona ★★★

(Lakota) oldest daughter.

First Impression: Some people describe Winona as a popular and cool girl with a great personality and an ability to get along with everyone. Others picture her as a dark-haired and small cutie who's perhaps a little unstable.

Gender Association: Used for girls

Popularity and Trend: Last ranked in the Top 1000 in the 1950s

Risk of Misspelling: Average

Risk of Mispronunciation: Fairly low

Famous Namesakes: Actress Winona Ryder; singer Wynonna Judd

Common Nicknames: Winnie

Common Variations: Wynonna

Consider This: Winona makes a strong first impression because this uncommon name recalls not one but two celebrities.

Winter ★★★

(English) winter.

First Impression: People say Winter may be cold, happy-go-lucky, or unique.

Gender Association: Used mostly for girls

Popularity and Trend: Never been ranked in Top 1000

Risk of Misspelling: Low

Risk of Mispronunciation: Low

Famous Namesakes: None

Common Nicknames: None

Common Variations: Wynter

Consider This: Winter doesn't rate as well as Autumn or Summer for two reasons: It's less common as a name and it's less favored as a season.

Yasmine ★★

(Persian) jasmine flower.

First Impression: Yasmine is seen as an articulate lawyer, a flirty makeup-counter salesclerk, or a sassy aerobics instructor.

Gender Association: Used for girls

Popularity and Trend: #588 (#418 in 2000)

Risk of Misspelling: Average

Risk of Mispronunciation: Fairly high

Famous Namesakes: Actress Yasmine Bleeth

Common Nicknames: None

Common Variations: Yasmin

Consider This: This name could be pronounced "YEZ-meen," "YAZ-meen," or "YAZ-min."

Yoko ★★★

(Japanese) good girl.

First Impression: Yoko is imagined to be an eccentric Asian artist with black hair, small stature, and plenty of quirks, much like Yoko Ono.

Gender Association: Used for girls

Popularity and Trend: Never been ranked in Top 1000

Risk of Misspelling: Low

Risk of Mispronunciation: Low

Famous Namesakes: Artist Yoko Ono

Common Nicknames: None

Common Variations: None

Consider This: Because of Yoko Ono, this name creates a distinct first impression, albeit an odd one.

Yolanda ★★★★

(Greek) violet flower.

First Impression: People say Yolanda uses her humor to speak her mind.

Gender Association: Used for girls

Popularity and Trend: Last ranked in the Top 1000 in the 1980s

Risk of Misspelling: Fairly low

Risk of Mispronunciation: Fairly low

Famous Namesakes: Gospel singer Yolanda Adams; singer Yolanda Perez

Common Nicknames: Yolie, Yone

Common Variations: Jolanda, Yolonda

Consider This: Yolanda is often identified as an African American or Latino name. Most people know to pronounce it "yoh-LAHN-dah."

Yvette ★

(French) a familiar form of Yvonne.

First Impression: Yvette comes across as a fashionable and cultured French sophisticate who's rail thin and model perfect.

Gender Association: Used for girls

Popularity and Trend: #913 (#622 in 2000)

Risk of Misspelling: Fairly high

Risk of Mispronunciation: Fairly high

Famous Namesakes: Model Yvette Nelson

Common Nicknames: None

Common Variations: Evette

Consider This: With a difficult French pronunciation ("ee-VET") and a snooty French image, Yvette is a problematic name.

Yvonne ★★

(French) young archer. (Scandinavian) yew wood; bow wood.

First Impression: Yvonne is primarily perceived as a bossy, pushy woman who's always in charge.

Gender Association: Used for girls

Popularity and Trend: Last ranked in the Top 1000 in the 1980s

Risk of Misspelling: Fairly high

Risk of Mispronunciation: Fairly high

Famous Namesakes: Actress Yvonne De Carlo

Common Nicknames: Vonna, Vonny, Yvette

Common Variations: Evonne

Consider This: Like Yvette, Yvonne may be hard to pronounce ("ee-VON"). It's less popular as well.

Zahara ★★★

(Swahili) a form of Zahra.

First Impression: Zahara is said to be an African model who's often quiet, shy, and reserved.

Gender Association: Used for girls

Popularity and Trend: Never been ranked in Top 1000

Risk of Misspelling: Average

Risk of Mispronunciation: Average

Famous Namesakes: Star kid Zahara Jolie-Pitt

Common Nicknames: None

Common Variations: None

Consider This: With its African origin, this name may be associated with African Americans. Also, some people will know to pronounce it "zah-HAR-ah," but others may mistake it for "zah-HAIR-ah."

Zaida ★★★

(Arabic) a form of Zada.

First Impression: Zaida is seen as a feisty, opinionated, and powerful intellectual.

Gender Association: Used for girls

Popularity and Trend: Never been ranked in Top 1000

Risk of Misspelling: Fairly high

Risk of Mispronunciation: Fairly high

Famous Namesakes: None

Common Nicknames: None

Common Variations: None

Consider This: This uncommon Arabic name creates a positive first impression. Pronunciation could be tricky, with both "ZAY-dah" and "ZAH-ee-dah" as options.

Zaza ★★★

(Hebrew) golden.

First Impression: This name makes people think of a generous, sassy, and witty woman.

Gender Association: Used for girls

Popularity and Trend: Never been ranked in Top 1000

Risk of Misspelling: Average

Risk of Mispronunciation: Average

Famous Namesakes: None

Common Nicknames: None

Common Variations: None

Consider This: People may think of Zsa Zsa Gabor when they hear this name, thanks to the similar spelling and sound.

Zelia ★★★

(Spanish) sunshine.

First Impression: People think Zelia has a zeal for work and life.

Gender Association: Used for girls

Popularity and Trend: Never been ranked in Top 1000

Risk of Misspelling: Fairly high

Risk of Mispronunciation: Fairly high

Famous Namesakes: Author Zélia Gattai; anthropologist Zelia Nuttall

Common Nicknames: None

Common Variations: None

Consider This: Like Zahara, Zaida, and Zaza, Zelia is an uncommon name that evokes a strong, positive image. Pronunciation could be problematic, though, with "ZEE-lee-ah," "ZEH-lee-ah," and even "SAY-lee-ah" as options.

Zena ★★

(Ethiopian) news. (Persian) woman. (Greek) a form of Xenia.

First Impression: Zena is envisioned as a buff and brave battler with mystical, strange powers, much like TV's *Xena: Warrior Princess*.

Gender Association: Used for girls

Popularity and Trend: Last ranked in the Top 1000 in the 1910s

Risk of Misspelling: Average

Risk of Mispronunciation: Average

Famous Namesakes: TV character Xena

Common Nicknames: None

Common Variations: Xena, Zina

Consider This: While the title character of TV's *Xena: Warrior Princess* is a strong female role model, you still need to think twice before naming your daughter after a wild TV character.

Zephyr ★★

(Greek) west wind.

First Impression: Zephyr is imagined to be an outgoing and energetic free spirit.

Gender Association: Used about equally for girls and boys

Popularity and Trend: Never been ranked in Top 1000

Risk of Misspelling: Average

Risk of Mispronunciation: Average

Famous Namesakes: None

Common Nicknames: None

Common Variations: None

Consider This: The main drawback to this name is its ambiguous gender association.

Zizi ★★

(Hungarian) a familiar form of Elizabeth.

First Impression: This name makes people think of a silly, happy, and adorable young woman.

Gender Association: Used for girls

Popularity and Trend: Never been ranked in Top 1000

Risk of Misspelling: Average

Risk of Mispronunciation: Average

Famous Namesakes: Ballerina Zizi Jeanmarie

Common Nicknames: None

Common Variations: None

Consider This: This nickname for Elizabeth is quite limiting as a given name. Also keep in mind that *zizi* is French slang for a certain part of male reproductive anatomy.

Zoe ★★★★

(Greek) life.

First Impression: Zoe is pictured as silly, playful, and downright nutty.

Gender Association: Used mostly for girls

Popularity and Trend: #54 (#82 in 2000)

Risk of Misspelling: Fairly low

Risk of Mispronunciation: Fairly low

Famous Namesakes: Radio personality Zoe Ball; actress Zoe Saldana

Common Nicknames: None

Common Variations: Zoey

Consider This: Zoe is a hot name on the rise, perhaps because it's so fun.

Zola ★★★★

(Italian) piece of earth.

First Impression: People feel this cool and unique name must belong to an equally cool and unique woman.

Gender Association: Used mostly for girls

Popularity and Trend: Last ranked in the Top 1000 in the 1940s

Risk of Misspelling: Fairly low

Risk of Mispronunciation: Low

Famous Namesakes: Olympian Zola Budd

Common Nicknames: None

Common Variations: Zolla

Consider This: Like many Z names, Zola sounds exotic, but that may or may not be a good fit for your daughter.

Profiles of
Boys' Names

Aaron ★★★★

(Hebrew) enlightened. (Arabic) messenger.

First Impression: Aaron is thought to be a smart but sweet bookworm who's tall and wears glasses.

Gender Association: Used mostly for boys

Popularity and Trend: #57 (#41 in 2000)

Risk of Misspelling: Fairly low

Risk of Mispronunciation: Low

Famous Namesakes: Biblical figure Aaron; actor Aaron Eckhart; singer Aaron Carter; politician Aaron Burr

Common Nicknames: None

Common Variations: Aarron, Aron

Consider This: Since the '70s, Aaron has been a perennial Top 100 name. However, its pronunciation is the same as Erin, a popular name for girls, which may cause gender confusion.

Abel ★★★★

(Hebrew) breath. (Assyrian) meadow. (German) a form of Abelard.

First Impression: People say Abel is moral and wise, but he's also a sad pushover.

Gender Association: Used for boys

Popularity and Trend: #338 (#352 in 2000)

Risk of Misspelling: Fairly low

Risk of Mispronunciation: Low

Famous Namesakes: Biblical figure Abel

Common Nicknames: Abe, Abie

Common Variations: Abell

Consider This: While the name Abel suffers a bit from the biblical allusion, it certainly doesn't suffer as much as Cain.

Abraham ★★★★★

(Hebrew) father of many nations.

First Impression: People associate the name Abraham with Abraham Lincoln and imagine a highly intelligent and trustworthy leader who's tall, dark, and bearded.

Gender Association: Used for boys

Popularity and Trend: #183 (#213 in 2000)

Risk of Misspelling: Fairly low

Risk of Mispronunciation: Fairly low

Famous Namesakes: Biblical figure Abraham; president Abraham Lincoln; psychologist Abraham Maslow

Common Nicknames: Abe, Abie, Bram

Common Variations: Ibrahim, Abram

Consider This: Abraham earns 5 stars, especially because it's highly versatile.

Abram ★★★★

(Hebrew) a form of Abraham.

First Impression: For many people, the name Abram conjures up an image of a self-assured, assertive, and wise man.

Gender Association: Used for boys

Popularity and Trend: #586 (#796 in 2000)

Risk of Misspelling: Fairly low

Risk of Mispronunciation: Fairly low

Famous Namesakes: Another name for biblical figure Abraham

Common Nicknames: Bram, Abe, Abie

Common Variations: Avram

Consider This: Abram is technically a short form of Abraham, but it still has fairly decent versatility with its many nicknames. Another plus is that most people will pronounce it correctly as "AY-bram."

Ace ★★★

(Latin) unity.

First Impression: People seem to think of Ace as a sweet, nice guy who loves to be the center of attention.

Gender Association: Used for boys

Popularity and Trend: #838 (first time ranked in Top 1000)

Risk of Misspelling: Low

Risk of Mispronunciation: Low

Famous Namesakes: Movie character Ace Ventura; musician Ace Frehley

Common Nicknames: None

Common Variations: None

Consider This: An unconventional name, Ace cracked the Top 1000 in 2006.

Adam ★★★★★

(Phoenician) man; mankind. (Hebrew) earth; man of the red earth.

First Impression: Adam is pictured as a physically fit and handsome man who's shy, kind, and intelligent.

Gender Association: Used for boys

Popularity and Trend: #64 (#45 in 2000)

Risk of Misspelling: Fairly low

Risk of Mispronunciation: Low

Famous Namesakes: Biblical figure Adam; actor Adam Sandler; singer Adam Ant; actor Adam West

Common Nicknames: None

Common Variations: Addam

Consider This: Like Aaron, Adam is a biblical name that's been quite popular for years.

Addison ★★★

(English) son of Adam.

First Impression: People think Addison is genuine, caring, and successful.

Gender Association: Used about equally for girls and boys

Popularity and Trend: #562 (#514 in 2000)

Risk of Misspelling: Fairly low

Risk of Mispronunciation: Low

Famous Namesakes: Poet Joseph Addison

Common Nicknames: None

Common Variations: Adison

Consider This: Addison loses points for gender association, given that it's used about equally for girls and boys.

Adler ★★★★

(German) eagle.

First Impression: Adler is pictured as a woodsy naturalist who's strong and tall and who carries himself with respectable authority.

Gender Association: Used for boys

Popularity and Trend: Never been ranked in Top 1000

Risk of Misspelling: Fairly low

Risk of Mispronunciation: Low

Famous Namesakes: Psychologist Alfred Adler

Common Nicknames: None

Common Variations: None

Consider This: Last names as first names are popular, but Adler is one that has never ranked in the Top 1000.

Adolf ★★

(German) noble wolf.

First Impression: People describe Adolf as a cruel and socially awkward control freak with Adolf Hitler's trademark moustache and lank dark hair.

Gender Association: Used for boys

Popularity and Trend: Last ranked in the Top 1000 in the 1910s

Risk of Misspelling: Fairly low

Risk of Mispronunciation: Average

Famous Namesakes: Nazi dictator Adolf Hitler

Common Nicknames: Dolf

Common Variations: Adolph, Adolfo, Adolphus

Consider This: Few names create such a negative impression as Adolf—and rightfully so. On top of that, pronunciation will be divided between "AA-dahlf" and "AY-dahlf."

Adon ★★

(Hebrew) Lord.

First Impression: Adon is a bit of a contradiction: Although people feel he's kind, chivalrous, and handsome, he doesn't have many friends.

Gender Association: Used for boys

Popularity and Trend: Never been ranked in Top 1000

Risk of Misspelling: Average

Risk of Mispronunciation: Fairly high

Famous Namesakes: Phoenician mythological figure Adon

Common Nicknames: None

Common Variations: Adonis

Consider This: People may have trouble with this Hebrew name, thinking it's pronounced "AY-don" instead of "AH-don."

Adrian ★★★★

(Greek) rich. (Latin) dark.

First Impression: People think of Adrian as the boy next door:

He's described as caring, wholesome, cheerful, and open.
Gender Association: Used mostly for boys
Popularity and Trend: #63 (#78 in 2000)
Risk of Misspelling: Average
Risk of Mispronunciation: Low
Famous Namesakes: Several popes named Adrian; baseball player Adrián Beltré; actor Adrien Brody; character Adrian Monk (*Monk*); actor Adrian Grenier
Common Nicknames: None
Common Variations: Adrien
Consider This: Choosing between Adrian and Aidan comes down to origins: Adrian has a classical Greek/Latin sound, while Aidan is purely Irish. However, Adrian's pronunciation is the same as that for Adrienne, a popular name for girls, which may cause gender confusion.

Adriel ★★★★
(Hebrew) member of God's flock.
First Impression: Friendly and determined, Adriel is considered someone you can count on.
Gender Association: Used for boys
Popularity and Trend: #707 (#916 in 2002)
Risk of Misspelling: Fairly low
Risk of Mispronunciation: Fairly low
Famous Namesakes: Biblical figure Adriel

Common Nicknames: None
Common Variations: Adrial
Consider This: Perhaps Adriel is a good substitution for Ariel, which is more often used as a girls' name. Most people will pronounce it correctly as "AY-dree-ell."

Ahmad ★★
(Arabic) most highly praised.
First Impression: Ahmad is described as a young Middle Easterner who's bossy and loud yet socially outgoing.
Gender Association: Used for boys
Popularity and Trend: #524 (#454 in 2000)
Risk of Misspelling: Fairly low
Risk of Mispronunciation: Average
Famous Namesakes: Football player Ahmad Rashad
Common Nicknames: None
Common Variations: Amad, Amahd
Consider This: Ahmad is used most often by Muslim families. Some people outside that culture may not realize it's pronounced "ah-MAHD."

Aidan ★★★★
(Irish) fiery.
First Impression: Aidan is described as a sensitive, caring guy who's always a good listener, much like *Sex and the City* character Aidan Shaw.

Gender Association: Used mostly for boys
Popularity and Trend: #44 (#114 in 2000)
Risk of Misspelling: Average
Risk of Mispronunciation: Low
Famous Namesakes: Actor Aidan Quinn; character Aidan Lynch (*Harry Potter* series)
Common Nicknames: None
Common Variations: Aiden, Aidon
Consider This: Both Aidan and Aiden are highly popular names, which will forever prompt the spelling question, "With an *a* or an *e*?"

Ajay ★★
(Punjabi) victorious; undefeatable.
First Impression: People see a nasty, bratty side to Ajay, but he'll likely charm you with his wit and sophistication.
Gender Association: Used for boys
Popularity and Trend: Never been ranked in Top 1000
Risk of Misspelling: Average
Risk of Mispronunciation: Fairly high
Famous Namesakes: Actor Ajay Devgan
Common Nicknames: None
Common Variations: Aj
Consider This: The correct pronunciation is "AH-jay," but people unfamiliar with this Punjabi name may pronounce it like the letters *A* and *J*.

Akeem ★★★

(Hebrew) a form of Joachim.

First Impression: People say Akeem may be quiet, but he always stands up for himself.

Gender Association: Used for boys

Popularity and Trend: Last ranked in the Top 1000 in the 1990s

Risk of Misspelling: Average

Risk of Mispronunciation: Average

Famous Namesakes: Character Prince Akeem (*Coming to America*); original name of basketball player Hakeem Olajuwon

Common Nicknames: None

Common Variations: Ahkeem

Consider This: Akeem is a Hebrew name, but because it's the original name of Hakeem Olajuwon, it may be identified as Muslim or African as well. It's pronunciation is mostly phonetic as "ah-KEEM," but it still could trip up those unfamiliar with it.

Aladdin ★★★★

(Arabic) height of faith.

First Impression: People imagine Aladdin as a sly, quick-thinking young man of Middle Eastern descent, much like Aladdin of *Arabian Nights*.

Gender Association: Used for boys

Popularity and Trend: Never been ranked in Top 1000

Risk of Misspelling: Fairly low

Risk of Mispronunciation: Low

Famous Namesakes: Character Aladdin (*Arabian Nights*)

Common Nicknames: Alaa

Common Variations: Aladden, Aladdyn

Consider This: Despite its folktale origins, the name Aladdin now mostly recalls a Disney cartoon, which may be limiting.

Albert ★★★★

(German, French) noble and bright.

First Impression: Most people think Albert is geeky and smart, probably because of the most famous namesake: Albert Einstein.

Gender Association: Used for boys

Popularity and Trend: #354 (#284 in 2000)

Risk of Misspelling: Low

Risk of Mispronunciation: Low

Famous Namesakes: Scientist Albert Einstein; humanitarian Albert Schweitzer; actor Albert Brooks; TV and movie character Fat Albert; baseball player Albert Pujols

Common Nicknames: Al, Bert, Albie

Common Variations: Alberto, Elbert

Consider This: Albert may score 4 stars, but be aware of the geeky first impression it creates.

Alberto ★★★★

(Italian) a form of Albert.

First Impression: People see Alberto as a Latino who's fun-loving, large, and confident.

Gender Association: Used for boys

Popularity and Trend: #315 (#270 in 2000)

Risk of Misspelling: Low

Risk of Mispronunciation: Low

Famous Namesakes: Skier Alberto Tomba; attorney general Alberto Gonzales

Common Nicknames: Berto, Al

Common Variations: Albert

Consider This: Alberto is a good choice for Italian or Latino families.

Alcott ★★

(English) old cottage.

First Impression: People envision Alcott as a snooty aristocrat who's ever so prim and proper.

Gender Association: Used for boys

Popularity and Trend: Never been ranked in Top 1000

Risk of Misspelling: Average

Risk of Mispronunciation: Fairly low

Famous Namesakes: None

Common Nicknames: None

Common Variations: Alcot, Allcott

Consider This: This English name takes on an English impression.

Alden ★★★

(English) old; wise protector.

First Impression: This name evokes an image of an elegant, well-mannered intellectual.

Gender Association: Used mostly for boys

Popularity and Trend: #811 (#854 in 2000)

Risk of Misspelling: Average

Risk of Mispronunciation: Average

Famous Namesakes: Mayflower Pilgrim John Alden

Common Nicknames: None

Common Variations: Aldon, Elden, Aldan

Consider This: There may be an problem with people pronouncing this name as both "AL-den" and "AHL-den."

Alec ★★★★

(Greek) a form of Alexander.

First Impression: People think Alec is a funny and cool charmer, much like actor Alec Baldwin.

Gender Association: Used for boys

Popularity and Trend: #328 (#156 in 2000)

Risk of Misspelling: Fairly low

Risk of Mispronunciation: Low

Famous Namesakes: Actor Alec Baldwin; actor Alec Guinness

Common Nicknames: Al

Common Variations: Alek, Aleck

Consider This: Alec has fallen in popularity this decade, and it's definitely less popular than Alex.

Alejandro ★★★

(Spanish) a form of Alexander.

First Impression: Alejandro is viewed as a colorful and kind character.

Gender Association: Used for boys

Popularity and Trend: #96 (#89 in 2000)

Risk of Misspelling: Fairly high

Risk of Mispronunciation: Fairly high

Famous Namesakes: Director Alejandro Amenábar; musician Alejandro Fernádez

Common Nicknames: None

Common Variations: None

Consider This: Alejandro is in the Top 100, though people outside the Latino culture should consider how it fits with their family name before choosing it. Also, those not familiar with Latino names may have a hard time pronouncing it: "ah-leh-HAHN-droh."

Alex ★★★★

(Greek) a form of Alexander.

First Impression: Folks think Alex is a class clown who's charming and smart, but he has the tendency to be too immature and cocky for his own good.

Gender Association: Used mostly for boys

Popularity and Trend: #67 (#62 in 2000)

Risk of Misspelling: Fairly low

Risk of Mispronunciation: Low

Famous Namesakes: Game show host Alex Trebeck; baseball player Alex Rodriguez; character Alex P. Keaton (*Family Ties*); author Alex Haley

Common Nicknames: Al, Lex

Common Variations: Alax, Allex, Aleks

Consider This: Alex is a fine name on its own, but consider the benefit of using it as a nickname for Alexander.

Alexander ★★★★★

(Greek) defender of mankind.

First Impression: Alexander is pictured as a caring protector and provider who's well liked as well as wise, like the great conqueror who shares his name.

Gender Association: Used mostly for boys

Popularity and Trend: #12 (#20 in 2000)

Risk of Misspelling: Fairly low

Risk of Mispronunciation: Low

Famous Namesakes: King Alexander the Great; inventor Alexander Graham Bell; poet Alexander Pope; Founding Father Alexander Hamilton

Common Nicknames: Al, Alec, Alex, Alexis, Alexei, Lex, Lexus, Xander, Sasha, Sandy

Common Variations: Alejandro, Alessandro, Alexandre

Consider This: With a near-perfect score, Alexander is a strong 5-star name with lots of versatility.

Alfonso ★★★

(Italian, Spanish) a form of Alphonse.

First Impression: Alfonso strikes people as a name for a macho Italian man who's arrogant and insecure, but at times funny and energetic.

Gender Association: Used for boys
Popularity and Trend: #552
(#489 in 2000)
Risk of Misspelling: Average
Risk of Mispronunciation: Average
Famous Namesakes: Actor Alfonso Ribeiro; baseball player Alfonso Soriano
Common Nicknames: Alf, Fonzie, Alfie, Fonso
Common Variations: Alfonse, Alphonse, Alphonso
Consider This: With "Alphonso" also in the mix, spelling could be a problem for this name.

Alfred ★★★

(English) elf counselor; wise counselor.

First Impression: People say Alfred is an awkward loner who's reserved and uptight, but smart and polite when he comes out of his shell.
Gender Association: Used for boys
Popularity and Trend: #755
(#577 in 2000)
Risk of Misspelling: Low
Risk of Mispronunciation: Low
Famous Namesakes: Director Alfred Hitchcock; character Alfred E. Neuman (*MAD*); character Alfred Pennyworth (*Batman*)
Common Nicknames: Alfie, Fred, Alf
Common Variations: Alfredo

Consider This: This old-fashioned name creates an awkward image, which is perhaps why it's not overly popular.

Alfredo ★★★

(Italian, Spanish) a form of Alfred.

First Impression: Alfredo is pictured as a respectful and clever poet who can quickly change from charming and flirtatious to jealous and sullen.
Gender Association: Used for boys
Popularity and Trend: #334
(#301 in 2000)
Risk of Misspelling: Fairly low
Risk of Mispronunciation: Fairly low
Famous Namesakes: Baseball player Alfredo Amézaga; singer Alfredo Kraus
Common Nicknames: Fredo
Common Variations: Alfred, Alfrido
Consider This: Like Alfonso and Alejandro, Alfredo is an ethnic name that needs to be considered for fit. Because most people are familiar with the Italian dish fettuccine alfredo, pronunciation should be relatively simple.

Ali ★★★

(Arabic) greatest. (Swahili) exalted.

First Impression: Ali is envisioned as a strong-willed, spontaneous, and handsome dark-haired man.
Gender Association: Used mostly for boys

Popularity and Trend: #360
(#380 in 2000)
Risk of Misspelling: Average
Risk of Mispronunciation: Fairly high
Famous Namesakes: Boxer Muhammad Ali; Sacha Baron Cohen character Ali G
Common Nicknames: None
Common Variations: Aly
Consider This: Two problems: One, Ali is an ethnic name that may fit some cultures better than others. Two, people may pronounce it as "AL-ee," like the nickname for the popular girls' name Alison, rather than as "ah-LEE."

Alistair ★★

(English) a form of Alexander.

First Impression: Alistair is viewed as a pompous aristocrat fond of playing evil pranks.
Gender Association: Used for boys
Popularity and Trend: Never been ranked in Top 1000
Risk of Misspelling: Average
Risk of Mispronunciation: Fairly high
Famous Namesakes: *Masterpiece Theatre* host Alistair Cooke; character Alistair "Mad Eye" Moody (*Harry Potter* series)
Common Nicknames: None
Common Variations: Allister, Alistaire
Consider This: This name may trip up many people when it comes to pronunciation. (Is it "AL-eh-ster," "AL-eh-stair," or "AL-eh-star"?)

Allen ★★★

(Irish) a form of Alan.

First Impression: Folks say Allen may be a tad on the dorky side, but he probably has more money than you.

Gender Association: Used for boys

Popularity and Trend: #283 (#251 in 2000)

Risk of Misspelling: Average

Risk of Mispronunciation: Low

Famous Namesakes: Poet Allen Ginsberg; basketball player Allen Iverson

Common Nicknames: Al

Common Variations: Alan, Alain, Allan, Alen

Consider This: Allen is usually a last name, while Alan is more popular and more established as a given name, which means people will likely misspell Allen on a daily basis.

Alphonse ★★

(German) noble and eager.

First Impression: Alphonse is imagined to be an unattractive but intelligent smarty-pants.

Gender Association: Used for boys

Popularity and Trend: Last ranked in the Top 1000 in the 1950s

Risk of Misspelling: Average

Risk of Mispronunciation: Fairly low

Famous Namesakes: Mobster Alphonse "Al" Capone; artist Alphonse Mucha

Common Nicknames: Alf, Alfie, Fonzie

Common Variations: Alphons, Alfonso, Alphonsus

Consider This: Both Alphonse and Alfonso have less-than-stellar first impressions.

Alvin ★★★

(Latin) white; light-skinned. (German) friend of elves.

First Impression: Most people think of Alvin as a computer geek who's as socially awkward as he is brainy.

Gender Association: Used for boys

Popularity and Trend: #513 (#469 in 2000)

Risk of Misspelling: Fairly low

Risk of Mispronunciation: Low

Famous Namesakes: Cartoon character Alvin the Chipmunk; choreographer Alvin Ailey

Common Nicknames: Alvy, Alvie

Common Variations: Alvyn, Alvan

Consider This: Like Allen and Albert, Alvin is identified as a nerdy name.

Amir ★★

(Hebrew) proclaimed. (Punjabi) wealthy; king's minister. (Arabic) prince.

First Impression: Amir is considered an unsympathetic individual driven by ambition and intelligence.

Gender Association: Used for boys

Popularity and Trend: #324 (#414 in 2000)

Risk of Misspelling: Average

Risk of Mispronunciation: Average

Famous Namesakes: Islamic title Amir al-Mu'minin; poker player Amir Vahedi

Common Nicknames: None

Common Variations: Aamir, Ameer

Consider This: While it does have Hebrew and Punjabi roots, Amir is often considered a Muslim name. Pronunciation ("ah-MEER") could be challenging for some people.

Amos ★★★

(Hebrew) burdened, troubled.

First Impression: People imagine Amos as polite, quiet, and kind.

Gender Association: Used for boys

Popularity and Trend: Last ranked in the Top 1000 in the 1990s

Risk of Misspelling: Fairly low

Risk of Mispronunciation: Average

Famous Namesakes: Cookie maker Wally "Famous" Amos; biblical figure Amos

Common Nicknames: None

Common Variations: Amose

Consider This: Although this is a relatively easy name to pronounce, you may hear slight differences between "AY-muhs," "AY-mess," and "AY-mohs."

Anders ★★★

(Swedish) a form of Andrew.

First Impression: Anders is regarded as a suave and serious metrosexual who's secretly self-conscious and lonely.

Gender Association: Used for boys

Popularity and Trend: #987 (first time ranked in Top 1000)

Risk of Misspelling: Low

Risk of Mispronunciation: Low

Famous Namesakes: Scientist Anders Celsius

Common Nicknames: Andy

Common Variations: None

Consider This: This Scandinavian name cracked the Top 1000 for the first time in 2006.

Andre ★★★★

(French) a form of Andrew.

First Impression: People think Andre is popular with the ladies because he's witty, cultured, and sure of himself.

Gender Association: Used for boys

Popularity and Trend: #207 (#197 in 2000)

Risk of Misspelling: Fairly low

Risk of Mispronunciation: Fairly low

Famous Namesakes: Tennis player Andre Agassi; wrestler André the Giant; rapper André 3000; actor Andre Braugher

Common Nicknames: Dre

Common Variations: Andrei

Consider This: This French name is sometimes used by African American families.

Andrew ★★★★★

(Greek) strong; manly; courageous.

First Impression: Andrew is seen as polite, goodhearted, and friendly.

Gender Association: Used for boys

Popularity and Trend: #8 (#7 in 2000)

Risk of Misspelling: Fairly low

Risk of Mispronunciation: Low

Famous Namesakes: Presidents Andrew Jackson and Andrew Johnson; composer Andrew Lloyd Webber; biblical figure Andrew

Common Nicknames: Andy, Drew

Common Variations: Anders, Andre, Andreas, Andruw

Consider This: The downside to this 5-star name is its overwhelming popularity, which might produce one or two Andrews in every grade-school class.

Andy ★★★

(Greek) a short form of Andrew.

First Impression: People may think Andy is a wimpy and puny guy with freckles and red hair, but he has all the qualities of a good friend: He's trustworthy, sweet, and amiable.

Gender Association: Used for boys

Popularity and Trend: #204 (#211 in 2000)

Risk of Misspelling: Low

Risk of Mispronunciation: Low

Famous Namesakes: Artist Andy Warhol; actor Andy Griffith; comedian Andy Ritcher; actor Andy Garcia; comedian Andy Kaufman

Common Nicknames: None

Common Variations: None

Consider This: Andy is a terrific nickname, but it's hard to take it seriously as a given name.

Angel ★★★★★

(Greek) angel. (Latin) messenger.

First Impression: Angel is described as a selfless, insightful, and meek man with a slight build and dark, good looks.

Gender Association: Used mostly for boys

Popularity and Trend: #31 (#67 in 2000)

Risk of Misspelling: Low

Risk of Mispronunciation: Low

Famous Namesakes: Character Angel (*Buffy the Vampire Slayer* and *Angel*); character Angel Dumott Schunard (*RENT*); jockey Angel Cordero, Jr.

Common Nicknames: None

Common Variations: Angelo

Consider This: Angel is a 5-star name, but keep gender association and cultural association in mind: This name is used mostly for boys in Latino families, but it's also used across cultures for girls.

Angelo ★★

(Italian) a form of Angel.

First Impression: People say Angelo is a tough, bad-tempered, and bossy Italian.

Gender Association: Used for boys

Popularity and Trend: #262 (#303 in 2000)

Risk of Misspelling: Fairly low

Risk of Mispronunciation: Fairly low

Famous Namesakes: Character Angelo (*Measure for Measure*); composer Angelo Badalamenti

Common Nicknames: None

Common Variations: Angel

Consider This: Like many Italian names, Angelo suffers from mobster stereotypes. Pronunciation may differ slightly between "ANN-jeh-loh" and "AHN-jeh-loh."

Angus ★★★

(Scottish) exceptional; outstanding.

First Impression: Most folks imagine Angus as a hefty Scot who's stoic and respectful.

Gender Association: Used for boys

Popularity and Trend: Last ranked in the Top 1000 in the 1920s

Risk of Misspelling: Fairly low

Risk of Mispronunciation: Fairly low

Famous Namesakes: Musician Angus Young; Celtic mythological figure Angus the Young; actor Angus T. Jones

Common Nicknames: Gus

Common Variations: Aeneas, Ennis

Consider This: Because it's so strongly linked to its Scottish origin, you may need to consider how well Angus fits your family's cultural background.

Ansel ★★★★

(French) follower of a nobleman.

First Impression: People see Ansel as a well-traveled and well-read photographer, just like photographer Ansel Adams.

Gender Association: Used for boys

Popularity and Trend: Last ranked in the Top 1000 in the 1910s

Risk of Misspelling: Fairly low

Risk of Mispronunciation: Fairly low

Famous Namesakes: Photographer Ansel Adams

Common Nicknames: None

Common Variations: Anselmo

Consider This: Because Ansel Adams's photographs capture the rugged beauty of the American West, this French name's image now has a distinct sense of adventure.

Anthony ★★★★

(Latin) praiseworthy. (Greek) flourishing.

First Impression: Folks see Anthony as an exuberant romantic with handsome, dark looks from his Italian or Mediterranean heritage.

Gender Association: Used mostly for boys

Popularity and Trend: #9 (#17 in 2000)

Risk of Misspelling: Low

Risk of Mispronunciation: Low

Famous Namesakes: Actor Anthony Hopkins; actor Anthony Perkins; actor Anthony Edwards; singer Anthony Kiedis

Common Nicknames: Tony

Common Variations: Antoine, Antony, Antonio

Consider This: Slowly but surely for over one hundred years, Anthony has inched up the Top 100 to the Top 10.

Antoine ★★★

(French) a form of Anthony.

First Impression: People say Antoine is a handsome Frenchman who's confident, loyal, and charming.

Gender Association: Used for boys

Popularity and Trend: #631 (#591 in 2000)

Risk of Misspelling: Average

Risk of Mispronunciation: Average

Famous Namesakes: Author Antoine de Saint-Exupéry; basketball player Antoine Walker

Common Nicknames: None

Common Variations: Antwon, Antwan

Consider This: This name is traditionally pronounced "ANN-twahn," but with the rise of the African American variation Antwan, some may pronounce it "ANT-wan."

Antonio ★★★★

(Italian) a form of Anthony.

First Impression: Like famous namesake Antonio Banderas, Antonio is described as a heroic, charming, and sweet Lothario with dark eyes, skin, and hair.

Gender Association: Used for boys

Popularity and Trend: #93 (#82 in 2000)

Risk of Misspelling: Fairly low

Risk of Mispronunciation: Fairly low

Famous Namesakes: Actor Antonio Banderas; composer Antonio Vivaldi; character Antonio (*The Merchant of Venice*)

Common Nicknames: Tino, Tonio, Tony

Common Variations: Anton, Antonyo

Consider This: Antonio is a 4-star name, but be aware that it may work for some cultures better than others. Also, keep it mind that it creates a Lothario image, which is flattering but perhaps limiting.

Archie ★★★

(German, English) a familiar form of Archer, Archibald.

First Impression: People think of Archie as either a goofy and freckled redhead, like the eponymous character of *Archie* comics, or a balding husband who's narrow-minded but loyal, like Archie Bunker of TV's *All in the Family*.

Gender Association: Used for boys

Popularity and Trend: Last ranked in the Top 1000 in the 1980s

Risk of Misspelling: Fairly low

Risk of Mispronunciation: Low

Famous Namesakes: Character Archie Bunker (*All in the Family*); character Archie Andrews (*Archie*); football player Archie Manning

Common Nicknames: None

Common Variations: Archee, Archey

Consider This: As the first impression shows, this name relates to two namesakes who inspire mixed reactions.

Argus ★★★

(Danish) watchful, vigilant.

First Impression: Argus is pictured as a burly and boisterous Scot with a big laugh and a bigger yell when he's feeling surly.

Gender Association: Used for boys

Popularity and Trend: Never been ranked in Top 1000

Risk of Misspelling: Fairly low

Risk of Mispronunciation: Low

Famous Namesakes: Character Argus Filch (*Harry Potter* series); Greek mythological figure Argus

Common Nicknames: Gus

Common Variations: Argos, Arguss

Consider This: Apparently people hear "Argus" and think "Angus," because this Danish name evokes the stereotypical lovable-but-surly Scot.

Arlen ★★

(Irish) pledge.

First Impression: Arlen is said to be a frail, aging Southerner who's timid and insecure despite his vast wealth.

Gender Association: Used for boys

Popularity and Trend: Last ranked in the Top 1000 in the 1960s

Risk of Misspelling: Fairly low

Risk of Mispronunciation: Low

Famous Namesakes: Senator Arlen Specter; football player Arlen Harris

Common Nicknames: None

Common Variations: Arlan, Arlin

Consider This: Although people identify Arlen as a Southern name, it lacks charm due to its old image.

Armand ★

(Latin, German) a form of Herman.

First Impression: People say Armand is an unattractive yet conceited slickster who talks too fast and wears designer suits.

Gender Association: Used for boys

Popularity and Trend: Last ranked in the Top 1000 in the 1970s

Risk of Misspelling: Fairly high

Risk of Mispronunciation: Fairly high

Famous Namesakes: Actor Armand Assante; designer Armand Diradourian; character Armand (*The Vampire Chronicles*)

Common Nicknames: Mando

Common Variations: None

Consider This: The silent *d* makes Armand tricky to spell and pronounce.

Armando ★★★

(Spanish) a form of Armand.

First Impression: Armando is seen as a passionate and dashing bodice ripper with suave Latin looks.

Gender Association: Used for boys

Popularity and Trend: #264 (#237 in 2000)

Risk of Misspelling: Average

Risk of Mispronunciation: Average

Famous Namesakes: Baseball player Armando Benítez

Common Nicknames: Mando

Common Variations: Armondo

Consider This: As with Antonio, Armando's suave, handsome image is both a blessing and a curse.

Armen ★★★★

(Hebrew) a form of Armon.

First Impression: People think Armen is highly intelligent and good with numbers.

Gender Association: Used for boys

Popularity and Trend: Never been ranked in Top 1000

Risk of Misspelling: Average

Risk of Mispronunciation: Low

Famous Namesakes: TV personality Armen Keteyian

Common Nicknames: None

Common Variations: Armon, Armin

Consider This: Armen is a simpler, more straightforward alternative to Armand.

Arnie ★★

(German) a familiar form of Arnold.

First Impression: Arnie is pictured as either a nerd with thick glasses or a country boy with a love for beer and tobacco.

Gender Association: Used for boys

Popularity and Trend: Last ranked in the Top 1000 in the 1960s

Risk of Misspelling: Fairly low

Risk of Mispronunciation: Low

Famous Namesakes: Nickname for Arnold Palmer and Arnold Schwarzenegger

Common Nicknames: None

Common Variations: Arney, Arny

Consider This: Although Arnold isn't a winning name, it's still better than its nickname, Arnie.

Arnold ★★★

(German) eagle ruler.

First Impression: People imagine Arnold as a bespectacled, clumsy geek who's a dubious used-car salesman.

Gender Association: Used for boys

Popularity and Trend: Last ranked #763 in 2000

Risk of Misspelling: Low

Risk of Mispronunciation: Low

Famous Namesakes: Actor and California governor Arnold Schwarzenegger; golfer Arnold Palmer; character Arnold Jackson (*Diff'rent Strokes*)

Common Nicknames: Arnie, Arno

Common Variations: Arnaldo, Arnoldo

Consider This: Arnold suffers from an awkward first impression, and its exit from the Top 1000 suggests it's out of date.

Aron ★★★

(Hebrew) a form of Aaron.

First Impression: Folks regard Aron as a warm, approachable, self-assured guy with a strong build and sparkling eyes.

Gender Association: Used for boys

Popularity and Trend: #640 (#597 in 2000)

Risk of Misspelling: Fairly high

Risk of Mispronunciation: Average

Famous Namesakes: Another name for biblical figure Aaron

Common Nicknames: None

Common Variations: Aaron, Aren, Arin

Consider This: Spelling "Aron" could be a hassle when everyone expects it to be "Aaron." Pronunciation may be tricky, too: Some say "AIR-on," and others say "ARR-on." Lastly, because the "AIR-on" pronunciation is the same as Erin, a popular name for girls, it may cause gender confusion.

Arsen ★

(Greek) a form of Arsenio.

First Impression: When people hear Arsen, they imagine an arsonist who's slow, lazy, and sneaky.

Gender Association: Used for boys

Popularity and Trend: Never been ranked in Top 1000

Risk of Misspelling: Fairly high

Risk of Mispronunciation: Low

Famous Namesakes: None

Common Nicknames: None

Common Variations: Arsenio

Consider This: Forget that it's a form of Arsenio—people will forever associate Arsen with *arson*. They'll probably spell it *arson*, too.

Arthur ★★★★

(Irish) noble; lofty hill. (Scottish) bear. (English) rock. (Icelandic) follower of Thor.

First Impression: People picture Arthur as a studious and science-minded intellectual.

Gender Association: Used for boys

Popularity and Trend: #377 (#316 in 2000)

Risk of Misspelling: Fairly low

Risk of Mispronunciation: Low

Famous Namesakes: Legendary figure King Arthur; character Arthur Bach (*Arthur*); tennis player Arthur Ashe; playwright Arthur Miller

Common Nicknames: Art, Artie

Common Variations: Arther, Arturo

Consider This: Arthur is an upstanding name, but it does sound old-fashioned.

Arturo ★★★★

(Italian) a form of Arthur.

First Impression: Arturo is said to be a dark-haired and handsome character who's smooth and suave.

Gender Association: Used for boys

Popularity and Trend: #323 (#291 in 2000)

Risk of Misspelling: Average

Risk of Mispronunciation: Average

Famous Namesakes: Boxer Arturo Gatti; character Maximillian Arturo (*Sliders*); jazz musician Arturo Sandoval

Common Nicknames: Art, Artie

Common Variations: Arthuro, Artur

Consider This: Surprisingly, Arturo is more popular than Arthur, even though it may be more suited to some cultures than others.

Asher ★★★★★

(Hebrew) happy; blessed.

First Impression: Asher is thought to be funny, sweet, and well liked.

Gender Association: Used for boys

Popularity and Trend: #252 (#579 in 2000)

Risk of Misspelling: Low

Risk of Mispronunciation: Low

Famous Namesakes: Biblical figure Asher

Common Nicknames: Ash

Common Variations: Ashir

Consider This: Asher is surging up the popularity charts, perhaps as an alternative to Ashton, which has less clear gender association.

Ashton ★★★

(English) ash-tree settlement.

First Impression: To most people, Ashton is a condescending, conceited, cocky, and competitive preppy from an old-money family.

Gender Association: Used mostly for boys

Popularity and Trend: #121 (#254 in 2000)

Risk of Misspelling: Fairly low

Risk of Mispronunciation: Low

Famous Namesakes: Actor Ashton Kutcher

Common Nicknames: Ash

Common Variations: Ashten, Ashtin

Consider This: Ashton peaked at #76 in 2004, but it's slipped a bit since then. Today, it's used equally for boys and girls, which may pose a problem for parents searching for names with clear gender associations.

Aubrey ★★★

(German) noble; bearlike.

First Impression: People describe Aubrey as a sweet-natured, smart, and proper Southern gentleman.

Gender Association: Used mostly for girls

Popularity and Trend: Last ranked #844 in 2000

Risk of Misspelling: Average

Risk of Mispronunciation: Average

Famous Namesakes: Writer John Aubrey

Common Nicknames: Aube

Common Variations: Aubre, Aubry

Consider This: Despite its positive first impression, Aubrey's main drawback is that it's used more often as a girls' name. Another disadvantage is its somewhat challenging pronunciation as "AW-bree" instead of "AW-bray."

Auden ★★

(English) old friend.

First Impression: Auden is seen as a dainty poet and dreamer—perhaps because of English-born poet W. H. Auden.

Gender Association: Used for boys

Popularity and Trend: Never been ranked in Top 1000

Risk of Misspelling: Average

Risk of Mispronunciation: Average

Famous Namesakes: Poet W. H. Auden

Common Nicknames: None

Common Variations: Audan, Audin

Consider This: This name has a poetic, dreamy quality, no doubt inspired by poet namesake W. H. Auden.

August ★★★★

(Latin) a form of Augustine, Augustus.

First Impression: People see August as the creative type—perhaps an actor or writer—who's gentle, compassionate, and handsome.

Gender Association: Used mostly for boys

Popularity and Trend: #618 (#613 in 2000)

Risk of Misspelling: Low

Risk of Mispronunciation: Low

Famous Namesakes: Playwright August Wilson

Common Nicknames: Augie, Gus

Common Variations: Auguste, Augusto, Augustus

Consider This: August is breezier and more fun than Augustus, yet it's sufficiently solid as a given name.

Augustus ★★★★

(Latin) majestic; venerable.

First Impression: Folks consider Augustus a wise, powerful man who commands respect.

Gender Association: Used for boys

Popularity and Trend: #831 (#955 in 2000)

Risk of Misspelling: Fairly low

Risk of Mispronunciation: Low

Famous Namesakes: Emperor Augustus; character Augustus Gloop (*Charlie and the Chocolate Factory*)

Common Nicknames: Augie, Gus

Common Variations: Agustus, August

Consider This: According to the first impression, Augustus is a weighty name, which is something to consider before bestowing it on a baby.

Aurek ★★

(Polish) golden-haired.

First Impression: Aurek is considered a kingly name for a leader who's mysterious and odd.

Gender Association: Used for boys

Popularity and Trend: Never been ranked in Top 1000

Risk of Misspelling: Fairly high

Risk of Mispronunciation: Fairly high

Famous Namesakes: None

Common Nicknames: None

Common Variations: Aurec

Consider This: People may not know to pronounce this unusual name as "AWE-rek."

Austin ★★★★★

(Latin) a form of Augustine.

First Impression: People imagine Austin is gentle, caring, and loyal, and he also has a great sense of humor.

Gender Association: Used mostly for boys

Popularity and Trend: #41 (#23 in 2000)

Risk of Misspelling: Low

Risk of Mispronunciation: Low

Famous Namesakes: Film character Austin Powers

Common Nicknames: None

Common Variations: None

Consider This: Created as a short form of Augustine, Austin has been a Top 100 name for a generation.

Avery ★★★

(English) a form of Aubrey.

First Impression: Avery comes across as very intelligent, self-assured, and popular.

Gender Association: Used mostly for girls

Popularity and Trend: #212 (#245 in 2000)

Risk of Misspelling: Fairly low

Risk of Mispronunciation: Fairly low

Famous Namesakes: Actor Avery Brooks; basketball coach Avery Johnson

Common Nicknames: None

Common Variations: Avrey

Consider This: While Avery is a relatively popular name for boys, it's more often used for girls. And although it is commonly pronounced "AY-vuh-ree," some say "AY-vree."

Axel ★★

(Latin) axe. (German) small oak tree; source of life. (Scandinavian) a form of Absalom.

First Impression: People say Axel is a tough, raunchy, and self-centered rock star with long, greasy hair and a slender face, likely thanks to Guns N' Roses frontman Axl Rose.

Gender Association: Used for boys

Popularity and Trend: #295 (#364 in 2000)

Risk of Misspelling: Average

Risk of Mispronunciation: Low

Famous Namesakes: Character Axel Foley (*Beverly Hills Cop*); singer Axl Rose

Common Nicknames: Ax

Common Variations: Axl, Axell

Consider This: While most people find Axl Rose to be a negative influence, perhaps a metalhead would disagree. Either way, people may misspell Axel as "Axl."

Bailey ★★

(French) bailiff, steward.

First Impression: Folks imagine Bailey as lively, playful, charming, happy, and loving.

Gender Association: Used mostly for girls

Popularity and Trend: #635 (#202 in 2000)

Risk of Misspelling: Average

Risk of Mispronunciation: Low

Famous Namesakes: Comic strip character Beetle Bailey; character Bailey Salinger (*Party of Five*); football player Champ Bailey

Common Nicknames: Bail

Common Variations: Baylee, Bayley

Consider This: Bailey is used more often for girls, which may explain why it's falling so quickly in popularity for boys.

Ballard ★

(German) brave; strong.

First Impression: Ballard comes across as a snobby, tall, and incredibly rich sophisticate.

Gender Association: Used for boys

Popularity and Trend: Never been ranked in Top 1000

Risk of Misspelling: Average

Risk of Mispronunciation: Fairly low

Famous Namesakes: Singer Hank Ballard

Common Nicknames: None

Common Variations: Balard

Consider This: For whatever reason, Ballard gives a snooty first impression.

Bane ★

(Hawaiian) a form of Bartholomew.

First Impression: People describe Bane as a needy, arrogant man who aches to be the center of attention.

Gender Association: Used for boys

Popularity and Trend: Never been ranked in Top 1000

Risk of Misspelling: Fairly low

Risk of Mispronunciation: Average

Famous Namesakes: Character Bane (*Batman*)

Common Nicknames: None

Common Variations: Bain

Consider This: Unless people are aware of its Hawaiian origins, this name will evoke the word *bane* and all its negative associations.

Barak ★★★

(Hebrew) lightning bolt.

First Impression: Many imagine Barak as an intelligent, confident, and charismatic African American politician, likely thanks to political star Barack Obama.

Gender Association: Used for boys

Popularity and Trend: Never been ranked in Top 1000

Risk of Misspelling: Fairly high

Risk of Mispronunciation: Average

Famous Namesakes: Biblical figure Barak; senator Barack Hussein Obama

Common Nicknames: None

Common Variations: Barack, Barrak

Consider This: Thanks to the popularity of Barack Obama, most people will know to pronounce this "bah-ROCK," but a few may still say "bah-RACK" or "BAR-ak."

Baron ★★

(German, English) nobleman, baron.

First Impression: Baron is pictured as a mean, humorless man with a large build and an overbearing demeanor.

Gender Association: Used for boys

Popularity and Trend: Last ranked in the Top 1000 in the 1970s

Risk of Misspelling: Low

Risk of Mispronunciation: Low

Famous Namesakes: Basketball player Baron Davis; WWI pilot Manfred "The Red Baron" von Richthofen

Common Nicknames: None

Common Variations: Barron

Consider This: Perhaps because of the Red Baron lore, this name has a negative, intimidating image.

Barrett ★★

(German) strong as a bear.

First Impression: Barrett is viewed as a snobby, know-it-all pansy spoiled by his posh upbringing.

Gender Association: Used mostly for boys

Popularity and Trend: #762 (#982 in 2000)

Risk of Misspelling: Average

Risk of Mispronunciation: Low

Famous Namesakes: Singer Barrett Strong; football player Barrett Brooks

Common Nicknames: Bar, Barry

Common Variations: Barret, Baret

Consider This: Although it's climbing in popularity, Barrett (like Ballard) has a snooty, rich come-off.

Barry ★★★

(Welsh) son of Harry. (Irish) spear, marksman. (French) gate, fence.

First Impression: Barry sounds like bear, which maybe why people think of him as a big, cuddly teddy bear who's sweet, witty, and talented.

Gender Association: Used for boys

Popularity and Trend: Last ranked #678 in 2000

Risk of Misspelling: Fairly low

Risk of Mispronunciation: Low

Famous Namesakes: Baseball player Barry Bonds; singer Barry Manilow; director Barry Levinson; baseball player Barry Zito

Common Nicknames: None

Common Variations: Barrie

Consider This: Being compared to a teddy bear is nice, but the association may make it hard to be taken seriously.

Bart ★★

(Hebrew) a short form of Bartholomew, Barton.

First Impression: People say Bart is either a nerdy, awkward bookworm with big glasses and pimples, or a lazy and rude tough guy with a beer belly and bald spot.

Gender Association: Used for boys

Popularity and Trend: Last ranked in the Top 1000 in the 1980s

Risk of Misspelling: Low

Risk of Mispronunciation: Low

Famous Namesakes: Character Bart Simpson (The Simpsons); football player Bart Starr; pirate Bartholomew "Black Bart" Roberts; gymnast Bart Conner

Common Nicknames: None

Common Variations: Bartel

Consider This: One may think incorrigible cartoon character Bart Simpson would influence this name's image, especially considering the name has been off the Top 1000 since *The Simpsons* began airing in 1987. But people have their own negative images of this name.

Bartholomew ★★

(Hebrew) son of Talmaí.

First Impression: Bartholomew is considered rich and successful, but he's a bit of a weird introvert who's heavy and unattractive.

Gender Association: Used for boys

Popularity and Trend: Last ranked in the Top 1000 in the 1910s

Risk of Misspelling: Average

Risk of Mispronunciation: Fairly low

Famous Namesakes: Biblical figure Bartholomew; character Bartholomew "Bart" Simpson (*The Simpsons*)

Common Nicknames: Bart

Common Variations: Bartel, Barthelemy

Consider This: Bartholomew defines *outdated*: It hasn't appeared on the Top 1000 for nearly one hundred years.

Barton ★★★★

(English) barley town; Bart's town.

First Impression: Barton seems to be a name for a smart and good-humored country boy with rugged good looks.

Gender Association: Used for boys

Popularity and Trend: Last ranked in the Top 1000 in the 1980s

Risk of Misspelling: Fairly low

Risk of Mispronunciation: Low

Famous Namesakes: Film character Barton Fink

Common Nicknames: Bart

Common Variations: Barrton

Consider This: Barton's image is even more countrified than Bart's.

Basil ★★

(Greek, Latin) royal, kingly.

First Impression: People imagine Basil as a snooty and stuffy upper-class Brit who's well educated but dull.

Gender Association: Used for boys

Popularity and Trend: Last ranked in the Top 1000 in the 1960s

Risk of Misspelling: Average

Risk of Mispronunciation: Average

Famous Namesakes: Eastern Orthodox saint Basil of Caesarea; cartoonist Basil Wolverton

Common Nicknames: Bas

Common Variations: Basile, Basal, Basel

Consider This: Because this name has been off the radar for decades, people may unknowingly pronounce it "BAYZ-ill," like the herb, rather than "BAZ-ill."

Baul ★★

(Gypsy) snail.

First Impression: Folks picture Baul as a forthright and courageous man with Herculean strength that makes him clumsy.

Gender Association: Used for boys

Popularity and Trend: Never been ranked in Top 1000

Risk of Misspelling: Average

Risk of Mispronunciation: Fairly low

Famous Namesakes: None

Common Nicknames: None

Common Variations: None

Consider This: Baul is an unusual name that will likely garner unusual reactions.

Beaman ★★★

(English) beekeeper.

First Impression: Beaman seems like a fancy, rich man who's trustworthy and discreet.

Gender Association: Used for boys

Popularity and Trend: Never been ranked in Top 1000

Risk of Misspelling: Average

Risk of Mispronunciation: Low

Famous Namesakes: None

Common Nicknames: None

Common Variations: None

Consider This: Beaman is another example of a last name as first name that hasn't yet caught on.

Beau ★★★

(French) handsome.

First Impression: People imagine Beau as a masculine, muscular guy who has a shy, quiet, and even timid side deep down.

Gender Association: Used for boys

Popularity and Trend: #438 (#465 in 2000)

Risk of Misspelling: Average

Risk of Mispronunciation: Fairly low

Famous Namesakes: Actor Beau Bridges; fashion icon Beau Brummel

Common Nicknames: None

Common Variations: Bo

Consider This: Bo and Beau are both 3-star names, but when it comes to spelling, people may confuse them. Of the two, Beau is a bit harder to pronounce, though most people are familiar enough with the name to get it right.

Ben ★★★

(Hebrew) a short form of Benjamin.

First Impression: Most agree that Ben is a sweet, dark-haired boy.

Gender Association: Used for boys

Popularity and Trend: #555 (#561 in 2000)

Risk of Misspelling: Low

Risk of Mispronunciation: Low

Famous Namesakes: Actor Ben Affleck; actor Ben Stiller; actor Ben Kingsley; actor Ben Stein; singer Ben Folds

Common Nicknames: Benny

Common Variations: Benn

Consider This: Like most nicknames, Ben is a great option when paired with Benjamin, but it's not nearly as versatile.

Benjamin ★★★★★

(Hebrew) son of my right hand.

First Impression: Benjamin is described as a considerate, smart, and charismatic athlete who likes to have a good time.

Gender Association: Used for boys

Popularity and Trend: #24 (#26 in 2000)

Risk of Misspelling: Fairly low

Risk of Mispronunciation: Low

Famous Namesakes: Founding Father Benjamin Franklin; actor Benjamin Bratt

Common Nicknames: Ben, Benjy, Benny

Common Variations: Benjamen, Benjimin

Consider This: Benjamin earns a near-perfect score, especially because it's so versatile.

Bennett ★★★★

(Latin) little blessed one.

First Impression: People imagine Bennett as a studious, mathematically brilliant prep schooler who's arrogant and serious.

Gender Association: Used mostly for boys

Popularity and Trend: #369 (#441 in 2000)

Risk of Misspelling: Average

Risk of Mispronunciation: Low

Famous Namesakes: Singer Tony Bennett

Common Nicknames: Ben, Benny

Common Variations: Benett, Bennet, Benet

Consider This: Bennett has a studious image, making it a "smart" alternative to Benjamin. Spelling may be an problem, though, because of its many variations.

Benny ★★

(Hebrew) a familiar form of Benjamin.

First Impression: Benny is pictured as a carefree, good-natured partier who may strike some as immature and overindulged.

Gender Association: Used for boys

Popularity and Trend: #962 (#836 in 2000)

Risk of Misspelling: Fairly low

Risk of Mispronunciation: Low

Famous Namesakes: Musician Benny Goodman; comedian Benny Hill

Common Nicknames: None

Common Variations: Bennie

Consider This: A diminutive form of Benjamin, Benny scores lower than Ben because it's more casual.

Benson ★★★★

(Hebrew) son of Ben.

First Impression: People say Benson is a refined and smart—if not snooty—African American butler, much like the popular '80s TV character played by Robert Guillaume.

Gender Association: Used for boys

Popularity and Trend: Never been ranked in Top 1000

Risk of Misspelling: Fairly low

Risk of Mispronunciation: Low

Famous Namesakes: Character Benson DuBois (*Benson*)

Common Nicknames: Ben, Benny

Common Variations: Bensen

Consider This: If you like Benjamin but want something less popular, Benson is a good pick.

Bentley ★★★

(English) moor; coarse grass meadow.

First Impression: Bentley is viewed as a tall, stuffy snob who's well mannered and proper but often morose.

Gender Association: Used for boys

Popularity and Trend: Never been ranked in Top 1000

Risk of Misspelling: Fairly low

Risk of Mispronunciation: Low

Famous Namesakes: Singer Dierks Bentley; auto entrepreneur Walter Owen Bentley

Common Nicknames: Lee, Bent

Common Variations: Bentlee

Consider This: Giving your son the same name as a luxury car may raise some eyebrows, especially if a Bentley is well out of your price range.

Berk ★★

(Turkish) solid; rugged.

First Impression: Berk is seen as a weird outcast who gets into trouble but can talk himself out of it.

Gender Association: Used for boys

Popularity and Trend: Never been ranked in Top 1000

Risk of Misspelling: Fairly high

Risk of Mispronunciation: Low

Famous Namesakes: None

Common Nicknames: None

Common Variations: Burke, Burk, Birk

Consider This: Most people won't realize Berk is a Turkish name; instead, they'll think it an odd way to spell "Burke."

Bern ★★

(German) a short form of Bernard.

First Impression: Bern is regarded as quiet and smart, and depending on how his day is going, he can be either grouchy or kind.

Gender Association: Used for boys

Popularity and Trend: Never been ranked in Top 1000

Risk of Misspelling: Average

Risk of Mispronunciation: Low

Famous Namesakes: Character Lord Bern (*The Voyage of the Dawn Treader*)

Common Nicknames: None

Common Variations: Berne

Consider This: Bern is a fun nickname for Bernard, but it would be an odd name by itself. Some may assume it's spelled like the word *burn*.

Bernard ★★★

(German) brave as a bear.

First Impression: Bernard is pictured as a one-of-a-kind character who's bookish but messy.

Gender Association: Used for boys

Popularity and Trend: #945 (#654 in 2000)

Risk of Misspelling: Fairly low

Risk of Mispronunciation: Low

Famous Namesakes: Several saints named Bernard; playwright George Bernard Shaw

Common Nicknames: Bernie, Bern

Common Variations: Barnard, Bernardino, Bernardo

Consider This: Bernard is relatively easy to spell and pronounce, and it's highly versatile; however, don't overlook its plummeting popularity.

Bert ★★

(German, English) bright, shining.

First Impression: Like the *Sesame Street* Muppet of the same name, Bert is seen as uptight and argumentative with a nerdy persona.

Gender Association: Used for boys

Popularity and Trend: Last ranked in the Top 1000 in the 1980s

Risk of Misspelling: Average

Risk of Mispronunciation: Low

Famous Namesakes: Character Bert (*Sesame Street*); baseball player Bert Blyleven; actor Burt Reynolds

Common Nicknames: Bertie

Common Variations: Burt

Consider This: The name Bert will always call to mind the cranky *Sesame Street* character. The spelling, however, may be confused with "Burt."

Bilal ★

(Arabic) chosen.

First Impression: People say Bilal is a stubborn and odd Middle Easterner who's irritatingly talkative.

Gender Association: Used for boys

Popularity and Trend: Never been ranked in Top 1000

Risk of Misspelling: Average

Risk of Mispronunciation: Average

Famous Namesakes: Singer Bilal

Common Nicknames: Bila

Common Variations: Bilale, Bilel

Consider This: Bilal is most often used by Muslim families, and spelling and pronunciation ("BIH-lahl") may be unfamiliar

to some people outside that culture.

Bill ★★★★

(German) a short form of William.

First Impression: Bill is seen as generous, neighborly, dependable, and smart.

Gender Association: Used for boys

Popularity and Trend: Last ranked in the Top 1000 in the 1990s

Risk of Misspelling: Low

Risk of Mispronunciation: Low

Famous Namesakes: President Bill Clinton; comedian Bill Cosby; actor Bill Murray; Microsoft founder Bill Gates; showman William "Buffalo Bill" Cody

Common Nicknames: Billy

Common Variations: Will

Consider This: While Bill does have a positive image, it's still best used as a nickname for William. But if you're choosing between Bill and Will, Will is the more popular choice.

Billy ★★

(German) a familiar form of Bill, William.

First Impression: Most people think Billy is a hick who's quick to help others and quick to tell mischievous jokes.

Gender Association: Used mostly for boys

Popularity and Trend: #473 (#385 in 2000)

Risk of Misspelling: Fairly low

Risk of Mispronunciation: Low

Famous Namesakes: Outlaw Billy the Kid; actor Billy Bob Thorton; singer Billy Joel; actor Billy Crystal; actor Billy Baldwin

Common Nicknames: None

Common Variations: Billie, Willie, Willy

Consider This: Surprisingly, Billy—one of the most casual nicknames for William—is a relatively popular given name.

Bjorn ★★

(Scandinavian) a form of Bernard.

First Impression: People tend to picture Bjorn as a model or movie star with stunning, exotic features.

Gender Association: Used for boys

Popularity and Trend: Last ranked in the Top 1000 in the 1980s

Risk of Misspelling: Fairly high

Risk of Mispronunciation: Fairly high

Famous Namesakes: Tennis player Björn Borg; musician Björn Ulvaeus

Common Nicknames: None

Common Variations: None

Consider This: Bjorn is a distinctly Scandinavian name (with a challenging pronunciation: "bee-YORN"), which means you need to consider how it fits with your last name.

Blade ★★

(English) knife, sword.

First Impression: Folks think Blade is a rough and violent punk who's physically imposing.

Gender Association: Used for boys

Popularity and Trend: Never been ranked in Top 1000

Risk of Misspelling: Low

Risk of Mispronunciation: Low

Famous Namesakes: Movie and comic book character Blade

Common Nicknames: None

Common Variations: None

Consider This: Blake and Blaine are much better alternatives to Blade, due to its violent tone.

Blaine ★★★★

(Irish) thin, lean. (English) river source.

First Impression: Blaine is thought to be an all-around good person with a tender heart.

Gender Association: Used mostly for boys

Popularity and Trend: #572 (#455 in 2000)

Risk of Misspelling: Fairly low

Risk of Mispronunciation: Low

Famous Namesakes: Magician David Blaine; golfer Blaine McCallister

Common Nicknames: Laine

Common Variations: Blain, Blane

Consider This: Blaine may not be very popular, but its first impression is much better than Blake's.

Blake ★★★

(English) attractive; dark.

First Impression: Blake is seen as a spoiled rich kid living on daddy's money.

Gender Association: Used mostly for boys

Popularity and Trend: #97 (#80 in 2000)

Risk of Misspelling: Low

Risk of Mispronunciation: Low

Famous Namesakes: Poet William Blake; comedian Blake Clark; character Blake Carrington (*Dynasty*)

Common Nicknames: None

Common Variations: Blakely

Consider This: Blake's only downside is its snooty first impression.

Bo ★★★

(English) a form of Beau, Beauregard. (German) a form of Bogart.

First Impression: People think Bo is an easygoing, uncomplicated country boy who works with his hands, much like Bo Duke of TV's *The Dukes of Hazzard*.

Gender Association: Used mostly for boys

Popularity and Trend: #771 (#975 in 2000)

Risk of Misspelling: Average

Risk of Mispronunciation: Low

Famous Namesakes: Athlete Bo Jackson; singer Bo Didley; character Bo Duke (*The Dukes of Hazzard*); singer Bo Bice

Common Nicknames: None

Common Variations: Beau

Consider This: While Bo Duke is a good ol' boy, urbanites should think twice about choosing such a rural name.

Bob ★★★

(English) a short form of Robert.

First Impression: Bob is pictured as an average, ordinary guy with average intelligence, average looks, and average friendliness.

Gender Association: Used for boys

Popularity and Trend: Last ranked in the Top 1000 in the 1980s

Risk of Misspelling: Low

Risk of Mispronunciation: Low

Famous Namesakes: Senator Bob Dole; entertainer Bob Hope; singer Bob Dylan; game show host Bob Barker; singer Bob Marley

Common Nicknames: Bobby

Common Variations: Bobby, Rob

Consider This: As the first impression indicates, Bob is middle of the road, which makes it limiting as a given name and perhaps even as a nickname.

Bobby ★★★

(English) a familiar form of Bob, Robert.

First Impression: People view Bobby as a jolly, goofy, and friendly brown-haired boy.
Gender Association: Used for boys
Popularity and Trend: #480 (#363 in 2000)
Risk of Misspelling: Fairly low
Risk of Mispronunciation: Low
Famous Namesakes: Singer Bobby Brown; basketball coach Bobby Knight; politician Bobby Kennedy; chess master Bobby Fischer; hockey player Bobby Orr
Common Nicknames: None
Common Variations: Bobbie
Consider This: Just like Billy, casual nickname Bobby is a surprisingly popular given name. In fact, they're only a few spots away from each other on the Top 1000 list.

Bond ★★★★

(English) tiller of the soil.
First Impression: People say Bond is a cocky and charming flirt who's tan and buff, much like the character James Bond.
Gender Association: Used for boys
Popularity and Trend: Never been ranked in Top 1000
Risk of Misspelling: Low
Risk of Mispronunciation: Low
Famous Namesakes: Movie and book character James Bond
Common Nicknames: None
Common Variations: None
Consider This: James Bond may be a thrilling namesake, but your son will likely grow tired of people saying things like "shaken, not stirred" when they meet him.

Boris ★★

(Slavic) battler, warrior.
First Impression: People perceive Boris as a burly, Russian brute who isn't very smart and isn't very attractive.
Gender Association: Used for boys
Popularity and Trend: Last ranked in the Top 1000 in the 1970s
Risk of Misspelling: Fairly low
Risk of Mispronunciation: Low
Famous Namesakes: Russian politician Boris Yeltsin; tennis player Boris Becker; actor Boris Karloff
Common Nicknames: None
Common Variations: Boriss
Consider This: Boris suffers from the stereotype of an oafish, burly Russian.

Brad ★★★★

(English) a short form of Bradford, Bradley.
First Impression: Brad is described as a sexy, muscular guy who's kind, outgoing, and smart, much like Hollywood hunk Brad Pitt.
Gender Association: Used for boys
Popularity and Trend: #897 (#631 in 2000)
Risk of Misspelling: Low
Risk of Mispronunciation: Low
Famous Namesakes: Actor Brad Pitt; football player Brad Johnson
Common Nicknames: None
Common Variations: None
Consider This: Brad has steadily declined in popularity since the '70s, while parents prefer the more formal Bradley.

Braden ★★★

(English) broad valley.
First Impression: People say Braden can be caring, but he can sometimes cause trouble.
Gender Association: Used for boys
Popularity and Trend: #141 (#204 in 2000)
Risk of Misspelling: Fairly high
Risk of Mispronunciation: Fairly low
Famous Namesakes: Baseball player Braden Looper
Common Nicknames: None
Common Variations: Bradyn, Braiden, Brayden
Consider This: Braden has a glut of popular variations, which forces your son to either correct people or spell out his name for the rest of his life. Also, pronunciation could be unclear for the handful who mistakenly say "BRAA-den" instead of "BRAY-den."

Bradford ★★★

(English) broad river crossing.
First Impression: People imagine Bradford is a tall and muscular athlete who's cocky and snobby.

Gender Association: Used for boys

Popularity and Trend: Last ranked in the Top 1000 in the 1990s

Risk of Misspelling: Fairly low

Risk of Mispronunciation: Low

Famous Namesakes: Colonist William Bradford

Common Nicknames: Brad, Ford

Common Variations: Braddford

Consider This: Both Bradford and Bradley have questionable first impressions, but in the end, Bradford loses out in popularity.

Bradley ★★★

(English) broad meadow.

First Impression: Bradley is pictured as geeky yet still hunky.

Gender Association: Used mostly for boys

Popularity and Trend: #188 (#131 in 2000)

Risk of Misspelling: Fairly low

Risk of Mispronunciation: Low

Famous Namesakes: Actor Bradley Cooper; actor Bradley Whitford; senator Bill Bradley

Common Nicknames: Brad

Common Variations: Bradlee

Consider This: Even with Bradley's geekish vibe, pairing it with Brad as a nickname will make it more appealing.

Brady ★★★

(Irish) spirited. (English) broad island.

First Impression: Brady is considered take-charge and arrogant, but he's made a fortune in finance.

Gender Association: Used mostly for boys

Popularity and Trend: #105 (#190 in 2000)

Risk of Misspelling: Fairly low

Risk of Mispronunciation: Low

Famous Namesakes: Baseball player Brady Anderson; TV's *The Brady Bunch*; football player Brady Quinn; football player Tom Brady

Common Nicknames: None

Common Variations: Bradey, Braidy

Consider This: It's surprising that star quarterback Tom Brady doesn't seem to affect this name's first impression.

Bram ★★

(Scottish) bramble, brushwood. (Hebrew) a form of Abraham, Abram.

First Impression: Bram is viewed as a bookish pushover who's better at helping others than helping himself.

Gender Association: Used for boys

Popularity and Trend: Never been ranked in Top 1000

Risk of Misspelling: Average

Risk of Mispronunciation: Average

Famous Namesakes: Author Bram Stoker

Common Nicknames: None

Common Variations: Abram, Bramm, Brahm

Consider This: When people read this name, some may think it's pronounced so it rhymes with *lamb*, and when they hear it, some may think it's spelled "Brahm."

Brandon ★★★

(English) beacon hill.

First Impression: Brandon is seen as a snobbish yuppie who carries on like a spoiled only child.

Gender Association: Used mostly for boys

Popularity and Trend: #27 (#12 in 2000)

Risk of Misspelling: Average

Risk of Mispronunciation: Low

Famous Namesakes: Actor Brandon Routh; actor Brandon Lee; character Brandon Walsh (*Beverly Hills, 90210*)

Common Nicknames: Brand, Bran

Common Variations: Brandan, Brandyn, Branden

Consider This: Brandon is a highly popular name, but it has many variations that will confound spelling.

Brant ★★★★

(English) proud.

First Impression: Brant is said to be a friendly, fun-loving class clown with a lanky body and a big smile.

Gender Association: Used for boys

Popularity and Trend: Last ranked #984 in 2000

Risk of Misspelling: Fairly low

Risk of Mispronunciation: Low
Famous Namesakes: Satirist Sebastian Brant
Common Nicknames: Bran
Common Variations: Brandt, Brantley
Consider This: Brant is a unique alternative to Brent.

Brayden ★★★★
(English) a form of Braden.
First Impression: People say Brayden could be a preppy brainiac, a motivated athlete, or an outdoorsy farmhand.
Gender Association: Used for boys
Popularity and Trend: #79 (#199 in 2000)
Risk of Misspelling: Average
Risk of Mispronunciation: Low
Famous Namesakes: Actor Eric Braeden
Common Nicknames: None
Common Variations: Braden, Bradyn, Braiden
Consider This: Brayden may be the most popular form of Braden, but the other variations are prevalent enough to cause spelling trouble. At the very least, it's quite easy to pronounce.

Breck ★★★
(Irish) freckled.
First Impression: The name Breck makes people picture a kind and friendly free spirit.

Gender Association: Used about equally for girls and boys
Popularity and Trend: Never been ranked in Top 1000
Risk of Misspelling: Fairly low
Risk of Mispronunciation: Low
Famous Namesakes: Director Breck Eisner
Common Nicknames: Breckie
Common Variations: Brecken, Breckin
Consider This: Breck has unclear gender association, which may or may not be a plus.

Brendan ★★★★
(Irish) little raven. (English) sword.
First Impression: People imagine Brendan is warmhearted, dependable, honest, and fun.
Gender Association: Used for boys
Popularity and Trend: #185 (#101 in 2000)
Risk of Misspelling: Average
Risk of Mispronunciation: Low
Famous Namesakes: Actor Brendan Fraser; saint Brendan of Clonfert; hockey player Brendan Shanahan
Common Nicknames: Bren
Common Variations: Brenden, Brendon, Brendyn
Consider This: Brendan may not be as popular as Brandon, but it does inspire a better first impression. Like Braden and Brandon, though, it has many variations that make spelling a challenge.

Brent ★★★★
(English) a form of Brenton.
First Impression: Folks agree that Brent enjoys hunting and fishing much more than shopping at busy malls.
Gender Association: Used for boys
Popularity and Trend: #481 (#318 in 2000)
Risk of Misspelling: Low
Risk of Mispronunciation: Low
Famous Namesakes: Actor Brent Spiner; sportscaster Brent Musburger
Common Nicknames: None
Common Variations: Brenton
Consider This: Brent is more popular than Brant, but it's not quite as popular as Brett.

Brett ★★★★
(Scottish) from Great Britain.
First Impression: Brett is viewed as a great friend for playing sports or just hanging out.
Gender Association: Used mostly for boys
Popularity and Trend: #304 (#163 in 2000)
Risk of Misspelling: Fairly low
Risk of Mispronunciation: Low
Famous Namesakes: Singer Brett Michaels; football player Brett Favre; hockey player Brett Hull; wrestler Brett Hart
Common Nicknames: None
Common Variations: Bret

Consider This: Brett benefits from sporty namesakes like Brett Favre and Brett Hull.

Brian ★★★★★
(Irish, Scottish) strong; virtuous; honorable.
First Impression: Brian strikes people as polite, caring, and intelligent.
Gender Association: Used for boys
Popularity and Trend: #72 (#43 in 2000)
Risk of Misspelling: Average
Risk of Mispronunciation: Low
Famous Namesakes: Skater Brian Boitano; football player Brian Urlacher; singer Brian Wilson; singer Brian McKnight; singer Brian Setzer
Common Nicknames: Bri
Common Variations: Bryan, Brien
Consider This: Brian is a 5-star name, but because Bryan is so popular, there may be some spelling problems.

Brock ★★★
(English) badger.
First Impression: Brock is considered confident to the point of being a smarmy jerk.
Gender Association: Used for boys
Popularity and Trend: #261 (#268 in 2000)
Risk of Misspelling: Fairly low
Risk of Mispronunciation: Low
Famous Namesakes: Wrestler Brock Lesnar; actor Brock Peters; football player Brock Edwards
Common Nicknames: None
Common Variations: Broc, Brockton
Consider This: If you're looking for a masculine name, Brock is it—but be aware that it may come on too strong.

Brooklyn ★★
(English) a combination of Brook + Lynn.
First Impression: Brooklyn makes people think of an energetic and fun guy who can be rough and intimidating.
Gender Association: Used mostly for girls
Popularity and Trend: Never been ranked in Top 1000
Risk of Misspelling: Low
Risk of Mispronunciation: Low
Famous Namesakes: Star kid Brooklyn Beckham
Common Nicknames: None
Common Variations: None
Consider This: This name will likely cause gender confusion, given that it's used more often as a girls' name.

Bruce ★★★
(French) brushwood thicket; woods.
First Impression: People think Bruce may be sweet and simple or tough and brutish.
Gender Association: Used for boys
Popularity and Trend: #482 (#432 in 2000)
Risk of Misspelling: Low
Risk of Mispronunciation: Low
Famous Namesakes: Singer Bruce Springsteen; actor Bruce Willis; martial artist Bruce Lee; football player Bruce Smith
Common Nicknames: None
Common Variations: None
Consider This: Bryce has surpassed Bruce in popularity, suggesting that Bruce is a more uncommon choice.

Bryan ★★★★
(Irish) a form of Brian.
First Impression: Bryan is seen as a strong-willed go-getter who loves to be the center of attention.
Gender Association: Used for boys
Popularity and Trend: #66 (#70 in 2000)
Risk of Misspelling: Average
Risk of Mispronunciation: Low
Famous Namesakes: Singer Bryan Adams; statesman William Jennings Bryan; director Bryan Singer
Common Nicknames: Bry
Common Variations: Brian, Brien
Consider This: While "Brian" is thought to be the proper spelling, Bryan has surpassed it in popularity, which creates spelling challenges in both cases.

Bryce ★★★★

(Welsh) a form of Brice.

First Impression: Bryce is pictured as a determined leader who's smart and energetic, but perhaps too demanding.

Gender Association: Used mostly for boys

Popularity and Trend: #109 (#92 in 2000)

Risk of Misspelling: Average

Risk of Mispronunciation: Low

Famous Namesakes: Football player Bryce Fisher

Common Nicknames: Bry

Common Variations: Brice

Consider This: As Bryan is to Brian, the variation Bryce is more popular than the proper form Brice.

Bryson ★★★★★

(Welsh) son of Brice.

First Impression: Bryson is a great combination of personality and looks.

Gender Association: Used for boys

Popularity and Trend: #176 (#269 in 2000)

Risk of Misspelling: Fairly low

Risk of Mispronunciation: Low

Famous Namesakes: Singer Peabo Bryson; author Bill Bryson

Common Nicknames: Bry, Bryce

Common Variations: Brysen

Consider This: Bryson is a surprising 5-star name with many upsides.

Bud ★★★

(English) brother; friend.

First Impression: People see Bud as a dumb hick, but he makes up for it with his soft heart and friendly ways.

Gender Association: Used for boys

Popularity and Trend: Last ranked in the Top 1000 in the 1960s

Risk of Misspelling: Low

Risk of Mispronunciation: Low

Famous Namesakes: Baseball commissioner Bud Selig; comedian Bud Abbott; character Bud Bundy (*Married...with Children*)

Common Nicknames: Buddy

Common Variations: None

Consider This: Like Buddy, Bud's image is formed by the literal meaning of the word *buddy* and by rural, working-class connotations.

Buddy ★★★

(American) a familiar form of Bud.

First Impression: Buddy is regarded as either a sweet friend or a dim redneck.

Gender Association: Used for boys

Popularity and Trend: Last ranked in the Top 1000 in the 1980s

Risk of Misspelling: Low

Risk of Mispronunciation: Low

Famous Namesakes: Singer Buddy Holly; actor Buddy Ebsen; singer Buddy Guy; actor Buddy Hackett

Common Nicknames: None

Common Variations: None

Consider This: Although Buddy and Bud are lackluster choices, Buddy has more namesakes.

Butch ★★

(American) a short form of Butcher.

First Impression: Everyone says Butch is a big, burly bully who's none too bright.

Gender Association: Used for boys

Popularity and Trend: Last ranked in the Top 1000 in the 1960s

Risk of Misspelling: Low

Risk of Mispronunciation: Low

Famous Namesakes: Robber Butch Cassidy

Common Nicknames: None

Common Variations: None

Consider This: Even if you predict your son will someday be rough-and-tough enough for the nickname Butch, don't even think about making it his given name.

Byron ★★★

(French) cottage. (English) barn.

First Impression: Most people say Byron is a lonely, bullied misfit, but perhaps because of Don Juan poet Lord Byron's influence, some also see a noble and poetic side to Byron.

Gender Association: Used for boys

Popularity and Trend: #523 (#438 in 2000)

Risk of Misspelling: Fairly low
Risk of Mispronunciation: Low
Famous Namesakes: Poet Lord Byron; golfer Byron Nelson
Common Nicknames: None
Common Variations: Byran
Consider This: Byron has the same dorky vibe as Myron, but because of namesake Lord Byron, it also has a poetic sensibility.

Caden ★★★★
(American) a form of Kadin.
First Impression: Caden is seen as either a successful businessman or a beach bum.
Gender Association: Used for boys
Popularity and Trend: #91 (#239 in 2000)
Risk of Misspelling: Average
Risk of Mispronunciation: Fairly low
Famous Namesakes: None
Common Nicknames: Cade, Cay
Common Variations: Cayden, Cadan, Cadyn, Caiden
Consider This: Caden would be a 5-star name if it weren't for the spelling woes caused by the gamut of popular variations. As with Braden, a handful of people may mispronounce it "CAD-en" instead of "CAY-den."

Caesar ★★★
(Latin) long-haired.
First Impression: Caesar is seen as strong both physically and mentally.

Gender Association: Used for boys
Popularity and Trend: Last ranked in the Top 1000 in the 1910s
Risk of Misspelling: Fairly low
Risk of Mispronunciation: Fairly low
Famous Namesakes: Emperor Julius Caesar; "Dog Whisperer" Cesar Millan; activist César Chávez; comedian Sid Caesar
Common Nicknames: None
Common Variations: Ceasar, Cesar
Consider This: Caesar (pronounced "SEE-zer") hasn't been popular for nearly a century, but Cesar (pronounced "sez-ZAR" or "say-ZAR") is quite popular—especially with Latino families.

Cain ★★
(Hebrew) spear; gatherer.
First Impression: Cain is thought to be spiteful and murderous, like the biblical Cain, or hardworking and smart.
Gender Association: Used for boys
Popularity and Trend: Never been ranked in Top 1000
Risk of Misspelling: Fairly low
Risk of Mispronunciation: Low
Famous Namesakes: Biblical figure Cain
Common Nicknames: None
Common Variations: Caine, Kane, Cayne, Kayne
Consider This: It's notable that Cain has never made the Top 1000 list, indicating how strong of a

negative first impression the "Cain and Abel" story makes.

Caleb ★★★★★
(Hebrew) dog; faithful. (Arabic) bold, brave.
First Impression: Most people say Caleb is an extremely dedicated and hardworking man who's caring as well as charismatic.
Gender Association: Used for boys
Popularity and Trend: #34 (#38 in 2000)
Risk of Misspelling: Fairly low
Risk of Mispronunciation: Fairly low
Famous Namesakes: Biblical figure Caleb; character Caleb (*East of Eden*)
Common Nicknames: Cal, Cale, Caley
Common Variations: Kaleb
Consider This: Most people may not realize how versatile Caleb can be with so many nicknames.

Calvin ★★★★
(Latin) bald.
First Impression: Calvin is seen as thoughtful and trustworthy, and his sense of humor makes him popular with others.
Gender Association: Used for boys
Popularity and Trend: #220 (#214 in 2000)
Risk of Misspelling: Fairly low
Risk of Mispronunciation: Low
Famous Namesakes: Designer Calvin Klein; comic strip *Calvin and*

Hobbes; president Calvin Coolidge; theologian John Calvin

Common Nicknames: Cal, Calv, Vinny

Common Variations: Kalvin

Consider This: The fun, casual nickname Cal provides a nice balance for the formal tone of Calvin.

Cameron ★★★★

(Scottish) crooked nose.

First Impression: Cameron is thought to be a tall, blond actor with an active, outdoorsy lifestyle.

Gender Association: Used mostly for boys

Popularity and Trend: #52 (#31 in 2000)

Risk of Misspelling: Fairly low

Risk of Mispronunciation: Low

Famous Namesakes: Director Cameron Crowe

Common Nicknames: Cam

Common Variations: Camren, Kameron, Camryn

Consider This: This spelling is sometimes used as a girls' name, although it's more popular as a boys' name. However, its pronunciation is virtually the same as that for Camryn, a popular name for girls, which may cause gender confusion.

Campbell ★★★★

(Latin, French) beautiful field. (Scottish) crooked mouth.

First Impression: People can't decide if Campbell is a sophisticated

professional who's well dressed and well spoken or if he's a rugged rancher in cowboy hat and boots.

Gender Association: Used mostly for boys

Popularity and Trend: Never been ranked in Top 1000

Risk of Misspelling: Fairly low

Risk of Mispronunciation: Fairly low

Famous Namesakes: Actor Bruce Campbell; football player Earl Campbell; singer Glen Campbell; actor Campbell Scott

Common Nicknames: Cam

Common Variations: Kampbell

Consider This: It's hard to say why people think of Campbell as either a businessman or a cowboy, but either way, they see this name in a positive light.

Carey ★★

(Greek) pure. (Welsh) castle; rocky island.

First Impression: People don't know if Carey is a boy or a girl, and they also can't decide if Carey is a bookworm or a joker.

Gender Association: Used about equally for girls and boys

Popularity and Trend: Last ranked in the Top 1000 in the 1990s

Risk of Misspelling: Average

Risk of Mispronunciation: Low

Famous Namesakes: Tattoo artist Carey Hart; actor Drew Carey;

sportscaster Harry Carey; actor Jim Carrey; actor Cary Grant

Common Nicknames: None

Common Variations: Cary, Karey

Consider This: This particular spelling is no longer in the Top 1000 for boys or girls, and most variations of Carey are used nearly exclusively for girls.

Carl ★★★★

(German, English) a form of Carlton. A form of Charles.

First Impression: Carl is pictured as a sociable guy, even though he's a tad bit geeky.

Gender Association: Used for boys

Popularity and Trend: #429 (#304 in 2000)

Risk of Misspelling: Fairly low

Risk of Mispronunciation: Low

Famous Namesakes: Astronomer Carl Sagan; athlete Carl Lewis; psychiatrist Carl Jung; racecar driver Carl Edwards

Common Nicknames: None

Common Variations: Karl, Carle

Consider This: Carlos is more popular than Carl, though Carl fits a wider range of cultures.

Carlo ★★★★

(Italian) a form of Carl, Charles.

First Impression: Carlo is viewed as gregarious, self-assured, and ambitious—qualities that make him a natural flirt.

Gender Association: Used for boys

Popularity and Trend: #937
(#901 in 2000)
Risk of Misspelling: Fairly low
Risk of Mispronunciation: Low
Famous Namesakes: Director Carlo
Ponti
Common Nicknames: None
Common Variations: Karlo
Consider This: Like Carl and Carlos,
this name also has an outgoing
come-off.

Carlos ★★★★★
(Spanish) a form of Carl, Charles.
First Impression: People view Carlos as
a chatty, outgoing, and energetic
man of Latino descent.
Gender Association: Used for boys
Popularity and Trend: #70
(#66 in 2000)
Risk of Misspelling: Fairly low
Risk of Mispronunciation: Low
Famous Namesakes: Comedian Carlos
Mencia; musician Carlos Santana;
baseball player Carlos Delgado
Common Nicknames: Carlito, Los
Common Variations: Karlos
Consider This: Carlos is one of many
Latino names in the Top 100.

Carlton ★★★
(English) Carl's town.
First Impression: Carlton is seen as a
well-dressed snob who's spoiled
and pompous.
Gender Association: Used for boys
Popularity and Trend: Last ranked
#749 in 2000

Risk of Misspelling: Fairly low
Risk of Mispronunciation: Low
Famous Namesakes: Baseball player
Steve Carlton; baseball player
Carlton Fisk; character Carlton
Banks (*The Fresh Prince of Bel Air*)
Common Nicknames: Carl
Common Variations: Carleton, Karlton
Consider This: The first impression
for this name likely comes from
character Carlton Banks of TV's
The Fresh Prince of Bel Air.

Carmel ★★
(Hebrew) vineyard, garden.
First Impression: Carmel is described
as a warmhearted and religious
man who's probably less
informed than he should be.
Gender Association: Used mostly
for girls
Popularity and Trend: Never been
ranked in Top 1000
Risk of Misspelling: Fairly low
Risk of Mispronunciation: Average
Famous Namesakes: None
Common Nicknames: Mel
Common Variations: Carmelo, Karmel
Consider This: Latinos pronounce this
name "car-MEL," but most others
pronounce it "CAR-mel." Either
way, this name is used mostly
for girls.

Carrick ★★★
(Irish) rock.
First Impression: Carrick is regarded
as a sporty smarty who's

outgoing and witty with
freckles and red hair.
Gender Association: Used for boys
Popularity and Trend: Never been
ranked in Top 1000
Risk of Misspelling: Average
Risk of Mispronunciation: Average
Famous Namesakes: None
Common Nicknames: Rick
Common Variations: None
Consider This: Pronunciation could be
an problem if people pronounce
this name "CAR-rick" instead of
"CARE-rick."

Carson ★★★★★
(English) son of Carr.
First Impression: People picture Carson
as a confident, fit guy.
Gender Association: Used mostly
for boys
Popularity and Trend: #87
(#119 in 2000)
Risk of Misspelling: Fairly low
Risk of Mispronunciation: Low
Famous Namesakes: Talk show host
Johnny Carson; talk show host
Carson Daly; football player
Carson Palmer
Common Nicknames: None
Common Variations: Carsen, Karsen,
Karson
Consider This: Like Carter, Carson is
a last name as first name that's
quite popular.

Carter ★★★★★

(English) cart driver.

First Impression: People say Carter is intelligent, charismatic, and warm, much like *ER* character John Carter.

Gender Association: Used mostly for boys

Popularity and Trend: #75 (#152 in 2000)

Risk of Misspelling: Low

Risk of Mispronunciation: Low

Famous Namesakes: President Jimmy Carter; character Dr. John Carter (*ER*); Declaration of Independence signer Carter Braxton

Common Nicknames: Cart

Common Variations: None

Consider This: Carter is climbing up the popularity list, now making its way into the Top 100.

Casey ★★★

(Irish) brave.

First Impression: Casey is imagined to be strong-willed, playful, and energetic.

Gender Association: Used about equally for girls and boys

Popularity and Trend: #308 (#193 in 2000)

Risk of Misspelling: Fairly low

Risk of Mispronunciation: Low

Famous Namesakes: Baseball player Casey Stengel; golfer Casey Martin; actor Casey Affleck; poem "Casey at the Bat"

Common Nicknames: Case

Common Variations: Kacey, Kasey

Consider This: Casey is used about equally for boys and girls, which creates a gender association problem.

Casper ★★★

(Persian) treasurer. (German) imperial.

First Impression: Casper is pictured as a kindhearted boy who's pale, shy, and somewhat strange—perhaps like Casper the Friendly Ghost.

Gender Association: Used for boys

Popularity and Trend: Last ranked in the Top 1000 in the 1930s

Risk of Misspelling: Fairly low

Risk of Mispronunciation: Low

Famous Namesakes: Character Casper the Friendly Ghost; actor Casper Van Dien

Common Nicknames: Cass

Common Variations: Kasper

Consider This: Although the first impression makes a connection to Casper the Friendly Ghost, the name Casper dropped off the Top 1000 before the character was introduced.

Cecil ★★

(Latin) blind.

First Impression: People say Cecil is a name for a skinny, wimpy British aristocrat.

Gender Association: Used for boys

Popularity and Trend: Last ranked in the Top 1000 in the 1990s

Risk of Misspelling: Fairly low

Risk of Mispronunciation: Average

Famous Namesakes: Director Cecil B. Demille; baseball player Cecil Fielder

Common Nicknames: Cece

Common Variations: Cecilio, Cecill

Consider This: Brits pronounce this name "SESS-ill," while Yanks prefer "SEE-sill," which may pose problems either way you go.

Cedric ★★★

(English) battle chieftain.

First Impression: The name Cedric makes people think of a witty, clever, and distinguished preppy.

Gender Association: Used for boys

Popularity and Trend: #595 (#464 in 2000)

Risk of Misspelling: Fairly low

Risk of Mispronunciation: Fairly low

Famous Namesakes: Comedian Cedric the Entertainer

Common Nicknames: Rick

Common Variations: Cederic, Cedrick

Consider This: Cedric seems like a lofty name for a battle chieftain, but consider whether it's too heavy for a young boy.

Chad ★★★★

(English) warrior. A form of Chadwick.

First Impression: Chad is seen as an athletic, good-looking blond who's independent and persistent.
Gender Association: Used for boys
Popularity and Trend: #375 (#235 in 2000)
Risk of Misspelling: Low
Risk of Mispronunciation: Low
Famous Namesakes: Actor Chad Allen; actor Chad Lowe
Common Nicknames: None
Common Variations: None
Consider This: Chad scores well for many reasons, but it's slipping in popularity.

Chance ★★★★
(English) a form of Chancellor, Chauncey.
First Impression: People picture Chance as a rowdy risk taker who's cocky and clever.
Gender Association: Used mostly for boys
Popularity and Trend: #273 (#212 in 2000)
Risk of Misspelling: Low
Risk of Mispronunciation: Low
Famous Namesakes: None
Common Nicknames: Chancey
Common Variations: Chanse
Consider This: Chance and Chase are two of the few noun names for boys, whereas there are many for girls.

Chandler ★★★★
(English) candle maker.
First Impression: Folks say Chandler is goofy, sarcastic, and sweet with brown hair, much like character Chandler Bing of TV's *Friends*.
Gender Association: Used mostly for boys
Popularity and Trend: #402 (#174 in 2000)
Risk of Misspelling: Fairly low
Risk of Mispronunciation: Low
Famous Namesakes: Character Chandler Bing (*Friends*)
Common Nicknames: None
Common Variations: Chandlar
Consider This: This name peaked when *Friends* peaked in the late '90s, but it's gradually fallen in popularity since then.

Charles ★★★★★
(German) farmer. (English) strong and manly.
First Impression: Charles conjures up the image of a brilliant but stodgy man who gained wealth and power with his strong, decisive will.
Gender Association: Used for boys
Popularity and Trend: #60 (#51 in 2000)
Risk of Misspelling: Low
Risk of Mispronunciation: Low
Famous Namesakes: British prince Charles; author Charles Dickens; basketball player Charles Barkley; pilot Charles Lindbergh; broker Charles Schwab
Common Nicknames: Chuck, Charlie, Chas, Chip
Common Variations: None
Consider This: Charles scores high, thanks in part to its simple spelling and pronunciation and lots of nicknames to choose from.

Charlie ★★★
(German, English) a familiar form of Charles.
First Impression: People see Charlie as kind, cheerful, and smart.
Gender Association: Used mostly for boys
Popularity and Trend: #337 (#452 in 2000)
Risk of Misspelling: Fairly low
Risk of Mispronunciation: Low
Famous Namesakes: Actor Charlie Sheen; actor Charlie Chaplin; character Charlie Brown (*Peanuts*); singer Charlie Daniels
Common Nicknames: None
Common Variations: Charley, Charly
Consider This: Charlie is relatively popular on its own, but this nickname for Charles is hard to take seriously as a given name.

Charlton ★★★
(English) a form of Carlton.
First Impression: Charlton comes across as dignified and stoic to some, but egotistical and inflexible to others.

Gender Association: Used for boys
Popularity and Trend: Never been
 ranked in Top 1000
Risk of Misspelling: Fairly low
Risk of Mispronunciation: Fairly low
Famous Namesakes: Actor Charlton
 Heston
Common Nicknames: Charlie
Common Variations: Charleton
Consider This: Charlton's first impres-
 sion gets mixed reactions, but it
 fairs slightly better than Carlton's.

Chase ★★★★★
(French) hunter.
First Impression: People describe
 Chase as an energized, playful,
 and outgoing athlete who's
 passionate about living life to
 the fullest.
Gender Association: Used mostly
 for boys
Popularity and Trend: #83
 (#77 in 2000)
Risk of Misspelling: Low
Risk of Mispronunciation: Low
Famous Namesakes: Actor Chevy
 Chase; baseball player Chase
 Utley
Common Nicknames: None
Common Variations: Chace, Chaise,
 Chayce
Consider This: Like Chance, Chase is
 a noun name, but it's much more
 popular than Chance because it
 makes a much more positive first
 impression.

Chester ★★★
(English) a form of Rochester.
First Impression: Chester is seen as a
 meek geek who keeps to his
 books and studies.
Gender Association: Used for boys
Popularity and Trend: Last ranked in
 the Top 1000 in the 1990s
Risk of Misspelling: Low
Risk of Mispronunciation: Low
Famous Namesakes: President Chester
 A. Arthur; singer Chester
 Bennington
Common Nicknames: Chet
Common Variations: Cheston
Consider This: A Top 1000 dropout,
 Chester carries a distinctly geeky
 image.

Chet ★★
(English) a short form of Chester.
First Impression: People think Chet is
 arrogant, rude, and not very
 bright.
Gender Association: Used for boys
Popularity and Trend: Last ranked in
 the Top 1000 in the 1980s
Risk of Misspelling: Low
Risk of Mispronunciation: Low
Famous Namesakes: Singer Chet
 Atkins; musician Chet Baker
Common Nicknames: None
Common Variations: None
Consider This: Chet evokes a strong,
 clear first impression, though it's
 not a good one.

Chris ★★★
(Greek) a short form of Christian,
 Christopher.
First Impression: People see Chris as
 kind and trusting as well as
 funny and smart.
Gender Association: Used mostly
 for boys
Popularity and Trend: #358
 (#395 in 2000)
Risk of Misspelling: Fairly low
Risk of Mispronunciation: Low
Famous Namesakes: Comedian Chris
 Rock; singer Chris Isaak;
 basketball player Chris Webber;
 singer Chris Cornell
Common Nicknames: None
Common Variations: Cris, Kris
Consider This: Chris is a terrific nick-
 name, but it doesn't have nearly
 as much versatility and gravitas
 as Christopher or Christian.

Christian ★★★★★
(Greek) follower of Christ;
 anointed.
First Impression: Folks imagine
 Christian has a big, generous
 heart and handsome, alluring
 looks.
Gender Association: Used mostly
 for boys
Popularity and Trend: #21
 (#22 in 2000)
Risk of Misspelling: Fairly low
Risk of Mispronunciation: Low

Famous Namesakes: Actor Christian Bale; actor Christian Slater; designer Christian Dior; basketball player Christian Laettner

Common Nicknames: Chris, Kit

Common Variations: Christien, Cristian, Kristian

Consider This: With its strong religious tone, Christian is nearly as popular as Christopher.

Christopher ★★★★★

(Greek) Christ-bearer.

First Impression: People say Christopher is an educated man who's superfriendly and quick to help others.

Gender Association: Used mostly for boys

Popularity and Trend: #7 (#5 in 2000)

Risk of Misspelling: Fairly low

Risk of Mispronunciation: Low

Famous Namesakes: Actor Christopher Reeve; character Christopher Robin (*Winnie-the-Pooh*); actor Christopher Walken; actor Christopher Atkins

Common Nicknames: Chris, Topher, Kit

Common Variations: Christofer, Cristofer, Cristopher, Kristopher, Christophe

Consider This: Christopher is a 5-star name, despite the facts that it's perhaps *too* popular as a Top 10 name and that there are many variations that could affect spelling ease.

Chuck ★★★

(American) a familiar form of Charles.

First Impression: Chuck may be mousy, but many think he's nice as can be.

Gender Association: Used for boys

Popularity and Trend: Last ranked in the Top 1000 in the 1970s

Risk of Misspelling: Low

Risk of Mispronunciation: Low

Famous Namesakes: Singer Chuck Berry; actor Chuck Norris; rapper Chuck D; pilot Chuck Yeager

Common Nicknames: Chuckie

Common Variations: None

Consider This: Although Chuck sounds like a tough, macho name and has Chuck Norris as a namesake, it has a surprisingly meek and mild image.

Clarence ★★

(Latin) clear; victorious.

First Impression: Clarence is described as a doofy and timid mama's boy.

Gender Association: Used for boys

Popularity and Trend: #818 (#616 in 2000)

Risk of Misspelling: Fairly low

Risk of Mispronunciation: Low

Famous Namesakes: Supreme Court justice Clarence Thomas; singer Clarence Carter; lawyer Clarence Darrow

Common Nicknames: Clare

Common Variations: Clarance, Clarrance

Consider This: Clarence is a nerdy name that seems dated.

Clark ★★★★

(French) cleric; scholar.

First Impression: Some people describe Clark as a caring, trustworthy square who seems to lack common sense, like Superman's alter ego, Clark Kent. Others describe him as a dashing, distinguished, and romantic charmer, like silver-screen star Clark Gable.

Gender Association: Used for boys

Popularity and Trend: #696 (#764 in 2000)

Risk of Misspelling: Fairly low

Risk of Mispronunciation: Low

Famous Namesakes: Character Clark Kent (*Superman*); actor Clark Gable; TV personality Dick Clark; explorer William Clark

Common Nicknames: None

Common Variations: Clarke

Consider This: For the last few years, Clark has risen and fallen in popularity, though it always remains in the bottom half of the Top 1000.

Claude ★★

(Latin, French) lame.

First Impression: Claude is regarded as a standoffish and overly ambitious Frenchman.

Gender Association: Used mostly for boys

Popularity and Trend: Last ranked in the Top 1000 in the 1990s

Risk of Misspelling: Low

Risk of Mispronunciation: Low

Famous Namesakes: Composer Claude Debussy; artist Claude Monet; actor Jean-Claude Van Damme

Common Nicknames: None

Common Variations: Claudio, Claudius

Consider This: Having been out of the Top 1000 for years, Claude has an old-fashioned feel to it.

Clay ★★★★

(English) clay pit.

First Impression: People say Clay is a talented musician who's confident, calm, kind, and cute, much like *American Idol* winner Clay Aiken.

Gender Association: Used for boys

Popularity and Trend: #708 (#397 in 2000)

Risk of Misspelling: Low

Risk of Mispronunciation: Low

Famous Namesakes: Boxer Cassius Clay, birth name of Muhammad Ali; singer Clay Aiken; statesman Henry Clay

Common Nicknames: None

Common Variations: Klay

Consider This: While Clay Aiken affects the first impression, his success hasn't kept this name's popularity from tumbling.

Clayton ★★★★

(English) town built on clay.

First Impression: People think Clayton is an intellectual who's straight-laced and businesslike.

Gender Association: Used for boys

Popularity and Trend: #226 (#151 in 2000)

Risk of Misspelling: Fairly low

Risk of Mispronunciation: Low

Famous Namesakes: Character Clayton (Disney's *Tarzan*); actor Clayton Moore; bassist Adam Clayton

Common Nicknames: Clay

Common Variations: Klayton, Clayten

Consider This: If you like the name Clay, perhaps use it as a nickname for Clayton, which is much more popular and versatile.

Cletus ★

(Greek) illustrious.

First Impression: People imagine Cletus is the epitome of a countrified hick.

Gender Association: Used for boys

Popularity and Trend: Last ranked in the Top 1000 in the 1950s

Risk of Misspelling: Average

Risk of Mispronunciation: Fairly low

Famous Namesakes: Character Cletus the Slack-Jawed Yokel (*The Simpsons*); character Cletus Hogg (*The Dukes of Hazzard*)

Common Nicknames: None

Common Variations: Cletis

Consider This: As the first impression so clearly indicates, Cletus is the epitome of a hick.

Cliff ★★★★

(English) a short form of Clifford, Clifton.

First Impression: Cliff is pictured as a popular physician—perhaps because of Dr. Cliff Huxtable of TV's *The Cosby Show*.

Gender Association: Used for boys

Popularity and Trend: Last ranked in the Top 1000 in the 1980s

Risk of Misspelling: Low

Risk of Mispronunciation: Low

Famous Namesakes: Actor Cliff Robertson; character Cliff Huxtable (*The Cosby Show*); character Cliff Clavin (*Cheers*)

Common Nicknames: None

Common Variations: Kliff

Consider This: No longer in the Top 1000, Cliff is rarely used as a given name.

Clifford ★★★

(English) cliff at the river crossing.

First Impression: Clifford is misunderstood: He comes across as annoying and loud, but he really means to be sweet, silly, and playful.

Gender Association: Used for boys
Popularity and Trend: Last ranked #753 in 2000
Risk of Misspelling: Fairly low
Risk of Mispronunciation: Low
Famous Namesakes: Book and cartoon character Clifford the Big Red Dog
Common Nicknames: Cliff, Ford
Common Variations: Klifford
Consider This: Not only is Cliff out of the Top 1000, but so is Clifford—perhaps because parents think of Clifford the Big Red Dog.

Clint ★★★★

(English) a form of Clinton.
First Impression: People imagine Clint as a rugged, stone-faced, and confident gunslinger, not unlike many of the Western characters actor Clint Eastwood has portrayed.
Gender Association: Used for boys
Popularity and Trend: Last ranked #917 in 2000
Risk of Misspelling: Low
Risk of Mispronunciation: Low
Famous Namesakes: Actor Clint Eastwood; singer Clint Black; actor Clint Howard
Common Nicknames: None
Common Variations: Klint
Consider This: Sort out your feelings about Clint Eastwood before you choose this name, because it's impossible to separate its image from his.

Clinton ★★★

(English) hill town.
First Impression: Clinton is described as a slick and powerful man that people like in spite of his lying and womanizing ways, perhaps like a certain former American president.
Gender Association: Used for boys
Popularity and Trend: #844 (#634 in 2000)
Risk of Misspelling: Fairly low
Risk of Mispronunciation: Low
Famous Namesakes: President Bill Clinton; singer George Clinton
Common Nicknames: Clint
Common Variations: Clinten, Klinton
Consider This: Just as with Clint, sort out your feelings about Bill (and Hillary) Clinton before you choose this name.

Clyde ★★

(Welsh) warm.
First Impression: Clyde is viewed as a lumbering farmhand who's tough and gruff in his old age.
Gender Association: Used for boys
Popularity and Trend: Last ranked in the Top 1000 in the 1990s
Risk of Misspelling: Fairly low
Risk of Mispronunciation: Low
Famous Namesakes: Robber Clyde Barrow; basketball player Clyde Drexler
Common Nicknames: Cly
Common Variations: Klyde

Consider This: Clyde's first impression suggests it's out of fashion, as does the fact that it's a Top 1000 dropout.

Cody ★★

(English) cushion.
First Impression: People describe Cody as a manipulative, spoiled, and bratty blond.
Gender Association: Used mostly for boys
Popularity and Trend: #106 (#60 in 2000)
Risk of Misspelling: Fairly low
Risk of Mispronunciation: Low
Famous Namesakes: Showman William "Buffalo Bill" Cody; star kid Cody Gifford
Common Nicknames: None
Common Variations: Codey, Kodey, Kody, Koty, Coty
Consider This: You'd think Cody would have a rugged Western image, but the first impression is just the opposite.

Colby ★★★

(English) dark; dark-haired.
First Impression: Colby is seen as a cute blond with a button nose, but he's also a stuffy snob.
Gender Association: Used mostly for boys
Popularity and Trend: #271 (#233 in 2000)
Risk of Misspelling: Fairly low
Risk of Mispronunciation: Low

Famous Namesakes: CIA director William E. Colby; hockey player Colby Armstrong

Common Nicknames: None

Common Variations: Kolby

Consider This: Colby could be a nice alternative to Cole, but you can expect comments such as, "You must like cheese."

Cole ★★★★

(Latin) cabbage farmer. (English) a form of Colbert, Coleman. (Greek) a form of Nicholas.

First Impression: Cole is thought to be a rugged man who can be moody but is caring overall.

Gender Association: Used for boys

Popularity and Trend: #84 (#71 in 2000)

Risk of Misspelling: Fairly low

Risk of Mispronunciation: Low

Famous Namesakes: Composer Cole Porter; singer Nat "King" Cole; designer Kenneth Cole

Common Nicknames: None

Common Variations: Kohl, Kole

Consider This: Although traditionally a nickname, Cole seems strong enough to be a given name, thanks to its popularity.

Colin ★★★

(Irish) young cub. (Greek) a form of Nicholas.

First Impression: Colin is said to be intelligent, dryly funny, and confident to the point of being cocky.

Gender Association: Used for boys

Popularity and Trend: #111 (#117 in 2000)

Risk of Misspelling: Average

Risk of Mispronunciation: Average

Famous Namesakes: Actor Colin Farrell; comedian Colin Quinn; actor Colin Firth; secretary of state Colin Powell

Common Nicknames: None

Common Variations: Collin

Consider This: Colin makes a positive first impression, but there are two common ways to pronounce this name: "CAH-len" and "COH-len."

Collin ★★★

(Scottish) a form of Colin, Collins.

First Impression: Some people think Collin is handsome yet dumb, pigheaded, and boring. Others see a more positive side to him, saying he's cheerful and gregarious.

Gender Association: Used for boys

Popularity and Trend: #181 (#129 in 2000)

Risk of Misspelling: Average

Risk of Mispronunciation: Fairly low

Famous Namesakes: Singer Collin Raye; actor Collin Chou

Common Nicknames: None

Common Variations: Colin

Consider This: Collin is a popular variation, but people will likely spell it "Colin."

Connor ★★★★

(Scottish) wise. (Irish) a form of Conan.

First Impression: Connor is pictured as an articulate and friendly joker who's sly and quick on his feet.

Gender Association: Used mostly for boys

Popularity and Trend: #53 (#50 in 2000)

Risk of Misspelling: Fairly low

Risk of Mispronunciation: Low

Famous Namesakes: Character Connor MacLeod (*Highlander*)

Common Nicknames: None

Common Variations: Conor, Konner, Connor

Consider This: Connor is quite popular, perhaps because of the last name as first name trend.

Conrad ★★

(German) brave counselor.

First Impression: People say Conrad is a conniving, manipulative sleaze with dark hair and pale skin.

Gender Association: Used for boys

Popularity and Trend: #788 (#709 in 2000)

Risk of Misspelling: Fairly low

Risk of Mispronunciation: Low

Famous Namesakes: Author Joseph Conrad; hotel founder Conrad Hilton; actor Conrad Bain

Common Nicknames: Connie

Common Variations: Konrad

Consider This: If you find yourself drawn to the name Conrad, it may be smart to turn your attention to Connor instead.

Constantine ★★★★
(Latin) firm, constant.

First Impression: Constantine is considered an intelligent and trustworthy man with stubborn—almost arrogant—determination.

Gender Association: Used for boys

Popularity and Trend: Last ranked in the Top 1000 in the 1980s

Risk of Misspelling: Fairly low

Risk of Mispronunciation: Fairly low

Famous Namesakes: Emperor Constantine the Great; character John Constantine (*Constantine* and *Hellblazer*)

Common Nicknames: Connie, Constant, Costa

Common Variations: Constantino, Konstantine

Consider This: Versatility raises Constantine to 4 stars, but its low popularity nevertheless suggests it's an old-fashioned name.

Cooper ★★★★
(English) barrel maker.

First Impression: Cooper is pictured as a wild and rambunctious risk taker who drives fast and lives for stressful situations.

Gender Association: Used mostly for boys

Popularity and Trend: #113 (#240 in 2000)

Risk of Misspelling: Low

Risk of Mispronunciation: Low

Famous Namesakes: Actor Gary Cooper; reporter Anderson Cooper

Common Nicknames: Coop

Common Variations: None

Consider This: Cooper would be a 5-Star name if it weren't for its wild first impression.

Corbin ★★
(Latin) raven.

First Impression: People feel Corbin is so wholesome and nice, he's boring.

Gender Association: Used mostly for boys

Popularity and Trend: #289 (#292 in 2000)

Risk of Misspelling: Fairly low

Risk of Mispronunciation: Low

Famous Namesakes: Actor Corbin Bernsen; actor Corbin Bleu

Common Nicknames: None

Common Variations: Corban, Korbin

Consider This: Corbin is a moderately popular name, hanging in around #300 for several years.

Corey ★★★
(Irish) hollow.

First Impression: Corey is viewed as a goofy, silly, and entertaining guy who's fun to be around.

Gender Association: Used mostly for boys

Popularity and Trend: #234 (#149 in 2000)

Risk of Misspelling: Average

Risk of Mispronunciation: Low

Famous Namesakes: Actor Corey Haim; actor Corey Feldman

Common Nicknames: None

Common Variations: Cori, Cory, Korey, Kory

Consider This: Although Corey is considered the proper spelling of this name, there are many variations that may cause spelling problems.

Cornelius ★★★
(Greek) cornel tree. (Latin) horn colored.

First Impression: People think of Cornelius as a nerdy, inventive, and slightly crazy brainiac who wears suspenders to hold up his pants on his skinny build.

Gender Association: Used for boys

Popularity and Trend: #939 (#791 in 2000)

Risk of Misspelling: Average

Risk of Mispronunciation: Fairly low

Famous Namesakes: Entrepreneur Cornelius Vanderbilt; character Cornelius Fudge (*Harry Potter* series)

Common Nicknames: Corny, Nelius, Nellie

Common Variations: Kornelius

Consider This: With its mad-scientist image, it's no wonder Cornelius is on the verge of falling out of the Top 1000. Most people, however, will know to pronounce it "cor-NEE-lee-us."

Cory ★★★

(Latin) a form of Corey. (French) a form of Cornell. (Greek) a form of Corydon.

First Impression: Cory is depicted as a cute, fair-haired guy who's sweet and kind when he's not filled with anxiety.

Gender Association: Used mostly for boys

Popularity and Trend: #431 (#227 in 2000)

Risk of Misspelling: Average

Risk of Mispronunciation: Low

Famous Namesakes: Baseball player Cory Lidle; character Cory Matthews (*Boy Meets World*); character Cory Baxter (*Cory in the House*)

Common Nicknames: None

Common Variations: Corey, Korey, Kory

Consider This: Cory will likely be confused for Corey on a daily basis.

Coty ★

(French) slope, hillside.

First Impression: Coty gives the impression of a dirty, greasy jerk who isn't very bright.

Gender Association: Used for boys

Popularity and Trend: Last ranked in the Top 1000 in the 1990s

Risk of Misspelling: Average

Risk of Mispronunciation: Fairly low

Famous Namesakes: French President René Coty

Common Nicknames: None

Common Variations: Kody, Koty, Cody

Consider This: Because *t* and *d* sound so similar—and because Cody is much more popular—people will probably mistake Coty for Cody.

Craig ★★★★

(Irish, Scottish) crag; steep rock.

First Impression: People imagine Craig as fast paced and hardworking—traits he developed during his military service.

Gender Association: Used for boys

Popularity and Trend: #548 (#339 in 2000)

Risk of Misspelling: Fairly low

Risk of Mispronunciation: Low

Famous Namesakes: Talk show host Craig Kilborn; actor Craig T. Nelson; actor Daniel Craig

Common Nicknames: None

Common Variations: Kraig

Consider This: Craig has a certain rugged vibe, perhaps because of the "rocky" meaning and its hard consonant sounds.

Curt ★★★★

(Latin) a form of Courtney, Curtis.

First Impression: Curt is seen as a philosophical deep thinker.

Gender Association: Used for boys

Popularity and Trend: Last ranked in the Top 1000 in the 1980s

Risk of Misspelling: Average

Risk of Mispronunciation: Low

Famous Namesakes: Baseball player Curt Schilling

Common Nicknames: None

Common Variations: Kurt

Consider This: Although Curt is a short form of Curtis, it isn't nearly as popular—despite a more positive first impression and pitcher Curt Schilling as a namesake.

Curtis ★★★

(Latin) enclosure. (French) courteous.

First Impression: People think Curtis is an annoying and insecure guy.

Gender Association: Used for boys

Popularity and Trend: #339 (#265 in 2000)

Risk of Misspelling: Fairly low

Risk of Mispronunciation: Low

Famous Namesakes: Singer Curtis Mayfield; football player Curtis Martin; rapper Curtis "50 Cent" Jackson

Common Nicknames: Curt

Common Variations: Kurtis

Consider This: Curtis has an unfortunate first impression, so it may be smart to pair it with Curt, a pleasant nickname.

Cyrus ★★★

(Persian) sun.

First Impression: Cyrus is pictured as a good-tempered gentleman with a creative and intellectual flair, but his talents make him a bit egocentric.

Gender Association: Used for boys

Popularity and Trend: #515 (#541 in 2000)

Risk of Misspelling: Average

Risk of Mispronunciation: Fairly low

Famous Namesakes: Singer Billy Ray Cyrus; inventor Cyrus McCormick

Common Nicknames: Cy

Common Variations: Syrus

Consider This: It may not be overly popular, but it's been holding steady: Cyrus has been in the middle tier of the Top 1000 for several years.

Dakota ★★★★

(Dakota) friend; partner; tribal name.

First Impression: Dakota is considered a people-person, but he's also a nature lover.

Gender Association: Used mostly for boys

Popularity and Trend: #172 (#88 in 2000)

Risk of Misspelling: Low

Risk of Mispronunciation: Low

Famous Namesakes: None

Common Nicknames: None

Common Variations: Dakoda, Dakotah

Consider This: Dakota may be used more for boys than girls, but the popularity of actress Dakota Fanning may reverse that trend.

Dale ★★★★

(English) dale, valley.

First Impression: People say Dale's a popular and fun-loving guy with a great sense of humor.

Gender Association: Used mostly for boys

Popularity and Trend: #745 (#536 in 2000)

Risk of Misspelling: Low

Risk of Mispronunciation: Low

Famous Namesakes: Racecar drivers Dale Earnhardt, Sr. and Dale Earnhardt, Jr.; racecar driver Dale Jarrett; character Dale (*Chip 'n' Dale*)

Common Nicknames: Daley

Common Variations: None

Consider This: Even though the first impression doesn't suggest it, some people may consider Dale to be a Southern name, thanks to three namesakes from NASCAR racing.

Dalton ★★★

(English) town in the valley.

First Impression: Most people regard Dalton as an opinionated and rude Southern rancher whose shrewd business sense has made him rich and powerful.

Gender Association: Used mostly for boys

Popularity and Trend: #199 (#91 in 2000)

Risk of Misspelling: Low

Risk of Mispronunciation: Low

Famous Namesakes: Chemist John Dalton; actor Timothy Dalton

Common Nicknames: Dalt

Common Variations: None

Consider This: Dalton has fallen about one hundred places this decade, but it's still a relatively popular name.

Damian ★★

(Greek) tamer; soother.

First Impression: With the character from horror film *The Omen* firmly in mind, people say Damian is a demonic and cunning devil who wears black and gets away with evil.

Gender Association: Used for boys

Popularity and Trend: #136 (#205 in 2000)

Risk of Misspelling: Average

Risk of Mispronunciation: Low

Famous Namesakes: Singer Damian Marley; character Father Damien

Karras (*The Exorcist*); singer Damien Rice; character Damien Thorn (*The Omen*)

Common Nicknames: None

Common Variations: Damien

Consider This: Some parents either don't know about *The Omen* connection—or don't care about it—because Damian is rising in popularity. In fact, at #196 Damien is also popular, which means spelling may be a problem with Damian.

Dan ★★★

(Vietnamese) yes. (Hebrew) a short form of Daniel.

First Impression: Most people think of Dan as an old newsman who's smart, trustworthy, and humorous—but perhaps a little dull. Maybe they're thinking of anchorman Dan Rather?

Gender Association: Used for boys

Popularity and Trend: Last ranked #945 in 2000

Risk of Misspelling: Low

Risk of Mispronunciation: Low

Famous Namesakes: News anchor Dan Rather; vice president Dan Quayle; actor Dan Ackroyd; football player Dan Marino

Common Nicknames: Danny

Common Variations: None

Consider This: Dan is infrequently used as a given name, as indicated in its drop from the Top 1000.

Daniel ★★★★★

(Hebrew) God is my judge.

First Impression: Daniel is envisioned as a tall, athletic man with a handsome smile.

Gender Association: Used mostly for boys

Popularity and Trend: #6 (#9 in 2000)

Risk of Misspelling: Low

Risk of Mispronunciation: Low

Famous Namesakes: Biblical figure Daniel; actor Daniel Day-Lewis; frontiersman Daniel Boone; actor Daniel Radcliffe; actor Daniel Craig

Common Nicknames: Dan, Danny

Common Variations: None

Consider This: It's no wonder Daniel is so popular—it scores nearly perfectly. The only downside may be that it's *too* popular.

Danny ★★★★

(Hebrew) a familiar form of Daniel.

First Impression: Danny is pictured as a cheeky, red-haired, Irish joker.

Gender Association: Used for boys

Popularity and Trend: #307 (#287 in 2000)

Risk of Misspelling: Fairly low

Risk of Mispronunciation: Low

Famous Namesakes: Actor Danny Glover; actor Danny DeVito; actor Danny Bonaduce; actor Danny Masterson

Common Nicknames: None

Common Variations: Dannie

Consider This: Danny scores fairly well on paper, but in real life, people will always assume your son's "real" name is Daniel.

Dante ★★★

(Latin) lasting, enduring.

First Impression: People think of Dante as a cultured and dashing flirt with alluring, Italian looks.

Gender Association: Used for boys

Popularity and Trend: #291 (#247 in 2000)

Risk of Misspelling: Average

Risk of Mispronunciation: Average

Famous Namesakes: Poet Dante Alighieri; football player Daunte Culpepper; football player Dante Hall

Common Nicknames: None

Common Variations: Dantae, Daunte

Consider This: Dante seems to fit with some cultures, like Italian and African American, better than others. In addition, spelling could be a problem because there are several variations of this name.

Darby ★★★

(Irish) free. (English) deer park.

First Impression: Oddly enough, people think Darby is either a gangly übergeek or a hunky party animal.

Gender Association: Used mostly for girls

Popularity and Trend: Last ranked in the Top 1000 in the 1970s

Risk of Misspelling: Low

Risk of Mispronunciation: Low

Famous Namesakes: Character Darby O'Gill (*Darby O'Gill and the Little People*); musician Darby Crash; cartoonist Darby Conley

Common Nicknames: Darb

Common Variations: None

Consider This: The biggest problem to point out is that Darby is most often used as a girls' name.

Darius ★★★★

(Greek) wealthy.

First Impression: Darius strikes people as a polite, respectful, and handsome African American who's daring and strong.

Gender Association: Used for boys

Popularity and Trend: #280 (#220 in 2000)

Risk of Misspelling: Average

Risk of Mispronunciation: Average

Famous Namesakes: Basketball player Darius Miles; singer Darius Rucker

Common Nicknames: Daris

Common Variations: Darious

Consider This: Greek in origin, Darius is often used by African American families. It can be pronounced "DARE-ee-us" or "dah-RYE-us," which could create problems.

Darren ★★★

(Irish) great. (English) small; rocky hill.

First Impression: People aren't sure whether Darren is goofy, bold, arrogant, outgoing, or spiritual.

Gender Association: Used for boys

Popularity and Trend: #361 (#297 in 2000)

Risk of Misspelling: Fairly low

Risk of Mispronunciation: Low

Famous Namesakes: Actor Darren McGavin; football player Darren Sharper; director Darren Aronofsky

Common Nicknames: Dare

Common Variations: Daren, Darron

Consider This: It's hard to put a finger on Darren's image, which may or may not be a plus.

Darrion ★

(Irish, English) a form of Darren.

First Impression: People find Darrion to be a physically imposing jock with a tough mean streak.

Gender Association: Used mostly for boys

Popularity and Trend: Last ranked #868 in 2000

Risk of Misspelling: Fairly high

Risk of Mispronunciation: Fairly low

Famous Namesakes: Football player Darrion Scott

Common Nicknames: None

Common Variations: Darien, Darion

Consider This: As one of many variations of Darren, Darrion is hard to distinguish from Darien or Darion when it comes to spelling.

Darrius ★★★

(Greek) a form of Darius.

First Impression: Folks see Darrius as a footloose, happy charmer who's tall, strong, and most likely African American.

Gender Association: Used for boys

Popularity and Trend: #930 (#676 in 2000)

Risk of Misspelling: Fairly high

Risk of Mispronunciation: Average

Famous Namesakes: Singer Darrius Willrich

Common Nicknames: Daris

Common Variations: Darius

Consider This: Compare the first impressions of Darrius and Darius to see which you prefer. The extra *r* in Darrius will create spelling problems.

Darryl ★★

(French) a form of Darrell.

First Impression: Darryl is imagined to be a dumb oddball who remains overly confident and outgoing despite his shortcomings.

Gender Association: Used for boys

Popularity and Trend: #773 (#551 in 2000)

Risk of Misspelling: Fairly high

Risk of Mispronunciation: Low

Famous Namesakes: Baseball player Darryl Strawberry; comedian Darryl Hammond; hockey player Darryl Sutter

Common Nicknames: None

Common Variations: Daryl, Darrell

Consider This: Still in the Top 1000, Darryl is slightly more popular than Daryl. Spelling will be an problem, though, because Darrell is the most popular variation of the bunch.

Daryl ★★★

(French) a form of Darrell.

First Impression: Daryl is thought to be a kindhearted and laid-back hick with a toothpick in his mouth.

Gender Association: Used mostly for boys

Popularity and Trend: Last ranked #738 in 2000

Risk of Misspelling: Fairly high

Risk of Mispronunciation: Low

Famous Namesakes: Singer Daryl Hall

Common Nicknames: None

Common Variations: Darryl, Darrell

Consider This: Unlike Darryl, Daryl has a rural association that may or may not fit with your family's lifestyle. But it shares Darryl's spelling problem.

Dave ★★★★

(Hebrew) a short form of David, Davis.

First Impression: People imagine Dave as a caring, lovable, and dependable person who makes a great friend.

Gender Association: Used for boys

Popularity and Trend: Last ranked in the Top 1000 in the 1990s

Risk of Misspelling: Low

Risk of Mispronunciation: Low

Famous Namesakes: Writer Dave Barry; singer Dave Matthews; comedian Dave Chappelle; actor Dave Foley

Common Nicknames: Davey

Common Variations: None

Consider This: Dave scores well, but people will assume it's a nickname for David.

David ★★★★★

(Hebrew) beloved.

First Impression: David is pictured with a tall, athletic build, and he's known to be caring and thoughtful with a quiet confidence that makes him a good leader.

Gender Association: Used mostly for boys

Popularity and Trend: #13 (#16 in 2000)

Risk of Misspelling: Low

Risk of Mispronunciation: Low

Famous Namesakes: Talk show host David Letterman; actor David Schwimmer; actor David Spade; singer David Bowie; biblical figure David

Common Nicknames: Dave, Davy

Common Variations: None

Consider This: There's little downside to David—it scores a nearly perfect 5 stars.

Deangelo ★★★★

(Italian) a combination of the prefix De + Angelo.

First Impression: Deangelo is said to be an intelligent, approachable, and fun-loving African American.

Gender Association: Used for boys

Popularity and Trend: #794 (#649 in 2000)

Risk of Misspelling: Average

Risk of Mispronunciation: Average

Famous Namesakes: Singer D'Angelo; football player DeAngelo Williams

Common Nicknames: Dang, Angelo

Common Variations: D'angelo, Dangelo

Consider This: Deangelo is often used by African American families.

Deman ★

(Dutch) man.

First Impression: The name Deman looks an awful lot like *demon*, which must be why people imagine Deman as an evil and selfish troublemaker with devilish features.

Gender Association: Used for boys

Popularity and Trend: Never been
ranked in Top 1000
Risk of Misspelling: Fairly high
Risk of Mispronunciation: Fairly high
Famous Namesakes: Military
intelligence pioneer Ralph Van
Deman
Common Nicknames: None
Common Variations: None
Consider This: Pronunciation is a
huge problem because there are
many ways one could pronounce
this uncommon Dutch name.
("DAY-mahn" seems to be the
best guess.)

Dennis ★★★

(Greek) a follower of Dionysus,
the god of wine.
First Impression: People think Dennis
is a geeky and bespectacled
know-it-all who tends to be
conceited.
Gender Association: Used for boys
Popularity and Trend: #313
(#252 in 2000)
Risk of Misspelling: Fairly low
Risk of Mispronunciation: Low
Famous Namesakes: Comedian
Dennis Leary; basketball player
Dennis Rodman; character
Dennis Mitchell (*Dennis the
Menace*); actor Dennis Quaid
Common Nicknames: Den, Denny
Common Variations: Denis
Consider This: It's somewhat surpris-
ing that people don't associate

this name with bratty Dennis the
Menace; instead, they see it as a
nerdy name.

Denny ★★★

(Greek) a familiar form of Dennis.
First Impression: People say Denny
always has friends around, despite
the fact he's immature and a
little grungy.
Gender Association: Used for boys
Popularity and Trend: Last ranked in
the Top 1000 in the 1980s
Risk of Misspelling: Low
Risk of Mispronunciation: Low
Famous Namesakes: Singer Denny
Doherty; football coach Denny
Green; Denny's restaurant
Common Nicknames: Den
Common Variations: None
Consider This: As a Top 1000
dropout, Denny is rarely used as
a given name, but it is a nice
nickname for Dennis.

Denver ★★★★

(English) green valley.
First Impression: With the moun-
tainous beauty of the capital of
Colorado as inspiration, Denver
is seen as free spirited and
rugged.
Gender Association: Used mostly
for boys
Popularity and Trend: Last ranked
#894 in 2000
Risk of Misspelling: Low
Risk of Mispronunciation: Low

Famous Namesakes: Singer John
Denver; actor Bob Denver; actor
Denver Pyle
Common Nicknames: Den, Denny
Common Variations: None
Consider This: Outdoorsy types may
consider this place name a more
unique and rugged alternative to
Dennis.

Derek ★★★★

(German) a form of Theodoric.
First Impression: People think Derek
is congenial, fun, and very
handsome.
Gender Association: Used for boys
Popularity and Trend: #159
(#121 in 2000)
Risk of Misspelling: Fairly low
Risk of Mispronunciation: Low
Famous Namesakes: Character Dr.
Derek Shepherd (*Grey's Anatomy*);
baseball player Derek Jeter;
character Derek Zoolander
(*Zoolander*)
Common Nicknames: None
Common Variations: Derrek, Derrick
Consider This: After being in the Top
100 through the '70s, '80s, and
into the '90s, Derek has now
settled in the Top 200.

Desmond ★★★★

(Irish) from south Munster.
First Impression: The name Desmond
makes people think of a good-
natured charmer who's intelligent and confident.

Gender Association: Used for boys

Popularity and Trend: #464
(#375 in 2000)

Risk of Misspelling: Fairly low

Risk of Mispronunciation: Low

Famous Namesakes: Football player Desmond Clark; humanitarian Desmond Tutu; character Desmond Hume (*Lost*)

Common Nicknames: Desi

Common Variations: Desmon, Dezmond

Consider This: Though Irish in origin, Desmond has been adopted by African Americans.

Devin ★★★

(Irish) poet.

First Impression: People say Devin has dark, good looks that mask his proud and deceitful personality.

Gender Association: Used mostly for boys

Popularity and Trend: #100
(#69 in 2000)

Risk of Misspelling: Average

Risk of Mispronunciation: Low

Famous Namesakes: Football player Devin Hester; basketball player Devin Harris

Common Nicknames: Dev, Devy

Common Variations: Devon, Devyn

Consider This: Like Devlin, Devin's image has a devilish connotation. Unlike Devlin, Devin is quite popular at #100. However, Devon is also very popular,

which creates some spelling confusion.

Devlin ★★

(Irish) brave, fierce.

First Impression: Devlin is regarded as an untrustworthy and devilish trickster of Irish ancestry.

Gender Association: Used for boys

Popularity and Trend: Never been ranked in Top 1000

Risk of Misspelling: Fairly low

Risk of Mispronunciation: Low

Famous Namesakes: Poet Denis Devlin

Common Nicknames: Dev

Common Variations: Devlyn

Consider This: Being so similar to the word *devil* certainly affects this name's image.

Dexter ★★★

(Latin) dexterous, adroit. (English) fabric dyer.

First Impression: Some people think Dexter is sweet, but others find him to be an annoying brown-noser.

Gender Association: Used for boys

Popularity and Trend: #913
(#756 in 2000)

Risk of Misspelling: Fairly low

Risk of Mispronunciation: Low

Famous Namesakes: Singer Dexter Holland; character Dexter (*Dexter's Laboratory*); character Dexter Morgan (*Dexter*)

Common Nicknames: Dex, Deck

Common Variations: Dextar

Consider This: The creators of the cartoon *Dexter's Laboratory* were right on target when they named their geeky scientist character.

Dick ★★★

(German) a short form of Frederick, Richard.

First Impression: Many see Dick as a mean jerk, but others say he's a high-spirited and well-known man.

Gender Association: Used for boys

Popularity and Trend: Last ranked in the Top 1000 in the 1960s

Risk of Misspelling: Low

Risk of Mispronunciation: Low

Famous Namesakes: TV personality Dick Clark; vice president Dick Cheney; actor Dick Van Dyke; sportscaster Dick Vitale

Common Nicknames: Dicky

Common Variations: Dickens

Consider This: Dick's many pejorative connotations have hurt its popularity both as a given name and even as a nickname. Dick creates a major playground teasing alert.

Diego ★★★★

(Spanish) a form of Jacob, James.

First Impression: Diego is described as a serious and thoughtful man with dark features and a Spanish or Latino heritage.

Gender Association: Used for boys

Popularity and Trend: #56
(#147 in 2000)

Risk of Misspelling: Fairly low
Risk of Mispronunciation: Fairly low
Famous Namesakes: Artist Diego Rivera; soccer player Diego Maradona; actor Diego Luna
Common Nicknames: None
Common Variations: None
Consider This: Like many Latino names, Diego's popularity has grown.

Dimitri ★★

(Russian) a short form of Demetrius.
First Impression: This name calls to mind a magnetic ladies' man who isn't ready to settle down.
Gender Association: Used for boys
Popularity and Trend: Last ranked #733 in 2000
Risk of Misspelling: Fairly high
Risk of Mispronunciation: Average
Famous Namesakes: Chemist Dmitri Mendeleev
Common Nicknames: None
Common Variations: Dmitri
Consider This: This name's pronunciation ("dee-MEE-tree") may be a challenge for some people. Spelling may be troublesome, too, with Dmitri as another option.

Dirk ★★★

(German) a form of Derek, Theodoric.
First Impression: People picture Dirk as either a studious science geek with snooty arrogance or a dim-witted jock with a sweet disposition.
Gender Association: Used for boys
Popularity and Trend: Last ranked in the Top 1000 in the 1980s
Risk of Misspelling: Fairly low
Risk of Mispronunciation: Fairly low
Famous Namesakes: Basketball player Dirk Nowitzki; character Dirk Diggler (*Boogie Nights*)
Common Nicknames: None
Common Variations: Dirke
Consider This: Dirk is a short form of Derek, but it's not nearly as popular.

Dominic ★★★★★

(Latin) belonging to the Lord.
First Impression: People think Dominic is an arty, smart, and determined man with very handsome Italian looks.
Gender Association: Used for boys
Popularity and Trend: #85 (#118 in 2000)
Risk of Misspelling: Average
Risk of Mispronunciation: Low
Famous Namesakes: Saint Dominic; actor Dominic Monaghan
Common Nicknames: Dom, Nick
Common Variations: Dominick, Dominik
Consider This: While Dominic has traditionally been an Italian name, today it's suitable for any culture. Spelling will be tricky, though, because it has many variations.

Don ★★★

(Scottish) a short form of Donald.
First Impression: Don is depicted as rough around the edges, but people love him anyway.
Gender Association: Used for boys
Popularity and Trend: Last ranked #828 in 2000
Risk of Misspelling: Low
Risk of Mispronunciation: Low
Famous Namesakes: Legendary figure Don Juan; actor Don Johnson; baseball player Don Mattingley; actor Don Knotts
Common Nicknames: Donnie
Common Variations: Donn
Consider This: Don is a logical nickname for Donald, but it's rarely used as a given name. Plus, its pronunciation can be mistaken for Dawn, a traditional name for girls, which may cause gender confusion.

Donald ★★★★

(Scottish) world leader; proud ruler.
First Impression: People picture Donald as an intelligent, successful, and talented man.
Gender Association: Used for boys
Popularity and Trend: #303 (#217 in 2000)
Risk of Misspelling: Low
Risk of Mispronunciation: Low
Famous Namesakes: Tycoon Donald Trump; actor Donald Sutherland;

secretary of defense Donald Rumsfeld; cartoon character Donald Duck

Common Nicknames: Don, Donny

Common Variations: Donal

Consider This: Donald rates fairly well, but it's slipping in popularity.

Donovan ★★★★

(Irish) dark warrior.

First Impression: People depict Donovan as a freewheeling, intelligent, and well-liked hippie, likely thanks to groovy '60s British pop star Donovan.

Gender Association: Used for boys

Popularity and Trend: #198 (#206 in 2000)

Risk of Misspelling: Fairly low

Risk of Mispronunciation: Low

Famous Namesakes: Football player Donovan McNabb; singer Donovan

Common Nicknames: Don

Common Variations: Donavan

Consider This: With its rising popularity, Donovan may be a contemporary alternative to Donald.

Dorcas ★

(Hebrew) gazelle.

First Impression: Dorcas gives the impression of a strange man who tries too hard to fit in with people who treat him poorly.

Gender Association: Used for boys

Popularity and Trend: Never been ranked in Top 1000

Risk of Misspelling: Fairly high

Risk of Mispronunciation: Fairly low

Famous Namesakes: Biblical figure Dorcas

Common Nicknames: None

Common Variations: None

Consider This: Playground teasing alert: It would be cruel to give your son a name that sounds as though it has *dork* right in it.

Dorian ★★★

(Greek) from Doris, Greece.

First Impression: Dorian is viewed as a handsome man who's so overly dramatic, he can be aggravating.

Gender Association: Used mostly for boys

Popularity and Trend: #469 (#399 in 2000)

Risk of Misspelling: Fairly low

Risk of Mispronunciation: Low

Famous Namesakes: Dorian Gray (*The Picture of Dorian Gray*)

Common Nicknames: Dorey

Common Variations: Dorien, Dorrian

Consider This: As the first impression suggests—and as anyone familiar with Oscar Wilde's *The Picture of Dorian Gray* knows—this name has an overly dramatic flair.

Douglas ★★★★

(Scottish) dark river, dark stream.

First Impression: Nearly everyone says Douglas is a driven, smart, and assertive—if not aggressive—perfectionist.

Gender Association: Used for boys

Popularity and Trend: #365 (#274 in 2000)

Risk of Misspelling: Fairly low

Risk of Mispronunciation: Low

Famous Namesakes: Actor Douglas Fairbanks; general Douglas A. Macarthur; actors Kirk and Michael Douglas

Common Nicknames: Doug, Dougie

Common Variations: Douglass

Consider This: Douglas is a lot like Donald: They're both falling in popularity.

Doyle ★★★

(Irish) a form of Dougal.

First Impression: People can't decide if Doyle is an adventurous class clown or an introverted nerd.

Gender Association: Used for boys

Popularity and Trend: Last ranked in the Top 1000 in the 1980s

Risk of Misspelling: Fairly low

Risk of Mispronunciation: Low

Famous Namesakes: Musician Doyle Lawson; author Arthur Conan Doyle; author Roddy Doyle; poker player Doyle Brunson

Common Nicknames: Doy

Common Variations: None

Consider This: Because it's so uncommon, Doyle seems to give off an "oddball" vibe.

Drake ★★★★

(English) dragon; owner of the inn with the dragon trademark.

First Impression: Drake is said to be a spoiled man from a wealthy family—but he also has the determination to become powerful on his own.
Gender Association: Used for boys
Popularity and Trend: #239 (#261 in 2000)
Risk of Misspelling: Low
Risk of Mispronunciation: Low
Famous Namesakes: Explorer Francis Drake; actor Drake Hogestyn
Common Nicknames: None
Common Variations: Drago
Consider This: Drake has an upper-class connotation, much like Blake.

Drew ★★★★

(Welsh) wise. (English) a form of Andrew.
First Impression: People think Drew is sweet, caring, and friendly.
Gender Association: Used mostly for boys
Popularity and Trend: #205 (#188 in 2000)
Risk of Misspelling: Fairly low
Risk of Mispronunciation: Low
Famous Namesakes: Actor Drew Carey; football player Drew Brees; football player Drew Bledsoe
Common Nicknames: None
Common Variations: Dru, Drewe
Consider This: One, consider using Drew as a nickname for Andrew

for more versatility. Two, because of actress Drew Barrymore, there's some gender association confusion.

Dudley ★★★

(English) common field.
First Impression: Most people say Dudley is a sensitive but boring nerd.
Gender Association: Used for boys
Popularity and Trend: Last ranked in the Top 1000 in the 1960s
Risk of Misspelling: Fairly low
Risk of Mispronunciation: Low
Famous Namesakes: Actor Dudley Moore; cartoon character Dudley Do-Right
Common Nicknames: Dud, Duddy
Common Variations: None
Consider This: Although it's not as bad as Dorcas, your child is vulnerable to teasing with a "dud" name like Dudley.

Duff ★★★

(Scottish) dark.
First Impression: The name Duff conjures up images of heavy metal bassist Duff McKagan and his thin, long-haired, leather-clad looks. Others believe the name Duff belongs to an intellectual.
Gender Association: Used for boys
Popularity and Trend: Never been ranked in Top 1000
Risk of Misspelling: Low

Risk of Mispronunciation: Low
Famous Namesakes: Duff beer from *The Simpsons*; rock musician Duff McKagan
Common Nicknames: None
Common Variations: Duffy
Consider This: If you really want to call your son Duff, make it a special nickname. It's not well suited for use as a given name.

Duncan ★★★★

(Scottish) brown warrior.
First Impression: Duncan is regarded as a friendly, jolly guy who's down to earth but bashful around the opposite sex.
Gender Association: Used for boys
Popularity and Trend: #654 (#448 in 2000)
Risk of Misspelling: Low
Risk of Mispronunciation: Low
Famous Namesakes: Character Duncan MacLeod (*Highlander: The Series*); character Duncan (*Macbeth*); actor Michael Clarke Duncan; basketball player Tim Duncan
Common Nicknames: Dunn, Dunc
Common Variations: None
Consider This: Although it rates well in other categories, Duncan isn't very popular. Can it be because of the association with Dunkin' Donuts?

Dunn ★★

(Scottish) a form of Duncan.

First Impression: Dunn is imagined to be an unusual and mysterious guy with broad shoulders and a tall frame.

Gender Association: Used for boys

Popularity and Trend: Never been ranked in Top 1000

Risk of Misspelling: Fairly low

Risk of Mispronunciation: Low

Famous Namesakes: Football player Warrick Dunn; musician Ronnie Dunn

Common Nicknames: None

Common Variations: Dunne

Consider This: Dunn is not—and may never be—included in the list of surnames that are popular as given names.

Dustin ★★★★

(German) valiant fighter. (English) brown rock quarry.

First Impression: Most people describe Dustin as a happy, fun-loving guy who's easy to befriend.

Gender Association: Used mostly for boys

Popularity and Trend: #259 (#148 in 2000)

Risk of Misspelling: Fairly low

Risk of Mispronunciation: Low

Famous Namesakes: Actor Dustin Hoffman

Common Nicknames: Dusty

Common Variations: Dusten

Consider This: Dustin is falling in popularity much like Donald and Douglas, though it's still the most popular of the three.

Dusty ★★★

(English) a familiar form of Dustin.

First Impression: When people hear the name Dusty, they think of a dirty and dumb redneck who likes to ride ATVs, leaving a big cloud of dust behind him.

Gender Association: Used mostly for boys

Popularity and Trend: Last ranked in the Top 1000 in the 1990s

Risk of Misspelling: Low

Risk of Mispronunciation: Low

Famous Namesakes: Wrestler Dusty Rhodes

Common Nicknames: None

Common Variations: None

Consider This: Dusty suffers from the stereotypical redneck image.

Dwayne ★★

(Irish) dark.

First Impression: Dwayne is pictured as a lanky, dark-skinned yokel with simple, backwoods ways.

Gender Association: Used for boys

Popularity and Trend: #610 (#539 in 2000)

Risk of Misspelling: Average

Risk of Mispronunciation: Fairly low

Famous Namesakes: Character Dwayne Wayne (*A Different World*); wrestler and actor Dwyane "The Rock" Johnson; basketball player Dwyane Wade

Common Nicknames: None

Common Variations: Duane

Consider This: Although the first impression paints an image of a yokel, Dwayne is often used by African American families.

Dwight ★★

(English) a form of DeWitt.

First Impression: People say Dwight is a dimwitted hick who's lazy and dull.

Gender Association: Used for boys

Popularity and Trend: Last ranked #768 in 2000

Risk of Misspelling: Fairly low

Risk of Mispronunciation: Fairly low

Famous Namesakes: President Dwight Eisenhower; singer Dwight Yoakam; baseball player Dwight Gooden

Common Nicknames: Ike

Common Variations: None

Consider This: Like Dwayne, Dwight has a redneck association that's less than positive.

Dylan ★★★★

(Welsh) sea.

First Impression: People think of Dylan as a cheerful, playful guy, but he's also loyal and caring.

Gender Association: Used mostly for boys

Popularity and Trend: #26
(#24 in 2000)
Risk of Misspelling: Fairly low
Risk of Mispronunciation: Low
Famous Namesakes: Singer Bob
Dylan; poet Dylan Thomas;
actor Dylan McDermott
Common Nicknames: None
Common Variations: Dillon
Consider This: This popular name
has a cheerful image and is
almost trouble free.

Earl ★★★★
(Irish) pledge. (English) nobleman.
First Impression: Earl is considered an
older man who's a doting, sweet
father.
Gender Association: Used for boys
Popularity and Trend: #993
(#712 in 2000)
Risk of Misspelling: Low
Risk of Mispronunciation: Low
Famous Namesakes: Supreme Court
justice Earl Warren; actor James
Earl Jones; character Earl Hickey
(*My Name Is Earl*)
Common Nicknames: None
Common Variations: Errol, Earle
Consider This: Despite a positive
first impression, Earl may be
over the hill.

Ed ★★
(English) a short form of Edgar,
Edsel, Edward.

First Impression: Ed is thought to be
an awkward and bashful blue-
collar man.
Gender Association: Used for boys
Popularity and Trend: Last ranked in
the Top 1000 in the 1970s
Risk of Misspelling: Low
Risk of Mispronunciation: Low
Famous Namesakes: TV personality
Ed Sullivan; talking horse Mr. Ed;
talk show host Ed McMahon;
actor Ed Harris; character Ed
Stevens (*Ed*)
Common Nicknames: Eddie
Common Variations: None
Consider This: Although it's a
common name, Ed's image may
be too old for a small child.

Eddie ★★★
(English) a familiar form of Edgar,
Edsel, Edward.
First Impression: Several comedians
share this name, including Eddie
Murphy, so people definitely see
Eddie as a funny guy.
Gender Association: Used for boys
Popularity and Trend: #395
(#350 in 2000)
Risk of Misspelling: Fairly low
Risk of Mispronunciation: Low
Famous Namesakes: Actor Eddie
Murphy; singer Eddie Vedder;
actor Eddie Arnold; musician
Eddie Van Halen
Common Nicknames: None
Common Variations: Eddy

Consider This: More appealing than
Ed, Eddie still seems too informal
as a given name; it lacks Edward's
versatility.

Edgar ★★★★
(English) successful spearman.
First Impression: Edgar is pictured as
melancholy, somber, intelligent,
and mysterious, much like poet
Edgar Allan Poe.
Gender Association: Used for boys
Popularity and Trend: #171
(#177 in 2000)
Risk of Misspelling: Fairly low
Risk of Mispronunciation: Low
Famous Namesakes: Poet Edgar Allan
Poe; musician Edgar Winter;
baseball player Edgar Martinez
Common Nicknames: Ed, Eddie
Common Variations: Edgard
Consider This: Given its rising
popularity, Edgar has quirky
appeal despite its murky first
impression.

Edmund ★★★
(English) prosperous protector.
First Impression: The name Edmund
conjures up the image of a snooty
and well-educated professional
who's tall, dark, and impeccably
dressed.
Gender Association: Used for boys
Popularity and Trend: Last ranked in
the Top 1000 in the 1990s
Risk of Misspelling: Fairly low
Risk of Mispronunciation: Low

Famous Namesakes: Poet Edmund
Spenser; explorer Edmund
Hillary; politician Edmund
Muskie; character Edmund
Pevensie (*The Chronicles of Narnia*)
Common Nicknames: Ed, Eddie
Common Variations: Edmond,
Edmundo, Edmun
Consider This: Off the Top 1000 for
over a decade, Edmund's poor
first impression may explain its
unpopularity.

Eduardo ★★★

(Spanish) a form of Edward.
First Impression: Eduardo is
considered either a romantic
gentleman or a pugnacious
fighter.
Gender Association: Used for boys
Popularity and Trend: #126
(#124 in 2000)
Risk of Misspelling: Fairly high
Risk of Mispronunciation: Fairly high
Famous Namesakes: Actor Eduardo
Yanez; actor Eduardo Palomo;
baseball player Eduardo Perez
Common Nicknames: Eddie, Duardo
Common Variations: Estuardo
Consider This: Eduardo probably
won't fit well with families that
aren't of Latino heritage.

Edward ★★★★★

(English) prosperous guardian.
First Impression: People describe
Edward as a wealthy and well-
bred man who's gentle yet deter-
mined.
Gender Association: Used for boys
Popularity and Trend: #143
(#108 in 2000)
Risk of Misspelling: Low
Risk of Mispronunciation: Low
Famous Namesakes: British prince
Edward; actor Edward Norton;
journalist Edward R. Murrow;
film character Edward
Scissorhands
Common Nicknames: Ed, Eddie, Audie
Common Variations: Eduard, Edvard
Consider This: This classic name is a
solid choice, but its popularity is
losing steam.

Edwin ★★★★

(English) prosperous friend.
First Impression: Edwin makes people
think of a bookish Brit prone to
stuffy gallantry.
Gender Association: Used for boys
Popularity and Trend: #158
(#196 in 2000)
Risk of Misspelling: Fairly low
Risk of Mispronunciation: Low
Famous Namesakes: Writer Edwin
Muir; singer Edwin McCain
Common Nicknames: Ed, Win
Common Variations: None
Consider This: Despite its boring
image, Edwin's rising popularity
may actually make it a cooler
alternative to Edward.

Eldon ★★

(English) holy hill. A form of
Elton.
First Impression: Eldon seems like a
name for an old loner who's
geeky but sweet and shy.
Gender Association: Used for boys
Popularity and Trend: Last ranked in
the Top 1000 in the 1970s
Risk of Misspelling: Fairly low
Risk of Mispronunciation: Low
Famous Namesakes: Actor Elden
Henson
Common Nicknames: None
Common Variations: Elden, Elton
Consider This: Eldon seems to be an
old, stuffy name, and its poor
image reflects that depiction.

Eli ★★★★

(Hebrew) uplifted. A form of Elijah,
Elisha.
First Impression: People picture Eli as
a caring and sensitive man faith-
ful to God.
Gender Association: Used mostly
for boys
Popularity and Trend: #139
(#236 in 2000)
Risk of Misspelling: Fairly low
Risk of Mispronunciation: Fairly low
Famous Namesakes: Director Eli
Roth; inventor Eli Whitney;
football player Eli Manning
Common Nicknames: None
Common Variations: Ely

Consider This: Like Elias and Elijah, Eli has growing appeal for girls, too—a problem if you want a name associated only with boys.

Elias ★★★

(Greek) a form of Elijah.

First Impression: Elias is said to be a strange and dark troublemaker.

Gender Association: Used for boys

Popularity and Trend: #186 (#242 in 2000)

Risk of Misspelling: Average

Risk of Mispronunciation: Average

Famous Namesakes: Writer Elias Canetti; actor Elias Koteas; another name for biblical figure Elijah

Common Nicknames: Eli

Common Variations: Ellias, Ellis

Consider This: Although growing in popularity, Elias seems less attractive than Elijah. Pronunciation can be a problem, with some saying "eh-LYE-as" and others saying "ee-LEE-as."

Elijah ★★★★★

(Hebrew) a form of Eliyahu.

First Impression: Elijah is said to be a moral and faithful man, like the biblical prophet of the same name.

Gender Association: Used mostly for boys

Popularity and Trend: #29 (#52 in 2000)

Risk of Misspelling: Fairly low

Risk of Mispronunciation: Fairly low

Famous Namesakes: Biblical figure Elijah; actor Elijah Wood

Common Nicknames: Eli, Elia

Common Variations: Elias, Elijha

Consider This: Elijah's rise in popularity reflects its solid appeal. It's easier to spell and pronounce than Elias, most likely because people are more familiar with the name.

Elliot ★★★

(English) a form of Eli, Elijah.

First Impression: Elliot is described as a book-smart and shy guy whose weak, skinny build isn't fit for athletics.

Gender Association: Used for boys

Popularity and Trend: #372 (#468 in 2000)

Risk of Misspelling: Average

Risk of Mispronunciation: Low

Famous Namesakes: Lawman Eliot Ness; writer T. S. Eliot; character Elliott (*E. T.*)

Common Nicknames: Eli

Common Variations: Eliot

Consider This: Elliot is a good choice if you think Elijah is too popular. Spelling could be a problem, however, because Eliot is also an option.

Ellis ★★★

(English) a form of Elias.

First Impression: Ellis strikes people as a gracious and kind bookworm who's always in the middle of a good read.

Gender Association: Used mostly for boys

Popularity and Trend: #783 (#786 in 2000)

Risk of Misspelling: Fairly low

Risk of Mispronunciation: Low

Famous Namesakes: Designer Perry Ellis

Common Nicknames: None

Common Variations: None

Consider This: Many parents are naming their daughters Ellis, which may some day cross it off the lists of parents expecting sons.

Elmer ★★★

(English) noble; famous.

First Impression: Elmer is pictured as a dimwitted, old farmer who's timid, quiet, and silly, much like Looney Tune character Elmer Fudd.

Gender Association: Used for boys

Popularity and Trend: #907 (#864 in 2000)

Risk of Misspelling: Low

Risk of Mispronunciation: Low

Famous Namesakes: Character Elmer Fudd (*Looney Tunes*); book character Elmer Gantry

Common Nicknames: None

Common Variations: Elmo

Consider This: It's surprising that this old-fashioned name is still on the Top 1000 list. Elmer's most famous namesake is likely to sink this name, eventually.

Elmo ★★★

(Greek) lovable, friendly. (Italian) guardian. (Latin) a form of Anselm. (English) a form of Elmer.

First Impression: People say Elmo is a silly, cuddly red Muppet who's happy all the time.

Gender Association: Used for boys

Popularity and Trend: Last ranked in the Top 1000 in the 1950s

Risk of Misspelling: Low

Risk of Mispronunciation: Low

Famous Namesakes: Character Elmo (*Sesame Street*); comedy singer Elmo Shropshire; Saint Elmo

Common Nicknames: None

Common Variations: None

Consider This: Despite being a beloved Muppet, Elmo's most famous namesake hasn't made this name appealing to parents.

Elton ★★★

(English) old town.

First Impression: Elton is imagined to be a shy and nerdy man who prefers books to people.

Gender Association: Used for boys

Popularity and Trend: Last ranked in the Top 1000 in the 1990s

Risk of Misspelling: Fairly low

Risk of Mispronunciation: Low

Famous Namesakes: Singer Elton John; basketball player Elton Brand

Common Nicknames: None

Common Variations: Eldon

Consider This: Elton John may have had an influence on this name a generation ago, but apparently not today.

Elvin ★★

(English) a form of Alvin.

First Impression: People think Elvin is a nerdy genius who's tiny with elflike ears.

Gender Association: Used for boys

Popularity and Trend: Last ranked in the Top 1000 in the 1990s

Risk of Misspelling: Fairly low

Risk of Mispronunciation: Low

Famous Namesakes: Basketball player Elvin Hayes; musician Elvin Bishop

Common Nicknames: None

Common Variations: Alvin

Consider This: Elvin's poor image and drop in popularity may make it a risky choice.

Elvis ★★★★

(Scandinavian) wise.

First Impression: People imagine Elvis as a talented entertainer who's cool, slick, and exciting, much like Elvis Presley, the king of rock 'n' roll.

Gender Association: Used for boys

Popularity and Trend: #761 (#593 in 2000)

Risk of Misspelling: Low

Risk of Mispronunciation: Low

Famous Namesakes: Singer Elvis Presley; singer Elvis Costello; skater Elvis Stojko

Common Nicknames: None

Common Variations: None

Consider This: Despite Elvis Presley's star power, the name's popularity is slipping. Parents wonder will Elvis Presley's image overpower their child's. Could be.

Emerson ★★★★

(German, English) son of Emery.

First Impression: Emerson is pictured as a well-read, kind, and classy man.

Gender Association: Used for boys

Popularity and Trend: #539 (#911 in 2000)

Risk of Misspelling: Fairly low

Risk of Mispronunciation: Low

Famous Namesakes: Racecar driver Emerson Fittipaldi; writer Ralph Waldo Emerson

Common Nicknames: None

Common Variations: Emmerson

Consider This: Emerson's skyrocketing popularity makes it a good choice for trend-setting parents.

Emery ★★★

(German) industrious leader.

First Impression: Emery is viewed as a bright and studious bookworm who's likable yet shy.

Gender Association: Used mostly for boys

Popularity and Trend: Last ranked in the Top 1000 in the 1970s

Risk of Misspelling: Fairly low

Risk of Mispronunciation: Low

Famous Namesakes: Hockey player Ray Emery

Common Nicknames: None

Common Variations: Emory

Consider This: Emery doesn't have quite the appeal that Emerson has, which may make it a more unique alternative.

Emil ★★★

(Latin) flatterer. (German) industrious.

First Impression: People think Emil is studious and bookish, but he also loves quiet, refined sports like golf.

Gender Association: Used for boys

Popularity and Trend: Last ranked in the Top 1000 in the 1980s

Risk of Misspelling: Average

Risk of Mispronunciation: Fairly high

Famous Namesakes: Baseball player Emil Brown; artist Emil Nolde

Common Nicknames: Milo

Common Variations: Emile, Emilio

Consider This: Emil isn't as trendy as Emilio, but it may fit better with last names not of Latino origin.

Emilio ★★★

(Italian, Spanish) a form of Emil.

First Impression: People imagine Emilio as either a controlling, foul-mouthed man or a thoughtful and suave gentleman.

Gender Association: Used for boys

Popularity and Trend: #298 (#347 in 2000)

Risk of Misspelling: Average

Risk of Mispronunciation: Average

Famous Namesakes: Actor Emilio Estevez; musician Emilio Estéfan

Common Nicknames: None

Common Variations: Emil

Consider This: Although its popularity is on the rise, Emilio probably won't fit well with last names not of Latino origin. Also, those not familiar with Latino names may not realize it's pronounced "eh-MEE-lee-oh."

Emmanuel ★★★★

(Hebrew) God is with us.

First Impression: Emmanuel is described as a serene and religious man with quiet strength.

Gender Association: Used for boys

Popularity and Trend: #166 (#195 in 2000)

Risk of Misspelling: Average

Risk of Mispronunciation: Average

Famous Namesakes: Actor Emmanuel Lewis; birth name of biblical figure Jesus Christ

Common Nicknames: Manuel, Manny

Common Variations: Emanuel, Immanuel

Consider This: Like many names with biblical origins, Emmanuel is a solid choice even though its spelling and pronunciation may be challenging to some.

Emmett ★★★

(German) industrious; strong. (English) ant.

First Impression: Emmett is seen as a young man who's polite, kind, and somewhat of a mama's boy.

Gender Association: Used for boys

Popularity and Trend: #569 (#739 in 2000)

Risk of Misspelling: Average

Risk of Mispronunciation: Low

Famous Namesakes: Character Emmett "Doc" Brown (*Back to the Future*); football player Emmitt Smith

Common Nicknames: None

Common Variations: Emmet, Emmitt

Consider This: Emmett's modest rise in popularity may not overcome its lukewarm first impression. It also has a spelling problem because some people may expect it to be spelled "Emmitt."

Ennis ★★

(Greek) mine. (Scottish) a form of Angus.

First Impression: Ennis is envisioned as serious and studious, stoic and shy.

Gender Association: Used for boys

Popularity and Trend: Last ranked in the Top 1000 in the 1920s

Risk of Misspelling: Average

Risk of Mispronunciation: Average

Famous Namesakes: Character Ennis Del Mar (*Brokeback Mountain*)

Common Nicknames: None

Common Variations: None

Consider This: This old-fashioned name doesn't seem to be making a comeback anytime soon. Although it looks like "EN-iss," it's pronounced "EEN-iss," which could trip up some people.

Enrique ★★★

(Spanish) a form of Henry.

First Impression: Thanks to pop singer Enrique Iglesias, people think of Enrique as a romantic Latino musician who has a flashy style.

Gender Association: Used for boys

Popularity and Trend: #281 (#221 in 2000)

Risk of Misspelling: Fairly high

Risk of Mispronunciation: Fairly high

Famous Namesakes: Singer Enrique Iglesias; actor Enrique Murciano

Common Nicknames: Quiqui

Common Variations: None

Consider This: Perhaps Enrique Iglesias's disappearance from the spotlight explains this name's dip in popularity. Those not familiar with Latino names may find the pronunciation a bit difficult: "en-REE-kay."

Ephraim ★★★

(Hebrew) fruitful.

First Impression: Ephraim is well rounded: He's considered a talented and curious man who's patient and committed as well as religious.

Gender Association: Used for boys

Popularity and Trend: Last ranked in the Top 1000 in the 1900s

Risk of Misspelling: Fairly high

Risk of Mispronunciation: Average

Famous Namesakes: Biblical figure Ephraim

Common Nicknames: None

Common Variations: None

Consider This: Ephraim hasn't been ranked in the Top 1000 for over a century. That doesn't make pronunciation any easier, with both "EF-ram" and "EEF-rem" as options.

Eric ★★★★

(Scandinavian) ruler of all. (English) brave ruler. (German) a form of Frederick.

First Impression: Eric is seen as a kind and loving man who's emotionally supportive.

Gender Association: Used for boys

Popularity and Trend: #77 (#42 in 2000)

Risk of Misspelling: Average

Risk of Mispronunciation: Low

Famous Namesakes: Singer Eric Clapton; actor Eric Bana; explorer Erik the Red; hockey player Eric Lindros; character Eric Foreman (*That 70s Show*)

Common Nicknames: None

Common Variations: Erik, Erich, Erick

Consider This: Although Eric is the most popular variation, Erik and Erick are both in the Top 200, making spelling a challenge for this seemingly simple name.

Ernest ★★★

(English) earnest, sincere.

First Impression: Ernest is primarily thought to be a goofy-looking dweeb who gets bullied by his peers.

Gender Association: Used for boys

Popularity and Trend: #723 (#512 in 2000)

Risk of Misspelling: Fairly low

Risk of Mispronunciation: Low

Famous Namesakes: Author Ernest Hemingway; actor Ernest Borgnine; character Ernest P. Worrel (*Ernest Goes to Jail*)

Common Nicknames: Ernie

Common Variations: Earnest, Ernesto, Ernst

Consider This: A poor image does nothing to help Ernest's appeal.

Ernie ★★★

(English) a familiar form of Ernest.

First Impression: People imagine Ernie in one of two ways: He's either a lonely, depressed man who's a wimpy pushover, or he's a generous and caring guy with a down-to-earth sense of humor.

Gender Association: Used for boys

Popularity and Trend: Last ranked in the Top 1000 in the 1980s

Risk of Misspelling: Low

Risk of Mispronunciation: Low

Famous Namesakes: Character Ernie (*Sesame Street*); comedian Ernie Kovacs; golfer Ernie Els

Common Nicknames: None

Common Variations: None

Consider This: Although Ernie's first impression fares slightly better than Ernest's, this name still has little appeal.

Ervin ★★

(English) sea friend. A form of Irving, Irwin.

First Impression: People think Ervin is a quirky, gangly dork with a funny walk, an obnoxious laugh, and glasses.

Gender Association: Used for boys

Popularity and Trend: Last ranked in the Top 1000 in the 1990s

Risk of Misspelling: Average

Risk of Mispronunciation: Low

Famous Namesakes: Basketball player Ervin Johnson; basketball player Earvin "Magic" Johnson

Common Nicknames: Erv

Common Variations: Earvin, Irvin

Consider This: Not even Earvin "Magic" Johnson can save Ervin from a dated, nerdy image.

Ethan ★★★★

(Hebrew) strong; firm.

First Impression: People consider Ethan to be reserved, compassionate, and down to earth.

Gender Association: Used for boys

Popularity and Trend: #4 (#25 in 2000)

Risk of Misspelling: Fairly low

Risk of Mispronunciation: Fairly low

Famous Namesakes: Actor Ethan Hawke; revolutionary Ethan Allen; director Ethan Coen; character Ethan Hunt (*Mission: Impossible*)

Common Nicknames: None

Common Variations: Ethen

Consider This: Ethan's popularity has skyrocketed, which means you may find an Ethan in every day-care and kindergarten class.

Eugene ★★

(Greek) born to nobility.

First Impression: Eugene is said to be a dorky bookworm who's shy, if not stuck-up.

Gender Association: Used for boys

Popularity and Trend: #647 (#504 in 2000)

Risk of Misspelling: Fairly low

Risk of Mispronunciation: Low

Famous Namesakes: Playwright Eugene O'Neill; politician Eugene McCarthy; actor Eugene Levy

Common Nicknames: Gene, Gino

Common Variations: Eugenio

Consider This: Eugene may never shake its nerdy image.

Evan ★★★★

(Irish) young warrior. (English) a form of John.

First Impression: Evan is regarded as a handsome man who's impulsive and self-indulgent.

Gender Association: Used mostly for boys

Popularity and Trend: #42 (#55 in 2000)

Risk of Misspelling: Fairly low

Risk of Mispronunciation: Low

Famous Namesakes: Reality-TV star Evan Marriott; skater Evan Lysacek; singer Evan Dando; character Evan Baxter (*Evan Almighty*)

Common Nicknames: None

Common Variations: Evin, Ewan, Owen

Consider This: This popular name is still on the rise. However, it's not a name that is exclusively used for boys.

Ewan ★★

(Scottish) a form of Eugene, Evan.

First Impression: Ewan is pictured as a novelist, poet, or actor.

Gender Association: Used for boys

Popularity and Trend: Never been ranked in Top 1000

Risk of Misspelling: Fairly high

Risk of Mispronunciation: Fairly high

Famous Namesakes: Actor Ewan McGregor
Common Nicknames: None
Common Variations: None
Consider This: An unusual alternative to Evan, this name may soon break into the Top 1000. But even with namesake Ewan McGregor in the spotlight, many people may not know it's pronounced "YOO-an."

Ezekiel ★★★
(Hebrew) strength of God.
First Impression: People describe Ezekiel as a deeply religious man who's quiet, wise, and studious.
Gender Association: Used for boys
Popularity and Trend: #269 (#358 in 2000)
Risk of Misspelling: Fairly high
Risk of Mispronunciation: Average
Famous Namesakes: Biblical figure Ezekiel
Common Nicknames: Zeke
Common Variations: Ezequiel
Consider This: This biblical name may be unique enough to appeal to some but not to others. There's also a pronunciation problem because some pronounce it with four syllables ("ee-ZEE-kee-yul") and others only use three ("ee-ZEEK-yul").

Ezra ★★★
(Hebrew) helper; strong.
First Impression: Ezra conjures up the image of a harsh and selfish man without many friends.
Gender Association: Used for boys
Popularity and Trend: #340 (#435 in 2000)
Risk of Misspelling: Low
Risk of Mispronunciation: Low
Famous Namesakes: Poet Ezra Pound; biblical figure Ezra
Common Nicknames: None
Common Variations: None
Consider This: The popularity of this name is still on the rise, but consider its harsh image before you join the parade.

Fabian ★★★
(Latin) bean grower.
First Impression: People say Fabian is a gorgeous but conceited European who's popular and outgoing.
Gender Association: Used for boys
Popularity and Trend: #272 (#285 in 2000)
Risk of Misspelling: Fairly low
Risk of Mispronunciation: Fairly high
Famous Namesakes: Singer Fabian
Common Nicknames: Fabio
Common Variations: Fabien
Consider This: Its steadily increasing popularity suggests that some find Fabian appealing. People who have never heard Fabian sing may not know the name is pronounced "FAY-bee-en."

Fabio ★★
(Latin) a form of Fabian. (Italian) a short form of Fabiano.
First Impression: Everybody agrees Fabio is handsome but arrogant, passionate but cheesy, and buff but dumb.
Gender Association: Used for boys
Popularity and Trend: Never been ranked in Top 1000
Risk of Misspelling: Low
Risk of Mispronunciation: Fairly low
Famous Namesakes: Model Fabio Lanzoni
Common Nicknames: None
Common Variations: None
Consider This: Heartthrob Fabio Lanzoni hasn't enchanted many people to this name. But because of him, most people know this name is pronounced "FAH-bee-oh" instead of "FAB-ee-oh."

Ferdinand ★★★
(German) daring, adventurous.
First Impression: Ferdinand calls to mind an upper-class man who's elegant, introspective, and self-possessed.
Gender Association: Used for boys
Popularity and Trend: Last ranked in the Top 1000 in the 1960s
Risk of Misspelling: Fairly low
Risk of Mispronunciation: Low

Famous Namesakes: Explorer Ferdinand Magellan; archduke Franz Ferdinand; Filipino president Ferdinand Marcos

Common Nicknames: Nando

Common Variations: Fernando

Consider This: Ferdinand's image may be quietly elegant, but it seems to have been *too* quiet to capture parents' attention.

Fergus ★★

(Irish) strong; manly.

First Impression: Fergus is thought to be intellectual and ambitious, but that ambition makes him manipulative and sneaky.

Gender Association: Used for boys

Popularity and Trend: Never been ranked in Top 1000

Risk of Misspelling: Fairly low

Risk of Mispronunciation: Low

Famous Namesakes: Comic character Fergus McDuck; legendary Scottish king Fergus Mór

Common Nicknames: None

Common Variations: None

Consider This: Fergus's poor image seems to have kept it off the Top 1000 throughout the decades.

Ferguson ★★

(Irish) son of Fergus.

First Impression: Ferguson is viewed as a know-it-all showoff.

Gender Association: Used for boys

Popularity and Trend: Never been ranked in Top 1000

Risk of Misspelling: Fairly low

Risk of Mispronunciation: Low

Famous Namesakes: Talk show host Craig Ferguson; poker player Chris "Jesus" Ferguson

Common Nicknames: None

Common Variations: None

Consider This: Like Fergus, Ferguson's image seems to have prevented more families from choosing it.

Fernando ★★★

(Spanish) a form of Ferdinand.

First Impression: Fernando is described as a macho and annoying braggart who's suave and strong-willed.

Gender Association: Used for boys

Popularity and Trend: #151 (#150 in 2000)

Risk of Misspelling: Fairly low

Risk of Mispronunciation: Average

Famous Namesakes: Baseball player Fernando Valenzuela; actor Fernando Lamas; character Fernando (*Saturday Night Live*)

Common Nicknames: Nando

Common Variations: Ferdinand

Consider This: Fernando's steady ranking suggests it's a popular choice for Latino parents, despite its poor first impression. There may be a slight pronunciation problem if some people say "fer-NAN-doh" and others say "fer-NAHN-doh."

Fidel ★★

(Latin) faithful.

First Impression: Fidel is pictured as a heartless dictator who's strong-willed, smart, and masculine.

Gender Association: Used for boys

Popularity and Trend: Last ranked #882 in 2000

Risk of Misspelling: Fairly low

Risk of Mispronunciation: Fairly low

Famous Namesakes: Cuban president Fidel Castro

Common Nicknames: None

Common Variations: None

Consider This: Fidel Castro's negative image has limited this name's use. But because Castro is so well known, most people should find it relatively easy to spell and pronounce Fidel.

Finnegan ★★★

(Irish) light-skinned; white.

First Impression: People find this name fit for a gregarious, cheerful Irishman who has a great sense of humor as well as a short temper.

Gender Association: Used for boys

Popularity and Trend: #779 (#888 in 2005)

Risk of Misspelling: Average

Risk of Mispronunciation: Fairly low

Famous Namesakes: Character Finnegan (*Finnegan's Wake*)

Common Nicknames: Finn

Common Variations: None

Consider This: With its lively image and growing popularity, Finnegan should appeal to trendy parents. Most people will know to pronounce it "FIN-ah-gen."

Fletcher ★★★★

(English) arrow featherer, arrow maker.

First Impression: Fletcher is described as a quiet but friendly guy who opens up once you get to know him.

Gender Association: Used for boys

Popularity and Trend: Last ranked in the Top 1000 in the 1970s

Risk of Misspelling: Low

Risk of Mispronunciation: Low

Famous Namesakes: Character Irwin Fletcher (*Fletch*); *Bounty* mutineer Fletcher Christian

Common Nicknames: Fletch

Common Variations: None

Consider This: Fletcher hasn't been popular since the '70s, and its image doesn't suggest a comeback anytime soon.

Floyd ★★

(English) a form of Lloyd.

First Impression: Floyd is depicted as a slow, goofy, and strange man who's not very attractive.

Gender Association: Used for boys

Popularity and Trend: Last ranked in the Top 1000 in the 1990s

Risk of Misspelling: Fairly low

Risk of Mispronunciation: Low

Famous Namesakes: Band Pink Floyd; boxer Floyd Patterson; cyclist Floyd Landis

Common Nicknames: None

Common Variations: None

Consider This: Floyd's negative first impression has kept it off the Top 1000 for years.

Flynn ★★

(Irish) son of the red-haired man.

First Impression: This name calls to mind a nerdy young man who's quite smart but also quite weird.

Gender Association: Used for boys

Popularity and Trend: Never been ranked in Top 1000

Risk of Misspelling: Fairly low

Risk of Mispronunciation: Low

Famous Namesakes: Actor Errol Flynn

Common Nicknames: None

Common Variations: None

Consider This: Although neither has been ranked, Fynn seems a better choice than Flynn, because it makes a more favorable impression.

Ford ★★

(English) river crossing. A form of names ending in "ford."

First Impression: People perceive Ford as coldhearted, rough, and self-centered.

Gender Association: Used for boys

Popularity and Trend: Last ranked in the Top 1000 in the 1920s

Risk of Misspelling: Low

Risk of Mispronunciation: Low

Famous Namesakes: Industrialist Henry Ford; president Gerald Ford; character Ford Fairlane (*The Adventures of Ford Fairlane*)

Common Nicknames: None

Common Variations: None

Consider This: Despite its strong namesakes, Ford's image is extremely unattractive.

Forrest ★★★

(French) forest; woodsman.

First Impression: Forrest is described as a gifted, caring, and sometimes goofy boy who loves the wilderness.

Gender Association: Used mostly for boys

Popularity and Trend: Last ranked #696 in 2000

Risk of Misspelling: Fairly high

Risk of Mispronunciation: Low

Famous Namesakes: Film and book character Forrest Gump; actor Forrest Whitaker

Common Nicknames: None

Common Variations: Forest

Consider This: Forrest has dropped off the ranking charts, but its positive image may appeal to outdoorsy parents. However, spelling could be problematic for those expecting it to be spelled like the word *forest*.

Francis ★★★

(Latin) free; from France.

First Impression: Francis calls to mind a sweet, loving man.

Gender Association: Used mostly for boys

Popularity and Trend: #561 (#436 in 2000)

Risk of Misspelling: Fairly low

Risk of Mispronunciation: Low

Famous Namesakes: Director Francis Ford Coppola; philosopher Francis Bacon; saint Francis of Assisi

Common Nicknames: Fran, Franco, Frank

Common Variations: Francisco, Francois

Consider This: This classic name has dropped in popularity, but it's still a solid choice for traditionalists. However, its pronunciation is the same as that for Frances, a traditional name for girls, which may cause gender confusion.

Frank ★★

(English) a short form of Francis, Franklin.

First Impression: People see Frank as either a sloppy old man or a socially inept techie with a strange sense of humor.

Gender Association: Used for boys

Popularity and Trend: #245 (#208 in 2000)

Risk of Misspelling: Low

Risk of Mispronunciation: Low

Famous Namesakes: Singer Frank Sinatra; singer Frank Zappa; architect Frank Lloyd Wright; football player Frank Gifford; baseball player Frank Thomas

Common Nicknames: Frankie

Common Variations: Franc

Consider This: Frank is a common name, but it has a decidedly negative and old image. On the playground, Frank may be called "Frankfurter."

Franklin ★★★

(English) free landowner.

First Impression: People think Franklin is smart to the point of being nerdy, and proud to the point of being arrogant.

Gender Association: Used for boys

Popularity and Trend: #439 (#449 in 2000)

Risk of Misspelling: Fairly low

Risk of Mispronunciation: Low

Famous Namesakes: President Franklin Roosevelt; Founding Father Benjamin Franklin; president Franklin Pierce

Common Nicknames: Frank, Frankie

Common Variations: Franklyn

Consider This: An old-fashioned name, Franklin seems too dowdy despite its slight increase in popularity.

Fred ★★★

(German) a short form of Alfred, Frederick, Manfred.

First Impression: Fred is pictured as a kindhearted, dependable, and hardworking everyman.

Gender Association: Used for boys

Popularity and Trend: Last ranked #960 in 2000

Risk of Misspelling: Low

Risk of Mispronunciation: Low

Famous Namesakes: Character Fred Flintstone (*The Flintstones*); actor Fred Astaire; singer Fred Durst; golfer Fred Couples

Common Nicknames: Freddie

Common Variations: Fredd

Consider This: This classic has dropped off the charts. Although it makes a fine first impression, perhaps the name seems dated.

Freddie ★★

(German) a familiar form of Frederick.

First Impression: Freddie is pictured as a scrawny, dorky kid who is unpopular with the cool crowd, but his true friends think he's great fun.

Gender Association: Used mostly for boys

Popularity and Trend: Last ranked #932 in 2000

Risk of Misspelling: Average

Risk of Mispronunciation: Low

Famous Namesakes: Actors Freddie Prinze, Sr. and Freddie Prinze, Jr.; singer Freddie Mercury; singer Freddie Jackson; character

Freddy Krueger (*Nightmare on Elm Street*)

Common Nicknames: None

Common Variations: Freddy

Consider This: Even less formal than Fred, Freddie seems unappealing. "Freddy" is also a popular spelling, which may cause confusion.

Frederick ★★★

(German) peaceful ruler.

First Impression: People regard Frederick as an authoritative and standoffish man who's refined but pompous.

Gender Association: Used for boys

Popularity and Trend: #483 (#396 in 2000)

Risk of Misspelling: Average

Risk of Mispronunciation: Fairly low

Famous Namesakes: Abolitionist Frederick Douglass; several kings named Frederick

Common Nicknames: Fred, Freddie, Dick, Rick, Eric, Fritz

Common Variations: Federico, Fredrick, Frederic, Friedrich

Consider This: Pronunciation is a slight problem because both "FRED-er-ick" and "FRED-rick" are options. Spelling is also something to consider because there are so many variations of this name.

Frick ★★★

(English) bold.

First Impression: People say Frick is either selfish and mean, goofy and fun, unusual and weird, loving and nice, quiet and lonely, or stupid and slow.

Gender Association: Used for boys

Popularity and Trend: Never been ranked in Top 1000

Risk of Misspelling: Low

Risk of Mispronunciation: Low

Famous Namesakes: Art patron Henry Clay Frick

Common Nicknames: None

Common Variations: None

Consider This: This is a unique name that comes across as "odd," not "cool." It also comes across as the PG version of the R-rated *F* word.

Fritz ★★★

(German) a familiar form of Frederick.

First Impression: Some say Fritz is reserved and gentle, but others imagine he's egotistical and forceful.

Gender Association: Used for boys

Popularity and Trend: Last ranked in the Top 1000 in the 1970s

Risk of Misspelling: Fairly low

Risk of Mispronunciation: Low

Famous Namesakes: Vice president Walter "Fritz" Mondale; cartoon character Fritz the Cat; writer Fritz Leiber

Common Nicknames: None

Common Variations: None

Consider This: Fritz will probably fit best with last names of Germanic origin.

Fynn ★★★

(Ghanaian) Geography: another name for the Offin River in Ghana.

First Impression: Fynn is described as a soft-spoken and well-mannered man who's not without charm and humor.

Gender Association: Used for boys

Popularity and Trend: Never been ranked in Top 1000

Risk of Misspelling: Fairly high

Risk of Mispronunciation: Low

Famous Namesakes: Author and character Fynn (*Mister God, This Is Anna*)

Common Nicknames: None

Common Variations: Finn

Consider This: If you're looking for a cutting-edge name, Fynn's positive image may make it a unique winner. Its spelling could be a downside, though, because people will likely expect it to be "Finn."

Gabe ★★★

(Hebrew) a short form of Gabriel.

First Impression: Gabe is said to be charismatic and sly with a dry sense of humor.

Gender Association: Used for boys

Popularity and Trend: Never been ranked in Top 1000

Risk of Misspelling: Low

Risk of Mispronunciation: Low

Famous Namesakes: Actor Gabe Kaplan; baseball player Gabe Kapler

Common Nicknames: None

Common Variations: None

Consider This: Gabe is a common nickname, so people may assume Gabriel is the given name.

Gabriel ★★★★★

(Hebrew) devoted to God.

First Impression: Gabriel is thought to be a helpful and watchful man who's serene, smart, and mysterious.

Gender Association: Used mostly for boys

Popularity and Trend: #28 (#44 in 2000)

Risk of Misspelling: Fairly low

Risk of Mispronunciation: Low

Famous Namesakes: Archangel Gabriel; actor Gabriel Bryne; writer Gabriel José García Márquez; singer Juan Gabriel; singer Peter Gabriel

Common Nicknames: Gabe, Gabby, Riel

Common Variations: Gabrial

Consider This: Gabriel is undoubtedly a strong name worthy of 5 stars.

Gage ★★★★

(French) pledge.

First Impression: Folks imagine that Gage has a strong, confident personality—he's outgoing, popular, witty, and also caring.

Gender Association: Used mostly for boys

Popularity and Trend: #156 (#166 in 2000)

Risk of Misspelling: Fairly low

Risk of Mispronunciation: Low

Famous Namesakes: General Thomas Gage

Common Nicknames: None

Common Variations: Gaige

Consider This: Gage could break into the Top 100 in the next few years.

Gareth ★★★

(Welsh) gentle. (Irish) a form of Garrett.

First Impression: The jury is still out on Gareth: He may be a soccer star or a chess-playing nerd.

Gender Association: Used for boys

Popularity and Trend: Never been ranked in Top 1000

Risk of Misspelling: Fairly low

Risk of Mispronunciation: Average

Famous Namesakes: Arthurian figure Gareth

Common Nicknames: Garth, Gar

Common Variations: None

Consider This: Gareth is a popular name in the United Kingdom, but not here. Some people may pronounce it "GARE-eth," but others pronounce it "GAR-eth."

Garrett ★★★★

(Irish) brave spearman.

First Impression: People think Garrett is an ambitious and strong-willed go-getter.

Gender Association: Used for boys

Popularity and Trend: #138 (#74 in 2000)

Risk of Misspelling: Average

Risk of Mispronunciation: Fairly low

Famous Namesakes: Actor Brad Garrett; lawman Pat Garrett; actor Garrett Hedlund

Common Nicknames: Gar

Common Variations: Garet, Garret, Gareth

Consider This: With its solidly positive image, Garrett is a great choice. Spelling is a slight problem, though, with the possibility of some people forgetting to double the *r* and/or the *t*.

Garrison ★★★★

(English) Garry's son. (French) troops stationed at a fort; garrison.

First Impression: Garrison is said to be a combination of intelligence, fun, and gentlemanly politeness.

Gender Association: Used for boys

Popularity and Trend: #895 (#667 in 2000)

Risk of Misspelling: Low

Risk of Mispronunciation: Low

Famous Namesakes: Radio personality Garrison Keillor

BOYS • PAGE 252

Common Nicknames: None
Common Variations: None
Consider This: Despite its falling popularity, Garrison's image is still appealing.

Garth ★★★★

(Scandinavian) garden, gardener. (Welsh) a form of Gareth.
First Impression: Garth is pictured as a country boy with old-fashioned values and a stocky build.
Gender Association: Used for boys
Popularity and Trend: Last ranked in the Top 1000 in the 1980s
Risk of Misspelling: Low
Risk of Mispronunciation: Low
Famous Namesakes: Singer Garth Brooks; character Garth Algar (*Wayne's World*)
Common Nicknames: None
Common Variations: None
Consider This: Garth Brooks has been out of the spotlight for several years, which may explain this name's waning popularity.

Gary ★★★

(German) mighty spearman. (English) a form of Gerald.
First Impression: People perceive Gary as a warm family man who's smart, friendly, and easygoing, but his plain looks gives him low self-esteem.
Gender Association: Used for boys
Popularity and Trend: #350 (#275 in 2000)

Risk of Misspelling: Average
Risk of Mispronunciation: Low
Famous Namesakes: Actor Gary Cooper; comedian Garry Shandling; actor Gary Coleman; politician Gary Hart
Common Nicknames: None
Common Variations: Garry
Consider This: Gary was a Top 100 name from the '30s to the '80s, but it doesn't seem to be a common choice today. The spelling may be confused with "Garry."

Gavin ★★★★

(Welsh) white hawk.
First Impression: Gavin is seen as compassionate, popular, and fun, but he may come across as pretentious.
Gender Association: Used for boys
Popularity and Trend: #38 (#85 in 2000)
Risk of Misspelling: Fairly low
Risk of Mispronunciation: Low
Famous Namesakes: Actor Gavin MacLeod; singer Gavin DeGraw; singer Gavin Rossdale
Common Nicknames: None
Common Variations: Gaven
Consider This: The popularity of this Top 100 name continues to increase.

Gaylord ★★★

(French) merry lord; jailer.
First Impression: People picture Gaylord as a wimpy but well-to-do British man.

Gender Association: Used for boys
Popularity and Trend: Last ranked in the Top 1000 in the 1950s
Risk of Misspelling: Low
Risk of Mispronunciation: Low
Famous Namesakes: Character Gaylord Focker (*Meet the Parents*); baseball player Gaylord Perry; gymnast Mitch Gaylord
Common Nicknames: None
Common Variations: None
Consider This: It doesn't seem surprising that Gaylord hasn't been ranked for over a half-century.

Gene ★★★

(Greek) a form of Eugene.
First Impression: People think Gene is a moody man who's sometimes mean and hard to please, although sometimes he's jovial and kind.
Gender Association: Used for boys
Popularity and Trend: Last ranked in the Top 1000 in the 1990s
Risk of Misspelling: Fairly low
Risk of Mispronunciation: Low
Famous Namesakes: Actor Gene Autrey; actor Gene Hackman; musician Gene Simmons; actor Gene Kelly; writer Gene Roddenberry
Common Nicknames: None
Common Variations: None
Consider This: Gene certainly seems more appealing than its long form, Eugene. However, its

pronunciation is the same as that for Jean, a name often used for girls, which may cause gender confusion.

George ★★★
(Greek) farmer.

First Impression: People see George as a gangly, acne-prone nerd who plays a mean game of chess.

Gender Association: Used for boys

Popularity and Trend: #153 (#130 in 2000)

Risk of Misspelling: Low

Risk of Mispronunciation: Low

Famous Namesakes: Presidents George H. W. Bush and George W. Bush; president George Washington; actor George Clooney; comedian George Burns; boxer George Foreman

Common Nicknames: Georgy

Common Variations: Georgio, Jorge

Consider This: George is a classic name with a less-than-stellar image.

Gerald ★★★
(German) mighty spearman.

First Impression: Here's a contrast: People say Gerald is either obnoxious and socially inept or smart and quietly authoritative.

Gender Association: Used for boys

Popularity and Trend: #544 (#383 in 2000)

Risk of Misspelling: Average

Risk of Mispronunciation: Low

Famous Namesakes: President Gerald Ford; actor Gerald McRainey; singer Gerald Levert

Common Nicknames: Gary, Gerry, Jerry

Common Variations: Geraldo, Jerald

Consider This: Its ambivalent image may make this classic name an unlikely choice. Also, its spelling may be confused for "Jerald."

Geraldo ★
(Italian, Spanish) a form of Gerald.

First Impression: People think Geraldo is loud, opinionated, and sensationalistic.

Gender Association: Used for boys

Popularity and Trend: Never been ranked in Top 1000

Risk of Misspelling: Fairly high

Risk of Mispronunciation: Fairly high

Famous Namesakes: TV personality Geraldo Rivera; baseball player Geraldo Guzman

Common Nicknames: None

Common Variations: None

Consider This: A negative image hurts Geraldo, a name whose pronunciation may work best with Latino family names. Some people may not realize it's "her-AHL-do," not "jer-AHL-do."

Gerard ★★★
(English) brave spearman.

First Impression: Some people think of Gerard as a wild and crazy

partier. Others say he's shy, nervous, and clumsy.

Gender Association: Used for boys

Popularity and Trend: Last ranked #823 in 2000

Risk of Misspelling: Fairly low

Risk of Mispronunciation: Fairly low

Famous Namesakes: Actor Gérard Depardieu; poet Gerard Hopkins; actor Gerard Butler

Common Nicknames: Gerry

Common Variations: Gerardo

Consider This: Gerard's mixed image makes it appealing to some, but unappealing to others. Most people will likely pronounce it correctly as "je-RARD."

Gideon ★★★
(Hebrew) tree cutter.

First Impression: People think Gideon is a geeky bookworm who's soft-spoken with a tall, slender frame.

Gender Association: Used for boys

Popularity and Trend: #591 (#891 in 2000)

Risk of Misspelling: Fairly low

Risk of Mispronunciation: Fairly low

Famous Namesakes: Biblical figure Gideon; character Dr. Ben Gideon (*Gideon's Crossing*)

Common Nicknames: None

Common Variations: Gedeon, Gidon

Consider This: The popularity of this old-fashioned name is rising, but it's a name without a short form or a familiar form. Name your

boy Gideon; that's what he'll
be called.

Gilbert ★★★

(English) brilliant pledge; trustworthy.

First Impression: Gilbert is described
as a rich and spoiled geek who's
greedy and grumpy.

Gender Association: Used for boys

Popularity and Trend: #658
(#527 in 2000)

Risk of Misspelling: Low

Risk of Mispronunciation: Low

Famous Namesakes: Comedian
Gilbert Gottfried; dramatist
W. S. Gilbert; character Gilbert
Grape (*What's Eating Gilbert
Grape*)

Common Nicknames: Bert, Gil

Common Variations: Gilberto

Consider This: Gilbert's negative
image may explain why more
parents aren't choosing it.

Gino ★★

(Greek) a familiar form of Eugene.
(Italian) a short form of names
ending in "gene," "gino."

First Impression: People say Gino is a
temperamental guy who can be
suave and even amiable when he
isn't being cocky and brash.

Gender Association: Used for boys

Popularity and Trend: Last ranked
#902 in 2000

Risk of Misspelling: Fairly low

Risk of Mispronunciation: Fairly low

Famous Namesakes: Football player
Gino Toretta; singer Gino Vanelli

Common Nicknames: None

Common Variations: None

Consider This: Despite its lackluster
image, Gino may appeal to parents of Greek or Italian descent.
Most people know it's pronounced "JEE-noh."

Giuseppe ★

(Italian) a form of Joseph.

First Impression: Giuseppe is considered a nomad of sorts, letting
his wise, mystic ways lead him
from place to place.

Gender Association: Used for boys

Popularity and Trend: Last ranked in
the Top 1000 in the 1980s

Risk of Misspelling: High

Risk of Mispronunciation: High

Famous Namesakes: Composer
Giuseppe Verdi; director
Giuseppe Tornatore

Common Nicknames: None

Common Variations: None

Consider This: This ethnic name
doesn't have broad appeal. Pronounced "jeh-SEP-ee," it's a
challenge to say or to spell.

Glen ★★

(Irish) a form of Glendon.

First Impression: Most people imagine
Glen as a hardworking businessman who needs to be in control
and cares too much about
appearances.

Gender Association: Used for boys

Popularity and Trend: Last ranked
#769 in 2000

Risk of Misspelling: Average

Risk of Mispronunciation: Low

Famous Namesakes: Singer Glen
Campbell; musician Glenn
Miller; basketball player Glen
Rice; movie *Glengarry Glen Ross*

Common Nicknames: None

Common Variations: Glenn, Glyn

Consider This: A lukewarm image
doesn't explain Glen's declining
popularity. Perhaps the name's
association with musicians like
Glenn Miller and Glen Campbell
date it. Plus, its spelling may be
confused for "Glenn."

Godfrey ★★★

(Irish) God's peace. (German) a
form of Jeffrey.

First Impression: Godfrey calls to
mind a distinguished, tea-
drinking gentleman who's a
bookish loner.

Gender Association: Used for boys

Popularity and Trend: Last ranked in
the Top 1000 in the 1920s

Risk of Misspelling: Fairly low

Risk of Mispronunciation: Fairly low

Famous Namesakes: Comedian
Godfrey; radio personality
Arthur Godfrey

Common Nicknames: None

Common Variations: Gottfried

Consider This: Godfrey hasn't been
ranked for nearly a century,

which suggests it's old-fashioned. That said, most people know it's pronounced "GOD-free" and not "GOD-fray."

Gomer ★★

(Hebrew) completed, finished. (English) famous battle.

First Impression: Gomer is imagined to be a clumsy and goofy hick, much like TV character Gomer Pyle.

Gender Association: Used for boys

Popularity and Trend: Never been ranked in Top 1000

Risk of Misspelling: Low

Risk of Mispronunciation: Fairly low

Famous Namesakes: Character Gomer Pyle (*The Andy Griffith Show* and *Gomer Pyle, U.S.M.C.*)

Common Nicknames: None

Common Variations: None

Consider This: When people call someone Gomer, they're not praising his intellect. 'Nuff said.

Gordon ★★★

(English) triangular-shaped hill.

First Impression: People describe Gordon as a goofy, skinny computer geek who sometimes acts lighthearted and sometimes acts immature.

Gender Association: Used for boys

Popularity and Trend: #900 (#641 in 2000)

Risk of Misspelling: Low

Risk of Mispronunciation: Low

Famous Namesakes: Comic book character Flash Gordon; radio personality G. Gordon Liddy; singer Gordon Lightfoot; racecar driver Jeff Gordon

Common Nicknames: Gord, Gordy

Common Variations: None

Consider This: Sharply dropping popularity plus a poor image make Gordon a bad choice.

Grady ★★★★

(Irish) noble; illustrious.

First Impression: People see Grady as a sincere, kind, and easygoing farm boy.

Gender Association: Used for boys

Popularity and Trend: #475 (#746 in 2000)

Risk of Misspelling: Low

Risk of Mispronunciation: Low

Famous Namesakes: Baseball player Grady Sizemore

Common Nicknames: None

Common Variations: None

Consider This: Grady's popularity is rising, and its down-home image may appeal to many parents.

Graham ★★★

(English) grand home.

First Impression: Graham reminds people of a bookish but friendly Brit who's classy and gentle.

Gender Association: Used for boys

Popularity and Trend: #430 (#406 in 2000)

Risk of Misspelling: Fairly low

Risk of Mispronunciation: Fairly low

Famous Namesakes: Writer Graham Greene; actor Graham Greene; inventor Alexander Graham Bell; singer Graham Nash

Common Nicknames: None

Common Variations: Graeme

Consider This: Although Graham's popularity is slipping, its refined image is a plus. There may be subtle differences in pronunciation, with some saying it as one syllable and others saying it as two.

Grant ★★★★

(English) a form of Grantland.

First Impression: Grant is thought to be a natural leader who gets things done.

Gender Association: Used mostly for boys

Popularity and Trend: #155 (#123 in 2000)

Risk of Misspelling: Low

Risk of Mispronunciation: Low

Famous Namesakes: Actor Hugh Grant; actor Cary Grant; football player Grant Wistrom; president Ulysses S. Grant

Common Nicknames: None

Common Variations: None

Consider This: If you're looking for a solid name with a solid image, Grant is a good choice.

Grayson ★★★★

(English) bailiff's son.

First Impression: People describe Grayson as a refined man who's polite and caring.

Gender Association: Used mostly for boys

Popularity and Trend: #218 (#313 in 2000)

Risk of Misspelling: Fairly low

Risk of Mispronunciation: Low

Famous Namesakes: Character Dick Grayson (*Batman*); actor Grayson McCouch

Common Nicknames: Gray, Sonny

Common Variations: Greyson

Consider This: Grayson's positive image is boosting the name's popularity.

Greg ★★★★

(Latin) a short form of Gregory.

First Impression: Greg is pictured as flirty and impish, but he has a big heart.

Gender Association: Used for boys

Popularity and Trend: Last ranked in the Top 1000 in the 1990s

Risk of Misspelling: Fairly low

Risk of Mispronunciation: Low

Famous Namesakes: Actor Greg Kinnear; golfer Greg Norman; diver Greg Louganis; character Greg Montgomery (*Dharma & Greg*); cyclist Greg LeMonde

Common Nicknames: None

Common Variations: Gregg

Consider This: This name has several star athletes among its famous namesakes, but less popularity than you'd imagine.

Gregory ★★★★

(Latin) vigilant watchman.

First Impression: People think Gregory is wise, compassionate, and respected.

Gender Association: Used for boys

Popularity and Trend: #208 (#138 in 2000)

Risk of Misspelling: Fairly low

Risk of Mispronunciation: Low

Famous Namesakes: Actor Gregory Peck; actor Gregory Hines; character Gregory House (*House, M.D.*); several popes named Gregory

Common Nicknames: Greg

Common Variations: Greggory, Gregor

Consider This: This classic name isn't as popular as it once was, but it's still a solid contender.

Griffin ★★★★

(Latin) hooked nose.

First Impression: Griffin is pictured as a cool guy with deep intelligence, an easygoing attitude, and a magnetic personality.

Gender Association: Used for boys

Popularity and Trend: #254 (#231 in 2000)

Risk of Misspelling: Fairly low

Risk of Mispronunciation: Low

Famous Namesakes: Actor Griffin Dunne; talk show host Merv Griffin; actor Eddie Griffin; the Griffin family (*Family Guy*)

Common Nicknames: None

Common Variations: Griffen

Consider This: Griffin has a stellar image, and it's relatively popular.

Grimshaw ★★

(English) dark woods.

First Impression: Most people suspect Grimshaw is a miserly, moody, and depressed outcast.

Gender Association: Used for boys

Popularity and Trend: Never been ranked in Top 1000

Risk of Misspelling: Fairly low

Risk of Mispronunciation: Fairly low

Famous Namesakes: Chess expert Walter Grimshaw

Common Nicknames: None

Common Variations: None

Consider This: This unique name's grim sound and grim image severely limit its popularity.

Grover ★★

(English) grove.

First Impression: Grover is viewed as a grumpy, grouchy guy who's also nerdy.

Gender Association: Used for boys

Popularity and Trend: Last ranked in the Top 1000 in the 1970s

Risk of Misspelling: Low

Risk of Mispronunciation: Low

Famous Namesakes: President Grover
Cleveland; musician Grover
Washington; character Grover
(*Sesame Street*)
Common Nicknames: None
Common Variations: None
Consider This: Most parents are
unlikely to name their child
after a Muppet.

Gunther ★

(Scandinavian) battle army;
warrior.
First Impression: Some people see
Gunther as a methodical, burly
German. Others see him as a
dorky but sensitive nerd.
Gender Association: Used for boys
Popularity and Trend: Never been
ranked in Top 1000
Risk of Misspelling: Average
Risk of Mispronunciation: Fairly high
Famous Namesakes: Character
Gunther (*Friends*); football coach
Gunther Cunningham
Common Nicknames: None
Common Variations: Gunnar, Gunner,
Gunter
Consider This: It's unlikely this name
will increase in popularity with
an unpleasant image and an awk-
ward traditional pronunciation
("GOON-ter") that is often
mispronounced "GUN-ther."

Guy ★★★★

(Hebrew) valley. (German) warrior.
(French) guide.

First Impression: Guy is imagined to
be a clever, if not brilliant, man
with a caring and helpful heart.
Gender Association: Used for boys
Popularity and Trend: #989
(#811 in 2000)
Risk of Misspelling: Low
Risk of Mispronunciation: Fairly low
Famous Namesakes: Actor Guy
Pierce; musician Guy Lombardo;
director Guy Ritchie; conspirator
Guy Fawkes
Common Nicknames: None
Common Variations: Guido
Consider This: Guy is a short name
with a lot of appeal. Most will
pronounce it like the English
word *guy*, but another pronunciation is "gee" with a hard *G*
sound (as in Gomer) rather than
a soft *G* sound (as in George).

Gwidon ★

(Polish) life.
First Impression: Gwidon is described
as a rude and mean loner.
Gender Association: Used for boys
Popularity and Trend: Never been
ranked in Top 1000
Risk of Misspelling: Fairly high
Risk of Mispronunciation: Fairly high
Famous Namesakes: None
Common Nicknames: None
Common Variations: None
Consider This: People don't seem to
warm to this unique name, pro-
nounced "GWEE-don," nor to
its loner image.

Habib ★★

(Arabic) beloved.
First Impression: Habib is perceived as
a caring and responsible people
pleaser.
Gender Association: Used for boys
Popularity and Trend: Never been
ranked in Top 1000
Risk of Misspelling: Fairly high
Risk of Mispronunciation: Fairly high
Famous Namesakes: Diplomat Philip
Habib
Common Nicknames: None
Common Variations: Habîb
Consider This: Habib is a good choice
for parents who want to showcase
their Arabic lineage. Those out-
side the culture may not know
to pronounce it "ha-BEEB."

Hakim ★

(Arabic) wise. (Ethiopian) doctor.
First Impression: Hakim is described
as a thug with an attitude.
Gender Association: Used for boys
Popularity and Trend: Never been
ranked in Top 1000
Risk of Misspelling: Fairly high
Risk of Mispronunciation: Fairly high
Famous Namesakes: Allah title al-
Hakim; basketball player
Hakeem Olajuwon; basketball
player Hakim Warrick
Common Nicknames: None
Common Variations: Hakeem
Consider This: Hakim's cold first
impression doesn't help its score.

Just as with Habib, some people may not know to pronounce it "ha-KEEM."

Ham ★★
(Hebrew) hot.

First Impression: People describe Ham as a piggish, rude, and dorky man.

Gender Association: Used for boys

Popularity and Trend: Never been ranked in Top 1000

Risk of Misspelling: Low

Risk of Mispronunciation: Low

Famous Namesakes: Biblical figure Ham

Common Nicknames: None

Common Variations: None

Consider This: It's difficult to separate the porcine product from this moniker.

Hank ★★
(American) a familiar form of Henry.

First Impression: Many people see Hank as a simple-minded fellow in a small, rural town.

Gender Association: Used for boys

Popularity and Trend: Last ranked in the Top 1000 in the 1980s

Risk of Misspelling: Low

Risk of Mispronunciation: Low

Famous Namesakes: Baseball player Hank Aaron; actor Hank Azaria; singers Hank Williams, Sr. and Hank Williams, Jr.; baseball player Hank Blalock

Common Nicknames: None

Common Variations: None

Consider This: Some parents may find Hank's down-home image detrimental, despite its likable famous namesakes.

Hans ★★
(Scandinavian) a form of John.

First Impression: Hans is imagined to be a Nordic or German man who's caring and generous but not very bright.

Gender Association: Used for boys

Popularity and Trend: Last ranked in the Top 1000 in the 1990s

Risk of Misspelling: Fairly low

Risk of Mispronunciation: Average

Famous Namesakes: Composer Hans Zimmer; author Hans Christian Andersen; character Hans Moleman (*The Simpsons*); character Han Solo (*Star Wars*)

Common Nicknames: None

Common Variations: Hansel

Consider This: This name may fit best with Scandinavian or Germanic surnames. The correct pronunciation is "hahnz," but some mistakenly pronounce it "hanz."

Harley ★★
(English) hare's meadow; army meadow.

First Impression: Harley is described as a gruff, nasty, and rebellious biker.

Gender Association: Used about equally for girls and boys

Popularity and Trend: #522 (#446 in 2000)

Risk of Misspelling: Low

Risk of Mispronunciation: Low

Famous Namesakes: Motorcycle manufacturer Harley-Davidson

Common Nicknames: None

Common Variations: None

Consider This: There's no separating Harley from its motorcycle namesake. Plus, just as many girls receive this name as boys—a potential negative if you want a name exclusively associated with boys.

Harmon ★★★★
(English) a form of Herman.

First Impression: People describe Harmon as a loyal, strong-hearted, and very good-looking military man.

Gender Association: Used for boys

Popularity and Trend: Last ranked in the Top 1000 in the 1950s

Risk of Misspelling: Low

Risk of Mispronunciation: Low

Famous Namesakes: Actor Mark Harmon; baseball player Harmon Killebrew

Common Nicknames: None

Common Variations: None

Consider This: Harmon has a great image, but it may come across as old-fashioned.

Harold ★★★

(Scandinavian) army ruler.

First Impression: Harold is thought to be a quiet nerd who keeps to himself and keeps his mind on his work.

Gender Association: Used for boys

Popularity and Trend: #652 (#535 in 2000)

Risk of Misspelling: Fairly low

Risk of Mispronunciation: Low

Famous Namesakes: Character Harold Chasen (*Harold and Maude*); director Harold Ramis; actor Harold Perrineau; character Harold Lee (*Harold and Kumar Go to White Castle*)

Common Nicknames: Harry, Hal

Common Variations: Harald, Heraldo

Consider This: This classic name has versatility, but not an image many parents will go for.

Harrison ★★★★

(English) son of Harry.

First Impression: People see Harrison as a hardworking and stoic man who's rugged and masculine.

Gender Association: Used for boys

Popularity and Trend: #232 (#184 in 2000)

Risk of Misspelling: Low

Risk of Mispronunciation: Low

Famous Namesakes: Actor Harrison Ford; musician George Harrison; presidents William Henry Harrison and Benjamin Harrison

Common Nicknames: Harris, Harry

Common Variations: None

Consider This: Harrison is a strong name with strong namesakes.

Harry ★★★

(English) a familiar form of Harold, Henry.

First Impression: Harry is seen as an older gentleman who's quick with a joke and a smile.

Gender Association: Used for boys

Popularity and Trend: #593 (#513 in 2000)

Risk of Misspelling: Low

Risk of Mispronunciation: Low

Famous Namesakes: Film and book character Harry Potter; magician Harry Houdini; president Harry S. Truman; British prince Harry; film character "Dirty" Harry Callahan

Common Nicknames: None

Common Variations: None

Consider This: Harry has been slipping in popularity for decades, and even Prince Harry and the *Harry Potter* series haven't been able to reverse the trend.

Harvey ★★★

(German) army warrior.

First Impression: Harvey is considered an awkward nerd who's smart, quiet, and sweet.

Gender Association: Used for boys

Popularity and Trend: Last ranked in the Top 1000 in the 1990s

Risk of Misspelling: Low

Risk of Mispronunciation: Low

Famous Namesakes: Producer Harvey Weinstein; actor Harvey Keitel; play and film *Harvey*; radio personality Paul Harvey

Common Nicknames: None

Common Variations: None

Consider This: While sweet, this old-fashioned name may be too dated.

Hayden ★★★★★

(English) hedged valley.

First Impression: Hayden is thought to be a charming and cheerful man who's tall, chiseled, and beautiful.

Gender Association: Used mostly for boys

Popularity and Trend: #73 (#128 in 2000)

Risk of Misspelling: Fairly low

Risk of Mispronunciation: Low

Famous Namesakes: Actor Hayden Christensen; character Hayden Fox (*Coach*); activist Tom Hayden

Common Nicknames: None

Common Variations: Haiden, Haydn

Consider This: If you're looking for a trendy name, check out Hayden's rising popularity.

Heath ★★★★

(English) heath.

First Impression: Most people say Heath is strong, masculine, and thoughtful.

Gender Association: Used for boys

Popularity and Trend: #786
(#851 in 2000)
Risk of Misspelling: Low
Risk of Mispronunciation: Low
Famous Namesakes: Actor Heath
Ledger; football player Heath
Miller
Common Nicknames: None
Common Variations: None
Consider This: Namesake Heath
Ledger gives this name a boost.

Hector ★★★★
(Greek) steadfast.
First Impression: Folks think Hector
is a manly Latino who's caring,
kindhearted, and dedicated to
his family.
Gender Association: Used for boys
Popularity and Trend: #175
(#185 in 2000)
Risk of Misspelling: Low
Risk of Mispronunciation: Low
Famous Namesakes: Greek
mythological figure Hector;
actor Hector Elizondo
Common Nicknames: None
Common Variations: None
Consider This: Although climbing up
the rankings, Hector may fit best
with Latino surnames. Keep in
mind: the Latino pronunciation
is "hec-TOR."

Henry ★★★★★
(German) ruler of the household.
First Impression: Henry reminds
people of a scholarly professor—

perhaps a reference to Henry
Higgins of *My Fair Lady.*
Gender Association: Used for boys
Popularity and Trend: #95
(#126 in 2000)
Risk of Misspelling: Fairly low
Risk of Mispronunciation: Low
Famous Namesakes: British king
Henry VIII; actor Henry Fonda;
industrialist Henry Ford; secretary
of state Henry Kissinger; author
Henry Miller
Common Nicknames: Hank, Harry,
Heinz
Common Variations: Heinrich, Henri
Consider This: This classic name has
broken into the Top 100, and its
erudite image is attractive.

Herbert ★★★
(German) glorious soldier.
First Impression: People think Herbert
is a generally nice and respectful
man who can't overcome his
shyness.
Gender Association: Used for boys
Popularity and Trend: Last ranked
#964 in 2000
Risk of Misspelling: Low
Risk of Mispronunciation: Low
Famous Namesakes: President
Herbert Hoover
Common Nicknames: Herb
Common Variations: Heriberto
Consider This: Herbert may sound
too elderly for some.

Herman ★★★
(Latin) noble. (German) soldier.
First Impression: People feel Herman
is fearful and nervous because he
gets picked on so often.
Gender Association: Used for boys
Popularity and Trend: Last ranked in
the Top 1000 in the 1990s
Risk of Misspelling: Low
Risk of Mispronunciation: Low
Famous Namesakes: Author Herman
Melville; character Herman
Munster (*The Munsters*); band
Herman's Hermits
Common Nicknames: None
Common Variations: Harman
Consider This: Like Herbert, Herman
may be too outdated for today's
parents.

Herschel ★★
(Hebrew) a form of Hershel.
First Impression: Some view Herschel
as a mild-mannered and dorky
outcast who's scrawny and slight.
Thinking of football player
Herschel Walker, other people
feel he's athletic and strong.
Gender Association: Used for boys
Popularity and Trend: Last ranked in
the Top 1000 in the 1960s
Risk of Misspelling: Average
Risk of Mispronunciation: Fairly low
Famous Namesakes: Football player
Herschel Walker
Common Nicknames: None
Common Variations: Hershel

Consider This: Herschel could sound too ethnic for some, but it may appeal to others who want a traditional Hebrew name. Pronunciation is fairly clear: "HER-shul."

Hilario ★★
(Spanish) a form of Hilary.
First Impression: People say Hilario is a funny clown with a big mouth, an amusing laugh, a lot of confidence.
Gender Association: Used for boys
Popularity and Trend: Last ranked in the Top 1000 in the 1910s
Risk of Misspelling: Fairly high
Risk of Mispronunciation: Fairly high
Famous Namesakes: Basketball player Nene Hilario
Common Nicknames: None
Common Variations: None
Consider This: Although Hilario looks like the word *hilarious*, many people may not know the traditional Spanish pronunciation is "ee-LAR-ee-oh" with a silent *h*.

Holden ★★★
(English) hollow in the valley.
First Impression: Holden is pictured as a nervous, increasingly crazy man who's smart and wealthy but mostly an outcast.
Gender Association: Used for boys
Popularity and Trend: #384 (#453 in 2000)
Risk of Misspelling: Low
Risk of Mispronunciation: Low
Famous Namesakes: Character Holden Caufield (*The Catcher in the Rye*); actor William Holden
Common Nicknames: None
Common Variations: None
Consider This: *The Catcher in the Rye* may always affect this name's image.

Homer ★★★
(Greek) hostage; pledge; security.
First Impression: People picture Homer as a beer-guzzling, donut-eating simpleton who is, for the most part, funny and nice.
Gender Association: Used for boys
Popularity and Trend: Last ranked in the Top 1000 in the 1980s
Risk of Misspelling: Low
Risk of Mispronunciation: Low
Famous Namesakes: Philosopher Homer; character Homer Simpson (*The Simpsons*)
Common Nicknames: None
Common Variations: Homar, Homero
Consider This: The popularity of *The Simpsons* may deter many parents from Homer, despite its famous philosophical namesake.

Horace ★★★★
(Latin) keeper of the hours.
First Impression: Horace is said to be a supportive and friendly dad who loves children and is a great role model.
Gender Association: Used for boys
Popularity and Trend: Last ranked in the Top 1000 in the 1980s
Risk of Misspelling: Fairly low
Risk of Mispronunciation: Low
Famous Namesakes: Poet Horace; basketball player Horace Grant; politician Horace Greeley
Common Nicknames: None
Common Variations: Horacio
Consider This: Horace has a super image, but it sounds ancient to most people.

Houston ★★★★
(English) hill town.
First Impression: Houston is pictured as a rancher who's masculine and sexy in his Stetson hat and Wrangler jeans.
Gender Association: Used for boys
Popularity and Trend: #837 (#777 in 2000)
Risk of Misspelling: Low
Risk of Mispronunciation: Low
Famous Namesakes: Statesman Sam Houston; basketball player Allan Houston
Common Nicknames: None
Common Variations: Huston
Consider This: Place names are hot for some parents, but this one seems to be cooling.

Howard ★★★
(English) watchman.
First Impression: Howard is viewed as a middle-aged salesman who's

friendly and talkative, but his stories go nowhere.

Gender Association: Used for boys

Popularity and Trend: #836 (#664 in 2000)

Risk of Misspelling: Low

Risk of Mispronunciation: Low

Famous Namesakes: Radio personality Howard Stern; tycoon Howard Hughes; sportscaster Howard Cosell; comic book character Howard the Duck

Common Nicknames: Howie

Common Variations: None

Consider This: A lukewarm image and declining popularity don't help Howard.

Hubert ★★★

(German) bright mind; bright spirit.

First Impression: Hubert is imagined to be a quiet genius with great love for *Star Trek* and comic books, which means he has a great big imagination.

Gender Association: Used for boys

Popularity and Trend: Last ranked in the Top 1000 in the 1980s

Risk of Misspelling: Low

Risk of Mispronunciation: Low

Famous Namesakes: Vice president Hubert H. Humphrey

Common Nicknames: Hubie, Hugh

Common Variations: Hobart, Huberto

Consider This: Hubert has a bright meaning and a contemporary,

though odd, image. But like Herbert and Herman, it's not finding many takers.

Hugh ★★★

(English) a form of Hubert.

First Impression: People say Hugh is a self-assured and friendly man who's tall and thin.

Gender Association: Used for boys

Popularity and Trend: #994 (#906 in 2000)

Risk of Misspelling: Fairly low

Risk of Mispronunciation: Fairly low

Famous Namesakes: Actor Hugh Grant; *Playboy* founder Hugh Hefner; actor Hugh Jackman

Common Nicknames: Huey

Common Variations: Hugo

Consider This: Even though Hugh's popularity is waning, its dashing famous namesakes may still make it enticing. Although it's not phonetic, most people know it's pronounced "hyoo."

Hugo ★★★

(Latin) a form of Hugh.

First Impression: Hugo is thought to be funny and goofy, boisterous and outspoken—but not overly intelligent.

Gender Association: Used for boys

Popularity and Trend: #371 (#400 in 2000)

Risk of Misspelling: Fairly low

Risk of Mispronunciation: Fairly low

Famous Namesakes: Actor Hugo Weaving; designer Hugo Boss; author Victor Hugo

Common Nicknames: None

Common Variations: Hugh

Consider This: Hugo seems less suave than Hugh, but it's vastly more popular. Most people will pronounce it "HYOO-goh," but some cultures pronounce it "YOO-goh."

Humphrey ★★★

(German) peaceful strength.

First Impression: People say Humphrey is a smart aleck but also a man's man.

Gender Association: Used for boys

Popularity and Trend: Never been ranked in Top 1000

Risk of Misspelling: Fairly low

Risk of Mispronunciation: Fairly low

Famous Namesakes: Actor Humphrey Bogart; vice president Hubert H. Humphrey

Common Nicknames: None

Common Variations: None

Consider This: Humphrey has never been ranked, even though it's the name of one of Hollywood's most famous leading men. Nearly everyone will know it's pronounced "HUM-free."

Hunter ★★★★

(English) hunter.

First Impression: While many see Hunter as a kind, laid-back guy, others imagine him as compassionate and loyal with rugged, manly looks.

Gender Association: Used mostly for boys

Popularity and Trend: #54 (#35 in 2000)

Risk of Misspelling: Low

Risk of Mispronunciation: Low

Famous Namesakes: Writer Hunter S. Thompson; wrestler "Triple H" Hunter Hearst Helmsley; baseball player Jim "Catfish" Hunter

Common Nicknames: None

Common Variations: None

Consider This: This trendy name's popularity has lost a little steam, which has a benefit—now it isn't "too popular."

Hussein ★

(Arabic) little; handsome.

First Impression: People describe Hussein as a corrupt and remorseless man who's evil and untrustworthy.

Gender Association: Used for boys

Popularity and Trend: Never been ranked in Top 1000

Risk of Misspelling: Average

Risk of Mispronunciation: Average

Famous Namesakes: Iraqi president Saddam Hussein; senator Barack Hussein Obama

Common Nicknames: None

Common Variations: Hussain

Consider This: This name undeniably evokes images of former dictator Saddam Hussein. Like Adolf, this isn't a name that's likely to become popular within the next decade or five.

Ian ★★★

(Scottish) a form of John.

First Impression: Folks say Ian can be quick-witted and friendly, but he can also be conceited and smug.

Gender Association: Used mostly for boys

Popularity and Trend: #81 (#73 in 2000)

Risk of Misspelling: Average

Risk of Mispronunciation: Average

Famous Namesakes: Author Ian Fleming; actor Ian McKellan; actor Ian Ziering; actor Ian Somerhalder

Common Nicknames: None

Common Variations: Ean

Consider This: Despite its undecided image, Ian is still in the Top 100. Pronunciation ("EE-en") could be a bit tricky for some, and spelling could be as well.

Ignatius ★

(Latin) fiery, ardent.

First Impression: Ignatius is pictured as a brainy geek who spends too much time obsessing over school and fantasy books, and his feeble social life reflects that obsession.

Gender Association: Used for boys

Popularity and Trend: Last ranked in the Top 1000 in the 1930s

Risk of Misspelling: Fairly high

Risk of Mispronunciation: Fairly high

Famous Namesakes: Saint Ignatius of Loyola

Common Nicknames: Iggy

Common Variations: Ignacio

Consider This: This old-fashioned name may be too unique—and its image too negative—for today's parents.

Ike ★★

(Hebrew) a familiar form of Isaac.

First Impression: Many people think Ike is a quiet guy who lacks friends as well as confidence.

Gender Association: Used for boys

Popularity and Trend: Last ranked in the Top 1000 in the 1950s

Risk of Misspelling: Low

Risk of Mispronunciation: Low

Famous Namesakes: Singer Ike Turner; president Dwight "Ike" Eisenhower; football player Ike Taylor; football player Ike Hilliard

Common Nicknames: None

Common Variations: None

Consider This: A half-century has passed since "Ike" Eisenhower was president, making this name seem dated.

Ira ★★★

(Hebrew) watchful.

First Impression: Ira is seen as a good person who sometimes has bad days.

Gender Association: Used mostly for boys

Popularity and Trend: Last ranked in the Top 1000 in the 1990s

Risk of Misspelling: Low

Risk of Mispronunciation: Low

Famous Namesakes: Lyricist Ira Gershwin; author Ira Levin

Common Nicknames: None

Common Variations: None

Consider This: Although ranked in the Top 1000 just a decade ago, Ira may be too old-fashioned today.

Irving ★★★

(Irish) handsome. (Welsh) white river. (English) sea friend.

First Impression: People think Irving is the smart, studious, and shy type.

Gender Association: Used for boys

Popularity and Trend: Last ranked #838 in 2000

Risk of Misspelling: Average

Risk of Mispronunciation: Low

Famous Namesakes: Songwriter Irving Berlin; football player Michael Irving; writer Washington Irving

Common Nicknames: Irv

Common Variations: Erving, Ervin, Ervine, Irvin

Consider This: Like Ira, Irving has a dated feel to it. Also, its spelling may be confused with "Erving."

Isaac ★★★★★

(Hebrew) he will laugh.

First Impression: Isaac is considered a very smart and caring gentleman.

Gender Association: Used for boys

Popularity and Trend: #48 (#53 in 2000)

Risk of Misspelling: Average

Risk of Mispronunciation: Fairly low

Famous Namesakes: Biblical figure Isaac; singer and actor Isaac Hayes; scientist Isaac Newton; designer Isaac Mizrahi; author Isaac Asminov

Common Nicknames: Ike, Izzy

Common Variations: Isaak, Isac

Consider This: As with other biblical names, Isaac has strong appeal. Even with its double *a* spelling, which could confuse a few people, it's still a 5-star name.

Isaiah ★★★★

(Hebrew) God is my salvation.

First Impression: Isaiah is best described as an all-around good person.

Gender Association: Used for boys

Popularity and Trend: #40 (#47 in 2000)

Risk of Misspelling: Fairly high

Risk of Mispronunciation: Fairly low

Famous Namesakes: Biblical figure Isaiah; basketball player Isaiah Thomas; movie *Losing Isaiah*

Common Nicknames: None

Common Variations: Isiah

Consider This: Isaiah's somewhat challenging spelling keeps it from being a 5-star name, but it's a solid choice nonetheless. Most people know to pronounce it "eye-ZAY-ah."

Israel ★★★★

(Hebrew) prince of God; wrestled with God.

First Impression: Israel is regarded as a laid-back, crunchy hippie who has bold moments of risk taking.

Gender Association: Used for boys

Popularity and Trend: #203 (#244 in 2000)

Risk of Misspelling: Fairly low

Risk of Mispronunciation: Average

Famous Namesakes: Rabbi Menasseh Ben Israel; football player Israel Idonije

Common Nicknames: Izzy

Common Variations: Isreal

Consider This: Place names are hit-or-miss, but this place name seems to be a hit. Pronunciation could be "IZ-ree-el" or "IZ-ray-el."

Ittamar ★

(Hebrew) island of palms.

First Impression: Ittamar is seen as a Middle Eastern recluse with swarthy features and a short frame.

Gender Association: Used for boys
Popularity and Trend: Never been ranked in Top 1000
Risk of Misspelling: Fairly high
Risk of Mispronunciation: Fairly high
Famous Namesakes: Biblical figure Aaron's son Ithamar
Common Nicknames: None
Common Variations: Itamar, Ittmar, Ithamar
Consider This: This biblical name has yet to catch on. Pronunciation will be challenging: "ee-TAH-mahr."

Ivan ★★★

(Russian) a form of John.
First Impression: Most people think Ivan is a very polite man who's big and burly.
Gender Association: Used for boys
Popularity and Trend: #127 (#153 in 2000)
Risk of Misspelling: Fairly low
Risk of Mispronunciation: Fairly low
Famous Namesakes: Russian czar Ivan the Terrible; baseball player Ivan Rodriguez
Common Nicknames: Vanya
Common Variations: None
Consider This: Ivan's popularity is rising. Many may pronounce it "EYE-ven," but others will use the traditional "ee-VON."

Jack ★★★★★

(American) a form of Jacob, John.
First Impression: People picture Jack as a jovial and funny guy who loves to create mischief.
Gender Association: Used for boys
Popularity and Trend: #35 (#46 in 2000)
Risk of Misspelling: Low
Risk of Mispronunciation: Low
Famous Namesakes: Actor Jack Nicholson; golfer Jack Nicklaus; actor Jack Black; president John "Jack" Kennedy; character Captain Jack Sparrow (*Pirates of the Caribbean*)
Common Nicknames: Jackie
Common Variations: Jock
Consider This: This fun name's popularity is increasing, but it's not "too regular" yet.

Jackson ★★★★★

(English) son of Jack.
First Impression: Jackson is thought to be good-looking, kind, and smart.
Gender Association: Used mostly for boys
Popularity and Trend: #36 (#72 in 2000)
Risk of Misspelling: Fairly low
Risk of Mispronunciation: Low
Famous Namesakes: Artist Jackson Pollock; singer Jackson Browne; president Andrew Jackson; singer Michael Jackson
Common Nicknames: Jax, Jack
Common Variations: Jaxon
Consider This: A popular and more formal alternative to Jack, you may find Jackson's versatility appealing.

Jacob ★★★★

(Hebrew) supplanter, substitute.
First Impression: Jacob is pictured as a nice suburban kid who gets along with everybody.
Gender Association: Used mostly for boys
Popularity and Trend: #1 (#1 in 2000)
Risk of Misspelling: Fairly low
Risk of Mispronunciation: Low
Famous Namesakes: Biblical figure Jacob; singer Jakob Dylan; character Jacob Marley (*A Christmas Carol*)
Common Nicknames: Cobi, Jack, Jake, Jock
Common Variations: Jakob, Jacoby, Jacques
Consider This: A name doesn't become number one without reason. But while its appeal is undeniable, Jacob may be overused.

Jacques ★★

(French) a form of Jacob, James.
First Impression: People think Jacques is a Frenchman who's seductive, intriguing, and arty.
Gender Association: Used for boys
Popularity and Trend: Last ranked in the Top 1000 in the 1990s

Risk of Misspelling: Fairly high
Risk of Mispronunciation: Fairly high
Famous Namesakes: Explorer Jacques Cousteau; character Jacques Clouseau (*The Pink Panther*); chef Jacques Pépin; French president Jacques Chirac
Common Nicknames: Coco
Common Variations: None
Consider This: Jacques is classically French, and it may not fit with non-French surnames. Also, some people may have a hard time with the traditional "zhock" pronunciation and instead pronounce it "jocks" or "jock."

Jaden ★★★★

(Hebrew) a form of Jadon.
First Impression: Jaden is viewed as a stylish and creative designer and art teacher.
Gender Association: Used mostly for boys
Popularity and Trend: #88 (#154 in 2000)
Risk of Misspelling: Average
Risk of Mispronunciation: Fairly low
Famous Namesakes: Star kid Jaden Smith
Common Nicknames: None
Common Variations: Jadon, Jayden
Consider This: Jaden will be tricky to spell, considering Jayden is even more popular at #50. Pronunciation ("JAY-den") shouldn't be much of a problem.

Jagger ★★

(English) carter.
First Impression: Jagger makes people think of a rebellious and untrustworthy brute with rocker Mick Jagger's looks: a thin body, full lips, and wild clothes.
Gender Association: Used for boys
Popularity and Trend: Never been ranked in Top 1000
Risk of Misspelling: Fairly low
Risk of Mispronunciation: Fairly low
Famous Namesakes: Singer Mick Jagger
Common Nicknames: None
Common Variations: None
Consider This: This name's image is associated with Mick Jagger's, and probably will be for some time.

Jake ★★★★

(Hebrew) a short form of Jacob.
First Impression: Jake is viewed by most as a fun, popular, and strong-villed guy.
Gender Association: Used for boys
Popularity and Trend: #107 (#96 in 2000)
Risk of Misspelling: Low
Risk of Mispronunciation: Low
Famous Namesakes: Actor Jake Gyllenhaal; football player Jake Plummer; football player Jake Delhomme; baseball player Jake Peavy
Common Nicknames: None
Common Variations: None

Consider This: Like Jack, this name is short but solid.

Jamal ★★★

(Arabic) handsome.
First Impression: Jamal is thought to be an African American athlete who's extroverted and popular, but he can also have an attitude.
Gender Association: Used for boys
Popularity and Trend: #504 (#366 in 2000)
Risk of Misspelling: Fairly low
Risk of Mispronunciation: Fairly low
Famous Namesakes: Football player Jamal Lewis; basketball player Jamal Mashburn
Common Nicknames: Jam
Common Variations: Jamaal
Consider This: Jamal is often viewed as an African American or Muslim name.

James ★★★★★

(Hebrew) supplanter, substitute. (English) a form of Jacob.
First Impression: James is pictured as a warmhearted and approachable brown-haired man who's studious and respectful.
Gender Association: Used mostly for boys
Popularity and Trend: #16 (#18 in 2000)
Risk of Misspelling: Low
Risk of Mispronunciation: Low
Famous Namesakes: Biblical figure James; actor James Woods; actor

James Earl Jones; singer James Taylor; film and book character James Bond

Common Nicknames: Jaime, Jay, Jem, Jim

Common Variations: Seamus

Consider This: Classic James earns its 5-star rating: It's versatile and popular, and it conveys a solid image.

Jamie ★★

(English) a familiar form of James.

First Impression: Jamie is thought to have an ugly face and an ugly personality to match.

Gender Association: Used for boys

Popularity and Trend: #583 (#501 in 2000)

Risk of Misspelling: Fairly low

Risk of Mispronunciation: Low

Famous Namesakes: Actor Jamie Foxx; comedian Jamie Kennedy; chef Jamie Oliver; poker player Jamie Gold

Common Nicknames: None

Common Variations: Jaime

Consider This: For such a friendly sounding alternative to James, Jamie has a surprisingly unpleasant image.

Jamison ★★★★

(English) son of James.

First Impression: People think Jamison is an honest and well-educated romantic who writes thoughtful poems and songs.

Gender Association: Used mostly for boys

Popularity and Trend: #534 (#629 in 2000)

Risk of Misspelling: Average

Risk of Mispronunciation: Fairly low

Famous Namesakes: Basketball player Antawn Jamison

Common Nicknames: Jamie

Common Variations: Jameson, Jamieson

Consider This: If you want an alternative to James, Jamison seems to be a preferred choice. Spelling may be a problem, though, because "Jameson" is more popular.

Jan ★

(Dutch, Slavic) a form of John.

First Impression: Some think Jan is loud and talkative, but to others, he's quiet and shy.

Gender Association: Used mostly for boys

Popularity and Trend: #751 (#835 in 2000)

Risk of Misspelling: Average

Risk of Mispronunciation: Fairly high

Famous Namesakes: Composer Jan Hammer; artist Jan Vermeer; football player Jan Stenerud

Common Nicknames: None

Common Variations: None

Consider This: Pronounced "YAHN," this name has pronunciation and spelling problems. Pronounced "jan," it has gender association problems. Either way, Jan won't attract many parents.

Jared ★★★

(Hebrew) a form of Jordan.

First Impression: Jared is pictured as a thin, tall, and dark-haired kid who can't harness his intelligence.

Gender Association: Used for boys

Popularity and Trend: #137 (#56 in 2000)

Risk of Misspelling: Average

Risk of Mispronunciation: Low

Famous Namesakes: Subway spokesperson Jared Fogel; actor Jared Leto; basketball player Jared Jeffries

Common Nicknames: None

Common Variations: Jarad, Jarrod

Consider This: Jared has several common variations affecting spelling—and a poor image doesn't mitigate that problem.

Jarl ★★

(Scandinavian) earl, nobleman.

First Impression: People agree Jarl is a burly, scruffy, and rugged country boy.

Gender Association: Used for boys

Popularity and Trend: Never been ranked in Top 1000

Risk of Misspelling: Fairly high

Risk of Mispronunciation: Fairly high

Famous Namesakes: None

Common Nicknames: None

Common Variations: None

Consider This: Because it's one letter different from the classic name Carl, Jarl may be considered a mistake too often. Pronunciation is also a problem, with few people realizing it's pronounced "yarl."

Jason ★★★★★

(Greek) healer.

First Impression: Jason has everything going for him: He's described as handsome, popular, caring, funny, bright, and confident.

Gender Association: Used for boys

Popularity and Trend: #55 (#39 in 2000)

Risk of Misspelling: Fairly low

Risk of Mispronunciation: Low

Famous Namesakes: Actor Jason Priestly; basketball player Jason Kidd; baseball player Jason Giambi; singer Jason Mraz; actor Jason Alexander

Common Nicknames: Jase, Jay

Common Variations: Jayson, Jaysen

Consider This: This classic name was a huge hit a generation ago, and it still stands the test of time.

Jasper ★★★★

(French) brown, red, or yellow ornamental stone. (English) a form of Casper.

First Impression: Jasper is considered personable, goofy, extraordinarily gifted, and downright odd.

Gender Association: Used mostly for boys

Popularity and Trend: #568 (#592 in 2000)

Risk of Misspelling: Low

Risk of Mispronunciation: Low

Famous Namesakes: Character Jasper Beardley (*The Simpsons*); artist Jasper Johns; author Jasper Fforde

Common Nicknames: None

Common Variations: None

Consider This: A quirky image and rising popularity may soon put Jasper on the map.

Javier ★★

(Spanish) owner of a new house.

First Impression: People view Javier as a Latino fellow who's headstrong, macho, and fun-loving.

Gender Association: Used for boys

Popularity and Trend: #162 (#155 in 2000)

Risk of Misspelling: Fairly high

Risk of Mispronunciation: Fairly high

Famous Namesakes: Baseball player Javier Vázquez; actor Javier Bardem; baseball player Javier Valentín

Common Nicknames: None

Common Variations: Javiero

Consider This: Distinctly ethnic, Javier may fit only with last names of Latino origin. Also, pronunciation can be a problem for those who don't realize it's "hah-vee-AIR."

Jay ★★★★

(French) blue jay. (English) a form of James, Jason.

First Impression: Most people think Jay is a nice guy, but a few disagree.

Gender Association: Used for boys

Popularity and Trend: #351 (#328 in 2000)

Risk of Misspelling: Low

Risk of Mispronunciation: Low

Famous Namesakes: Talk show host Jay Leno; actor Jay Mohr; actor Jay Hernandez; rapper Jay-Z; character Jay (*Jay and Silent Bob Strike Back*)

Common Nicknames: None

Common Variations: Jae, Jaye

Consider This: This short name seems like a fairly solid choice, but it may be best used as a nickname for any *J* name.

Jayden ★★★★

(Hebrew) a form of Jadon. (American) a form of Jayde.

First Impression: Folks think Jayden is a popular, confident, and spunky guy to whom girls flock.

Gender Association: Used mostly for boys

Popularity and Trend: #50 (#194 in 2000)

Risk of Misspelling: Average

Risk of Mispronunciation: Fairly low

Famous Namesakes: Star kid Jayden James Federline

Common Nicknames: Jay

Common Variations: Jadon, Jaden

Consider This: Spelling will be confounded by the variation Jaden, but Jayden is easier to pronounce.

Jed ★★★

(Hebrew) a form of Jedidiah. (Arabic) hand.

First Impression: Most people say Jed is a hillbilly who does things in his own scatterbrained way.

Gender Association: Used for boys

Popularity and Trend: Last ranked in the Top 1000 in the 1980s

Risk of Misspelling: Low

Risk of Mispronunciation: Low

Famous Namesakes: Character Jed Bartlet (*West Wing*); character Jed Clampett (*The Beverly Hillbillies*)

Common Nicknames: None

Common Variations: None

Consider This: This name sounds strong, but thanks to Jed Clampett, people seem to closely connect it to hillbillies.

Jedidiah ★★

(Hebrew) friend of God, beloved of God.

First Impression: People say Jedidiah is a strict, withdrawn, and deeply religious old man who shies away from society.

Gender Association: Used for boys

Popularity and Trend: Last ranked in the Top 1000 in the 1990s

Risk of Misspelling: Average

Risk of Mispronunciation: Average

Famous Namesakes: Alternate name for biblical figure King Solomon; explorer Jedidiah Smith

Common Nicknames: Jed

Common Variations: Jebediah

Consider This: Because this name is such a mouthful ("jed-ah-DYE-ah"), consider pairing it with its nickname, Jed.

Jeff ★★★★

(English) a short form of Jefferson, Jeffrey.

First Impression: People think Jeff is mischievous, funny, and always original.

Gender Association: Used for boys

Popularity and Trend: Last ranked #929 in 2000

Risk of Misspelling: Fairly low

Risk of Mispronunciation: Low

Famous Namesakes: Actor Jeff Bridges; racecar driver Jeff Gordon; comedian Jeff Foxworthy; actor Jeff Goldblum; rapper DJ Jazzy Jeff

Common Nicknames: None

Common Variations: Geoff

Consider This: A classic nickname, Jeff is best used as a short form of Jefferson or Jeffrey.

Jefferson ★★★★

(English) son of Jeff.

First Impression: People believe Jefferson is an intellectual and logical African American, but they aren't sure whether he's slick talking and womanizing or straight-laced and stuffy.

Gender Association: Used for boys

Popularity and Trend: #642 (#716 in 2000)

Risk of Misspelling: Low

Risk of Mispronunciation: Low

Famous Namesakes: President Thomas Jefferson; Confederate president Jefferson Davis; character George Jefferson (*The Jeffersons*)

Common Nicknames: Jeff

Common Variations: None

Consider This: Jefferson has the versatility that Jeff lacks, but it also has an ambiguous image.

Jeffrey ★★★

(English) divinely peaceful.

First Impression: Most think of Jeffrey as a congenial and honest man, but others imagine him as a self-centered and bratty liar.

Gender Association: Used for boys

Popularity and Trend: #180 (#104 in 2000)

Risk of Misspelling: Average

Risk of Mispronunciation: Fairly low

Famous Namesakes: Actor Jeffrey Tambor

Common Nicknames: Jeff

Common Variations: Geoffrey, Jefferey, Jeffry

Consider This: Jeffrey has the versatility and popularity that Jeff lacks, but it lacks a strong positive image. Spelling may be in question, too, because there are many variations.

Jeremiah ★★★★

(Hebrew) God will uplift.

First Impression: Jeremiah creates the image of a lanky and loving egghead.

Gender Association: Used for boys

Popularity and Trend: #71 (#103 in 2000)

Risk of Misspelling: Fairly low

Risk of Mispronunciation: Fairly low

Famous Namesakes: Film character Jeremiah Johnson; biblical figure Jeremiah

Common Nicknames: Jem

Common Variations: Jermiah

Consider This: This traditional name is quickly gaining popularity. Most people will know to pronounce it "jer-ah-MY-ah."

Jeremy ★★★

(English) a form of Jeremiah.

First Impression: Many see Jeremy as a popular and charming guy who's honest and sweet. Others think he's quick-tempered and cruel.

Gender Association: Used for boys

Popularity and Trend: #123 (#84 in 2000)

Risk of Misspelling: Fairly low

Risk of Mispronunciation: Fairly low

Famous Namesakes: Actor Jeremy Irons; actor Jeremy Piven; football player Jeremy Shockey; supercross racer Jeremy McGrath

Common Nicknames: None

Common Variations: None

Consider This: Although Jeremy is still quite popular, Jeremiah seems to be the preferred choice for parents. Also, Jeremy has a minor pronunciation problem with some saying "JER-ah-mee" and others saying "JER-mee."

Jeriah ★★★

(Hebrew) Jehovah has seen.

First Impression: People believe Jeriah is a caring, happy, and considerate man who's good at listening and big on smiling.

Gender Association: Used for boys

Popularity and Trend: Never been ranked in Top 1000

Risk of Misspelling: Average

Risk of Mispronunciation: Average

Famous Namesakes: Biblical figure Jeriah

Common Nicknames: None

Common Variations: None

Consider This: This biblical name appears to be too unique for most parents to handle. Pronunciation ("jer-EYE-ah") and spelling may be unclear to some.

Jermaine ★★★

(French) a form of Germain. (English) sprout, bud.

First Impression: Folks agree that Jermaine is handsome, friendly, and intelligent.

Gender Association: Used mostly for boys

Popularity and Trend: #474 (#444 in 2000)

Risk of Misspelling: Fairly low

Risk of Mispronunciation: Low

Famous Namesakes: Singer Jermaine Jackson; boxer Jermain Taylor; singer Jermaine Dupri; basketball player Jermaine O'Neal

Common Nicknames: None

Common Variations: Jermain

Consider This: With its pleasant image and middling popularity, Jermaine may be a decent choice.

Jerome ★★★

(Latin) holy.

First Impression: People can't agree on whether Jerome is loud and flirty or quiet and gentle.

Gender Association: Used for boys

Popularity and Trend: #577 (#495 in 2000)

Risk of Misspelling: Fairly low

Risk of Mispronunciation: Fairly low

Famous Namesakes: Football player Jerome Bettis

Common Nicknames: Jerry

Common Variations: Gerome

Consider This: Jerome is less appealing than Jeremiah or Jeremy.

Jerry ★★

(German) mighty spearman. (English) a familiar form of Jerald, Jerard.

First Impression: Jerry is imagined to be an annoying, gossipy pest who's cloddish and homely.
Gender Association: Used for boys
Popularity and Trend: #318 (#264 in 2000)
Risk of Misspelling: Fairly low
Risk of Mispronunciation: Low
Famous Namesakes: Comedian Jerry Lewis; comedian Jerry Seinfeld; singer Jerry Garcia; football player Jerry Rice; talk show host Jerry Springer
Common Nicknames: None
Common Variations: Gerry
Consider This: It's a bit surprising that this common nickname doesn't have a better first impression.

Jesse ★★★★
(Hebrew) wealthy.
First Impression: People find Jesse to be energetic, fun, and daring—although he's smart enough to exercise caution when necessary.
Gender Association: Used mostly for boys
Popularity and Trend: #102 (#90 in 2000)
Risk of Misspelling: Average
Risk of Mispronunciation: Low
Famous Namesakes: Activist Jesse Jackson; outlaw Jesse James; athlete Jesse Owens; governor and wrestler Jesse Ventura
Common Nicknames: Jess

Common Variations: Jessy, Jessie
Consider This: A strong image makes Jesse a strong candidate. However, its pronunciation is the same as Jessie, a name often used for girls, which may cause gender confusion.

Jesus ★★★★
(Hebrew) a form of Joshua.
First Impression: Most can't separate this name from Jesus Christ: They say Jesus is a forgiving, gentle, and holy bearded man who sacrifices himself. Many also say he's likely Latino.
Gender Association: Used mostly for boys
Popularity and Trend: #74 (#76 in 2000)
Risk of Misspelling: Low
Risk of Mispronunciation: Average
Famous Namesakes: Biblical figure Jesus Christ; baseball player Jesús Alou; band Jesus Jones
Common Nicknames: None
Common Variations: Jésus
Consider This: Latino families often use the name Jesus (pronounced "HAY-zoos"), but other cultures seem to avoid it.

Jibril ★★
(Arabic) archangel of Allah.
First Impression: People aren't sure if Jibril is loud and glad to be the center of attention, or if he's quiet and glad to be a loner.

Gender Association: Used for boys
Popularity and Trend: Never been ranked in Top 1000
Risk of Misspelling: Fairly high
Risk of Mispronunciation: Fairly high
Famous Namesakes: Islamic archangel Jibril
Common Nicknames: None
Common Variations: Jabril
Consider This: An ambiguous image and foreign feel may make this unique name too unappealing.

Jim ★★
(Hebrew, English) a short form of James.
First Impression: Jim is imagined to be an unhappy and harsh man who doesn't speak much.
Gender Association: Used for boys
Popularity and Trend: Last ranked in the Top 1000 in the 1990s
Risk of Misspelling: Low
Risk of Mispronunciation: Low
Famous Namesakes: Actor Jim Carrey; actor Jim Belushi; football player Jim Kelly; singer Jim Morrison
Common Nicknames: Jimbo, Jimmy
Common Variations: None
Consider This: Not as popular as Jimmy or James, Jim's unpleasant image could be a limitation.

Jimmy ★★★
(English) a familiar form of Jim, James.

First Impression: For some, Jimmy is a kind but timid fellow. Others imagine he's a wild, goofy, and fun-loving guy who's up for anything.
Gender Association: Used for boys
Popularity and Trend: #325 (#272 in 2000)
Risk of Misspelling: Fairly low
Risk of Mispronunciation: Low
Famous Namesakes: Actor Jimmy Smits; football coach Jimmy Johnson; actor Jimmy Stewart; singer Jimmy Buffett; president Jimmy Carter
Common Nicknames: None
Common Variations: Jimi
Consider This: Jimmy, a traditional nickname, may be too informal as a given name.

Jock ★★

(American) a familiar form of Jacob.
First Impression: When most people hear the name Jock, they understandably think of a husky athlete with big muscles.
Gender Association: Used for boys
Popularity and Trend: Never been ranked in Top 1000
Risk of Misspelling: Low
Risk of Mispronunciation: Low
Famous Namesakes: None
Common Nicknames: None
Common Variations: None

Consider This: Too often used as slang for an athlete, Jock may not be taken seriously as a given name.

Joe ★★★★

(Hebrew) a short form of Joseph.
First Impression: People imagine Joe as kindhearted, fun, and lovable—which, coupled with his handsome good looks, makes him popular with girls.
Gender Association: Used for boys
Popularity and Trend: #370 (#315 in 2000)
Risk of Misspelling: Fairly low
Risk of Mispronunciation: Low
Famous Namesakes: Football player Joe Namath; football player Joe Montana; baseball player Joe DiMaggio; singer Joe Cocker; actor Joe Pesci
Common Nicknames: Joey
Common Variations: Jo
Consider This: For such a common name, Joe has an uncommonly good image

Joel ★★★★★

(Hebrew) God is willing.
First Impression: This name reminds people of a caring, loyal man who makes his own decisions and never takes the easy way out.
Gender Association: Used for boys
Popularity and Trend: #124 (#112 in 2000)
Risk of Misspelling: Low
Risk of Mispronunciation: Low

Famous Namesakes: Biblical figure Joel; singer Joel Madden; singer Billy Joel; director Joel Schumacher
Common Nicknames: None
Common Variations: None
Consider This: Although Joel's popularity has fallen slightly, its solid image makes it a contender.

Joey ★★★

(Hebrew) a familiar form of Joe, Joseph.
First Impression: Joey evokes an image of a dark-featured, handsome man who's fun-loving, bright, and sweet.
Gender Association: Used mostly for boys
Popularity and Trend: #537 (#488 in 2000)
Risk of Misspelling: Low
Risk of Mispronunciation: Low
Famous Namesakes: Singer Joey Ramone; actor Joey Bishop; character Joey Tribbiani (Friends); football player Joey Harrington
Common Nicknames: None
Common Variations: None
Consider This: Joey has a positive image, but its informality suggests that versatile Joseph may be a better option.

Johann ★★★

(German) a form of John.
First Impression: Johann is said to be a gentlemanly and traditional man

who may very well be a genius, especially when it comes to music.
Gender Association: Used for boys
Popularity and Trend: Never been ranked in Top 1000
Risk of Misspelling: Fairly high
Risk of Mispronunciation: Fairly high
Famous Namesakes: Composer Johann Strauss; composer Johann Sebastian Bach; baseball player Johan Santana
Common Nicknames: Anno, Hanno
Common Variations: Johan, Johannes
Consider This: Although it's never been ranked, this traditional, ethnic name may appeal to families of German or Scandinavian heritage. Anyone outside the culture may not realize it's pronounced "YOH-hahn."

John ★★★★

(Hebrew) God is gracious.
First Impression: John is described as a levelheaded and hardworking all-American guy.
Gender Association: Used for boys
Popularity and Trend: #20 (#14 in 2000)
Risk of Misspelling: Fairly low
Risk of Mispronunciation: Low
Famous Namesakes: Biblical figure John the Baptist; president John F. Kennedy; actor John Wayne; singer John Lennon; presidents John Adams and John Quincy Adams

Common Nicknames: Johnny
Common Variations: Jon, Hans, Sean, Juan, Jack
Consider This: This classic 5-star name has a solid image and is a lot more versatile than you might imagine.

Johnny ★★★

(Hebrew) a familiar form of John.
First Impression: People think Johnny is a fun-loving partier who can be too irresponsible and immature.
Gender Association: Used for boys
Popularity and Trend: #237 (#234 in 2000)
Risk of Misspelling: Fairly low
Risk of Mispronunciation: Low
Famous Namesakes: Singer Johnny Cash; actor Johnny Depp; lawyer Johnny Cochrane; talk show host Johnny Carson; baseball player Johnny Damon
Common Nicknames: None
Common Variations: Johnie, Jonny
Consider This: Johnny's informality may prevent you from choosing it as a given name, but it makes a great nickname.

Jonah ★★★★

(Hebrew) dove.
First Impression: Jonah is considered a compassionate and perceptive churchgoer who's quiet and polite.
Gender Association: Used for boys

Popularity and Trend: #170 (#192 in 2000)
Risk of Misspelling: Low
Risk of Mispronunciation: Low
Famous Namesakes: Biblical figure Jonah
Common Nicknames: None
Common Variations: None
Consider This: Biblical names are gaining in popularity, and Jonah is no exception.

Jonas ★★★★

(Hebrew) he accomplishes. (Lithuanian) a form of John.
First Impression: Jonas is described as a religious minister or youth counselor with exceptional interpersonal skills.
Gender Association: Used for boys
Popularity and Trend: #357 (#526 in 2000)
Risk of Misspelling: Low
Risk of Mispronunciation: Low
Famous Namesakes: Researcher Jonas Salk
Common Nicknames: None
Common Variations: None
Consider This: Like Jonah, this traditional name creates a religious impression, though this name is a bit more uncommon.

Jonathan ★★★★

(Hebrew) gift of God.
First Impression: People imagine Jonathan as a considerate and clever jock with a great smile.

Gender Association: Used mostly
 for boys

Popularity and Trend: #22
 (#21 in 2000)

Risk of Misspelling: Fairly low

Risk of Mispronunciation: Low

Famous Namesakes: Author Jonathan
 Swift; actor Jonathan Winters;
 actor Jonathan Taylor Thomas;
 book character Jonathan
 Livingston Seagull

Common Nicknames: Jon, Jonny

Common Variations: Johnathan,
 Jonathen

Consider This: Jonathan is an example
 of a strong, stable name.

Jordan ★★★★

(Hebrew) descending.

First Impression: Folks think Jordan
 may seem carefree because of
 his cool, playful personality and
 good sense of humor. But they
 soon realize he's wise, sensitive,
 and kind.

Gender Association: Used mostly
 for boys

Popularity and Trend: #46
 (#36 in 2000)

Risk of Misspelling: Fairly low

Risk of Mispronunciation: Low

Famous Namesakes: Basketball player
 Michael Jordan; singer Jordan
 Knight

Common Nicknames: Jordy

Common Variations: Jorden, Jordon

Consider This: This popular name has
 a lot going for it, but its ambiguous gender association may deter
 some parents from choosing it.

Jorge ★★★

(Spanish) a form of George.

First Impression: Jorge is seen as a
 loving family man who's Latino
 with dark hair and eyes.

Gender Association: Used for boys

Popularity and Trend: #120
 (#107 in 2000)

Risk of Misspelling: Fairly high

Risk of Mispronunciation: Fairly high

Famous Namesakes: Author Jorge
 Luis Borges; baseball player
 Jorge Posada; actor Jorge Garcia

Common Nicknames: None

Common Variations: George

Consider This: This name's unique
 pronunciation ("HORE-hay")
 may be a challenge to those not
 of Latino heritage.

Jose ★★★★

(Spanish) a form of Joseph.

First Impression: Jose is described as a
 Latino man who's lighthearted,
 happy, and fun to be around.

Gender Association: Used mostly
 for boys

Popularity and Trend: #32
 (#34 in 2000)

Risk of Misspelling: Average

Risk of Mispronunciation: Average

Famous Namesakes: Singer José
 Feliciano; singer José Carreras;

baseball player José Canseco;
 baseball player José Vizcaíno

Common Nicknames: Che, Pepe

Common Variations: José

Consider This: Jose's positive image
 makes it a perfect choice for
 Latino families.

Joseph ★★★★★

(Hebrew) God will add, God will
 increase.

First Impression: People picture
 Joseph as a dependable, honest,
 and hardworking man.

Gender Association: Used mostly
 for boys

Popularity and Trend: #11
 (#8 in 2000)

Risk of Misspelling: Fairly low

Risk of Mispronunciation: Low

Famous Namesakes: Biblical figure
 Joseph; religious leader Joseph
 Smith; actor Joseph Fiennes; Nez
 Perce leader Chief Joseph; Soviet
 leader Joseph Stalin

Common Nicknames: Joey, Jody, Joe

Common Variations: Josef

Consider This: A classic name, Joseph
 is a solid, versatile choice.

Josh ★★★★

(Hebrew) a short form of Joshua.

First Impression: People say Josh is a
 gorgeous guy who's outgoing,
 cool, and always fun.

Gender Association: Used for boys

Popularity and Trend: #714
 (#821 in 2000)

Risk of Misspelling: Low
Risk of Mispronunciation: Low
Famous Namesakes: Actor Josh Hartnett; actor Josh Duhamel; actor Josh Brolin; singer Josh Groban; actor Josh Lucas
Common Nicknames: None
Common Variations: None
Consider This: If you name your son Josh, people will likely assume his "real" name is Joshua.

Joshua ★★★★★
(Hebrew) God is my salvation.
First Impression: Joshua is depicted as a patient, soft-spoken man who loves to help others.
Gender Association: Used mostly for boys
Popularity and Trend: #3 (#4 in 2000)
Risk of Misspelling: Low
Risk of Mispronunciation: Low
Famous Namesakes: Biblical figure Joshua; actor Joshua Jackson
Common Nicknames: Josh
Common Variations: None
Consider This: Joshua may be "too popular," but it has a caring image plus a light-hearted nickname.

Josiah ★★★★
(Hebrew) fire of the Lord.
First Impression: People imagine Josiah as a God-fearing, caring, and patient man.
Gender Association: Used for boys

Popularity and Trend: #117 (#181 in 2000)
Risk of Misspelling: Fairly low
Risk of Mispronunciation: Fairly low
Famous Namesakes: Biblical figure Josiah
Common Nicknames: None
Common Variations: Josias
Consider This: Like many biblical names, Josiah is rising fast on the popularity charts. Most people will realize it's pronounced "joh-SYE-ah."

Juan ★★★
(Spanish) a form of John.
First Impression: Juan is regarded as a smooth-talking Latino that some people say is sweet and loving and other people see as a womanizer.
Gender Association: Used for boys
Popularity and Trend: #61 (#48 in 2000)
Risk of Misspelling: Average
Risk of Mispronunciation: Average
Famous Namesakes: Singer Juan Gabriel; Spanish king Juan Carlos; racecar driver Juan Pablo Montoya; legendary character Don Juan; baseball player Juan González
Common Nicknames: None
Common Variations: None
Consider This: Juan is a Top 100 name, but it may not fit with surnames that aren't of Spanish or Latino origin. Most people will know to pronounce it "wahn."

Judd ★★★
(Hebrew) a form of Judah.
First Impression: People may think Judd is a slow, gullible hillbilly, but he's friendly and he puts others first.
Gender Association: Used for boys
Popularity and Trend: Last ranked in the Top 1000 in the 1980s
Risk of Misspelling: Fairly low
Risk of Mispronunciation: Low
Famous Namesakes: Actor Judd Nelson; actor Judd Hirsch
Common Nicknames: None
Common Variations: Jud
Consider This: With a hillbilly image, Judd may be a dud for urban parents.

Jude ★★★★★
(Latin) a form of Judah, Judas.
First Impression: Jude is pictured as an introspective and introverted man with a creative flair for music and art.
Gender Association: Used for boys
Popularity and Trend: #330 (#679 in 2000)
Risk of Misspelling: Low
Risk of Mispronunciation: Low
Famous Namesakes: Biblical figure Jude; actor Jude Law; song "Hey Jude"; character Jude Fawley (*Jude the Obscure*)
Common Nicknames: None
Common Variations: Judah

Consider This: Jude's great image and rising popularity may land it on your short list.

Jules ★★★

(French) a form of Julius.

First Impression: Some people see Jules as bubbly and friendly, but others see him as articulate and reserved.

Gender Association: Used for boys

Popularity and Trend: Last ranked in the Top 1000 in the 1950s

Risk of Misspelling: Fairly low

Risk of Mispronunciation: Fairly low

Famous Namesakes: Author Jules Verne; character Jules Winnfield (*Pulp Fiction*)

Common Nicknames: None

Common Variations: None

Consider This: It's been a long time since this friendly name was popular.

Julian ★★★

(Greek, Latin) a form of Julius.

First Impression: People think Julian is a charismatic, classy, and clever aristocrat who at times can be self-absorbed.

Gender Association: Used mostly for boys

Popularity and Trend: #65 (#87 in 2000)

Risk of Misspelling: Fairly low

Risk of Mispronunciation: Fairly low

Famous Namesakes: Singer Julian Lennon; actor Julian McMahon; musician Julian Marley

Common Nicknames: None

Common Variations: Julien

Consider This: This charming name is gaining popularity. There could be a minor gender association problem, however, because Julian is sometimes used as a variation of the girls' name Julianne.

Julio ★★

(Hispanic) a form of Julius.

First Impression: Julio is regarded as a dark and handsome flirt.

Gender Association: Used for boys

Popularity and Trend: #240 (#256 in 2000)

Risk of Misspelling: Fairly high

Risk of Mispronunciation: Fairly high

Famous Namesakes: Singer Julio Iglesias; winemaker Julio Gallo; boxer Julio César Chávez; baseball player Julio Franco

Common Nicknames: None

Common Variations: Julius

Consider This: This ethnic name has its charm, although it may not fit well with surnames not of Latino or Spanish origin. Those not familiar with Latino names may not know to pronounce it "HOO-lee-oh."

Julius ★★★

(Greek, Latin) youthful, downy bearded.

First Impression: Julius is described as an individualistic, jovial, conceited rich boy who loves a glass of wine—or three.

Gender Association: Used for boys

Popularity and Trend: #319 (#483 in 2000)

Risk of Misspelling: Fairly low

Risk of Mispronunciation: Fairly low

Famous Namesakes: Emperor Julius Caesar; basketball player Julius "Dr. J" Irving; character Dr. Julius Hibbert (*The Simpsons*)

Common Nicknames: None

Common Variations: Jules

Consider This: Julius's popularity is climbing despite its over-the-top image.

Justin ★★★★

(Latin) just, righteous.

First Impression: Justin strikes people as sweet, personable, and handsome.

Gender Association: Used mostly for boys

Popularity and Trend: #45 (#19 in 2000)

Risk of Misspelling: Fairly low

Risk of Mispronunciation: Low

Famous Namesakes: Singer Justin Timberlake; singer Justin Guarini; actor Justin Long; baseball player Justin Morneau

Common Nicknames: None

Common Variations: Justan, Justino

Consider This: Justin's solid image will likely continue to bolster it even as its popularity declines.

Kadar ★★
(Arabic) powerful.

First Impression: Kadar is seen as a brilliant but quiet intellectual who's logical, serious, and humorless.

Gender Association: Used for boys

Popularity and Trend: Never been ranked in Top 1000

Risk of Misspelling: Average

Risk of Mispronunciation: Fairly high

Famous Namesakes: Hungarian prime minister János Kádár

Common Nicknames: None

Common Variations: None

Consider This: Kadar's spelling and pronunciation ("KAH-dur") may be tricky for some.

Kale ★★★
(Arabic) a form of Kahlil. (Hawaiian) a form of Carl.

First Impression: Kale is pictured as an islander who loves the water, beach, and big waves.

Gender Association: Used for boys

Popularity and Trend: #766 (#987 in 2000)

Risk of Misspelling: Average

Risk of Mispronunciation: Average

Famous Namesakes: Kasey Kahne's brother Kale Kahne

Common Nicknames: None

Common Variations: Kalen, Kayle

Consider This: A fairly unusual name with a cool image, Kale is attracting more and more parents. Many will pronounce it phonetically as "cayle," but the Hawaiian pronunciation is "KAY-lay."

Kane ★
(Welsh) beautiful. (Irish) tribute. (Japanese) golden. (Hawaiian) eastern sky. (English) a form of Keene.

First Impression: Kane strikes people as a smart and hardworking businessman.

Gender Association: Used mostly for boys

Popularity and Trend: #701 (#594 in 2000)

Risk of Misspelling: Average

Risk of Mispronunciation: Average

Famous Namesakes: Character Charles Foster Kane (*Citizen Kane*); wrestler Kane

Common Nicknames: None

Common Variations: Kain, Cain

Consider This: More common as a surname, Kane doesn't score well as a given name. Like Kale, its Hawaiian pronunciation ("KAH-nay") is quite different than its phonetic pronunciation ("kayn").

Kareem ★★
(Arabic) noble; distinguished.

First Impression: Most people describe Kareem as a lanky, African American basketball player who's fun to be around.

Gender Association: Used for boys

Popularity and Trend: #713 (#619 in 2000)

Risk of Misspelling: Average

Risk of Mispronunciation: Fairly low

Famous Namesakes: Basketball player Kareem Abdul-Jabbar; skater Kareem Campbell

Common Nicknames: None

Common Variations: Karim

Consider This: Basketball legend Kareem Abdul-Jabbar seems to cast his long shadow on this name's image. Basketball fans and families of Arabic descent may consider it.

Karl ★★
(German) a form of Carl.

First Impression: People say Karl is a gangly geek whose intelligence and formal manners make him an outsider.

Gender Association: Used for boys

Popularity and Trend: #769 (#564 in 2000)

Risk of Misspelling: Average

Risk of Mispronunciation: Low

Famous Namesakes: Philosopher Karl Marx; basketball player Karl Malone; political advisor Karl Rove; actor Karl Urban

Common Nicknames: None

Common Variations: Carl

Consider This: A geeky image and possible spelling problems limit Karl's popularity.

Keaton ★★★

(English) where hawks fly.

First Impression: Keaton is pictured as neat, clean, and conservatively dressed.

Gender Association: Used mostly for boys

Popularity and Trend: #382 (#353 in 2000)

Risk of Misspelling: Fairly low

Risk of Mispronunciation: Fairly low

Famous Namesakes: Actor Buster Keaton; actor Michael Keaton; the Keaton family (*Family Ties*)

Common Nicknames: None

Common Variations: Keyton

Consider This: A familiar surname, Keaton may be squeaky-clean enough for some parents to consider it as a given name.

Keelan ★★★

(Irish) little; slender. A form of Kellen.

First Impression: People think Keelan is smart and studious, but the rest of his personality is a mystery.

Gender Association: Used for boys

Popularity and Trend: Never been ranked in Top 1000

Risk of Misspelling: Average

Risk of Mispronunciation: Low

Famous Namesakes: None

Common Nicknames: None

Common Variations: Keilan, Kelan

Consider This: This unique name has yet to be ranked, and people seem unsure of its first impression. It's easy to pronounce, but spelling could be a bit tricky with so many variations.

Keenan ★★★

(Irish) little Keene.

First Impression: People imagine Keenan as an outgoing, polite, and funny African American with a nice smile.

Gender Association: Used for boys

Popularity and Trend: #607 (#532 in 2000)

Risk of Misspelling: Average

Risk of Mispronunciation: Low

Famous Namesakes: Actor Keenen Ivory Wayans; actor Kenan Thompson; football player Keenan McCardell; singer Maynard James Keenan

Common Nicknames: None

Common Variations: Keenen, Keanan, Keynan, Kienan

Consider This: This name's image owes a lot to comedian Keenen Ivory Wayans. Like Keelan, it's easy to pronounce but harder to spell because of its variations.

Keene ★★★

(German) bold; sharp. (English) smart.

First Impression: Folks say Keene could be a hardworking business-man or a nerdy teacher's pet.

Gender Association: Used for boys

Popularity and Trend: Never been ranked in Top 1000

Risk of Misspelling: Average

Risk of Mispronunciation: Low

Famous Namesakes: Band Keane

Common Nicknames: None

Common Variations: Keane, Kane, Kean

Consider This: A lukewarm image and possible spelling problems limit the appeal of this name.

Keith ★★★★

(Welsh) forest. (Scottish) battle place.

First Impression: Keith makes people think of a reliable, caring, and spirited fellow with a fun sense of humor.

Gender Association: Used for boys

Popularity and Trend: #277 (#222 in 2000)

Risk of Misspelling: Low

Risk of Mispronunciation: Low

Famous Namesakes: Musician Keith Richards; musician Keith Moon; sportscaster Keith Jackson; singer Keith Urban; TV personality Keith Olbermann

Common Nicknames: None

Common Variations: None

Consider This: Keith's popularity may have sagged, but this classic name nevertheless still seems a solid choice.

Kellan ★★★★

(Irish) a form of Kellen.

First Impression: Kellan is said to be an all-around great person who's loving, helpful, friendly, and smart.

Gender Association: Used mostly for boys

Popularity and Trend: Never been ranked in Top 1000

Risk of Misspelling: Average

Risk of Mispronunciation: Low

Famous Namesakes: Actor Kellan Lutz; football players Kellen Winslow, Sr. and Kellen Winslow, Jr.

Common Nicknames: Kel

Common Variations: Kellen

Consider This: Kellan hasn't been ranked, but close variation Kellen—ranked #526 in 2006, up from #749 in the '90s—seems like the better choice. Because Kellan is less popular, it is more likely to be misspelled.

Kelly ★★★

(Irish) warrior.

First Impression: Kelly is seen to love life, and everyone loves Kelly. But he may be too upbeat for some people's tastes.

Gender Association: Used mostly for girls

Popularity and Trend: Last ranked #803 in 2000

Risk of Misspelling: Fairly low

Risk of Mispronunciation: Low

Famous Namesakes: Surfer Kelly Slater; actor Gene Kelly; gangster George "Machine Gun" Kelly; singer R. Kelly; Australian outlaw Ned Kelly

Common Nicknames: None

Common Variations: Kelley

Consider This: Kelly has a good image, but it's used more for girls than boys.

Kelsey ★

(Scandinavian) island of ships.

First Impression: Many people think of Kelsey as an unruly, hyper guy who's self-centered and untrustworthy.

Gender Association: Used mostly for girls

Popularity and Trend: Last ranked in the Top 1000 in the 1990s

Risk of Misspelling: Fairly low

Risk of Mispronunciation: Low

Famous Namesakes: Actor Kelsey Grammer

Common Nicknames: None

Common Variations: Kelcey

Consider This: Kelsey is used more girls than boys, and given its poor image, parents may avoid it altogether.

Kelvin ★★★★

(Irish, English) narrow river.

First Impression: People imagine Kelvin is generous, caring, and strong spirited.

Gender Association: Used for boys

Popularity and Trend: #434 (#389 in 2000)

Risk of Misspelling: Average

Risk of Mispronunciation: Low

Famous Namesakes: Scientist William Thomson, First Baron Kelvin

Common Nicknames: None

Common Variations: None

Consider This: This seemingly stuffy name has a surprisingly great image. Although there's a slight difference in pronunciation, it may be confused for Calvin.

Ken ★★★★

(Japanese) one's own kind. (Scottish) a form of Kendall, Kendrick, Kenneth.

First Impression: People picture Ken with sandy blond hair and a friendly, bubbly personality.

Gender Association: Used for boys

Popularity and Trend: Last ranked in the Top 1000 in the 1990s

Risk of Misspelling: Fairly low

Risk of Mispronunciation: Low

Famous Namesakes: Doll character Ken Carson; baseball player Ken Griffey, Jr.; *Jeopardy!* champion Ken Jennings; actor Ken Watanabe; producer Ken Burns

Common Nicknames: Kenny
Common Variations: Kenn
Consider This: Although this name isn't used often as a given name, Ken's warm image suggests it's an excellent nickname for Kendall and Kenneth.

Kendall ★★
(English) valley of the river Kent.
First Impression: People believe Kendall is feisty and spunky—perhaps even bossy.
Gender Association: Used mostly for girls
Popularity and Trend: #573 (#359 in 2000)
Risk of Misspelling: Average
Risk of Mispronunciation: Fairly low
Famous Namesakes: Basketball player Kendall Gill
Common Nicknames: Ken
Common Variations: Kendal, Kendel, Kendell
Consider This: Kendall has a feisty image, but it's also used more for girls than boys, a fact that may deter some parents. When it comes to spelling, some people may confuse this name with "Kendell."

Kenley ★★
(English) royal meadow.
First Impression: With his happy-go-lucky personality, Kenley is considered harmless, but he may be a sneaky thief.

Gender Association: Used about equally for girls and boys
Popularity and Trend: Never been ranked in Top 1000
Risk of Misspelling: Average
Risk of Mispronunciation: Low
Famous Namesakes: None
Common Nicknames: Ken
Common Variations: None
Consider This: This unusual name is used for as many girls as it is for boys.

Kenneth ★★★★★
(Irish) handsome. (English) royal oath.
First Impression: People say Kenneth is friendly, attentive, funny, smart, energetic, well-to-do, and even lucky.
Gender Association: Used for boys
Popularity and Trend: #128 (#94 in 2000)
Risk of Misspelling: Low
Risk of Mispronunciation: Low
Famous Namesakes: Actor Kenneth Branagh; lawyer Kenneth Starr; designer Kenneth Cole
Common Nicknames: Ken, Kenny
Common Variations: None
Consider This: Here's a strong, solid name with versatility and appeal.

Kenny ★★★
(Scottish) a familiar form of Kenneth.
First Impression: People picture Kenny as a geek who loves

schoolwork, especially his computer science classes.
Gender Association: Used for boys
Popularity and Trend: #498 (#431 in 2000)
Risk of Misspelling: Low
Risk of Mispronunciation: Low
Famous Namesakes: Sportscaster Kenny Mayne; singer Kenny Rogers; musician Kenny G; singer Kenny Loggins; singer Kenny Chesney
Common Nicknames: None
Common Variations: None
Consider This: Traditionally a nickname, Kenny may be informal, but it has a solid image.

Kent ★★★★
(Welsh) white; bright. (English) a form of Kenton.
First Impression: Kent is seen as a strong and in-charge community leader who's part of the country club set.
Gender Association: Used for boys
Popularity and Trend: Last ranked #772 in 2000
Risk of Misspelling: Low
Risk of Mispronunciation: Low
Famous Namesakes: Character Clark Kent (*Superman*); character Kent Brockman (*The Simpsons*); baseball player Jeff Kent; baseball player Kent Hrbek
Common Nicknames: None
Common Variations: Kenton

Consider This: Kent is a strong name with a strong image, though its popularity has slipped.

Kermit ★★★★

(Irish) a form of Dermot.

First Impression: Most people think Kermit is short and scrawny—but huggable.

Gender Association: Used for boys

Popularity and Trend: Last ranked in the Top 1000 in the 1970s

Risk of Misspelling: Low

Risk of Mispronunciation: Low

Famous Namesakes: Character Kermit the Frog (*Sesame Street* and *The Muppet Show*); basketball player Kermit Washington; Theodore Roosevelt's son Kermit Roosevelt

Common Nicknames: None

Common Variations: None

Consider This: Kermit the Frog is still the most famous Kermit out there, which may leave your child open to teasing.

Kerry ★★★

(Irish) dark; dark-haired.

First Impression: Kerry is viewed as a fun guy with a good head on his shoulders.

Gender Association: Used mostly for girls

Popularity and Trend: Last ranked in the Top 1000 in the 1990s

Risk of Misspelling: Fairly high

Risk of Mispronunciation: Low

Famous Namesakes: Senator John Kerry; football player Kerry Collins; baseball player Kerry Wood

Common Nicknames: None

Common Variations: Keary

Consider This: Despite its great image, Kerry has a few drawbacks: It's a name that's used more for girls than boys. Also, spelling will be difficult because people may confuse it for Carey—not to mention the glut of girls' variations.

Kevin ★★★★★

(Irish) handsome.

First Impression: Kevin comes across as an easygoing and popular guy who's always joking and having fun.

Gender Association: Used for boys

Popularity and Trend: #37 (#32 in 2000)

Risk of Misspelling: Fairly low

Risk of Mispronunciation: Low

Famous Namesakes: Actor Kevin Costner; actor Kevin Spacey; actor Kevin Bacon; basketball player Kevin Garnett; basketball player Kevin McHale

Common Nicknames: None

Common Variations: Kevyn, Kevan

Consider This: This popular name has a lot going for it, though there's no short form or familiar form for variety.

Kieran ★★★

(Irish) little and dark; little Keir.

First Impression: Kieran is pictured as a fun, competitive guy, but he's also thoughtful, intelligent, and sensitive to others.

Gender Association: Used mostly for boys

Popularity and Trend: #566 (#528 in 2000)

Risk of Misspelling: Average

Risk of Mispronunciation: Average

Famous Namesakes: Actor Kieran Culkin

Common Nicknames: Keir, Kier, Kern

Common Variations: Keiran, Kieren

Consider This: Here's an Irish name with a great image that's less common than Kevin and Kenneth.

Kim ★★★

(English) a short form of Kimball.

First Impression: Most people see Kim as quiet, shy, thoughtful, and quite kind—but a few people think of him as active and popular.

Gender Association: Used mostly for girls

Popularity and Trend: Last ranked in the Top 1000 in the 1980s

Risk of Misspelling: Low

Risk of Mispronunciation: Low

Famous Namesakes: North Korean leaders Kim Il Sung and Kim Jong Il; South Korean president Kim Dae Jung

Common Nicknames: None
Common Variations: Kimball
Consider This: Kim is overwhelmingly used for more girls than boys.

King ★★★

(English) king.
First Impression: King is seen as a popular and hip punk rocker who usually acts like a tough jerk.
Gender Association: Used for boys
Popularity and Trend: #896 (Last ranked in the Top 1000 in the 1950s)
Risk of Misspelling: Low
Risk of Mispronunciation: Low
Famous Namesakes: Activist Dr. Martin Luther King, Jr.; musician B. B. King; author Stephen King
Common Nicknames: None
Common Variations: Kingston
Consider This: This name's image isn't fit for a king.

Kipp ★★

(English) pointed hill.
First Impression: Kipp is viewed as a snobby and self-centered preppy, but he somehow manages to be friendly and happy every now and then.
Gender Association: Used for boys
Popularity and Trend: Last ranked in the Top 1000 in the 1960s
Risk of Misspelling: Average
Risk of Mispronunciation: Low
Famous Namesakes: Singer Kip Winger; character Kip Dynamite

(*Napoleon Dynamite*); baseball player Kip Wells
Common Nicknames: None
Common Variations: Kip
Consider This: This quirky short name hasn't been ranked since the '60s, and parents may find it dated. Spelling will be a problem if people expect it to have only one *p*.

Kirk ★★★★

(Scandinavian) church.
First Impression: Kirk calls to mind an optimistic and excitable guy with a generous heart and sweet intentions.
Gender Association: Used for boys
Popularity and Trend: Last ranked #848 in 2000
Risk of Misspelling: Low
Risk of Mispronunciation: Low
Famous Namesakes: Character Captain James T. Kirk (*Star Trek*); actor Kirk Cameron; actor Kirk Douglas; basketball player Kirk Hinrich
Common Nicknames: None
Common Variations: Kirklin, Kirkland
Consider This: It's a bit surprising that Kirk, with its positive image, has fallen out of the Top 1000.

Kiros ★★

(Greek) a form of Kyros.
First Impression: People picture Kiros as a strong, physically fit man with dark skin, hair, and eyes.

Gender Association: Used for boys
Popularity and Trend: Never been ranked in Top 1000
Risk of Misspelling: Fairly high
Risk of Mispronunciation: Fairly high
Famous Namesakes: None
Common Nicknames: None
Common Variations: None
Consider This: This name has a strong image, but people pronounce it several ways: "KYE-rohs," "KEE-rohs," "KYE-ross," and "KEE-ross."

Kohana ★★★

(Lakota) swift.
First Impression: Kohana strikes people as a nice, polite, and upstanding Hawaiian boy.
Gender Association: Used for boys
Popularity and Trend: Never been ranked in Top 1000
Risk of Misspelling: Average
Risk of Mispronunciation: Average
Famous Namesakes: None
Common Nicknames: None
Common Variations: None
Consider This: Like Kiros, Kohana is unranked. Unlike Kiros, however, this name has a nice first impression. It's pronunciation is mostly phonetic: "koh-HAH-nah."

Kris ★★

(Greek) a form of Chris.
First Impression: Most people say Kris is considerate and sweet, as well as charming and artistic. But

sometimes he seems to be self-centered and secretive.

Gender Association: Used mostly for boys

Popularity and Trend: Last ranked in the Top 1000 in the 1980s

Risk of Misspelling: Average

Risk of Mispronunciation: Low

Famous Namesakes: Singer Kris Kristofferson; legendary character Kriss Kringle; football player Kris Jenkins

Common Nicknames: None

Common Variations: Chris

Consider This: Kris is quite a lot less common than Chris, which may cause spelling problems.

Kurt ★★★

(Latin, German, French) a form of Kurtis.

First Impression: Kurt is seen as a dopey bookworm who's very sweet underneath his shyness.

Gender Association: Used for boys

Popularity and Trend: Last ranked #610 in 2000

Risk of Misspelling: Fairly low

Risk of Mispronunciation: Low

Famous Namesakes: Actor Kurt Russell; singer Kurt Cobain; author Kurt Vonnegut; racecar driver Kurt Busch; football player Kurt Warner

Common Nicknames: None

Common Variations: Curt, Kirt, Kurtis

Consider This: A meek image along with a lack of popularity may give you pause about Kurt.

Kyle ★★★★

(Irish) narrow piece of land; place where cattle graze. (Yiddish) crowned with laurels.

First Impression: Kyle is pictured as a gorgeous but dumb jock who's rowdy with his frat brothers and charming with the ladies.

Gender Association: Used mostly for boys

Popularity and Trend: #80 (#37 in 2000)

Risk of Misspelling: Fairly low

Risk of Mispronunciation: Low

Famous Namesakes: Actor Kyle Chandler; actor Kyle MacLachlan; racecar driver Kyle Petty; football player Kyle Boller

Common Nicknames: Ky

Common Variations: Kile

Consider This: Kyle doesn't have a stellar image, so it may not last much longer in the Top 100.

Lamar ★★

(German) famous throughout the land. (French) sea, ocean.

First Impression: Lamar is viewed as a driven and successful guy, but he's too abrasive to be popular.

Gender Association: Used for boys

Popularity and Trend: #672 (#639 in 2000)

Risk of Misspelling: Fairly low

Risk of Mispronunciation: Fairly low

Famous Namesakes: Basketball player Lamar Odom; football player Lamar Gordon

Common Nicknames: None

Common Variations: Lamarr, Lemar

Consider This: Lamar may not win a popularity contest, but the name is still listed in the Top 1000.

Lance ★★★★

(German) a form of Lancelot.

First Impression: People describe Lance as a noble, caring, and outgoing athlete.

Gender Association: Used for boys

Popularity and Trend: #321 (#267 in 2000)

Risk of Misspelling: Low

Risk of Mispronunciation: Low

Famous Namesakes: Cyclist Lance Armstrong; singer Lance Bass; baseball player Lance Johnson; magician Lance Burton

Common Nicknames: None

Common Variations: Lancelot

Consider This: Cyclist Lance Armstrong is hard to separate from this name's image, which seems to be a plus.

Landon ★★★★

(English) open, grassy meadow.

First Impression: Landon is regarded as an only child with over-achieving parents who push him too hard, which makes him an obsessive workaholic.

Gender Association: Used mostly
for boys

Popularity and Trend: #49
(#200 in 2000)

Risk of Misspelling: Fairly low

Risk of Mispronunciation: Low

Famous Namesakes: Actor Michael
Landon; soccer player Landon
Donovan

Common Nicknames: None

Common Variations: Landan

Consider This: Even though Landon's
image may be worrisome, its
popularity is skyrocketing.

Lane ★★★

(English) narrow road.

First Impression: People envision Lane
as a driven, powerful guy with a
perfect body and perfect face.

Gender Association: Used mostly
for boys

Popularity and Trend: #322
(#296 in 2000)

Risk of Misspelling: Fairly low

Risk of Mispronunciation: Low

Famous Namesakes: Actor Nathan
Lane; singer Layne Staley

Common Nicknames: None

Common Variations: Layne, Laine

Consider This: Lane is a simple name
with an attractive image.

Laramie ★

(French) tears of love.

First Impression: Laramie is depicted
as a cowboy who lives out West
and enjoys long horse rides.

Gender Association: Used mostly
for girls

Popularity and Trend: Never been
ranked in Top 1000

Risk of Misspelling: Average

Risk of Mispronunciation: Average

Famous Namesakes: None

Common Nicknames: None

Common Variations: None

Consider This: Despite its rugged
image, more girls than boys
receive this name. People will
likely know it's pronounced
"LAIR-ah-mee."

Larry ★★★

(Latin) a familiar form of Lawrence.

First Impression: Larry is imagined to
be a nerdy, goofy fellow who's
tall, heavy, and not very attractive
with a unibrow and glasses.

Gender Association: Used for boys

Popularity and Trend: #381
(#280 in 2000)

Risk of Misspelling: Low

Risk of Mispronunciation: Low

Famous Namesakes: Character Larry
Sanders (*The Larry Sanders Show*);
TV personality Larry King;
comedian Larry the Cable Guy;
basketball player Larry Bird

Common Nicknames: None

Common Variations: None

Consider This: This nickname is
now slightly more popular than
Lawrence. Compare their very
different images before you make
a choice.

Lars ★★

(Scandinavian) a form of Lawrence.

First Impression: When people think
of Lars, they imagine a big, burly,
and pale-skinned German.

Gender Association: Used for boys

Popularity and Trend: Last ranked in
the Top 1000 in the 1980s

Risk of Misspelling: Average

Risk of Mispronunciation: Average

Famous Namesakes: Musician Lars
Ulrich

Common Nicknames: None

Common Variations: None

Consider This: Lars certainly has
strengths, but it may fit best
with Scandinavian surnames.
Also, there's a slight pronunciation problem with both "lahrs"
and "larz" as options.

Lawrence ★★

(Latin) crowned with laurel.

First Impression: People say Lawrence
is a shrewd and snooty man
who's quite pompous and tries
to impress others with little-
known facts.

Gender Association: Used for boys

Popularity and Trend: #407
(#323 in 2000)

Risk of Misspelling: Average

Risk of Mispronunciation: Low

Famous Namesakes: Soldier T. E.
Lawrence, known as Lawrence of
Arabia; actor Martin Lawrence;

author D. H. Lawrence; TV personality Lawrence Welk

Common Nicknames: Larry, Loren, Lorne

Common Variations: Laurence, Lars

Consider This: This traditional name has a less-than-stellar image, but its versatility is undeniable. Spelling may be confused for "Laurence."

Lee ★★

(English) a form of Farley, Leonard, and names containing "lee."

First Impression: Lee is seen as an imaginative geek who loves role-playing games and writes fantasy stories.

Gender Association: Used mostly for boys

Popularity and Trend: #613 (#471 in 2000)

Risk of Misspelling: Fairly low

Risk of Mispronunciation: Low

Famous Namesakes: Actor Lee Marvin; CEO Lee Iacocca; general Robert E. Lee; golfer Lee Trevino

Common Nicknames: None

Common Variations: Leigh

Consider This: This short, simple name's popularity is slipping. Plus, its pronunciation is the same as Leigh, a popular name for girls, which may cause gender confusion.

Leif ★★★

(Scandinavian) beloved.

First Impression: Leif is pictured as a funny, easygoing guy that everyone wants to be around.

Gender Association: Used mostly for boys

Popularity and Trend: Last ranked in the Top 1000 in the 1980s

Risk of Misspelling: Average

Risk of Mispronunciation: Fairly high

Famous Namesakes: Explorer Leif Ericson; singer Leif Garrett

Common Nicknames: None

Common Variations: None

Consider This: A great image bolsters Leif's appeal, but its various pronunciations ("leaf," "layf," "life") may be a turnoff.

Lenny ★★

(German) a familiar form of Leonard.

First Impression: Most people think Lenny is an awkward, shy bookworm who has no friends.

Gender Association: Used for boys

Popularity and Trend: Last ranked in the Top 1000 in the 1980s

Risk of Misspelling: Fairly low

Risk of Mispronunciation: Low

Famous Namesakes: Singer Lenny Kravitz; character Lenny Leonard (*The Simpsons*); character Lennie Small (*Of Mice and Men*); comedian Lenny Bruce; basketball player Lenny Wilkens

Common Nicknames: None

Common Variations: Lennie

Consider This: Lenny is very informal. An unappealing image doesn't help it, either.

Leo ★★★

(Latin) lion. (German) a short form of Leon, Leopold.

First Impression: Leo is described as a good-humored, attractive man who enjoys drinking and women—but shouldn't necessarily be trusted with either.

Gender Association: Used for boys

Popularity and Trend: #236 (#390 in 2000)

Risk of Misspelling: Low

Risk of Mispronunciation: Low

Famous Namesakes: Author Leo Tolstoy; actor Leonardo "Leo" DiCaprio

Common Nicknames: None

Common Variations: None

Consider This: Leo's popularity is rapidly increasing, but the name doesn't have a clean-cut image.

Leon ★★★★

(Greek, German) a form of Leonard, Napoleon.

First Impression: People think Leon is a friendly, talkative fellow who's very smart and very funny.

Gender Association: Used for boys

Popularity and Trend: #505 (#503 in 2000)

Risk of Misspelling: Low

Risk of Mispronunciation: Fairly low
Famous Namesakes: Boxer Leon Spinks; revolutionary Leon Trotsky; singer Leon Russell
Common Nicknames: Lee
Common Variations: Leondre
Consider This: Although it has modest popularity, Leon has all the pluses parents want. Most times it will be pronounced "LEE-ahn," but some cultures may pronounce it "lay-OHN."

Leonard ★★★

(German) brave as a lion.
First Impression: Leonard comes across as a socially awkward introvert.
Gender Association: Used for boys
Popularity and Trend: #614 (#508 in 2000)
Risk of Misspelling: Fairly low
Risk of Mispronunciation: Low
Famous Namesakes: Composer Leonard Bernstein; actor Leonard Nimoy; poet and singer Leonard Cohen
Common Nicknames: Lee, Leo, Leon, Len, Lennie, Lon
Common Variations: Lenard
Consider This: Leonard's versatility is great, even though its image isn't.

Leroy ★★★

(French) king.
First Impression: Folks think Leroy could be cranky, mean, and intimidating, or he could be poised, polite, and articulate.

Gender Association: Used for boys
Popularity and Trend: #956 (#722 in 2000)
Risk of Misspelling: Fairly low
Risk of Mispronunciation: Fairly low
Famous Namesakes: Song "Bad, Bad Leroy Brown"; football player LeRoy Bulter
Common Nicknames: Roy
Common Variations: Elroy
Consider This: A questionable image may be hurting this name's popularity. Also, pronunciation is a small problem, with most people saying "LEE-roy" but a few saying "luh-ROY."

Leslie ★★

(Scottish) gray fortress.
First Impression: Leslie is seen as a selfless, kind man whose refined manners can come across as snobbish to some.
Gender Association: Used mostly for girls
Popularity and Trend: Last ranked in the Top 1000 in the 1990s
Risk of Misspelling: Average
Risk of Mispronunciation: Fairly low
Famous Namesakes: Actor Leslie Howard; actor Leslie Nielsen
Common Nicknames: Les
Common Variations: Lesley
Consider This: Parents name their daughters Leslie more often than they do their sons. Lesley is a popular variation, which will create spelling troubles as well.

Lester ★★★

(Latin) chosen camp. (English) from Leicester, England.
First Impression: Lester is viewed as a soft-spoken geek—or a bully who terrorizes geeks.
Gender Association: Used for boys
Popularity and Trend: Last ranked in the Top 1000 in the 1990s
Risk of Misspelling: Low
Risk of Mispronunciation: Low
Famous Namesakes: Musician Lester Young; character Lester Burnham (*American Beauty*)
Common Nicknames: Les
Common Variations: None
Consider This: Lester's negative image will cause most parents to consider other options.

Levi ★★★★

(Hebrew) joined in harmony.
First Impression: Most people see Levi as a Californian surfer.
Gender Association: Used for boys
Popularity and Trend: #135 (#172 in 2000)
Risk of Misspelling: Fairly low
Risk of Mispronunciation: Fairly low
Famous Namesakes: Clothing manufacturer Levi Strauss; biblical figure Levi
Common Nicknames: Lev
Common Variations: Levin
Consider This: This biblical name is gaining popularity. Because of Levi's jeans, nearly everyone will know how to pronounce it.

Lewis ★★★

(Welsh) a form of Llewellyn.
(English) a form of Louis.

First Impression: Lewis is considered a studious bookworm who's almost always kind, gentle, and compassionate.

Gender Association: Used for boys

Popularity and Trend: #678 (#573 in 2000)

Risk of Misspelling: Average

Risk of Mispronunciation: Low

Famous Namesakes: Explorer Meriwether Lewis; comedian Lewis Black; author Lewis Carroll; author C. S. Lewis; boxer Lennox Lewis

Common Nicknames: Lew, Lewy

Common Variations: Louis

Consider This: With this less common alternative to Louis, spelling will be a problem.

Lex ★★

(English) a short form of Alexander.

First Impression: People say Lex is a criminal genius who's rich, sneaky, and worldly, much like Superman's nemesis, Lex Luthor.

Gender Association: Used for boys

Popularity and Trend: Never been ranked in Top 1000

Risk of Misspelling: Low

Risk of Mispronunciation: Low

Famous Namesakes: Character Lex Luthor (*Superman*); wrestler Lex Luger

Common Nicknames: None

Common Variations: None

Consider This: Many parents will have a tough time giving Lex two thumbs up.

Liam ★★★

(Irish) a form of William.

First Impression: Liam is thought to be a worldly and well-read Irishman who's strong and handsome with green eyes and dimples.

Gender Association: Used for boys

Popularity and Trend: #98 (#140 in 2000)

Risk of Misspelling: Fairly low

Risk of Mispronunciation: Fairly low

Famous Namesakes: Actor Liam Neeson; singer Liam Gallagher

Common Nicknames: None

Common Variations: Liem

Consider This: This increasingly popular variation of William entered the Top 100 for the first time in 2006, and it's likely to keep rising.

Lincoln ★★

(English) settlement by the pool.

First Impression: Lincoln is described as an unfortunate blend of arrogance, power, wealth, and rudeness.

Gender Association: Used for boys

Popularity and Trend: #300 (#711 in 2000)

Risk of Misspelling: Fairly low

Risk of Mispronunciation: Low

Famous Namesakes: President Abraham Lincoln; character Lincoln Burrows (*Prison Break*); football player Lincoln Kennedy

Common Nicknames: Linc

Common Variations: None

Consider This: You'd think Lincoln's image would resemble a certain legendary president, but the connection is in name only. Its negative image hasn't quelled this name's popularity, though.

Lionel ★★★

(French) lion cub.

First Impression: People say Lionel is intelligent, caring, and usually silent.

Gender Association: Used for boys

Popularity and Trend: Last ranked #997 in 2000

Risk of Misspelling: Fairly low

Risk of Mispronunciation: Fairly low

Famous Namesakes: Singer Lionel Richie; actor Lionel Barrymore; soccer player Lionel Messi

Common Nicknames: None

Common Variations: None

Consider This: Lionel has fallen out of the Top 1000, and it may project too meek an image. There may be slight differences in pronunciation because some say "LYE-eh-nel" and others say "LYE-nel."

Lister ★★★

(English) dyer.

First Impression: Lister comes across as a quiet and gentle loner.

Gender Association: Used for boys

Popularity and Trend: Never been ranked in Top 1000

Risk of Misspelling: Low

Risk of Mispronunciation: Low

Famous Namesakes: Surgeon Joseph Lister

Common Nicknames: None

Common Variations: None

Consider This: This unusual name's image hasn't won over parents yet, and it probably won't anytime soon.

Llewellyn ★

(Welsh) lionlike.

First Impression: Llewellyn is seen as a loony eccentric who's either chock-full of attitude or conservative and reserved.

Gender Association: Used for boys

Popularity and Trend: Last ranked in the Top 1000 in the 1940s

Risk of Misspelling: Fairly high

Risk of Mispronunciation: Fairly high

Famous Namesakes: Actor Desmond Llewelyn; several Welsh kings named Llewelyn

Common Nicknames: None

Common Variations: Lewis

Consider This: Llewellyn's "lionlike" meaning is offset by its weak image and its challenging spelling and pronunciation ("loo-WELL-en").

Lloyd ★★

(Welsh) gray-haired; holy.

First Impression: Lloyd is depicted as a highly intelligent guy who's hyperactive and hypersensitive.

Gender Association: Used for boys

Popularity and Trend: Last ranked #922 in 2000

Risk of Misspelling: Average

Risk of Mispronunciation: Fairly low

Famous Namesakes: Actor Lloyd Bridges; character Lloyd Christmas (*Dumb and Dumber*)

Common Nicknames: None

Common Variations: Floyd

Consider This: A poor image and tricky, double *l* spelling may cause parents to skip this name.

Logan ★★★★★

(Irish) meadow.

First Impression: People say Logan is adventurous and daring when it comes to surfing, but he's laid-back and relaxed when it comes to life.

Gender Association: Used mostly for boys

Popularity and Trend: #19 (#40 in 2000)

Risk of Misspelling: Fairly low

Risk of Mispronunciation: Low

Famous Namesakes: Character Logan Echolls (*Veronica Mars*); character Logan, also known as Wolverine (*X-Men*)

Common Nicknames: None

Common Variations: Logen

Consider This: A surge in popularity gives Logan trendy appeal.

Lonnie ★★★

(German, Spanish) a familiar form of Alonso.

First Impression: Lonnie is thought to be extremely friendly, laid-back, and cool.

Gender Association: Used for boys

Popularity and Trend: Last ranked #825 in 2000

Risk of Misspelling: Average

Risk of Mispronunciation: Low

Famous Namesakes: Basketball player Lonny Baxter; musician Lonny Mack

Common Nicknames: Lon

Common Variations: Lonny

Consider This: Lonnie is informal, and people aren't using it with any regularity these days. Even as a nickname, Lonny seems to be more popular.

Lorenzo ★★★

(Italian, Spanish) a form of Lawrence.

First Impression: People describe Lorenzo as a strong and confident man who tends to be smarmy and melodramatic.

Gender Association: Used for boys

Popularity and Trend: #301
(#314 in 2000)
Risk of Misspelling: Fairly low
Risk of Mispronunciation: Fairly low
Famous Namesakes: Actor Lorenzo Lamas; football player Lorenzo Neal; ALD patient Lorenzo Odone and movie *Lorenzo's Oil*
Common Nicknames: Renzo
Common Variations: Larenzo
Consider This: Lorenzo may work best with Latino surnames. It's mostly phonetic, however, pronounced "lore-EN-zoh."

Lorne ★★★

(Latin) a form of Lawrence.
First Impression: Lorne is regarded as kind, good natured, and dependable—all traits that make him a popular leader.
Gender Association: Used for boys
Popularity and Trend: Last ranked in the Top 1000 in the 1970s
Risk of Misspelling: Average
Risk of Mispronunciation: Fairly low
Famous Namesakes: Producer Lorne Michaels; actor Lorne Green
Common Nicknames: None
Common Variations: None
Consider This: Lorne hasn't been popular for decades; it sounds dated.

Louis ★★★★

(German) famous warrior.
First Impression: People believe Louis has a prominent ethnic background, but they can't decide whether it's French, Greek, Italian, or Welsh.
Gender Association: Used for boys
Popularity and Trend: #326
(#279 in 2000)
Risk of Misspelling: Fairly low
Risk of Mispronunciation: Average
Famous Namesakes: Several kings named Louis; designer Louis Vuitton; musician Louis Armstrong; author Louis L'Amour; actor Louis Gosset, Jr.
Common Nicknames: Lou, Louie
Common Variations: Lewis, Luis
Consider This: This classic spelling fares better than "Lewis," even if pronunciation ("LOO-iss" or "LOO-ee") is a problem.

Lowell ★★

(French) young wolf. (English) beloved.
First Impression: Many picture Lowell as a mechanic, electrician, or some other laborer who works with his hands.
Gender Association: Used for boys
Popularity and Trend: Last ranked in the Top 1000 in the 1980s
Risk of Misspelling: Average
Risk of Mispronunciation: Fairly low
Famous Namesakes: Decorator Christopher Lowell; baseball player Mike Lowell
Common Nicknames: None
Common Variations: Lovell
Consider This: Lowell may be too old-fashioned to be a good choice.

Luc ★★

(French) a form of Luke.
First Impression: Luc comes across as a suave, sophisticated, and sexy Frenchman.
Gender Association: Used for boys
Popularity and Trend: Never been ranked in Top 1000
Risk of Misspelling: Fairly high
Risk of Mispronunciation: Average
Famous Namesakes: Basketball player Luc Longley; hockey player Luc Robitaille; director Luc Besson
Common Nicknames: None
Common Variations: Luke
Consider This: Challenging spelling may deter you from this French version of Luke.

Lucas ★★★★★

(German, Irish, Danish, Dutch) a form of Lucius.
First Impression: Some people see Lucas as a mischievous joker who's tall, dark, and smart. Other people, however, believe he's a quiet and brooding artist.
Gender Association: Used for boys
Popularity and Trend: #59
(#83 in 2000)
Risk of Misspelling: Fairly low
Risk of Mispronunciation: Low
Famous Namesakes: Director George Lucas; actor Lucas Black; actor Josh Lucas

Common Nicknames: Luc
Common Variations: Lucus, Lukas
Consider This: Rising popularity and an intriguing image may give Lucas the pop you're looking for.

Luis ★★

(Spanish) a form of Louis.

First Impression: People describe Luis as a goofy, clumsy Latino who can be colorful and lively in one light and sly, sneaky, and loud mouthed in another.
Gender Association: Used for boys
Popularity and Trend: #62 (#49 in 2000)
Risk of Misspelling: Fairly high
Risk of Mispronunciation: Fairly high
Famous Namesakes: Director Luis Valdez; baseball player Luis Gonzalez; singer Luis Miguel; baseball player Luis Castillo
Common Nicknames: None
Common Variations: None
Consider This: Pronounced "loo-EES" rather than "LOO-ee" or "LOO-iss," challenging pronunciation may make Luis a safe bet only for Latino families. Spelling may be a problem for some as well.

Luke ★★★★★

(Latin) a form of Lucius.

First Impression: Luke is pictured as a muscular and tall athlete who's personable and always ready to party down.
Gender Association: Used for boys

Popularity and Trend: #43 (#59 in 2000)
Risk of Misspelling: Fairly low
Risk of Mispronunciation: Low
Famous Namesakes: Biblical figure Luke; actor Luke Perry; actor Luke Wilson; character Luke Skywalker (*Star Wars*)
Common Nicknames: Lucky
Common Variations: Luc, Luka, Lukas
Consider This: Like other biblical names, Luke is very popular.

Luther ★★★

(German) famous warrior.

First Impression: Luther comes across as a sweet and shy fellow who'd rather listen to a conversation than participate in one.
Gender Association: Used for boys
Popularity and Trend: Last ranked in the Top 1000 in the 1990s
Risk of Misspelling: Low
Risk of Mispronunciation: Low
Famous Namesakes: Theologian Martin Luther; singer Luther Vandross; activist Martin Luther King, Jr.
Common Nicknames: None
Common Variations: Lothar
Consider This: Off the Top 1000 for nearly a decade, Luther may seem passé.

Lyle ★★★

(French) island.

First Impression: People say Lyle is a friendly Southern country singer

with a gangly body and plain looks.
Gender Association: Used for boys
Popularity and Trend: Last ranked in the Top 1000 in the 1990s
Risk of Misspelling: Low
Risk of Mispronunciation: Low
Famous Namesakes: Singer Lyle Lovett; football player Lyle Alzado
Common Nicknames: None
Common Variations: None
Consider This: People associate this name with Lyle Lovett, which could be a good or a bad thing, depending on your music tastes.

Lyndon ★★★

(English) linden hill.

First Impression: Lyndon is seen as a powerful, straightforward professional.
Gender Association: Used for boys
Popularity and Trend: Last ranked in the Top 1000 in the 1960s
Risk of Misspelling: Average
Risk of Mispronunciation: Low
Famous Namesakes: President Lyndon B. Johnson; political thinker Lyndon LaRouche
Common Nicknames: Lynn
Common Variations: Linden, Lynden
Consider This: It's not surprising Lyndon last peaked in popularity when LBJ was president.

Mack ★★★

(Scottish) a short form of names beginning with "Mac" and "Mc."

First Impression: People not only imagine Mack driving a Mack Truck, but they also picture him looking like one.

Gender Association: Used for boys

Popularity and Trend: Last ranked in the Top 1000 in the 1980s

Risk of Misspelling: Fairly low

Risk of Mispronunciation: Low

Famous Namesakes: Song "Mack the Knife"; baseball player Connie Mack; football player Mack Strong

Common Nicknames: None

Common Variations: Macklin, Mac

Consider This: Mack may be an attractive name if you have a big-truck fetish, but it probably won't fare well if you don't.

Malcolm ★★★

(Scottish) follower of Saint Columba who Christianized North Scotland. (Arabic) dove.

First Impression: Folks believe Malcolm is a strong activist leader with passionate purposefulness.

Gender Association: Used for boys

Popularity and Trend: #545 (#368 in 2000)

Risk of Misspelling: Average

Risk of Mispronunciation: Fairly low

Famous Namesakes: Activist Malcolm X; actor Malcolm-Jamal Warner; actor Malcolm McDowell; character Malcolm Wilkerson (*Malcolm in the Middle*)

Common Nicknames: None

Common Variations: Malcom

Consider This: Malcolm's popularity is waning, despite its strong first impression. Spelling could be a little tricky for those who forget the silent *l*.

Malik ★★

(Punjabi) lord, master. (Arabic) a form of Malachi.

First Impression: Malik is imaged to be one of these: an intimidating tough guy, a perfectionist student at the top of his class, an earthy tree-hugger, an arty introvert, or a dynamic athlete.

Gender Association: Used for boys

Popularity and Trend: #290 (#176 in 2000)

Risk of Misspelling: Fairly high

Risk of Mispronunciation: Fairly high

Famous Namesakes: Actor Malik Yoba; basketball player Malik Rose; Allah title al-Malik

Common Nicknames: None

Common Variations: Maleek, Malek

Consider This: This ethnic name has enjoyed moderate popularity over the last several years. However, some people may not know to pronounce it "MAH-leek" when they see it. Its spelling is a problem as well.

Mandek ★

(Polish) a form of Herman.

First Impression: Mandek is said to be a quiet loner whose unusual and somewhat geeky ways make him socially inept and unpopular.

Gender Association: Used for boys

Popularity and Trend: Never been ranked in Top 1000

Risk of Misspelling: Average

Risk of Mispronunciation: Fairly low

Famous Namesakes: None

Common Nicknames: None

Common Variations: None

Consider This: Mandek's loner image isn't likely to boost its nonexistent popularity. However, its pronunciation is mostly phonetic ("MAN-deck").

Manuel ★★★★

(Hebrew) a form of Emmanuel.

First Impression: People find Manuel to be a caring and loving Latino who's a wonderful friend.

Gender Association: Used for boys

Popularity and Trend: #164 (#159 in 2000)

Risk of Misspelling: Average

Risk of Mispronunciation: Average

Famous Namesakes: Panamanian leader Manuel Noriega; makeup artist Jay Manuel

Common Nicknames: Mango, Manny

Common Variations: Emmanuel

Consider This: A common name, Manuel enjoys a great image. However, it may not fit well with family names not of Latino or Spanish origin. It can be pronounced "MAN-yoo-ell" or "MAHN-well."

Marc ★★★★

(French) a form of Mark. (Latin) a form of Marcus.

First Impression: Marc is thought to be sexy and jovial.

Gender Association: Used for boys

Popularity and Trend: #408 (#228 in 2000)

Risk of Misspelling: Average

Risk of Mispronunciation: Low

Famous Namesakes: Singer Marc Anthony; designer Marc Jacobs; football player Marc Bulger

Common Nicknames: None

Common Variations: Mark, Marcus, Marco

Consider This: A variation of Mark, Marc's less popular spelling could cause problems.

Marcel ★★

(French) a form of Marcellus.

First Impression: People think Marcel is a shy guy who's small, plain, and insecure.

Gender Association: Used for boys

Popularity and Trend: #957 (#750 in 2000)

Risk of Misspelling: Fairly low

Risk of Mispronunciation: Fairly low

Famous Namesakes: Mime Marcel Marceau; writer Marcel Proust; artist Marcel Duchamp

Common Nicknames: None

Common Variations: Marcellus

Consider This: Marcel may sound strange with last names that aren't French. Pronunciation ("mar-SELL") should be easy for most people, however.

Marco ★★★★

(Italian) a form of Marcus.

First Impression: Marco is viewed as a strong-minded, ambitious man who achieves his goals.

Gender Association: Used for boys

Popularity and Trend: #206 (#182 in 2000)

Risk of Misspelling: Fairly low

Risk of Mispronunciation: Low

Famous Namesakes: Explorer Marco Polo; racecar driver Marco Andretti

Common Nicknames: Marc

Common Variations: Marko, Marcus, Marc

Consider This: Marco may work best with Italian or Latino family names.

Marcus ★★★★

(Latin) martial, warlike.

First Impression: Marcus is pictured as talented, intelligent, and trustworthy.

Gender Association: Used for boys

Popularity and Trend: #112 (#99 in 2000)

Risk of Misspelling: Fairly low

Risk of Mispronunciation: Low

Famous Namesakes: Emperor Marcus Aurelius; Roman statesman Marcus Brutus; football player Marcus Allen; model Marcus Schenkenberg

Common Nicknames: Marc

Common Variations: Marco, Marcos, Mark, Markus

Consider This: Echoing its image, Marcus seems to be a name you can count on.

Mario ★★★★

(Italian) a form of Marino.

First Impression: People say Mario is an adventurous, brave, and hyperactive Italian man.

Gender Association: Used for boys

Popularity and Trend: #178 (#167 in 2000)

Risk of Misspelling: Fairly low

Risk of Mispronunciation: Fairly low

Famous Namesakes: Video game character Mario; actor Mario Lopez; racecar driver Mario Andretti; mayor Mario Cuomo; football player Mario Williams

Common Nicknames: None

Common Variations: None

Consider This: Nintendo gamers will recognize their pint-size hero in this name's image, and parents of Latino or Italian heritage may also find this name a winner. Pronunciation ("MAHR-ee-oh") should be easy for most people.

Marion ★★★

(French) bitter; sea of bitterness.

First Impression: Marion is seen as an intelligent and eloquent African American man who's funny, caring, and a big flirt.

Gender Association: Used mostly for girls

Popularity and Trend: Last ranked in the Top 1000 in the 1990s

Risk of Misspelling: Fairly low

Risk of Mispronunciation: Fairly low

Famous Namesakes: Mayor Marion Barry; basketball player Shawn Marion; Marion Morrison, a.k.a. John Wayne

Common Nicknames: None

Common Variations: Marian, Mariano

Consider This: Marion has a stellar image, but ambiguous gender association may cause trouble.

Mark ★★★

(Latin) a form of Marcus.

First Impression: Many people think Mark is a helpful, caring guy who's perfect to bring home to Mom and perfect family-man material.

Gender Association: Used for boys

Popularity and Trend: #129 (#79 in 2000)

Risk of Misspelling: Fairly low

Risk of Mispronunciation: Low

Famous Namesakes: Biblical figure Mark; actor Mark Wahlberg; baseball player Mark McGwire; author Mark Twain; Roman statesman Mark Anthony

Common Nicknames: None

Common Variations: Marc, Marcus, Marko

Consider This: Unlike many other biblical names, Mark's popularity is falling.

Marlon ★★★★

(French) a form of Merlin.

First Impression: People picture Marlon as a deep-sea fisherman—most likely because *Marlon* and *marlin* sound the same.

Gender Association: Used for boys

Popularity and Trend: #508 (#506 in 2000)

Risk of Misspelling: Fairly low

Risk of Mispronunciation: Low

Famous Namesakes: Actor Marlon Brando; actor Marlon Wayans; singer Marlon Jackson

Common Nicknames: None

Common Variations: Marlin

Consider This: If you don't mind the occasional fish joke, Marlon is a great catch. Keep in mind, though, this name is used more often for girls than for boys.

Marshall ★★★★

(French) caretaker of the horses; military title.

First Impression: People say Marshall is a talented and successful rapper who has gone far in life.

Gender Association: Used for boys

Popularity and Trend: #417 (#344 in 2000)

Risk of Misspelling: Low

Risk of Mispronunciation: Low

Famous Namesakes: Singer Marshall Crenshaw; Supreme Court justice Thurgood Marshall; rapper Marshall Mathers, also known as Eminem; football player Marshall Faulk

Common Nicknames: Marsh

Common Variations: Marshal

Consider This: Even though he goes by Eminem, Marshall Mathers influences this name in a big way.

Martin ★★★★

(Latin, French) a form of Martinus.

First Impression: Martin is depicted as a reliable and mild-mannered man who's polite and well liked by his peers.

Gender Association: Used for boys

Popularity and Trend: #200 (#175 in 2000)

Risk of Misspelling: Fairly low

Risk of Mispronunciation: Fairly low

Famous Namesakes: Actor Martin Sheen; director Martin Scorsese; actor Martin Short; actor Martin Lawrence; civil rights leader Martin Luther King, Jr.; theologian Martin Luther

Common Nicknames: Marty

Common Variations: Marten, Martino

Consider This: While its boring image may tarnish Martin for you, its versatility may attract you. Most people will pronounce it "MAR-tin," but some cultures may pronounce it "MAR-teen."

Marty ★★

(Latin) a familiar form of Martin.

First Impression: People believe Marty is a chubby class clown who can be childish, annoying, and dim-witted.

Gender Association: Used mostly for boys

Popularity and Trend: Last ranked in the Top 1000 in the 1990s

Risk of Misspelling: Low

Risk of Mispronunciation: Low

Famous Namesakes: Character Marty McFly (*Back to the Future*); actor Marty Feldman; character Marty Piletti (*Marty*)

Common Nicknames: None

Common Variations: None

Consider This: A negative image may make Marty unattractive as either a given name *or* a nickname.

Marvin ★★★

(English) lover of the sea.

First Impression: Marvin is seen as a whiny, dorky guy who's smart but boring.

Gender Association: Used for boys

Popularity and Trend: #346 (#341 in 2000)

Risk of Misspelling: Low

Risk of Mispronunciation: Low

Famous Namesakes: Actor Lee Marvin; singer Marvin Gaye; character Marvin the Martian (*Looney Tunes*); boxer Marvin Hagler; football player Marvin Harrison

Common Nicknames: Marv

Common Variations: Mervin

Consider This: It's surprising that a name popularized by macho guys like Lee Marvin and Marvin Hagler would make a dorky first impression.

Mason ★★★★

(French) stone worker.

First Impression: Mason is described as a rich, aloof man who has time only for other rich people and who throws lavish parties simply because he can.

Gender Association: Used mostly for boys

Popularity and Trend: #39 (#64 in 2000)

Risk of Misspelling: Low

Risk of Mispronunciation: Low

Famous Namesakes: Book and TV character Perry Mason; surveyor Charles Mason of the Mason-Dixon Line; comedian Jackie Mason

Common Nicknames: Mase

Common Variations: Maison, Mayson

Consider This: Mason's popularity is surging, despite a richy-rich image.

Mateo ★★★

(Spanish) a form of Matthew.

First Impression: People imagine Mateo is kindhearted, noble, and generous.

Gender Association: Used for boys

Popularity and Trend: #274 (#429 in 2000)

Risk of Misspelling: Fairly high

Risk of Mispronunciation: Fairly high

Famous Namesakes: Character Mateo Santos (*All My Children*)

Common Nicknames: None

Common Variations: None

Consider This: This unique name has a great image and skyrocketing popularity, but its challenging pronunciation ("mah-TAY-oh") and spelling may be deterrents.

Mathias ★★

(German, Swedish) a form of Matthew.

First Impression: Mathias is pictured as an intellectual medical researcher, doctor, or pharmacist who's still a mama's boy.

Gender Association: Used for boys

Popularity and Trend: #741 (#947 in 2003)

Risk of Misspelling: Average

Risk of Mispronunciation: Average

Famous Namesakes: Biblical figure Matthias

Common Nicknames: None

Common Variations: Matthias, Mathis, Matias

Consider This: A biblical name with rising popularity, Mathias's fairly challenging pronunciation ("mah-THYE-us" or "mah-TEE-us") and spelling ("Mathias," "Matthias," or "Matias") may cause problems.

Matt ★★★

(Hebrew) a short form of Matthew.

First Impression: Most people say Matt is softhearted, considerate, and cheery. But some think he may be a liar and a cheat.

Gender Association: Used for boys

Popularity and Trend: Last ranked in the Top 1000 in the 1980s

Risk of Misspelling: Low

Risk of Mispronunciation: Low

Famous Namesakes: Actor Matt Damon; actor Matt LeBlanc; football player Matt Hasselbeck; cartoonist Matt Groening; TV personality Matt Lauer

Common Nicknames: Matty

Common Variations: None

Consider This: A familiar nickname, Matt isn't as versatile as Matthew.

Matthew ★★★★★

(Hebrew) gift of God.

First Impression: Matthew is described as a caring and friendly guy who's tall and fit.

Gender Association: Used mostly for boys

Popularity and Trend: #5 (#3 in 2000)

Risk of Misspelling: Fairly low

Risk of Mispronunciation: Low

Famous Namesakes: Actor Matthew Perry; biblical figure Matthew; actor Matthew Broderick; actor Matthew McConaughey

Common Nicknames: Matt, Matty

Common Variations: Mathew, Mathias

Consider This: Matthew has the image and versatility you may be seeking, but it may be *too* popular.

Maurice ★★★

(Latin) dark-skinned; moor; marshland.

First Impression: People say Maurice is an old Frenchman who's fun loving, goodhearted, and extroverted.

Gender Association: Used for boys

Popularity and Trend: #400 (#345 in 2000)

Risk of Misspelling: Average

Risk of Mispronunciation: Average

Famous Namesakes: Singer Maurice Gibb; writer Maurice Sendak; hockey player Maurice Richard

Common Nicknames: Maury, Morrie, Morris, Moss

Common Variations: Mauricio, Morris

Consider This: Maurice has an old image, but it has great versatility. It can be pronounced as "MOR-iss" or "mor-EESE," and may cause spelling problems, too.

Max ★★★

(Latin) a short form of Maximilian, Maxwell.

First Impression: Max makes people think of a rough bad boy who has no manners, but is very popular with women—probably because he's masculine and handsome.

Gender Association: Used for boys

Popularity and Trend: #160 (#164 in 2000)

Risk of Misspelling: Low

Risk of Mispronunciation: Low

Famous Namesakes: TV character Max Headroom; movie character Mad Max; sportscaster Max Kellerman; actor Max von Sydow; boxer Max Schmeling

Common Nicknames: Maxy

Common Variations: None

Consider This: People may assume Max is short for Maximilian or Maxwell.

Maximilian ★★

(Latin) greatest.

First Impression: People say Maximilian is a powerful, wealthy, and arrogant man.

Gender Association: Used for boys

Popularity and Trend: #348 (#391 in 2000)

Risk of Misspelling: Fairly high

Risk of Mispronunciation: Average

Famous Namesakes: Actor Maximilian Schell; character Professor Maximilian P. Arturo (*Sliders*)

Common Nicknames: Max, Maxy

Common Variations: Maximilien, Maximo

Consider This: If it sounds as though *million* is part of your name, people can't help but think you're rich. But there aren't quite a million ways to misspell this name.

Maxwell ★★★★★

(English) great spring.

First Impression: Maxwell is pictured as an intelligent man who's rich, dapper, and confident, not to mention tall, dark, and handsome.

Gender Association: Used for boys

Popularity and Trend: #149 (#113 in 2000)

Risk of Misspelling: Low

Risk of Mispronunciation: Low

Famous Namesakes: Character Maxwell Smart (*Get Smart*)

Common Nicknames: Max, Maxy

Common Variations: None

Consider This: With a decent image and solid popularity, Maxwell seems the best of the "Max" family.

Maynard ★★

(English) powerful; brave.

First Impression: Most people see Maynard as an unsure and shy bookworm.

Gender Association: Used for boys

Popularity and Trend: Last ranked in the Top 1000 in the 1960s

Risk of Misspelling: Average

Risk of Mispronunciation: Average

Famous Namesakes: Singer Maynard James Keenan; character Maynard G. Krebs (*The Many Loves of Dobie Gillis*)

Common Nicknames: None

Common Variations: Maynor

Consider This: Maynard hasn't been popular since the '60s, and it's not likely to be popular again any time soon.

Melvin ★★★

(Irish) armored chief. (English) mill friend; council friend.

First Impression: Overwhelmingly, Melvin strikes people as a nerdy and awkward fellow with a non-existent social life.

Gender Association: Used for boys

Popularity and Trend: #425 (#459 in 2000)

Risk of Misspelling: Low

Risk of Mispronunciation: Low

Famous Namesakes: Chemist Melvin Calvin; director Melvin Van Peebles; baseball player Melvin Mora

Common Nicknames: Mel, Vinny

Common Variations: Malvin

Consider This: Despite its negative image, Melvin has become more popular over the last few years.

Merlin ★★★★

(English) falcon.

First Impression: People describe Merlin as a powerful, mysterious, and, of course, magical old mentor.

Gender Association: Used for boys

Popularity and Trend: Last ranked in the Top 1000 in the 1960s

Risk of Misspelling: Low

Risk of Mispronunciation: Low

Famous Namesakes: Arthurian figure Merlin; football player Merlin Olson

Common Nicknames: Merle

Common Variations: Marlon, Merlino

Consider This: It's not magic—people associate Merlin with the magician from the King Arthur legend. Whether that's a boon or a bane depends on your preference for legendary lore.

Mervin ★★★

(Irish) a form of Marvin.

First Impression: Mervin is thought to be a smart but socially awkward nerd who's shy and quiet most of the time.

Gender Association: Used for boys

Popularity and Trend: Last ranked in the Top 1000 in the 1970s

Risk of Misspelling: Fairly low

Risk of Mispronunciation: Low

Famous Namesakes: Talk show host Mervyn "Merv" Griffin

Common Nicknames: Merv

Common Variations: Mervyn

Consider This: Like Melvin and Marvin, this name seems to project *social misfit*.

Michael ★★★★

(Hebrew) who is like God?

First Impression:, People think Michael is a sweet, caring, loyal, and trusting family man.

Gender Association: Used mostly for boys

Popularity and Trend: #2 (#2 in 2000)

Risk of Misspelling: Fairly low

Risk of Mispronunciation: Low

Famous Namesakes: Biblical figure Michael; basketball player Michael Jordan; singer Michael Jackson; actor Michael J. Fox; filmmaker Michael Moore

Common Nicknames: Mike, Mikey, Mick, Mickey

Common Variations: Micah, Mikhail, Micheal, Miguel

Consider This: This solid, classic name is undeniably versatile, but it may be too popular for some parents' taste.

Miguel ★★★

(Portuguese, Spanish) a form of Michael.

First Impression: Miguel is pictured as a Latino man who's smooth talking and street-smart.

Gender Association: Used for boys

Popularity and Trend: #89 (#86 in 2000)

Risk of Misspelling: Average

Risk of Mispronunciation: Average

Famous Namesakes: Baseball player Miguel Tejada; author Miguel de Cervantes; baseball player Miguel Cabrera; boxer Miguel Cotto

Common Nicknames: None

Common Variations: Migel

Consider This: This Top 100 name fits well with last names of Latino origin. Those not familiar with Latino names may not know to pronounce it "mee-GELL."

Mike ★★★

(Hebrew) a short form of Michael.

First Impression: People tend to think of Mike as a popular guy who's smart and sweet.

Gender Association: Used for boys

Popularity and Trend: #680 (#599 in 2000)

Risk of Misspelling: Low

Risk of Mispronunciation: Low

Famous Namesakes: Boxer Mike Tyson; actor Mike Myers; TV personality Mike Wallace; baseball player Mike Piazza; rapper Mike Jones

Common Nicknames: Mikey

Common Variations: None

Consider This: While Mike has a likable image, it is more informal and less versatile than Michael.

Mikhail ★★

(Greek, Russian) a form of Michael.

First Impression: People say Mikhail is a Russian man who's interesting, confident, and intense.

Gender Association: Used for boys

Popularity and Trend: Last ranked in the Top 1000 in the 1990s

Risk of Misspelling: Fairly high

Risk of Mispronunciation: Fairly high

Famous Namesakes: Dancer Mikhail Baryshnikov; Soviet leader Mikhail Gorbachev

Common Nicknames: None

Common Variations: Mikail, Mikhael

Consider This: With famous Russian namesakes Mikhail Gorbachev and Mikhail Baryshnikov, this name is loaded with ethnic association. Sometimes it's pronounced "mih-KALE," but the traditional pronunciation is "mee-KAH-eel."

Miles ★★★★

(Greek) millstone. (Latin) soldier. (German) merciful. (English) a form of Michael.

First Impression: People think Miles is a debonair and stylish fellow, much like Miles Davis, the cool king of jazz.

Gender Association: Used for boys

Popularity and Trend: #202 (#257 in 2000)

Risk of Misspelling: Average

Risk of Mispronunciation: Low

Famous Namesakes: Musician Miles Davis; Pilgrim Miles Standish

Common Nicknames: None
Common Variations: Myles
Consider This: Hip parents should like this name's hip image. But because Myles is also fairly popular, misspelling is possible.

Milt ★★

(English) a short form of Milton.
First Impression: Some people see Milt as brainy and awkward. Others see him as a macho man who's showy and full of himself.
Gender Association: Used for boys
Popularity and Trend: Never been ranked in Top 1000
Risk of Misspelling: Low
Risk of Mispronunciation: Low
Famous Namesakes: Musician Milt Hinton; basketball player Milt Palacio
Common Nicknames: None
Common Variations: None
Consider This: People differ in their views on this name, but the name is unlikely to grow popular soon.

Milton ★★★

(English) mill town.
First Impression: Some people say Milton is a bookish, lonely geek. Others say he's a hilarious comedian.
Gender Association: Used for boys
Popularity and Trend: #845 (#652 in 2000)
Risk of Misspelling: Low

Risk of Mispronunciation: Low
Famous Namesakes: Comedian Milton Berle; poet John Milton; baseball player Milton Bradley; game designer Milton Bradley
Common Nicknames: Milt
Common Variations: None
Consider This: Comedy legend Milton Berle gives this name's image some allure, but he hasn't been on TV for decades.

Mitch ★★

(English) a short form of Mitchell.
First Impression: Everyone sees Mitch as a beefy and bulky guy.
Gender Association: Used for boys
Popularity and Trend: Last ranked in the Top 1000 in the 1970s
Risk of Misspelling: Low
Risk of Mispronunciation: Low
Famous Namesakes: Comedian Mitch Hedberg; sportswriter Mitch Albom; singer Mitch Miller
Common Nicknames: None
Common Variations: None
Consider This: Compare the image of Mitch and Mitchell. What a difference *ell* makes.

Mitchell ★★

(English) a form of Michael.
First Impression: Mitchell is thought to be a serious, boring fellow.
Gender Association: Used for boys
Popularity and Trend: #275 (#132 in 2000)

Risk of Misspelling: Fairly low
Risk of Mispronunciation: Low
Famous Namesakes: Hairstylist Paul Mitchell; musician Mitch Mitchell
Common Nicknames: Mitch
Common Variations: Mitchel
Consider This: Mitchell ranked in the Top 100 throughout the '90s, but it's on its way down.

Montgomery ★★★

(English) rich man's mountain.
First Impression: People describe Montgomery as a studious Southern gent.
Gender Association: Used mostly for boys
Popularity and Trend: Last ranked in the Top 1000 in the 1960s
Risk of Misspelling: Fairly low
Risk of Mispronunciation: Fairly low
Famous Namesakes: Band Montgomery Gentry; actor Montgomery Cliff; character C. Montgomery Burns (*The Simpsons*); character Montgomery Montgomery (*Lemony Snickett*)
Common Nicknames: Monty
Common Variations: None
Consider This: This name definitely has Southern charm. There may be a slight difference in pronunciation with some saying "mont-GUM-er-ee" and others saying "mont-GUM-ree."

Monty ★★★

(English) a familiar form of Montgomery.

First Impression: Most people picture Monty as a hilarious and quirky British cutup.

Gender Association: Used for boys

Popularity and Trend: Last ranked in the Top 1000 in the 1980s

Risk of Misspelling: Fairly low

Risk of Mispronunciation: Low

Famous Namesakes: Comedy troupe Monty Python; game show host Monty Hall; golfer Colin "Monty" Montgomerie; film *The Full Monty*

Common Nicknames: None

Common Variations: Monte

Consider This: Much of this name's image comes from the legendary Monty Python comedy troupe. If you love its zany antics, you may love this name.

Morgan ★★★

(Scottish) sea warrior.

First Impression: Morgan is seen as a vibrant and popular fellow who loves life.

Gender Association: Used mostly for girls

Popularity and Trend: #366 (#332 in 2000)

Risk of Misspelling: Fairly low

Risk of Mispronunciation: Low

Famous Namesakes: Actor Morgan Freeman; filmmaker Morgan Spurlock; financier J. P. Morgan; baseball player Joe Morgan

Common Nicknames: None

Common Variations: Morgen

Consider This: Although Morgan's image is great, some parents may not like the fact it's used for more girls than boys.

Morris ★★★

(Latin) dark-skinned; moor; marshland. (English) a form of Maurice.

First Impression: Morris is depicted as an ordinary older man who's fairly kind, fairly meek, fairly smart, and thoroughly dull.

Gender Association: Used for boys

Popularity and Trend: Last ranked in the Top 1000 in the 1990s

Risk of Misspelling: Fairly low

Risk of Mispronunciation: Low

Famous Namesakes: Artist William Morris; cat-food mascot Morris the Cat

Common Nicknames: Moss, Morey

Common Variations: Moris

Consider This: Morris's image may be just too dull to make it a good choice.

Morton ★★

(English) town near the moor.

First Impression: People think Morton is a reserved guy who's quite intelligent but afraid to take risks.

Gender Association: Used for boys

Popularity and Trend: Last ranked in the Top 1000 in the 1950s

Risk of Misspelling: Fairly low

Risk of Mispronunciation: Low

Famous Namesakes: Football player Johnnie Morton; composer Morton Feldman; musician Jelly Roll Morton

Common Nicknames: Mort, Morty

Common Variations: Morten

Consider This: A milquetoast image may convince many parents not to roll the dice on Morton.

Moses ★★★★★

(Hebrew) drawn out of the water. (Egyptian) son, child.

First Impression: People think of Moses as a generous and respectful man with strong values, much like the biblical Moses.

Gender Association: Used for boys

Popularity and Trend: #445 (#461 in 2000)

Risk of Misspelling: Fairly low

Risk of Mispronunciation: Fairly low

Famous Namesakes: Biblical figure Moses; basketball player Moses Malone; star kid Moses Martin

Common Nicknames: Moe, Moss

Common Variations: Moishe, Moises

Consider This: Not quite as popular as other biblical names, Moses is definitely getting some attention lately, thanks to star kid Moses Martin.

Muhammed ★★★

(Arabic) a form of Muhammad.

First Impression: Muhammed is described as a faithful Muslim who's compassionate and strong-minded.

Gender Association: Used for boys

Popularity and Trend: Never been ranked in Top 1000

Risk of Misspelling: Average

Risk of Mispronunciation: Average

Famous Namesakes: Islamic figure Muhammad; boxer Muhammad Ali; football player Mushin Muhammad

Common Nicknames: None

Common Variations: Muhammad, Mohammad, Mohammed

Consider This: Although his name is spelled differently, the Islamic prophet Muhammad overwhelmingly influences this name's image. There may be some pronunciation differences with both "muh-HAH-med" and "moo-HAH-med" as options.

Murray ★★

(Scottish) sailor.

First Impression: Murray is said to be a loner with a knack for science and math but absolutely no social skills.

Gender Association: Used for boys

Popularity and Trend: Last ranked in the Top 1000 in the 1970s

Risk of Misspelling: Fairly low

Risk of Mispronunciation: Fairly low

Famous Namesakes: Actor Bill Murray; baseball player Eddie Murray; character Murray Slaughter (*The Mary Tyler Moore Show*); actor F. Murray Abraham

Common Nicknames: None

Common Variations: Murry

Consider This: Most parents probably won't find Murray's geeky image pleasing.

Myles ★★★★

(Latin) soldier. (German) a form of Miles.

First Impression: People say Myles is a brilliant booklover as well as a kind, true friend.

Gender Association: Used for boys

Popularity and Trend: #311 (#290 in 2000)

Risk of Misspelling: Average

Risk of Mispronunciation: Low

Famous Namesakes: NCAA president Myles Brand

Common Nicknames: None

Common Variations: Miles

Consider This: This variation of Miles doesn't stand up quite as well as the original, but it's a solid alternative nonetheless. Spelling will be a problem for both.

Myron ★★

(Greek) fragrant ointment. (Polish) a form of Miron.

First Impression: Myron is regarded as an awkward, bespectacled brainiac who loves chess and role-playing games.

Gender Association: Used for boys

Popularity and Trend: Last ranked #923 in 2000

Risk of Misspelling: Fairly low

Risk of Mispronunciation: Low

Famous Namesakes: Sculptor Myron

Common Nicknames: Ron

Common Variations: Miron

Consider This: Myron's unflattering image limits its appeal.

Nathan ★★★★★

(Hebrew) a form of Nathaniel.

First Impression: Most people feel Nathan is a funny, happy, and off-the-wall guy who's kind-hearted and clever.

Gender Association: Used for boys

Popularity and Trend: #23 (#30 in 2000)

Risk of Misspelling: Fairly low

Risk of Mispronunciation: Low

Famous Namesakes: Actor Nathan Lane; patriot Nathan Hale; biblical figure Nathan; actor Nathan Fillion

Common Nicknames: Nate, Nat

Common Variations: Nathen

Consider This: This classic name has stood the test of time and is gaining in popularity. It may be *too* popular soon, but for now it seems a solid choice.

Nathaniel ★★★★

(Hebrew) a form of Nathanael.

First Impression: People think Nathaniel is faithful, loving, and wise.

Gender Association: Used for boys

Popularity and Trend: #69 (#61 in 2000)

Risk of Misspelling: Fairly low

Risk of Mispronunciation: Fairly low

Famous Namesakes: Biblical figure Nathanael; writer Nathaniel Hawthorne

Common Nicknames: Nate, Nat, Nathan

Common Variations: Nathanael, Nethaniel

Consider This: This variation of Nathanael is more popular and easier to spell than its root name. It's also a meatier alternative to Nathan.

Navin ★★★

(Hindi) new, novel.

First Impression: Navin is perceived to be a mild-mannered and pleasant fellow with lots of creativity.

Gender Association: Used for boys

Popularity and Trend: Never been ranked in Top 1000

Risk of Misspelling: Average

Risk of Mispronunciation: Average

Famous Namesakes: Character Navin R. Johnson (*The Jerk*); actor Naveen Andrews (*Lost*)

Common Nicknames: None

Common Variations: Naveen

Consider This: Navin has yet to be ranked, but its great image may soon propel it onto the charts. Those familiar with *The Jerk* will pronounce it "NAV-in," but those familiar with the name's Hindi origins will pronounce it "nah-VEEN."

Neal ★★

(Irish) a form of Neil.

First Impression: Neal is seen as a very smart but stubborn man who borders on fussiness.

Gender Association: Used for boys

Popularity and Trend: Last ranked #892 in 2000

Risk of Misspelling: Average

Risk of Mispronunciation: Low

Famous Namesakes: Singer Neal McCoy; astronaut Neil Armstrong; playwright Neil Simon; radio personality Neal Boortz

Common Nicknames: None

Common Variations: Neil

Consider This: Not as popular as Neil, its original form, Neal will likely be confused for the traditional spelling.

Nelson ★★★

(English) son of Neil.

First Impression: Nelson is considered either the one who gets bullied or the one who does the bullying.

Gender Association: Used for boys

Popularity and Trend: #447 (#417 in 2000)

Risk of Misspelling: Low

Risk of Mispronunciation: Low

Famous Namesakes: Politician Nelson Rockefeller; activist Nelson Mandela; character Nelson Muntz (*The Simpsons*); the Ozzie and Harriet Nelson family

Common Nicknames: Nellie

Common Variations: Nels

Consider This: Despite having a Nobel Peace Prize winner as a namesake, Nelson's image is not particularly peaceful.

Nicholas ★★★★★

(Greek) victorious people.

First Impression: People say Nicholas is charming, personable, and attractive.

Gender Association: Used mostly for boys

Popularity and Trend: #17 (#6 in 2000)

Risk of Misspelling: Fairly low

Risk of Mispronunciation: Low

Famous Namesakes: Actor Nicholas Cage; author Nicholas Sparks; saint Nicholas; czar Nicholas I

Common Nicknames: Nick, Claus, Cole, Nico, Nicky

Common Variations: Nicholai, Nicolas, Nickolas, Nikolas

Consider This: This strong, versatile name has a great image and is worthy of its 5 stars.

Nick ★★★★

(English) a short form of Dominic, Nicholas.

First Impression: Nick is described as a good-looking and goofy guy who loves sports, animals, and children.

Gender Association: Used for boys

Popularity and Trend: #820 (#767 in 2000)

Risk of Misspelling: Low

Risk of Mispronunciation: Low

Famous Namesakes: Singer Nick Carter; singer Nick Lachey; actor Nick Nolte; golfer Nick Faldo

Common Nicknames: Nicky

Common Variations: None

Consider This: Even though the image is solid, Nick may work better as a nickname than as a given name.

Nigel ★★

(Latin) dark night.

First Impression: People imagine Nigel is an attractive but wimpy Brit.

Gender Association: Used for boys

Popularity and Trend: #709 (#576 in 2000)

Risk of Misspelling: Fairly low

Risk of Mispronunciation: Fairly low

Famous Namesakes: Actor Nigel Bruce; musician Nigel Kennedy

Common Nicknames: None

Common Variations: None

Consider This: Nigel may be a popular name elsewhere in the world, but it has a wimpy image here. Most people will pronounce it correctly as "NYE-jehl."

Noah ★★★★

(Hebrew) peaceful, restful.

First Impression: Noah is believed to be a noble, hardworking, and godly man.

Gender Association: Used mostly for boys

Popularity and Trend: #15 (#27 in 2000)

Risk of Misspelling: Low

Risk of Mispronunciation: Low

Famous Namesakes: Biblical figure Noah; lexicographer Noah Webster; actor Noah Wyle; basketball player Joakim Noah

Common Nicknames: None

Common Variations: None

Consider This: The biblical figure Noah seems to flood people's minds when they hear this name. Its surging popularity is in sync with other biblical names.

Nodin ★★

(Native American) wind.

First Impression: This name makes people picture a quiet, introverted dork with a nasally voice, a chubby body, and Norwegian heritage.

Gender Association: Used for boys

Popularity and Trend: Never been ranked in Top 1000

Risk of Misspelling: Fairly low

Risk of Mispronunciation: Fairly low

Famous Namesakes: None

Common Nicknames: None

Common Variations: None

Consider This: This unusual name may not win over many parents, given its introverted image. At least it's pronounced phonetically: "NOH-din."

Noel ★★★

(French) day of Christ's birth

First Impression: Noel is depicted as an intelligent chap with a talent for music, poetry, and art.

Gender Association: Used mostly for boys

Popularity and Trend: #448 (#407 in 2000)

Risk of Misspelling: Fairly low

Risk of Mispronunciation: Fairly low

Famous Namesakes: Writer Noel Coward; musician Noel Gallagher

Common Nicknames: None

Common Variations: None

Consider This: Noel has a sophisticated vibe, and its consistently moderate popularity suggests parents are taking note. However, this spelling can have two pronunciations: "NOH-el," which is used more for boys, and "noh-ELL," which is used more for girls.

Nolan ★★★★

(Irish) famous; noble.

First Impression: People say Nolan has a tough, stubborn competitive streak, which he most likely channels into sports.

Gender Association: Used for boys

Popularity and Trend: #145 (#180 in 2000)

Risk of Misspelling: Fairly low

Risk of Mispronunciation: Low

Famous Namesakes: Baseball player Nolan Ryan; director Christopher Nolan; hockey player Owen Nolan

Common Nicknames: None

Common Variations: Nolen

Consider This: Nolan Ryan gives this name a competitive, sporty image that's growing in popularity.

Norman ★★★

(French) Norseman.

First Impression: Most people think Norman is a chess-club nerd who's bashful but kind; however, others say he's a creepy serial killer.

Gender Association: Used for boys

Popularity and Trend: Last ranked #671 in 2000

Risk of Misspelling: Low

Risk of Mispronunciation: Low

Famous Namesakes: Artist Norman Rockwell; character Norman Bates (*Psycho*); writer Norman Mailer; general Norman Schwarzkopf; golfer Greg Norman

Common Nicknames: Norm

Common Variations: None

Consider This: People who've seen *Psycho* may have a hard time selecting this name for their child.

Norton ★★

(English) northern town.

First Impression: Folks say Norton is a brainy dweeb with glasses and a penchant for science.

Gender Association: Used for boys

Popularity and Trend: Last ranked in the Top 1000 in the 1930s

Risk of Misspelling: Low

Risk of Mispronunciation: Low

Famous Namesakes: Actor Edward Norton; character Ed Norton (*The Honeymooners*)

Common Nicknames: None

Common Variations: None

Consider This: Norton works better as a surname.

Obert ★★

(German) wealthy; bright.

First Impression: There isn't a clear image of Obert's personality, but everyone sees him as an overweight fellow with glasses.

Gender Association: Used for boys

Popularity and Trend: Never been ranked in Top 1000

Risk of Misspelling: Average

Risk of Mispronunciation: Average

Famous Namesakes: None

Common Nicknames: Bert

Common Variations: None

Consider This: Obert has never been a Top 1000 name, which is probably why it has an ambiguous image. Most people will pronounce it "OH-bert," but a few may pronounce it "OH-bairt."

Octavius ★★

(Latin) a form of Octavio.

First Impression: People think Octavius is a masterful leader who's strong-willed, serious, and confident.

Gender Association: Used for boys

Popularity and Trend: Never been ranked in Top 1000

Risk of Misspelling: Average

Risk of Mispronunciation: Average

Famous Namesakes: Legendary Briton king Octavius; character Doctor Otto Octavius (*Spider-Man*)

Common Nicknames: None

Common Variations: Octavious

Consider This: This powerful image is inspired by Octavius, the legendary king of the Britons, or perhaps even Octavian, the Roman emperor. Spelling and pronunciation may be a challenge for some, however.

Og ★★

(Aramaic) king.

First Impression: People agree Og is thick, tall, ugly, and bald.

Gender Association: Used for boys

Popularity and Trend: Never been ranked in Top 1000

Risk of Misspelling: Fairly low

Risk of Mispronunciation: Fairly low

Famous Namesakes: Biblical figure Og; inspirational figure Og Mandino; Celtic mythological figure Angus Og

Common Nicknames: None

Common Variations: None

Consider This: Even though it's a biblical name, Og hasn't won over many folks. On the plus side, it's fairly easy to spell and pronounce.

Oliver ★★★★★

(Latin) olive tree. (Scandinavian) kind; affectionate.

First Impression: Many say Oliver is charming, fun, smart, and attractive.

Gender Association: Used for boys

Popularity and Trend: #173 (#305 in 2000)

Risk of Misspelling: Low

Risk of Mispronunciation: Low

Famous Namesakes: Book and play character Oliver Twist; director Oliver Stone; general Oliver North; British lord protector Oliver Cromwell; comedian Oliver Hardy

Common Nicknames: Ollie

Common Variations: Olivier

Consider This: Oliver's popularity has skyrocketed recently, and its positive image makes it a solid choice.

Ollie ★★★

(English) a familiar form of Oliver.

First Impression: Ollie is perceived as a silly, happy, and upbeat fellow.

Gender Association: Used about equally for girls and boys

Popularity and Trend: Last ranked in the Top 1000 in the 1970s

Risk of Misspelling: Fairly low

Risk of Mispronunciation: Fairly low

Famous Namesakes: Skateboarder Alan "Ollie" Gelfand; basketball player Kevin Ollie

Common Nicknames: None

Common Variations: Olly

Consider This: A likable nickname for Oliver, Ollie may be too informal as a given name. Plus, just as many girls have this name as boys.

Omar ★★★

(Arabic) highest; follower of the Prophet. (Hebrew) reverent.

First Impression: Omar is thought to be a charismatic and popular dark-skinned man.

Gender Association: Used for boys

Popularity and Trend: #131 (#146 in 2000)

Risk of Misspelling: Average

Risk of Mispronunciation: Average

Famous Namesakes: Actor Omar Sharif; poet Omar Khayyám; actor Omar Epps; baseball player Omar Vizquel

Common Nicknames: None

Common Variations: Omarr

Consider This: Omar projects a charming image, and its foreign aura sets it apart. Few people will have trouble pronouncing it "OH-mar."

Orien ★★

(Latin) visitor from the east.

First Impression: Many people think Orien is moody, mean, and hard to like.

Gender Association: Used for boys

Popularity and Trend: Never been ranked in Top 1000

Risk of Misspelling: Fairly high

Risk of Mispronunciation: Fairly high

Famous Namesakes: Basketball player Orien Greene

Common Nicknames: Rien

Common Variations: None

Consider This: Based on its "eastern" meaning, Orien is pronounced "ORE-ee-en." But without that clue, people may think it's pronounced like the name Orion. Either way, spelling could be a problem.

Orlando ★★★★

(German) famous throughout the land. (Spanish) a form of Roland.

First Impression: People imagine Orlando is courteous and kind but also an intense actor who's talented and creative, much like actor Orlando Bloom.

Gender Association: Used for boys

Popularity and Trend: #356 (#401 in 2000)

Risk of Misspelling: Fairly low

Risk of Mispronunciation: Fairly low

Famous Namesakes: Actor Orlando Bloom; comedian Orlando Jones; singer Tony Orlando; Shakespearean character Orlando; book character Orlando

Common Nicknames: Lando

Common Variations: None

Consider This: This classic name has gotten a definite boost from Orlando Bloom's popularity.

Orson ★★★★

(Latin) bearlike.

First Impression: Orson is seen as an old grandfather who's stocky and balding.

Gender Association: Used for boys

Popularity and Trend: Never been ranked in Top 1000

Risk of Misspelling: Fairly low

Risk of Mispronunciation: Low

Famous Namesakes: Director and actor Orson Welles; TV personality Orson Bean

Common Nicknames: Sonny

Common Variations: Orsino, Orsen

Consider This: Orson has never been ranked, and it may be because people picture a grandpa, not a child, when they hear or read it.

Oscar ★★★

(Scandinavian) divine spearman.

First Impression: Oscar is described as grouchy, likely thanks to Oscar the Grouch of *Sesame Street* fame.

Gender Association: Used for boys

Popularity and Trend: #118 (#122 in 2000)

Risk of Misspelling: Fairly low

Risk of Mispronunciation: Low

Famous Namesakes: Character Oscar the Grouch (*Sesame Street*); writer Oscar Wilde; boxer Oscar de la Hoya; businessman Oscar Mayer

Common Nicknames: None

Common Variations: Oskar

Consider This: This traditional name is making a comeback in spite of its grouchy image.

Oswald ★★

(English) God's power; God's crest.

First Impression: Oswald is viewed as a weirdo rejected by society, despite his riches and fame.

Gender Association: Used for boys

Popularity and Trend: Last ranked in the Top 1000 in the 1930s

Risk of Misspelling: Fairly low

Risk of Mispronunciation: Fairly low

Famous Namesakes: Assassin Lee Harvey Oswald; character Oswald Lee Harvey (*The Drew Carey Show*)

Common Nicknames: Oz, Ozzie, Waldo

Common Variations: Oswaldo

Consider This: Oswald may have great versatility, but its terrible image and notorious namesake make it a 2-star name.

Otis ★★

(Greek) keen of hearing. (German) son of Otto.

First Impression: People see Otis as an old, overweight man.

Gender Association: Used for boys

Popularity and Trend: Last ranked in the Top 1000 in the 1990s

Risk of Misspelling: Fairly low

Risk of Mispronunciation: Fairly low

Famous Namesakes: Singer Otis Redding; inventor Elisha Otis

Common Nicknames: None

Common Variations: Ottis

Consider This: This old-fashioned name may have had a resurgence a decade ago, but it seems passé today. Most people will know to pronounce it "OH-tiss."

Otto ★★

(German) rich.

First Impression: Otto is said to be a chubby German who's dumb but funny.

Gender Association: Used for boys

Popularity and Trend: Last ranked in the Top 1000 in the 1970s

Risk of Misspelling: Fairly low

Risk of Mispronunciation: Fairly low

Famous Namesakes: German statesman Otto von Bismark; director Otto Preminger; character Otto Mann (*The Simpsons*)

Common Nicknames: None

Common Variations: None

Consider This: If you like palindromes, you may find Otto attractive. Although the *O* has a different sound than it does in Otis, most people will know to pronounce it "AH-toh."

Ottokar ★★

(German) happy warrior.

First Impression: Some people think Ottokar is helpful, moral, and heroic. But others believe he's an introverted loner.

Gender Association: Used for boys

Popularity and Trend: Never been ranked in Top 1000

Risk of Misspelling: Fairly high

Risk of Mispronunciation: Average

Famous Namesakes: Bohemian king Ottokar I

Common Nicknames: Otto

Common Variations: None

Consider This: Although it's pronounced much like Otto, Ottokar ("AH-toh-car") may be hard for some people to say or spell because it's so unfamiliar.

Owen ★★★★★

(Irish) born to nobility; young warrior. (Welsh) a form of Evan.

First Impression: People think Owen is a very intelligent, very nice, and very entertaining guy.

Gender Association: Used for boys

Popularity and Trend: #58 (#145 in 2000)

Risk of Misspelling: Low

Risk of Mispronunciation: Low

Famous Namesakes: Actor Owen Wilson; actor Clive Owen; hockey player Owen Nolan; Welsh hero Owen Glendower

Common Nicknames: None

Common Variations: None

Consider This: Owen is moving up the Top 100 list with a great first impression.

Oz ★★★

(Hebrew) a form of Osborn, Oswald.

First Impression: People think Oz is a one-of-a-kind man who's quirky, creative, and funky.

Gender Association: Used about equally for girls and boys

Popularity and Trend: Never been ranked in Top 1000

Risk of Misspelling: Fairly low

Risk of Mispronunciation: Low

Famous Namesakes: Director Frank Oz; book and movie character Wizard of Oz

Common Nicknames: Ozzie

Common Variations: None

Consider This: Thanks to L. Frank Baum's books and the beloved *Wizard of Oz* movie, this name's image is a bit strange and magical. Also, the name is used for both genders about equally.

Pablo ★★★★

(Spanish) a form of Paul.

First Impression: Most think Pablo is a Latino artist who's a creative free spirit.

Gender Association: Used for boys

Popularity and Trend: #292 (#298 in 2000)

Risk of Misspelling: Average

Risk of Mispronunciation: Average

Famous Namesakes: Artist Pablo Picasso; drug lord Pablo Escobar; writer Pablo Neruda; baseball player Pablo Ozuna; actor Pablo Montero

Common Nicknames: None

Common Variations: None

Consider This: It's natural that Pablo Picasso figures into this name's image. Art lovers and Latino families may choose this name. However, those unfamiliar with Latino names may not know to pronounce it "PAH-bloh."

Paddy ★★★

(Irish) a familiar form of Padraic, Patrick.

First Impression: Paddy is seen as an easygoing guy, and he finds it easy to go along with what others say.

Gender Association: Used for boys
Popularity and Trend: Never been ranked in Top 1000
Risk of Misspelling: Fairly low
Risk of Mispronunciation: Low
Famous Namesakes: Writer Paddy Chayefsky; musician Paddy Moloney
Common Nicknames: None
Common Variations: None
Consider This: Despite its likable image, this prototypical Irish name's informality makes it more appropriate for use as a nickname than a given name. Plus, its pronunciation is very close to Patty, a traditional nickname for girls, which may cause gender confusion.

Palmer ★★

(English) palm-bearing pilgrim.
First Impression: People say Palmer is a snobby, smarmy, and materialistic yuppie, but, boy, is he well dressed.
Gender Association: Used mostly for boys
Popularity and Trend: Last ranked in the Top 1000 in the 1940s
Risk of Misspelling: Low
Risk of Mispronunciation: Low
Famous Namesakes: Golfer Arnold Palmer; football player Carson

Palmer; character David Palmer (24)
Common Nicknames: None
Common Variations: None
Consider This: Palmer's snobby image may limit its appeal.

Paolo ★★

(Italian) a form of Paul.
First Impression: Paolo is pictured as a sexy Italian smooth talker.
Gender Association: Used for boys
Popularity and Trend: Never been ranked in Top 1000
Risk of Misspelling: Fairly high
Risk of Mispronunciation: Fairly high
Famous Namesakes: Artist Paolo Veronese
Common Nicknames: None
Common Variations: None
Consider This: Paolo has a definite ethnic vibe and an alluring image, but its challenging pronunciation ("POW-loh") and spelling may limit its selection to Italians.

Park ★★

(Chinese) cypress tree. (English) a form of Parker.
First Impression: Park is imagined to be a wealthy heir who's spoiled, snobby, and self-centered.
Gender Association: Used for boys
Popularity and Trend: Never been ranked in Top 1000
Risk of Misspelling: Low
Risk of Mispronunciation: Low

Famous Namesakes: Baseball player Chan-ho Park
Common Nicknames: None
Common Variations: None
Consider This: Parker is a better choice than this nickname.

Parker ★★★★

(English) park keeper.
First Impression: People imagine Parker as a rich, flaxen-haired WASP who's smart, dry humored, and sociable.
Gender Association: Used mostly for boys
Popularity and Trend: #116 (#127 in 2000)
Risk of Misspelling: Low
Risk of Mispronunciation: Low
Famous Namesakes: Character Parker Lewis (*Parker Lewis Can't Lose*); game makers Parker Brothers; actor Parker Stevenson; character Peter Parker (*Spider-Man*)
Common Nicknames: Park
Common Variations: None
Consider This: Despite its WASPy image, Parker's popularity is rising.

Pascale ★★

(French) born on Easter or Passover.
First Impression: People say Pascale is a talented artist who's either loud and talkative or solemn and quiet.
Gender Association: Used for boys

Popularity and Trend: Never been ranked in Top 1000
Risk of Misspelling: Average
Risk of Mispronunciation: Fairly low
Famous Namesakes: Thinker Blaise Pascal
Common Nicknames: None
Common Variations: Pascal
Consider This: This unusual name certainly has an artistic aura. Although it's French, it's fairly easy to pronounce: "pas-CALL."

Pat ★★

(Native American) fish. (English) a short form of Patrick.
First Impression: Pat evokes the image of a sincere and reliable fellow with a plump physique.
Gender Association: Used about equally for girls and boys
Popularity and Trend: Last ranked in the Top 1000 in the 1970s
Risk of Misspelling: Low
Risk of Mispronunciation: Low
Famous Namesakes: Singer Pat Boone; actor Pat Morita; politician Pat Buchanan; sportscaster Pat Summerall; game show host Pat Sajak
Common Nicknames: None
Common Variations: None
Consider This: Pat's dull image, combined with its ambiguous gender association, may convince you to strike it from your short list.

Patrick ★★★★

(Latin) nobleman.
First Impression: Patrick is pictured as either a sparkling personality, or he's as dull as they come.
Gender Association: Used for boys
Popularity and Trend: #110 (#68 in 2000)
Risk of Misspelling: Fairly low
Risk of Mispronunciation: Low
Famous Namesakes: Actor Patrick Stewart; saint Patrick; basketball player Patrick Ewing; actor Patrick Swayze; hockey player Patrick Roy
Common Nicknames: Pat, Paddy
Common Variations: Padraic, Patric
Consider This: A traditional name, Patrick's versatility may be irresistible, even if its image isn't.

Paul ★★★★★

(Latin) small.
First Impression: Paul is described as kind, compassionate, dependable, and humble.
Gender Association: Used for boys
Popularity and Trend: #134 (#100 in 2000)
Risk of Misspelling: Low
Risk of Mispronunciation: Low
Famous Namesakes: Biblical figure Paul; singer Paul McCartney; actor Paul Newman; singer Paul Simon; patriot Paul Revere
Common Nicknames: Paulie
Common Variations: Paolo, Paulino

Consider This: Going against the current trend, this biblical name's popularity isn't rising. Yet its stellar image still makes it a solid choice.

Payton ★★

(English) a form of Patton.
First Impression: Payton gives the impression of a football player who's resourceful, driven, and businesslike, much like NFL quarterback Peyton Manning.
Gender Association: Used mostly for girls
Popularity and Trend: #267 (#219 in 2000)
Risk of Misspelling: Average
Risk of Mispronunciation: Fairly low
Famous Namesakes: Football player Walter Payton; football player Peyton Manning
Common Nicknames: None
Common Variations: Peyton
Consider This: Football fans may love Payton, even though it's actually used more for girls than boys. Spelling will likely be confused for "Peyton."

Pedro ★★★

(Spanish) a form of Peter.
First Impression: Pedro is depicted as a short Latino who's entertaining, generous, and kind.
Gender Association: Used for boys
Popularity and Trend: #219 (#210 in 2000)

Risk of Misspelling: Average

Risk of Mispronunciation: Average

Famous Namesakes: Director Pedro Almodóvar; character Pedro Sanchez (*Napoleon Dynamite*); baseball player Pedro Martínez

Common Nicknames: None

Common Variations: None

Consider This: A popular and solid choice for Latino families, Pedro may not fit well with surnames of other origins. Most people will pronounce it correctly as "PAY-droh."

Percy ★★

(French) a familiar form of Percival.

First Impression: People think Percy is snobby, fussy, bossy, spoiled, wimpy, whiny, *and* dorky.

Gender Association: Used for boys

Popularity and Trend: Last ranked in the Top 1000 in the 1980s

Risk of Misspelling: Fairly low

Risk of Mispronunciation: Low

Famous Namesakes: Poet Percy Bysshe Shelley; singer Percy Sledge; character Percy Weasley (*Harry Potter* series)

Common Nicknames: None

Common Variations: None

Consider This: With such an unpleasant image, it's no wonder parents are avoiding Percy.

Perry ★★

(English) a form of Peregrine, Peter.

First Impression: Some think Perry is a snob, but others think he's all right.

Gender Association: Used mostly for boys

Popularity and Trend: #958 (#684 in 2000)

Risk of Misspelling: Fairly low

Risk of Mispronunciation: Fairly low

Famous Namesakes: Singer Perry Como; football player William "The Refrigerator" Perry; book and TV character Perry Mason; designer Perry Ellis; actor Matthew Perry

Common Nicknames: None

Common Variations: Parry

Consider This: Perry is poised to slide off the Top 1000 list, where it may become a unique "find."

Pete ★★

(English) a short form of Peter.

First Impression: Most folks think Pete is a scrawny, nerdy, and obnoxious teacher's pet.

Gender Association: Used for boys

Popularity and Trend: Last ranked in the Top 1000 in the 1990s

Risk of Misspelling: Low

Risk of Mispronunciation: Low

Famous Namesakes: Baseball player Pete Rose; musician Pete Townshend

Common Nicknames: Petey

Common Variations: None

Consider This: Pete has fallen out of the Top 1000, but Peter is still a good bet.

Peter ★★★★

(Greek, Latin) small rock.

First Impression: Is Peter dry or dashing? People describe him as one or the other.

Gender Association: Used for boys

Popularity and Trend: #167 (#125 in 2000)

Risk of Misspelling: Low

Risk of Mispronunciation: Low

Famous Namesakes: Biblical figure Peter; news anchor Peter Jennings; book and movie character Peter Pan; character Peter Parker (*Spider-Man*); actor Peter O'Toole

Common Nicknames: Pete, Petey

Common Variations: Peder, Pieter

Consider This: Peter's image can be either positive or negative. Nonetheless, it's a versatile name with solid popularity.

Philip ★★★

(Greek) lover of horses.

First Impression: Philip is pictured as a rude, egomaniacal, and spoiled aristocrat.

Gender Association: Used for boys

Popularity and Trend: #343 (#255 in 2000)

Risk of Misspelling: Fairly low

Risk of Mispronunciation: Fairly low

Famous Namesakes: Biblical figure Philip; British prince Philip; football player Philip Rivers

Common Nicknames: Flip, Phil

Common Variations: Felipe, Philipe, Phillip

Consider This: Philip's popularity is falling, but it's still a classic name. Spelling (is it one *l* or two?) and pronunciation (is it "fee-LEEP" or "FILL-up"?) could be slight problems.

Phineas ★★

(English) a form of Pinchas.

First Impression: Phineas is thought to be quite intelligent and thoughtful, but he's also quite sensitive.

Gender Association: Used for boys

Popularity and Trend: Never been ranked in Top 1000

Risk of Misspelling: Fairly high

Risk of Mispronunciation: Fairly high

Famous Namesakes: Greek mythological figure Phineas; showman Phineas Taylor "P. T." Barnum; star kid Phinnaeus Moder

Common Nicknames: Finn

Common Variations: Fineas, Phinnaeus

Consider This: Julia Roberts's son, Phinnaeus, introduced a form of this name to the masses, but it still seems too unique for average folk. Pronunciation ("FIN-ee-as") and spelling are challenging.

Pierce ★★

(English) a form of Peter.

First Impression: People say Pierce is a snob who flaunts his money and is quite full of himself.

Gender Association: Used mostly for boys

Popularity and Trend: #549 (#498 in 2000)

Risk of Misspelling: Fairly low

Risk of Mispronunciation: Low

Famous Namesakes: President Franklin Pierce; actor Pierce Brosnan; character "Hawkeye" Pierce (*M*A*S*H*); actor David Hyde Pierce

Common Nicknames: None

Common Variations: Pearce, Piers, Peirce

Consider This: Pierce's snobby image may be the cause of its falling popularity.

Pierre ★★

(French) a form of Peter.

First Impression: Pierre is thought to be a French sophisticate who's worldly and elegant.

Gender Association: Used for boys

Popularity and Trend: Last ranked #926 in 2000

Risk of Misspelling: Average

Risk of Mispronunciation: Average

Famous Namesakes: Canadian prime minister Pierre Trudeau; designer Pierre Cardin; baseball player Juan Pierre

Common Nicknames: None

Common Variations: None

Consider This: Pierre hasn't won over many parents during the last several years. Pronunciation is also a problem; not every one knows to pronounce it "pee-AIR." (Folks from South Dakota may say "PEER.")

Pin ★★★

(Vietnamese) faithful boy.

First Impression: Some say Pin is timid, nervous, and withdrawn; others see him as lighthearted, easygoing, and strong.

Gender Association: Used for boys

Popularity and Trend: Never been ranked in Top 1000

Risk of Misspelling: Low

Risk of Mispronunciation: Low

Famous Namesakes: None

Common Nicknames: None

Common Variations: None

Consider This: This Vietnamese name may seem strange to people of other backgrounds. It is easy to say and spell, however.

Poni ★★

(Scottish) a form of Pony.

First Impression: Poni is seen as a strange goofball who loves silly jokes.

Gender Association: Used for boys

Popularity and Trend: Never been ranked in Top 1000

Risk of Misspelling: Fairly high

Risk of Mispronunciation: Fairly low
Famous Namesakes: None
Common Nicknames: None
Common Variations: Pony
Consider This: This name is too silly for most people, and a child named Poni will likely be teased. On top of that, spelling will be challenging because people will assume it's "Pony."

Porter ★★★★

(Latin) gatekeeper.
First Impression: Most see Porter as an accommodating and loyal friend.
Gender Association: Used mostly for boys
Popularity and Trend: #476 (#804 in 2000)
Risk of Misspelling: Low
Risk of Mispronunciation: Low
Famous Namesakes: Singer Porter Wagoner; character Porter (Payback); composer Cole Porter
Common Nicknames: None
Common Variations: None
Consider This: With a solid image and easy spelling and pronunciation, it's no wonder Porter's popularity has surged in the new millennium.

Preston ★★★

(English) priest's estate.
First Impression: Preston seems to be a geek who's as pretentious and snooty as he is studious.
Gender Association: Used for boys

Popularity and Trend: #114 (#142 in 2000)
Risk of Misspelling: Low
Risk of Mispronunciation: Low
Famous Namesakes: Character Preston Burke (Grey's Anatomy); singer Billy Preston
Common Nicknames: None
Common Variations: None
Consider This: Despite Preston's pretentious image, its popularity keeps rising.

Prince ★★

(Latin) chief; prince.
First Impression: People imagine Prince as a raunchy and arrogant singer.
Gender Association: Used for boys
Popularity and Trend: #825 (#887 in 2000)
Risk of Misspelling: Low
Risk of Mispronunciation: Low
Famous Namesakes: Singer Prince; star kid Prince Michael Joseph Jackson
Common Nicknames: None
Common Variations: None
Consider This: Rock icon Prince definitely leaves his mark on this name's image. If you're not a fan, there's no strong reason to choose it.

Pryor ★★

(Latin) head of the monastery; prior.

First Impression: This name creates an image of a stuffy, pompous preppy.
Gender Association: Used for boys
Popularity and Trend: Never been ranked in Top 1000
Risk of Misspelling: Average
Risk of Mispronunciation: Low
Famous Namesakes: Comedian Richard Pryor; baseball player Mark Prior
Common Nicknames: None
Common Variations: Prior
Consider This: Pryor seems better suited as a surname than a given name. People may expect it to be spelled "Prior."

Purdy ★★

(Hindi) recluse.
First Impression: People believe this hillbilly is anal-retentive, prudish, and overly sensitive.
Gender Association: Used for boys
Popularity and Trend: Never been ranked in Top 1000
Risk of Misspelling: Average
Risk of Mispronunciation: Low
Famous Namesakes: None
Common Nicknames: None
Common Variations: None
Consider This: Despite its Hindi origin, this name has an unflattering downhome image, because "purdy" is an exaggerated way to pronounce the word pretty with a Southern accent.

Quentin ★★★

(Latin) fifth. (English) queen's town.

First Impression: Quentin is viewed as a lanky academic with quirky creativity and overachieving discipline.

Gender Association: Used for boys

Popularity and Trend: #347 (#325 in 2000)

Risk of Misspelling: Fairly low

Risk of Mispronunciation: Low

Famous Namesakes: Director Quentin Tarantino; author Quentin Crisp; football player Quentin Jammer

Common Nicknames: None

Common Variations: Quinten, Quenten

Consider This: Quirky may be another good way to describe Quentin, and its moderate popularity suggests parents who like quirkiness find it attractive.

Quincy ★★★★

(French) fifth son's estate.

First Impression: People say Quincy is a dedicated and high-achieving man who's educated, prudent, and patriotic.

Gender Association: Used mostly for boys

Popularity and Trend: #489 (#507 in 2000)

Risk of Misspelling: Fairly low

Risk of Mispronunciation: Low

Famous Namesakes: President John Quincy Adams; music producer Quincy Jones; character Dr. Quincy (*Quincy, M.E.*); football player Quincy Morgan

Common Nicknames: Quinn

Common Variations: Quincey

Consider This: John Quincy Adams was the sixth American president, but he's likely the first person who comes to mind when people hear this name. The name's positive image may account for its rising popularity.

Quinlan ★★★

(Irish) strong; well shaped.

First Impression: Quinlan is seen as a tiny man with dark features and a gentle, calm manner.

Gender Association: Used for boys

Popularity and Trend: Never been ranked in Top 1000

Risk of Misspelling: Fairly low

Risk of Mispronunciation: Low

Famous Namesakes: Baseball player Robb Quinlan; star kid Quinlin Stiller

Common Nicknames: Quinn

Common Variations: None

Consider This: Quinlan has yet to break into the Top 1000, and its average image doesn't help it.

Quinn ★★★★

(Irish) a form of Quincy, Quinlan, Quinten.

First Impression: People say Quinn is well mannered, sweet, and sincere.

Gender Association: Used mostly for boys

Popularity and Trend: #282 (#311 in 2000)

Risk of Misspelling: Fairly low

Risk of Mispronunciation: Low

Famous Namesakes: Basketball coach Quin Snyder; actor Aidan Quinn; actor Anthony Quin

Common Nicknames: None

Common Variations: Quin

Consider This: Of all the names that begin "Quin-," this one has the greatest appeal. Spelling could be a minor problem for those who forget to double the *n*.

Quintin ★★

(Latin) a form of Quentin.

First Impression: Most call Quintin a nerdy science guy who's shy, wimpy, and boyish.

Gender Association: Used for boys

Popularity and Trend: #651 (#570 in 2000)

Risk of Misspelling: Fairly low

Risk of Mispronunciation: Fairly low

Famous Namesakes: Football player Quintin Mikell

Common Nicknames: Quinn

Common Variations: Quinten, Quentin

Consider This: This form of Quentin doesn't score as well as the root spelling. Because they're so similar, spelling and pronunciation may be affected.

Raheem ★★★

(Punjabi) compassionate God.

First Impression: Raheem is considered an ambitious, daring, and confident leader.

Gender Association: Used mostly for boys

Popularity and Trend: Last ranked #919 in 2000

Risk of Misspelling: Average

Risk of Mispronunciation: Fairly low

Famous Namesakes: Character Radio Raheem (*Do the Right Thing*)

Common Nicknames: None

Common Variations: Raheim

Consider This: Raheem has a foreign flavor and a good image. Although it's largely phonetic ("rah-HEEM"), spelling and pronunciation may still challenge some.

Ralph ★★★

(English) wolf counselor.

First Impression: People think Ralph is a sweet but goofy nerd who's unintentionally funny and a little dumb.

Gender Association: Used for boys

Popularity and Trend: #764 (#586 in 2000)

Risk of Misspelling: Fairly low

Risk of Mispronunciation: Average

Famous Namesakes: Activist Ralph Nader; designer Ralph Lauren; character Ralph Wiggum (*The Simpsons*); poet Ralph Waldo Emerson

Common Nicknames: Ralphie

Common Variations: Rolf, Rafe

Consider This: This classic name can be pronounced "rayf" or "rahlf," but most people will pronounce it "ralf."

Ramon ★★★

(Spanish) a form of Raymond.

First Impression: Ramon is described as a happy and excited ladies' man with a Latin heritage and a big smile.

Gender Association: Used for boys

Popularity and Trend: #367 (#319 in 2000)

Risk of Misspelling: Average

Risk of Mispronunciation: Fairly high

Famous Namesakes: Baseball player Ramon Hernandez

Common Nicknames: None

Common Variations: None

Consider This: This name has ethnic flavor—if pronounced "rah-MOAN" or "ray-MOAN." Pronounced "RAY-mun," the name loses its foreign feel, but it may fit with more family names.

Randolph ★★

(English) shield wolf.

First Impression: Randolph reminds people of an arrogant and spoiled fellow from a well-to-do family.

Gender Association: Used for boys

Popularity and Trend: Last ranked in the Top 1000 in the 1990s

Risk of Misspelling: Fairly low

Risk of Mispronunciation: Low

Famous Namesakes: Actor Randolph Scott; publisher William Randolph Hearst

Common Nicknames: Randy

Common Variations: Randall, Randolf

Consider This: With a stuffy image and low popularity, Randolph would be a clear miss, if it weren't for its great versatility.

Randy ★★★

(English) a familiar form of Rand, Randall, Randolph.

First Impression: People imagine Randy likes to get loud and crazy in a fun, good-natured way.

Gender Association: Used mostly for boys

Popularity and Trend: #310 (#278 in 2000)

Risk of Misspelling: Low

Risk of Mispronunciation: Low

Famous Namesakes: TV personality Randy Jackson; actor Randy Quaid; singer Randy Travis; baseball player Randy Johnson; football player Randy Moss

Common Nicknames: None

Common Variations: None

Consider This: Randy has a more appealing image than its formal form, Randolph, but it lacks versatility.

Ranger ★★★★

(French) forest keeper.

First Impression: Ranger is regarded as an adventurous, outdoorsy man who works with horses and other animals.

Gender Association: Used for boys

Popularity and Trend: Never been ranked in Top 1000

Risk of Misspelling: Low

Risk of Mispronunciation: Low

Famous Namesakes: None

Common Nicknames: None

Common Variations: None

Consider This: This uncommon name describes a distinct occupation. Although it has a good image, it may be too off the beaten path for many folks.

Raphael ★★

(Hebrew) God has healed.

First Impression: People picture Raphael as a handsome Italian painter who's intelligent and unique.

Gender Association: Used for boys

Popularity and Trend: #681 (#621 in 2000)

Risk of Misspelling: Fairly high

Risk of Mispronunciation: Fairly high

Famous Namesakes: Artist Raphael Santi; archangel Raphael; baseball player Rafael Palmeiro

Common Nicknames: Rafi

Common Variations: Rapheal, Rafael

Consider This: While Italian master Raphael is a positive namesake, you need to consider whether that fact makes up for this name's challenging spelling and pronunciation. It can be pronounced "RAY-fee-ell," "RAH-fee-ell," or "rah-fay-ELL."

Rashad ★★

(Arabic) wise counselor.

First Impression: To some, Rashad comes across as intelligent and visionary. But to others, he's shy and reserved.

Gender Association: Used for boys

Popularity and Trend: #660 (#646 in 2000)

Risk of Misspelling: Fairly high

Risk of Mispronunciation: Fairly high

Famous Namesakes: Football player Ahmad Rashad; basketball player Rashad McCants

Common Nicknames: None

Common Variations: Rashaad

Consider This: Rashad may fit best with family names of Middle Eastern or African origin. Those outside the culture may not know to pronounce it "rah-SHAHD."

Raul ★★★

(French) a form of Ralph.

First Impression: People say Raul is a dark Latino man who's handsome, deep, and not a bit conceited.

Gender Association: Used for boys

Popularity and Trend: #255 (#223 in 2000)

Risk of Misspelling: Fairly high

Risk of Mispronunciation: Fairly high

Famous Namesakes: Actor Raúl Juliá; Cuban political figure Raúl Castro; baseball player Raúl Ibáñez

Common Nicknames: None

Common Variations: None

Consider This: Raul has an ethnic flair to go with its great image. However, spelling and pronunciation ("ra-OOL") may be problems.

Ray ★★★

(French) kingly, royal. (English) a form of Rayburn, Raymond.

First Impression: People think Ray is a used-car salesman with a pretty persuasive sales pitch.

Gender Association: Used for boys

Popularity and Trend: #560 (#516 in 2000)

Risk of Misspelling: Low

Risk of Mispronunciation: Low

Famous Namesakes: Actor Ray Romano; singer Ray Charles; boxers Sugar Ray Leonard and Sugar Ray Robinson; businessman Ray Kroc; author Ray Bradbury

Common Nicknames: None

Common Variations: None

Consider This: Ray definitely has a cheesy image, but its familiarity as a nickname may make it an attractive name in its own right.

Raymond ★★★★

(English) mighty; wise protector.

First Impression: Raymond is seen as a high-strung, loud-mouthed goof.

Gender Association: Used for boys

Popularity and Trend: #194 (#162 in 2000)

Risk of Misspelling: Fairly low

Risk of Mispronunciation: Low

Famous Namesakes: Actor Raymond Burr; sitcom *Everybody Loves Raymond*; author Raymond Chandler; character Raymond Babbitt (*Rain Man*)

Common Nicknames: Ray

Common Variations: Ramon, Reymond

Consider This: Apparently, everyone doesn't love Raymond's image.

Reese ★★★

(Welsh) a form of Reece.

First Impression: Reese is believed to be a fun-loving guy who's nice and always happy.

Gender Association: Used mostly for girls

Popularity and Trend: #433 (#419 in 2000)

Risk of Misspelling: Average

Risk of Mispronunciation: Low

Famous Namesakes: Character Reese Wilkerson (*Malcolm in the Middle*); baseball player Pee Wee Reese

Common Nicknames: None

Common Variations: Reece, Rhys

Consider This: Actress Reese Witherspoon has put this name on the map—for girls, that is. As a name for boys, Reese is falling. In addition, this spelling may be confused for "Reece" or "Rhys."

Reggie ★★★★

(English) a familiar form of Reginald.

First Impression: Reggie is said to be a kind and loving athlete.

Gender Association: Used mostly for boys

Popularity and Trend: Last ranked in the Top 1000 in the 1990s

Risk of Misspelling: Low

Risk of Mispronunciation: Low

Famous Namesakes: Baseball player Reggie Jackson; basketball player Reggie Miller; football player Reggie Bush

Common Nicknames: None

Common Variations: None

Consider This: With namesakes like Reggie Jackson, sports fans may consider this a great name for their sons, despite its lack of versatility.

Reginald ★★

(English) king's advisor.

First Impression: Reginald is pictured as an upper-crust Brit who's sophisticated and intelligent but also stuffy, snobby, and spoiled.

Gender Association: Used for boys

Popularity and Trend: #516 (#372 in 2000)

Risk of Misspelling: Fairly low

Risk of Mispronunciation: Fairly low

Famous Namesakes: Truck driver Reginald Denny

Common Nicknames: Reggie

Common Variations: Reginal

Consider This: Although Reginald has the versatility, its nickname, Reggie, clearly has the better image.

Regis ★★★

(Latin) regal.

First Impression: People see Regis as a loud gabber who's good-natured and outgoing.

Gender Association: Used for boys

Popularity and Trend: Last ranked in the Top 1000 in the 1950s

Risk of Misspelling: Fairly low

Risk of Mispronunciation: Fairly low

Famous Namesakes: TV personality Regis Philbin

Common Nicknames: None

Common Variations: None

Consider This: If you like watching Regis Philbin chat up famous guests, consider this name. If you don't, look elsewhere.

Rei ★

(Japanese) rule, law.

First Impression: Rei is considered either nice and thoughtful or moody and perplexing.

Gender Association: Used mostly for girls

Popularity and Trend: Never been ranked in Top 1000

Risk of Misspelling: Fairly high

Risk of Mispronunciation: Fairly high

Famous Namesakes: None

Common Nicknames: None

Common Variations: None

Consider This: Given its challenging spelling and pronunciation ("ray") and the fact that more girls than boys receive this name, Rei may not be a great choice.

Reid ★★★

(English) redhead.

First Impression: Reid is believed to be a preppy, professional WASP.

Gender Association: Used mostly for boys

Popularity and Trend: #422 (#439 in 2000)

Risk of Misspelling: Average

Risk of Mispronunciation: Fairly low

Famous Namesakes: Senator Harry Reid; football coach Andy Reid; actor Tim Reid

Common Nicknames: None

Common Variations: Reed

Consider This: Rising popularity could make Reid a good bet. Spelling could be confused with "Reed," however.

Reilly ★★

(Irish) a form of Riley.

First Impression: Most people imagine Reilly as a polite and sensitive person with a kind face.

Gender Association: Used about equally for girls and boys

Popularity and Trend: Last ranked #826 in 2000

Risk of Misspelling: Fairly high

Risk of Mispronunciation: Fairly low

Famous Namesakes: Actor Charles Nelson Reilly; writer Rick Reilly; actor John C. Reilly

Common Nicknames: None

Common Variations: Riley, Ryley

Consider This: People aren't sure if Reilly is a name for a girl or a boy, which isn't a plus if you want a name with clear gender association. People may not be sure how to spell it, either, given that there are so many variations of this name.

Rex ★★★

(Latin) king.

First Impression: Rex is seen as a successful workaholic who could be rude and uptight or talkative and charming.

Gender Association: Used for boys

Popularity and Trend: #814 (#911 in 2003)

Risk of Misspelling: Low

Risk of Mispronunciation: Low

Famous Namesakes: Actor Rex Harrison; critic Rex Reed; football player Rex Grossman

Common Nicknames: None

Common Variations: None

Consider This: This strong, short name isn't versatile, but it sure is easy to spell and say.

Reynard ★

(French) wise; bold, courageous.

First Impression: People suspect Reynard has never been married and still lives with his mother.

Gender Association: Used for boys

Popularity and Trend: Never been ranked in Top 1000

Risk of Misspelling: Average

Risk of Mispronunciation: Average

Famous Namesakes: Fable character Reynard the Fox

Common Nicknames: Rey

Common Variations: Raynard

Consider This: This unique name may attract Francophiles, but its poor image may push away all others. People may have some confusion, too, about whether to pronounce it "RAY-nard" or "RUH-nard."

Reynold ★★

(English) king's advisor.

First Impression: People agree Reynold is cold and uptight.

Gender Association: Used for boys

Popularity and Trend: Last ranked in the Top 1000 in the 1950s

Risk of Misspelling: Fairly low

Risk of Mispronunciation: Fairly low
Famous Namesakes: Actor Burt
   Reynolds; actor Ryan Reynolds
Common Nicknames: Rey
Common Variations: Reynaldo,
   Renaldo, Reynald
Consider This: An unflattering image
   may be why Reynold has been out
   of the Top 1000 since the '60s.

Rhett ★★★

(Welsh) a form of Rhys.
First Impression: Rhett is pictured as
   a charming and kind man who's
   handsome, romantic, and not
   afraid to take risks.
Gender Association: Used for boys
Popularity and Trend: #683
   (#675 in 2000)
Risk of Misspelling: Fairly low
Risk of Mispronunciation: Fairly low
Famous Namesakes: Character Rhett
   Bulter (*Gone with the Wind*);
   singer Rhett Akins; singer
   Rhett Miller
Common Nicknames: None
Common Variations: None
Consider This: Many folks can't seem
   to separate *Gone with the Wind*'s
   Rhett Butler from this name's
   image. If you love that book and
   movie, you should love this name.

Rhys ★

(Welsh) a form of Reece.
First Impression: Rhys is said to be
   one of the following: a dorky
   computer nerd, a wealthy and
weird Welshman, or an antisocial
loner who's often picked on by
bullies.
Gender Association: Used for boys
Popularity and Trend: #915
   (#977 in 2005)
Risk of Misspelling: Fairly high
Risk of Mispronunciation: Fairly high
Famous Namesakes: Writer Rhys
   Davies; actor Jonathan Rhys-
   Meyers; actor John Rhys-Davies
Common Nicknames: None
Common Variations: Reece, Reese
Consider This: Despite its tricky
   Welsh pronunciation ("reese")
   and quirky image—or perhaps
   because of them—Rhys's pop-
   ularity is rising.

Ricardo ★★★★★

(Portuguese, Spanish) a form of
Richard.
First Impression: Whether he's Cuban,
   Spanish, or Italian, Ricardo is
   depicted as suave, cool, and
   popular.
Gender Association: Used for boys
Popularity and Trend: #152
   (#134 in 2000)
Risk of Misspelling: Fairly low
Risk of Mispronunciation: Fairly low
Famous Namesakes: Actor Ricardo
   Montalbán; character Ricky
   Ricardo (*I Love Lucy*)
Common Nicknames: Rick, Ricky,
   Rico
Common Variations: None
Consider This: Ricardo has a defi-
   nite Latino flavor. Most people
   should know to pronounce it
   "ree-CAR-doh."

Richard ★★★

(English) a form of Richart.
First Impression: People say Richard is
   a man with bad judgment and a
   tendency to lie.
Gender Association: Used for boys
Popularity and Trend: #99
   (#65 in 2000)
Risk of Misspelling: Low
Risk of Mispronunciation: Fairly low
Famous Namesakes: President
   Richard Nixon; king Richard the
   Lionheart; actor Richard Gere;
   racecar driver Richard Petty;
   singer Little Richard
Common Nicknames: Dick, Richie,
   Rich, Rico, Rick, Ricky
Common Variations: Ricardo
Consider This: People still associate
   this name with former president
   Richard Nixon. Regardless,
   Richard's stellar versatility is
   undeniable. The most common
   pronunciation is "RICH-erd,"
   but other cultures may pronounce
   it "rih-SHARD" or "RICK-ard."

Rick ★★★

(German, English) a short form of
   Cedric, Frederick, Richard.
First Impression: Rick is described as a
   smart, friendly, and talented man.
Gender Association: Used for boys

Popularity and Trend: Last ranked #930 in 2000

Risk of Misspelling: Fairly low

Risk of Mispronunciation: Low

Famous Namesakes: Singer Rick James; singer Rick Springfield; singer Ric Ocasek

Common Nicknames: Ricky

Common Variations: Ric

Consider This: Rick has a much more positive image than its formal form, Richard.

Ricky ★★★★

(English) a familiar form of Richard, Rick.

First Impression: People say Ricky is a good-natured, smiling, and deeply empathetic man.

Gender Association: Used for boys

Popularity and Trend: #394 (#295 in 2000)

Risk of Misspelling: Fairly low

Risk of Mispronunciation: Low

Famous Namesakes: Singer Ricky Martin; character Ricky Ricardo (*I Love Lucy*); football player Ricky Williams; racecar driver Ricky Rudd; actor Ricky Gervais; actor Ricky Schroder

Common Nicknames: None

Common Variations: Rickey

Consider This: With a better image than Richard, this informal name's lack of versatility may not be a problem for some parents.

Rico ★

(Italian) a short form of Enrico. (Spanish) a familiar form of Richard.

First Impression: Rico is thought to be a self-confident and flirtatious slickster, but many say he's arrogant, promiscuous, and even chauvinistic.

Gender Association: Used for boys

Popularity and Trend: Last ranked in the Top 1000 in the 1990s

Risk of Misspelling: Average

Risk of Mispronunciation: Average

Famous Namesakes: Song "Rico Suave"; character Uncle Rico (*Napoleon Dynamite*)

Common Nicknames: None

Common Variations: Ric

Consider This: Rico's smarmy image may deter some parents from this ethnic nickname. Furthermore, it may not fit well with non-Latino last names, and some people outside the culture may not know to pronounce it "REE-coh."

Riley ★★★

(Irish) valiant.

First Impression: Riley is pictured as a carefree, happy, and rambunctious free spirit.

Gender Association: Used mostly for boys

Popularity and Trend: #101 (#109 in 2000)

Risk of Misspelling: Average

Risk of Mispronunciation: Low

Famous Namesakes: Character Chester A. Riley (*The Life of Riley*)

Common Nicknames: None

Common Variations: Reilly, Ryley

Consider This: Although Riley is used mostly for boys, it sounds like Reilly, which is used about equally for both genders. So spelling could be a problem.

Ringo ★★★

(Japanese) apple. (English) a form of Ring.

First Impression: Many think Ringo is fun-loving and musically inclined with a big nose and weird teeth, much like Beatle Ringo Starr.

Gender Association: Used for boys

Popularity and Trend: Never been ranked in Top 1000

Risk of Misspelling: Fairly low

Risk of Mispronunciation: Fairly low

Famous Namesakes: Singer Ringo Starr

Common Nicknames: None

Common Variations: None

Consider This: Beatles fans may want to consider John, Paul, or George first.

Robbie ★★★

(English) a familiar form of Robert.

First Impression: People describe Robbie as a Renaissance man who's observant and intelligent enough to excel in everything.

Gender Association: Used mostly for boys

Popularity and Trend: Last ranked in the Top 1000 in the 1990s

Risk of Misspelling: Average

Risk of Mispronunciation: Low

Famous Namesakes: Singer Robbie Williams; stuntman Robbie Knievel; singer Robbie Robertson; racecar driver Robbie Gordon; character Robbie Hart (*The Wedding Singer*)

Common Nicknames: None

Common Variations: Robby

Consider This: A great image makes Robbie attractive, but its informality may make it a better nickname than given name. Plus, spelling may be confused with "Robby."

Robert ★★★★★

(English) famous brilliance.

First Impression: People say Robert is kind, conscientious, and popular as well as successful, attractive, and smart.

Gender Association: Used mostly for boys

Popularity and Trend: #47 (#29 in 2000)

Risk of Misspelling: Low

Risk of Mispronunciation: Low

Famous Namesakes: Actor Robert Redford; actor Robert De Niro; singer Robert Plant; general Robert E. Lee

Common Nicknames: Rob, Robbie, Bert, Bob, Bobby, Robin

Common Variations: Roberto

Consider This: A solid image, strong popularity, and great versatility make Robert a 5-star name.

Roberto ★★★★

(Italian, Portuguese, Spanish) a form of Robert.

First Impression: Folks think Roberto is a dark-featured man who's loyal, sweet, and romantic.

Gender Association: Used for boys

Popularity and Trend: #215 (#187 in 2000)

Risk of Misspelling: Fairly low

Risk of Mispronunciation: Fairly low

Famous Namesakes: Director Roberto Benigni; designer Roberto Cavalli; baseball player Roberto Clemente; boxer Roberto Durán

Common Nicknames: Berto

Common Variations: None

Consider This: This variation of Robert has a good image and versatility, but it may fit better with Latino surnames.

Robin ★★

(English) a form of Robert.

First Impression: Most people think Robin is a good person, but others feel quite differently.

Gender Association: Used mostly for girls

Popularity and Trend: Last ranked in the Top 1000 in the 1990s

Risk of Misspelling: Fairly low

Risk of Mispronunciation: Low

Famous Namesakes: Legendary character Robin Hood; actor Robin Williams; singer Robin Gibb

Common Nicknames: Rob

Common Variations: Robyn

Consider This: The fact that Robin is used more for girls than boys may turn off some parents.

Rocco ★★

(Italian) rock.

First Impression: People believe Rocco is violent, crude, street-smart, and fierce.

Gender Association: Used for boys

Popularity and Trend: #490 (#730 in 2001)

Risk of Misspelling: Average

Risk of Mispronunciation: Average

Famous Namesakes: Actor Alex Rocco; chef Rocco DiSpirito; star kid Rocco Ritchie

Common Nicknames: Rocky

Common Variations: None

Consider This: Rocco John, son of pop icon Madonna, seems to have given this name's popularity a boost. Still, some people may not realize it's pronounced "ROCK-oh" rather than "ROH-coh."

Rock ★★

(English) a short form of Rockwell.

First Impression: Rock is pictured as a big, muscular wrestler who's tough, bullish, and not too smart.

Gender Association: Used for boys

Popularity and Trend: Last ranked in the Top 1000 in the 1960s

Risk of Misspelling: Low

Risk of Mispronunciation: Low

Famous Namesakes: Actor and wrestler Dwayne "The Rock" Johnson; actor Rock Hudson; comedian Chris Rock; singer Kid Rock

Common Nicknames: Rocky

Common Variations: Rockwell

Consider This: With a rather unflattering image and nearly nonexistent popularity, Rock seems like a poor choice.

Rocky ★★★

(American) a familiar form of Rocco, Rock.

First Impression: People describe Rocky as macho, stubborn, cocky, and powerful.

Gender Association: Used for boys

Popularity and Trend: #973 (#908 in 2000)

Risk of Misspelling: Low

Risk of Mispronunciation: Low

Famous Namesakes: Movie character Rocky Balboa; boxer Rocky Marciano; character Rocky the Flying Squirrel (*The Rocky and Bullwinkle Show*)

Common Nicknames: None

Common Variations: None

Consider This: If you want your child to be a boxer, Rocky is the name for you.

Rodney ★★★★

(English) island clearing.

First Impression: People say Rodney is a kind and friendly guy who's outgoing to the point of being rowdy and hyper.

Gender Association: Used for boys

Popularity and Trend: #449 (#343 in 2000)

Risk of Misspelling: Low

Risk of Mispronunciation: Low

Famous Namesakes: Comedian Rodney Dangerfield; taxi driver Rodney King; football player Rodney Peete

Common Nicknames: Rod

Common Variations: None

Consider This: This traditional name has decent spelling, pronunciation, and versatility.

Rodrigo ★★★

(Italian, Spanish) a form of Roderick.

First Impression: Rodrigo is overwhelmingly pictured as a Latino who's lively, carefree, and always ready to party.

Gender Association: Used for boys

Popularity and Trend: #363 (#384 in 2000)

Risk of Misspelling: Average

Risk of Mispronunciation: Average

Famous Namesakes: Baseball player Rodrigo López; actor Rodrigo Santoro

Common Nicknames: None

Common Variations: None

Consider This: Rodrigo's distinct image may make it a safe choice only for families of Latino or Spanish origin. Those unfamiliar with the culture may not know it's pronounced "rod-REE-goh."

Roger ★★★

(German) famous spearman.

First Impression: People think Roger is an older fellow with a few wrinkles, a receding hairline, and a shy demeanor.

Gender Association: Used for boys

Popularity and Trend: #453 (#373 in 2000)

Risk of Misspelling: Fairly low

Risk of Mispronunciation: Low

Famous Namesakes: Critic Roger Ebert; tennis player Roger Federer; baseball player Roger Clemens; runner Roger Bannister

Common Nicknames: None

Common Variations: Rodger

Consider This: Apparently, people picture someone like movie critic Roger Ebert rather than tennis star Roger Federer when they think of this name.

Roland ★★★★

(German) famous throughout the land.

First Impression: Roland is pictured as a respectful and caring man with a big belly and Nordic looks.

Gender Association: Used for boys

Popularity and Trend: #787
(#690 in 2000)

Risk of Misspelling: Fairly low

Risk of Mispronunciation: Fairly low

Famous Namesakes: Legendary character Roland

Common Nicknames: Rolle, Rollo

Common Variations: Rolando, Rowland

Consider This: A drop in popularity may mean parents are finding Roland too old-fashioned. Most people will pronounce it "ROH-lund," but a few may say "roh-LAHND."

Rolando ★★★

(Portuguese, Spanish) a form of Roland.

First Impression: People say Rolando is a flashy partier with a loud voice and even louder clothes.

Gender Association: Used for boys

Popularity and Trend: #571
(#518 in 2000)

Risk of Misspelling: Average

Risk of Mispronunciation: Average

Famous Namesakes: Singer Rolando Villazón

Common Nicknames: Olo, Lando, Rollo

Common Variations: None

Consider This: An ethnic variation of Roland, this name has great versatility. It will work best with Portuguese and Latino surnames. Pronunciation ("roh-LAHN-doh")

could trip up a few people, though.

Rollo ★★

(English) a familiar form of Roland.

First Impression: Rollo is seen as a bawdy but likable joker who loves to make others as jolly as he is.

Gender Association: Used for boys

Popularity and Trend: Never been ranked in Top 1000

Risk of Misspelling: Average

Risk of Mispronunciation: Average

Famous Namesakes: Viking ruler Rollo of Normandy

Common Nicknames: None

Common Variations: None

Consider This: This nickname for Roland has a good image, but it may be too informal as a given name. Also, there may be some confusion, with people pronouncing it "RAH-loh" as well as "ROH-loh."

Roman ★★★★

(Latin) from Rome, Italy. (Roma) gypsy; wanderer.

First Impression: Roman is described as a tall and muscular warrior.

Gender Association: Used for boys

Popularity and Trend: #209
(#321 in 2000)

Risk of Misspelling: Low

Risk of Mispronunciation: Low

Famous Namesakes: Director Roman Polanski; actor Roman Coppola;

character Roman Brady (*Days of Our Lives*)

Common Nicknames: Romy

Common Variations: Romany

Consider This: The image for Roman exudes confidence, and its popularity is rising.

Ron ★★★

(Hebrew) a short form of Aaron, Ronald.

First Impression: Ron reminds people of a witty and upbeat people pleaser.

Gender Association: Used for boys

Popularity and Trend: Last ranked in the Top 1000 in the 1990s

Risk of Misspelling: Low

Risk of Mispronunciation: Low

Famous Namesakes: Actor and director Ron Howard; radio personality Ron Reagan; basketball player Ron Artest; comedian Ron White

Common Nicknames: Ronnie

Common Variations: None

Consider This: A solid first impression may make Ron a great nickname, but Ronald is a lot more versatile as a given name.

Ronald ★★★★★

(Scottish) a form of Reginald. (English) a form of Reynold.

First Impression: Ronald is said to be self-sufficient, decisive, and determined.

Gender Association: Used for boys

Popularity and Trend: #251
(#203 in 2000)
Risk of Misspelling: Low
Risk of Mispronunciation: Low
Famous Namesakes: President Ronald
Reagan; mascot Ronald
McDonald
Common Nicknames: Ron, Ronnie
Common Variations: Ronaldo
Consider This: A strong image,
steady popularity, and good versatility make this classic name a
sure bet.

Ronnie ★

(Scottish) a familiar form of Ronald.
First Impression: People think Ronnie
is a pudgy country boy who's
obnoxious, slow, and snobby after
being spoiled most of his life.
Gender Association: Used mostly
for boys
Popularity and Trend: #563
(#482 in 2000)
Risk of Misspelling: Average
Risk of Mispronunciation: Low
Famous Namesakes: Singer Ronnie
Van Zant; football player Ronnie
Lott; football player Ronnie
Brown; singer Ronnie James Dio
Common Nicknames: None
Common Variations: Ronny
Consider This: For such a lighthearted
nickname, Ronnie's image is
weighed down with negativity.
With Ronny as another option,
spelling could be a problem, too.

Roosevelt ★★★

(Dutch) rose field.
First Impression: People describe
Roosevelt as a successful and
powerful leader who's charismatic, intelligent, and handsome.
Gender Association: Used for boys
Popularity and Trend: Last ranked in
the Top 1000 in the 1990s
Risk of Misspelling: Average
Risk of Mispronunciation: Average
Famous Namesakes: Presidents
Theodore Roosevelt and Franklin
Roosevelt; character Roosevelt
Franklin (*Sesame Street*); football
player Roosevelt Brown
Common Nicknames: None
Common Variations: None
Consider This: People think of former presidents Theodore and
Franklin D. Roosevelt when
hearing this name, which gives
it its strong image. Even with
the famous namesakes, though,
spelling and pronunciation could
be tricky for some.

Roscoe ★★

(Scandinavian) deer forest.
First Impression: Roscoe is pictured as
a tough guy who's strong-willed
and rugged.
Gender Association: Used for boys
Popularity and Trend: Last ranked in
the Top 1000 in the 1970s
Risk of Misspelling: Average
Risk of Mispronunciation: Fairly low
Famous Namesakes: Character Roscoe
P. Coltrane (*The Dukes of Hazzard*)
Common Nicknames: None
Common Variations: None
Consider This: A rugged image
may hurt this name with some
parents—but it may help it with
others. Most people will know
it's pronounced "RAHS-coh."

Ross ★★★★

(Latin) rose. (Scottish) peninsula.
(French) red.
First Impression: This name makes
people think of a geeky and
sensible guy who's friendly and
funny in a goofy way.
Gender Association: Used for boys
Popularity and Trend: #747
(#433 in 2000)
Risk of Misspelling: Low
Risk of Mispronunciation: Low
Famous Namesakes: Politician Ross
Perot; character Ross Geller
(*Friends*); character Dr. Doug
Ross (*ER*)
Common Nicknames: None
Common Variations: None
Consider This: Many think of Ross
Gellar of TV's *Friends* when they
hear this name. Given its falling
popularity, the name may have
lost its oomph when the show
went off the air.

Roy ★★★★

(French) king. A form of Royal,
Royce.

First Impression: Roy reminds people of a caring, devoted, and lanky cowboy, like famous cowboy Roy Rogers.

Gender Association: Used for boys

Popularity and Trend: #458 (#402 in 2000)

Risk of Misspelling: Low

Risk of Mispronunciation: Low

Famous Namesakes: Cowboy Roy Rogers; singer Roy Orbison; magician Roy Horn; baseball player Roy Campanella

Common Nicknames: None

Common Variations: None

Consider This: Roy's Old West feel may attract some people to this name—although fewer people are choosing it today than in years past.

Royce ★★★

(English) son of Roy.

First Impression: People say Royce could be a popular and friendly leader with a strong focus, or an antisocial and uppity snob with few friends.

Gender Association: Used for boys

Popularity and Trend: #901 (#884 in 2000)

Risk of Misspelling: Fairly low

Risk of Mispronunciation: Fairly low

Famous Namesakes: Businessman Henry Royce

Common Nicknames: Roy

Common Variations: None

Consider This: With its slightly pretentious come-off, Royce may fall out of the Top 1000 soon.

Ruben ★★★★

(Hebrew) a form of Reuben.

First Impression: People imagine Ruben as a heavyset African American who's friendly, caring, and generous.

Gender Association: Used for boys

Popularity and Trend: #227 (#207 in 2000)

Risk of Misspelling: Average

Risk of Mispronunciation: Fairly low

Famous Namesakes: Singer Ruben Studdard; basketball player Ruben Patterson

Common Nicknames: None

Common Variations: Reuben

Consider This: *American Idol* Ruben Studdard commands this name's image, and most people seem to approve, given its solid popularity. Spelling could be a problem, though, because of "Reuben."

Rudolph ★★★

(German) famous wolf.

First Impression: Rudolph is thought to be a suave and stately ladies' man or an annoying and dweeby know-it-all.

Gender Association: Used for boys

Popularity and Trend: Last ranked in the Top 1000 in the 1990s

Risk of Misspelling: Average

Risk of Mispronunciation: Low

Famous Namesakes: Actor Rudolph Valentino; character Rudolph the Red-Nosed Reindeer

Common Nicknames: Rudy, Dolph, Rolf

Common Variations: Rudolf

Consider This: This name may be old fashioned, but it has great versatility. Some may confuse the spelling with "Rudolf."

Rudy ★★★

(English) a familiar form of Rudolph.

First Impression: Many people think Rudy is a hardworking and helpful family man, leader, and role model.

Gender Association: Used for boys

Popularity and Trend: #628 (#557 in 2000)

Risk of Misspelling: Fairly low

Risk of Mispronunciation: Low

Famous Namesakes: Singer Rudy Vallee; inspirational figure Daniel "Rudy" Ruettiger; mayor Rudy Giuliani

Common Nicknames: None

Common Variations: Rudi

Consider This: Rudy has a more positive image than Rudolph, and it's a lot more popular—so this looks like the better choice, although it has less versatility.

Rufus ★★

(Latin) redhead.

First Impression: People picture Rufus as a loner and introvert with a dull personality and a dull wit, although some argue he's intelligent.

Gender Association: Used for boys

Popularity and Trend: Last ranked in the Top 1000 in the 1980s

Risk of Misspelling: Fairly low

Risk of Mispronunciation: Fairly low

Famous Namesakes: Singer Rufus Wainwright

Common Nicknames: None

Common Variations: Rufio

Consider This: Rufus hasn't been in the Top 1000 since the '80s, and its poor image may be the reason. Most people should know to pronounce it as "ROO-fuss."

Rush ★★

(French) redhead. (English) a form of Russell.

First Impression: People describe Rush as a blowhard who's very outspoken, pushy, and cynical.

Gender Association: Used for boys

Popularity and Trend: Last ranked in the Top 1000 in the 1900s

Risk of Misspelling: Low

Risk of Mispronunciation: Low

Famous Namesakes: Radio personality Rush Limbaugh; actor Geoffrey Rush

Common Nicknames: None

Common Variations: None

Consider This: Rush Limbaugh is this name's most famous namesake, but his fame hasn't prompted many parents to give it to their sons.

Ruskin ★★

(French) redhead.

First Impression: Folks say Ruskin is a rough and tough, rude and crude country boy with dirty, ruddy skin.

Gender Association: Used for boys

Popularity and Trend: Never been ranked in Top 1000

Risk of Misspelling: Fairly low

Risk of Mispronunciation: Fairly low

Famous Namesakes: Critic John Ruskin

Common Nicknames: None

Common Variations: None

Consider This: This unusual name has a rough vibe, which may explain why it's never caught on. Pronunciation ("RUSS-kin") and spelling are fairly easy, nonetheless.

Russell ★★★

(French) redhead; fox colored.

First Impression: Russell is pictured as a rude jerk who's competitive, cocky, and bossy.

Gender Association: Used for boys

Popularity and Trend: #404 (#320 in 2000)

Risk of Misspelling: Fairly low

Risk of Mispronunciation: Low

Famous Namesakes: Actor Russell Crowe; basketball player Bill Russell; music mogul Russell Simons; actor Kurt Russell

Common Nicknames: Rush, Russ, Rusty

Common Variations: Russel

Consider This: Russell's great versatility doesn't make up for its rude image.

Rusty ★★★

(French) a familiar form of Russell.

First Impression: Some people say Rusty is a laid-back and cool surfer. Others believe he's a blue-collar worker who didn't do well in school.

Gender Association: Used for boys

Popularity and Trend: Last ranked in the Top 1000 in the 1990s

Risk of Misspelling: Low

Risk of Mispronunciation: Low

Famous Namesakes: Racecar driver Rusty Wallace

Common Nicknames: None

Common Variations: Rustin

Consider This: Rusty may be too informal for some situations.

Ryan ★★★★

(Irish) little king.

First Impression: Ryan is seen as either an average guy who's funny and caring but bland, or a gifted athlete.

Gender Association: Used mostly for boys

Popularity and Trend: #14
(#13 in 2000)
Risk of Misspelling: Fairly low
Risk of Mispronunciation: Low
Famous Namesakes: Actor Ryan
O'Neal; TV personality Ryan
Seacrest; character Jack Ryan
(*The Hunt for Red October*); actor
Ryan Phillippe
Common Nicknames: None
Common Variations: Rian
Consider This: This very popular
name remains a solid choice.

Saburo ★★

(Japanese) third-born son.
First Impression: Saburo seems to be
an outspoken and opinionated
Latino whose anger sometimes
gets in the way of his nicer
qualities.
Gender Association: Used for boys
Popularity and Trend: Never been
ranked in Top 1000
Risk of Misspelling: Fairly high
Risk of Mispronunciation: Fairly high
Famous Namesakes: Japanese pilot
Saburo Sakai
Common Nicknames: None
Common Variations: None
Consider This: This unique name has
an Asian flavor that may appeal
to those with a penchant for the
Far East. Others may find it hard
to pronounce it correctly: "sah-
BOO-roh."

Sadler ★★★

(English) saddle maker.
First Impression: People describe
Sadler as a Western cowboy who's
tall and muscular.
Gender Association: Used for boys
Popularity and Trend: Never been
ranked in Top 1000
Risk of Misspelling: Fairly high
Risk of Mispronunciation: Low
Famous Namesakes: Racecar driver
Elliott Sadler
Common Nicknames: None
Common Variations: None
Consider This: This unusual name has
a cowboy image, but it may be
too horsy for some. Plus, its one
d may make spelling tricky.

Salvador ★★★

(Spanish) savior.
First Impression: Salvador is seen as a
dark-featured Spanish man with
great wealth and power.
Gender Association: Used for boys
Popularity and Trend: #390
(#330 in 2000)
Risk of Misspelling: Fairly low
Risk of Mispronunciation: Fairly low
Famous Namesakes: Artist Salvador
Dalí
Common Nicknames: Salvino
Common Variations: None
Consider This: People keen for
Salvador Dali's works may warm
to this name, which will fit best
with last names of Latino origin.

Few people will have trouble
spelling or pronouncing this
phonetic name.

Sam ★★★★

(Hebrew) a short form of Samuel.
First Impression: People think Sam is
a happy and likable guy who's
open-minded and full of helpful
advice.
Gender Association: Used for boys
Popularity and Trend: #463
(#462 in 2000)
Risk of Misspelling: Low
Risk of Mispronunciation: Low
Famous Namesakes: Actor Sam Elliot;
playwright Sam Shepard; patri-
otic figure Uncle Sam; character
Samwise "Sam" Gamgee (*The
Lord of the Rings*)
Common Nicknames: Sammy
Common Variations: None
Consider This: This short name has a
great image and modest popular-
ity, but it may not be formal
enough for some occasions. It
works great as a nickname for
Samuel.

Sammy ★★★

(Hebrew) a familiar form of
Samuel.
First Impression: Sammy is considered
a silly goofball who's likable and
confident, but a little brainless.
Gender Association: Used mostly
for boys

Popularity and Trend: #934 (#761 in 2000)
Risk of Misspelling: Fairly low
Risk of Mispronunciation: Low
Famous Namesakes: Entertainer Sammy Davis, Jr.; baseball player Sammy Sosa; singer Sammy Hagar; singer Sammy Kershaw
Common Nicknames: None
Common Variations: Sammie
Consider This: Sammy has a silly image, and its informality is a drawback.

Samson ★★★

(Hebrew) like the sun.
First Impression: First and foremost, people picture Samson as a muscular man with broad shoulders. From there, some say he's rough, crude, and dumb, but others say he's loyal, honest, and good-hearted.
Gender Association: Used for boys
Popularity and Trend: #887 (#899 in 2000)
Risk of Misspelling: Fairly low
Risk of Mispronunciation: Low
Famous Namesakes: Biblical figure Samson
Common Nicknames: Sam
Common Variations: Sampson
Consider This: Like other biblical names, Samson's popularity is rising, albeit more slowly than others.

Samuel ★★★★

(Hebrew) heard God; asked of God.
First Impression: Samuel is described as a respectful and thoughtful upper-class man.
Gender Association: Used mostly for boys
Popularity and Trend: #25 (#28 in 2000)
Risk of Misspelling: Fairly low
Risk of Mispronunciation: Fairly low
Famous Namesakes: Biblical figure Samuel; patriot Samuel Adams; author Samuel Clemens, also known as Mark Twain; actor Samuel L. Jackson
Common Nicknames: Sam, Sammy
Common Variations: Samual
Consider This: This classic name has always been popular—and its popularity keeps growing. You may notice a slight difference in pronunciation as some say "SAM-yool" and others say "SAM-yoo-ell."

Santiago ★★★

(Spanish) a form of James.
First Impression: Santiago is described as a Latino who loves dancing, playing drums, and wooing ladies.
Gender Association: Used for boys
Popularity and Trend: #231 (#360 in 2000)
Risk of Misspelling: Fairly high
Risk of Mispronunciation: Fairly high
Famous Namesakes: Character Santiago (*Old Man and the Sea*); baseball player Benito Santiago
Common Nicknames: None
Common Variations: None
Consider This: With rising popularity, Santiago has the charm that may fit best with Latino family names. Those unfamiliar with the culture may have trouble pronouncing it "sahn-tee-AH-goh."

Santos ★★

(Spanish) saint.
First Impression: Santos is thought to be a dark-haired Latino with sudden and intense mood swings: Sometimes he's happy-go-lucky and friendly, and other times he's angry and rude.
Gender Association: Used for boys
Popularity and Trend: #718 (#748 in 2000)
Risk of Misspelling: Average
Risk of Mispronunciation: Average
Famous Namesakes: Character Matthew Santos (*The West Wing*); baseball player Victor Santos
Common Nicknames: None
Common Variations: None
Consider This: Although Santos has a turbulent image, its popularity is rising. However, it may work best with surnames of Latino origin, and some may not know to pronounce it "SAHN-tohs."

Sarngin ★

(Hindi) archer; protector.

First Impression: People say Sarngin's image could be that of a sulker or a joke teller.

Gender Association: Used for boys

Popularity and Trend: Never been ranked in Top 1000

Risk of Misspelling: Fairly high

Risk of Mispronunciation: Fairly high

Famous Namesakes: None

Common Nicknames: None

Common Variations: None

Consider This: It's unlikely that this name will hit the mainstream soon. Its tricky spelling and pronunciation ("SAHRN-geen") don't help its chances.

Saul ★★★★

(Hebrew) asked for, borrowed.

First Impression: People think Saul is a wisecracking retiree who's full of wisdom and stories.

Gender Association: Used for boys

Popularity and Trend: #297 (#286 in 2000)

Risk of Misspelling: Fairly low

Risk of Mispronunciation: Fairly low

Famous Namesakes: Biblical figure Saul; writer Saul Bellow; musician Saul Hudson, also known as Slash; author John Saul

Common Nicknames: Solly

Common Variations: Sol

Consider This: In spite of its bright image, this biblical name is bucking the trend and falling in popularity.

Sawyer ★★★

(English) wood worker.

First Impression: Sawyer is viewed as an old-fashioned and sensitive romantic.

Gender Association: Used mostly for boys

Popularity and Trend: #247 (#458 in 2000)

Risk of Misspelling: Average

Risk of Mispronunciation: Average

Famous Namesakes: Book character Tom Sawyer; character Sawyer Ford (*Lost*); band Sawyer Brown

Common Nicknames: None

Common Variations: None

Consider This: Sawyer's namesakes all have Southern roots, so this increasingly popular name may be right for a Southern boy. Most people will pronounce it "SOY-yer," but a few may say "SAW-yer."

Schuyler ★

(Dutch) sheltering.

First Impression: People think of Schuyler as a brainy, blond boy who most likely reads up on all kinds of subjects even when he's out of school.

Gender Association: Used for boys

Popularity and Trend: Last ranked in the Top 1000 in the 1900s

Risk of Misspelling: High

Risk of Mispronunciation: High

Famous Namesakes: Vice president Schuyler Colfax

Common Nicknames: None

Common Variations: Schyler, Skyler, Skylar

Consider This: With its challenging spelling and pronunciation, more phonetic variations ("Skyler" or "Skylar") are probably better choices.

Scott ★★★

(English) from Scotland. A form of Prescott.

First Impression: Scott reminds people of a popular and charming playboy who's the life of the party.

Gender Association: Used for boys

Popularity and Trend: #253 (#158 in 2000)

Risk of Misspelling: Fairly low

Risk of Mispronunciation: Low

Famous Namesakes: Actor Scott Baio; singer Scott Weiland; writer F. Scott Fitzgerald; skater Scott Hamilton

Common Nicknames: Scotty

Common Variations: Scot

Consider This: Scott's life-of-the-party image seems to be attracting fewer parents.

Scotty ★★

(English) a familiar form of Scott.

First Impression: Most people see Scotty as snobby, snotty, sassy, and sissy.

Gender Association: Used for boys

Popularity and Trend: Last ranked in the Top 1000 in the 1990s

Risk of Misspelling: Fairly low

Risk of Mispronunciation: Low

Famous Namesakes: Character Montgomery "Scotty" Scott (*Star Trek*); basketball player Scottie Pippen

Common Nicknames: None

Common Variations: Scottie

Consider This: For such an innocent-sounding name, this nickname has a terrible image.

Seamus ★

(Irish) a form of James.

First Impression: On the outside, Seamus is seen as an Irishman who's crabby, odd, and not well liked. Those who aren't afraid of his mean demeanor and grizzled appearance find him to have a great sense of humor.

Gender Association: Used for boys

Popularity and Trend: #842 (#827 in 2000)

Risk of Misspelling: Fairly high

Risk of Mispronunciation: Fairly high

Famous Namesakes: Character Seamus Finnigan (*Harry Potter*); poet Seamus Heaney

Common Nicknames: None

Common Variations: Shamus

Consider This: This traditional Irish name has a crabby image as well as challenging spelling and pronunciation ("SHAY-muss") that may keep its popularity from rising much higher.

Sean ★★★

(Irish) a form of John.

First Impression: Some people think Sean is an easily distracted, energetic guy who loves life. Others think he's quiet, serious, and considerate.

Gender Association: Used mostly for boys

Popularity and Trend: #68 (#57 in 2000)

Risk of Misspelling: Average

Risk of Mispronunciation: Average

Famous Namesakes: Actor Sean Connery; actor Sean Penn; singer Sean Paul; rapper Sean Combs, also known as Diddy; football player Sean Salisbury

Common Nicknames: None

Common Variations: Shawn, Shaun, Shon

Consider This: Most people—but not all—know to pronounce this classic Irish name as "shahn." The popularity of phonetic variations (like Shawn) compounds the spelling problem.

Sebastian ★★★

(Greek) venerable. (Latin) revered.

First Impression: Some imagine Sebastian is arrogant, cocky, and perhaps even mean; but others say the opposite, that he's a laid-back pushover.

Gender Association: Used for boys

Popularity and Trend: #76 (#81 in 2000)

Risk of Misspelling: Average

Risk of Mispronunciation: Average

Famous Namesakes: Character Sebastian (*The Little Mermaid*); explorer Sebastian Cabot

Common Nicknames: None

Common Variations: Sabastian, Sabastien, Sebastien

Consider This: The popularity of this sophisticated name is rising, despite an ambiguous image. People will likely pronounce it "seh-BASS-chen," but some may opt for "seh-BASS-tee-en."

Senior ★★★

(French) lord.

First Impression: Folks say Senior as an old, gray man who's hunched over, frail, and hard of hearing.

Gender Association: Used for boys

Popularity and Trend: Never been ranked in Top 1000

Risk of Misspelling: Low

Risk of Mispronunciation: Low

Famous Namesakes: None

Common Nicknames: None

Common Variations: None
Consider This: Senior would seem a silly name for a small child.

Serge ★★

(Latin) attendant.

First Impression: Serge is described as a willful foreigner whose determination has the ability to sway others.

Gender Association: Used for boys

Popularity and Trend: Never been ranked in Top 1000

Risk of Misspelling: Fairly high

Risk of Mispronunciation: Fairly high

Famous Namesakes: Poet and songwriter Serge Gainsbourg; singer Serj Tankian

Common Nicknames: None

Common Variations: Sergei, Sergio

Consider This: The pronunciation of this ethnic name may not be intuitive to most people. The traditional pronunciation is "sairzh," not "surge."

Sergio ★★★

(Italian) a form of Serge.

First Impression: When people hear the name Sergio, they think of a dark-haired Italian man with an accent.

Gender Association: Used for boys

Popularity and Trend: #195 (#179 in 2000)

Risk of Misspelling: Fairly high

Risk of Mispronunciation: Fairly high

Famous Namesakes: Composer Sérgio Mendes; director Sergio Leone; golfer Sergio García

Common Nicknames: Serge

Common Variations: None

Consider This: With solid popularity and a distinct first impression, Sergio may be a good choice for families of Latino or Italian heritage. However, pronunciation could be a problem.

Seth ★★★★

(Hebrew) appointed.

First Impression: Most people think of Seth as a logical intellectual, even though he's perfectly built for athletics.

Gender Association: Used for boys

Popularity and Trend: #103 (#63 in 2000)

Risk of Misspelling: Low

Risk of Mispronunciation: Low

Famous Namesakes: Biblical figure Seth; actor Seth Green; character Seth Cohen (The OC); cartoon creator Seth MacFarlane

Common Nicknames: None

Common Variations: None

Consider This: An intellectual image may be why Seth remains popular.

Shakir ★★

(Arabic) thankful.

First Impression: Shakir is seen as a witty, outgoing, and personable African American man.

Gender Association: Used for boys

Popularity and Trend: Never been ranked in Top 1000

Risk of Misspelling: Fairly high

Risk of Mispronunciation: Fairly high

Famous Namesakes: Muslim scholar Zaid Shakir

Common Nicknames: None

Common Variations: Shakur

Consider This: People think of a fun-loving guy when they hear this name, but it may be too uncommon for many parents. The "shah-KEER" pronunciation may be challenging to some people as well.

Shane ★★★★

(Irish) a form of Sean.

First Impression: This name calls to mind a fun-loving man with a loud laugh, a big smile, and a mischievous twinkle in his eyes.

Gender Association: Used mostly for boys

Popularity and Trend: #179 (#116 in 2000)

Risk of Misspelling: Fairly low

Risk of Mispronunciation: Low

Famous Namesakes: Actor Shane West; movie and book character Shane; boxer Sugar Shane Mosley

Common Nicknames: None

Common Variations: Shayne

Consider This: Shane's warm image will likely keep this name popular.

Sharif ★★

(Arabic) honest; noble.

First Impression: People agree Sharif is a portly Middle Easterner who's well read and serious.

Gender Association: Used for boys

Popularity and Trend: Never been ranked in Top 1000

Risk of Misspelling: Fairly high

Risk of Mispronunciation: Fairly high

Famous Namesakes: Egyptian actor Omar Sharif

Common Nicknames: None

Common Variations: Shareef

Consider This: Sharif's unique spelling and pronunciation ("shah-REEF") may give people trouble.

Shavar ★★★

(Hebrew) comet.

First Impression: People view Shavar as a distant, distracted man who always has his head in the clouds.

Gender Association: Used for boys

Popularity and Trend: Never been ranked in Top 1000

Risk of Misspelling: Fairly low

Risk of Mispronunciation: Fairly low

Famous Namesakes: Actor Shavar Ross

Common Nicknames: None

Common Variations: None

Consider This: This name may be unusual, but its spelling and pronunciation are mostly phonetic.

Shawn ★★★

(Irish) a form of Sean.

First Impression: Shawn comes across as a great guy, but he keeps his shady side under wraps.

Gender Association: Used mostly for boys

Popularity and Trend: #169 (#135 in 2000)

Risk of Misspelling: Fairly high

Risk of Mispronunciation: Low

Famous Namesakes: Wrestler Shawn Michaels; actor Shawn Wayans; basketball player Shawn Kemp

Common Nicknames: None

Common Variations: Sean, Shaun, Shon

Consider This: A classic variation of Sean, this name's two-faced image may harm its appeal. Also, spelling will be a problem because there are so many ways you can spell this name.

Sheldon ★★

(English) farm on the ledge.

First Impression: Sheldon is thought to have a wealthy and sheltered upbringing that made him a loner who's very serious and not very social.

Gender Association: Used mostly for boys

Popularity and Trend: #843 (#623 in 2000)

Risk of Misspelling: Fairly low

Risk of Mispronunciation: Low

Famous Namesakes: Football player Sheldon Brown; writer Sidney Sheldon

Common Nicknames: Shel, Shelley

Common Variations: None

Consider This: Given its fairly unflattering image, perhaps it's no surprise Sheldon's popularity is falling.

Shepherd ★★★★

(English) shepherd.

First Impression: People think Shepherd is an easygoing and quiet suburbanite.

Gender Association: Used for boys

Popularity and Trend: Never been ranked in Top 1000

Risk of Misspelling: Fairly low

Risk of Mispronunciation: Low

Famous Namesakes: Character Dr. Derek Shepherd (*Grey's Anatomy*); singer Kenny Wayne Shepherd; playwright Sam Shepard

Common Nicknames: Shep

Common Variations: Shephard

Consider This: This common surname is still unusual as a given name.

Sherman ★★★

(English) sheep shearer; resident of a shire.

First Impression: Sherman is said to be a tough but dorky kid who's a popular target for fights.

Gender Association: Used for boys

Popularity and Trend: Last ranked in the Top 1000 in the 1990s

Risk of Misspelling: Low
Risk of Mispronunciation: Low
Famous Namesakes: Actor Sherman Hemsley; character Sherman McCoy (*Bonfire of the Vanities*); general William Tecumseh Sherman; singer Bobby Sherman
Common Nicknames: Sherm
Common Variations: None
Consider This: Parents seem to have lost interest in this Top 1000 dropout.

Sherrod ★★

(English) clearer of the land.
First Impression: Most say Sherrod is a bookish dork with thick specs. But others say he's a good-looking and romantic ladies' man.
Gender Association: Used for boys
Popularity and Trend: Never been ranked in Top 1000
Risk of Misspelling: Fairly high
Risk of Mispronunciation: Fairly high
Famous Namesakes: Comedian Sherrod Small; senator Sherrod Brown
Common Nicknames: None
Common Variations: None
Consider This: This unusual name has an unattractive combo of an ambiguous image plus challenging spelling and pronunciation ("SHUR-rod").

Sidney ★★★

(French) from Saint-Denis, France.
First Impression: People say Sidney is cool, collected, and perfectly poised.
Gender Association: Used mostly for girls
Popularity and Trend: #801 (#595 in 2000)
Risk of Misspelling: Fairly low
Risk of Mispronunciation: Low
Famous Namesakes: Actor Sidney Poitier; writer Sidney Sheldon; hockey player Sidney Crosby
Common Nicknames: Sid
Common Variations: Sydney
Consider This: Sidney is quite popular—for girls, that is. The sharp decline in its popularity may suggest that its use as a boy's name is over.

Silas ★★★★

(Latin) a form of Silvan.
First Impression: Silas is viewed as a cool, sexy guy who's very popular with women.
Gender Association: Used for boys
Popularity and Trend: #373 (#600 in 2000)
Risk of Misspelling: Fairly low
Risk of Mispronunciation: Fairly low
Famous Namesakes: Biblical figure Silas; book character Silas Marner; character Silas (*The Da Vinci Code*); character Silas Botwin (*Weeds*)
Common Nicknames: Si
Common Variations: Sylas
Consider This: Silas is another biblical name whose popularity is rising. The name's cool image may have powered the recent rise. Its pronunciation is mostly phonetic: "SYE-lus."

Simba ★★★★

(Swahili) lion. (Yao) a form of Lisimba.
First Impression: Simba creates an image of a confident and determined African man with curious intelligence.
Gender Association: Used for boys
Popularity and Trend: Never been ranked in Top 1000
Risk of Misspelling: Fairly low
Risk of Mispronunciation: Fairly low
Famous Namesakes: Character Simba (*The Lion King*)
Common Nicknames: None
Common Variations: None
Consider This: In many people's minds, there's only one Simba: the eponymous *Lion King*.

Simon ★★★

(Hebrew) he heard.
First Impression: Simon is considered arrogant, mean, and overpowering—like *Idol*-maker Simon Cowell.
Gender Association: Used for boys
Popularity and Trend: #246 (#263 in 2000)

Risk of Misspelling: Fairly low

Risk of Mispronunciation: Fairly low

Famous Namesakes: Biblical figure Simon; character Simon (*Alvin and the Chipmunks*); singer Simon LeBon; TV personality Simon Cowell; singer Paul Simon

Common Nicknames: Si, Simmy

Common Variations: Symon, Simeon

Consider This: Despite a negative image, Simon's popularity has improved as *American Idol* has become a popular TV show.

Sinclair ★

(French) prayer.

First Impression: People think Sinclair is a wealthy, stuffy, and pretentious bookworm.

Gender Association: Used mostly for girls

Popularity and Trend: Never been ranked in Top 1000

Risk of Misspelling: Average

Risk of Mispronunciation: Average

Famous Namesakes: Writer Sinclair Lewis; writer Upton Sinclair

Common Nicknames: None

Common Variations: Sinclaire

Consider This: Sinclair is traditionally used more for girls than boys, and its stuffy image is unlikely to prompt parents to give it to their sons.

Skipper ★★★★

(Scandinavian) shipmaster.

First Impression: Skipper is considered either a shy nerd who's awkward with women or an all-American jock who's well liked and preppy.

Gender Association: Used for boys

Popularity and Trend: Never been ranked in Top 1000

Risk of Misspelling: Low

Risk of Mispronunciation: Low

Famous Namesakes: Character Skipper Jonas Grumby (*Gilligan's Island*)

Common Nicknames: Skip, Skippie

Common Variations: None

Consider This: Skipper refers to the captain of a ship, but it also refers to the captain or coach of any team—hence the jock image.

Skyler ★★★★

(Dutch) a form of Schuyler.

First Impression: People describe Skyler as having Nordic looks and a bright, beautiful smile.

Gender Association: Used mostly for boys

Popularity and Trend: #270 (#229 in 2000)

Risk of Misspelling: Fairly low

Risk of Mispronunciation: Fairly low

Famous Namesakes: Football player Skyler Green

Common Nicknames: None

Common Variations: Skylar

Consider This: Although this phonetic variation of Schuyler fares better than the original, its popularity is falling.

Slade ★★★

(English) a form of Sladen.

First Impression: Slade is perceived as a bold and daring go-getter who's calm under pressure. But some people say he's also boastful and pompous.

Gender Association: Used for boys

Popularity and Trend: Never been ranked in Top 1000

Risk of Misspelling: Low

Risk of Mispronunciation: Low

Famous Namesakes: Musician Chris Slade; singer Isaac Slade

Common Nicknames: None

Common Variations: Sladen

Consider This: This unusual name has an ambiguous first impression, which may not win you over.

Slater ★★

(English) roof slater.

First Impression: Slater appears to be a violent, mean, and stubborn man with whom people no doubt have a hard time communicating.

Gender Association: Used for boys

Popularity and Trend: Never been ranked in Top 1000

Risk of Misspelling: Low

Risk of Mispronunciation: Low

Famous Namesakes: Actor Christian Slater; character A. C. Slater

(*Saved by the Bell*); surfer Kelly Slater

Common Nicknames: None
Common Variations: None
Consider This: Slater's image is troubled, which may explain why it's never made the Top 1000.

Soloman ★★★

(Hebrew) a form of Solomon.
First Impression: Soloman is said to be intelligent, introspective, and strong-willed.
Gender Association: Used for boys
Popularity and Trend: Never been ranked in Top 1000
Risk of Misspelling: Fairly high
Risk of Mispronunciation: Fairly low
Famous Namesakes: Biblical figure Solomon
Common Nicknames: None
Common Variations: Solaman, Solomon
Consider This: Although Soloman has yet to be ranked, its root form, Solomon, has ranked in the middle of the Top 1000 for years. Being an obscure variation creates spelling trouble, though.

Spencer ★★★★

(English) dispenser of provisions.
First Impression: Spencer is depicted as the kind of guy you'd want your daughter to marry.
Gender Association: Used mostly for boys

Popularity and Trend: #182 (#98 in 2000)
Risk of Misspelling: Fairly low
Risk of Mispronunciation: Low
Famous Namesakes: Actor Spencer Tracy; poet Edmund Spenser; racecar driver Jimmy Spencer
Common Nicknames: Spence
Common Variations: Spenser
Consider This: Despite a pleasing image, this name has slipped in popularity in the last few years.

Stanislav ★★★

(Slavic) a form of Stanislaus.
First Impression: This name gives the impression of a responsible, honest, and hardworking man.
Gender Association: Used for boys
Popularity and Trend: Never been ranked in Top 1000
Risk of Misspelling: Fairly high
Risk of Mispronunciation: Fairly high
Famous Namesakes: Actor Stanislav Ianevski; hockey player Stanislav Chistov
Common Nicknames: Slava, Stan
Common Variations: None
Consider This: With its great image, perhaps Stanislav is a good choice for families of Eastern European or Russian origin. However, most people outside those cultures will not know it's pronounced "STAH-nee-slahf," and spelling will be quite challenging as well.

Stanley ★★★

(English) stony meadow.
First Impression: Stanley's described as an authoritative academic who's kind yet serious.
Gender Association: Used for boys
Popularity and Trend: #600 (#505 in 2000)
Risk of Misspelling: Low
Risk of Mispronunciation: Low
Famous Namesakes: Director Stanley Kubrick; actor Stanley Tucci; character Stanley Kowalski (*A Streetcar Named Desire*); musician Ralph Stanley
Common Nicknames: Stan
Common Variations: None
Consider This: Stanley has a rather academic image, and its falling popularity may reflect that fact.

Steel ★★

(English) like steel.
First Impression: People say Steel is as macho, mean, and strong as his name suggests.
Gender Association: Used for boys
Popularity and Trend: Never been ranked in Top 1000
Risk of Misspelling: Fairly low
Risk of Mispronunciation: Low
Famous Namesakes: TV character Remington Steele
Common Nicknames: None
Common Variations: Steele
Consider This: Because this name's hard-as-nails image makes big

demands, you may not want to burden your son with it.

Stefan ★

(German, Polish, Swedish) a form of Stephen.

First Impression: People think Stefan is an arrogant and intelligent brooder who quietly conjures up conniving thoughts that shouldn't be trusted.

Gender Association: Used for boys

Popularity and Trend: #878 (#571 in 2000)

Risk of Misspelling: Average

Risk of Mispronunciation: Fairly high

Famous Namesakes: Tennis player Stefan Edberg

Common Nicknames: Stef

Common Variations: Steffan, Stephen

Consider This: Most Americans will likely pronounce this name as "STEF-ahn" or "STEF-en," but Europeans say "SHTEH-fahn" and "STAY-fahn." Similar-sounding name Stephen may be a better choice.

Stefano ★★

(Italian) a form of Stephen.

First Impression: This tall, curly-haired Italian is pictured as a sommelier in a gourmet restaurant.

Gender Association: Used for boys

Popularity and Trend: Never been ranked in Top 1000

Risk of Misspelling: Average

Risk of Mispronunciation: Average

Famous Namesakes: Character Stefano DiMera (*Days of Our Lives*); singer Giuseppe Di Stefano

Common Nicknames: Stef

Common Variations: None

Consider This: This uncommon name has a foreign flair and is a good choice if you want your son to appear sophisticated. Most people will pronounce it "STEH-fah-noh," but some may say "STEE-fah-no."

Stephen ★★★★

(Greek) crowned.

First Impression: Stephen is pictured as an educated professional, like a doctor or surgeon.

Gender Association: Used for boys

Popularity and Trend: #165 (#95 in 2000)

Risk of Misspelling: Average

Risk of Mispronunciation: Average

Famous Namesakes: Author Stephen King; actor Stephen Baldwin; saint Stephen

Common Nicknames: Steve, Stevie

Common Variations: Steven, Stefan, Stefano

Consider This: Here's a classic name with an intellectual image, but its popularity is waning. Perhaps its two pronunciations ("STEEV-en" and "STEF-en") are the problem. Spelling could also be a culprit, because "Stephen" can be confused with "Steven."

Sterling ★★★

(English) valuable; silver penny. A form of Starling.

First Impression: Sterling strikes people as a cunning and elusive spy who's smart, sophisticated, and smooth.

Gender Association: Used mostly for boys

Popularity and Trend: #784 (#568 in 2000)

Risk of Misspelling: Fairly low

Risk of Mispronunciation: Fairly low

Famous Namesakes: Actor Sterling Hayden; racecar driver Sterling Martin; football player Sterling Sharpe

Common Nicknames: None

Common Variations: Stirling

Consider This: Sterling's image is sophisticated, but its popularity is falling.

Steve ★★★

(Greek) a short form of Stephen, Steven.

First Impression: Some people think Steve is a loud, funny, and gregarious guy who's quirky and sweet. Others say he's a mean and stubborn misfit who thinks only of himself.

Gender Association: Used for boys

Popularity and Trend: #532 (#394 in 2000)

Risk of Misspelling: Low
Risk of Mispronunciation: Low
Famous Namesakes: Actor Steve McQueen; actor Steve Martin; actor Steve Harvey; basketball player Steve Nash; talk show host Steve Allen
Common Nicknames: Stevie
Common Variations: None
Consider This: Steve has an ambiguous image and falling popularity. Its limited versatility doesn't help it, either.

Steven ★★★★★

(Greek) a form of Stephen.
First Impression: Steven is seen as a charming, easygoing guy with a good heart.
Gender Association: Used for boys
Popularity and Trend: #90 (#54 in 2000)
Risk of Misspelling: Average
Risk of Mispronunciation: Low
Famous Namesakes: Director Steven Spielberg; singer Steven Tyler; football player Steven Jackson; actor Steven Segal
Common Nicknames: Steve, Stevie
Common Variations: Stephen, Stefan, Stephan
Consider This: While more popular than Stephen, this name's popularity is declining, and spelling will still be a problem. It's still a 5-star name, though.

Stevie ★★

(English) a familiar form of Stephen, Steven.
First Impression: People say Stevie is a kind and considerate guy who loves to volunteer.
Gender Association: Used mostly for girls
Popularity and Trend: Last ranked in the Top 1000 in the 1990s
Risk of Misspelling: Low
Risk of Mispronunciation: Low
Famous Namesakes: Singer Stevie Wonder; singer Stevie Ray Vaughan; skateboarder Stevie Williams
Common Nicknames: None
Common Variations: None
Consider This: Although Stevie has a good image, it has two major strikes against it: It's mainly used for girls, and it's very informal.

Stuart ★★★

(English) caretaker, steward.
First Impression: Stuart is pictured as a socially challenged nerd whose intellect makes him great at studies, but whose scrawny frame makes him terrible at sports.
Gender Association: Used for boys
Popularity and Trend: Last ranked #665 in 2000
Risk of Misspelling: Average
Risk of Mispronunciation: Fairly low
Famous Namesakes: Sportscaster Stuart Scott; book and movie character Stuart Little; actor Stuart Townsend; character Stuart Smalley (*Staurday Night Live*)
Common Nicknames: Stu, Stuey
Common Variations: Stewart
Consider This: Stuart's nerdy image is a major downside. So is the fact that the spelling can be confused with "Stewart."

Sullivan ★★★

(Irish) black-eyed.
First Impression: Some say Sullivan is quiet, well mannered, and book smart. Others say he's timid, dull, and naïve.
Gender Association: Used mostly for boys
Popularity and Trend: #916 (#990 in 2002)
Risk of Misspelling: Fairly low
Risk of Mispronunciation: Fairly low
Famous Namesakes: Variety show host Ed Sullivan; composer Arthur Sullivan
Common Nicknames: Sully
Common Variations: None
Consider This: This traditional surname is a cool given name, which has cracked the Top 1000. The image is ambiguous, but spelling and pronunciation ("SULL-eh-van") should be fairly easy for most people.

Sundeep ★★★

(Punjabi) light; enlightened.

First Impression: Sundeep is described as a warm, affectionate, and philosophical man.

Gender Association: Used for boys

Popularity and Trend: Never been ranked in Top 1000

Risk of Misspelling: Fairly low

Risk of Mispronunciation: Fairly low

Famous Namesakes: Bollywood composer Sandeep Chowta

Common Nicknames: None

Common Variations: Sandeep

Consider This: Sundeep has a definite Eastern feel as well as a solid image. Families of Punjabi or Indian heritage may consider it a good choice. As a plus, it's pronounced just as it's spelled: "SUN-deep."

Sutherland ★★★★

(Scandinavian) southern land.

First Impression: People picture Sutherland as a wealthy, polite, and distinguished Southern professional.

Gender Association: Used for boys

Popularity and Trend: Never been ranked in Top 1000

Risk of Misspelling: Fairly low

Risk of Mispronunciation: Fairly low

Famous Namesakes: Actors Donald Sutherland and Kiefer Sutherland

Common Nicknames: None

Common Variations: None

Consider This: A traditional surname, Sutherland may soon appear in the Top 1000 if Southern parents pick up on it.

Sylvester ★★★★

(Latin) forest dweller.

First Impression: Sylvester is described as a caring man with a loud voice and a friendly smile.

Gender Association: Used for boys

Popularity and Trend: Last ranked in the Top 1000 in the 1990s

Risk of Misspelling: Fairly low

Risk of Mispronunciation: Low

Famous Namesakes: Actor Sylvester Stallone; character Sylvester J. Pussycat (*Looney Tunes*)

Common Nicknames: Sly

Common Variations: Silvester

Consider This: Don't overlook the fact that a cartoon cat and a man who plays cartoonish characters are Sylvester's most famous namesakes, and that most people named Sylvester are called "Sly."

Tad ★★★

(Welsh) father. (Greek, Latin) a form of Thaddeus.

First Impression: People think Tad is a fun partier with boyish charm and a rich father who bought his son's way into a prestigious college.

Gender Association: Used for boys

Popularity and Trend: Last ranked in the Top 1000 in the 1980s

Risk of Misspelling: Fairly low

Risk of Mispronunciation: Low

Famous Namesakes: Character Tad Hamilton (*Win a Date with Tad Hamilton!*); Abraham Lincoln's son Tad Lincoln; author Tad Williams

Common Nicknames: Taddy

Common Variations: Tadd

Consider This: Tad has a pretentious come-off, yet it seems informal at the same time.

Tan ★★

(Burmese) million. (Vietnamese) new.

First Impression: Some say Tan is an easygoing, relaxed fellow who's likable and cool. Others contend he's a selfish, jerky know-it-all who's secretly insecure.

Gender Association: Used for boys

Popularity and Trend: Never been ranked in Top 1000

Risk of Misspelling: Average

Risk of Mispronunciation: Fairly high

Famous Namesakes: Composer Tan Dun

Common Nicknames: None

Common Variations: None

Consider This: Tan (usually pronounced "TAHN") is common in some Asian cultures, but for Western folks, it probably looks like *tan*, the name of a brownish color.

Tanner ★★★★

(English) leather worker; tanner.

First Impression: Tanner is pictured as a happy and boyish suburban kid who's friendly and caring.

Gender Association: Used mostly for boys

Popularity and Trend: #142 (#93 in 2000)

Risk of Misspelling: Low

Risk of Mispronunciation: Low

Famous Namesakes: Artist Henry Ossawa Tanner; character Danny Tanner (*Full House*)

Common Nicknames: Tan, Tanny

Common Variations: None

Consider This: Tanner has dropped out of the Top 100, but its popularity—and image—are still sound.

Tariq ★★

(Arabic) conqueror.

First Impression: Tariq is envisioned as a quiet observer who may be shy but is more likely laconic.

Gender Association: Used for boys

Popularity and Trend: Last ranked #648 in 2000

Risk of Misspelling: Fairly high

Risk of Mispronunciation: Fairly high

Famous Namesakes: Iraqi official Tariq Aziz; football player Tarik Glenn

Common Nicknames: None

Common Variations: Tarek

Consider This: Challenging spelling and pronunciation ("TAH-rick" or "TAH-reek") may dissuade some people from this foreign-sounding name.

Tate ★★★

(Scandinavian, English) cheerful. (Native American) long-winded talker.

First Impression: Tate is thought to be a naïve and easily manipulated guy with an athletic lifestyle and lots of charm.

Gender Association: Used mostly for boys

Popularity and Trend: #412 (#437 in 2000)

Risk of Misspelling: Low

Risk of Mispronunciation: Low

Famous Namesakes: Poet Allen Tate; actor Tate Donavan; actor Larenz Tate; commercial character Terry Tate

Common Nicknames: None

Common Variations: None

Consider This: With easy spelling and pronunciation, this short name is creeping up the Top 1000.

Taylor ★★★

(English) tailor.

First Impression: Taylor is seen as a handsome blond who's wealthy and spoiled.

Gender Association: Used mostly for girls

Popularity and Trend: #222 (#136 in 2000)

Risk of Misspelling: Fairly low

Risk of Mispronunciation: Low

Famous Namesakes: President Zachary Taylor; singer Taylor Hicks; football player Fred Taylor; singer James Taylor

Common Nicknames: Taye

Common Variations: Tayler

Consider This: Taylor has an upper-crust image. It's a name parents are more likely to give to girls than boys.

Ted ★★★

(English) a short form of Edward, Edwin, Theodore.

First Impression: Ted is considered a jolly, outgoing, and sometimes boisterous man.

Gender Association: Used for boys

Popularity and Trend: Last ranked in the Top 1000 in the 1990s

Risk of Misspelling: Low

Risk of Mispronunciation: Low

Famous Namesakes: Actor Ted Danson; tycoon Ted Turner; senator Ted Kennedy; singer Ted Nugent; baseball player Ted Williams

Common Nicknames: Teddy

Common Variations: None

Consider This: Although Ted is less cutesy than Teddy, it may be better used as a nickname for Theodore or Edward than as a given name by itself.

Teddy ★★★★

(English) a familiar form of Edward, Theodore.

First Impression: Teddy is described as a huggable, squeezable, and lovable guy who's chubby with dark hair and a big smile.

Gender Association: Used for boys

Popularity and Trend: Last ranked in the Top 1000 in the 1990s

Risk of Misspelling: Low

Risk of Mispronunciation: Low

Famous Namesakes: President Theodore "Teddy" Roosevelt; singer Teddy Pendergrass; singer Teddy Geiger; boxing trainer Teddy Atlas

Common Nicknames: None

Common Variations: None

Consider This: Because people can't separate Teddy, the name, from teddy, the stuffed animal, it may be best used as a nickname rather than a given name.

Terrell ★★★

(German) thunder ruler.

First Impression: People say Terrell is an African American athlete—most likely a football player—who's tough mentally as well as physically.

Gender Association: Used for boys

Popularity and Trend: #520 (#409 in 2000)

Risk of Misspelling: Average

Risk of Mispronunciation: Average

Famous Namesakes: Football player Terrell Owens; football player Terrell Davis

Common Nicknames: Terry

Common Variations: Terel, Terrelle

Consider This: The famous football players bearing this name dominate its image. But those players pronounce the name differently ("TAH-rell" and "TARE-uhl"), which may cause problems whichever way you go. Spelling could be a problem as well.

Terrence ★★★

(Latin) smooth.

First Impression: Terrence is perceived as an African American whose moods can range from fun-loving to clingy to arrogant to angry in an instant.

Gender Association: Used for boys

Popularity and Trend: #538 (#486 in 2000)

Risk of Misspelling: Average

Risk of Mispronunciation: Fairly low

Famous Namesakes: Actor Terrence Howard; singer Terence Trent D'Arby; actor Terrence Mann

Common Nicknames: Terry

Common Variations: Terrance

Consider This: Terrence has a volatile image, and that may be the reason its popularity is falling. Spelling will be affected by the variation Terrance.

Terry ★★★

(English) a familiar form of Terrence.

First Impression: Terry is seen as a funny, boisterous man that many see as a clown or a free spirit. People believe he's friendly and caring for the most part, but he can be selfish and immature at times.

Gender Association: Used mostly for boys

Popularity and Trend: #446 (#331 in 2000)

Risk of Misspelling: Low

Risk of Mispronunciation: Low

Famous Namesakes: Writer Terry Brooks; wrestler Terry Bollea, also known as Hulk Hogan; football player Terry Bradshaw; football coach Terry Bowden

Common Nicknames: None

Common Variations: None

Consider This: With an ambiguous image and falling popularity, Terry may work best as a nickname rather than a given name.

Tevin ★★★

(American) a combination of the prefix Te + Kevin.

First Impression: Tevin is considered a playful and impish practical joker with an attractive smile. He's known to be so mischievous that you can't really trust him, but deep down, he's a friendly and decent person.

Gender Association: Used for boys
Popularity and Trend: Last ranked #800 in 2000
Risk of Misspelling: Fairly low
Risk of Mispronunciation: Fairly low
Famous Namesakes: Singer Tevin Campbell
Common Nicknames: None
Common Variations: Tevan
Consider This: A unique variation of Kevin, Tevin's popularity may have peaked years ago.

Thaddeus ★★★

(Greek) courageous. (Latin) praiser.
First Impression: Thaddeus is regarded as a charming and suave gentleman with a winning personality.
Gender Association: Used for boys
Popularity and Trend: #998 (#762 in 2000)
Risk of Misspelling: Average
Risk of Mispronunciation: Average
Famous Namesakes: Biblical figure Thaddeus
Common Nicknames: Thad
Common Variations: Thadeus
Consider This: Old-fashioned Thaddeus has a suave image, but its popularity has plummeted. Pronunciation ("THAD-ee-us") and spelling could confuse some people.

Thanos ★

(Greek) nobleman; bear-man.
First Impression: Thanos is described as a troublemaker who's quick to anger.
Gender Association: Used for boys
Popularity and Trend: Never been ranked in Top 1000
Risk of Misspelling: Fairly high
Risk of Mispronunciation: Fairly high
Famous Namesakes: None
Common Nicknames: None
Common Variations: None
Consider This: This unique name has Greek flavor, but a problematic first impression, spelling, and pronunciation ("THAY-nose," "THAA-nose," or "THAH-nose").

Theo ★★★★

(English) a short form of Theodore.
First Impression: People think Theo is a responsible and sensible African American who comes from a good family and has a good head on his shoulders.
Gender Association: Used for boys
Popularity and Trend: Last ranked in the Top 1000 in the 1930s
Risk of Misspelling: Low
Risk of Mispronunciation: Fairly low
Famous Namesakes: Art dealer Theo van Gogh; character Theo Huxtable (*The Cosby Show*); baseball executive Theo Epstein; hockey player Theo Fleury
Common Nicknames: None

Common Variations: None
Consider This: Theo Huxtable from *The Cosby Show* clearly influences this name's positive image. Despite that fact, it hasn't been popular since the '30s.

Theodore ★★★★

(Greek) gift of God.
First Impression: Theodore strikes people as a name for an intelligent and savvy politician who reads people well.
Gender Association: Used for boys
Popularity and Trend: #296 (#312 in 2000)
Risk of Misspelling: Fairly low
Risk of Mispronunciation: Fairly low
Famous Namesakes: President Theodore Roosevelt; character Theodore (*Alvin and the Chipmunks*); poet Theodore Roethke; hockey player José Theodore
Common Nicknames: Theo, Ted, Teddy, Telly
Common Variations: Theodor
Consider This: Theodore Roosevelt was a memorable American president, and this name's image bears resemblance to him. But its versatility is a big draw, too.

Thomas ★★★★★

(Greek, Aramaic) twin.
First Impression: Thomas is considered mature, distinguished, and scholarly.

Gender Association: Used for boys
Popularity and Trend: #51
  (#33 in 2000)
Risk of Misspelling: Fairly low
Risk of Mispronunciation: Low
Famous Namesakes: President
  Thomas Jefferson; revolutionary
  Thomas Paine; biblical figure
  Thomas; inventor Thomas
  Edison; saint Thomas Aquinas
Common Nicknames: Tom, Tommy
Common Variations: Tomas
Consider This: Despite this classic
  name's great versatility, spelling,
  and pronunciation, Thomas's
  popularity is slipping.

Thornton ★★

(English) thorny town.
First Impression: People think
  Thornton is a snooty, rich preppy
  who's skinny, lanky, and pale.
Gender Association: Used for boys
Popularity and Trend: Last ranked in
  the Top 1000 in the 1930s
Risk of Misspelling: Low
Risk of Mispronunciation: Fairly low
Famous Namesakes: Actor Billy Bob
  Thornton; playwright Thornton
  Wilder; hockey player Joe
  Thornton
Common Nicknames: None
Common Variations: None
Consider This: A familiar surname,
  Thornton's less-than-flattering
  first impression has kept it off
  the Top 1000 for decades.

Tim ★★★

(Greek) a short form of Timothy.
First Impression: Most folks love Tim,
  but a few aren't won over by his
  goofy ways.
Gender Association: Used for boys
Popularity and Trend: Last ranked in
  the Top 1000 in the 1980s
Risk of Misspelling: Low
Risk of Mispronunciation: Low
Famous Namesakes: Actor Tim Allen;
  singer Tim McGraw; basketball
  player Tim Duncan; actor Tim
  Robbins; character Tiny Tim
  Cratchit (*A Christmas Carol*)
Common Nicknames: Timmy
Common Variations: None
Consider This: Tim hasn't been pop-
  ular as a given name for a gener-
  ation, but versatile Timothy is
  still in the Top 100.

Timmy ★★

(Greek) a familiar form of Timothy.
First Impression: Timmy is considered
  a scrawny, fragile boy who's quiet,
  timid, and happy to stay out of
  the spotlight.
Gender Association: Used for boys
Popularity and Trend: Last ranked in
  the Top 1000 in the 1990s
Risk of Misspelling: Fairly low
Risk of Mispronunciation: Low
Famous Namesakes: Character
  Timmy (*Lassie*); character
  Timmy (*South Park*)
Common Nicknames: None

Common Variations: Timmie
Consider This: Timmy is an okay
  name when your son is a young
  boy, but it doesn't work as well
  when he's a grown man.

Timothy ★★★★★

(Greek) honoring God.
First Impression: People think Timothy
  is creative, spontaneous, smart,
  and outgoing.
Gender Association: Used for boys
Popularity and Trend: #94
  (#58 in 2000)
Risk of Misspelling: Fairly low
Risk of Mispronunciation: Low
Famous Namesakes: Biblical figure
  Timothy; actor Timothy Hutton;
  actor Timothy Dalton; psychol-
  ogist Timothy Leary
Common Nicknames: Tim, Timmy
Common Variations: Timmothy
Consider This: Despite its great image,
  Timothy's popularity is slipping.
  Nevertheless, this versatile name
  still ranks in the Top 100.

Titus ★★★

(Greek) giant. (Latin) hero. A form
of Tatius.
First Impression: Titus is depicted as a
  muscular, manly, and confident
  leader.
Gender Association: Used for boys
Popularity and Trend: #550
  (#633 in 2000)
Risk of Misspelling: Fairly low
Risk of Mispronunciation: Fairly low

Famous Namesakes: Biblical figure Titus; play character Titus Andronicus; Roman emperor Titus; comedian Christopher Titus

Common Nicknames: None

Common Variations: Tito

Consider This: Titus has some powerful namesakes, so you may find it overwhelming for a small boy. Also, most people will pronounce it correctly as "TYE-tus," but mispronunciation could lead to embarrassing results.

Tobias ★★★
(Hebrew) God is good.

First Impression: Tobias is described as a loyal, friendly guy who's soft-hearted and hard bodied.

Gender Association: Used for boys

Popularity and Trend: #484 (#589 in 2000)

Risk of Misspelling: Average

Risk of Mispronunciation: Average

Famous Namesakes: Biblical figure Tobias; character Tobias Fünke (*Arrested Development*); actor Tobias Menzies

Common Nicknames: Toby

Common Variations: None

Consider This: Tobias's first impression coveys sensitivity and strength, and its increasing popularity suggests people are aware of that fact. Most people know to pronounce it "toh-BYE-us."

Toby ★★★★
(Hebrew) a form of Tobias.

First Impression: Toby is seen as a sweet, spunky guy who may or may not be gainfully employed.

Gender Association: Used for boys

Popularity and Trend: #509 (#538 in 2000)

Risk of Misspelling: Fairly low

Risk of Mispronunciation: Low

Famous Namesakes: Singer Toby Keith; actor Tobey Maguire; skiier Toby Dawson

Common Nicknames: None

Common Variations: Tobey

Consider This: Toby may not be as versatile as Tobias, but its most famous namesake, Tobey Maguire, projects a friendly image.

Todd ★★★
(English) fox.

First Impression: Todd is viewed as an incredibly smart preppy who's tall and lean.

Gender Association: Used for boys

Popularity and Trend: #653 (#426 in 2000)

Risk of Misspelling: Fairly low

Risk of Mispronunciation: Low

Famous Namesakes: Actor Todd Bridges; hockey player Todd Bertuzzi; designer Todd Oldham; singer Todd Rundgren; football player Todd Heap

Common Nicknames: None

Common Variations: Tod

Consider This: Todd has a smart, preppy image, but several famous namesakes are jocks. Its popularity has been sinking for years.

Tom ★★★
(English) a short form of Thomas, Tomas.

First Impression: Everyone agrees Tom is loud, silly, and famous for laughing too much.

Gender Association: Used for boys

Popularity and Trend: Last ranked in the Top 1000 in the 1990s

Risk of Misspelling: Fairly low

Risk of Mispronunciation: Low

Famous Namesakes: Actor Tom Hanks; actor Tom Cruise; football player Tom Brady; actor Tom Selleck; singer Tom Petty

Common Nicknames: Tommy

Common Variations: Thom

Consider This: Check out the image of this name. It's hard to take Tom seriously as a given name when you compare it to Thomas.

Tomlin ★★★
(English) little Tom.

First Impression: Tomlin comes across as a sweet fellow who's soft-spoken, conservative, passive, and, unfortunately, dull.

Gender Association: Used for boys

Popularity and Trend: Never been ranked in Top 1000

Risk of Misspelling: Fairly low

Risk of Mispronunciation: Low

Famous Namesakes: Singer Chris Tomlin
Common Nicknames: Tom, Tommy
Common Variations: None
Consider This: This unique name has a rather dull image.

Tommy ★★★

(Hebrew) a familiar form of Thomas.
First Impression: People say Tommy could be a hyper jock, a rude snob who likes only the popular crowd, or the wholesome kid next door.
Gender Association: Used for boys
Popularity and Trend: #460 (#307 in 2000)
Risk of Misspelling: Fairly low
Risk of Mispronunciation: Low
Famous Namesakes: Musician Tommy Lee; designer Tommy Hilfiger; actor Tommy Lee Jones; character Tommy Pickles (*Rugrats*)
Common Nicknames: None
Common Variations: Tommie
Consider This: Tommy's informality strongly suggests it depicts a boy, not a man—a fact that may present problems for your son in adulthood.

Tony ★★★

(Greek) flourishing. (Latin) praiseworthy. (English) a short form of Anthony. A familiar form of Remington.
First Impression: People think of Tony as an Italian who's friendly, charismatic, and popular.
Gender Association: Used for boys
Popularity and Trend: #329 (#282 in 2000)
Risk of Misspelling: Fairly low
Risk of Mispronunciation: Low
Famous Namesakes: Character Tony Soprano (*The Sopranos*); racecar driver Tony Stewart; singer Tony Bennett; skateboarder Tony Hawk; British prime minister Tony Blair
Common Nicknames: None
Common Variations: Toni
Consider This: Tony has a solid image, but it isn't as versatile as Anthony for use as a given name.

Tracy ★★

(Greek) harvester. (Latin) courageous. (Irish) battler.
First Impression: Many people say Tracy is a spunky and funny comedian (perhaps like former *Saturday Night Live* cast member Tracy Morgan). But others imagine he's meek, quiet, and unremarkable.
Gender Association: Used mostly for girls
Popularity and Trend: Last ranked in the Top 1000 in the 1990s
Risk of Misspelling: Fairly low
Risk of Mispronunciation: Low
Famous Namesakes: Actor Tracy Morgan; singer Tracy Lawrence; basketball player Tracy McGrady; comic character Dick Tracy
Common Nicknames: Trace
Common Variations: Tracey
Consider This: Far more girls than boys are named Tracy, and this fact probably keeps it out of the Top 1000 for boys' names.

Travis ★★★

(English) a form of Travers.
First Impression: Travis is thought to be a rowdy cowboy or country hick who's loud and mean.
Gender Association: Used for boys
Popularity and Trend: #163 (#115 in 2000)
Risk of Misspelling: Low
Risk of Mispronunciation: Low
Famous Namesakes: Singer Travis Tritt; character Travis Bickle (*Taxi Driver*); musician Travis Barker; baseball player Travis Hafner; singer Randy Travis
Common Nicknames: None
Common Variations: Trevis
Consider This: Travis Tritt's rough 'n' tough image may strongly influence this name's image, which could be too rowdy for some.

Trayton ★★★

(English) town full of trees.
First Impression: Trayton is described as an intellectual, geeky young man who could master any

subject—which is precisely why he's so confused.

Gender Association: Used for boys

Popularity and Trend: Never been ranked in Top 1000

Risk of Misspelling: Fairly low

Risk of Mispronunciation: Low

Famous Namesakes: None

Common Nicknames: Tray

Common Variations: Treyton

Consider This: Trayton's image focuses on indecision, but based on the name's popularity data, most parents have made up their minds not to use it.

Tremaine ★★★★

(Scottish) house of stone.

First Impression: People picture Tremaine as a tall African American man with tremendous athletic talent.

Gender Association: Used for boys

Popularity and Trend: Last ranked in the Top 1000 in the 1990s

Risk of Misspelling: Average

Risk of Mispronunciation: Fairly low

Famous Namesakes: Basketball player Tremaine Fowlkes; book character Johnny Tremain; director Jeff Tremaine

Common Nicknames: Tre

Common Variations: Tremane

Consider This: Tremaine has an athletic image, but it's fallen out of the Top 1000.

Trent ★★★★

(Latin) torrent, rapid stream. (French) thirty.

First Impression: Trent is pictured as goodhearted, buff, handsome, sporty, wealthy, outgoing, funny, popular, and good at just about everything he does.

Gender Association: Used for boys

Popularity and Trend: #287 (#232 in 2000)

Risk of Misspelling: Low

Risk of Mispronunciation: Low

Famous Namesakes: Singer Trent Reznor; senator Trent Lott; football player Trent Green; character Trent Walker (*Swingers*)

Common Nicknames: None

Common Variations: Trenton

Consider This: With a great image and easy spelling and pronunciation, Trent should be more popular than it is.

Trenton ★★★

(Latin) town by the rapid stream.

First Impression: The name Trenton calls to mind a quiet loner who overcompensates for his shyness by acting like a bully and a punk.

Gender Association: Used for boys

Popularity and Trend: #192 (#178 in 2000)

Risk of Misspelling: Fairly low

Risk of Mispronunciation: Low

Famous Namesakes: Basketball player Trenton Hassell

Common Nicknames: Trent

Common Variations: Trenten

Consider This: Like Trent, this name's popularity is dropping. Unlike Trent, however, Trenton hasn't dropped much, though its loner image isn't appealing.

Trevor ★★★

(Irish) prudent. (Welsh) homestead.

First Impression: Trevor is said to be a kind, likable guy who's unkempt and lazy.

Gender Association: Used for boys

Popularity and Trend: #125 (#75 in 2000)

Risk of Misspelling: Fairly low

Risk of Mispronunciation: Fairly low

Famous Namesakes: Basketball player Trevor Ariza; boxer Trevor Berbick; baseball player Trevor Hoffman

Common Nicknames: Trev

Common Variations: Trever

Consider This: Trevor's likeable-but-lazy image may be dimming its considerable popularity.

Trey ★★★

(English) three; third.

First Impression: Trey is depicted as a large, buff athlete who's strong-willed to the point of being obstinate and rough edged to the point of being criminal.

Gender Association: Used for boys

Popularity and Trend: #250 (#215 in 2000)

Risk of Misspelling: Fairly low

Risk of Mispronunciation: Low

Famous Namesakes: Singer Trey Anastasio; cartoon creator Trey Parker; sportscaster Trey Wingo

Common Nicknames: None

Common Variations: Tray, Tre

Consider This: Trey's rough image may repel some parents.

Tristan ★★★★

(Welsh) bold.

First Impression: Tristan reminds people of a very handsome blond man who's compassionate, well loved, and charming.

Gender Association: Used mostly for boys

Popularity and Trend: #86 (#105 in 2000)

Risk of Misspelling: Average

Risk of Mispronunciation: Fairly low

Famous Namesakes: Arthurian figure Tristan of Cornwall; character Tristan Ludlow (*Legends of the Fall*)

Common Nicknames: None

Common Variations: Tristen, Tristin, Trystan, Tristian

Consider This: Tristan has broken into the Top 100, and it may be the positive namesake from the film *Legends of the Fall* that's responsible for the rise. However, with so many popular variations, Tristan may be hard to spell.

Troy ★★★

(Irish) foot soldier. (French) curly-haired. (English) water.

First Impression: People picture Troy as a toned, model-like pretty boy who's smarmy, snobby, and egotistical.

Gender Association: Used mostly for boys

Popularity and Trend: #229 (#225 in 2000)

Risk of Misspelling: Low

Risk of Mispronunciation: Low

Famous Namesakes: Football player Troy Aikman; singer Cowboy Troy; football player Troy Polamalu; character Troy McClure (*The Simpsons*)

Common Nicknames: None

Common Variations: None

Consider This: Troy has a pretentious first impression, but its fairly solid popularity suggests it's still on many parents' short lists.

Tucker ★★★

(English) fuller, tucker of cloth.

First Impression: Tucker is considered either slow as an ox or smart as a fox.

Gender Association: Used for boys

Popularity and Trend: #260 (#288 in 2000)

Risk of Misspelling: Low

Risk of Mispronunciation: Low

Famous Namesakes: Actor Chris Tucker; TV personality Tucker Carlson; entrepreneur Preston Tucker

Common Nicknames: Tuck

Common Variations: None

Consider This: It may have an ambiguous image, but Tucker is rising modestly in popularity.

Ty ★★★

(English) a short form of Tyler, Tyrone, Tyrus.

First Impression: Most people think Ty is a friendly, likable guy who's outgoing, vivacious, and carefree. Other people think he's serious and emotionless.

Gender Association: Used mostly for boys

Popularity and Trend: #210 (#259 in 2000)

Risk of Misspelling: Fairly low

Risk of Mispronunciation: Fairly low

Famous Namesakes: Baseball player Ty Cobb; singer Ty Herndon; football player Ty Law; TV personality Ty Pennington

Common Nicknames: None

Common Variations: None

Consider This: Despite its informality, Ty keeps gaining in popularity.

Tyler ★★★★

(English) tile maker.

First Impression: Tyler is pictured as a blond, fit cutie who's playful, friendly, and outgoing. But some people think this upper-middle-class preppy is snobby, self-centered, and childish.

Gender Association: Used mostly for boys

Popularity and Trend: #18 (#10 in 2000)

Risk of Misspelling: Fairly low

Risk of Mispronunciation: Low

Famous Namesakes: President John Tyler; character Tyler Durden (*Fight Club*); singer Steven Tyler

Common Nicknames: Ty

Common Variations: Tylar, Tylor

Consider This: Although still in the Top 25, Tyler's popularity has slipped. The name's attractive image has some snobby undertones.

Tymon ★★

(Polish) a form of Timothy. (Greek) a form of Timon.

First Impression: Some find Tymon to be shy, quiet, and passive. Others describe him as stubborn and proud.

Gender Association: Used for boys

Popularity and Trend: Never been ranked in Top 1000

Risk of Misspelling: Average

Risk of Mispronunciation: Average

Famous Namesakes: Musician Tymon Dogg; play *Timon of Athens*; character Timon (*The Lion King*)

Common Nicknames: Ty

Common Variations: Timon

Consider This: Tymon hasn't broken into the Top 1000, perhaps because of its somewhat challenging pronunciation ("tee-MON" or "tye-MON"?). Spelling is also a problem.

Tyree ★★★

(Scottish) island dweller.

First Impression: Tyree comes across as an African American man who's hardworking, competitive, and assertive.

Gender Association: Used mostly for boys

Popularity and Trend: #700 (#493 in 2000)

Risk of Misspelling: Average

Risk of Mispronunciation: Fairly low

Famous Namesakes: Author Omar Tyree; football player David Tyree

Common Nicknames: Ty

Common Variations: Tyre

Consider This: Despite its deep drop in the rankings, Tyree has a positive image. While pronunciation is phonetic, some may stress the first syllable and others may stress the second.

Tyrel ★★

(American) a form of Terrell.

First Impression: People picture Tyrel as an African American basketball or football player who may be a fun-loving, likable prankster, but who may also be an angry, untrustworthy bully.

Gender Association: Used for boys

Popularity and Trend: Last ranked in the Top 1000 in the 1990s

Risk of Misspelling: Average

Risk of Mispronunciation: Average

Famous Namesakes: Boxer Tyrell Biggs; singer Steve Tyrell

Common Nicknames: Ty

Common Variations: None

Consider This: Tyrel's ambiguous image leaves some room for improvement, which may be why it hasn't ranked in the Top 1000 in several years.

Tyrone ★★★

(Greek) sovereign. (Irish) land of Owen.

First Impression: Tyrone reminds people of a muscular guy who's arrogant, insensitive, and thuggish.

Gender Association: Used for boys

Popularity and Trend: #575 (#411 in 2000)

Risk of Misspelling: Fairly low

Risk of Mispronunciation: Fairly low

Famous Namesakes: Singer Tyrone Davis; football player Tyrone Williams; football player Tyrone Carter

Common Nicknames: Ty

Common Variations: None

Consider This: Tyrone has an arrogant first impression, and its slipping popularity may mean parents are realizing that fact. Most people

know to pronounce the name
"tye-ROHN."

Tyson ★★★
(French) son of Ty.

First Impression: Tyson is described as a physically formidable African American heavyweight boxer who's mentally slow and tormented by anger, insecurity, and maybe even insanity.

Gender Association: Used for boys

Popularity and Trend: #276 (#335 in 2000)

Risk of Misspelling: Fairly low

Risk of Mispronunciation: Fairly low

Famous Namesakes: Boxer Mike Tyson; model Tyson Beckford; basketball player Tyson Chandler

Common Nicknames: Ty

Common Variations: Tysen

Consider This: This name reflects the image of notorious boxer Mike Tyson. You'd think most parents would not want this violent man as a namesake for their sons, so it's hard to understand why the name's popularity is rising.

Ulysses ★★
(Latin) wrathful. A form of Odysseus.

First Impression: Ulysses is considered a wise and bold man who's fond of travel and adventure.

Gender Association: Used for boys

Popularity and Trend: Last ranked #776 in 2000

Risk of Misspelling: Fairly high

Risk of Mispronunciation: Average

Famous Namesakes: Character Ulysses, Latinized name for Odysseus (*The Odyssey*); novel *Ulysses*; president Ulysses S. Grant

Common Nicknames: None

Common Variations: Ulyses

Consider This: When they see it, many people will correctly pronounce this classic name "yoo-LISS-eez." But when they hear it, spelling the name could be a challenge.

Upton ★★
(English) upper town.

First Impression: People describe Upton as a snooty and pretentious spoiled brat who's geeky and boring.

Gender Association: Used for boys

Popularity and Trend: Never been ranked in Top 1000

Risk of Misspelling: Low

Risk of Mispronunciation: Low

Famous Namesakes: Author Upton Sinclair

Common Nicknames: None

Common Variations: None

Consider This: An uncommon name, Upton doesn't have an appealing image—a fact that may keep it uncommon.

Vance ★★★
(English) thresher.

First Impression: Vance is thought to be a self-absorbed and high-maintenance jock off the court, but on the court, he's a team player.

Gender Association: Used for boys

Popularity and Trend: #719 (#916 in 2001)

Risk of Misspelling: Low

Risk of Mispronunciation: Low

Famous Namesakes: Actor Courtney B. Vance; baseball player Dazzy Vance

Common Nicknames: None

Common Variations: None

Consider This: This straightforward name is rising in popularity despite its lackluster image.

Vaughn ★★★
(Welsh) small.

First Impression: The images of Vaughn are plentiful: People think he's a funny, outgoing prankster; a pushy go-getter; a cultured aristocrat; a sweet gentleman; a deep thinker; or a moody narcissist.

Gender Association: Used for boys

Popularity and Trend: #734 (#916 in 2000)

Risk of Misspelling: Average

Risk of Mispronunciation: Fairly low

Famous Namesakes: Golfer Vaughn Taylor; actor Vince Vaughn;

baseball player Mo Vaughn; singer Stevie Ray Vaughan

Common Nicknames: None

Common Variations: Vaughan, Von

Consider This: A common surname, Vaughn is catching on as a given name. Spelling could trip up some folks, however.

Vernon ★★★

(Latin) springlike; youthful.

First Impression: People agree Vernon is skinny and lanky, but they can't decide if he's a shy bookworm or a backwoods farmer.

Gender Association: Used for boys

Popularity and Trend: Last ranked #843 in 2000

Risk of Misspelling: Fairly low

Risk of Mispronunciation: Fairly low

Famous Namesakes: Businessman Vernon Jordan; baseball player Vernon Wells; football player Vernon Davis

Common Nicknames: Vern

Common Variations: Vernen

Consider This: Vernon has an old-fashioned sound, and its lack of popularity suggests it may stay in the past.

Vic ★★

(Latin) a short form of Victor.

First Impression: People think Vic is a rude, arrogant, and grouchy guy who keeps to himself.

Gender Association: Used for boys

Popularity and Trend: Last ranked in the Top 1000 in the 1960s

Risk of Misspelling: Fairly low

Risk of Mispronunciation: Low

Famous Namesakes: Singer Vic Damone; actor Vic Morrow

Common Nicknames: None

Common Variations: Vick

Consider This: Vic's image is unlovable, so it may not be a good choice even as a nickname.

Victor ★★★★

(Latin) victor, conqueror.

First Impression: Victor is pictured as a commanding leader who's masculine, worldly, and strong-willed.

Gender Association: Used for boys

Popularity and Trend: #104 (#97 in 2000)

Risk of Misspelling: Fairly low

Risk of Mispronunciation: Fairly low

Famous Namesakes: Author Victor Hugo; actor Victor Garber; musician Victor Borge; book and movie character Victor Frankenstein

Common Nicknames: Vic

Common Variations: Viktor

Consider This: Despite its powerful image, this classic name left the Top 100 in 2004 for the first time since the '70s. Most Americans will pronounce it "VICK-ter," but other cultures may pronounce it "VEEK-ter."

Vijay ★★

(Hindi) victorious.

First Impression: An Indian man, Vijay is said to be a tech-savvy computer programmer.

Gender Association: Used for boys

Popularity and Trend: Never been ranked in Top 1000

Risk of Misspelling: Fairly high

Risk of Mispronunciation: Fairly high

Famous Namesakes: Golfer Vijay Singh; tennis player Vijay Amritraj

Common Nicknames: None

Common Variations: None

Consider This: This unique name may fit best with surnames of Indian origin. Most people don't realize it's pronounced "vee-JAY."

Vince ★★★★

(English) a short form of Vincent.

First Impression: Vince is described as a dark-haired Italian who's warm, witty, and driven.

Gender Association: Used for boys

Popularity and Trend: Last ranked in the Top 1000 in the 1990s

Risk of Misspelling: Low

Risk of Mispronunciation: Low

Famous Namesakes: Actor Vince Vaughn; football coach Vince Lombardi; character Vince Chase (*Entourage*); football player Vince Young; singer Vince Neil

Common Nicknames: Vinny

Common Variations: None

Consider This: Vince isn't as versatile or popular as Vincent, but it has a slightly more positive first impression.

Vincent ★★★★

(Latin) victor, conqueror.

First Impression: Some people imagine Vincent as a tender parent or friend. Others see him as creepy; still others as arty.

Gender Association: Used mostly for boys

Popularity and Trend: #108 (#120 in 2000)

Risk of Misspelling: Fairly low

Risk of Mispronunciation: Low

Famous Namesakes: Artist Vincent van Gogh; actor Vincent Price; character Vincent Vega (*Pulp Fiction*); hockey player Vincent Lecavalier

Common Nicknames: Vince, Vinny

Common Variations: Vincente

Consider This: This classic name has staying power: It has ranked in or near the Top 100 for over a hundred years.

Vinny ★★

(English) a familiar form of Calvin, Melvin, Vincent.

First Impression: Most people think Vinny is tough, pigheaded, and possibly abusive. Others think he's quiet and shy with a mild temperament.

Gender Association: Used for boys

Popularity and Trend: Never been ranked in Top 1000

Risk of Misspelling: Fairly low

Risk of Mispronunciation: Low

Famous Namesakes: Football player Vinny Testaverde; character Vinny LaGuardia Gambini (*My Cousin Vinny*); baseball player Vinny Castilla

Common Nicknames: None

Common Variations: Vinnie

Consider This: It's surprising that this common nickname for Vincent has never ranked in the Top 1000. The name's ambiguous image may be holding it back.

Virgil ★★

(Latin) rod bearer, staff bearer.

First Impression: Virgil is viewed as literate, contemplative, poetic—and downright nerdy.

Gender Association: Used for boys

Popularity and Trend: Last ranked in the Top 1000 in the 1990s

Risk of Misspelling: Fairly low

Risk of Mispronunciation: Fairly low

Famous Namesakes: Roman poet Virgil; lawman Virgil Earp

Common Nicknames: None

Common Variations: Vergil

Consider This: Virgil is an old-fashioned name that probably won't make a comeback any time soon.

Vito ★★

(Latin) a form of Vittorio.

First Impression: People imagine Vito is a powerful Italian mob boss who's dangerous yet businesslike, much like *The Godfather* Vito Corleone.

Gender Association: Used for boys

Popularity and Trend: Last ranked in the Top 1000 in the 1980s

Risk of Misspelling: Average

Risk of Mispronunciation: Average

Famous Namesakes: Character Vito Corleone (*The Godfather*); mobster Vito Rizzuto

Common Nicknames: None

Common Variations: None

Consider This: This very Italian name hasn't been in the Top 1000 since the last *Godfather* film premiered.

Vladimir ★★

(Russian) famous prince.

First Impression: People see Vladimir as a determined and confident Russian leader who ranges from dominant to militant to tyrannical to evil.

Gender Association: Used for boys

Popularity and Trend: Never been ranked in Top 1000

Risk of Misspelling: Fairly high

Risk of Mispronunciation: Average

Famous Namesakes: Russian president Vladimir Putin; Soviet leader Vladimir Lenin; author

Vladimir Nabokov; baseball player Vladimir Guerrero

Common Nicknames: Vlad

Common Variations: None

Consider This: Vladimir has yet to break into the Top 1000. Perhaps its challenging spelling and pronunciation are factors. Although Russians pronounce it "VLAHD-ah-meer," non-Russians are likely to say "VLAD-ah-meer."

Wade ★★★

(English) ford; river crossing.

First Impression: Some say Wade is a defiant, rude troublemaker. Others say he's a dependable, honest friend.

Gender Association: Used for boys

Popularity and Trend: #551 (#474 in 2000)

Risk of Misspelling: Low

Risk of Mispronunciation: Low

Famous Namesakes: Baseball player Wade Boggs; basketball player Dwayne Wade

Common Nicknames: None

Common Variations: None

Consider This: Wade is a snap to pronounce and spell, but it's fallen to the bottom half of the Top 1000. An ambiguous image isn't helping the name's popularity.

Wallace ★★★

(English) from Wales.

First Impression: People believe Wallace is studious, articulate, and thoughtful as well as skinny, tall, and bespectacled.

Gender Association: Used for boys

Popularity and Trend: Last ranked in the Top 1000 in the 1990s

Risk of Misspelling: Fairly low

Risk of Mispronunciation: Low

Famous Namesakes: Racecar driver Rusty Wallace; character Wallace (*Wallace and Gromit*); Scottish patriot William Wallace; basketball player Ben Wallace

Common Nicknames: Wally

Common Variations: Wallis

Consider This: Wallace has brave, athletic, and quirky famous namesakes, but that hasn't kept it in the Top 1000.

Walter ★★★★

(German) army ruler, general. (English) woodsman.

First Impression: Walter is described as an inquisitive thinker who loves reading, chess, bird watching, and other old-fashioned activities.

Gender Association: Used for boys

Popularity and Trend: #355 (#308 in 2000)

Risk of Misspelling: Low

Risk of Mispronunciation: Low

Famous Namesakes: News anchor Walter Cronkite; football player Walter Payton; actor Walter Matthau; vice president Walter Mondale; explorer Walter Raleigh

Common Nicknames: Wally, Walt

Common Variations: Walther

Consider This: This classic name may have an upstanding image, but it has falling popularity. Perhaps this is a reflection of the fact that none of the five famous namesakes are now doing what made them famous.

Warren ★★

(German) general; warden; rabbit hutch.

First Impression: As a kid, Warren is seen as a nerdy, mousy bookworm who's always on the honor roll. As an older man, he's probably an uptight fuddy-duddy who's snobbish and boring.

Gender Association: Used for boys

Popularity and Trend: #506 (#440 in 2000)

Risk of Misspelling: Fairly low

Risk of Mispronunciation: Low

Famous Namesakes: President Warren Harding; actor Warren Beatty; football player Warren Moon; rapper Warren G; singer Warren Zevon

Common Nicknames: None

Common Variations: Warrin

Consider This: Warren has a poor first impression, so it's surprising the name is still ranked in the middle of the Top 1000.

Waylon ★★★

(English) land by the road.

First Impression: Waylon is depicted as an unsophisticated but confident country singer, much like legendary country singer Waylon Jennings.

Gender Association: Used for boys

Popularity and Trend: #547 (#753 in 2002)

Risk of Misspelling: Fairly low

Risk of Mispronunciation: Low

Famous Namesakes: Singer Waylon Jennings; character Waylon Smithers (*The Simpsons*); actor Waylon Payne

Common Nicknames: None

Common Variations: Wayland

Consider This: Perhaps retro country fans fondly remember the glory days of Waylon Jennings, and they're the reason why this name's popularity is rising.

Wayne ★★

(English) wagon maker.

First Impression: People think Wayne is grumpy and fussy, and he often feels pestered.

Gender Association: Used for boys

Popularity and Trend: #645 (#509 in 2000)

Risk of Misspelling: Low

Risk of Mispronunciation: Low

Famous Namesakes: Hockey player Wayne Gretzky; singer Wayne Newton; actor Wayne Brady; character Wayne Campbell (*Wayne's World*); character Bruce Wayne (*Batman*)

Common Nicknames: None

Common Variations: None

Consider This: Maybe people are finding fault with Wayne's image, which may explain why its popularity has dropped recently.

Wendell ★★

(German) wanderer. (English) good dale, good valley.

First Impression: Wendell is pictured as a bookish, brainy guy who's frail, antisocial, overly sensitive, and vision impaired.

Gender Association: Used for boys

Popularity and Trend: Last ranked in the Top 1000 in the 1990s

Risk of Misspelling: Fairly low

Risk of Mispronunciation: Fairly low

Famous Namesakes: Poet Oliver Wendell Holmes, Sr., and Supreme Court justice Oliver Wendell Holmes, Jr.

Common Nicknames: None

Common Variations: Wendall

Consider This: Wendell's unappealing first impression may explain why it hasn't been popular since the '90s.

Wesley ★★★

(English) western meadow.

First Impression: Wesley is seen as a vibrant, popular, and amusing guy who's as smart as he is kind.

Gender Association: Used mostly for boys

Popularity and Trend: #190 (#171 in 2000)

Risk of Misspelling: Fairly low

Risk of Mispronunciation: Average

Famous Namesakes: Actor Wesley Snipes; theologian John Wesley; actor Wesley Jonathan

Common Nicknames: Wes

Common Variations: Wesly, Westley

Consider This: Wesley has been a Top 200 name for over a hundred years, but seems to be slipping, despite its great image. Pronunciation will be divided, with some saying "WESS-lee" and some saying "WEZ-lee."

Weston ★★★

(English) western town.

First Impression: People say Weston inherited a great deal of wealth from his grandfather, but he's also a powerful entrepreneur in his own right.

Gender Association: Used for boys

Popularity and Trend: #380 (#398 in 2000)

Risk of Misspelling: Fairly low

Risk of Mispronunciation: Fairly low

Famous Namesakes: Photographer Edward Weston; actor Michael Weston

Common Nicknames: West, Wes

Common Variations: Westin

Consider This: While similar-sounding Wesley is becoming less popular, Weston is becoming more popular.

Wilbert ★★★

(German) brilliant; resolute.

First Impression: Everyone agrees Wilbert is a humorous and gregarious fellow who's rotund and a little clumsy.

Gender Association: Used for boys

Popularity and Trend: Last ranked in the Top 1000 in the 1990s

Risk of Misspelling: Average

Risk of Mispronunciation: Fairly low

Famous Namesakes: Baseball player Wilbert Robinson

Common Nicknames: Will, Bert, Willie

Common Variations: Wilburt

Consider This: Wilbert has a humorous image and good versatility. But the combination of "Will" and "Bert" in a single name doesn't seem to be clicking.

Wilbur ★★★

(English) wall fortification; bright willows.

First Impression: Wilbur is viewed as a nerdy older gent who's quiet and easily intimidated.

Gender Association: Used for boys

Popularity and Trend: Last ranked in the Top 1000 in the 1980s

Risk of Misspelling: Average

Risk of Mispronunciation: Low

Famous Namesakes: Aviator Wilbur Wright; character Wilbur (*Charlotte's Web*)

Common Nicknames: Will, Willie

Common Variations: Wilber

Consider This: Wilbur has an old-fashioned sound and an old image. No wonder it hasn't been in the Top 1000 for a generation. Like Wilbert and Wilburt, Wilber and Wilbur may be confused when it comes to spelling.

Wiley ★

(English) willow meadow.

First Impression: Wiley comes across as a dirty, sneaky schemer who's always in trouble unless he has constant supervision.

Gender Association: Used for boys

Popularity and Trend: Last ranked in the Top 1000 in the 1970s

Risk of Misspelling: Fairly low

Risk of Mispronunciation: Average

Famous Namesakes: Aviator Wiley Post; football player Marcellus Wiley; cartoon character Wile E. Coyote

Common Nicknames: None

Common Variations: None

Consider This: Wiley's untrustworthy image makes it a name many parents won't choose. The name is pronounced "WHY-lee," but some people may pronounce it "WILL-ee."

Wilfred ★★★

(German) determined peacemaker.

First Impression: Wilfred is considered an outdoorsy guy who loves fishing, hunting, and nature in general.

Gender Association: Used for boys

Popularity and Trend: Last ranked in the Top 1000 in the 1970s

Risk of Misspelling: Fairly low

Risk of Mispronunciation: Fairly low

Famous Namesakes: Actor Wilford Brimley

Common Nicknames: Will, Fred, Willie

Common Variations: Wilfredo

Consider This: Wilfred is very versatile, but having peaked in the '30s, it's also dated.

Will ★★★★

(English) a short form of William.

First Impression: Will is said to be friendly, loving, funny, and handsome.

Gender Association: Used for boys

Popularity and Trend: #533 (#510 in 2000)

Risk of Misspelling: Low

Risk of Mispronunciation: Low

Famous Namesakes: Actor Will Smith; actor Will Ferrell; character Will Truman (*Will & Grace*); humorist Will Rogers

Common Nicknames: Willie

Common Variations: Wil

Consider This: People may expect Will to be short for William and not be a given name, but the name has a warm image and can stand on its own.

Willard ★★★

(German) determined and brave.

First Impression: People think Willard is a meek fellow who's overweight, old, and a bit of a hermit.

Gender Association: Used for boys

Popularity and Trend: Last ranked in the Top 1000 in the 1980s

Risk of Misspelling: Fairly low

Risk of Mispronunciation: Fairly low

Famous Namesakes: TV personality Willard Scott; actor Fred Willard

Common Nicknames: Will, Willie

Common Variations: None

Consider This: With an image that conveys stodginess, perhaps folks are avoiding this name on purpose.

William ★★★★★

(English) a form of Wilhelm.

First Impression: People describe William as a royal, noble prince who's kind, altruistic, and a smart college student.

Gender Association: Used mostly for boys

Popularity and Trend: #10 (#11 in 2000)

Risk of Misspelling: Low

Risk of Mispronunciation: Low

Famous Namesakes: Playwright William Shakespeare; legendary hero William Tell; prince William; author William Faulkner; musician will.i.am

Common Nicknames: Will, Bill, Willie, Billy, Liam

Common Variations: Vilhelm, Willem

Consider This: Not surprisingly, people associate William with the United Kingdom's Prince William. Also not surprising is this classic name's 5-star ranking.

Willie ★★

(German) a familiar form of William.

First Impression: This name evokes the image of a scrawny, mischievous guy who's always smiling and having fun.

Gender Association: Used mostly for boys

Popularity and Trend: #514 (#410 in 2000)

Risk of Misspelling: Average

Risk of Mispronunciation: Low

Famous Namesakes: Singer Willie Nelson; baseball player Willie Mays; character Willy Wonka (*Charlie and the Chocolate Factory*); character Willy Loman (*Death of a Salesman*)

Common Nicknames: None

Common Variations: Willy

Consider This: Willie's lack of versatility keeps it from scoring as well as William or Will. In addition, spelling may be confused because Willy is a popular variation.

Willis ★★★

(German) son of Willie.

First Impression: People think of Willis as a gray-haired, short retiree who's shy and quietly funny.

Gender Association: Used for boys

Popularity and Trend: Last ranked in the Top 1000 in the 1990s

Risk of Misspelling: Fairly low

Risk of Mispronunciation: Low

Famous Namesakes: Actor Bruce Willis; character Willis Jackson (*Diff'rent Strokes*); baseball player Dontrelle Willis; football player Willis McGahee

Common Nicknames: Will, Willie

Common Variations: None

Consider This: An old-man image may be the primary reason Willis fell out of the Top 1000 in the early '90s.

Wilson ★★★★

(English) son of Will.

First Impression: Some people describe Wilson as a grouchy and mean old man. Others imagine him as a friendly, intelligent blond with surfer looks and a handsome smile.

Gender Association: Used for boys

Popularity and Trend: #512
(#525 in 2000)

Risk of Misspelling: Low

Risk of Mispronunciation: Low

Famous Namesakes: President Woodrow Wilson; character George Wilson (*Dennis the Menace*); character Wilson the volleyball (*Cast Away*); actors Owen Wilson and Luke Wilson

Common Nicknames: Will, Willie

Common Variations: None

Consider This: This common surname has an ambiguous image, but it's nevertheless rising in popularity.

Winston ★★★★

(English) friendly town; victory town.

First Impression: People associate Winston with a gruff, extremely bright, pipe-smoking British politician.

Gender Association: Used for boys

Popularity and Trend: #879
(#707 in 2000)

Risk of Misspelling: Fairly low

Risk of Mispronunciation: Fairly low

Famous Namesakes: British prime minister Winston Churchill; jeweler Harry Winston

Common Nicknames: Win, Winnie

Common Variations: Winton, Winsten

Consider This: Thank Winston Churchill for this name's image. But even his influence hasn't kept Winston's popularity from slipping.

Wood ★★★★

(English) a form of Elwood, Garwood, Woodrow.

First Impression: Wood is described as an intelligent thinker who loves the outdoors and the solitude it offers.

Gender Association: Used for boys

Popularity and Trend: Never been ranked in Top 1000

Risk of Misspelling: Low

Risk of Mispronunciation: Low

Famous Namesakes: Actor Elijah Wood; artist Grant Wood; musician Ron Wood

Common Nicknames: Woody

Common Variations: None

Consider This: Most people won't realize Wood is a name. Nevertheless, its solid image may persuade some trendy parents not to pulp it.

Wyatt ★★★★

(French) little warrior.

First Impression: Wyatt is said to be a brave, rugged Westerner who's tough and mean.

Gender Association: Used for boys

Popularity and Trend: #82
(#111 in 2000)

Risk of Misspelling: Fairly low

Risk of Mispronunciation: Fairly low

Famous Namesakes: Lawman Wyatt Earp

Common Nicknames: None

Common Variations: None

Consider This: Wyatt's popularity is skyrocketing. Most people will know to pronounce it "WYE-ett."

Xander ★★★

(Greek) a form of Alexander.

First Impression: Despite his bookish personality, Xander is most often pictured as a lanky guy with tattoos, piercings, and spiked hair.

Gender Association: Used for boys

Popularity and Trend: #278
(#927 in 2000)

Risk of Misspelling: Fairly high

Risk of Mispronunciation: Fairly high

Famous Namesakes: Character Xander Cage (*xxx*); actor Xander Berkeley; character Xander Harris (*Buffy the Vampire Slayer*)

Common Nicknames: None

Common Variations: Zander

Consider This: Xander has made a *huge* leap in popularity over the past few years. Still, the trendy *X* will make pronunciation ("ZAN-der") and spelling troublesome.

Xavier ★★★

(Arabic) bright. (Basque) owner of the new house.

First Impression: Xavier is pictured as big, manly, and tough.

Gender Association: Used mostly for boys

Popularity and Trend: #78
(#102 in 2000)

Risk of Misspelling: Average

Risk of Mispronunciation: Fairly high

Famous Namesakes: Saint Francis Xavier; character Professor Charles Xavier (*X-Men*)

Common Nicknames: None

Common Variations: Zavier

Consider This: Xavier recently broke into the Top 100, despite several pronunciation options: "ZAYV-yur," "ZAY-vee-yur," "eks-ZAYV-yur," or "eks-ZAY-vee-yur."

Xerxes ★★

(Persian) ruler.

First Impression: Xerxes is said to be as eccentric as he is physically strong.

Gender Association: Used for boys

Popularity and Trend: Never been ranked in Top 1000

Risk of Misspelling: Fairly high

Risk of Mispronunciation: Fairly high

Famous Namesakes: Persian king Xerxes the Great; opera character Xerxes, also known as Serse

Common Nicknames: None

Common Variations: None

Consider This: While Xander and Xavier are hot, Xerxes has yet to break into the Top 1000. Its two *x*'s probably make its spelling and pronunciation ("ZERK-zees") tough for most folks.

Yakov ★

(Russian, Hebrew) a form of Jacob.

First Impression: People picture Yakov as a vodka-loving Russian who's high-strung and strong willed.

Gender Association: Used for boys

Popularity and Trend: Never been ranked in Top 1000

Risk of Misspelling: Fairly high

Risk of Mispronunciation: Fairly high

Famous Namesakes: Comedian Yakov Smirnoff

Common Nicknames: None

Common Variations: None

Consider This: Yakov may work best with Eastern European surnames. People may not know the Russian pronunciation is "YAHK-ahf" and the Hebrew pronunciation is "YAH-ah-kove."

Yoshi ★★

(Japanese) adopted son.

First Impression: People say Yoshi is a mild-mannered and shy fellow who's kindhearted and smiley.

Gender Association: Used for boys

Popularity and Trend: Never been ranked in Top 1000

Risk of Misspelling: Fairly high

Risk of Mispronunciation: Fairly high

Famous Namesakes: Dinosaur character Yoshi (*Super Mario World*); Japanese actor Yoshi Kato

Common Nicknames: None

Common Variations: None

Consider This: A solid image promotes Yoshi, but it may fit well only with surnames of Japanese origin. Also, some may know it's pronounced "YOH-shee," but others may struggle with the pronunciation.

Zachariah ★★★

(Hebrew) God remembered.

First Impression: Zachariah is seen as a wise, educated man who's also kind and thoughtful.

Gender Association: Used for boys

Popularity and Trend: #420 (#374 in 2000)

Risk of Misspelling: Average

Risk of Mispronunciation: Average

Famous Namesakes: Biblical figure Zechariah; book *Z for Zachariah*

Common Nicknames: Zach

Common Variations: Zacharia, Zacheriah, Zackariah

Consider This: Bucking the current trend, this biblical name has dropped in popularity. Perhaps its spelling and pronunciation ("zack-ah-RYE-ah") are too cumbersome.

Zachary ★★★★

(Hebrew) a form of Zachariah.

First Impression: Zachary is described as a warm, considerate guy with blond good looks and a flirty attitude.

Gender Association: Used mostly for boys

Popularity and Trend: #33 (#15 in 2000)

Risk of Misspelling: Average

Risk of Mispronunciation: Fairly low

Famous Namesakes: President Zachary Taylor

Common Nicknames: Zach

Common Variations: Zacary, Zachery, Zachory, Zackary

Consider This: Zachary has so many variations, spelling will be a problem. Also, there's a minor pronunciation difference between those who pronounce it "ZACK-a-ree" and those who pronounce it "ZACK-ree."

Zane ★★★★
(English) a form of John.

First Impression: Zane is seen as either tellin' jokes or bustin' broncos. He seems to be hunky and sweet—on that, people agree.

Gender Association: Used for boys

Popularity and Trend: #243 (#246 in 2000)

Risk of Misspelling: Fairly low

Risk of Mispronunciation: Low

Famous Namesakes: Actor Billy Zane; baseball player Zane Smith; author Zane Grey

Common Nicknames: None

Common Variations: Zain, Zayne

Consider This: Zane isn't versatile, but it's relatively easy to say and spell, and it's fairly popular.

Zedekiah ★★★
(Hebrew) God is mighty and just.

First Impression: Zedekiah is thought to be a quiet, humble, and simple man with great spiritual faith and wisdom.

Gender Association: Used for boys

Popularity and Trend: Never been ranked in Top 1000

Risk of Misspelling: Fairly high

Risk of Mispronunciation: Fairly high

Famous Namesakes: Biblical figure Zedekiah

Common Nicknames: Zed

Common Variations: None

Consider This: This biblical name's challenging spelling and pronunciation ("zed-ah-KYE-ah") may keep you at bay.

Zeke ★★★
(Hebrew) a form of Ezekiel, Zachariah, Zachary, Zechariah.

First Impression: People believe Zeke is a loud, wild guy who loves surprises and spontaneity.

Gender Association: Used for boys

Popularity and Trend: Never been ranked in Top 1000

Risk of Misspelling: Fairly low

Risk of Mispronunciation: Fairly low

Famous Namesakes: None

Common Nicknames: None

Common Variations: Zeek

Consider This: This uncommon name has a fun, positive image, but perhaps people expect it to be a nickname rather than a given name.

Zeno ★★★
(Greek) cart; harness.

First Impression: Most of the time, Zeno comes across as a friendly guy, but sometimes his wild side can get out of hand.

Gender Association: Used for boys

Popularity and Trend: Never been ranked in Top 1000

Risk of Misspelling: Average

Risk of Mispronunciation: Average

Famous Namesakes: Byzantine emperor Flavius Zeno

Common Nicknames: None

Common Variations: None

Consider This: An intriguing image characterizes this unusual name, but its similarity to the word *zero* may be holding it back. Pronunciation may differ between "ZEE-noh" and "ZEN-oh."

Zephyr ★★★
(Greek) west wind.

First Impression: Zephyr is seen as an outgoing and energetic free spirit.

Gender Association: Used about equally for girls and boys

Popularity and Trend: Never been ranked in Top 1000

Risk of Misspelling: Average

Risk of Mispronunciation: Average

Famous Namesakes: Song "The Zephyr Song"

Common Nicknames: None

Common Variations: None

Consider This: Zephyr has a delightful image, but the fact that it's used for an equal number of boys and girls may cause some confusion.

Also from Meadowbrook Press

100,000+ Baby Names is the #1 baby name book and is the most complete guide for helping you name your baby. It contains over 100,000 popular and unusual names from around the world, complete with origins, meanings, variations, and famous namesakes. It also includes the most recently available top 100 names for girls and boys, as well as over 300 helpful lists of names to consider and avoid.

Baby Bites combines everything parents need to know about feeding babies and toddlers in one book. Part nutrition guide, part recipe book, this is the most comprehensive baby nutrition book on the market. Informative subjects include breastfeeding, formula-feeding, first-food purées, and table foods. Facts and practical tips help parents understand their baby's nutritional needs and prepare tasty food that encourages healthy eating habits and avoids health problems.

Breastfeeding with Confidence is a practical guide to breastfeeding that's designed to provide new mothers with the practical skills and confidence they need to have a positive breastfeeding experience. Internationally known lactation expert Sue Cox explains both the art and the method of breastfeeding, and addresses the fact that making milk comes naturally but breastfeeding is a learned skill. She provides invaluable information, advice, resources, and encouragement for new mothers.

The Toddler's Busy Book, ***The Preschooler's Busy Book***, ***The Arts and Crafts Busy Book***, and ***The Wiggle & Giggle Busy Book*** each contain 365 activities (one for each day of the year) for your children, using items found around the home. The books offer parents and child-care providers fun reading, math, and science activities that will stimulate a child's natural curiosity. They also provide great activities for indoor play during even the longest stretches of bad weather!

**We offer many more titles written to delight, inform, and entertain.
To order books with a credit card or browse our full
selection of titles, visit our website at:**

www.meadowbrookpress.com

or call toll free to place an order, request a free catalog, or ask a question:

1-800-338-2232

Meadowbrook Press • 5451 Smetana Drive • Minnetonka, MN • 55343